Cultural Psychiatry and Medical Anthropology

An Introduction and Reader

Edited by

ROLAND LITTLEWOOD
&
SIMON DEIN

THE ATHLONE PRESS
London & New Brunswick, NJ

First published in 2000 by
THE ATHLONE PRESS
1 Park Drive, London NW11 7SG
and New Brunswick, New Jersey

British Library Cataloguing in Publication Data
*A catalogue record for this book is available
from the British Library*

ISBN 0 485 11527 1 HB
0 485 12139 5 PB

Library of Congress Cataloging-in-Publication Data

Littlewood, Roland.
  Cultural psychiatry and medical anthropology : an introduction and reader/Roland
Littlewood and Simon Dein.
    p. cm.
  Includes bibliographical references and index.
  ISBN 0-485-12139-5 (pbk. : alk. paper) – ISBN 0-485-11527-1 (cloth : alk. paper)
  1. Cultural psychiatry. I. Dein, Simon, 1959- II. Title.

RC455.4.E8 L58 2000
616.89–dc21

99-044634

Distributed in The United States, Canada and South America by
Transaction Publishers
390 Campus Drive
Somerset, New Jersey 08873

Typeset by Acorn Bookwork, Salisbury, Wiltshire
Printed and bound in Great Britain by
Bookcraft (Bath) Ltd

Contents

Preface

Cultural psychiatry, like social anthropology itself, is best approached through reading the original papers rather than attempting to digest a textbook. (Not that there is yet such a thing in this area.) We have offered here a number of texts, some well known and already influential, others less so; all, we would claim, have some claim to 'canonical' status as influential or simply representative texts. They have been read with our postgraduate students in anthropology and in psychiatry at University College London over a number of years. We have preferred to recommend classic ethnographic and readable selections rather than the drier critical synopsis typical of much recent work. Each text is accompanied by a short commentary with suggestions on later research and on further reading, and an introductory chapter provides a short historical overview. We intend that the texts selected are fairly accessible but the reader new to anthropology might like to have available a short dictionary of anthropology or one of the introductions to the discipline such as those of Evans-Pritchard, Leach, Lienhardt, Beattie, Pocock, or I. M. Lewis. For the anthropologist without psychiatry, a small medical students' textbook on psychiatry might be helpful for reference, but do not expect much in these books on cultural, or indeed social, psychiatry.

R. L., S. D.
UCL 1998

Acknowledgements

Chapter 1, the introduction, is modified from the *International Journal of Social Psychiatry*, 42(4) (1996): 245–68.

Chapter 2 is a paper presented by Dr G. M. Beard of New York at the American Neurological Association Report of the Committee of Nominations (1880).

Chapter 3 appears in S. Hirsch and M. Shepherd (eds) *Themes and Variations in European Psychiatry* (1974), pp. 3–6. It is reproduced with the kind permission of John Wright and Sons.

Chapter 4 appears in *Medicine, Magic and Religion*, the Fitzpatrick Lectures delivered before the Royal College of Physicians of London in 1915–16 by W. H. R. Rivers with a preface by G. Elliot Smith. It was published in London by Kegan Paul, Trench, Trubner & Co.

Chapter 5 appears in the *International Journal of Psycho-analysis*, VI, Pt 2 (April 1925): 109–30.

Chapter 6 appears in M. Mauss, *Sociology and Psychology: Essays*, trans. B. Brewster (1979). It is reproduced with the kind permission of Routledge & Kegan Paul.

Chapter 6 appears in the *British Journal of Medical Psychology*, IX, Pt III (1929): 187–202.

Chapter 8 appears as Chapter 14 of *Culture and Experience*, ed. A. Irving Hallowell (1974), pp. 266–76. It is reproduced with the kind permission of the University of Pennsylvania Press. It was originally published in the *American Sociological Review* VII (1941): 869–81.

Chapter 9 appears in the *Bulletin of the History of Medicine*, 14 (1943): 30–68.

Chapter 10 appears in *Structural Anthropology*, Vol. 1, ed. C. Lé-Strauss (1968), pp. 186–205. It is reproduced with the kind permission of Penguin Books.

Chapter 11 appears in the *Journal of Mental Sciences*, 97 (1951): 313–37. It is reproduced with the kind permission of the Royal College of Psychiatrists.

Chapter 12 appears in the quarterly *Journal of Studies on Alcohol*, 1 (1954): 220–237. It is reproduced with the kind permission of Rutgers University Press.

A modified version of Chapter 13 appears in G. Devereux, *Basic*

Problems of Ethnopsychiatry, trans. B. Miller Gulati and G. Devereux (1980). It is reproduced with the kind permission of the University of Chicago Press. Most of the chapter appeared first in an article entitled 'Normal & Abnormal' in J. Casagrande and T. Galwin (eds) *Some uses of Anthropology, Theoretical and Applied* (Washington, DC: 1956). A few pages appeared first in a note entitled 'Shamans as Neurotics' *American Anthropologist*, 63 (1961): 1058–90.

Chapter 14 appears in *American Anthropologist*, 6(59) (1957): 1046–66 and is reproduced with the kind permission of the American Anthropological Association.

Chapter 15 appears in *Psychiatry*, 23 (1961): 1–17 and is reproduced with the kind permission of the Guilford Press.

Chapter 16 appears in A. Kiev (ed.) *Magic, Faith & Healing* (1964). It is reproduced with the kind permission of the Free Press.

Chapter 17 appears as Chapter 2 in M. Hammer and K. Salinger (eds) *Psychopathology* (1971). It is reproduced with the kind permission of John Wiley & Sons.

A Note on Terminology

The term to designate our area of interest has varied, in part determined by subject-matter, in part by theoretical focus. Kraepelin used 'comparative psychiatry' (*vergleichende Psychiatrie*), as have Yap and Murphy more recently for their comprehensive textbooks. Social anthropologists have not usually found it profitable to use a particular label, although the term 'medical anthropology' became popular in the 1960s to designate the social anthropology of health and illness. The influence of psychoanalysis on American anthropology in the 1930s resulted in an approach generally known as 'culture and personality'; more recently this has been termed 'psychoanalytical anthropology' or even 'psychological anthropology', here overlapping with more empirical accounts of systems of psychological knowledge, otherwise known as 'cognitive anthropology', 'semantic anthropology', or the 'anthropology of the person'. By the 1950s North American psychiatrists were using the term 'transcultural psychiatry' or 'cross-cultural psychiatry' to designate comparisons of rates and symptomatology across different societies. The 'new cross-cultural psychiatry' advocated by Kleinman is often known in the United States simply as 'cultural psychiatry', emphasising that Western psychopathology is no less culturally constructed than any other. British anthropologists who use 'culture' in a more extended sense than their American counterparts, to include all social and political processes in a given society, have no preferred term although some use 'psychiatry and anthropology'; in Britain 'transcultural psychiatry', although still carrying connotations of the older comparative studies, has increasingly come to refer to a psychiatric commitment to minority ethnic groups. To an extent this has been replaced by 'antiracist psychiatry'.

CHAPTER ONE

Introduction

As with any other social fact, one can interpret an illness as somehow characteristic of the particular society in which it is found. Such specificity has been a continuing problem for comparative studies in psychiatry. Can those patterns recognised by medicine as 'culture-bound syndromes' be fully explained through an understanding of one particular society? Or should these patterns be subsumed under more universal categories? Or, more modestly, be placed in groups whose members merely demonstrate some family resemblances to each other? Can we argue both – local specification and superordinate category – when a 'behavioural syndrome appearing in widely differing cultures takes on local meaning so completely that it appears uniquely suited to articulate important dimensions of each local culture, as though it had sprung naturally from that environment' (Good and Good 1992: 257)?

Whether some general category adequately subsumes a characteristic local experience is fundamental for any human science. The case of medicine is complicated by its claim to demonstrate biological reality – so that individual illnesses can be identified as instances of some natural category that exists 'out there' independently of any local interests in which it appears embedded, our own included. The question recalls anthropology's debates, less as to whether *tabu* or segmentary alliance are categories that transcend local particularities, than as to whether sexual avoidance of close kin by non-human primates is homologous to incest prohibition or whether it is merely analogous, primate sexual 'avoidance' then being an inappropriate extrapolation from our human concerns.

As psychiatry developed into a clinical speciality in late eighteenth-century Europe, doctors recognised that certain of the concerns which (by analogy with physical disease) they now examined as sicknesses could appear more commonly in one country rather than in another. Psychiatry took up existing speculations on a nation's 'manners' and 'spirit': in his *Poétique* of 1561, the Italian humanist Julius Scaliger had identified the character of his compatriots as 'cuctatores, irrisores, factiosi'. Britain was described by its physicians as a country particularly liable to the *morbus anglicus* (despair and suicide) as a consequence of its climate (cold and wet), its diet (beef) and the pace of its commercial life (fast), all contributing to the vulnerabilities of the national character (melancholic) (Cheyne 1734). Illnesses like melancholia, spleen, or neurasthenia were

1

recognised as the cost of accepting new public responsibilities by men of the emerging middle classes in the period of early industrialisation and extending political representation. Other psychological sicknesses – hysteria and moral retardation – were rather a distressing inability to accept such responsibility, an outward manifestation of the weaker bodily or moral constitution of European workers, criminals and women, or of African slaves and colonised peoples when they were threatened with the possibility of similar obligation (Brigham 1832). Mental illnesses were taken as characteristic of life in one or other nation or social stratum: such as Beard's 'Jumping Frenchmen' (Chapter 2) more immediately to be understood as the manifestation of occupation, age, gender, temperament, habit, bodily constitution and physical environment, as individuals variously conformed to or neglected their immediate obligations (Boudin 1857). Or more generally through some idiom which tried to put together those obligations and sentiments, social organisation and history, modes of sustenance and technical knowledge, individual character and family life, rituals and symbolisations which seemed to characterise a particular society: what has become known as its 'culture'.

'Culture' became accepted as a term to place together all those characteristics attributable to living in a particular society, through the acquiring of which a child, like a plant in a nursery, was cultivated into maturity. Johann Herder proposed that national cultures resemble plants, each distinct and destined to grow in its own way. The mystical *Naturphilosophie* placed together culture, myth, personality, community and environment as all inherently related and shaped to transcendent 'primordial images' (*Urbilden*). Whether human groups could be said each to have a separate biological (or divine) origin still remained debated, but 'culture' was generally placed in opposition to the existing term 'nature'; once the physical world created by divine action, nature now denoted those features of human life that were found in other living beings – physical form and function, growth and reproduction; or which, more specifically were shared only with animals – including the passions, sexuality, violence and even such propensities as benevolence and sociality, all natural attributes that could be found in human societies in differing degrees (Collingwood 1945; Thomas 1983).

Maurice and Jean Bloch (1980) have suggested that the term 'nature' carries a number of related meanings for contemporary Europeans: the archaic and the chronologically presocial; our internal bodily processes; the universal and inevitable order of the organic and inorganic; and (identified and imagined) primitive peoples. By contrast 'culture' argued for the moral and aesthetic moulding of natural growth, for a precarious binding of that which was more elemental and basic but which still sought expression in human life. Non-Europeans and European proletarians, like

bourgeois women and children inaccessible to culture or still to be cultivated, remained 'in a state of nature' (Michaelis 1814). Harraway has
argued recently (1989: 13) that in the early industrial period Europeans
took as nature 'only the material of nature appropriated, preserved,
enslaved, exalted or otherwise made flexible for disposal by culture in the
logic of capitalist colonialism'. Culture was not only an historical process
in human time but, like nature, something which could be accumulated for
use, and thus commodified. The more culture, the less significant was
nature in human society: and the converse. As in the earliest Christian
schema, nature in herself was independent of willed intention but she
could be mastered by man's agency; the development of civilisation
demonstrated that European men had gradually acquired dominion over
nature, both as an industrial resource 'out there', as raw material or slaves,
but also in their own bodies: as Francis Bacon had put it, in a 'truly
masculine birth of time [in which men] would conquer and subdue Nature'
(quoted in Easlea 1980: 247). And if they had eventually learnt that they
could not control the natural depredation of their bodies' diseases by an
act of magical speech or sorcery or even by divine supplication, they could
perhaps effect bodily healing through culture's technical power over
nature.

The actual relationship between nature and culture – what we might
now consider rather as modes of explanation taken as concrete entities –
was and remains problematic. Different professional disciplines developed
to specialise in each: what in German scholarship became known as the
natural and moral (human) sciences. The pervasive notion of a hierarchy
within nature – initially ordered as the Creator's Great Chain of Being,
later as an unfolding evolutionary struggle – placed together what we still
distinguish as the biological and the moral into a unitary schema: certain
races had particularly high rates of one sort of psychological illness or
another through their position in the evolutionary chain and their ability
(or their failure) to dominate their nature. If melancholy was the fruit of
European civilisation's gradual accumulation of culture and self-conscious-
ness, then primitive mental illness – a lack of control over instinct and
impulsivity – was demonstrated by tribal peoples (Madden 1857). Yet
one's 'psychic energy' a measure of health, reflected the number of the
(newly discovered) brain cells. If biological and cultural were variously
elided in different ways, the common conclusion was that 'culture' was
primarily an attribute of Europeans, a function of their 'development'.
Illnesses like Down's mongolism or mass hysteria warned Europeans of
their possible degeneration to an earlier and more protean nature (ibid;
Morel 1860).

FORM AND CONTENT

Clinical psychiatry developed as an academic discipline in the nineteenth-century hospital and clinics of Europe where the new industrial order had confined those recognised as insane, and the majority of hospitalised patients still remain diagnosed as psychotic – as demonstrating diseases which, if pathological changes in the brain cannot readily be demonstrated, are at least presumed to be present (e.g. Schneider 1959). And which reduce responsibility and thus legal accountability. The scientific ambitions of hospital medicine, and its identification of an illness which corresponded to what was popularly recognised as chronic insanity (and which in the early twentieth century came to be known as schizophrenia), tended to make the predominant understanding of mental illness the medical (e.g. Gaskell 1860). When the new 'nervous specialists' and 'alienists' were called to deal with patterns of distress or unusual behaviour among people who could not be obviously recognised as physically diseased or insane, they were faced with a practical issue of deciding if the patient was responsible for his or her symptoms; and whether he or she was accountable when making a will or giving evidence in a court of law, or could be expected to take responsibility for criminal acts or for rearing the children. If the patient was a member of the upper or middling classes, some disease-like category such as hysteria or nervous prostration (neurasthenia) might be advanced which minimised his or her responsibility for the condition itself but not for other actions (e.g. Beard 1881). Doctors in private practice realised that to challenge a patient's own ascription of illness too radically was to lose the client, as sardonically illustrated by Molière and Proust. When deciding accountability for criminal acts where the individual claimed to be ill, doctors might, or might not, hold the prisoner accountable; decisions had to be made as to whether the illness was 'real', that is, caused by physical changes that were independent of the prisoner's awareness and whose actions were unintended, or feigned, as it might be among those awaiting trial or sentence. The simulation of insanity under such circumstances might itself be considered an illness, yet not one that should provide exculpation for past crimes (Ganser 1897).

Not every person who was diagnosed as having a particular mental illness reported exactly the same experiences. To deal with variations in the symptoms between individuals, everyday clinical psychiatry still makes a distinction between the essential *pathogenic* determinants of a mental disorder – those biological processes which are held to be necessary and sufficient to cause it – and the *pathoplastic* personal and cultural variations in the pattern (Birnbaum 1923). These two are still distinguished in everyday clinical practice by the particularly nineteenth-century German distinction between form and content. To distinguish form from content was once a virtually ubiquitous practice in comparative studies in art, history, ethnology, literary criticism, or archaeology, indeed in the humanities in general; but in those areas it has been superseded by looser thematic, mimetic, or emergent approaches: in part because of the inevitable uncertainty over deciding what was properly form and what content, together with the problem of justifying whether one or the other was somehow more fundamental, whether (ontologically) in a pattern's historical appearance or in its immediate causation, or (epistemologically) in its observed configuration and analytical typology. It has been argued that the form/content dichotomy is facilitated by Indo-European subject-predicate syntax, or more specifically that it is characteristic of the scientific method whose advances have been fuelled by the analysis of apparent wholes through the underlying natural properties of their presumed parts, together with an empiricist theory of linguistic realism in which names simply label distinct entities such as diseases that are already present in the external world (Yap 1974; Lewontin, Rose and Kamin 1984; Good and Good 1982). To which we might add the modern imperative to concretise experience; so our experience of hotness, translated into temperature, became something like a natural entity which, like the idea of manic-depression, could easily be rated as a linear scale (Littlewood 1994).

The form/content dichotomy continues in psychiatry as a medical proxy for distinguishing the biological (which doctors aim to explain) from the cultural (which they can only seek to understand) (Jaspers 1963). It has seemed most applicable when abnormal experiences and actions were associated with a recognised and presumably ubiquitous physical disease such as a brain or thyroid tumour, anaemia, and traumatic or vascular damage to the brain. The hallucinations which were experienced during the delirium of the brain-damaged alcoholic are taken as directly reflecting the biological form which is expressed through an insignificant content which reflects their particular character and the standard preoccupations of their society. Thus, looking at persecutory ideas in the West Indies, one study in the 1960s argued that for the local Blacks, paranoid suspicions (the form) were directed against their relatives and neighbours (the content), following local ideas of sorcery in an egalitarian village community; whilst for the White Creoles, preoccupied with retaining control as a precarious elite, the phantom poisoners were identified among the surrounding Black population (Weinstein 1962).

But to distinguish form from content was problematic when there were no evident biological changes, and thus where the distinction had to be made on the basis of the patient's symptoms as presented to the physician. Hallucinations and delusions contrary to shared everyday reality were nearly always regarded as primary and thus biological; their particular themes had even less bearing on the cause (and thus treatment) of the disease than the way patients might understand pain had any significance for ascertaining the origins of the pain. To take an example from the German psychiatrist Emil Kraepelin: that a patient said he was the Kaiser rather than Napoleon (that is, the content) was of little clinical value compared with the fact of a delusion of grandiose identification (the form). Now this left the intersubjective cultural world fairly redundant in psychiatric illness as it was observed in the hospital; except in as much as a society might facilitate one or other physical cause – as patterns of drinking might encourage alcohol-induced dementia, or local conceptions of risk increase the likelihood of traumatic accidents, or in a less direct way through a society's transformation of the physical environment and thus of human biology through genetic selection (as with sickle cell anaemia). If cultural values could thus sometimes cause disease through transforming natural causes, they could not cause serious mental illness directly in the way that Christianity, Islam and popular understandings might still identify moral turpitude as the immediate cause of insanity.

The form/content schema worked fairly smoothly in European mental hospitals where the scope of what counted as clinical observation was limited by the institutional context, but by the beginning of the twentieth century psychiatry had begun to extend its interests to the peoples of the colonial empires. Many local patterns which suggested novel types of mental illness had been previously recorded by travellers, missionaries and colonial administrators, sometimes indeed as illnesses but often as examples of the criminal perversity of native life, or just as picturesque if rather troublesome oddities. Most notable among these was *amok* (Oxley 1849), a Malay word which has passed into the English language for indiscriminate and unmotivated violence against others (Chapter 17). In one of the first discussions of the problems of comparing psychiatric illness across societies, Kraepelin in 1904, after a trip to Java during which he collected accounts of amoks and also observed hospitalised patients, suggested that the characteristic symptoms of a particular mental illness – those which one could find everywhere in the world – were the essential pathogenic ones that directly reflected its physical cause (Chapter 3). Yet, as he noted, 'reliable comparison is of course only possible if we are able to draw distinctions between identifiable illnesses'. This proved difficult given the variety of local patterns together with the intention, which Kraepelin enthusiastically shared, to fit them into the restricted number of categories already identified in European hospitals.

Eugen Bleuler, the Swiss psychiatrist who coined the term 'schizophrenia', argued that those symptoms by which we can distinguish this illness form other patterns directly reflect the underlying biological process (Bleuler 1911). This coalesced with Kraepelin's idea that the characteristic features are the universal ones, to produce the still current model of psychiatric illness which may be described as something like a Russian doll: the essential biological determinants which specify an illness are surrounded by a confusing series of cultural and idiosyncratic envelopes which have to be picked away in diagnosis to reveal the real disease. As Kraepelin's pupil Karl Birnbaum (1923) put it, these pathoplastic envelopes give 'content, colouring and contour to individual illnesses whose basic form and character have already been biologically established'. Wittgenstein (1958) critically likened the same sort of approach in the psychological sciences to our picking away the leaves off an artichoke in a hopeless attempt to uncover some real artichoke, on the assumption that – to use the anthropologist Clifford Geertz's (1986) sarcastic aphorism – 'culture is icing, biology cake. ... Difference is shallow, likeness deep.' The medical observer was to focus on those symptoms which seem distinguishing and characteristic, and thus biologically determining: symptoms notably elusive in psychiatry where anxiety, irritation, insomnia, anorexia, depression, self-doubt and suicidal preoccupations are common to virtually all identified illnesses, and which themselves shade into everyday experience. Such common features tend to be ignored in diagnostic practice, more by an act of faith in the Kraepelin–Birnbaum model than through an empirical consideration of all the available evidence. And even the statistical attempt to develop a nomenclature favoured by epidemiologists in the 1980s resulted in circular and quite varied arguments about categorisation and universality. Psychiatric illnesses have not been shown to fit neatly bounded monothetic categories (which supposedly 'carve nature at the joint' as Young [1995] puts it), so multivariate analysis of a multitude of possible symptoms produces rather different schemata for classification, depending on the statistical procedure, on whether one includes or omits shared symptoms, and indeed on what is to count as a symptom.

Psychiatric diagnostic categories are ideally monothetic – that is, they have robust core symptoms which specify that diagnosis and no other. Yet it is perhaps only for schizophrenia that psychiatrists can agree on any defining symptoms which are not found in other illnesses: the 'first-rank' symptoms described by the younger Schneider (1959). Yet these are found in only a half of identified schizophrenic patients in Britain and are 'overridden' by evidence of organic brain disease as seen at post-mortem (which them becomes the principal diagnosis). The form/content (pathogenic/pathoplastic) model in comparative psychiatry (like its associated 'category fallacy' (Kleinman 1988) which presumes the European core symptoms everywhere) does seem to produce useful conclusions where there is evidence of invariant biological change which may be said to 'determine' behaviour and experience in a unique way such that they do not seem to occur without it. Examples would be delirium tremens and possibly Gilles de la Tourette's syndrome (although behaviours recalled

Tourette's are found with other types of brain lesions and with severe anxiety, and with the experimentally induced hyperstartle response and such social institutions as latah, which encourages hyperstartling).

The World Health Organisation's International Pilot Study of Schizophrenia (IPSS) produced evidence in the 1970s that a similar core schizophrenic pattern (following Schneider's criteria) can be identified in widely differing societies. What it did not show was the extent of the cultural contribution to the illness, supposedly one of the intentions of the study, as Kleinman (1988) has observed; emphasis on the core group, which was shown to have comparable rates across cultures, ignored the cases at the edges where there was a much greater difference in rates, such as a three-fold difference between Denmark and India for a 'broad' category of schizophrenic similar to that actually used in British psychiatric practice. The core symptoms of schizophrenia thus appeared to be a *manifestation* of an underlying disease process; taking a wider category of schizophrenia suggests alternatively that schizophrenic symptoms might also be understood as a *response* to a variety of insults, whether neurological or social. Examining stable societies rather than groups of refugees or communities in the midst of civil upheavals will emphasise intra-personal biological differences in the aetiology of schizophrenia. (This is analogous to the finding that, when studying affluent societies, genetic associations appear most salient in looking at differences in height, for we have already controlled for one environmental source of variation – nutrition.) Nevertheless, the similarity of core symptoms and rates found across societies in the IPSS argues that we are unlikely to be able to explain all instances of schizophrenia by a more cultural and political understanding as was assumed by anthropologists like Gregory Bateson and by the British anti-psychiatrists of the 1960s. Cultural considerations of the IPSS results have been limited to speculating on the prognosis of an illness whose origin is taken as primarily biological: vague generalisations about industrialisation (Cooper and Sartorius 1977), or possible correlation with unemployment in capitalist economies (Warner 1985), or differences in relatives' affective responses to a person with schizophrenia (Leff et al. 1987).

The so-called 'neo-Kraepelinian' (Young 1995) diagnostic systems of the 1980s and 1990s such as DSM-III to DSM-IV, which are a reaction against the earlier classification's hypothetic psychodynamics, maintain a hierarchy of diagnostic significance: passivity experiences are still more important in specifying a diagnosis of schizophrenia than are depressive experiences. The local understandings of illness which a society shared were ignored by the colonial doctors who, as in Europe, restricted themselves to examination of those admitted to prison or later to the psychiatric hospital (Fisher 1985; McCulloch 1994). When faced with patients from a society or minority group with which they are unfamiliar,

British and American psychiatrists still complain of the culturally confusing factors which obscure the elusive disease process. With European patients in a predominantly European society they have fewer problems in finding universal categories because 'culture' is always there, tacit, to be implicitly omitted in what counted as the clinical assessment, for, being fairly uniform, it does not contribute to variability between patients. Indeed, any differences within the shared social context of Western patterns, say between women and men, have been ignored until recently in favour of biological or bio-psychological aetiologies to explain variation (and thence 'causation'). Thus there could not seem to be anything immediately 'cultural' in those patterns identified particularly in the West – eating disorders, panic reactions, phobias, self-harm, or shoplifting (Littlewood and Lipsedge 1987). And thus these could be easily presumed to be world-wide patterns. Socially appropriate ways of experiencing and demonstrating distress, like everyday notions of personhood and responsibility, have not been taken as causal, for what appeared as a constant could not determine a variable such as illness. Ignoring the full range of symptoms across society and their relationship to the patients' own beliefs and expectations (and to the therapeutic context) did not seem inappropriate for practice within apparently homogeneous societies, because there doctor–patient interactions and the process of diagnosis were already significant and taken-for-granted aspects of daily life. Diagnostic decisions were followed by generally accepted patterns of social response – by medication, hospital admission and on occasion suspension of civil rights.

COLONIAL PSYCHIATRY

It was when they took their diagnostic systems with them to their colonies at the beginning of the twentieth century that psychiatrists first recognised some of these difficulties (Chapter 11). Dysphoric moods and unusual actions were locally recognised in Africa or Asia, not necessarily as something recalling a physical illness but often as part of totally different patterns of social classifications and order – as spirit possession or rituals of mourning, or in the course of initiation, sorcery and warfare. Those patterns that recalled the psychoses of the West seemed generally recognised as unwelcome but not always as akin to sickness (Rivers 1924; see chapter 4). yet, when colonial doctors turned to writing reports and academic communications, local understandings of self and illness which now seem to us analogous to psychiatric theories were described, not as self-contained, meaningful and functional conceptions in themselves, but rather as inadequate approximations to Western scientific knowledge. At times, however, the understandings of small-scale rural societies, like the more recognisably medical traditions of India and China, cut dramatically across European experience. The anthropologist Charles Seligman (1929; see Chapter 7) who had trained as a doctor reported that there seemed to have been nothing in New Guinea before European contact which could be said to resemble schizophrenia: as cases analogous to schizophrenia have been later identified by psychiatrists, he has been criticised for what is known as 'the Seligman error' – missing a universal illness because local understandings and social response did not allow it to appear objectivised through social extrusion as in a Western hospital but rather incorporated it into some shared institution where it lay unremarked by the medical observer. And similarly, Amerindian and circum-polar patterns of healing, religious inspiration and leadership, in which election to the shamanic role might be signalled by a sudden illness, accident or other troubling experience, were said to mask underlying schizophrenia (Devereux 1956; see Chapter 13).

Patterns like amok or piblokto ('arctic hysteria') were initially taken as rather odd – generally simpler – variants of the psychiatric disorders described in Europe. Mental illness in Java, said Kraepelin (1904), showed 'broadly the same clinical picture as we see in our country ... The overall similarity far outweighed the deviant features.' Individuals locally regarded as amoks were thus really demonstrating epilepsy or perhaps catatonic schizophrenia (ibid.). But what were to be taken as these 'deviant features', and what was being compared with what? Presumably what counted was the form of the illness, the basis for categorisation of the pattern as some clinical entity. If one looked, for instance, at a Malay patient who had an unjustified belief that she was being persecuted by her neighbours, then her delusion was the form, and the neighbours provided the content, but the persecution seemed variously one or the other. That she was deluded is important for arguing that she is mentally ill; the neighbours are of no diagnostic significance. But that her delusions were persecutory might or might not matter, depending on the selected illness. The assumptions made by Kraepelin in his studies in Java remain the dominant paradigms in comparative psychiatry. How similar do patterns have to be before we can say that we are talking about the same pattern? How do we distinguish between those features that appear to be generally the same and those that vary? And what are our units of categorisation going to be when deciding sameness and difference, normality and pathology? Does something like 'depression' occur everywhere? Or perhaps just a less specific experience such as 'distress'?

Textbooks of cultural psychiatry have generally argued that locally recognised patterns like amok are 'not new diagnostic entities: they are in fact similar to those already known in the West' (Kiev 1972). This equivalence has often been extraordinarily optimistic. To take one pattern which attracted comment because of its exotic salience, *windigo*, the 'cannibal-compulsion' syndrome of the North American Ojibwa and Inuit, was locally described as an individual's becoming possessed by a cannibalistic vampire and then attacking other people in an attempt to devour them. Windigo was identified by psychiatrists confidently but quite variously with patterns as disparate as depression, schizophrenia, hysteria and anxiety. Similarly, amok was explained not only as the local manifestation of either epilepsy or schizophrenia, but as malaria, syphilis, cannabis psychosis, sunstroke, mania, hysteria, depression, disinhibited aggression and anxiety (ibid.). *Latahs*, women of the Malay Peninsula who uttered obscene remarks when startled and who parodied the speech and actions of others apparently without intent (O'Brien 1883; see Chapter 17) were identified as demonstrating a 'psychosis [or] hysteria, arctic hysteria, reactive psychosis, startle reaction, fright neurosis, hysterical psychosis [or] hypnoid state' (Kiev 1972). Identifying symptoms rather than the local context meant that amok and latah have generally been regarded not as autonomous cultural institutions, but simply as erroneous Malay explanations that shaped one single universal disease, although the psychiatric observers disagreed radically as to which disease this might be. The extent to which such patterns could be fitted into a universal schema depended on how far the medical observer was prepared to stretch a known psychiatric category, and thus on the preferred theoretical model. By the 1970s, Weston La Barre and Georges Devereux, psychoanalysts who were much less attached to purely biomedical arguments, had gone further in including as instances of schizophrenia a wide variety of local institutions – possession states, shamanism, prophecy, millennial religions and indeed, for La Barre (1970), social change in general. They argued not just that schizophrenia might typically appear in these social institutions but that the institutions exemplified schizophrenic experiences (Littlewood 1993b): everyday culture in non-Western societies could be understood, as it were, as insanity spread out thin (Chapter 13; cf. Chapter 7).

If psychiatrists of the colonial period remained puzzled about the cultural encrustations they saw adhering to the essential symptoms, they could be struck by the opposite: 'barrenness of the clinical picture. ... In more primitive culture schizophrenia is "a poor imitation of Europeans forms"' (cited by Yap 1951; Chapter 11). Culturally obscured, or simply a primitive form, in neither case did culture determine anything but rather acted as a sort of indeterminant soup which passively filled in or distorted the biological matrix. And yet 'culture' itself could be a proxy for biological 'race'. Categorisations of illness, professional or popular, are adjacent to other social classifications – to those of character, ethnicity, gender, the natural world and historical experience – on which they draw and which they plagiarise. There is a distinction between universal biology and the variant culture which constrained it, yet by the end of the nineteenth century descriptive psychiatry was increasingly influenced by social Darwinism's idea of racial biology in which, while humans were agreed to have a common origin, neurological, psychological, social and moral variations were all considered as reflections of each other at a particular level on the linear scale of 'development'. Young (1995) has proposed the term 'the normalisation of pathology' for the Victorian topology (associated particularly with the neurologist Jackson [1884] and thence found in Rivers and Freud) that saw the central nervous system, like the colonial order, as organised in a series of levels of control in which the 'higher' could generally override the 'lower'. (Jackson's analogy was a rider and a horse). Hysteria was recognised as dysfunctional at the 'lower' level, and Kraepelin (1904; see Chapter 3) explained the unusual symptomatology of mental illness among the Javanese as reflecting their 'lower stage of intellectual development'. Variations in what doctors called the 'presentation' of an illness in different societies have been attributed until recently not just to particular historical and political experiences, as we might have expected from the 'pathoplastic' model, but to the existence of a fairly uniform primitive mentality (nature predominating over culture) which was shared with European children and with the 'degenerate', 'regressed' and 'retarded' adult European and which manifested symptoms characteristic of a loss of higher control: 'hyperidic states', 'catastrophic reactions' and 'malignant anxiety', 'simple responses available to psychologically disorganised individuals' and 'primitive reactions corresponding to outbursts of psychopathic persons in developed countries' (all in Kiev 1972). Not altogether unrelated physiological explanations attributed *piblokto* ('arctic hysteria') and *kayak angst* to the developed mind reflecting on 'the stillness and the sense of impending doom that are so characteristic of the Arctic climate' (ibid.)

DEPRESSION

This topological psychology of linear development, put together with the assumption that symptoms observed in Europe were somehow more real and less obfuscated by cultural values, led to the common argument that depression did not yet occur in non-Europeans for its essential Western characteristics of self-blame (a consequence of mature selfhood) was not observed (Carothers 1953). The absence of depression was sometimes directly attributed to a less evolved brain where the 'primitive layers' predominated (Vint 1932), an idea which might have had (but actually didn't) implications for the Colonial Office as J. C. Carothers (1954) recommended when it considered the possibility of independence for colonial Africa. The assumption was made that feelings of guilt were less often associated with depression in the non-Western world than in the West (Field 1960). Guilty self-accusations of the type found in clinical depression in Europe had in fact been identified in colonial Africa in the 1930s, not by doctors in the colonial hospitals but by an anthropologist looking at witchcraft and the distribution of shrines (Field 1960). Reactions which recall Western depression and parasuicide are now frequently described in small-scale, non-industrialised communities (Chapter 15), but the issue depends, not only on the frequency with which people with less socially disturbing problems may come to the hospital to be treated and thus studied, or on medical failure to empathise with another's experience, or on a rather cursory epidemiology based on colonial hospital statistics, but on what one means by 'depression'. Is it something like the misery which we might identify in various situations of loss or bereavement, or the pattern of rather physical experiences such as loss of interest, waking up early, and poor appetite, which are recognised as clinical depression (and which appear likely to be universal), or else some more specific expressed sentiment of Judaeo-Christian guilt and a wish to die? Greater psychiatric familiarity with the experience of personal distress in the former colonies has suggested that 'depression' may be simply a variant of widespread patterns of what we might term dysphoric mood which in depression is represented through a particularly Western moral psychology which assumes an autonomous self as the invariant locus of experience, memory and agency. When looking across societies, a more common experience of everyday distress than 'depression' (which figures a phenomenological sinking downwards of the once active self into an inertia for which we remain responsible: Littlewood 1994), may be one of depletion and the loss of something essential which has been taken out of the self – a pattern well glossed in various Latin American idioms of 'soul loss' (Shweder 1985). For a long time it has been assumed that the Africans and Asians did not experience depression. 'Naturally most of the race are carefree, live in the "here and now" with a limited capacity to recall or profit by experiences of the past. Sadness and depression have little part in his psychological make up' (Bevis 1921). Carothers was castigated by Frantz Fanon for his description of Africans as lobotomised Europeans, happy-go-lucky, feckless children unburdened by the pressure of civilisation. Depression required refinement. Depression was believed to be rare among black Americans and Africans until the 1960s (Prince 1968) and to occur only in cultures which were recognised as having the ability to introspect and verbalise emotions.

A current area of concern is the cultural universality and structuring of depressions (Sartorius 1983) and the continued debate on somatisation (the cultural patterning of psychological disorder into a language of disorder of mainly physical symptoms and signs [Kleinman 1986]). This idea can be traced back to Henry Maudsley: 'The sorrow that has no vent in tears makes other organs weep' (cited by McDougall 1989: 139). The medical idea of somatisation goes back to Freud and Breuer's model of hysteria which suggested that certain localised physical symptoms could be the expression of a particular intra-psychic conflict. What are the non-western analogues of depression? Kleinman has argued for neurasthenia, a term coined by the New York neurologist George Beard in 1891 to describe what he then referred to as the American Disorder because of its assumed prevalence in the United States, to be rediagnosed as major depressive disorder (Kleinman 1986).

THE CULTURE-BOUND SYNDROMES

In the 1950s, following revulsion at German psychiatric 'eugenics' under the Nazis, the social and medical sciences gradually discarded the ideas of biological evolution and psychological development as explanations for differences of experiences and action between contemporary societies. All societies were now recognised as each having 'a culture' in similar ways, and biological differences between groups as a whole – that between men and women still excepted – could not explain their different types of mental illness. The recognition that many non-Western illnesses could no longer be subsumed as primitive forms of universal categories led comparative psychiatry (or, as it now generally came to be called, cultural psychiatry) to propose a new sort of illness altogether whose study did not entail the biological form/cultural content dichotomy. Patterns like amok and latah, which had recalled the idea of psychological illness in Europe yet remained unclassifiable, came to be known as 'culture-bound syndromes' (Yap 1951, 1974; see Chapter 11). They were usually episodic and dramatic reactions, limited to a particular society where they were locally identified as distinct patterns of action very different from those of everyday life. And, we might now note, they had been of colonial concern because they were bizarre, outrageous, or frankly troublesome. Less dramatic patterns of distress – personal withdrawal from shared activities, troubling thought, chronic pain, bereavement, despondency – which did not come to the attention of the colonial administration or the local police were generally ignored until the development of medical anthropology in the 1980s (Chapter 8).

A larger number of such 'culture-bound' illnesses have now been catalogued (e.g. Simons and Hughes 1985) as distinctive and consistent patterns, transmitted to each generation in a continuing cultural tradition, and they are taken as closely related to a society's distinctive understanding of self and its prescribed norms. (By the 1990s, they were recognised in the American Psychiatric Association's fourth *Diagnostic and Statistical*

Manual.) Thus, however high the incidence of reactions like grief or terror might be in war-torn communities, they were not regarded as culture-specific unless they continued in some consistently recognisable form in successive generations as part of an enduring identity. What exactly was it that was 'bound' in culture-bound syndromes? Had 'culture' now aspired to the master status of 'biology' in the international nosology? There is a continuing debate about what the category refers to: usually restricted to a pattern found only in the society in question and which symbolises and represents fundamental local concerns, on occasion it has been applied to apparently universal and biologically understood illnesses which are shaped, distinguished and treated in a local content (on the changing applications of the term see Ritenbaugh 1982; Littlewood and Lipsedge 1987; Lee 1996; Littlewood 1996). Thus one might include *kifafa, malkadi* and *moth madness*, locally recognised patterns in Tanzania, Trinidad and among the Navaho which closely recall the medical description of epilepsy (Neutra *et al.* 1977; Littlewood 1993b). A locally recognised reaction in New Guinea, *kuru*, however, was once regarded as a culture-bound syndrome akin to hysteria, but no longer, given the likely role of a slow virus identified in its aetiology. (And this has made it even more exotic through recognition that it could be transmitted through cannibalism.) Patterns like kuru or the restricted abilities of senescence, or such apparently motivated patterns as homicide and rape, the deliria of malnutrition or alcohol intoxication, or the use of other psychoactive substances, have certainly been regarded as characteristic of a particular society (Chapter 12) but are seldom described as 'culture-bound' because they appear potentially available in any society or else do not immediately recall European 'mental illness'. Yet, if these patterns persisted – like the alcohol abuse, *anomic depression* and suicide consequent on the relocation of Native Americans on to reservations – they were taken as manifestations of 'American Indian culture', ignoring the political relationship between coloniser and native, and thus the context of the psychiatric observation. 'New illnesses' identified by more sophisticated epidemiological techniques in urban populations or through the expansion of psychiatric observation to a wide population have been termed 'culture-change' or 'acculturation illnesses' exemplified by the *brain-fag syndrome* identified in West African students (Prince 1960; Littlewood 1984, 1995).

Perhaps the most developed arguments on the cultural specificity of psychopathology have concerned *latah* (Chapter 17). In 1968 Hildred Geertz called attention to the 'latah paradox': whilst this rich cultural phenomenon seemed 'tailor-made for the Javanese', she noted remarkably similar patterns in a variety of East Asian societies from Siberia to the Malay-Indonesian archipelago. Against medical explanations that latahs – women responding to minimal but conventionalised stimuli with exaggerated startles, passive obedience and obscenities, and with imitation of others' words and actions – were demonstrating a 'pre-psychological' (that is, a universal physiological) response, Geertz suggested it could be completely explained by Javanese concerns. In reply, Ronald Simons (1980) argued from Malay instances that latah is a locally elicited expression of the mammalian capacity to startle, a potential on which a society can then elaborate additional features, out of which shared repertoire individual latahs, usually subdominant women, then develop their own characteristic pattern, whether we take this as spontaneous or simulated. He noted similarities between obscenities in different societies and hypothesised that these were 'neurologically coded in some special way'. Simons has been criticised in turn by psychodynamic commentators for ignoring the significance of teasing in Malay child-rearing, whilst Kenny (1983), arguing that latah represents an inversion of the symbolic code, distinguishes his own emphasis on the 'culture-specific explanation of a meaning potential implicit in a limited human repertoire of concepts pertaining to order, disorder and self-identity' from Simons' 'culture-specific exploitation of a neurophysiological potential'. Simons (1983) ripostes with a critique of the unverifiable nature of psychodynamic interpretations, and of the anthropological tendency to over-interpretation. Against Kenny he quotes informants that almost anybody can be turned into a latah provided she is adequately teased and argues that the pattern once established can then be elicited by a neutral stimulus quite independent of its situational meaning, and that anyway symbolic truths are more often elaborations of locally identified biological phenomena than anthropologists are prepared to admit.

As with other patterns of psychiatric interest, the latah question seems to be one of arguing how much the sensorimotor properties of an embodied 'natural symbol' may be said to constrain its meaning and deployment. As Kenny (1983) puts it, 'Perhaps there is no problem here at all, and latah in its cross-cultural distribution no more of a paradox than is the fact that all people have hands, but only some cultures have exploited the fact in requiring them to be shaken in formal greeting. If that is the case, then the latah performance is taken out of the province of biomedical reductionism and is seen as what I take to be its true light – as theatre.' Are there 'fracture lines' given in advance by physiology, or are we talking, as Kenny does, of intentional 'parodies' of everyday social roles? Can we distinguish the two? In much of comparative psychiatry it is difficult to propose convincingly any universal pattern, leading us to circular debates on the appropriate multivariate analysis of lists of 'symptoms' obtained in different societies in order to determine a presumed biological specification of the identified experience. Further problems come when a pattern seems to disappear from a society altogether – sometimes, as with the phenomenon of multiple personality, then to reappear – or else to transform itself into what we as observers take as a rather different pattern, a particular difficulty when professional Western medicine, the analytical procedure, itself becomes part of the local circumstances through which the pattern is reproduced. Thus the well-known rituals of rebellion of southern Africa have been said by Loudon (1959) to be replaced among Zulu women by neurotic illnesses presenting to the medical clinic, which, although they demonstrate a quite different context, experience, local complementarity between the sexes. Amok, once a standardised demonstration of retributive justice (Chapter 17), has now become recognised in South-East Asia as a purely medical problem. What then remains our identified pattern? What aspect of it is considered to change, and what are the determinants of such change?

PSYCHOANALYTICAL INFLUENCES

If local patterns were distinguished as 'culture-bound' by the European psychiatrist only in that they occurred in (other) cultures, how then did a culture lead to illness? Did 'culture' mean simply shared conceptualisations so that the psychiatrist could identify local concerns and sentiments either in the type of person who was vulnerable, or else in the actual symptoms which represented the culture in a way that recalled seventeenth- and eighteenth-century ideas of a national character? Or could 'culture' be located in social and biological stresses which occurred in a particular society but were not necessarily recognised in it (Chapter 6)? And anyway how could such an illness be distinguished from the other cultural patterns in which it was embedded? A later question, reserved for the 1980s, was whether to extend the category to illnesses such as eating disorders which were apparently only to be found in European societies (Littlewood and Lipsedge 1987; Lee 1996).

In part, the continuing problem of 'culture' for psychiatrists lay in its double-edged connotations. 'Culture' was still a valued commodity, that constraint on nature which distinguished human from animal, educated Europeans from primitive (and which often referred to 'high culture' alone [Williams 1958]). Yet for Western psychiatrists establishing their discipline as a medical specialty 'culture' remained secondary to scientific biological reality. As frank biological racism became disreputable after the Second World War, and its unifying idiom of 'development' separated out into the distinct fields of child psychology, economics and technology, the psychological differences between European and non-European could again be perceived only in rather uncertain 'cultural' terms: as a medical proxy for the other's 'difference' (or even for the lingering idea of 'race') and which still immersed the individual in some undifferentiated other, now less their biological level than their way of life. As medicine had little idea of how to deal with 'culture', it drew on other disciplines, particularly psychoanalysis and social anthropology, which claimed to be able to relate the interests of medicine to the intersubjective social world in a more empirical and humanistic way than had evolutionary medicine. The new cultural psychiatrists generally held appointments in Western university departments, away from the poorly funded and intellectually marginal concerns of colonial psychiatrists who still remained close to popular Western ideas of race (e.g. Carothers 1954). Psychoanalysts and anthropologists interested in providing a 'cultural psychiatry' of local patterns in British Africa based on intensive fieldwork in local communities were seldom interested in examining hospital statistics, unlike the epidemiologists associated with the World Health Organisation who until recently have preferred to stick with the presumed biomedical universals, and thus with the form/content idioms of hospital psychiatry.

Particularly in the United States where a strong inclinations towards psychoanalysis was apparent in medicine and the social sciences from the 1930s, psychiatrists emphasised the similarity of local illnesses to the 'modal personality' which an individual developed in his or her culture (Ruth Benedict and Abram Kardiner). The affected person was now not so much suffering from something that recalled a medical disease with a bit of culture tacked on, as demonstrating in an exaggerated form those psychological conflicts established in the course of childhood socialisation. So windigo (the Ojibwa cannibal-compulsion psychosis) was interpreted as a local preoccupation with food in a hostile environment, fuelled by residues of infantile resentment at the mother for the early weaning necessitated by the scarcity of food. After an indulgent childhood, the young boy was precipitated into early adulthood by brutal tests of self-reliance and encouraged to fast to attain ultrahuman powers. Dependence on his parents was replaced by a precarious dependence on spirits which encouraged solitary self-reliance in hunting. The mother, feared and hated for her violent rejection of her son, returned to possess him in the form of the windigo (Parker 1960).

Psychoanalytically orientated anthropologists proposed in this sort of way that any culture was a dynamic compromise between conflicting interests – ecological, physiological and psychological between self and others, parents and children, men and women. Symptoms, dreams, religious symbols and social institutions could all be taken as aspects of the same conflicts refracted through an individual's psychological functioning (Seligman 1928). Was the European observer now to take the locally identified illness as the expression of such conflicts in unconscious motivations: as a society's symptoms? Or, given the incorporation of personal conflicts into local institutions, was the 'illness' to be considered as a type of collective psychological adjustment, indeed as a sort of healing? Psycho-analysis agreed with psychiatry that one could distinguish problem, causation and treatment (Seligman 1928), but differed as to how to go about it. Devereux, perhaps the most sophisticated psychoanalytical anthropologist, eventually proposed that institutions like shamanism (which had often been taken as employing altered states of consciousness to facilitate something akin to Western psychotherapy [Janet 1925] were themselves the expression of psychological disturbances in what he called the 'ethnic unconscious': disturbances which could then be enhanced by a society to produce 'ethnic psychoses' as he called these pathological institutions (Devereux 1970; see Chapter 13). Criticising the medical historian Edwin Ackernecht (1943; see Chapter 9) who had argued for a clear distinction between local cultural meaning and medical terminology, Devereux (1956: 24) argued that the local healing of unconscious social conflicts simply exacerbated them: 'there exist societies so enmeshed in a vicious circle that everything they do to save themselves only causes them to sink deeper into the quicksand'. The British biological psychiatrist William Sargant, an ex-Methodist who had taken to arguing that religious ecstasy and spirit possession were a type of brainwashing, emphasised the cathartic function of culture-specific patterns which allowed the individual, when in a state dissociated consciousness, to express socially forbidden inclinations in a non-threatening and relatively sanctioned manner – as if they were half-way between an 'illness' and its 'treatment' (Sargant 1973). Like Devereux, he still regarded it as all distinctly unhealthy. Alternatively, Weston La Barre, Ari Kiev and Thomas Scheff took the cathartic expression of hidden desires as a resolution rather than an exacerbation of cultural conflicts – as something closer to healing.

This all got rather circular and, like hospital psychiatry, ignored local conceptions of healing (Chapter 10) in favour of Western schemata of normality and illness. Paralleling the earlier assumption that non-Western pathologies were masked or incomplete forms, non-Western healing was now taken as an elementary version of psychoanalytical therapy but one which employed 'suggestion' rather than 'insight' (Frank 1961; Kiev 1964). What remained constant in all this was the conviction, however muted, that Western categories were still the appropriate way to frame the question; and that these provided universal criteria by which one could agree that certain local patterns were justifiably termed dysfunctional or maladaptive (e.g. Doi 1971). On rare occasions analysts carried out something approaching formal psychoanalysis with their African and Amerindian informants (Sachs 1937; Devereux 1951; Laubscher 1937), even if they presumed Freudian ideals of psychological maturity to be universally valid. Few of the classic culture-bound syndromes were not at some time explained as the projection of unconscious fantasies and thwarted incestuous wishes, as the consequence of traumatic weaning, or simply as the overwhelming existential anxiety of tribal societies which followed from their unsophisticated psychology (e.g. Roheim 1950; Devereux 1956).

Eliding the conventional distinction between pathology as an individual phenomenon and treatment as a social response, the cost to the psycho-analysts was, as Ackernecht had warned, 'the wholesale pathologisation of cultures'. Equivalence between modal personality, characteristic personal illness and social structure led to an interpretation of small-scale communities as paranoid, obsessive, or whatever – even if the implication of these terms was evidently less 'strong' than the clinical usage from which they derived (e.g. Benedict 1935; Lambo 1955). During and after the Second World War, American psychoanalysts were funded to study the 'cultural pathologies' of enemy nations (Benedict 1946). Psychoanalysts still subscribed to those positivist ideals of the late nineteenth century which had sought a moral understanding of human society in science rather than in religion; like the French neurologists under whom he had studied, Freud had explained the medieval persecution of Europe's witches on the ground that they had really been suffering from mental illness, and psycho-analysts like Devereux took with them the assumption that spirit posses-sion was a variant of hysteria when they turned to look at non-European cultures. The universality of the Oedipus complex even in procreation was a matter of particular interest (following Malinowski 1927); not unlike the hospital psychiatrist Kraepelin, the psychoanalysts took a European pattern for which theories had been elaborated as the basic form which other societies then manifested as masked or incomplete (e.g. Jones 1924; see Chapter 5). And they tended to the evolutionary idioms of late nineteenth-century psychiatry, if in a less biologised way, still arguing developmental parallels between archaic ancestor, contemporary primitive, child and neurotic, all as early, arrested, or regressed levels characterised by an infantile psychology in which 'psychic omnipotence' and 'magical thinking' trailed behind the advancing line of mature rationality. Nor, with rare exceptions (Sachs 1937), was colonial power of much psychoanalytical interest, whether as the rather unusual site for their observations, or – occasional comments on the perils of imitating primitives for the Whites apart (Jung 1930) – as itself pathogenic (cf. Mannoni 1950; Fanon 1952; Loudon 1959).

More recently, local illnesses have been regarded by psychiatrists influ-enced by anthropology less as diseases or unconscious conflicts than as particularly salient everyday sensibilities and values of exaggerated idioms of distress (Kleinman 1988): as with the Hindu *suchi-bar* ('purity mania') and the related *ascetic syndrome*, or the Taiwanese *shen k'uei* and Japanese *taijin kyosusho* ('interpersonal phobia'). If these had been termed pathological or maladaptive by Western psychiatry, it was because normative institutions – Brahmanical obligations to avoid certain foods of inappropriate familiarity – were taken too enthusiastically by certain individuals, resulting in anxieties or interpersonal problems which could be recognised as disproportionate both in the local context and by Western psychiatric observers. Or alternatively, recalling the psychoanalytical view, the patterns represent in the individual a conflict or contradiction between the local institutions themselves: thus it has been argued that the continuing antagonism between the values of sexuality and asceticism in India generated the 'purity syndromes' (Malhotra and Wig 1975). Or else, as Sargant had argued, personal conflicts are expressed in limited contravention of role-specific norm in fairly standardised situations, and it is these contraventions that had been identified, correctly or otherwise, as pathologies. It has been suggested that all cultures have such loopholes which are themselves 'socially reinforced and have the same structural characteristics as other behavioural norms in the system'; and that at least in the case of the latah and amok, we should employ a less medical term than 'syndrome': perhaps something like 'stylised expressive traditional behaviours' for those deviant patterns that are fairly standardised and limited in time, but which, whilst they certainly contravene everyday behaviour, are somehow culturally condoned to allow the expression of apparently repressed but not uncommon sentiments (Carr 1978). This does push the psychiatrist's normative question back even further, but if deviance (or pathology) is sometimes locally condoned or even encouraged, what is the frame by which one should term it deviant? The lingering Western presumption of pathology, or some local 'Don't do this but if you must, do it this way'? As with the earlier colonial psychiatry, the idea of a 'culture' has, however, remained one which is fairly homogenous, with values and social order accepted in the same way by all members: a model which followed the idea of a tightly bounded society once sought by colonial officers and anthropologists, which ignored any unequal distinction of knowledge and power, of local contestation or global change (Littlewood 1984, 1995).

One area of interest for cultural psychiatry is the mode of action of symbolic therapies, i.e. therapy based on words, myths and ritual. Scholarly interest has shifted from mechanism to meaning. Traditional healing had originally been seen as an incomplete form of Western psychotherapy providing partial and temporary relief by 'primitive' mechanisms such as reassurance, suggestion, imitation, catharsis and projection (Lawrence 1910; Janet 1925; Gregory 1939; Kiev 1964; Torrey 1971). This could be contrasted with the lasting insight offered by Western psychoanalysis. Frank, in his influential *Persuasion and Healing* (1961), provided a model of healing based on the attainment of a new perspective by the patient leading to moralisation. Subsequent writers emphasise a shared understanding held by patients and healers, a cultural congruence between experience of illness and its symbolic representation which is deployed in the process of healing (Bourguignon 1976; Torrey 1971; Kleinmann and Sung 1979; Dow 1986; Good and Good (1986; and Kirmayer 1993). In his paper 'The effectiveness of symbols', Lévi-Strauss (1967; see Chapter 10), like Turner (1964; see Chapter 16), emphasises this shared understanding. The healing involves a Cuna shaman who recites a myth to a woman in obstructed labour where his narrative creates a metaphorical landscape that represents the sufferer's physical and existential plight. Emotions are conceptualised by Lévi-Strauss as mediators between social symbols and the body. Healing ultimately results through catharsis (Scheff 1979). The most recent formulations of healing now emphasise performance and the changes in experience (Desjarlais 1993; Laderman 1991; Kapferer 1993; Roseman 1991; and Csordas 1994 [see Chapter 16]). These authors examine the particular genres through which healing occurs (music, narrative, movement)

THE LIMITS OF CULTURAL PSYCHIATRY

Hospital psychiatrists and those inclined to psychoanalysis both argued for unitary theories of the phenomena once observed by missionaries, army doctors and colonial administrators, even if they disagreed as to what any such unity comprised: universally recognisable disease entity, exaggeration of norm, cultural conflict, social change, sanctioned rejection of the norm or even therapeutic response. Social anthropologists have objected that their error was to use a medical grid which inevitably objectified social action as disease entity. Rather, one should start by simply describing a society in its own terms, for societies are not traditional residues of some forgotten past which is passing away but always constitute themselves anew in their chosen memories and actions. If the term 'culture-bound syndrome' is to retain value only as a concept of local sickness, whether or not psychiatry recognises it as akin to Western disease, what then is to count as a 'concept of sickness'? Social scientists are hardly immune from comparing one society with another to obtain regularities and general patterns, and in order to do that, they too define apparently analogous domains in each – whether those of social structure, kinship, religion, or intoxication (Chapter 12). And those domains inevitably drive from Western ideas and terminology. Another society then simply comes to be read as an aggregate of such areas of comparison which have a structured and causal relationship to each other (Littlewood 1991). The comparative problem is hardly unique to medicine. As the British anthropologist Edward Evans-Pritchard is said to have observed: 'If social anthropology is anything it is a comparative discipline – and that is impossible.' It is not that psychiatry's inevitable grid, pathology, is necessarily inappropriate for comparing what looks to the European like 'suffering' or 'madness' in different societies, but pathology is just one possible grid and one that carries with it particular assumptions about normality and abnormality, which explicitly ignore considerations of power and of context of observation. And what is observed, and how 'observation' itself might shape it.

The evolutionary schema did offer one mode of comparison by placing societies (and illnesses) as states of transformation along an historical spectrum driven by certain processes. Few social anthropologists, some sociobiologists, Freudians and Marxists, perhaps excepted, would now subscribe to the idea of an unilinear human development through which local institutions and mentalities are to be understood as determined by underlying processes, whether those of evolutionary selection or of the relations of production. Whilst it is still argued that the insights offered by psychoanalysts may provide a useful perspective when trying to understand psychological experience in non-European societies (e.g. Doi 1971; Kakar 1978), others have argued that Freud's followers have little to contribute to the critical or social sciences for they offer a moralised version of common-sense Western assumptions about the inevitability of European rationality with entrepreneurial autonomy as 'health' or psychoanalytically orientated anthropologists such as Melford Spiro and Gananath Obeyesekere – the ethnographic monographs written by anthropologists now place little emphasis on the early childhood experiences which the psychoanalysts had argued were significant in generating culture. They take particular patterns of child-rearing as the manifestation rather than the cause of social knowledge. The assumption that non-Europeans thought is less rational has been superseded by recognition that all societies employ both deductive and inductive logic, both concrete and abstract reasoning, but that they do so within the limits that are determined by their own social interests. Societies differ psychologically not in their capabilities but in their modes of thought – through cognition and categorisations of space and time, the sexes and the natural world, their understandings of causality and individia, and which are encoded in their systems of representation, particularly language. What was once regarded as primitive (magical) thinking on the origins of sickness or misfortune appears now as a focus on the moral 'why' rather than the technical 'how', for societies differ in the focus of their immediate interests and practised knowledge. Indeed, in terms of the everyday understanding of sickness, Western medicine is less efficacious in relieving distress through its emphasis on the proximate mechanisms of misfortune, leaving the individual with chronic or serious illness little help in answering 'Why me?' (Kleinman 1988). In the case of severe mental illness we might note that Western psychiatry remains unable to offer its own patients any understanding, technical or moral, in terms of everyday knowledge (or, indeed, even of biology).

To recognise some other's pattern as especially 'cultural' is to assume a privileged perspective concerning it, whether colonial hubris or academic analysis. By the mid-1980s culture-specific illnesses had become recognised by critics as psychiatry's 'twilight zone' (Hughes 1985), 'what other people have, not us' (Hahn 1985). Medical interest in isolated and disembodied exotic patterns was seen to have directed attention from more immediate questions of economic development, poverty, exploitation, or nutrition, besides providing yet another justification of the otherness of non-Europeans, and one which ignored the role of Western medicine once in facilitating imperial expansion and now in the global marketing of untested pharmaceutical drugs.

How directly relevant had psychiatry been to imperialism? Both evidently developed in the same period. They shared certain modes of reasoning: we might note, for instance, affinities between the scientific objectification of illness experience as disease and the objectification of people as chattel slaves and colonial manpower, or the topological parallels between the nervous system and the colonial order. Both argued for an absence of 'higher' functions or sense of personal responsibility among patients and non-Europeans. The extent, however, to which any elaborated set of ideas which might be termed 'imperial psychiatry' provided a rationale for colonialism in British Africa or India is debatable: in a recent review we have argued that the evidence is meagre (Littlewood 1993a; cf. McCulloch 1994). With remarkably few exceptions (Laubscher 1937; Tooth 1950; Carothers 1953), the small number of colonial psychiatrists barely participated in the debates I have outlined above. Segregated facilities, of course (Lugard 1929; Ernst 1991); prejudice and neglect, undoubtedly, but hardly practicable ideologies for racial or cultural inferiority. One possible exception was the common medical assumption in the 1940s that too rapid social change (that is, access to schools and wage labour) was causing an increase in African psychiatric illness (Tooth 1950; Carothers 1953), but this increase was often explained by others as a better access to hospital services. This argument could of course be turned on its head by arguing that it was colonisation, not 'change', that was pathogenic (Mannoni 1950). Whilst the few colonial psychiatrists were quite tangential to the making of Colonial Office policy (and were themselves rather 'marginal' individuals within both British and colonial society: McCulloch 1994), in the francophone colonies and in Haiti, local Black psychiatrists developed radical critiques of European domination to argue for a distinct 'African identity' as against the settlers, and one which was couched in terms of *ethnopsychiatry* (Mars 1946; Fanon 1952). Ethnographers like W. H. R. Rivers (1924) and Bronislaw Malinowski (1927), aspects of whose work developed into what was to become medical anthropology, whilst they relied on missionary evidence and colonial office support, did not significantly influence British policy in Africa or elsewhere (Goody 1995). If diseases in the colonies were of any political interest to the metropolis, the concern was not madness but the acute infections which threatened to deprive the imperial administration of its labour force (Lyons 1992), or else the psychological health of the colonists themselves (Price 1913; Culpin 1953; Littlewood 1985; Ernst 1991; Barrell 1991).

By contrast, in the United States, psychiatry was deployed extensively during the nineteenth and twentieth centuries to justify what one may term the internal colonisation of Amerindians and African-Americans (Haller 1970). This was not simply because of the greater political influence of medicine in the United States. In the early stages of imperial expansion, domination is explicitly economic or military, and any necessary justification rests simply on evident technical or administrative superiority, sometimes manifest destiny, security of trade or the historical requirements of civilisation; only when dominated peoples 'inside the walls' threaten to achieve some sort of equality do apologies appear couched as a discourse on primitive pathology or biological inferiority (Littlewood and Lipsedge 1982). To an extent we may argue that Europe prepared to abandon her settlements well before equality threatened (except for the significant instances of Kenya, Algeria and the French Caribbean: on which see Vint 1932; Carothers 1954; Fanon 1952), and before colonial administrations had established much beyond a basic mental hospital for the native criminally insane. (Space prevents consideration here of the special case of South Africa [Littlewood 1993a].) In North America, arguments in favour of the emancipation of slaves had appeared by the time of Independence only to be countered by medical justifications for continued servitude which invoked such novel diseases as *drapetomania* (the impulse to escape) (Brigham 1832) or even, as argued by Bejamin Rush (1799), that African ancestry was itself an attenuated disease; justifications which became even more necessary for White supremacy after Emancipation. Among Native Americans, for whom collective political action was impossible after they were dispersed on reservations at the 'boundary' of the European state, twentieth-century administrators and medical officers developed increasingly psychological – and thence psychopathological – explanations to explain their high rates of suicide, alcoholism and general failure to participate in national life: the internalisation of the frontier as Andreas Heinz has put it.

Contemporary anthropologists have proposed that all illnesses may be said to be 'culture-bound' in that our adaptation to illness experience is always socially prescribed, whilst human behaviour can never be taken in independence from human action. The classic 'cultural syndromes' still remain as tilillating relief in the margins of psychiatric textbooks in the 1990s. Often the hearsay repetition of previous descriptions, travellers' tales and missionary anxieties, frequently in their most bizarre form, they distort local significance and context in providing a voyeuristic image of the other. The windigo cannibal-compulsion has now been recognised as psychiatric folklore, a 'near mythical syndrome' with perhaps three reported instances and one which has never been observed by Europeans (Neutra *et al.* 1977). Similar doubts have been cast on the evidence for *voodoo death* ('pointing the bone') in which awareness that one had been ensorcered apparently precipitated sudden death through 'a fatal spirit of despondency' (Jarvis [1872] cited by Mauss 1927 [see Chapter 6]; Eastwell 1982). Psychiatrists concerned with establishing basic mental health services in post-colonial Africa and Asia have deplored the endless collecting of novel syndromes 'by a host of short-term visitors [producing] a wealth of data about some strange ritual of an obscure tribe, analysed with style and erudition, but without comment on general trends particularly as they relate to the more mundane aspects of clinical psychiatry' (German 1972; but compare the psychiatrist De Jong 1987). For those concerned with establishing basic medical services and providing humane treatment in situations of poverty and exploitation, debates on the cultural specificity of suffering may appear otiose.

And yet 'culture-bound syndromes' represent salient instances of a particular community's dilemmas, as extreme if sometimes contentious representations of human distress in its distinctive milieu. To essentialise such social dramas as medical diseases in independence of everyday meanings or other experiences of distress, or in independence of the political context of our observation, is to render them exotic curiosities. To ignore them altogether is to render human adversity bland and familiar, to affirm that the European's experience alone is true, and thus to naturalise the patterns of Western psychiatric illnesses, to conform them as transcending our intentions, as necessary and immutable.

It may be reasonably objected that the very idea of culture-specific pathology is redundant, not just in the normative assumptions which give rise to the idea of 'pathology' for any domain (whether biological, psychological, or social), but as a residue of colonial reading of local practices as medico-legal problems (*amok*), superstition (*dhat*), hysteria (spirit possession), or other neuroses (*piblokto*, *latah*): patterns which then were rather optimistically fitted into the nosology of European medicine. For 'We predicate of the thing what lies in the method of representation. Impressed by the possibility of a comparison, we think we are perceiving a state of affairs of the highest generality' (Wittgenstein 1958: para. 105). Two related questions remain in dispute: (1) the distinctiveness which by definition any local syndrome must demonstrate relative to the ease with which it can be placed in a more general category; and whether such a category is to be derived from its symptomatology (the current psychiatric preference), from its biological correlates (Simons and Hughes 1985), or else from some more sociological criterion such as local understanding or political context (Littlewood and Lipsedge 1987); (2) what actually constitutes culture-binding – whether the 'syndrome' is just the local recognition of a global reality (*amok* properly being the psychotic illness schizophrenia), or an inappropriate demonstration of shared sentiments (the *dhat* syndrome as an excessive male concern with South Asian notions of purity and semen loss), or the adult's representation of traumatic childhood experience (psychoanalytical interpretations of the probably factitious Ojibwa *witigo*), or the manifestation of collective tensions in certain pivotal individuals (Somali *sar*, Lewis 1969) or the conventional resolution of such identified tensions (*ibid.*), or individual self-mastery against particular constraints (Sudanese *zar*, Boddy 1989). The same pattern may be variously identified as norm, illness, aetiology, or treatment, as resistance or performance. Restricting ourselves to the local ethnography may allow us to avoid categorisation but it hardly facilitates cross-cultural comparison: surely one of medicine's imperatives, as well as anthropology's.

REFERENCES

Ackernecht, E. (1943) 'Psychopathology, primitive medicine and primitive culture', *Bulletin of the History of Medicine*, 14: 30–68.

Barrell, J. (1991) *The Infection of Thomas De Quincey: A Psychopathology of Imperialism*. New Haven, CT: Yale University Press.

Beard, G. M. (1881) *American Nervousness: Its Causes and Consequences*. New York: Putnam.

Benedict, R. (1935) *Patterns of Culture*. London: Routledge & Kegan Paul.

Benedict, R. (1946) *The Chrysanthemum and the Sword: Patterns of Japanese Culture*. Boston, MA: Houghton Mifflin.

Bevis, W. M. (1921) 'Psychological traits of the southern Negro with observations as to some of his psychoses', *American Journal of Psychiatry*, 1: 69–78.

Birnbaum, K. (1923) 'Der Aufbau der Psychosen'. Translated as 'The Making of a Psychosis' in S. R. Hirsch and M. Shepherd (eds) (1974) *Themes and Variation in European Psychiatry*. Bristol: Wright.

Bleuler, E. (1911) *Dementia Praecox*. New York: International Universities Press.

Bloch, M. and Bloch, J. (1980) 'Women and the dialectics of nature'. In C. MacCormack and M. Strathern (eds), *Nature, Culture, Gender*. Cambridge: Cambridge University Press.

Boddy, J. (1989) *Words and Alien Spirits: Woman, Men and the Zar Cult in Northern Sudan*. Madison, WI: University of Wisconsin Press.

Boudin, J. (1857) *Traité de Géographie et de Statistiques Médicales et des Maladies Endémiques*. Paris: Baillière.

Bourdieu, P. (1977) *Outline of a Theory of Practice*. Cambridge: Cambridge University press.

Bourguignon, E. (1976) 'The effectiveness of religious healing movements: a review of recent literature', *Transcultural Psychiatric Research Review*, 13: 5–21.

Brigham, A. (1832) *Remarks on the Influence of Mental Cultivation upon Health*. Hartford, NY: Huntingdon.

Brown, T. M. (1985) 'Descartes, dualism and psychosomatic medicine'. In W. F. Bynum, R. Porter and M. Shepherd (eds) *The Anatomy of Madness*, Vol. 1. London: Tavistock.

Carothers, J. C. (1953) *The African Mind in Health and Disease*. Geneva: World Health Organisation.

Carothers, J. C. (1954) *The Psychology of Mau Mau*. Nairobi: Government Printers.

Carr, J. E. (1978) 'Ethno-behaviourism and the culture-bound syndromes: the case of amok', *Culture, Medicine and Psychiatry*, 2: 269–93.

Cheyne, G. (1734) *The English Malady*, cited in V. Skultans (1979) *English Madness: Ideas on Insanity 1580–1890*. London: Routledge & Kegan Paul.

Collingwood, R. G. (1945) *The Idea of Nature*. Oxford: Clarendon Press.

Cooper, J. E. and Sartorius, N. (1977) 'Cultural and temporal variation in schizophrenia: a speculation on the importance of industrialisation', *British Journal of Psychiatry*, 130: 50–5.

Csordas, T. J. (1994) *The Sacred Self: A Cultural Phenomenology of Charismatic Healing*. Berkeley: University of California Press.

Culpin, M. (1953) 'Neurasthenia in the tropics', *The Practitioner*, 85: 146–54.

De Jong, J. T. V. M. (1987) *A Descent into African Psychiatry*. Amsterdam: Royal Tropical Institute.

Desjarlais, R. (1993) *Body and Emotion*. Philadelphia, PA: University of Pennsylvania Press.

Devereux, G. (1951) *Reality and Dream: Psychotherapy of a Plains Indian*. New York: International Universities Press.

Devereux, G. (1956) 'The normal and abnormal: the key problem in psychiatric anthropology'. Reprinted (trans.) in Devereux 1970.

Devereux, G. (1970). *Essais d'Ethnopsychiatrie Générale*. Paris: Gallimard.

Doi, T. (1971) *Amae no Kozo*. Trans. as *The Anatomy of Dependence*. Tokyo: Kodansha.

Dow, J. (1986) 'Universal aspects of symbolic healing: a theoretical synthesis', *American Anthropologist* 88: 56–7.

Easlea, B. (1980) *Witch Hunting, Magic and the New Philosophy: An Introduction to the Debates of the Scientific Revolution 1450–1750*. Sussex: Harvester.

Eastwell, H. D. (1982) 'Voodoo death and the mechanism for the despatch of the dying in East Arnhem', *American Anthropologist*, 84: 5–18.

Ernst, W. (1991) *Mad Tales from the Raj: The European Insane in British India*. London: Routledge.

Evans-Pritchard, E. E. (1940) *The Nuer*. Oxford: Oxford University Press.

Fanon, F. (1952) *Peau Noir, Masques Noirs*. Paris: Seuil.

Field, M. J. (1960) *Search for Security: An Ethno-Psychiatric Study of Rural Ghana*. London: Faber & Faber.

Fisher, L. E. (1985) *Colonial Madness: Mental Health in the Barbadian Social Order*. New Brunswick, NJ: Rutgers University Press.

Frank, J. D. (1961) *Persuasion and Healing: A Comparative Study of Psychotherapy*. New York: Schocken.

Fumaroli, M. (1996) 'A Scottish Voltaire: John Barclay and the character of nations', *Times Literary Supplement*, 19 January: 16–17.

Ganser, S. J. M. (1897) 'A peculiar hysterical state'. Translated in S. R. Hirsch and

M. Shepherd (Eds) (1974) *Themes and Variation in European Psychiatry.* Bristol: Wright.

Gaskell, S. (1860) 'On the want of better provisions for the labouring and middle classes when attacked or threatened with insanity', *Journal of Mental Science*, 6: 321–7.

Geertz, C. (1986) 'Anti-anti-relativism', *American Anthropologist*, 86: 263–78.

Geertz, H. (1968) 'Latah in Java: a theoretical paradox', *Indonesia*, 3: 93–104.

German, A. A. (1972) 'Aspects of clinical psychiatry in sub-Saharan Africa', *British Journal of Psychiatry*, 121: 461–79.

Gilman, S. L. (185) *Difference and Pathology: Stereotypes of Sexuality, Race and Madness.* Ithaca, NY: Cornell University Press.

Good, B. J. and Good, M.-J. D. (1982) 'Towards a meaning-centred analysis of popular illness categories'. In A. Marsella and G. M. White (eds) *Cultural Conceptions of Mental Health and Therapy.* Dordrecht: Reidel.

Good, B. and Good, M. (1986) 'The cultural context of diagnosis and therapy: a view from medical anthropology'. In M. Miranda and H. Kitano (eds) *Mental Health Research Practice in Minority Communities: Development of Culturally Sensitive Training Programmes.* Washington, DC: Department of Health and Human Services.

Good, B. and Good, M.-J. D. (1992) 'The comparative study of Greeko-Islamic medicine: the integration of medical knowledge into real symbolic contexts'. In C. Leslie and A. Young (eds), *Paths to Asian Medical Knowledge.* Berkeley: University of California Press.

Goody, J. (1995) *The Expansive Moment: Anthropology in Britain and Africa 1918–1970.* Cambridge: Cambridge University Press.

Greenless, T. D. (1895) 'Insanity among the natives of South Africa', *Journal of Mental Science*, 41, 697–708.

Gregory, M. (1939) *Psychotherapy, Scientific & Religious.* London: Macmillan.

Hahn, R. A. (1985) 'Culture-bound syndromes unbound', *Social Science and Medicine*, 21: 165–80.

Haller, J. S. (1970) 'The physician versus the Negro: medical and anthropological concepts of race in the nineteenth century', *Bulletin of the History of Medicine*, 44: 154–67.

Harraway, D. (1989) *Primate Visions: Gender, Race and Nature in the World of Modern Science.* New York: Routledge.

Hughes, C. C. (1985) 'Culture-bound or construct-bound?' In Simons and Hughes (1985).

Jackson, J. H. (1884) *Croonian Lectures on the Evolution and Dissolution of the Nervous System.* Cambridge: Cambridge University Press.

Janet, P. (1925) *Psychological Healing: A Historical and Cultural Study.* London: Allen & Unwin.

Jaspers, K. (1963) *General Psychopathology*, 7th edn, trans. M. Hamilton. Manchester: Manchester University press.

Jones, E. (1924) 'Mother-right and the sexual ignorance of savages'. Reprinted in E. Jones (1974) *Psycho-myths, Psycho-history: Essays in Applied Psychoanalysis.* New York: Stonehill.

Jung, C. G. (1930) 'Your Negroid and Indian behaviour', *Forum*, 83: 193–9.

Kakar, S. (1978) *The Inner World: A Psychoanalytical Study of Childhood and Society in India.* Delhi: Oxford University press.

Kapferer, B. (1993) *A Celebration of Demons: Exorcism and the Aesthetics of Healing in Sri Lanka.* Oxford: Berg.

Kenny, M. (183) 'Paradox lost: the latah problem revisited', *Journal of Nervous and Mental Disease*, 171: 159–67.

Kiev, A. (1964) 'The study of folk psychiatry'. In A. Kiev (ed.) *Magic, Faith and Healing: Studies in Primitive Psychiatry Today*. New York: Free Press.

Kiev, A. (1972) *Transcultural Psychiatry*. Harmondsworth, Mx: Penguin.

Kirmayer, L. (1993) 'Healing and the invention of metaphor: the effectiveness of symbols revisited', *Culture, Medicine and Psychiatry*, 17: 161–95.

Kleinman, A. (1986) *Social Origins of Distress and Disease: Depression, Neurasthenia and Pain in Modern China*. New Haven, CT: Yale University Press.

Kleinman, A. (1988) *Rethinking Psychiatry: From Cultural Category to Personal Experience*. New York: Free Press.

Kleinman, A. and Sung, L. H. (1979) 'Why do indigenous practitioners successfully heal?', *Social Science and Medicine*, 13: 7–26.

Kraepelin, E. (1904) 'Vergleichende Psychiatrie'. Trans. as 'Comparative psychiatry', in S. R. Hirsch and M. Shepherd (eds) (1974) *Themes and Variation in European Psychiatry*, Bristol: Wright.

La Barre, W. (1970) *The Ghost Dance: Origins of Religion*. London: Allen & Unwin.

Laderman, C. (1991) *Taming the Winds of Desire: Psychology, Medicine and Aesthetics in Malay Shamanistic Performances*. Berkeley: University of California Press.

Lambo, T. A. (1955) 'The role of cultural factors in paranoid psychoses among the Yoruba tribe', *Journal of Mental Science*, 101: 239–66.

Laubscher, B. J. F. (1937) *Sex, Custom and Psychopathology: A Study of South African Pagan Natives*. London: Routledge.

Lawrence, R. M. (1910) *Primitive Psychotherapy and Quackery*. London: Constable.

Lee, S. (1996) 'Reconsidering the status of anorexia nervosa as a Western culture-bound syndrome', *Social Science and Medicine*, 42: 21–34.

Leff, J. et al. (1987) 'Influence of relatives' expressed emotion on the course of schizophrenia in Chandigarh', *British Journal of Psychiatry*, 151: 166–73.

Lévi-Strauss, C. (1967) 'The effectiveness of symbols'. In *Structural Anthropology*. New York: Doubleday.

Lewis, I. M. (1969) 'Spirit possession in Northern Somaliland'. In J. Beattie and J. Middleton (eds) *Spirit Mediumship and Society in Africa*. London: Routledge & Kegan Paul.

Lewontin, R. C., Rose, S. and Kamin, L. J. (1984) *Not in Our Genes: Biology, Ideology and Human Nature*. New York: Pantheon.

Littlewood, R. (1984) 'La migration des syndromes liés á la culture', *Psychopathologie Africaine*, 20(1): 5–16.

Littlewood, R. (1985) 'Jungle madness: some observations on expatriate psychopathology', *International Journal of Social Psychiatry*, 31(3): 194–7.

Littlewood, R. (1991) 'Against pathology: the new psychiatry and its critics', *British Journal of Psychiatry*, 159: 696–702.

Littlewood, R. (1992) 'DSM-IV and culture: Is the classification intentionally valid?', *Psychiatric Bulletin*, 16: 257–61.

Littlewood, R. (1993a) 'Ideology, camouflage or contingency? Racism in British psychiatry', *Transcultural Psychiatric Research Review*, 30: 243–90.

Littlewood, R. (1993b) *Pathology and Identity: The Work of Mother Earth in Trinidad*. Cambridge: Cambridge University Press.

Littlewood, R. (1993c) 'Culture-bound syndromes: cultural comments'. In J. E.

Mezzich, A. Kleinman, H. Fabrega and D. Parron (eds) *Working Papers for the DSM-IV Cultural Committee*. New York: American Psychiatric Press.

Littlewood, R. (1994) 'Verticality as the idiom for mood and disorder: a note on an eighteenth-century representation', *British Medical Anthropology Review*, (n.s.) 2(1): 44–8.

Littlewood, R. (1995) 'Psychopathology and personal agency: modernity, culture change and eating disorder in South Asian societies', *British Journal of Medical Psychology*, 68: 45–63.

Littlewood, R. (1996) 'Ethnopsychiatry'. In A. Barnard and J. Spencer (eds) *Encyclopaedic Dictionary of Social and Cultural Anthropology*. London: Routledge.

Littlewood, R. and Lipsedge, M. (1982) *Aliens and Alienists: Ethnic Minorities and Psychiatry*. Harmondsworth, Mx: Penguin.

Littlewood, R. and Lipsedge, M. (1987) 'The butterfly and the serpent', *Culture, Medicine and Psychiatry*, 11: 289–335.

Loudon, J. (1959) 'Psychogenic disorder and social conflict among the Zulu'. In M. K. Opler (ed.) *Culture and Mental Health*. New York: Macmillan.

Lugard, F. D. (1929) *The Dual Mandate in British Tropical Africa*. Edinburgh: Blackwood.

Lyons, M. (1992) *The Colonial Disease: A Social History of Sleeping Sickness in Northern Zaire 1900–1940*. Cambridge: Cambridge University Press.

McCulloch, J. (1994) *Colonial Psychiatry and the African Mind*. Cambridge: Cambridge University Press.

McDougall, I. (1989) *Theatres of the Body*. London: Free Association Books.

Madden, R. R. (1857) *Phantasmata: Or, Illusions and Fanaticisms of Protean Forms Productive of Great Evils*. London: Newby.

Malhotra, H. K. and Wig, T. (1975) 'Dhat syndrome: a culture-bound sex neurosis', *Archives of Sexual Behaviour*, 4: 519–28.

Malinowski, B. (1927) *Sex and Repression in Savage Society*. London: Routledge.

Mangan, J. A. (ed.) (1993) *The Imperial Curriculum: Racial Images and Education in the Colonial Experience*. London: Routledge.

Mannoni, O. (1950 *Psychologie de la colonisation*. Paris: Seuil.

Mars, L. (1946) *La Lutte contre la folie*. Port-au-Prince: Imprimerie de l'Etat.

Mauss, M. (1926) 'The physical effect on the individual of the idea of death suggested by the collectivity;. Translated in M. Mauss (1979) *Society and Psychology*. London: Routledge & Kegan Paul.

Michaelis, J. D. (1814) *Commentaries on the Law of Moses* (trans). London: Rivington.

Morel, B. A. (186) *Traité des Maladies Mentales*. Paris: Masson.

Neutra, R., Levy, J. E. and Parker, D. (1977) 'Cultural expectations versus reality in Navaho seizure patterns and sick roles', *Culture, Medicine and Psychiatry*, 1: 255–75.

O'Brien, H. A. (1883) 'Latah', *Journal of the Royal Asiatic Society (Straits Branch)*, 11: 143–53.

Oxley, T. (1849) 'Malay amoks', *Journal of the Indian Archipelago and Eastern Asia*, 3: 532–3.

Parker, S. (1960) 'The windigo psychosis', *American Anthropologist*, 62: 602–55.

Price, G. B. (1913) 'Discussion on the causes of invaliding from the tropics', *British Medical Journal*, ii: 1290–7.

Prince, R. (1960) 'The "brain-fag" syndrome in Nigerian students', *Journal of Mental Science* 106: 559–70.

Prince, R. (1968) 'The changing pattern of depressive syndromes in Africa', *Canadian Journal of African Studies*, 1: 177–92.

Richardson, A. and Hofkosh, S. (eds) (1996) *Romanticism, Race and Imperial Culture*. Indianapolis: Indiana University Press.

Ritenbaugh, C. (1982) 'Obesity as a culture-bound syndrome', *Culture, Medicine and Psychiatry* 6: 347–64.

Rivers, W. H. R. (1924) *Medicine, Magic and Religion*. London: Kegan Paul, Trench & Trubner.

Roheim, G. (1950) *Psychoanalysis and Anthropology: Culture, Personality and the Unconscious*. New York: International University Press.

Roseman, M. (1991) *Temiar Music and Medicine*. Berkeley: University of California Press.

Rush, B. (1799) 'Observations intended to favour a supposition that the black colour (as it is called) of the Negroes is derived from the leprosy', *Transactions of the American Philosophical Society*, 4: 289–297.

Sachs, W. (1937) *Black Hamlet*. London: Bles.

Sargant, W. (1973) *The Mind Possessed: From Ecstasy to Exorcism*. London: Heinemann.

Sartorius, N. (1983) *Depressive Disorders in Different Cultures*. Geneva: World Health organisation.

Scheff, T. (1979) *Catharsis in Healing, Ritual and Drama*. Berkeley: University of California Press.

Schneider, K. (1959) *Clinical Psychopathology*, (5th edn, trans.). New York: Grune & Stratton.

Seligman, C. G. (1928) 'The unconscious in relation to anthropology', *British Journal of Psychology*, 18: 373–87.

Seligman, C. G. (1929) 'Sex, temperament, conflict and psychosis in a Stone Age population', *British Journal of Medical Psychology*, 9: 187–228.

Shweder, R. A. (1985) 'Menstrual pollution, soul loss and the comparative study of emotions'. In A. Kleinman and B. Good (Eds) *Culture and Depression*. Berkeley: California University Press.

Simons, R. C. (1980) 'The resolution of the latah paradox', *Journal of Nervous and Mental Disease*, 168: 195–206.

Simons, R. C. (1983) 'Latah II: problems with a purely symbolic interpretation', *Journal of Nervous and Mental Disease* 171: 168–715.

Simons, R. C. (1985) 'Nature and nurture. Belief and behaviour in the culture-bound syndromes'. In Simons and Hughes (1985).

Simons, R. C. and Hughes, C. C. (eds) (1985) *The Culture-Bound Syndromes: Folk Illnesses of Psychiatric and Anthropological Interest*. Dordrecht: Reidel.

Thomas, K. (1983) *Man and the Natural World: Changing Attitudes in Britain 1500–1800*. London: Allen lane.

Tooth, G. (1950) *Studies in Mental Illness in the Gold Coast*. Colonial Research Publication No. 6. London: HMSO.

Torrey, E. F. (1971) *The Mind Game: Witchdoctors and Psychiatrists*. New York: Emerson Hall.

Turner, V. (1964) An Ndembu doctor in practice. In A. Kiev (ed.) *Magic, Faith and Healing*. New York: Free Press.

Vint, F. W. (1932) 'A preliminary note on the cell content of the prefrontal cortex of the East African native', *East African Medical Journal*, 9: 30–55.

Warner, R. (1985) *Recovery from Schizophrenia: Psychiatry and Political Economy*. New York: Routledge & Kegan Paul.

Weinstein, E. (1962) *Cultural Aspects of Delusion*. New York: Free Press.

Williams, E. A. (1994) *The Physical and the Moral: Anthropology, Physiology and Philosophical Medicine in France 1750–1850*. Cambridge: Cambridge University Press.

Williams, R. (1958) *Culture and Society 1780–1950*. London: Chatto & Windus.

Wing, J. K. (1978) *Reasoning about Madness*. Oxford: Oxford University Press.

Wittgenstein, L. (1958) *Philosophical Investigations*. Oxford: Blackwell.

Yap, P. M. (1951) 'Mental diseases peculiar to certain cultures', *Journal of Mental Sciences*. 97: 313–37.

Yap, P. M. (1974) *Comparative Psychiatry: A Theoretical Framework*. Toronto: Toronto University press.

Young, A. (1993) Making facts and marking time in psychiatric research: an essay on the anthropology of scientific knowledge. Unpublished ms.

Young, A. (1995) *The Harmony of Illusions; Inventing Post-Traumatic Stress Disorder*. Princeton, NJ: Princeton University Press.

FURTHER GENERAL READING

Desjarlais, R. R. (1992) *Body and Emotion: The Aesthetics of Illness and Healing in the Nepal Himalayas*. Philadelphia: University of Pennsylvania Press.

A lively and readable introduction to more phenomenological readings of the ethnography of illness.

Good, B. (1994) *Medicine, Rationality and Experience: An Anthropological Perspective*. Cambridge: Cambridge University Press.

A 'state of the art' approach to medical anthropology, emphasising narrative and phenomenological approaches.

Kleinman, A. (1986) *Social Origins of Distress and Disease: Depression, Neurasthenia and Pain in Modern China*. New haven, CT: Yale University Press.

Study of the fate of the diagnosis of neurasthenia in and after the Cultural Revolution, and its relation to the Western concept of depression.

Kleinman, A. (1988) *Rethinking Psychiatry: From Cultural Category to Personal Experience*. New York: Free Press.

A critique of current social and epidemiological psychiatry from the perspective of the 'new cross-cultural psychiatry'.

Kleinman, A. and Good, B. (eds) (1985) *Culture and Depression: Studies in the Anthropology and Cross-Cultural Psychiatry of Affect and Disorder*. Berkeley: University of California Press.

Historical and cross-cultural studies in the idea of and experience of depression, suggesting the Western medical concept has limited cross-cultural relevance.

Littlewood, R. (1993) *Pathology and Identity: The Work of Mother Earth in Trinidad*. Cambridge: Cambridge University Press.

Detailed study of the old idea of mental illness and creativity, through the study of a new Caribbean religion.

Loudon, J. (ed.) (1976) *Social Anthropology and Medicine*. London: Academic Press.

Essays in British medical anthropology: a representative selection of papers from the mid-1970s.

Lutz, C. (1988) *Unnatural Emotions: Everyday Sentiments on a Micronesia Atoll and their Challenge to Western Theory*. Chicago: Chicago University Press.

The detailed ethnopsychology of a Micronesian island, pointing out the resonances with and differences from our accepted psychological and medical theories.

Marsella, A. J. and White, S. M. (eds) (1982) *Cultural Conceptions of Mental Health and Therapy*. Dordrecht: Reidel.

Essays on the conceptualisation of mental illness and its analogues in different societies.

Murphy, H. B. M. (1982) *Comparative Psychiatry*. Berlin: Springer.

Survey of cultural psychiatry with particular emphasis on broadly psychodynamic explanations.

Simons, R. C. and Hughes, C. C. (eds) (1985) *The Culture-Bound Syndromes: Folk Illnesses of Psychiatric and Anthropological Interest*. Dordrecht: Reidel.

Review of culture-specific illnesses with a particular interest in classification using a new schema of 'taxa'.

Wallace, E. R. (1983) *Freud and Anthropology*. new York: International University Press.

Survey of the interrelationship between psychoanalysis and social anthropology.

Widiger, T. A. et al. (eds) (1997) *DSM-IV Source Book*, Volume 3. Washington, DC: American Psychiatric Association.

Contains a review of the cultural background for illnesses listed in the latest version of the *American Diagnostic and Statistical Manual* (DSM). This was the first version of DSM seriously to attempt the inclusion of cultural data.

CHAPTER TWO

Experiments with the 'Jumpers' or 'Jumping Frenchmen' of Maine (1880)
George Beard

Beard, the American neurologist who described neurasthenia (nervous disability) in 1869, briefly outlines here a pattern of behaviour in the United States which he only partly understands as 'cultural', although he makes comparisons with contemporary religious revivalism and medieval 'servant-girl hysteria'. Indeed the individuals studied apparently had no French ancestry. Simons and Hughes (1985) argue that the Jumpers were an example of the 'startle matching taxon', local illnesses like latah (Malaysia) and imu (Japan) being local cultural elaborations of the mammalian startle response followed by imitation of the words or actions of others.

Dr Beard remarked, that two years before he had made a verbal statement upon this subject to the American Neurological Association, but at that time had not seen any case and derived his facts from conversation and correspondence with those who had requested him to scientifically investigate the subject. In this month of June he had visited Moosehead Lake and found the jumpers and experimented with them, taking care to eliminate the six sources of error that complicate all experiments with living human beings. He found that what had been claimed was true and more than true. One of the jumpers while sitting in his chair with a knife in his hand was told to throw it, and he threw it quickly, so that it stuck in a beam opposite; at the same time he repeated the order to throw it, with cry or utterance of alarm resembling that of hysteria or epilepsy. He also threw away his pipe when filling it with tobacco when he was slapped upon the shoulder. Two jumpers standing near each other were told to strike, and they struck each other very forcibly. One jumper when standing by a window, was suddenly commanded by a person on the other side of the window, to jump, and he jumped straight up half a foot from the floor, repeating the order. When the commands are uttered in a quick loud voice the jumper repeats the order. When told to strike, he strikes, when told to throw it, he throws it, whatever he has in his hands. Dr Beard tried this power of repetition with the first part of the first line of Virgil's Aeneid and the first part of the first line of Homer's Iliad, and out-of-the-way words in the English language, with which the jumper could not be familiar, and he repeated or echoed the sound of the word as it came to him, in a quick, sharp voice, at the same time he jumped, or struck, or threw, or raised his shoulders, or made some other violent muscular motion. They could not help repeating the word or sound that came from the person that ordered them any more than they could help striking, dropping, throwing, jumping, or starting; all of these phenomena were indeed but parts of the general condition known as jumping. It was not necessary that the sound should come from a human being: any sudden or unexpected noise, as the explosion of a gun or pistol, the falling of a window, or the slamming of a door, provided it be unexpected and loud enough, would cause these jumpers to exhibit some one or all of these phenomena. One of these jumpers came very near cutting his 'throat' while shaving on hearing a door slam. They had been known to strike their fists against a red-hot stove; they had been known to jump into the fire and into water; they could not help striking their best friend; if near them, when ordered. The noise of a steam-whistle was especially obnoxious to them. One of these jumpers when taking some bromide of sodium in a tumbler, was told to throw it and he dashed the tumbler upon the floor. It was dangerous to startle them in any way when they had an axe or knife in their hand. All of the jumpers agree that it tires them to be jumped and they dread it, but they were constantly annoyed by their companions.

This disease was analogous to the mental or physical hysteria, the so-called servant-girl hysteria which was so often observed during the epidemics of the middle ages. It was a trancoidal condition: a temporary trance induced by reflex irritation, and the emotion of fear. In a certain sense we were all jumpers; an alarm of fire in a crowded building would have the same effect upon very many of us, producing trance with convulsive movements. An approximative analogue to these phenomena of 'jerks', as they were called, as to be found in certain religious revivals, and the 'holy rollers', those who under religious excitement rolled upon the floor, as observed in northern New Hampshire. In two respects this phenomenon of jumping was different from any analogue here given: *first*, the temporariness and momentariness of the phenomenon: it was all over in a second, and then the man was ready to be jumped again. in the mesmeric trance, which was a very good analogue of this condition, the entranced subject remained in that condition a long while, or at the will of the operator. Simply pointing with the finger at one of these jumpers, if done quickly and decidedly, would have the same effect as striking him: some persons were mesmerised in the same way. *Second*, it differed from the analogues in the persistence of the liability. The religious jerkers and holy rollers were victims of a condition that passed away after a time, while the jumper's liability to jump was a life-long condition from which they never recovered. One thing was certain, that these jumpers were not nervous: the phenomenon was not a symptom of neurasthenia, and in this it agreed with the servant-girl hysteria epidemic of the middle ages, with the jerkers and with the phenomenon of the 'holy rollers'. Psychologically, these jumpers were modest, quiet, retiring, deficient in power of self-assertion and push. They were not half French so far as Dr Beard could learn, and in this respect he had been misinformed. They were strong and capable of doing hard physical work, and some of them could read and write and were as intelligent as the class to which they belonged. Jumping was hereditary and ran in families: there were fifteen cases in four families. Women were rarely jumpers, young children four or five years of age might begin to jump; two such children were in one family. The disease was epidemic and restricted mostly to the northern part of New Hampshire, Maine, and Canada, although cases had been reported among the Malays upon the other side of the globe. This disease was probably an evolution of tickling: the habit of tickling each other in the woods.

In regard to prognosis Dr Beard said, once a jumper, always a jumper. Dr Beard tried bromisation in one case without any very great effect. Psychologically this subject was of the highest conceivable interest in its relation to trance, the involuntary life, the departments of science that are now exciting the attention of the ablest neurologists in the world. Dr Beard claimed that his theory of trance, as explained in his work upon that subject, explained this phenomenon of jumping. The most incredible fact connected with the whole subject was not the existence of the phenomena above described, but that they had not been previously observed by science.

INTRODUCTION: REFERENCE

Simons, A. C. and Hughes, C. C. (1985) *The Culture-Bound Syndromes: Folk Illnesses of Psychiatric and Anthropological Interest.* Dordrecht: Reidel.

CHAPTER THREE

Comparative Psychiatry[1] (1904)

Emil Kraepelin

In the Introduction we have already referred to this paper which ushered in something we can understand as cultural psychiatry. Kraepelin (1856–1926) was Professor of Psychiatry at Heidelberg and then Munich, and undertook his trip to Java in 1904. From our contemporary viewpoint he relies too easily on racial biology. Now largely celebrated as the person who first distinguished what we now call schizophrenia (dementia praecox) from manic-depressive psychosis through their symptomatic differences, he was also prone to authoritarian judgements on political and historical issues, a matter which has given rise to much retrospective criticism (Shepherd 1995).

Comparative psychiatry, which involves the observation of mental disorders in different groups of people, enables us to examine a number of factors – sex, for example, or age, or occupational class. There are two basic ways in which comparative studies may help to advance our knowledge. On the one hand they can throw light on the causes of mental disorder, and on the other they provide a means of determining the influence which the patient's personality exerts on the particular form his illness assumes. So far almost all such studies have been limited to different groups within the same nation. We therefore do not know whether and in which respects the psychiatric morbidity of the French, English, or Italian nations differs from our own. Reliable companion is, of course, only possible if we are able to draw clear distinctions between identifiable illnesses, as well as between clinical states: moreover, our clinical concepts vary so widely that for the foreseeable future such comparison is possible only if the observations are made by one and the same observer. For this reason the data so far accumulated on mental disorders in foreign nations are valid in only a few respects, but the differences to be expected are so great that comparisons of this kind ought to be particularly fruitful and the findings which they yield ought to be reliable.

I therefore decided personally to conduct one such investigation in the asylum of Buitenzorg, in Java, where I was fortunate enough not only to enjoy the most friendly co-operation of the Director, Dr Hofmann, but also to find particularly favourable conditions for achieving my goal. I was thus able, in spite of great inherent difficulties, to show clearly that results can be obtained, and to demonstrate the lines on which this can be done.

The first question that arose was whether tropical climate and consequent dietary differences appreciably affect the clinical case material encountered. This question may be answered in the negative. The European patients cared for in Buitenzorg showed broadly the same clinical pictures as we see in our own country. Senile dementia is practically unknown among them, but this is accounted for by the special conditions of colonial service.

Among the external causes of mental disorder, drinking and other similar habits are of outstanding importance. Since the natives of Java drink no beverages which affect their mental state, alcoholic disorders are unknown. There were no illnesses caused by opium in the asylum. Not (as Dr Ellis, director of the asylum there, confirmed) were there any in Singapore, where the population is largely Chinese and where the use of opium is very widespread. Chewing of sirih, which is very common, does not appear to produce any sort of general disturbance. It is doubtful whether malaria affects the mental hospital population to any appreciable degree; at any rate there is no sure evidence of a higher rate of malarial psychoses.

One fact may be considered of particular interest. Out of 370 native-born patients there was not one case of progressive paralysis or cerebral syphilis, while among 50 male European patients there were eight, two of which had not been definitely confirmed. The military finding that syphilis is only about one-fifth as common in native-born soldiers as in European soldiers is hardly enough to explain the extent of this difference, especially since similar findings in other countries support the view that Europeans are particularly liable to develop a luetic paralysis. One is led to suppose that this may be due to deep-seated differences: these might be racial characteristics, or it might be a question of organic damage which makes the European less able than the native-born to withstand the effect of lues on the brain and on cerebral vessels. Apart from the tropical climate itself, alcohol might also well be a contributing factor.

Turning to those illnesses for which no known external cause has so far been established, we found dementia praecox, as we delineate it today, to be very common. This, of course, raises the question of how far this illness constitutes a clinical entity. It is possible that if it were divided into smaller groups, differences might emerge between the morbidity of the native-born and of the European population which we are not yet in a position to recognise. Manic-depressive insanity is decidedly less frequent in the native population than among Europeans, although it does occur. On the other hand, states which we may, with a greater or lesser degree of certainty, call 'psychic epilepsy' are relatively frequent.

Comparison between the native and the European populations is made more difficult in all these instances by the fact that the clinical symptomatology, while broadly in agreement with that seen here, presents certain very noteworthy differences in individual instances. This could contribute to settling the much disputed question of the part played by personal disposition in determining the particular form of a mental disorder. Of the numerous forms of dementia praecox encountered among Javanese not one of the symptoms common among Europeans was missing, but they were all much less florid, less distinctively marked. In particular, the catatonic phenomena found in native-born patients were rarely pronounced; auditory hallucinations, which are so frequent in our patients, played a very minor role; systematic delusional attenuated states were either absent altogether or present in an attenuated form. The illness was hardly ever preceded by a depressive phase, and states of violent excitement were likewise uncommon. It was also rare for illnesses to progress to those very severe forms of dementia which fill our asylums at home and which were also frequently seen in the European population of Java. The end state was usually one of vague, silly confusion, with no very striking outward accompaniments.

It is, of course, an open question whether the underlying processes there are basically the same as those which produce similar clinical pictures in our hospitals at home. Perhaps it will be possible to settle the matter by anatomical studies, but from the clinical point of view, based on a comparison between the phenomena of disease which I found there and those with which I was familiar at home, the overall similarity far outweighed the deviant features. It almost looked as though the differences might be explained as a shift in the frequency of occurrence of individual species of generic illness. The cases which preponderate at home are comparatively rare over there, and vice versa. It is therefore not unreasonable to suppose that these differences may be due to the different ways in which the sick brain reacts. In particular the relative absence of delusions among the Javanese might be related to the lower stage of intellectual development attained, and the rarity of auditory hallucinations might reflect the fact that speech counts far less than it does with us and that thoughts tend to be governed more by sensory images.

Such considerations are supported by the further observations that manic-depressive illness, although unmistakably present, was found in a variety of clinically deviant forms. Depression, when it did occur, was usually only mild and fleeting, and feelings of guilt were never experienced. Manic excitement too was a great deal less marked and more uniform than we are accustomed to see here. Moderately severe, short-lived recurrent states of excitement were fairly frequent; their regular course and gradual abatement were more or less the same as occasionally we encounter here. It was sometimes difficult to interpret the clinical symptoms because the phenomena were too indefinite.

The illnesses which we ascribe particularly to Malaysian races are, of course, *amok* and *latah*. Here too it may be suggested that they are just special forms of illnesses which we know, but forms that are peculiar to the peoples in question. Latah is essentially the release of imitative automatism, with coprolalia: it is brought on by sudden pleasurable excitement, and the patient remains completely rational. Its short-lived course recalls similar observations which we have occasionally made on hysterics at home. Amok, on the other hand, is not a unitary disease, but a general term used to describe wild, instinctive deeds of violence performed in a state of clouded consciousness. In some cases it represents the onset of catatonia, in which case it does not differ from some of our own patients who suddenly make attempts on their life or try to kill other people. In most cases, however, the symptomatology was in keeping with that seen in psychic epilepsy. Other more or less distinct forms of epilepsy were also found. There were, however, isolated cases which, in spite of many clinical similarities, could not be equated entirely with epileptic twilight states. It must for the present remain an open question whether these states represent specific illnesses: here too one might suggest, perhaps, the possibility of larval malarial attacks.

At all events there are at present no compelling grounds for assuming that the natives of Java suffer from new and unknown forms of insanity, particularly when we remember that even in Europe we encounter numerous cases which cannot easily be accommodated within accepted clinical groups. On the other hand, however, the illness with which we are familiar undergo changes in Java which we can with some justification attribute to the patients' racial characteristics. Comparative psychiatric research here offers rich rewards and deserves the attention of investigators far beyond the medical field. If racial characteristics are reflected in a nation's religion and customs, in its spiritual and artistic achievements, in its political activity and in its historical development, they must also find expression in the frequency and clinical forms of its mental disorders, especially those which have no external cause. The study of mental disorders has afforded us deep insights into the workings of our individual mental lives, and we may correspondingly hope that the psychiatric study of a nation will further our understanding of its psychological make-up. In this sense comparative psychiatry is perhaps destined to be an important adjunct of ethnic psychology.

INTRODUCTION: REFERENCE

Shepherd, M. (1995) 'Two faces of Emil Kraepelin', *British Journal of Psychiatry*, 167: 174–83.

NOTES

1. 'Vergleichende Psychiatrie' (1904), *Zentbl. Nervenheilk. Psychiat.*, 27: 433–7. Translated by H. Marshall.

CHAPTER FOUR

Medicine, Magic and Religion (1924)
W. H. R. Rivers

Rivers (1864–1922) is remembered by anthropologists as the founder of the 'genealogical method' in kinship studies (Slobodin 1978), and by psychologists and psychiatrists for his work on shell-shock in the First World War and for his acceptance of a modified Freudian theory. His lectures on what we would now call medical anthropology were given in 1915 to the Royal College of Physicians and were collected together after his death by G. Elliot Smith, his colleague at University College London. Although the work was produced for a medical audience, Rivers closely argues the interrelationship of the 'medical' and the 'religious' in the cases he discusses. Despite his evolutionary assumptions, he leaves us with a strong case for the rationality of the practices he describes. The extract begins at the start of Chapter II.

In the first chapter I dealt especially with the relations between medicine and magic, using the latter term for two kinds of processes: that in which disease is ascribed to direct human agency, and that in which the methods of treatment involve no element of appeal to higher powers, in spite of the fact that disease is ascribed to the action of spiritual beings.

PROCESSES OF DIAGNOSIS AND PROGNOSIS

It may have been noted that little was said about the processes of diagnosis and prognosis. Although the nature of the belief in causation directly determines the mode of treatment, the discovery of the cause usually needs no special rite. It is inferred immediately by the patient or his friends from their knowledge of acts, on the part of the patient, which would have offended a man or spirit believed to have the power of inflicting disease.

Where definite rites are performed for the purpose of diagnosis these often have a religious character, even where the treatment appears to be entirely of a magical order. Thus, in Murray Island, in Torres Straits, disease is believed to occur by the action of certain men who, through their possession of objects called *zogo* and their knowledge of the appropriate rites, have the power of inflicting disease. Thus, one *zogo* is believed

43

to make people lean and hungry and at the same time to produce dysentery; another will produce constipation, and a third insanity.

When anyone falls ill the patient may know at once whom he has offended, so that no special process of diagnosis is necessary, but often the patient or his friends have recourse to certain men who own a shrine called *tomog zogo*, where a process of divination is carried out. This shrine consists of a number of stones and shells arranged so as to form an irregular plan of the island.[1] The place is visited at daybreak by those who have special knowledge. If a lizard comes out of one of the shells, the house or village which that shell represents will indicate the abode of the person by whom the sickness has been produced. If two lizards come from different shells and fight, the shell from which the victorious lizard has emerged would represent the abode of the sorcerer. This shrine was also consulted for the purpose of prognosis, a dead lizard being a sign of the death of the patient. Various other forms of divination are practised. In Murray Island, and still more in the western islands of the Torres Straits, the skulls of relatives are used for this purpose, the ghost to whom the skull belonged in life giving the desired information in a dream.[2]

In the case of the *tomog zogo* of Murray island we do not know enough of the attitude towards the animals who provide the material for diagnosis to enable us to say how far the process can be called religious, but the reference to the skulls of ancestors, which takes place in these and other islands of Torres Straits, certainly belongs to the category of religion, forming part of a religious cult of ancestors.

The cult of ancestors is still more definite in Melanesia. In many parts of that ethnographic province this cult provides an example of religion of a relatively high order, in which the elements of supplication and propitiation are clearly present. It may be noted that, here again, the appeal to the ghosts of ancestors may take place for the purpose of diagnosis in rites which have otherwise a definitely magical character.

Methods of prognosis are even more apt to have a purely religious character. Thus, when a chief in the island of Ambrim in the New Hebrides is gravely ill, little seems to be done by way of treatment; but the son or brother of the sick man takes a pig to a heap of stones called *worwor*, which had been built when the chief acquired his rank. After killing the pig on the *worwor* it is left there as a gift for the ghosts of the chief's ancestors. That night the ghost of the father of the sick man will talk to his son or brother in his sleep, and will say whether the sick man will or will not recover. In the latter case, the people may not be content with the adverse prognosis, but will kill a second pig of a kind more valuable than the first, in the hope of obtaining a more favourable answer. At the same time prayer is offered to the ancestor to allow the sick man to stay with his friends. The only treatment employed is to rub the sick man, but this is evidently of little account beside the strictly religious practices of divination by dream and of prayer, by which the people seek to discover, and, if need be, attempt to avert a fatal result.

It is, I think, a matter of interest that the aid of superhuman or divine powers should show itself so definitively in connection with prognosis. It is instructive that this difficult and uncertain art should, in such a people as the Melanesians, bring out more clearly than any other aspect of their leechcraft the close interdependence of medicine and religion.

DISEASE ATTRIBUTED TO INFRACTION OF TABOO

The close relation between the practice of medicine and the cult of the dead ancestors exists all through Melanesia, but probably the combined rites have nowhere reached a greater pitch of elaboration than in the western islands of the British Solomons, where the subject was carefully studied by Mr A. M. Hocart and myself some years ago. (I am greatly indebted to Mr Hocart for his permission to publish this preliminary extract from out joint work.)

In the little island of Mandegusu or Eddystone, where Mr Hocart and I spent several months, we found between the treatment of disease and certain religious practices, especially that of taboo, a connection so intimate that the account of medical practice is at the same time an account of taboo. The relation between the two is so close that it would be impossible to deal with one independently of the other. Nearly every disease which occurs in this little island is ascribed to the infraction of a taboo on the fruit of certain trees, especially the coconut and betel-vine, the taboo, as well as the sign by which it is known, being called *kenjo*. The process of *kenjo* has a large number of varieties, each variety being the property of a man or small group of men, the right to practise being acquired, partly by purchase from, partly through instruction by, one already in possession of the art. The knowledge thus acquired concerns a number of rites, one carried out when the taboo is imposed, another when it is removed, and still another to allow fruit taken from tabooed trees to be used. In addition, a number of rites are learnt, by means of which to cure or ameliorate the disease which falls on one who uses fruit from the tabooed trees without the performance of the rites which should accompany its removal. Each of these rites has a special name, *salanga* being that used for the therapeutic process. With certain exceptions, all belong to the same man or group of men. Thus, it is only a man who is able to impose or remove the taboo who is able to treat the disease produced by its infraction, and, as we shall see shortly, there is a close resemblance between the rites connected with the process of taboo and those of the more strictly medical kind. Mr Hocart and I found about a hundred examples of such conjoined processes of taboo and medicine, and obtained a record of more than sixty. The following is an example of one of these processes, namely, that connected with the taboo called *kirengge*, the infraction of which produces epilepsy and other convulsive seizures.

The sign of the *kenjo* is put up on or by the side of the tree or trees to be tabooed, and consists of several plants, the number of leaves or shoots of each plant being usually four, the sacred number of the island. The taboo sign of *kirengge* also includes a stone and a coral, both of which irritate the skin when touched, as well as the butterfly called *kirengge*, the common use of this word for the butterfly and epilepsy being due to the resemblance between the movements of the insect and those of the disease.

The leaves and other objects are put in a forked stick by the side of the tree to be protected with the following formula:–

'This is yours, ye spirits of the *kenjo*; this yours, ye four old women, four old women who knew the *kenjo*. Ye four old women in Mbakia, be favourable. Noemali, be favourable. Kiambakia, Tupombakia, Saemali, Mbukumenia. Grant my prayer against the man who steals the *kenjo*. Ye two *lipa*, grant my prayer.' The proper names mentioned in this formula are those of dead women, who one knew the process, while the fifth is that of a special *tomate* or ghost, the *tomate kirengee*, apparently a personification of epilepsy, derived perhaps from some dead man who suffered from the disease. The *lipa* is a special kind of fish.

If the owner of the tree wishes to use any of its fruit, four springs of a plant called *nyou* are swept over the fruit with the words, 'I sweep it down to throw it away. Do not return to this man. Go away to thy mother; go away to thy father. Go away.' These words indicate that some influence is thus removed from the fruit, and there is reason to believe that this influence is that of the *tomate* or ghost by whom epilepsy is believed to be produced.

If it is desired to remove the taboo altogether from the tree, the leaves and other objects making up the *kenjo* sign are thrown away in some unfrequented spot, so that there is no danger that it shall be trodden upon, a proceeding which is believed to have fatal results. When the *kenjo* is removed, the following formula is uttered: 'Depart and go to the sky, do not remain on earth, thou spirit of the *kenjo*. Depart. Be cooled in the fresh water. Depart, looking to the sun; depart, looking at the sky; go up and adhere to the thunder that sounds in the sky. Go back, not to return. Depart.'

When anyone suffers from epilepsy or other convulsive seizure which is recognised as *kirengge*, he and his friends consult one known to have the power of imposing the *kenio kirengge*.

This man visits the patient and strokes him from the head downwards with four leaves called *nyou*, some moss, soot and scrapings of wood, uttering the formula: 'Stroke away. Stroke down and away. Cease thou. Let the man live; do not return. They have given me a good ring.' The last clause of this formula and two in that used in removing the taboo refer to the fee, the chief money of the island consisting of arm-rings. The patient is then fumigated with the smoke of certain leaves, and the patient sniffs the smoke while the leech utters over him the words: 'be favourable, thou ancient woman. Thou new spirit. Ye four ancient women.' Leaves are then put round the neck of the patient with the words, 'Be favourable, thou. Favour this man. Let him live.' A fillet is then put round the head of the patient, and a girdle of leaves over his shoulder, with the words, 'Be favourable and let the fits cease.' After saying these words the leech leaves the patient, and goes away without looking back. This treatment is carried out on the last four days of the waning moon. It is performed on two successive days; then a day is left for the spirit or spirits of the *kenjo* to work, and then on the fourth day the rites are again performed, this setting aside of the third day for the action of the higher powers being a regular feature of the *salanga* process of a *kenjo*. At the end of four months the whole process is repeated.

At the end of the treatment four small puddings are burnt on a fire by the leech with the words, 'Here is the pudding for you, the spirit of *kirengge*. Be favourable. Let this man go. Let me not return hereafter.' Four other puddings are put in the thatch of the patient's house.

THE RELIGIOUS ELEMENT

The religious element in these rites is obvious. The note of supplication runs through all the formulas, which can definitely be regarded as prayers to beings who have the power to withhold that for which they are asked. The burnt-offering at the end of the whole proceedings has clearly a propitiatory character, and may also be regarded as a thank-offering to the ghostly being or beings through whose intervention the successful treatment has been brought about.

The special point of interest, however, in these proceedings is the intimate blending of the therapeutic process with the institution of taboo, which both in this and other parts of Melanesia has a definite religious character. Disease is held to be the result of the infraction of a taboo imposed in the name and under the sanction of the ghosts of the dead. Taking the fruit of trees so protected is not published by the offender's fellow men, but punishment comes directly from the higher powers without any human intervention. The rites of the leech are only the means by which the help of these higher powers is obtained. They are designed to remove the misfortune which has followed the breaking of the taboo, which must be regarded as a sin rather than a crime. Though I have called the human agent a leech he might more fitly or just as fitly be regarded as a priest, whose special privilege it is to call on the higher powers to remove the penalty which the sufferer has brought upon himself by his sacrilege. Though the arm-ring given as a fee is kept by the leech, it is regarded as given to the spirits through whose activity the cure is brought about.

In addition to their beliefs in the production of disease, by the ghosts who watch over tabooed trees, the natives of Eddystone Island also believe in a number of beings with special names, such as Mateana, Sea, Ilongo, Paro, Mbimbigo, to whom the power of producing disease is ascribed. These beings are personifications of natural phenomena such as thunder-bolts, shooting stars, and the rainbow, and most of them have special haunts, often associated with the presence of shrines. Intrusion on these haunts is one of the causes to which disease is ascribed; but these beings are believed to inflict disease quite apart from any offence on the part of the victim. The most frequent mechanism, however, by which they are believed to produce sickness is through the breaking of a taboo. When a man falls ill with symptoms ascribed to Mateana, it is supposed that the disease has been inflicted by Mateana, owing to the infraction of a special taboo associated with this being, and called *kenjo* Mateana. It is assumed that Mateana would not have afflicted the sufferer with fever if he had not broken the taboo associated with this being. It is probably that we have here an example of fusion between two different beliefs, one in the produc-tion of disease by a personification of the thunderbolt, and another according to which disease is ascribed to a transgression of the institution of taboo.

RELIGIOUS CHARACTER ACQUIRED BY MAGICAL PROCESS

I hope to deal with this process of fusion on another occasion. All that I need point out now is that both the elements in this process of fusion are clearly of a religious character. Two sets of belief concerning the causation and treatment of disease have been unified without in any way destroying the religious character of the product of the fusion. There are, however, examples in Eddystone Island in which a similar process of fusion has given a religious character to processes for the production of disease which would otherwise fall clearly into the category of magic. Thus, the breaking of one kind of taboo exposes the transgressor to the action of one of a number of men called *njiama*, whose powers closely resemble those ascribed in many parts of the world to the evil eye. One who breaks this taboo falls ill with a set of symptoms, which are believed to show the action of a *njiama*. In some of these cases blood gushes from the mouth of the patient, who dies at once, but in slighter cases there is a definite rite of treatment which follows lines similar to those of other curative rites connected with taboos.

The infraction of another *kenjo*, *kenjo mba*, brings as its consequence a disease ascribed to the action of a sorcerer called *mba*, who is believed to produce disease by acting on a fragment of food or an object which has been used by the person on whom it is intended to inflict illness, the case thus falling into the third category of magic described in my first lecture. The action of a *mba* can take place quite independently of the breaking of a taboo, but the tendency of the people to regard disease as a punishment for sin is so strong that a sorcerer is not supposed to be able to effect his purpose unless his victim puts himself in the wrong by breaking a taboo.

The acquirement of a religious character by a process which is primarily of a magical kind shows itself in another way in connection with the sorcery of Eddystone Island. When a person is afflicted with illness believed to be due to the action of a *mba*, the essential part of the treatment consists in the recovery of the fragment of food or other object, called *penupenu*, by means of which the sorcerer acts upon his victim. This *penupenu* may be recovered in two ways. In one the relatives of the patient go to a man reputed to have the power of divination in respect of this condition. The diviner holds up an arm-ring and recites the names of all the persons believed to possess magical powers, and when one of the names is mentioned the arm-ring begins to revolve. The person of the sorcerer having been thus revealed, the relatives visit him and accuse him of the deed. The suspected man may confess at once, and restore the hidden *penupenu* to his victim. If he refuses to confess he is suspended by one arm to the bough of a tree. As a rule a confession soon follows, but if there is long delay it is concluded that some mistake has been made in the divination by which the diagnosis was reached, and the suspended and suspected person is released. It may be noted that the patient in such a case will recover, because his mind is freed from the idea that his illness is due to the action of a sorcerer.

This mode of procedure departs from that proper to magic in the recourse to divination by the arm-ring, a process which definitely depends on the agency of an ancestral ghost. The suspension of the supposed sorcerer has the character of an ordeal, but with no obvious religious character. In the other mode of procedure in cases in which the action of a *mba* has been diagnosed, the religious character is evident. A man with especial knowledge and powers appeals to certain spirits called *tomate kuri*, who are believed to be able to find the *penupenu* in order to restore it to the sick man, the recovery of the *penupenu* being accompanied by rites similar to those by which the diseases incurred through breaking of a taboo are cured.

The religious character of the medical art is thus so strong in Eddystone

Island that procedures which are primarily of the same order as the magic of other places are both diagnosed and treated by means involving the supplication and propitiation of the spirits of the dead, who are the chief objects of the religious rites of the people. There seems to have been in action a process of unification whereby the most diverse modes of regarding disease, modes which clearly belong to wholly different categories elsewhere, have been brought under one head in respect of diagnosis and treatment. The same hold good to a certain extent of the beliefs in causation, in that it is held that the production of disease by human agency would not be effective unless the sufferer had rendered himself liable to such maleficent action by his transgression of a religious ordinance.

The close relation between religion and the production and cure of disease occurs in many parts of Melanesia. Thus, in those islands which possess the institution of totemism, disease is said to follow any infraction of totemic ordinances, such as killing or eating the totem. Since these ordinances have the nature of taboos, we are again brought into contact with the relation between medicine and taboo. In the New Hebrides, where taboo is especially associated with certain complex organisations in which men rise from rank to rank by the killing of pigs, the transgression of these taboos brings sickness in its train. This religious character of leechcraft does not, however, stand alone in Melanesia, but is often accompanied by magical practices of the most definite kind. In some places, as in the Banks and Torres Islands, and probably in New Britain and New Ireland, these take the place in the lives and thoughts of the people. In other parts the religious aspect of leechcraft is predominant, and, as we have already seen in Eddystone Island, this predominance may be so great that magic may become altogether subordinated to that view of disease according to which it is regarded as a punishment for sin.

INDEPENDENT OCCURRENCE OF DISEASE

I must now consider briefly those cases in which disease is believed to arise independently of any action on the part of human beings or of higher powers. This belief exists in many parts of Melanesia and New Guinea, and is probably universal, though it has attracted little notice beside the more striking customs which show the relation of leechcraft with magic and religion.

The diseases thus regarded are such as we are accustomed to group together as 'minor ailments'. It is especially when disease appears to threaten life that people begin to think of human or spiritual agency. As among ourselves, these 'minor ailments' are largely treated without the aid of any specialised practitioners, and by measures which correspond with our domestic remedies. Thus, Professor Seligman tells us[3] that, among the

Sinaugolo of New Guinea, a sorcerer is only consulted when ordinary treatment has been found of no avail.

In some cases the beliefs which underlie the treatment of the grave examples of disease are also concerned in the treatment of these minor ailments. Thus, in Eddystone Island, certain sores on the limbs which are believed to 'come of themselves' are yet treated by measures similar to those employed in diseases ascribed to the infraction of a taboo, and one such treatment is accompanied by a burnt-offering to spiritual beings, which offering forms a feature of the curative rites of a taboo.

Because certain cases of disease are not ascribed to direct human or spiritual agency, we must not conclude that they therefore fall within the domain of what we should call 'natural' causation. if we inquire into the beliefs concerning the causation of these minor ailments in such a place as Eddystone Island, we are told that they are believed to come of themselves and are not, therefore, the occasion of rites such as naturally follow disease ascribed to the neglect of religious injunctions. It would seem that these diseases attract little attention, and do not afford material for speculation. It is true that many of the troubles thus believed to 'come of themselves' are common and a source of great discomfort, though, as a rule, they do not threaten life. It is a question whether it is not their very frequency which takes them out of the magical and religious spheres. It is the exceptional, or at any rate the less habitual, incidents of life that tend to excite the speculations of mankind,[4] and occurrences so frequent in the tropics as the outbreak of sores on the limbs tends to remain without the circle of medico-religious interest, just as our own colds and other habitual ailments remain to a large extent without the scope of our own medicine.

VARIETY IN LEECHCRAFT

The belief in the occurrence of disease independently of human or spiritual agency introduces an element of variety into the leechcraft of savage peoples. Even when it is decided that some human or spiritual agency has been at work, there may still remain ample scope for variety in the treatment adopted. If we can judge by the following experience in Eddystone Island, such peoples as the Melanesians put their faith in many doctors, and are not content with one physician or one remedy.

A man who had acted as one of our assistants in this island fell ill with apical pneumonia. After he had been ill for a few days I heard that he was anxious to be treated by me, and I attended him for the rest of his illness. He was already being treated by a noted leech of the island, Kundakolo, to whom I owe much of my knowledge of Eddystone medicine. On one of my later visits another of our assistants, also a noted leech, who went with me, carried out a course of treatment consisting of rubbings, spittings, and prayers as soon as I had finished my interview, his treatment being designed to remedy the sweating which was at that time the chief cause of complaint. I thus knew during my attendance on the patient that I had two rivals in my art, but it was only after the patient had recovered that we learnt there had been at least a dozen. The first diagnosis had been that the patient was suffering from sorcery, or *mba*, and three different leeches were called upon in succession to carry out different forms of treatment for this condition. I then began my visits, but at the same time two other practitioners were called in, who performed two other 'cures' for sorcery. The diagnosis of *mba* was then given up, this being about the time of the crisis, and a woman then carried out the treatment for *njiama*, on the supposition that the patient had fallen under the spell of the evil eye. This was followed by a treatment assigned to cure a symptom ascribed to a being named Ave, whom we shall meet again shortly. This was followed by three separate 'cures' for a condition called *tagosoro*, usually produced by the action of the being called Mateana and Sea. As these were not wholly successful, the original diagnosis of *mba* was made the basis of the next treatment. A month later the patient was considering whether he would not call in another practitioner to treat him again for *tagosoro*, on account of his failure to recover his strength completely. At one stage of illness, when the patient was delirious and insisted on walking about naked, his friends had considered the propriety of calling in a practitioner skilled in the treatment for the infraction of *kenjo tuturu*, which has as a result a condition of insanity ascribed to beings, called *tuturu*, who live in the bush.

DIFFERENTIATION OF LEECH FROM PRIEST

The high degree of specialisation of medical function which exist in Eddystone Island may serve as an introduction to a subject I have until now left on one side. In the first chapter I stated that one of the means by which it is possible to distinguish medicine from magic and religion is an inquiry how far the leech is differentiated from the sorcerer and the priest. In the area with which I am specially dealing in these lectures, it may be said at once that there is little evidence of such differentiation. In Australia, New Guinea, and Melanesia, it would seem that the simpler remedies, of which I spoke just now, may be used by anyone, there being in this respect no differentiation of the leech from the general body of the people. Those who combine the practice of medicine with that of magical or religious rites usually acquire their art by a special process, either of initiation or instruction, and in Melanesia such knowledge has always to be purchased. The most complete instruction in any branch of medico-magical or medico-religious art is of no avail to the pupil unless money has passed from himself to his instructor. This instruction and purchase, however, nearly always include both the production and cure of disease, where disease is ascribed to human agency, and the power and knowledge to perform rites other than those of a curative nature where medicine is allied with religion.

In Eddystone Island, however, a distinct step has been taken towards the differentiation of the leech from the priest. A man who buys the knowledge which enables him to impose a taboo necessarily buys at the same time the knowledge of the process by means of which to treat the illness which follows infraction of the taboo. It does not follow, however, that he uses this part of his knowledge. Certain men of the island have acquired a special reputation for success in the application of remedies, such men being called *tinoni salanga*. In these *tinoni salanga* we have clearly present the beginning of the differentiation of the leech from the priest. It may be interesting to mention some of the conditions which seem to have brought about this distinction. One is that a *tinoni salanga* who wishes his treatment to be successful should use a special kind of shell-instrument, called a *rikerike*, with which to cut and scrape roots or other ingredients of his pharmacopoeia. One who steps over this instrument angers the *tomate* or ghostly ancestor from whom the leech derives his powers, the ghost showing his anger by the infliction of illness. Owing to the danger so incurred men who have bought the knowledge of a taboo will sometimes decline to use their knowledge of the associated treatment, and leave that part of their art to others willing to take the risk. Another deterrent is the need for sexual abstinence on the part of a leech, especially in certain rites, such as those for the cure of ulcers.

There is another indication that medicine in the strict sense of the term is becoming dissociated in Eddystone Island from the religious attitude. The influence of the being called Mateana shows itself in the occurrence of fever, pain, and weakness, this complex of symptoms being called *tagosoro*. At the present time there seems to be a distinct tendency to diagnose and treat *tagosoro* as a morbid entity, independently of any belief in the anger of Mateana or the transgression of a taboo. This was probably the case in the three treatments for *tagosoro* carried out on the patient I have already mentioned, while the treatment for symptoms ascribed to Ave may also have been of a similar nature. It is possible, however, that this modification of the leechcraft of Eddystone Island is due to recent European influence. This may also be true of the movement towards specialisation of the leech, for one of the first results of such external influence is to lower resistance to the dangers and hardships which so often accompany the religious and magical rites of savage man.

It must be noted that the widespread failure to distinguish the leech from the sorcerer or priest is not due to any failure in the specialisation of medical function itself. Indeed, the matter is rather the other way. Such people as the Papuan or Melanesian have carried the differentiation of medical function in some respects to a far higher pitch than even we have reached in our highly specialised medical art. In Eddystone Island the treatment of different diseases is so highly specialised that one man will treat rheumatism, another fever, a third epilepsy, and a fourth insanity, although in each case the cure of disease is intimately associated with certain religious functions. An example of similar specialisation in Torres Straits has already been given in this lecture, and still another example is found in the island of Tami on the north-eastern coast of New Guinea, where one man knows how to cure pain in the chest, another pain in the abdomen, a third rheumatism, and a fourth catarrh.[5] Specialism is thus present in a pre-eminent degree; but this specialism has taken a direction which has probably been antagonistic to the development of that kind of differentiation of social function which among ourselves, after centuries of progress, has made medicine a wholly independent department of social life.

EPIDEMIC DISEASE

A few special points remain for consideration. I have so far treated disease as if it were a condition which only affects individuals, and have said nothing of those cases of disease in which a whole population or a large portion of it suffers simultaneously from disease. I have not to consider what is the attitude of the peoples we are considering towards epidemic disease.

Here, as in individual cases of disease, we find medicine intimately blended with magic or religion. Among those peoples whose lives are dominated by magic, epidemics are ascribed to the action of sorcerers, but it is supposed that they are produced by the sorcery of members of some other village or some other island. I have recorded[6] a case from the Banks Islands, in which a man, who wished to injure a woman who had refused to marry him, held a bamboo containing certain ingredients so that the wind should carry its influence to the island where the woman was living. An epidemic illness which shortly followed was ascribed to his action. Payment was made to the sorcerer, who sent young coconuts to which he had imparted power (*mana*), and the milk of these coconuts was poured at the door of every sufferer, so that the epidemic might be stayed.

For an example of epidemic disease ascribed to the agency of higher powers, I may return to Eddystone Island. Here such disease is supposed to be due to the action of a being or beings, called Ave, whose coming is indicated by the presence of broken rainbows, shooting stars, red clouds, and showers of fine rain while the sun is shining. The symptoms of the disease usually produced by Ave are fever, headache, and cough. The Ave probably were spirits or ghosts associated with certain neglected shrines in Eddystone. Dysentery epidemics are ascribed to Ave from Ysabel.

When an epidemic ascribed to Ave visits the island the people appeal to one who knows the appropriate rites. This man, with certain companions, visits a now disused village. After uttering the names of certain ghosts, probably those of his predecessors in the knowledge of the rite, he proceeds: 'You, at the root of the sky, come down and depart. There is an end of the men, there is an end of the chiefs; an end of the chiefs' wives; an end of the chiefs' children. Come and depart thou, etc.,' the prayer ending with an exclamation like a bark, when all present shout. Then the root of turmeric is distributed, and all chew it and spit it about the path as they go towards the shore, making as much noise as possible, with the idea of driving away the Ave. When they reach the shore the leader in the ceremony folds a large leaf so as to make it like a canoe. In this imitation vessel he puts ashes, some of the leaf used in thatching a house, and five small shell ornaments called *ovala*. He then utters the following words: 'You! Go to Ysabel; go to Choiseul [neighbouring islands]. Do not stay in Mandegusu.' The canoe is then taken out to sea and put on the waves, so that it goes away from the island. It is believed to carry the Ave back to the place whence it came.

RELATIONS OF ECONOMICAL AND JURIDICAL NATURE

The chief object of this discussion has been to show the intimate relation of medicine with magic and religion among certain peoples who rank low in the scale of general culture. It may have been noticed that this tie carries with it other relations of an economical and juridical kind. Thus, the *kenjo* of Eddystone Island is not merely an example of an intimate blend between medicine and religion, but at the same time it involves the institution of private property. The people of Eddystone Island form a good example of communism in goods, large groups of persons owning land and certain other property in common. The process called *kenjo*, which we have so far studied in its relation to the social categories of medicine and religion, is also a means by which certain kinds of property – namely the fruit of certain trees – are kept for the special use of individual persons. It is a social practice by which a communistic people have progressed some way along the path of individualism.

The *kaia* rites of the Gazelle Peninsula and the Duke of York Island, which I described in the first chapter, offered another example of a similar process. The half-snake, half-human being called *kaia* is believed to abstract the soul of any person who takes fruit from the trees of the district it inhabits, persons from other districts being specially prone to suffer from its action. It is probable that the belief in the efficacy of this being is definitely fostered by the inhabitants of a district, as a means of protecting their property from the people of neighbouring districts. It would be very wrong to regard the institutions of the Solomon Islands and New Britain as inventions of the people in the interests of private property. The belief in the production of disease as a punishment for theft, however, provides a motive which tends to perpetrate the ideas and practices which bring medicine into so intimate a relation with religion. We have here only one of countless examples showing that among peoples of rude culture the distinction of social categories from one another is far more difficult than among ourselves. The religious character of the medical art among such peoples is only one example of the way in which religion and the religious attitude permeate every part of their social life. Religion among such people is not a matter for one day in the week, but influences every act of their daily lives.

THE PART PLAYED BY SUGGESTION

Another subject well illustrated by the proceedings described in this book is the evidence concerning the part played by suggestion in the production and cure of diseases among such people as the Papuans and Melanesians. There can be no question that such processes as I have recorded here are efficacious. Men who have offended one whom they believe to have magical powers sicken, and even die, as the direct result of their belief; and if the process has not gone too far they will recover if they can be convinced that the spell has been removed. Similarly, one who has intruded on the haunt of a ghost or spirit will suffer, it may be, fatal illness, because he believes that he has lost his soul; and he will recover after the performance of rites to which he ascribes the power of restoring the lost soul to his body. Doubtless, with this real factor of suggestion there is mixed up much deception, especially on the part of those to whose special knowledge the production and cure of disease is ascribed. If one falls ill with symptoms which by popular belief are ascribed to a sorcerer, or to some spirit whose influence is believed to be under the power of a priest, the sorcerer or priest is only too ready to accept the role ascribed to him to earn money and at the same time enhance his reputation for medico-magical or medico-religious powers.

At the same time there is reason to believe that he is not wholly a deceiver, but in some measure shares the general belief in his own powers. Even that degree of intimacy with those who practise medico-magical medico-religious arts which is possible to such a visitor as I have been among several peoples, is enough to show the sincerity and earnestness of many of these practitioners. I believe that, in many cases, it is the same among ourselves, and that a study of our own quacks and charlatans, with that amount of care which we devote to the Australian or the Melanesian leech, would show us the impostor far less than is usually supposed. Imposition there is, no doubt, but, if such a study were carried out from a psychological point of view, it would often reveal the enthusiast and the crank in even greater measure than the impostor.

Not only will the study of peoples of rude culture help us to estimate aright the part taken by fraud and deception in certain forms of the medical art of the civilised world, but, what is far more important, it will help us also to understand better the place taken by suggestion both in the production and the treatment of disease. From the psychological point of view the difference between the rude arts I have described in this book and much of our own medicine is not one of kind, but only of degree.

RATIONALITY OF THE LEECHCRAFT

The chief lesson, however, impressed upon us by the facts brought forward here, is one the importance of which reaches far beyond the limits of our special subject. This lesson is the rationality of the leechcraft of such peoples as the Papuan and the Melanesian. The practices of these peoples in relation to disease are not a medley of disconnected and meaningless customs, but are inspired by definite ideas concerning the causation of disease. Their modes of treatment follow directly from their ideas concerning etiology and pathology. From our modern standpoint we are able to see that these ideas are wrong. But the important point is that, however wrong may be the beliefs of the Papuan and Melanesian concerning the causation of disease, their practices are the logical consequence of those beliefs.

We may say even that these peoples practise an art of medicine which is in some respects more rational than our own, in that its modes of diagnosis and treatment follow more directly from their ideas concerning the causation of disease. According to the opinion of the civilised world, these ideas of causation are wrong, or contain but grains of truth here and there; but once grant these ideas, and the body of medical practice follows therefrom with a logical consistency which it may take us long to emulate in our pursuit of a medicine founded upon the sciences of physiology and psychology.

I tried to show, in the first chapter, that the concepts underlying the magical procedure of savage man have not the vague and indefinite character often assigned to them, but form clear and relatively concrete motives for the complex procedures of the sorcerer and leech. These concepts form the starting-point of his logical processes, and the general conclusion which can, I believe, be drawn from the facts before us, is that these logical processes are as definite as the premises from which they start.

There can be no greater hindrance to progress in our attempts to understand the mind of the man of lowly culture than the belief so widely held, that his actions are determined by motives having that vague and lawless character ascribed by many to the thought of savage man. There are even those who hold that such peoples as the Papuan and Melanesian have not yet reached the logical state of thought. I believe there is no single department of social life in which it cannot be shown that this view is false. I have elsewhere attempted a demonstration of its falsity in one department of social life.[8] I hope the facts brought forward here are sufficient to show that, in the department of his activity in which he endeavours to cope with disease, savage man is no illogical or prelogical creature, but that his actions are guided by reasoning as definite as that which we can claim for our own medical practices.

It must be noted, however, that the examples of leechcraft which have been recorded in this book have not always formed part of a strictly logical and consistent system. An instance from Eddystone Island is the way in which the causation of disease by such agencies as Mateana and Sea, as well as by the evil eye and sorcery, has become subservient to the ancestor-cult which underlies the *kenjo*. The indefiniteness of the beliefs connected with the being called Ave gives another instance from the same island. As an example from New Guinea may be mentioned the employment, by the Kai, of several remedies, such as bleeding and massage, which do not, so far as we now, immediately follow from their ideas concerning the causation of disease. Such cases lead us to a set of problems which I have left on one side in this book, problems which would lead us to a mode of studying early medicine too large to be included in the scope of this course of lectures – namely, the study of transformations suffered by medical beliefs and practices as the result of the contact and blending of peoples. I have dealt with two only of the methods by which social facts may be studied – the sociological and the psychological. I must leave the far more difficult problem of the historical relations of medicine, magic, and religion for another occasion.

INTRODUCTION: REFERENCE

Slobodin, R. (1978) *W. H. R. Rivers*. New York: Columbia University Press.

NOTES

1. *Report Cambridge Expedition to Torres Straits*, VI (1908): 261.
2. ibid., V: 362, and VI: 266.
3. *Journ. Anth Inst.*, XXXII (1902): 300.
4. Cf. W. H. R. Rivers, *Folk Lore*, XXIII (1912): 307.
5. In Neuhauss, *Deutsch Neu-Guinea*, Vol. III, p. 516.
6. *The History of Melanesian Society*, Vol. I, p. 158.
7. Lévy-Bruhl, *Les Fonctions Mentales dans les Sociétés Inférieures* (Paris: 1910).
8. 'The primitive conception of death', *Hibbert Journal*, X (1912): 393.

CHAPTER FIVE

Mother-Right and the Sexual Ignorance of Savages[1] (1925)

Ernest Jones

Jones (1879–1958) is particularly remembered as Freud's first British follower. In the 1920s he was involved in a dispute with the anthropologist Malinowski on the universality of the Oedipus complex, Malinowski having argued in Sex and Repression in Savage Society that in matrilineal societies, such as the Trobriands, the complex was associated not with the father but with the mother's brother as the main authority figure for the young boy. Here Jones refers back to certain nineteenth-century anthropological concerns with evolutionary development which we find in Freud's Totem and Taboo, to argue that the father–son complex is fundamental and that Malinowski ignores the son's sexual jealousy of his father (in favour of the authority role of the mother's brother). Malinowski had argued that the Trobrianders' apparent ignorance of the father's role in procreation meant that he could ignore that problem (Leach 1958). The debate still continues (Spiro 1982), although most anthropologists would probably adhere to something closer to Malinowski's position on the 'nuclear complex'.

I INTRODUCTION

Ever since the appearance, in 1861, of Bachofen's famous work *Das Mutterrecht* which was based largely on the study of classical literature, steadily increasing attention has been paid to the views of early man there revealed, until at the present day they constitute one of the central themes of anthropological interest. It may be said that subsequent research, although it has had to modify extensively some of his conclusions, has nevertheless amply confirmed many of them, and has shown that they hold good over a far larger field than he was able to investigate.

For reasons that will presently be indicated, however, the subject is apt to arouse intense emotional reactions, so that bias in the conclusions reached, and probably also in the observations made, is only too common.

59

There are certainly fanciful elements in some of the pictures drawn of what is alleged to have been the primordial 'matriarchal' state. A highly-coloured description of it will, for instance, be found in Vaerting's *The Dominant Sex*, where we are introduced to an extreme inversion of the relation between the sexes. According to the account given there, not only do the children belong solely to the mother, the father being quite unrelated to them either in blood or in kinship, but property belongs only to the women and is inherited only through them. The woman is the active wooer, has as many husbands or lovers as she pleases and as long as she pleases; she can at any time divorce her husband, but he cannot divorce her; he comes to her abode to live there as a guest; in fact, he exists only for the sexual pleasure he gives her, and the work he can do at her bidding, being in all other respects merely tolerated. The woman has a correspondingly dominant position in society, in counsel and in government. The description reads like a feminist's wish-fulfilment dream, a vision of a paradise out of which she has been driven by the protesting male, but to which she hopes one day to return.

Very little knowledge of sex psychology is needed to cast doubt on the authenticity of the account just mentioned, and the cold facts of anthropology only go to attenuate its ardour. Scepticism is at once aroused by the assumption that in savage times men were more docile than now, and that the growth of civilisation has been accompanied by a great increase in fierceness towards his womankind on the side of the brutal male. On the contrary, if one examines the institutions of existing savages, and still more of one submits these to an analytic scrutiny, one cannot resist the conclusion that these people have, in order to make social life possible at all, to maintain much more elaborate and formidable devices than we do in order to help them in securing some degree of control over their cruel and sadistic impulses, including those specifically directed against their women-folk; we may refer, for instance, to Reik's study of the pseudo-maternal couvade,[1] as well as to the general experience of explorers. One may appropriately quote here the following passage from Frazer's *Golden Bough*:[2]

> In order to dissipate misapprehensions which appear to be rife on this subject, it may be well to remind or inform the reader that the ancient and widespread custom of tracing descent and inheriting property through the mother alone does not any means imply that the government of tribes which observe the custom is in the hands of women; in short it should always be borne in mind that mother-kin does not mean mother-rule. On the contrary, the practice of mother-kin prevails most extensively amongst the lowest savages, with whom woman, instead

of being the ruler of man, is always his drudge and often little better than his slave. Indeed, so far is the system from implying any social superiority of women that it probably took its rise from what we should regard as their deepest degradation, to wit, from a state of society in which the relations of the sexes were so loose and vague that children could not be fathered on any particular man. When we pass from the purely savage state to that higher plane of culture in which the accumulation of property, and especially of landed property, had become a powerful instrument of social and political influence, we naturally find that wherever the ancient preference for the female line of descent has been retained, it tends to increase the importance and enhance the dignity of woman; and her aggrandisement is most marked in princely families, where she either herself holds royal authority as well as private property, or at least transmits them both to her consort or her children. But this social advance of women has never been carried so far as to place men as a whole in a position of political subordination to them. Even where the system of mother-kin in regard to descent and property has prevailed most fully, the actual government has generally, if not invariably, remained in the hands of men. Exceptions have no doubt occurred; women have occasionally arisen who by sheer force of character have swayed for a time the destinies of their people. But such exceptions are rare and their effects transitory; they do not affect the truth of the general rule that human society has been governed in the past and, human nature remaining the same, is likely to be governed in the future, mainly by masculine force and masculine intelligence.

There are few themes, if any, that arouse more emotional prejudice than the comparison of male and female, particularly if it includes the question of the respective parts played in life by the father and the mother. Without the insight gained into the characteristic complexes of men and women by means of psycho-analysis, it would be well-nigh hopeless to expect a really serious approach to impartiality, and even with the knowledge now at our service one cannot walk too warily in this delicate path.

The second difficulty is of a more material kind. It is the enormous complexity and almost endless variation in the phenomena themselves. A slight impression of this may be given by the following considerations. Anthropologists are agreed that the central, and perhaps the only essential one of the many phenomena grouped under the name of mother-right (*Mutterrecht*) is 'mother-kinship', i.e. the custom of reckoning descent through the female only; there is matrilineal descent, as it is called, and no patrilineal, or agnatic, descent.[3] This central feature is normally accompanied by a number of other characteristic ones, the chief of which will be mentioned presently, but the actual correlation found to exist among the various features is so extraordinarily irregular as to bewilder anyone who is seeking for any degree of order. The complications begin with what we have called the central feature, for the child does not necessarily belong to his mother's clan even if his descent is reckoned through the female; the totem who happened to impregnate his mother, to whose clan he therefore belongs, may be different from his mother's totem and clan. The descent itself may, of course, be matrilineal, patrilineal, or both together. The complexity increases as soon as we consider some of the connections between mother-kinship and the accompanying features.

1. *Authority.* – The term 'matriarchy' should be limited to the cases where there is true mother-rule, i.e. where the mother is the head of the household and disposes of the final authority over the children. This is extraordinarily rare, but when present constitutes the purest form of mother-right. Often the father is the head of the family and exercises the *potestas* – to use the legal term – as of course he mostly does where there is patrilineal descent. The most frequent case, however, and one so typical that its presence, even in an attenuated form, always makes one suspect the existence of mother-right (whether in the past or present), is that in which the *potestas* is wielded by the mother's brother, the child's maternal uncle; this is the so-called avunculate organisation. Other varieties are where the *potestas* is shared between the father and maternal uncle, according to the matters over which it is exercised, or where the uncle has authority over the son and the father over the daughter, or where the father has authority up to a given age and the uncle after this.

2. *Inheritance and Succession.* – With mother-right succession of rank (kingship, chieftainship, etc.) mostly, but not always, passes from a man to his sister's son, not to his wife's son; in other words, whether the rank can be held by a woman or not, it is often transmitted through the female, instead of, as with us, through the male. But again there is no rule about this. In Melanesia, for instance, where matrilineal descent mainly holds, succession is usually patrilineal.

The laws about inheritance (of property) are also extremely variable. The property may, very rarely, be held only by women; most typically it is transmitted to the sister's son, but there are instances of mother-right (as with the Malays of Moerong) where nevertheless the boy inherits from his father.

It should be borne in mind that there is no close correlation between the individual features just enumerated. Out of an endless number of illustrations one only need be quoted: in Torres Straits the *potestas* is avunculate, but the descent, inheritance and succession are all patrilineal.

3. *Residence*. – In the most extreme forms of mother-right the husband only visits his wife or else resides with her and her people (matrilocal marriage), in which case he is usually subject to the head of her household, her brother or uncle. Matrilocal marriage is nearly always accompanied by matrilineal descent, there being only two exceptions known to this rule. Patrilineal descent almost always involves patrilocal marriage, but the converse does not hold, for patrilocal marriage is often found with mother-kinship; Australian marriages, for instance, are mostly patrilocal, whereas mother-kinship is nearly as common with them as father-kinship.

The difficulties in correlating the institution of mother-right with the status of women accompanying it, whether high or low, with the level of civilisation in which it is found, and with the knowledge or certainty about paternity possessed by the peoples concerned will be mentioned in discussing the various hypotheses relating to the subject.

II EXPLANATIONS OF MOTHER-RIGHT

After these introductory remarks we may proceed to consider the main problems relating to mother-right, its general significance and the causes of its genesis and supersession. In doing so it will be seen that we at once impinge on some of the most fundamental problems of anthropology – those relating to the evolution of totemism and religion, of marriage and the family, as well as of other social institutions. To us the conception of a family where the father plays such a subordinate part, being to a great extent replaced by an uncle, certainly seems strange and needful of explanation. Yet many authorities, including McLennan, Spencer, Avebury, Frazer, and Hartland, find this state of affairs a perfectly natural one in an early stage of society, so that for them the greater problem would be to explain how it came to be superseded. They point to the more intimate connection between child and mother and the various uncertainties concerning the relationship of the father. Other authorities, on the other hand, regard the institution of mother-right as a secondary state of affairs to be accounted for by purely temporary circumstances. The causes for it may be either factors connected with the status of women, perhaps the part they are often supposed to have played in regard to agriculture, or more obscure ones of the kind that will be discussed below. The main hypotheses will next be considered in more detail.

The most obvious explanation for the existence of mother-right, one first put forward in 1757 by Schouten and since repeated by many travellers, is that it is due to uncertainty about the individuality of the father. As it has been cynically put, maternity is a question of fact, paternity a question of opinion. The slightest investigation, however, disposes of this view as being quite out of accord with the facts. There is no correlation at all between father-right and conjugal fidelity or between mother-right and infidelity.[4] On the one hand mother-right obtains, for instance, on the coast of West Africa and in Northern Abyssinia, where wifely fidelity is very strict, adultery exceedingly rare and often punished by death. On the other hand there is the far commoner state of affairs where conjugal morality is loose though father-right prevails. As Hartland puts it in connection with the Kafirs of the Hindu Kush, where the strictest father-right holds, 'that Kafir would be of a highly sporting disposition who ventured to stake much on the authenticity of any child of whom he was legally the father'.[5] More than this: among many patrilineal peoples the men appear to show the greatest indifference about their actual blood-relationship to their legal son, so long as they have one at all for the various ritualistic and economic purposes where a son is desirable, and an adopted son, or their wife's son by some other man, serves these purposes as well as one they have themselves begotten.

Closely akin to this hypothesis are those that postulate a specially close association between mother and child on account of either polygyny (Winterbottom) or polyandry (McLennan). Neither can be substantiated by reference to the actual facts.

A more subtle and interesting view, hinted at by McLennan over half a century ago in his *Primitive Marriage* and developed by Hartland in 1895 in his *Legend of Perseus*, is that mother-right represents a survival from a time when there was ignorance of the facts of procreation. If the father was not taught to play any necessary part in procreation, then it would seem to follow that the child's status could only be determined by the mother's, i.e. that there would be mother-right; and it is the essential presupposition of this hypothesis that mother-right necessarily preceded father-right throughout the world. It is true that mother-right is often found where the paternal role in procreation is fully understood; not only so, but, as Westermarck points out in this connection,[6] there are Australian tribes who have matrilineal descent in spite of their belief that the child is created solely by the father and merely nourished by the mother. Nevertheless there might well be psychological or sociological reasons why a given organisation should persist after the originating agent had ceased to operate, so that the considerations just adduced would not necessarily negative the hypothesis in question. We are thus led to investigate, as an essential preliminary in our enquiry, the much discussed topic of the sexual ignorance of savages.

The surmise expressed by Hartland in 1895 that sexual ignorance[7] may have played an important part in the development of social beliefs and institutions was within a few years brilliantly confirmed by Spencer and Gillen's discovery that there were still tribes in Australia, notably the interesting Aruntas, who were ignorant of the facts of paternal procreation.

The findings have been disputed by other field-workers, such as Strehlow and von Leonhardi, and the influences contravened by Westermarck, Heape, and Carveth Read. The question is not easily answered. Like all enquiries in the sphere of sexuality, the truth is peculiarly difficult to elicit and the fallacies unexpectedly numerous. The only field-worker who seems to have made a special study of these fallacies, and who exhibited remarkable acumen in dealing with them, is Malinowski. The account he gives of the sexual life of the Trobrianders, a Papuan-Melanesian race inhabiting an archipelago off the coast of New Guinea, is certainly the fullest extant, and its quality is such as to inspire great confidence in the correctness of his observations.[8] After a careful sifting of all the available data he comes to the definite conclusion that these natives have no knowledge whatever of the part played by semen in procreation. They appear to believe that pregnancy results only from a 'baloma', a spirit (usually female) of a dead person, inserting a spirit child, 'waiwaia', into the womb. They admit, however, that for this to happen it is necessary that the vagina be first opened up and this is, of course, usually done by sexual intercourse. Apparently the Australian Aruntas hold a similar view, that women are prepared in this way for the reception of the 'ratapas'. In making this belief more comprehensible Malinowski points out that the causal connection between intercourse and pregnancy is far from obvious to a race accustomed to frequent copulation from early childhood; the sexual act may take place hundreds of times before a single conception occurs. He has no doubts about the correctness of his observations and concludes: 'My firm conviction is that the ignorance of paternity is an original feature of primitive psychology, and that in all speculations about the origins of Marriage and the Evolution of Sexual Customs, we must bear in mind this fundamental ignorance.'[9]

If we accept these observations as correct, particularly Malinowski's careful investigations, as it seems to me we are bound to, then the question would appear to be settled. Nevertheless, the voice of scepticism refuses to be quieted. A number of other considerations strongly hint that even yet we are not at the end of the matter.

In the first place we have the indisputable fact that most savages all over the world, including those with mother-right, are fully aware of the part played by the man in procreation. This is proved not only by their own direct statements, but also by numerous practices based on the knowledge.[10] Then even the savages who are apparently ignorant in regard to paternal procreation yield hints that they nevertheless have some inklings of similar knowledge in other fields of thought. Thus the Intichiuma ceremonies of the Australian natives definitely imply some knowledge of the process of fertility in both animals and crops. A very curious feature observed by Malinowski among the Trobrianders, discussion of which will be reserved till later, points in the same direction: a Trobriander is horrified at the idea of physically resembling his mother, brother or sister, i.e. those who are thought to be his only blood-relatives, and is intensely insulted at the mere suggestion; he maintains, on the contrary, that he is the physical image of his father.

A psycho-analyst cannot fail to be struck by the unmistakeable symbolism these ignorant savages display when propounding their views on procreation, symbolism of so accurate a kind as to indicate at least an unconscious knowledge of the truth. Thus water plays a prominent part in regard to conception. The spirit-children, waiwaias, come from over the sea, often in a basket (like the womb symbol in which Moses arrived), they usually enter the woman's body when she is bathing in the sea, and the thing that has most carefully to be avoided by those who do not wish to conceive is the scum or froth of the sea – an obvious seminal symbol. In Australia impregnation may take place by stones, snakes or birds, well-known phallic symbols. The churinga nanja among the Aruntas are stone boulders connected with ancestors from whom the seed-spirit comes; in the Acheringa dream-world there are two ancestors for each child, not one, as might be expected, on the hypothesis of parthenogenesis.

Ideas of causality are known to be peculiarly difficult to unravel with savages, for they are often curiously different from our own. It is not easy to interpret, for instance, a belief that two causes are necessary for conception, an opening-up copulation and the introduction of spirit-children by a baloma. The natives say that the first of these allows the second, which is the essential one, to operate; but it is very well possible that the converse is the real meaning of the belief, i.e. that it is the influence of the baloma (the ancestral spirit) which permits the copulation to take effect. This multiplicity of causes is very common in regard to conception, for there are fewer topics that have more adjuvant agents associated with them, from bathing in holy water to the cure of barrenness by gynaecological curettage. The use of these agents, and the faith in them, may coexist with every degree of conscious awareness of the true agent in procreation; it would be absurd, for instance, to maintain that the Greeks were ignorant of the facts of procreation simply because their women practised various fertility rite and regarded the resultant offspring as the gift of the gods.

The argument put forward by Hartland and Malinowski to the effect that it must be hard to recognise the connection between frequent acts of copulation and rare ones of conception is not only incompatible with the simple fact that after all most peoples have recognised this connection, but has been penetratingly countered by Carveth Read on psychological grounds. he writes:[11] 'We must remember that the knowledge of animals and a great deal of the knowledge of savages and even of civilized people, is not of the discriminated, relational, propositional texture to which, under the influence of formal logic, we are apt to confine the name.' This is exactly in accord with what we find in the analysis of infantile mental life, where instinctive intuition plays a considerable part in divining the main outline at least of sexual knowledge. If a child of two years old can frame an image of genital coitus, and a year or so later connect it with the birth of another child, then the feat should certainly not be beyond the mentality of any adult savage.

III A PSYCHO-ANALYTICAL THEORY OF MOTHER-RIGHT

The foregoing considerations raise the question of whether the ignorance among these savages is after all so genuine and complete as it would appear. The curious combination of ignorance where one would reasonably expect knowledge and of half-knowledge is a phenomenon with which we are very familiar in other fields of thought.

Writers who are sceptical concerning the thorough-going nature of this ignorance have tended to regard it as something secondary or artificial, and a few have even propounded reasons for its occurrence. Thus Frazer, in speaking of the Australian belief that a 'ratapa' enters the womb at the moment of quickening, refers to the 'sick fancies of pregnant women'. Heape[12] expresses the following views:

> All the evidence we can bring to bear on the subject from a comparative point of view indicates that primitive man was not ignorant of this fundamental fact, and such evidence appears to me to be so strong that I consider it is irrefutable. Moreover, there is evidence that while these Australian savage people now declare their ignorance they still act in a variety of ways as if they knew the true facts. This being so, I maintain that the initial cause of this conceptional idea of totemism is due to a superstition which overrode instinctive knowledge of the facts; in other words, that the idea is not derived from ignorance but is a manufactured scheme, originating at a period in the history of man which is subsequent to his conception of superstitious fear of personal or individual spirits, and arising out of such superstition.

> It is thus I interpret the story of conceptional totemism; an impulse due to the sick fancies of the pregnant woman, due to fear or dread or desire, or all of them, has bred a superstition which necessitated the relinquishment of instinctive knowledge previously acquired, and all but buried it' – not quite buried, however; the Intichiuma ceremonies are performed just when

there is promise of a good breeding season, and thus necessity demands recognition of the truth; the Tully River[13] blacks grant that the breeding of animals, at any rate, is governed by the laws of Nature, while human beings are only exempt from the force of those laws because they are thereby confirmed in their belief of their superiority over the brute creation.

He suggests that the (purely conscious) motives why the natives maintain the beliefs they do is either to facilitate adultery[14] and condonement of it, or else to gratify the mother's hope of benefiting the child by conferring on it the qualities of some totemic spirit. These suggestions, however, evidently do not carry us far.

Carveth Read[15] makes a decided step forward in suggesting that the knowledge really present is only unconscious, having been 'repressed'; he speaks of its having been 'represented by the animistic philosophy and expelled from consciousness'. Malinowski, however, thinks that such knowledge cannot have been obliterated by any animistic superstructure because in determining 'descent' no importance is attached by these savages to blood-relationship.

When the question comes up of whether ideas are present in a state of repression, and, if so, what are likely to have been the reasons for the point, therefore, I propose to put forward an hypothesis along psycho-analytical lines, one which, if correct, would indicate that there is the closest collateral relationship between ignorance about paternal procreation on the one hand and the institution of mother-right on the other. My view is that both these phenomena are brought about by the same motive; in what chronological relation they stand to each other is another question altogether, which will be considered later. The motive, according to this view, in both cases is *to deflect the hatred towards his father felt by the growing boy.*

The following considerations may be adduced in support of this hypothesis. In the first place, it is known that of the two components of the primordial Oedipus complex – love for the mother and hatred for the father – the latter has played by far the more important part in leading to repression of the complex and in giving rise to the various complicated devices whereby this repression is brought about and maintained. The reason for this is evident, the dangerous rivalry between two murderous males with all its consequences. There is much reason to think that the ambivalent conflict between love and hate is sharper among savage peoples than among ourselves,[16] hence it is not surprising that they should possess more elaborate institutions subserving the function of guarding them from their repressed impulses; it is as though they had more reason than we to fear them, or less power of diverting them. As examples of institutions of this kind one may quote totemism and exogamy[17] on the one hand and the innumerable initiation ceremonies on the other.[18] (In accepting the view that the function in question is the essential one of these institutions one does not, of course, ignore the fact that they also subserve numerous other ones.)

It would seem to be the fashion at present among anthropologists to regard kinship and 'descent' as not necessarily having any close connection with blood-relationship. I am inclined to think that in so doing they are following a tendentious striving present among savages themselves. For it seems pretty plain that savages try in all sorts of ways to divorce the two matters,[19] although there is much reason to infer that fundamentally they attach an enormous, and even exaggerated, importance to blood-relationship. Not only is the child's social status determined by birth to a much greater extent than with us, but the central importance of birth to the savage mind is connection with the Oedipus complex has been made highly probable by Reik's brilliant work on puberty rites.[20] He showed there that the real significance of these rites is, by means of a complicated castration and birth symbolism, to annul the original birth by the mother and substitute for it an imaginary homosexual birth; the idea evidently being that attachment to the mother is due simply to the fact of being born of her, so that the only way to neutralise the incest tendencies that stand in the way of friendly relationship with other men is to nullify the supposed cause of them (birth) by a symbolic re-birth. If, according to savage theory, the maternal half of the Oedipus complex, the attachment to the mother, depends on the fact of being born of her, it is only reasonable to suppose that the same, *mutatis mutandis*, is equally true of the paternal half, the father-hate. At all events, as we shall see, savages appear to act on this assumption.

In unconsciously explaining incest tendencies as being due to the act of birth, savages would appear to indulge in the same 'retrospective fantasising' as our neurotics, who so often behave exactly like them in this respect, where we know the motive is to escape the guilt of infantile sexuality by substituting harmless thoughts about birth. Nevertheless, if Freud's hypothesis is substantiated about the inheritance of impulses dating from the primal horde, the savages and neurotics would prove to have some right on their side, though in a very indirect way. For in that event there would be some causal connection between birth, i.e. heredity, and the Oedipus complex.

Be this as it may, it is clear that any objectionable tendencies the source of which is imputed to the act of birth can most radically be countered by simply denying this act, as is done, for example, in the puberty rites. Now in the analysis of our neurotics we are very familiar with the wish-phantasy in which this happens in regard to the father. Many of them cherish, consciously or unconsciously, the idea that their 'father' had nothing to do with their conception or birth, this being entirely a matter between them and the mother. It is well known how extraordinarily widespread this myth of the Virgin Mother has been throughout the world, and there is every reason to think that it has generally the same significance as we find in the analysis of individuals.[21] The general belief evidently fulfils more than one deep-seated tendency; repudiation of the father's part in coitus and procreation, and consequently softening and deflection of the hatred against him, a consummation desired equally by son and father. This is what has happened where the institution of mother-right is combined with denial of paternal procreation. It might be said that just as the postural couvade is designed to protect the child from the father's hostility,[22] so the combination of mother-right and sexual ignorance protects both father and son from their mutual rivalry and hostility.

I should be inclined to bring into connection with this tendentious denial of paternal procreation the curious and unexpected finding recorded by Malinowski[23] that the topic of sexual intercourse between man and wife is regarded by the Trobrianders as highly indecent, although they are unusually free people in regard to sexual matters in general. This seems to represent a higher degree of the common aversion which most people feel in regard to the idea of parental coitus, and serves the same function of keeping at a distance the possibility of an Oedipus jealousy.

But the father is not so easily disposed of, a fact which might be used in support of Freud's suggestion that the inherited idea of the primal father is still actively alive in our unconscious. The father disappears from the scene only to reappear in a disguised form. The idea of the powerful and hated father is sacrificed in favour of an ancestral spirit, who in a supernatural manner impregnates the mother; for both the Australian ratapas and the Trobriand waiwaias emanate from ancestors, and no one who has had the opportunity of analysing a member of an ancient English family or an American with a passion for genealogy can fail to discover that forefathers are psychologically nothing but fathers at a slight remove. This elevated father is therefore the original powerful father in another guise. The idea corresponds with the deep belief that after all only the great father can procreate (or permit it by giving his sanction), with the added wish on the part of women to conceive of the father, as the Virgin Mary did.[24]

When put to the test of practice this way of treating the father does appear to achieve its aim of bringing about a far more intimate and friendly relationship between father and child than is usual in patrilineal societies. Among the Trobrianders, where the father has of course no authority whatever over his children, the society being matrilineal and the *potestas* devolving on the uncle, the father is described as being a 'beloved, benevolent friend'.[25] Malinowski writes as follows:[26]

Among the Melanesians, 'fatherhood', as we know, is a purely social relation. Now, part of this relation consists in his duty towards his wife's children; he is there 'to receive them into his arms', a phrase we have already quoted; he has to carry them about when on the march the mother is tired, and he has to assist in the nursing at home. He tends them in their natural needs, and cleanses them, and there are many stereotyped expressions in the native language referring to fatherhood and its hardships, and to the duty of filial gratitude towards him. A typical Trobriand father is a hard-working and conscientious nurse, in which he obeys the call of duty, expressed in social tradition. The fact is, however, that the father is always interested in the children, sometimes passionately so, and performs all his duties eagerly and fondly.

This solution of the father complex, however, was not always so easy, and with the obsessional ambivalence of savages room had to be found for an object towards whom could be directed the less amiable attitudes of awe, dread, respect and suppressed hostility which are inseparable from the idea of the father image. It will be remembered that it took Christian theology many centuries before they could afford to dispense with a devil (whom I have shown elsewhere to be a genetic counterpart of God) and allow themselves to face a God who would carry the responsibility for both good and evil. Similarly the savage had to be provided with a figure who would incorporate the disliked and feared attributes of the father image. In nearly all matrilineal societies, and in some that have partly passed over into the patrilineal form, the maternal uncle plays this part. It is he who wields over the children the direct *potestas*, he who is the main source of authority and discipline, from him that they inherit possessions and acquire various accomplishments, and often it is he who is responsible for their food and keep. Still, in the majority of cases he does not reside with the children, and often not even in the same village, while his relations with their mother are extremely formal and surrounded by taboos. Malinowski[27] contrasts the status of the two men as follows: 'To the father, therefore, the children look only for loving care and tender companionship. Their mother's brother represents the principle of discipline, authority and executive power within the family.' As might be expected, affection is not the most prominent feature in the relation between boy and uncle, though doubtless there is much companionship during the adolescent stage when the serious duties of life are being inculcated. Malinowski[28] describes this stage:

The father suffers at this time a temporary eclipse. The boy, who as a child was fairly independent and became the member of the small, juvenile republic, gains now on the one hand the additional freedom of the *bukumatula*, while on the other he becomes much more restricted by his various duties towards his *kada*, maternal uncle. He has less time and less interest left for the father. Later on, when friction with the maternal uncle makes its appearance, he turns, as a rule, to his father once more and their life friendship then becomes settled.

My suggestion is that the state of affairs just mentioned is an example of the process with which we are familiar in mythological studies under the name of 'decomposition', one common enough also in the psychoneuroses. it is one whereby various attributes can become detached from an original figure and incorporated in another one, which then personifies these attributes. In the present case, as in so many others, the process serves the function of unloading affect in a relationship where it might have unpleasant consequences and depositing it at a safer distance. The British Constitution has evolved a similar arrangement; in it the father of the country, the King, can do no wrong and so is immune from criticism, retaining only the affection and respect of his subjects. This was made possible, after the people refused to tolerate the system of absolute monarchy, by providing a counterpart, the Prime Minister, against whom all complaints, resentment and hostility could be directed; the volume of this opposition periodically and inevitably accumulates until he has to make way for a successor. A more subtle example has been analysed by Freud in his study of the 'taboo of virginity'.[29] He has shown that the custom of a bride being deflorated by someone other than the husband is to ensure that the resentment which this operation is apt to provoke shall be directed away from her future life-partner and precipitated elsewhere.

The two men being unconscious equivalents, it is not surprising that in some tribes the same name is applied to both, for instance, in Loangao, where the uncle is called Tate (= father).[30] A story recalled by Hartland[31] well illustrates the psychological complexity of the relationship. 'When a child dies or even meets with an accident unattended with fatal results, the mother's relatives, headed by her brother, turn out in force against the father. He must defend himself until he is wounded. Blood once drawn the combat ceases; but the attacking party plunders his house and appropriates everything on which hands can be laid, finally sitting down to a feast provided by the bereaved father.' The father is thus punished because his repressed hostile wishes have come true and the child has met with harm. Now this is in a patrilineal society – of Maoris – and the action taken by the maternal uncle points to an earlier avunculate and doubtless matrilineal social organisation. In this transition from one organisation one sees how the parts played by father and uncle respectively can change to the exact opposite. Mrs Seligman[32] informs me that in some Soudanese tribes a similar change can be observed to be at work, where the father is becoming dreaded and the uncle loved.

In this decomposition of the primal father into a kind and lenient actual father on the one hand, and a stern and moral uncle on the other, it is not chance that the latter person was chosen to fill this part. I will sketch the order of development here somewhat schematically. If we start with the primal trinity of father, mother, son, then in seeking for a surrogate to whom the jealous hatred felt for the father can become displaced there are two persons who naturally present themselves, the mother's father and her brother. The reason for this goes back to the mother's own incestuous attachments; her father and brother are also in a sense rivals of her son, though they are at a greater distance from him than his own father. It is therefore not surprising that the Oedipus legend can be paralleled by similar ones relating to the other men. Thus it was foretold of Acrisens that he would be killed by his daughter's son; and, in spite of all his efforts – first by isolating his daughter, Danae, and then by attempting to drown her and her son, Perseus, after Zeus had managed to evade the endeavours of her father to keep her a virgin – the prediction is verified: Perseus did kill his grandfather. Similar tales are related of other heroes besides Perseus, such as Cyrus, Gilgam, and Telephos.

We know from psycho-analytic work that the girl's attachment towards her father commonly becomes displaced on to her brother, just as the son displaces his mother-attachment on to his sister. The tendency towards filial and parental incest is thus exchanged for that towards brother–sister incest, which even today is much less taboo than the former and is often enough realised in actuality. As is well known, royal marriages between brother and sister were customary in ancient Egypt, and till our times in Hawaii,[33] though forbidden to commoners. It is thus comprehensible enough that jealous rivalry over the woman between nephew and uncle should duplicate that between son and father, or that the former psychological situation can replace the latter. The classical legend displaying this situation is, of course, the Tristan saga, particularly in its earlier versions. Before winning Isolde, Tristan logically kills her maternal uncle, Morolt (of course on other ostensible grounds), and, after she has espoused his own maternal uncle, Mark, he enters into rivalry with the latter; in the most recent version of the story, Thomas Hardy unveils the mask of benevolence that had been cast over Mark and lays bare the natural enmity between the two men. In the earliest versions of the Lancelot legend in the Arthurian cycle[34] there are plain indications of the same theme. In the first account it was Gawain who loved Guinevere, the wife of Arthur, his maternal uncle. In the later accounts his place is taken by Lancelot (who also usurped his position as the first Grail hero), but that the underlying themes is only disguised is shown by the circumstance that Lancelot's foster-mother was also Arthur's sister. At the end the original theme comes again to the surface, for it is another nephew, Mordred, who abducts Guinevere and kills his maternal uncle, Arthur. The further stage in repression, familiar to us in the Hamlet form of the Oedipus complex, can also be traced in the uncle–nephew relationship, the nephew avenging his uncle's murder; an example of this is the Otuel story in the Charlemagne cycle.[35] The most complete inversion is perhaps that of the Caucasian legend of Chopa,[36] for he avenges his maternal uncle, whom his father had slain, by attacking his own father.

We may now return to the Trobrianders. There, as with most matrilineal societies, there is an extraordinarily severe taboo against sexual relations between brother and sister, one which begins at the earliest age. It could not escape Malinowski's discernment that this taboo must be the expression of repressed incestuous tendencies, though he does not appear to have recognised the connection between this and the presence of an avunculate organisation; i.e. that the uncle, being the unconscious lover of the mother, is therefore the imaginary father of her children, and logically wields the *potestas* over them. He sees, however, that the uncle plays the negative part of the father in our civilisation, and formulates the following neat statement on the whole matter:[37] 'Applying to each society a terse, though rather crude formula, there is in our Society the repressed desire "to kill the father and marry the mother," while in the matrilineal complex of Melanesia, the wish is 'to' marry the sister and to kill the maternal uncle".' One striking piece of evidence he finds in support of this conclusion is a very typical set of myths among matrilineal peoples – corresponding with the European Oedipus myths – in which incest occurs between brother and sister and hatred between nephew and maternal uncle.[38]

Malinowski's conclusion is doubtless correct on the purely descriptive plane, but he goes on to use it as the basis of an extremely doubtful hypothesis in which he attempts to modify Freud's theory of the nuclear family complex. As is well known, the latter regards the relationship between father, mother and son as the prototype from which other more complicated relationships are derived. Malinowski, on the contrary, puts forward the view that the nuclear family complex varies according to the particular family structure existing in any community. According to him, a matrilineal family system arises, for unknown social and economic reasons, and then the repressed nuclear complex consists of brother and sister attraction, with nephew and uncle hatred; when this system is replaced by a patrilineal one, the nuclear complex becomes the familiar Oedipus one.

If attention is concentrated on the sociological aspects of the data, this will appear a very ingenious and perhaps even plausible suggestion. I would submit, however, that imperfect attention to the genetic aspects of the problem has led to a lack of what I have elsewhere called a 'dimensional perspective', i.e. a sense of value and proportion based on intimate knowledge of the unconscious, and that the opposite of Malinowski's conception is nearer the truth. It would seem more probable, in my opinion, that the matrilineal system with its avunculate complex arose in the way described above as a mode of defence against the primordial Oedipus tendencies than that it arose for unknown sociological reasons with then the avunculate complex as a necessary consequence and the Oedipus complex appearing only when the patrilineal system was subsequently introduced. The forbidden and unconsciously loved sister is only a substitute for the mother, as the uncle plainly is for the father. On Malinowski's hypothesis the Oedipus complex would be a late product; for the psycho-analyst it was the *fons et origo*.

IV   THE RELATION OF MOTHER-RIGHT TO FATHER-RIGHT

In 1861, the year Bachofen's famous work *Das Mutterrecht* appeared, an equally famous work was published by Sir Henry Maine, entitled *Primal Law*. In it he enunciated, largely on the basis of juristic studies in India, the view that the primal state of society must have been a patriarchal one. In the years that have elapsed since that date more historical and ethnological evidence and arguments, expounded especially by McLennan, Lewis Morgan, Lubbock and Hartland, have accumulated in favour of the first of these views, to the effect that the primal system of society (with or without a still earlier state of promiscuity) was a matrilineal one; and perhaps the majority of anthropologists to-day are inclined to support this view. It is at all events certain that mother-right is extremely widespread among savage races, and there is much reason to think that this was still more so 5,000 years ago.

A heated controversy has taken place over the question of whether father-right as we know it or mother-right as we find it among savages was the earlier system of the two. The view here represented is different from either. It is that the question has not been justly put, for the two alternatives mentioned do not exhaust the possibilities. We know from psychoanalytic work that there are often three mental layers where there appear to be only two. A perky conceitedness, for instance, is usually the compensatory reaction to a deep-seated sense of inferiority, but analysis shows that this in its turn is based on repressed narcissism. The first and the third layers are similar in their content, but they are not on that account to be identified. The present problem may well prove to be of a like nature.

Before developing this idea we may briefly review the opinion that have been expressed by other writers. Those who take the primal patriarchal view have to explain why mother-right ever came into existence, whereas for those who take the opposite view the question is rather why the primal mother-right was ever supplanted by father-right. The former tend to regard mother-right as a temporary and necessarily evanescent phase, and the chief explanation offered for its existence seems to be that it was dependent on the development of agriculture, where woman's work was found to be of special value; the correlation, however, between agriculture and mother-right is far from close enough to establish the connection.[39] The second set of writers, who often wax enthusiastic over the idyllic situation prevailing under mother-right, tend to regard this as the natural state of affairs and to take the view that women were driven from this paradise by brute force.[40] Hartland, for whom father-right is 'a purely artificial system',[41] says: 'The conclusion seems irresistible that father-right is traceable not to any change in savage or barbarous theories of blood-relationship, but to social and economical causes'.[42] Both he[43] and Rivers,[44] who, by the way, expresses no opinion about the relative antiquity of mother-right and father-right, would ascribe great importance in this connection to the violent immigrations of primitive times whereby the will of the conquered was imposed on the weaker.

The view advanced in this paper is based on the psycho-analytic recognition of the fundamental importance of the nuclear Oedipus complex. It is in accord neither with the idea of primitive promiscuity, nor with that of primal mother-right, nor even with that of patriarchy as we nowadays conceive it in its monogamic form. Far from being led by consideration of the subject, as Malinowski was, to abandon or revise Freud's conception of the 'primal horde' (Atkinson's 'cyclopean family'), it seems to me, on the contrary, that this conception furnishes the most satisfactory explanation of the complicated problems which we have been discussing. According to this, the system of mother-right, with its avunculate complex, represents one mode of defence among the many that have been adopted against the tendencies denoted by the term Oedipus complex. We cannot, of course, say whether it represents a necessary stage in the evolution towards the present patriarchal system; I see no reason why it should, and the fact that some of the lowest type of Australian savages, whose primitive instincts are hard enough to curb, find it possible to cope with them by an alternative method – that of taboo and the totemic system – might be quoted in support of the doubt. Nor is there any reason to suppose that the savage ignorance, or rather repression, of the facts to paternal procreation is a necessary accompaniment of mother-right, though it is evident that it must be a valuable support to the motives discussed above which led to the instituting of mother-right.

The patriarchal system, as we know it, betokens acknowledging of the supremacy of the father and yet the ability to accept this even with affection, without having to have recourse to a system either of mother-right or of complicated taboos. It means the taming of man, the gradual assimilation of the Oedipus complex. At last man could face his real father and live with him. Well might Freud say that the recognition of the father's place in the family signified the most important progress in cultural development.

So far as we can tell, the way in which this has been – at least partly – accomplished has been the replacement of hate by sublimated homosexuality, or murder thoughts by castration thoughts. The necessary price paid has been the diminished sexual potency of civilised man, with all the complicated consequences of this.

INTRODUCTION: REFERENCES

Leach, E. R. (1958) Virgin birth. *Journal of the Royal Anthropological Institute*, 88: 147–64.
Spiro, M. (1982) *Oedipus in the Trobriands*. Chicago: Chicago University Press.

NOTES

1. Reik, *Probleme der Religionspsychologie* (1919), Chap. II.
2. Frazer, *Adonis, Attis, Osiris*. Vol. II, pp. 208–9.
3. Rivers (*Hastings' Encyclopaedia of Religion and Ethics*: art. 'Mother-Right') would use the term 'mother-kinship' in a different and narrower sense, distinguishing it from matrilineal descent. For him, 'kinship' is much the same as our 'relationship' when used in a genealogical sense, though perhaps the actual conception of a blood-bond may not be always essential in the savage mind. In this strict sense mother-kinship probably never exists in a pure form, so that we may ignore it for our purpose; that is to say, there are no peoples where no kinship whatever is recognised between the child and his father (and the father's relatives). By descent, whether matrilineal or patrilineal, is meant the origin of the child that determines to which social group (moiety or clan) it shall belong. If this is determined by the status of the mother, we have matrilineal descent – which other writers denote by the term 'mother-kinship' – and this is the most essential feature of mother-right.
4. For a sufficiently full discussion of the point, see Hartland, *Primitive Society* (1921), pp. 12–17.
5. Hartland, *Primitive Paternity* (1909). Vol. I, p. 303.
6. Westermarck, *The History of Human Marriage*, 5th edn (1921). Vol. I, p. 294.
7. By 'sexual ignorance' I mean in this context particularly the ignorance that semen is the fertilising fluid.
8. Malinowski, 'Baloma; the spirits of the dead in the Trobriand Islands', *Journal of the Royal Anthropological Institute* (1916); 'The psychology of sex and the foundation of kinship in primitive societies' and 'Psycho-analysis and anthropology', both in *Psyche*, IV.
9. *Psyche*, IV: 128.
10. See Westermarck, op. cit., pp. 287, 288.
11. Carveth Read, 'No paternity', *Journal of the Royal Anthropological Institute*, XLVIII: 146.

12. Heape, *Sex Antagonism* (1913), pp. 103, 112.
13. Heape here quotes Roth: 'North Queensland ethnography', Bull. No. 5, p. 22.
14. He cites (p. 100) the Baganda custom of punishing adultery only when the banana tree is out of blossom, for otherwise the conception is ascribed to the latter. But as the banana tree blossoms all the year round – compare our saying 'when gorse is out bloom then kissing is out of fashion' – and the banana is an obvious phallic symbol, there would seem to be need for further investigation of the information gathered in respect of this custom.
15. Carveth Read, op. cit., p. 146.
16. One example is illustrated in Reik's interpretation of the postural couvade as a means of coping with the sadism aroused by the sight of the suffering wife.
17. See Freud, *Totem und Tabu* (1913).
18. See Reik, *Probleme der Religionspsycholgie* (1919), Chap. III.
19. This is perhaps one reason why mother-right so often persists, even when the facts of paternity are fully recognised.
20. ibid.
21. See Rank, *Der Mythus der Geburt des Heldens, 2nd edn (1922), and Ernest Jones, 'A psycho-analytic study of the Holy Ghost', Essays in Applied Psycho-Analysis* (1923), Chap. XIII.
22. Reik, op. cit.
23. Malinowski, *Psyche*, V: 207.
24. A contribution from the woman's side which may be compared with Frazer's remark (see above) about the sick fancies of pregnant women.
25. Malinowski, *Psyche*, IV: 298.
26. ibid: 304.
27. loc. cit.
28. op. cit. p. 324.
29. Freud, 'Taboo of virginity' (1918), *Collected Papers*, Vol. IV (1925).
30. Hartland, op. cit., p. 281.
31. ibid., p. 279.
32. Personal communication, for which I am much indebted.
33. Rivers, *Social Organization* (1924), p. 39.
34. See Jessie L. Weston's works, *Arthur and Guinevere, King Arthur and his Knights, The Legend of Sir Gawayne*, and *Lancelot du Lac*.
35. Ellis, *Specimens of Early English Metrical Romances* (1805), pp. 375 ff.
36. Cited by Hartland, op. cit., p. 271.
37. Malinowski, *Psyche*, V: 195.
38. ibid: 216.
39. See Westermarck, op. cit., p. 297.
40. One cannot refrain from wondering what part the infantile 'sadistic conception of coitus' may have played in the idea that men imposed 'father-right' on 'mother-right' by brute force.
41. Hartland, op. cit., Vol. II, p. 248.
42. ibid., p. 100.
43. idem: *Primitive Society* (1921), p. 161.
44. Rivers, op. cit., p. 97.

CHAPTER SIX

The Physical Effect on the Individual of the Idea of Death Suggested by the Collectivity (Australia, New Zealand) (1926)

Marcel Mauss

Marcel Mauss (1872–1956), the nephew of Emile Durkheim, collaborated with his uncle on numerous publications, notably Primitive Classification, and published articles in his journal Année Sociologique. Mauss is now remembered for his biosocial theories and his studies on magic, the gift, personhood and sacrifice. Here he re-examines an old chestnut of colonial folklore – the physical consequences (death) of understanding that one has been ensorcered. Mauss may be faulted for his assumption of the greater physical fortitude of the non-European and for his collection of anecdotes but his paper[1] makes a clear advance on Kraepelin's racial biology. Despite physiological interest by Cannon, more recent consideration on what is popularly known as 'voodoo death' emphasise the time taken to die after awareness of sorcery and suggest that death is due to starvation or self-deprivation of fluid (Lewis 1977; Eastwell 1982).

My study of the relations between psychology and sociology (Mauss 1924; pp. 1–33 above) was entirely one of method. But a method is justified only if it opens up a route, $\mu\acute{\alpha}\theta o\delta o\varsigma$, if it is a means of classifying facts hitherto resistant to classification. It is of interest only if it has a heuristic value. Let us therefore move on to positive work and show that behind the few assertions I allowed myself there were facts, in particular some which show the direct link in man between the physical, the psychological and the moral; i.e. the social.

I suggested to you that in a very large number of societies an obsession with death, purely social in origin, without any admixture of individual factors, was capable of such mental and physical ravages in the consciousness and the body of the individual that it led very quickly to his death, without any apparent or known lesions. And I promised to bring you documentation, a demonstration and, if not an analysis, at least an analytical project. Here they are, thrown into the debate and subject to your criticism. But first let us define the problem.

1   A DEFINITION OF THE COLLECTIVE SUGGESTION OF THE IDEA
OF DEATH

I shall not confuse these facts with facts which are indeed close to them
and which used to be grouped with them within the term *thanatomania.*
Suicide, in the societies we are going to study, is often the result of an
obsession of the same kind: the way the individual, in certain states of sin
or bewitchment, makes many attacks on his own life, especially in the land
of the Maori, demonstrates this persistent suggestion. The latter can thus
have precisely the same forms, yet has different consequences in the system
of facts that we are going to describe.[2] For in this case the will to cause
one's own death and the brutal act itself intervene. The influence of the
social on the physical has an obvious psychical mediator; it is the person
who destroys himself and the act is unconscious (*sic* – is 'conscious'
meant?).

The order of the facts that I wish to discuss with you is, from my point
of view and for my demonstration, far more striking. It consists of those
cases of death produced brutally, elementarily in many individuals, but
quite simply *because they known or believe* (which is the same thing) *that
they are going to die.*

However, among these latter facts there are grounds for distinguishing
those where this belief and this knowledge are – or may be – individual in
origin. It will soon be seen that, in the civilisations to be considered, such
facts are often confused with those that we envisage more precisely.
However, it is clear that if the individual is sick and believes he is going to
die, even if the disease is caused, according to him, by the witchcraft of
another or by his own sin (of commission or omission), it is arguable that
it is the idea of the disease that is the 'intermediate cause' of the (conscious
and subconscious) reasoning.

Hence we shall consider only those cases where the *subject who dies* does
not believe or know himself to be ill, *he only believes, for precise collective
causes, that he is in a state close to death.* This state generally coincides
with a break in his communion, either by magic or through sin, with the
sacred powers and things whose presence normally sustains him. His
consciousness is then completely invaded by ideas and sentiments which
are entirely of collective origin, which betray no physical disturbance.
Analysis is unable to hit on any element of will, choice or even voluntary
ideation on the part of the sufferer, or even of individual mental disturbance, other than the collective suggestion itself. This individual believes
himself to be bewitched or at fault and dies for this reason. These, therefore, are the kinds of events to which I shall confine my type of examination. Other facts, such as suicide occasioned or disease motivated by these
same states of sin or invultuation, are clearly less typical. In making my

study more difficult by such a detailed circumscription, I shall make it simpler, more impressive and more conclusive.

These facts are well known in many supposedly lower civilisations, but they seem uncommon or non-existent in our own. This upholds the point that they have a very marked social character; for they obviously depend on the presence or absence of a certain number of precise institutions and beliefs which have disappeared from the ranks of our society: witchcraft, prohibitions, taboos, etc. But however numerous and well known they may be among these peoples, they have not – I believe – yet been the object of any profound psychological and sociological study. (Max) Bartels (1893, pp. 10–13) and (Otto) Stoll (1904) quote a large number, but they mix them up with the others and go no further than the collection of facts borrowed from all sorts of peoples. However, these good old books are sufficient to give some idea of the wide spread of facts of this kind throughout mankind. Let us therefore proceed more methodologically; let us concentrate our study on two groups of facts from two groups of civilisations: one is the lowest possible, or rather the lowest known – the Australian; the other is already highly developed and has no doubt undergone many vicissitudes – that of the Maori, the Malayo-Polynesians of New Zealand. I shall restrict myself to a selection of facts from the collections that my late friend Hertz and I drew up.[3] It would have been easy to multiply these comparisons; especially in North America and in Africa (e.g. Casalis 1859, pp. 293–6 [and 1861, pp. 277–80]), facts of the same kind are common, and have indeed been well described by the older writers. But it is better to concentrate our attention on two types of facts which are close but distant enough from one another for comparison to be possible, and whose nature and functioning are well known both in themselves and in relation to the social environment and the individual.

A short description of the mental, physical and social conditions in which cases of this kind arise may be useful. (Paul) Fauconnet, for example, has given a fine account, in discussing responsibility in various societies (1920, pp. 247 ff.), and from Durkheim we have a fine description in relation to many Australian religious facts – funerary rituals *et al.* (1912, pp. 323–8; 1914, pp. 226–9) – of the violent impulses which inspire the groups, the violent fears and the reactions to which they may be prey. But these total seizures of the individual consciousnesses engendered in the group and by the group are not the only ones. The ideas then elaborated are maintained and reproduced in the individual under the permanent pressure of the group, of education, etc. On the most trivial occasion they unleash destruction or over-excite forces.

Even the intensity of these actions of the moral on the physical is all the more notable in that the latter is stronger, rougher and more animal-like in these peoples than it is among us. It is commonly observed both in

Australian ethnography and in many other ethnographies that a native's body has an astonishing physical resistance. This may be so either because of the effect of the sun and of life in a state of complete or near complete nakedness, because of the very low pollution of the environment and tools before the Europeans arrived, or because of certain peculiarities of the races selected precisely by this kind of life (in particular there may be physiological elements, sera and so on in their organisms which are different from those of weaker races, elements of the kind Eugen Fischer has begun to investigate, but with little success [see Fischer 1931, pp. 163–4]). Whatever the cause, even by comparison with African blacks, the Australian's organism is none the less distinguished by an astonishing resilience. The woman who has given birth returns immediately to her daily round, she gets up and walks after a few hours; serious flesh wounds heal very quickly; in a number of tribes a common punishment is to spear a woman or young man through the thigh; arm fractures are very quickly cured with light splints. All these cases are in marked contrast with other events. An individual is wounded, even slight; he has no chance of recovery if he believes the spear to be bewitched; he breaks some limb, and this starts to mend quickly only from the moment he has made his peace with the rules he violated, and so on. The extreme character of actions of this kind of the moral on the physical is obviously even more tangible in the cases where there is no wound, and which fall entirely within my scope.

New Zealand as an observational field is also rich in typical facts, although the New Zealanders already have finer physiologies which are less resistant to physical agents than the Australians. It is a commonplace in their ethnography, particularly the older ethnography, before the arrival of the Europeans and their smallpox, etc., which killed so many of them, to note their strength, their health, the rapidity with which wounds healed, their speed of recovery from illness, so long as their morale had not been undermined. But they interest us in other respects. The New Zealanders, like all Malayo-Polynesians, of all men are among the most subject to states of 'panic'. Everyone knows the Malay '*amok*': men (always men), even nowadays, and even in very large towns, avenge the death of one of their kin or an insult by setting out, 'running *amok*' and killing as many in their paths as they can until they themselves are struck down. New Zealand man and Malayo-Polynesian man in general is the prime example of this kind of emotionalism. It is here that, by a happy chance, Hertz found astonishing effects of the mechanisms of the moral consciousness to analyse. The Maori, in particular, present the high points of mental and physical potency with a moral and mystical cause, and also the low points of depression, for the same reasons. In Hertz's book (see p. 30 above) all the details of this demonstration are to be found, so I shall not go into it any further.

2   AUSTRALIAN TYPES OF FACTS

The Australians regard only the deaths we call violent as natural. A wound, a murder, a fracture are natural causes. Vendetta is unleashed less violently against the murderer than it is against the sorcerer. All other deaths have a magical or even religious origin.[4] Only in New Zealand do events of a moral or religious origin suggest to the individual the dominant idea that he is going to die, and even the bewitchings are ordinarily seen as intended primarily to make the victim commit a sin. On the contrary, in Australia the proportion is reversed. Cases in which death is caused by the idea that it is the fatal result of a sin are – to my knowledge – fairly uncommon, and I have found only a small number, mostly involving crimes affecting the totem, in particular eating it,[5] or else foods forbidden to age classes. Here are two fairly typical cases of the last, which Durkheim did not have to consider: 'If a young man or young woman of the Wakelbura tribe eats forbidden game ... they will become sick, and probably pine away and die, uttering the sounds peculiar to the creature in question' (Howitt, 1904, p. 769). It is the creature's spirit which has entered and killed them.[6] The other is one of those specific cases that concern us more closely (pp. 769–70):

> [Mr M'Alpine] had a Kurnai blackboy in his employ about 1856–7. The lad was strong and healthy until one day Mr M'Alpine found him ill. He explained that he had been doing what he ought not to have done, that he had 'stolen some female 'possum' before he was permitted to eat it; that the old men had found him out, and that he knew he would never grow up to be a man. He lay down under that belief, so to say, and never got up again, dying within three weeks.

Thus moral and religious causes can cause death among the Australians, too, by suggestion. This latter fact also serves as a bridge to cases of death with a purely magical origin. The old men threatened him. Besides, just as many of the deaths inflicted by magic are so inflicted during a vendetta, or as punishments[7] decreed by the (tribal) council, and are basically sanctions, the individual who believes that he is bewitched by these legal spells is also tainted morally, in the strict sense of the word, and the Australian facts overall are not so remote from the Maori facts overall as one might have thought. However, normally it is a question of magic. A man who thinks he is bewitched dies, that is the brute, and very frequent, fact. Let me refer to some eye-witness accounts, preferably old and well-observed ones, preferably during precise events or even those from naturalists and doctors. Before 1840 (James) Backhouse tells how a man at

Bourne Island believed he was bewitched and said he would die the following day; he did (1843, p. 105).[8] In the Kennedy district in 1865 at the Edens' house, an old Irish (*sic* – actually Scottish) maid complained to a black maid of her selfishness, saying, 'You too will die soon for being so cruel.' 'She stared for a minute ... then her hands fell ... the ghastly colour peculiar to blacks when under emotional feelings came over her face and, although we tried to rally her, and the poor woman was in despair at the effect of her words, it was to no purpose, she pined and pined, and in less than a month I dug her grave...' (Eden 1872, pp. 110–11).

Several early writers recount the fact in a more general way. In 1843, (F. Robert) Austin, the explorer of the Kimberley district, noted the astonishing vitality of the blacks and their astonishing and mortal susceptibility to the idea that they had been bewitched (Roth 1903, pp. 47, 49 [*sic* – actually p. 54?]). According to (Walter Wilson) Froggat, a naturalist, when 'a man hears that this (witchcraft) has been done to him he wastes away with fright' (1888, p. 654). A writer who made his observations around 1870 saw a man who had stated that he would die at a certain time and who died at that moment 'by the power of (his) imagination' (H.P. 1897, p. 100, col. 1). The Northern Victorian missionary, the Reverend (John) Bulmer, is very positive in general about certain tribes in which he saw cases of this kind (1888, p. 13 (*sic* – actually p. 16?]). In one of the most untouched tribes of Queensland another missionary specifies (is this a phrase of Anglo-Australian 'pidgin' or is it a fact?) that, if a counter-charm is not found, the blood 'goes bad' and the bewitched individual dies (Ward 1908, [pp. 119–20]).[9]

Cases where the individual even dies at a specified time have been noted. In other rather rare ones which fall outside the area of magic but still involve the social and the religious, when someone is haunted by the dead, the same thing is recorded. Backhouse also tells how a black from Molonbah died in two days: he had seen a dead 'white man' who told him he would die in this time (1843, p. 105 – about 1850 [*sic* – this seems to be a complete mis-reference]). In 1864, the murderer of the botanist Stevens [?] died of hunger in prison within a month. The dead man looked at him over his shoulder (Bride 1899).[10] A Dieri legend – a document of this kind is as valuable as any observation, to my mind – perfectly transcribed, tells how a divine ancestor, the Mura-Waruwondina, abandoned by his camp, wished to die and did die. He bewitched himself by the rite of the bone in the fire. The more he suffered, the happier he was. He ended as he had wished (Siebert 1910, p. 47, col. 2).

The study of the cure for these obsessions and illnesses is as revealing as the study of their fatal consequences. The individual recovers if the magical ceremony of exorcism, the counter-charm, acts, as unfailingly as he dies in the reverse circumstances (Newland 1890, p. 26). Two recent observers, one a doctor, tell how people die from the 'pointing-bones' among the Wongkonguru: they are very frightened. If this bone is rediscovered, the bewitched man gets better; if not, he gets worse. 'They distrust white man's medicine because it is not strong enough to cope with the poison of a bone' (Horne and Aiston 1924, pp. 150, 152). The story told to Sir (Walter) Baldwin Spencer, the great physiologist and anthropologist, by one of the Kakadu elders, a certain Mukalakki, should be read right through. As a young man he had accidentally eaten a certain snake forbidden to men of his age. An old man noticed this. 'Why have you eaten *kumali* (taboo food)? ... You are a little man ... you will be very ill,' he told him. Mukalakki was very frightened and said to the old man, 'What is it; shall I die?' The old man answered, 'Yes, by and by you very ill, you die.'[11] Fifteen years later Mukalakki fell very ill. An old medicine man asked him, 'What have you eaten?' He remembered and told the story. 'Today you die,' said the native doctor.[12] As the day wore on he became worse and worse. It took three men to hold him down. The spirit of the snake twisted around inside his body and, every now and then, came out through his forehead, hiss in his mouth, etc. It was terrifying. The natives went some way to seek the illustrious reincarnation of a celebrated medicine man. This man, named Morpun, arrived none too soon, for the convulsions of the snake and of Mukalakki grew more and more horrible. He sent everyone away and stood silently watching Mukalakki, saw the mystical serpent, caught it, put it into his dilly-bag or medicine-bag and took it back to his own country, where he put it into a water-hold and told it to stay there. Mukalakki 'felt intensely relieved. He perspired profusely, went to sleep and woke up all right in the morning. ... If it had not been for Morpun removing the snake, he must have died; and Morpun was the only man who could do this, etc.' (Spencer 1914, pp. 348–50).

Withnell, writing of tribes also in the North (the North-West this time), says that the '*tarlow*' (totem sanctuaries and ceremonies) have curative virtues of this sort, virtues which are effective even on the minds of young children (1901, p. 6). Fundamentally it is a question of demonstrating and re-establishing communion with the essential sacred thing. Thus the Dieri who believes he is bewitched saves himself by chanting the sacred song of his clan, of his ancestor, the *mura-wima* (Siebert 1910, p. 48, cols 1–2), and even the song of a certain ancestor made invincible.[13] A native's song of semi-Christian origin reported by Bulmer and composed at the burial of a converted black said that he was sheltered from death, since 'feel cheered I (by your) good helping spirit' (Bulmer 1888, p. 43). One of the finest ethnographers of Central Australia[14] supports the interpretation by Guyon[15] and Howitt of the Mindari ceremonies (of initiation and propitiation) and the rituals of counter-magic and *intichiuma*. Their meaning was to show men that they were at peace with the whole world (Worsnop 1890 [p. 27]).

These mentalities are completely steeped in this belief in the effectiveness of words, in the danger of sinister actions. They are also infinitely concerned with a kind of mysticism of the peace of the soul. And thus it is that the feeble trust in life either capsizes definitively or is restored to equilibrium by an auxiliary, magician or protective spirit, itself of a collective nature, like the loss of equilibrium itself.

3 NEW ZEALAND AND POLYNESIAN TYPES OF FACTS[16]

These descriptions also constitute a kind of common ground in the ethnography of the Maori and of all Polynesia. One of those most familiar with them, (Edward) Tregear, returned often to the subject (1893, pp. 71–3; 1904, pp. 20 ff.). The physical endurance of the Maori is extraordinary and renowned. No doubt it does not exceed that of our ancestors two thousand years ago, but the wounds that healed were extraordinary. Tregear cites some remarkable cases: e.g. a man who lived to a great age without a jaw; it had been carried away by a cannon-ball in 1863. This resistance contrasts strongly with the weakness in the case of diseases caused by sin or magic, or even by the one or the other without disease. The early and excellent author (John Jackson) Jarves describes in excellent terms the state thus induced: the result of being bewitched is death 'from want of exertion to live', through a 'fatal spirit of despondency', through 'an almost immovable apathy' (1872, pp. 20, 46, 191). A proverb of the Marquesas Islands, earlier than the arrival of the Europeans, said: 'We are sinners, we shall die.' An alternative dominates the entire consciousness, without any middle ground. On the one hand physical strength, gaiety, firmness, brutality and mental simplicity; on the other, without any transition, unlimited and unrestrained excitation by grief or insult,[17] or just as unlimited and unrestrained depression, and without any transition, lamentation at abandonment, despair and finally the suggestion of death.[18] (Alfred K.) Newman believes that the latter may even have an effect on the mortality rate. 'Unquestionably many Maoris die of slight ailments because when attacked they do not fight against the disease and strive to resist its ravages, but quietly coil their blankets round them, and lie down passively to die. They seem to have no pluck, and their friends look on in a listless do-nothing way, accepting their fate needlessly' (1882, p. 471). At any rate the Maori themselves classify the causes and their deaths in this way: (a) death by spirits (violation of taboo, magic, etc.); (b) death by war; (c) death by natural decay; (d) death by accident or suicide.[19] And they attribute the most importance to the first of these causes (Elsdon Best in Goldie 1904, pp. 2–3; cf. Best 1905, p. 222).

This system of beliefs is thus the same as in Australia. Only the results, and hence the intensity of the beliefs, are differently distributed. It is the purely moral and religious notions that predominate. Spells and witchcraft have the same role here as they do in Australia, but the Polynesian's morality, rich, tortuous and yet brutal and simple in its revolutions or through its effects, is the cause of the majority of deaths. At any rate, here are a few facts which prove the continuity of the two types.

First, although Polynesian totemism has largely disappeared, especially in New Zealand, it has left traces precisely in the manner in which certain causes of death are conceived. This is particularly so on Tonga, where (William) Mariner recounts how a man who had eaten a forbidden turtle got a swollen liver from it and died (Mariner and Martin 1817, Vol. 2, p. 133). But it is in Samoa above all that violated (totemic) taboos are avenged. The absorbed animal speaks and acts from inside him, destroys the man, eats him and he dies (Turner 1884, pp. 50–1).[20] Deaths by magic are also very frequent. Mariner tells how a woman (her spirit) haunted a young chief's mind. The *tohunga* told him that he would die in two days. He died (Mariner and Martin 1817, Vol. 1, pp. 110–11). Elsewhere it is a monster god who dies bewitched.[21] Deaths following on an omen are also common (Best 1898, p. 131).[22]

But what is common is essentially death by 'mortal sin', especially in Maori country. Moreover, the expression is their own. The innumerable descriptions are usually highly circumstantial and have many mythological alternatives: the soul is weighed down; it is bound, tied with ropes, nets and knots; it is absent; it is trapped; it is not the only spirit residing in the body; it has a neighbour haunting it; or it is blocked by an animal or thing which invades the body or the soul itself. All these expressions are familiar to the neurologist and psychologist, of course, but here they have a definite and common traditional and individual use.

But it is essential not to remove the effect too much from the cause. The Maori are very sophisticated in questions of morality or scruple. I shall set aside Hertz's fine analysis of these complicated and typical mechanisms and extract from it only two suggestions: death by magic is very often conceived, is often possible only as the result of a previous sin. Inversely, death by sin is often only the result of a spell which has made the victim sin.[23] Divination, omens, spirits ('*aitu*', '*atua*') may also be involved in the story.[24] They are true pangs of conscience that lead to the states of fatal depression[25] and are themselves caused by this magic of sin which causes the individual to feel himself to be in the wrong, to have been put in the wrong.[26] As it happens, we have a long study by a doctor on this set of facts. (W. H.) Goldie, assisted by one of the finest ethnographers, Elsdon Best, has theorised these facts, even comparatively.[27] In the chapter entitled 'Rapidly fatal melancholia', he says, people 'will themselves to death' (Goldie 1904, pp. 77, 81). Here are a few of the cases he quotes: Dr (later Sir) Batty Tuke knew an individual in good health and with a Herculean frame. He died in less than three days from this 'melancholia'. Another man was to all appearances well and 'certainly ... not suffering from any disease of the thoracic viscera', 'chagrined at life'; he said he was going to die, and die he did, within ten days. In most of the cases studied by this doctor the interval was three or four days.

Other facts are historical, taken from (Edward) Shortland, (Richard) Taylor and others. They took place publicly. On board the Governor's vessel, when the old chief Kukutai saw the North Cape and the cliff which is the door to the Land of the Dead, he propitiated the souls by throwing overboard the shirts, first of the men on board, including his ministers, then his own clothes; 'so great was his nervous prostration that grave fears were entertained that he might succumb' (Goldie 1904, p. 78).

But allow me to add, in addition to these concrete facts, some Maori literary documents. A famous song, that of Kikokko's daughter, well conveys the sentiments of the sick person.

> Bright sun! thou lingerest still,
> Adorning, with they yellow rays, famed
> Pukehinau's summit. Oh linger yet
> Awhile bright sun that we may set
> Together...
> Alas, thou (mother) canst not find a remedy
> The gods have otherwise decreed; Whiro (god of war and punishment) by his
> Axe has all my bones disjointed, and I am
> Torn asunder as a branch snapt from its
> Parent stem by some rude blast, and falling
> With a crash its rent in pieces...
>   I did it; I brought this death
> Upon myself (who comes from God – Hertz) and now
> As in a desert I'm bereft of every succour,
> Emaciated and forlorn, wracked with
> Pain of body and distress of mind.
> (Without soul, oppressed, exhausted – Hertz; and far better.)
>   I turn me
> Round to die.
> (That is why the body turns round to die – Hertz; and far better.)[28]

Here is Dr Goldie's conclusion (1904):

This fatalistic tendency which has been so often observed ... and which leads to death after a shorter or longer interval of deep depression and lack of desire to live, is due to the effects of superstitious fear acting on a peculiarly susceptible nervous system (p. 77).

No one, I think, has attempted to explain the rationale of death from this curious form of melancholia. The victim is popularly supposed to 'will himself to death', but we cannot seriously attribute the fatal issue to the will-force of the savage. The chief characteristic of the Maori mind is its instability. His mental equilibrium is at the mercy of a thousand daily incidents; he is the plaything of outside circumstances. His brain not having been subject to a prolonged course of moral and intellectual culture, he lacks that mental balance which is the characteristic of highly civilized peoples. He is incapable of governing himself; he will laugh or cry for the most futile reasons; explosions of joy or sadness may disappear with him in an instant ... (here Goldie cites many examples).

In that curious mental condition called 'South Sea Island Hysteria', the patient, after a preliminary period of depression, suddenly becomes violently excited, seizes a knife or some weapon, and rushes through the village slashing at everybody he meets and doing no end of damage, until he finally falls exhausted. If he cannot find a knife, he might rush to the ocean reef and fling himself into the water and swim for miles, until rescued or drowned. This violent hysterical excitement is common to all the islands, as is the opposite condition of sudden and profound mental depression.

There follows a description of the unfortunate results of a spiritualist séance after a funeral. One of the dead man's younger sisters heard his spirit, became excited, collapsed, decided to follow him and killed herself a few hours later.

Given, then, a people who are highly emotional, whose brain is in a state of unstable equilibrium, liable to excessive excitement or profound melancholy; who have no fear of death, and in whom the life-preserving instinct is feebly developed; who are deeply superstitious, attributing unlimited evil powers to their malignant gods and wicked sorcerers – when one possessing such mental attributes in a marked degree becomes convinced that he is the victim of a powerful god or *tohunga* (sorcerer), the excessive nervous shock renders the whole nervous system paretic; he offers no resistance to the stuporose condition which then supervenes; he becomes self-absorbed and dwells on the enormity of his sin and the utter hopelessness of his condition; he is the helpless victim of delusional melancholia. He is submerged by one overmastering delusion: he has offended the gods, he must die. There is an abeyance of interest in things external; the morbid state is most acutely centralized; there is great nervous depression; there is a loss of physical energy, and this secondary depression spreads gradually to all the organs: the vital functions are all depressed, the heart becomes depressed, the involuntary muscles become dormant, and finally there is a complete anergia or death. The unbalanced mind succumbs without a struggle to the severe mental shock of overwhelming superstitious fear. (pp. 81–2)

I quite simply offer this conclusion for your consideration. Its language is out of date from a medical point of view, but it has its importance and its value will no doubt be permanent.

Besides, it would be difficult to exaggerate the scale of these facts. I have quoted only a few out of those I know. let me come to an end. One of the most notable and most tragic cases is that of the Morioris of the Chatham Islands, conquered by the Maori in 1835 and reduced to twenty-five from the two thousand there had been. (Alexander) Shand, who lived among them and was their interpreter, tells how they were transported to the South Island and what their conquerors told them (1894, p. 79):

Some of the Maoris said of the Morioris, 'It was not the number we killed which reduced them, but after taking them as slaves, we frequently found them of a morning dead in their houses. It was the infringement of their own *tapus* (being compelled by the Maoris to do things which desecrated their *tapus*) which killed them. They were a very *tapu* people.'

And there is the famous passage from Job, still corresponding so profoundly to so many mentalities we call abnormal, but which were not abnormal in these civilisations:[29]

In dreams, in visions of the night,
when deepest sleep falls upon men,
while they sleep on their beds, God makes them listen,
and his correction strikes them with terror.
. . .
at the edge of the pit he holds him back alive
and stops him from crossing the river of death.
Or again, man learns his lessons on a bed of pain,

tormented by a ceaseless ague in his bones;
he turns from his food with loathing
and has no relish for the choicest meats;
his flesh hangs loose upon him,
his bones are loosened and out of joint,
his soul draws near to the pit,
his life to the ministers of death.

Those are the facts. I shall spare you any psychopathological or neuro-pathological discussion. All the witnesses, even the doctors, agree that there are no apparent lesions in these cases or any disturbance detectable by auscultation, etc. I do not know. Observations are urgently needed. Perhaps you could encourage them?

But for me as a sociologist it is enough to have pointed out to you a direction in which I have found numerous examples and – normal ones – at any rate frequent in their abnormality. This is what I promised you.

Moreover, they are of a kind I think should be studied very soon: the kind in which the social nature of man very directly intersects with his biological nature. The panic fear which completely disorganises conscious-ness up to and including what is called the instinct for self-preservation disorganises especially life it self. The psychological link is visible, firm: consciousness. But it is not very strong; the individual who is bewitched or in a state of mortal sin loses all control over his life, any choice, any independence, his whole personality.

In addition, these facts are also 'total' facts of the type I think should be studied. Not even a consideration of the psychical or rather of the psycho-organic is enough her, to describe the complex as a whole. The social also has to be considered. Conversely, the study of only that fragment of our life which is our life in society is not enough. Here we see how to place Durkheim's *homo duplex* into a more precise setting, and how his double nature is to be envisaged.

Finally, from this dual point of view, from the study of the totality of consciousness and that of the totality of behaviour, these facts are, I think, interesting. They oppose the 'totality' of those improperly called 'primitive' to the 'dissociation' of the sort of men we are, sensible of our persons and resistant to the collectivity. The instability of the whole character and life of an Australian or a Maori is plain to see. These collective or individual 'hysterias', as Goldie has also called them, are among us only questions of hospitals and country bumpkins. They have constituted the matrix from which our moral strength has slowly disengaged itself.

To close, may I mention once again that these facts confirm and extend the theory of anomic suicide that Durkheim expounded in a book which is a model of sociological demonstration (1897, 1952).

INTRODUCTION: REFERENCES

Eastwell, H. D. (1982) 'Voodoo death and the mechanism for the despatch of the dying in East Arnhem', *American Anthropologist*, 84: 5–18.

Lewis, G. (1977) 'Fear of death and the problem of death by suggestion'. In J. Blacking (ed.) *The Anthropology of the Body*. London: Academic Press.

NOTES

1. A communication to the Société de Psychologie presented in 1926, first published in the *Journal de Psychologie Normale et Pathologique*, 23 (1926): 653–69.

2. A few cases of this kind are to be found in (Sebald Rudolf) Steinmetz's excellent catalogue of African information (1907). See in particular the suicides through loss of prestige which are still frequent among us and in China, and which were so common in antiquity.

3. Hertz made a fine survey of most of the documentation published on New Zealand before the war. He was preparing a major study of sin and expiation in lower societies, the Introduction to which has been published (1922) and the rest of which I hope I can reconstruct from his excellent notes and the important fragments which remain of this great work. His introduction to this question was the notion of mortal sin. I have taken the liberty of sifting through this documentation. I myself have had occasion to look into these facts in connection with investigations into the origin of the belief in the effectiveness of words in Australia (Mauss 1904), and in this connection my own survey of ethnographic publications on the Australian natives is also fairly complete. However, I shall give details of only a small number of fairly obscure descriptions, leaving aside the well-known writers.

4. (Lucien) Lévy-Bruhl has studied these facts several times from the point of view of the notion of cause (1910, 1922, 1923, 1926).

5. Durkheim and I carefully collected these facts. A list can be found in Durkheim 1912, pp. 182, nn. 1–4 (cf. p. 184, n. 2); Durkheim 1914, p. 128, nn. 1–2, 129, nn. 1–2 (cf. p. 130, n. 2). They are found above all in the tribes of the Centre and the South, Narrinyeri, Encounter Bay tribe, etc. Let me specify that in the case of the taboo of the *yunbeai* (Parker 1905, p. 20), the latter is the individual totem, not the clan totem.

6. This case of haunting and possession is typical from my point of view (cf. Turner 1884 [pp. 17–18]) and also from the point of view of the relations between the individual and the powers that may become malignant and substitute their spirit for his own.

7. E.g. the description of the Arunta (Aranda) and Loritja (Kukatja) *kurdaitcha* in Strehlow 1907–13, Vol. 4, part 2, p. 20, etc.; magic as result of mourning, p. 34. Causes of suicide are rare in Australia. Strehlow tells us twice that they are unknown among the Arunta and Loritja: 'They cling too tightly to life.'

8. (*Sic* – the account in Backhouse refers to West Hunter or Barren Island and is slightly different: '...a man, who was ill at the time, stated, that he should die when the sun went down, and requested the other men would bring wood and form a pile. ... He became worse as the day progressed, and died before night.')

9. Observations made with (Nicholas) Hey, a collaborator of (Walter E.) Roth.

10. (*Sic* – the letters in this work all date form 1853–4 and the volume contains no reference to the incident or individuals mentioned.)
11. Here we have a curse duplicating the physico-moral sanction of the taboo.
12. Repetition of the curse.
13. Wadampa-wim a song (Siebert 1910, p. 48, col. 1).
14. (Thomas) Worsnop (1890) (who unfortunately wrote very little).
15. (*Sic.* 'Guyon' could be a misprint for Sidney Gason, Worsnop's informant, in Worsnop 1890, or more likely for Francis J. Gillen. Cf. Spencer and Gillen 1901, pp. 529–641, and Howitt 1904, pp. 212–30, 271–86, 347–51, 273–3.)
16. (The French text numbers this chapter as IV.)
17. To the point of murder or suicide, says (William) Colenso (1868 [p. 39]).
18. A résumé of the description by William Colenso (information gathered a bout 1840) (1868, pp. 39–44).
19. Thus they do not make the mistake of confusing suicide and fatal depression. But neither should one seek in these divisions – taken from the theologians of the Tuhoe tribe – more precision than actually exists. Thus wounds received in war are also the result of spells or sins.
20. (Beliefs especially of the Salevao.) In New Zealand, the idea seems to apply only to the sanctions of the cult of the lizard. Cf. Goldie 1904; p. 17.
21. Ngai Tahu tribe myth. H. T. (of Croisilles) 1901, p. 73.
22. On these deaths and hauntings etc., see White 1861 (or 1885; the subject is not discussed in this book of White's; but cf. White 1874, pp. 301–9) and Goldie 1904, p. 7.
23. On *makutu* (magic) and *pahunu* (induced sin), see Tregear 1904, pp. 201 ff.
24. Tuhoe tribes. Best 1898, pp. 119 ff. If the *atua*, the auxiliary spirit, is not strong, he 'wastes away'.
25. On *whakapahunu*, 'to cause to sin', see Best 1902, p. 81 (Tuhoe ((*sic* – this variety of magic is not mentioned here by Best); Best 1902–4, Vol. 11, p. 52: 'prick his conscience', i.e. the bewitched individual's.
26. On 'making sin' ('*whakahehe*') see Shortland 1854, p. 20 (*sic* – the subject is discussed on pp. 94 ff, under the name *makutu*).
27. Goldie 1904, pp. 78–9. The comparisons are taken from Andrew Lang (1887) (AtkinSon, Lang's nephew, on a Kaneka case (Vol. 1, p. 104); Fison and one of Howitt's informants on cases in Fiji and Australia (Vol. 1, pp. 105–6); Codrington on Melanesia (Vol. 1, p. 116). On p. 80, Goldie uses the term 'thanatomania' and says that cases 'might be cited *ad infinitum*'. In Hawaii, a magician to whom a European had said that he, too, was a wizard, died of weakness. In the Sandwich Islands (Hawaii) in 1847, during an epidemic, many succumbed not just to disease but to terror and this fatal melancholia. The epidemic was called *okuu* because people delivered (*okuu*) their souls to it and died. Similarly, in Fiji, when there is an epidemic, people become incapable of saving themselves or others; they are said to be '*taquaya*' (crushed, desperate, terrified), and have abandoned all hope for life.
28. Goldie's version (1904, p. 79) is not as good either as the complete text or as the translation in Davis 1855, p. 192 (text) and 191 (translation), neither above all is it as good as that which Hertz had prepared. Goldie leaves out the almost Euripidean appeal to the sun. (The text used here follows Davis with Hertz's corrections in brackets.) Another song describes possession by an animal implanted in the flesh by magic this time.
29. Job 33: 15–16, 18–22 (New English Bible 1970a, pp. 713–14. Mauss gives a different chapter and verses (32: 19, 21, cf. 17) and a text which differs in detail.

Here is a literal translation of the French: 'Then mighty God opens men's ears and in their punishment they are sealed. Let him save his soul from the pit and keep his life far from the sword. For the danger is that he will be destroyed in his flesh, in his bed, and the strength of his bones at the same time. Then his life is a horror to him and his soul no longer eats bread without disgust. He is consumed in his flesh (such that he is seen no more); and he is depressed in his bones such that he is seen no more. And his soul draws near the pit and his life near the things that produce death.')

BIBLIOGRAPHY

Backhouse, James (1843) *A Narrative of a Visit to the Australian Colonies.* London: Hamilton, Adams; New York: John L. Lindsay.

Bartels, Max (1893) *Die Medicin der Naturvölker: Ethnologische Beiträge zu Urgeschichte der Medicine.* Leipzig: Th. Grieben.

Best, Elsdon (1898) 'Omens and superstitious beliefs of the Maori', *Journal of the Polynesian Society* (Wellington), 7: 119–36, 233–43.

Best, Elsdon (1902) 'Maori magic: notes upon witchcraft, magic rites, and various superstitions as practised or believed in by the old-time Maori', *Transactions and Proceedings of the New Zealand Institute* (Wellington), 34: 69–98.

Best, Elsdon (1902–4) 'Notes on the art of war as conducted by the Maori of New Zealand, with accounts of various customs, rites, superstitions & c., pertaining to war, as practised and believed in by the ancient Maori', *Journal of the Polynesian Society* (Wellington), 11: 11–41, 47–75, 127–62, 219–46; 12: 32–84, 145–65, 193–210; 12: 1–19, 73–82.

Best, Elsdon (1905) 'Maori eschatology: the *Whare Potea* (House of Mourning) and its lore; being a description of many customs, beliefs, rites, etc., pertaining to death and burial among the Maori people, as also some account of native belief in a spiritual world', *Transactions and Proceedings of the New Zealand Institute* (Wellington), 38: 148–239.

Bride, Thomas Francis (ed.) (1899) *Letters from Victorian Pioneers.* Melbourne: Government Printer.

Bulmer, John (1888) 'Some account of the Aborigines of the Lower Murray, Wimmera, Gippsland and Maneroo', *Transactions and Proceedings of the Royal Geographical Society of Australasia (Victorian Branch)* (Melbourne), 5(1): 15–43.

Casalis, Eugène (1861) *The Basutos, or Twenty-three Years in South Africa.* London: James Nisbet.

Colenso, William (1868) 'On the Maori races of New Zealand', *Transactions and Proceedings of the New Zealand Institute* (Wellington) 1(3), Essays: 1–75.

Davis, Charles Oliver B. (1855) *Maori Mementoes; Being a Series of Addresses Presented by the Native People, to His Excellency Sir George Grey, K.C.B., F.R.S., Governor and High Commissioner of the Cape of Good Hope, and late Governor of New Zealand; With Introductory Remarks and Explanatory Notes, to which is Added a Small Collection of Laments, etc.* Auckland: Williamson & Wilson.

Durkheim, Émile (1897) *Le Suicide: étude de sociologie.* Paris: Alcan.

Durkheim, Émile (1912) *Les Formes élémentaires de la vie religieuse: le système totémique en Australie.* Paris: Alcan.

Durkheim, Émile (1914) *The Elementary Forms of the Religious Life: A Study in Religious Sociology.* trans. Joseph Ward Swain. London: Allen & Unwin; and New York: Macmillan.

Durkheim, Émile (1952) *Suicide: a Study in Sociology*, trans. John A. Spaulding and George Simpson. London: Routledge & Kegan Paul.

Eden, Charles H. (1872) *My Wife and I in Queensland: an Eight Years' Experience in the Above Colony, with Some Account of Polynesian labour*. London: Longman, Green.

Fauconnet, Paul (1920) *La Responsabilité: étude de sociologie* Paris: Alcan.

Fischer, Eugen (1931) 'Racial differences in mankind'. In Erwin Baur, Eugen Fischer and Fritz Leitz, *Human Heredity*, trans. Eden and Cedar Paul. London: Allen & Unwin; and New York: Macmillan, pp. 113–209.

Froggat, Walter Wilson (1888) 'Notes on the natives of West Kimberley, North-West Australia', *Proceedings of the Linnaean Society of New South Wales* (Sydney, 30 May 1888): 651–6.

Goldie, W. H. (1904) 'Maori medical lore: notes on the causes of disease and the treatment of the sick among the Maori people of New Zealand, as believed and practised in former times, together with some account of various ancient rites connected with the same' (with a preliminary note by Elsdon Best), *Transactions and Proceedings of the New Zealand Institute* (Wellington), 37: 1–120.

Hertz, Robert (1922) 'Le péché et l'expiation dans les sociétés primitives; Introduction', *Revue de l'Histoire des Religions* (Paris, 43 année), 86: 5–54.

Hertz, Robert (1929) *Mélanges de sociologie religieuse et de folklore*. Paris: Alcan.

Horne, G. and Aiston, G. (1924) *Savage Life in Central Australia*. London: Macmillan.

Howitt, Alfred William (1904) *The Native Tribes of South-East Australia*. London: Macmillan.

Jarves, James Jackson (1872) *History of the Hawaiian Island, Embracing their Antiquities, Mythology, Legends, Discovery by Europeans in the Sixteenth Century, Re-discovery by Cook, with their Civil, Religious and Political History, from the Earliest Traditionary Period to the year 1846*, 4th edn with an appendix. Honolulu: Henry M. Whitney (1st edn 1843).

Lang, Andrew (1887) *Myth, Ritual and Religion*, 2 vols. London: Longman, Green.

Lévy-Bruhl, Lucien (1910) *Les Fonctions mentales dans les sociétés inférieures*. Paris: Alcan.

Lévy-Bruhl, Lucien (1922) *La Mentalité primitive*. Paris: Alcan.

Lévy-Bruhl, Lucien (1923) *Primitive Mentality*, trans. Lilian A. Clare. London: Allen & Unwin.

Lévy-Bruhl, Lucien (1926) *How Natives Think* (*Les Fonctions mentales dans les sociétés inférieures*), trans. Lilian A. Clare. London: Allen & Unwin.

Mariner, William and Martin, John (1817) *An Account of the Natives of the Tonga islands in the South Pacific ocean with an Original Grammar and Vocabulary of their Language, Compiled and Arranged from the Extensive Communications of Mr. William Mariner, Several Years Resident on those Islands. By John Martin*, 2 vols. London: John Murray.

Lévy-Bruhl, Lucien Mauss, Marcel (1904) L'origine des pouvoirs magiques dans les sociétés australiennes, *Rapports Annuels de l'École Pratique des Hautes Études, Section des Sciences Religieuses* (paris): 1–55.

Lévy-Bruhl, Lucien Mauss, Marcel (1924) 'Rapports réels et pratiques de la psychologie et de la sociologie', *Journal de Psychologie Normale et Pathologique* (Paris: 21 année): 892–922.

New English Bible (1970a) *The New English Bible: The Old Testament*. London: Oxford University Press and Cambridge University press.

New English Bible (1970b) *The New English Bible: The New Testament*, 2nd edn. London: Oxford University Press and Cambridge University Press.

Newland, S. (1890) 'The Parkengees, or Aboriginal tribes on the Darling River', *Proceedings of the Royal Geographical Society of Australasia (South Australian Branch)* (Adelaide, 2) (session 1887–8): 20–32.

Newman, Alfred K. (1882) 'A study of the causes leading to the extinction of the Maori', *Transactions and Proceedings of the New Zealand Institute* (Wellington), 14 (1881): 459–77.

H.P. (1897) 'Information about Australian tribes', *Australasian Anthropological Journal* (Sydney), 1(5) (30 April 1897): 99–100.

Parker, K. Langloh (afterwards Catherine Somerville Stow) (1905) *The Euahlayi Tribe: A Study of Aboriginal Life in Australia*, Introduction by Andrew lang. London: Archibald Constable.

Roth, Walter Edmund (1903) 'Notes of savage life in the early days of West Australian settlement (based on reminiscences collected from F. Robert Austin ... discoverer of the Kimberley goldfields, West Australia)', *Proceedings of the Royal Society of Queensland* (Brisbane), 17(2): 45–69.

Shand, Alexander (1894) 'The Moriori people of the Chatham Islands: their traditions and history', *Journal of the Polynesian Society* (Wellington), 3: 76–92, 121–33, 187–98.

Shortland, Edward (1854) *Traditions and Superstitions of the New Zealanders with Illustrations of their Manners and Customs*. London: Longman, Brown, Green & Longman.

Siebert, Otto (1910) 'Sagen und Sitten der Dieri und Nachbarstämme in Zentral-Australien', *Globus, illustrierte Zeitschrift für Länder- und Völkerkunde* (Friedrich Vieweg, Brunswick), 97: 44–59.

Spencer, Sir Walter Baldwin (1914) *Native Tribes of the Northern Territory of Australia*. London: Macmillan.

Spencer, Sir Walter Baldwin and Gillen, Francis, J. (1901) *Native Tribes of Central Australia*. London: Macmillan.

Steinmetz, Sebald Rudolf (1907) 'Der Selbstmord bei den Afrikanischen Naturvölkern', *Zeitschrift für Sozialwissenschaft* (Deichert, Leipzig), 10: 298–304, 359–75.

Stoll, Otto (1904) *Suggestion und Hypnotismus in der Völkerpsychologie*, 2nd rev. edn. Leipzig: von Veit (1st edn, 1894).

Strehlow, Carl F. T. (1907–13) *Die Aranda- und Loritja-Stämme in zentral-Australien*, ed. Moritz Freiherr von Leonhardi, 5 vols. Frankfurt-am-Main: Städtisches Völker-Museum.

H.T. (1901) 'Short Traditions of the South Island of New Zealand', *Journal of the Polynesian Society* (Wellington), 10: 72–7.

Tregear, Edward (1893) 'Physical endurance' (of the Maori), *Journal of the Polynesian Society* (Wellington), 2: 71–3.

Tregear, Edward (1904) *The Maori Race*. Wanganui: A. D. Willis.

Turner, George (1884) *Samoa a Hundred Years Ago and Long Before, together with Notes on the Cults and Customs of Twenty-three other Islands in the Pacific*. London: Macmillan.

Ward, Arthur E. (1908) *The Miracle of Mapoon: or from Native Camp to Christian Village*. London: Moravian Missionary Agency, S. W. Partridge.

White, John (1861) *Lectures on Maori Customs and Superstitions*. Appendix to the *Journals of the House of Representatives of New Zealand* for 1861. Auckland, E.7, pp. 1–48.

White, John (1874) *Te Rou or The Maori at Home: a Tale Exhibiting the Social Life, Manners, Habits and Customs of the Maori Race in New Zealand prior to the Introduction of Civilization amongst them.* London: Sampson Low, Marston, Low & Searle.

White, John (1885) 'Maori customs and superstitions' (as White 1861). In Thomas Wayth Gudgeon, *The History and Doings of the Maoris from the Year 1820 to the Signing of the Treaty of Waitangi in 1840.* H. Brett, Auckland, pp. 95–225.

Withnell, John G. (1901) *The Customs and Traditions of the Aboriginal Natives of North Western Australia.* Roebourne, W. Australia: Hugh B. Geyer.

Worsnop, Thomas (1890) 'The pre-historic arts of the Aborigines of Australia', *Proceedings of the Royal Geographical Society of Australasia (South Australian Branch)* (Adelaide), 2 (session 1886–7): 9–32, plates A–J and map.

CHAPTER SEVEN

Temperament, Conflict and Psychosis in a Stone-Age Population[1] (1929)

C. G. Seligman

Seligman (1873–1940), Professor of anthropology at the London School of Economics, was a colleague of Rivers on the Cambridge University Torres Straits Expedition (1898) which is often cited as the start of British ethnographic fieldwork. Like Rivers, he was medically qualified. Seligman's assertion that serious mental illness was unknown in Papua-Melanesia has often been referred to as the 'Seligman error', mental illness being incorporated under certain social circumstances into institutions such as spirit possession, and hence not perceived; it nevertheless seems unlikely that Seligman as a doctor missed actual psychosis. The current opinion is generally that the International Pilot Study of Schizophrenia (WHO 1973) has shown that schizophrenia is universal and of approximately equal incidence (around 1 per cent lifetime risk).

The peoples referred to in this paper are the inhabitants of that part of Papua, or New Guinea, formerly known as British New Guinea but now officially entitled Papua, though actually constituting only about a quarter of the whole great island. Anthropologically the inhabitants of this restricted Papua fall into two great divisions, commonly termed Papuans and Papuo-Melanesians, presenting such considerable differences both in physique and mental make-up that it seems necessary not only to summarise the chief characteristics of each division but to note in every instance whether the individual concerned is Papuan or Melanesian. Further, in order to avoid confusion between Papua the Island, Papua the political unit, and the ethnic group called Papuan, I shall use the term Papuasian for any inhabitant of the Island, and Papuan and Melanesian (or Papuo-Melanesian, the first constituent of the word being geographical in sense) in their anthropological sense as outlined below.[2]

The Papuo-Melanesians are immigrants, inhabiting the south-eastern portion of the Territory and adjacent islands, and are, generally speaking, smaller, lighter coloured (skin coppery or some shade of *café-au-lait*) and not so invariable frizzly-haired as the Papuans. These Melanesians are again divided into two great branches – differing from each other physically and culturally – the Eastern and Western, the former commonly known as Massim. The Massim all speak a Melanesian language and have a highly specialised form of totemism with which is associated an advanced and very beautiful style of wood-carving. The Western Papua Melanesians are generally more mixed with Papuans, so that many tribes speak Papuan languages; culturally they vary more widely *inter se* than do the Massim, they are generally not totemic, and they have no characteristic art style that enables their work to be distinguished at a glance.

All Papuo-Melanesians can generally count as high as some hundreds, are often sea-going, and culturally may be considered more advanced than the Papuans. The latter are for the most part bigger, heavier men, the muscular processes on their bones are more developed, they are generally darker coloured, and, so far as I know, invariably have frizzly hair. They speak languages differing greatly from each other, but all non-Melanesian; many of their tribes have words for only two numerals – 1 and 2 – and scarcely count above 5. The Papuans are, generally speaking, less well known than the Papuo-Melanesians, and no doubt there is more variation in physical make-up within the Papuan division than there is within the Melanesian. Both diversions were only emerging from the stone age when I knew them. In 1899 I saw a whole fleet of dug-outs being constructed with stone adzes, and a more limited use of stone still persisted in 1904, though throughout this period stone tools were everywhere being replaced by iron. Ancestor worship occurs in both groups. Gods scarcely occur among the Melanesians (perhaps they are absent); they exist among the Papuans but probably their cults are not highly developed. The Melanesian tribes of the Central District of Papua are certainly the least religious of any primitive people I have met.

Of environmental factors those worth noting are the predominant vegetable diet (mitigated on the coast by a certain amount of fish), the general presence of malaria, not as a rule severe in adults though in some villages children die in large numbers and every child has a large spleen, the absence of syphilis but the widespread existence of yaws. As regard endocrine disturbances, I do not remember seeing goitre apart from cretinism; the latter is far from common, but Fröhlich's syndrome occurs as does achondroplasia. True dwarfs must be very uncommon; only one case was seen.

The predominance of Papuo-Melanesian subjects in the following notes does not necessarily signify that these are more liable to break down than are Papuans; that almost all my time was spent among Papuo-Melanesians may quite well account for this predominance, while the fact that the mass neuroses described by Dr Haddon and Mr Chinnery and by Mr Williams (*infra*, pp. 14–15) all occurred among Papuans does not suggest that the latter are less liable to suffer from the results of conflict between the old and the new.

Before discussing the abnormalities of individuals it seems well to record the wide range of variation in mental capacity existing among Papuo-Melanesians, a range which – ignoring undoubted genius – I have no doubt is as great as among ourselves. But while I am not prepared to state that genius exists among Papuaisians – the difficulty of estimating what constitutes genius in folk emerging from the stone age is obvious – it was clear that men of exceptional talent occurred, and that such men existed before the advent of the government, the missionary, or the trader. Outstanding talent, if not a share of something greater, cannot be denied to men such as Koapena, a former chief of Aroma, and Geboka Namo, who twenty-five years ago was recognised as the most influential man in the Rigo District, both men who, from the position of clan chiefs among thoroughly democratic peoples, raised themselves to that of acknowledged headman, whose word was law throughout their tribes.

In matters of art it was equally clear that certain folk had quite unusual talent, if not genius. Among the Massim, where many men are more or less expert wood-carvers and all are capable critics, there was a vast difference in the quality of the result produced, though here I did not see or hear of any one man whose work was commonly agreed to be greatly superior to that of his fellows.

It was otherwise as regards stone work; in 1904 I visited the 'quarry' at Suloga in the Woodlarks whence was obtained the stone from which adze blades – traded for hundreds of miles – were made. From the acres of flakes in the neighbourhood it was clear that work must have gone on for very many years, presumably centuries, yet there was but one name, Nevan, ever in the mouth of the local villagers when fine work and historic stones were discussed, and to this day his ceremonial blades are regarded over a great part of the eastern archipelago as priceless examples of the art, which have never been surpassed and probably have not been equalled.

But perhaps the term 'genius' may be most nearly applied to one Poa Oa, of Waima in the Roro-Mekeo District (Western Papuo-Melanesians), whose wood-carving was far superior to that of any other member of his group, numbering perhaps three to four hundred adult males. In certain of the Waima clans it is customary to carve a crocodile from six to twelve feet long upon the posts of the clan club-houses. This custom was still maintained at the time of my visit in 1904, and, as a club-house was then being built, the work of the Maoni Poa – admittedly the best carver of Waima at that time – was carefully examined and compared with surviving posts carved by his father. It needed no native to point out the infinite superiority of the work of Poa Oa, who was freely admitted to have been the finest wood-carver produced by Waima within the past six generations or so which constitute the historic period.

At the other end of the scale, imbeciles are relatively frequent. It is common enough in the Melanesian villages (my personal experience, be it remembered, is almost entirely of the Melanesian part of Papua) to see a loosely-knit adolescent, with his perineal bandage awry or absent, lolling shamelessly or uncouthly attempting to follow the movements of the dance. The general resemblance of such individuals to the 'village idiot' of our own country is undeniable.

Although the data are lacking for any adequate discussion of the psychical make-up (or idiosyncrasy, to use Dr Gillespie's recently suggested term) of the Papuasian, certain factors are so outstanding that they may fairly be given full weight. It has been a commonplace since Wallace's classical description of the character of the Papuan and his contrast with the Malay that the temper of the former is eager and merry, and that he is above all excitable, passionate and lacking in control.[3] To use the terminology introduced by Jung, the Papuasian is essentially extrovert.

The following instances – both from the Massim area – recorded by Mr A. M. Campbell, a former resident magistrate, are useful examples illustrating the limited self-control of these people.

> A man's wife cooked some food for their pig and ... placed it outside the house for the pig to eat. Her husband's dog came up and, chasing the pig away, began to eat the food. The woman then took up a small stone and threw it at the dog with the intention of driving it away. Her husband in a frenzy of passion immediately jumped up from the place where he had been sitting, and seizing a pointed stick drove it with such fatal effect into his wife's body that she expired on the spot.'[4]

Another case may be cited which shows the impulsive nature of some Papuasian murders.

> It is true I speared my wife. She came to me in my sleep and she awakened me. This was in the day when the sun was high; I was wild because of this and I rushed for my spear and I darted it at her. ... This woman was for all time talking and her tongue she never let it rest. Even as you see she must wake me from my sleep. I was angered, but I did not mean that she should die by my spear. She was a good woman but for one thing, her tongue, as I have said.

These examples indicate that the Massim is decidedly impulsive, and his behaviour when suddenly frightened, unless backed by large numbers of his fellows, confirms this view; he will usually run away from whatever frightened him without any attempt to investigate its nature, nor has he any feeling of shame for what we should regard as cowardice. His fellows recognise the overpowering influence of the impulse to fly, and, suffering from it in like circumstances themselves, regard it as undeserving of censure. And this same quality of impulsiveness may drive him to acts which show a reckless disregard for consequences even when he knows them well; in fact I am convinced that the basis of many an action in Papuasians is often an overpowering impulse, as in the following instance of a murder committed by a Massim, which the culprit knew would bring him to prison:

> I belong ... to a bush village. The woman who is now dead by my spear was a sorceress and she did bewitch my mother, wherefore my mother died, and I her son, seeing this woman one day at work in her garden said to myself – 'I will kill this woman' and therefore I came quietly upon her that she should not perceive me, and I took my spear and thrust it through her body. Then I took my tomahawk and cut her open with it. I did this because she had caused the death of my mother by her sorcery.

These instances, as well as that of the prisoner who bent outward a sheet of corrugated iron (*infra*, p. 12), may perhaps be considered to be in line with such 'explosive reactions' as in Europe are exemplified by prison-outbreaks, by episodes in the 'barbed-wire disease' of the Great War, and by sudden irresponsible acts under the influence of alcohol (cf. E. Kretschmer, *Medizinische Psychologie* [Leipzig: 1992], pp. 188–91).

As might be expected with so strong a tendency to impulsive action, it is recognised that the Papuo-Melanesian is strongly suggestible and therefore entertains an intense fear of sorcery. This fear has nothing to do with the dread of the supernatural; it is acute in folk whom I know well enough to assert that they have no belief in vengeful gods and no great fear of ghosts or ancestral spirits. The following instances reported by Mr A. M. Campbell both refer to the Massim; but I am prepared to say that they could be paralleled in every way among the Western Papuo-Melanesians of the Central Division of the Possession:

> A very intelligent youth, who had been for some time on a mission station, became very ill, and he at one came to the con-clusion that he was bewitched, and accordingly he set out to see

a renowned sorcerer, and, making him a handsome present of native valuables, asked him to remove the spell. This the sorcerer promised to do, but he also intimated to the youth that, although he would get no worse, still he would get no better, because the payment made was not sufficient to remove the spell entirely. The native returned to his home, and, as a matter of fact, remained in the state the sorcerer had predicted would be the case. At last he paid the sorcerer another visit, taking more presents with him which were accepted by the sorceror, who then remarked – 'Now you will get well and strong again.' Soon after this the boy began to improve, and in a short time had completely recovered his former good state of health.

In another case 'the sorcerer simply slapped the man on the back, at the same time saying to him – "Now you will die",' and the man did die within the course of a few days.[5]

Taking into account the impulsiveness and suggestibility of the Papuasian, it is not surprising that suicide is relatively common, but here the subject becomes more complicated than might at first be expected. Hasty suicides do occur: a woman will sometimes hang herself after a difference with husband or mother-in-law; often these quarrels have nothing to do with sexual matters, as in one case in which a Western Melanesian woman killed herself after rather prolonged bickering with her mother-in-law, due to the lack of intelligence shown by the younger (who hanged herself in her house) in managing her garden. Again, men have killed themselves from jealousy or in despair and disappointment, as in the instance of an escaped prisoner who rather than be again arrested hanged himself after having won back to his own district.

But besides these essentially impulsive suicides there are the ceremonial suicides of the Trobriand Islanders, described by Professor Malinowski, the like of which I do not doubt occur elsewhere among the Massim. An excellent example is the following:

Kama'i, a youth of about 16, had an intrigue with his cousin, the daughter of his mother's sister, a member of his own clan and so forbidden to him by the incest taboo.

> This had been known and generally disapproved of, but nothing was done until the girl's discarded lover, who had wanted to marry her ... took the initiative. ... Then one evening he insulted the culprit in public, accusing him in the hearing of the whole community of incest and hurling at him a certain expression intolerable to a native. For this there was only one remedy; only one means of escape remained to the unfortunate youth.

Next morning he put on festive attire and ornamentation, climbed a coco-nut palm and addressed the community, speaking from among the palm leaves and bidding them farewell. He explained the reasons for his desperate deed and also launched forth a veiled accusation against the man who had driven him to his death, upon which it became the duty of his clansmen to avenge him. Then he wailed aloud, as is the custom, jumped from a palm some sixty feet high and was killed on the spot. There followed a fight within the village in which the rival was wounded; and the quarrel was repeated during the funeral.

Such ceremonial suicides are explained by Malinowski as follows:

Two motives must be registered in the psychology of suicide: first there is always some sin, crime or passionate outburst to expiate, whether a breach of exogamous rules, or adultery, or an unjust injury done, or an attempt to escape one's obligations; secondly there is a protest against those who have brought this trespass to light, insulted the culprit in public, forced him into an unbearable situation. One of these two motives may be at times more prominent than the other, but as a rule there is a mixture of both in equal proportions. The person publicly accused admits his or her guilt, takes all the consequences, carries out the punishment upon his own person, but at the same time declares that he has been badly treated, appeals to the sentiment of those who have driven him to the extreme if they are his friends or relatives, or if they are his enemies appeals to the solidarity of his kinsmen, asking them to carry on a vendetta.[6]

I would add that in legend at any rate a sense of being wronged, even though to us the wrong does not seem very serious, is enough to drive the victim, a young girl, to ceremonial suicide by jumping from a lofty tree after she had arrayed herself in all her finery.[7]

I may conclude this short discussion on suicide by pointing out three facts:

(1) That although I know of no case on record from British New Guinea of the peculiar nostalgia leading in some cases to death of which there is evidence in other parts of Melanesia, a condition of similar apathy with a conviction of impending death having nothing to do with sorcery or illness occurs by no means uncommonly. I may cite an experience of my own. A Motu (West Melanesian) who had been with me some time was greatly disappointed by the boat we were travelling in heading away from home,

though, as I assured him, the extra delay could not be more than a couple of weeks. After a day or so he refused food, took no part in the work and amusements of his companions, and explained to me that he was going to die. It was only after continual rallying, and the somewhat forcible administration in effervescent form every two hours of the nastiest mixture the medicine chest allowed me to concoct, that he threw off his depression and decided to behave in a normal manner.

(2) Prolonged physical discomfort – I refer especially to chronic suppuration and its resulting enfeeblement and incapacity – is borne with an uncomplaining acceptance and amazing stoicism, and, so far as I am aware, never leads to suicide.

(3) Although the Papuasian is ready enough to kill himself as the result of quarrels with others, or when overwhelmingly shamed, he shows little or no resolve to involve others in his death. Nothing approaching the Malay *amok* has ever been noted in British New Guinea, even when the man about to commit suicide has a real or strongly held imaginary grievance against some other man.

To pass to definite pathological conditions:

One case of clinically true epilepsy was observed, and Dr Strong informs me that he has treated two individuals, who he does not doubt were epileptic, for severe burns due to rolling into the fire. It is perhaps interesting that the epileptic I was myself able to study was full sister of Ajuia Ova (Western Papuo-Melanesian), perhaps the most intelligent Papuasian I have met. She – Maba – was less vivacious than the ordinary girl, and though not an imbecile was far less intelligent than is usual. She was slow in her movements and a good deal fatter than most native women. She sat about the veranda of her brother's house all day and was practically exempt from work, her food being given her by her sister-in-law. I have several times seen Maba have a typical epileptic fit, but before I had done so her brother had described her attacks so clearly that there could be no doubt as to their nature. The fits begin with a tonic spasm – there is no preliminary cry and it was quite impossible to determine whether there was an aura or not; certainly Maba has never told her friends that she knew when an attack was coming on. In a fit the eyes are open and turned up, the mouth is clenched and the usual frothy saliva appears upon the lips. The fits appear to last three to four minutes, after which the patient regains consciousness and immediately goes to sleep, often appearing greatly astonished when she wakes up. These fits were first noticed when Maba was a small girl – perhaps about three to four years old. Typical post-epileptic automatism may occur, as when some two years before I saw her she was picked up by a fishing canoe at some distance from the shore. She could give no account of how she got into the sea, but when questioned she said she was Maba the sister of Ahuia. It was not clear how far she had swum, but when picked up she wore her petticoat, which is usually discarded by girls of her people when swimming. It was said that after a fit she would sometimes lie on the floor on her belly and strike the side of her head on the floor boards, often drawing blood; this movement was apparently quite unconscious.

No cases of true mental disorder were observed in the villages among natives leading their own normal life. It will make this paper more intelligible if I immediately state my opinion that apart from brief maniacal attacks which I shall presently record, the psychoses do not occur except as the result of the stresses set up by white influence, in other words, as the consequence of conflict of race, and that, as far as I have been able to discover, the result of such conflict is rather to set up a confusional condition than a systematised insanity, while no cases have been recorded which suggest manic-depressive insanity.

My own experiences then have been very largely negative. I naturally did not usually select natives or foreign Melanesians living in close contact with the white community as the subjects from whom to obtain anthropological information; indeed, looking back, I see that from the standpoint of the psychologist I should have paid more attention to these, but my deficiencies are to a considerable extent made good by the kindness of my old friend Dr W. M. Strong, now P.M.O. of the Territory, who has sent me valuable notes of cases coming under his personal observation.

I may first consider two patients with delusions, who had both been intimately associated with Europeans in responsible positions. In these they had earned a good deal of money, which when they broke down came to play a prominent part in their new systems of ideas.

About 1911 Dr Strong saw a native of Suau (Massim) at the Sumarai native hospital. He had been getting a large wage, about £6 a month, as head store boy at Buna among Papuans, i.e. among a people essentially foreign to him. He was clearly insane, and noisy at times, and believed that he owned thousands of pounds. 'I remember the orderly at the native hospital saying he had defaecated over the hospital verandah. On being remonstrated he had said, "It is not faeces, but money".' Dr Strong adds that there was no history of syphilis or reason to suppose that he had been infected, but that the condition reminded him of the delusions of grandeur in G.P.I.[8] Dr Strong also mentions another Massim whom he saw at Port Moresby, a particularly intelligent native who had been drawing a high salary, becoming obviously insane in a noisy way and with delusions of having much money. Both these cases died.[9]

With these two men may be grouped Navo, a native of the New Hebrides brought to Papua many years ago by the then Governor, Sir William MacGregor. When he came under Dr Strong's observation he was living a rather lonely life near Port Moresby and was suffering from progressive senile dementia, though at this time the condition was by no means extreme. Some fifteen years before he had something over a hundred pounds in the Treasury. He drew this amount bit by bit, but when it was all gone seemed unable to understand the fact and gradually began to complain that the Treasury was keeping large sums of his money from him. 'I think he was made worse by people teasing him and mischievously suggesting to him that the Treasury had much money of his.' His condition varied from time to time. Navo might well be classed as a senile paranoid dement.

The next case, though very incompletely reported, exhibits the effect of the conflict between old conditions and – since alcohol has been kept from the natives quite successfully – the most alien and disconcerting of the white man's imports into Papua, viz. his religion. Dr Strong had known a Melanesian as cook boy in the house of a married European at Port Moresby. He was a quiet youth, who had come to Port when young and untrained. About a couple of years later he was taken to Sydney, where he seems to have come intensely under missionary influence. It was reported that he had knelt down in the streets of Sydney to pray, and attracted a crowd. He was returned to New Guinea and examined by Dr Strong. 'He seemed in a more or less confused state, and his thoughts still seemed to run on missionary subjects, but I could not then have certified him as insane. I remember asking him what he would like to do, meaning did he wish to finish his signed-on time as cook and personal attendant, or go back to his village. He replied he would like to go and work for Mr Abel, the missionary at Samarai.' Samarai is the port of entry for the Eastern portion of the Possession; unfortunately I cannot say whether the boy knew Mr Abel personally.

Another instance which might be labelled reactive depression with hysterical features in which a missionary element entered was that of a Motu (Western Papuo-Melanesian) youth of about twenty-five from Port Moresby, whom I saw at the Mission station at Vatorata in 1898. Although well-developed and healthy looking and in spite of being long employed about the house, the patient was obviously nervous on entering a room; his thyroid cartilage worked up and down in his throat, he spoke in a lower voice than is usual among Papuasians and with something of a thrill in it and his conjunctivae were glistening and suffused with moisture. His illness began about five years before, when he lost a small trading vessel belonging to the mission, taking her out after being warned not to do so as there was a heavy sea on. On his return he was angrily remonstrated with by a very forcible and outspoken missionary, but he was not struck nor was physical violence threatened. He returned to his village, where he would sit for a long time with his head bent and his hands lying idle in his lap. Before this there was – according to his brother – a period of talkativeness. He abandoned cohabitation and took little notice of his child. He was not dirty in his habits, and, so far as could be learnt, took his food well. The melancholy condition lasted for about a year, getting gradually worse, until he never left his hut and seldom spoke; at this time he believed, or at any rate stated, that he could not walk. It may be assumed that his condition was undoubtedly fostered by the too sympathetic and pessimistic remarks of his neighbours. About this time he was discovered by Dr Lawes, who had him carried to his residence, where, on being quietly reasoned with, it was found that he could walk, stand, and talk. His condition slowly improved and in 1898, when he came under observation, he had begun to do light work about the house, but if left alone too long he was even then liable to fits of depression in which he would assume his old melancholic attitude.

Conditions of excitement, usually short but during their existence severe enough to be classed clinically as mania, are relatively frequent; kavakava sufficiently so to have a name (*kava*, lit. 'silly') in the Motu of the Central District, but I believe, though on this point I cannot be dogmatic, that they are commoner among Papuans than Melanesians. That the name is Melanesian is no argument against this, for even a quarter of a century ago Motu was something of a lingua franca throughout British new Guinea; moreover, Port Moresby – in the Melanesian part of the Territory – as headquarters of the government is also a police depot, where members of the Armed Native Constabulary from all over the Possession are drilled and stationed, and at the period during which I knew the country more Papuans than Melanesians enlisted in the A.N.C. It seems probable that some of these outbreaks are due to malaria, as when Dr Strong writes of a native in a condition of extreme maniacal excitement of a non-purposeful nature who succeeded in bending outward the sheet of corrugated iron forming the wall of his cell. The attack appeared to begin in the afternoon, and next morning he was normal.

In another class of case, again, I believe, commoner among Papuans than among Papuo-Melanesians, there is wild excitement and threats of assault on all and sundry. But in the instances I have in mind there is something a little unreal, 'a disproportion', as Dr Strong puts it, 'between the injury threatened and actually inflicted'; such cases might perhaps be regarded as dissocaitions without complete loss of self-control. It is by no means improbable that a desire – perhaps not entirely conscious – to draw the attention of the community enters into the causation of these attacks, and there is no doubt that they may occur repeatedly in the same individual, whose companions generally tie him up for a period. In answer to a question Dr Strong agrees with me that no serious injury is done during these attacks, which are generally more alarming to the white onlooker than to the natives.[10]

Instances where absurd things are done are probably slight dissociations, in which malaria may possibly be concerned. For many of these the native has the same explanation as the mediaeval European, viz. possession. Dr Strong writes of a Doura native (Western Papuo-Melanesian) accused of throwing stones on the roofs of European houses. On examination the answer was, 'Yes, a *dirava* (spirit) came and threw them', with the implication that the patient was merely the instrument. 'On another occasion a policeman (Papuan) was working with others cutting grass; at 5 o'clock, when orders were given to cease work, the policeman refused in an insulting manner. Some five days later he was brought before me and gave the explanation that a *dirava* had come and said things to him.' Dr Strong notes that previously the policeman had been a particularly smart, energetic, and keen constable, but after the event he changed completely. Probably this change in character was less due to the *dirava* than to the fact that in Dr Strong's absence a subordinate had treated the offence as serious and kept the constable in gaol.[11]

Another case noted by Dr Strong is the following:

One morning I told my orderly (Papuan) to stake some plants. He tied them up so outrageously badly that I spoke sharply to him. Contrary to his usual behaviour, he replied in a markedly insubordinate way to the effect that if I was always grumbling at him I had better send him away to be a policeman at Daru (Daru being the last place a sane north-eastern policeman cares to be sent to). I replied that if he did not behave and do what he was told I should send him to Daru as a prisoner. At the time I recognized his mental condition was abnormal. An hour or two later I found him with a temperature of over 102, and more or less unconscious. I diagnosed malaria, and after treatment he recovered, much as I should expect a malarial subject to recover. His recollection of my threat to send him to Daru seemed more or less vague, yet sufficiently definite for him to ask quite politely whether I was going to send him there. I said 'No,' but he must behave, etc. He replied, yes, of course he quite understood that. This man was of the Maisin tribe, normally polite and obedient but very sensitive of criticism, and on another occasion seemed unduly upset at some trivial rebuke....

So far I have been concerned only with the aberrations of individuals, and I would again stress that the more serious cases I have recorded have been men who had been submitted to rather intense forms of European influence. But the matter can be carried a stage further. While we have no knowledge of any form of mass neurosis or so-called contagious hysteria during the early days of Papuan settlement, in 1917 Chinnery and Haddon[12] were able to chronicle no less than five new religions, characterised by dissociation and the rapid spread typical of mass suggestion. To these must be added a sixth, described at length by F. E. Williams.[13] On of these, 'the Baigona cult', concerned especially with snakes and to a less extent with other reptiles, bears no obvious trace of white influence (to judge by the short account given by Haddon and Chinnery) but might as I believe, have arisen as a variant of local belief at any time. As to the five remaining cults, it seems probable that they have come into existence under the stress of conflict due to white influence; in two of them there is definite evidence of their hybrid origin and of the clash of Christianity with the old cult of the dead which seems to be the essential point of all New Guinea beliefs. Thus in the Kekesi rites one Bia represented himself as the earthly agent of a spirit calling itself Kekesi, and gave the following account of the origin of the movement:

> Early in November 1914 I and my friend Yavevi were returning to Manau from Buna. We slept at the point opposite Mitre Rock. During the night I was visited by the spirit of a man named Boinumbai, who died a long time ago at Gauoro village. I was told by this spirit that a very powerful spirit named Kekesi watched over all the people from the Mitre Rock (Kekesi) and controlled their food supply. Kekesi was a friend of Jesu Kerisu (Jesus Christ) and was able to see all that happened. ... A few nights later Boinumbai's spirit again visited me at Manau, and with it came the spirit that Boinumbai introduced as Kekesi, the big chief of food and a strong spirit, 'all the same as Jesu Kerisu and Government,' whom he told me to listen carefully to and to take notice of.[14]

One of the five new cults described by Chinnery and Haddon is scarcely a cult in the same sense as the others they describe. Moreover, though I do not know how much stress should be laid on this, the folk affected were Massim, not Papuans as in the other instances recorded. A prophet – one Tokerua – arose who as the result of an interview with a spirit by night appeared in the morning 'his face ... transfigured', and looking 'like a man whose wits had left him'. His message was that during the following moon there would be thunder and a great rain, with a gale of untold fury; then would come an earthquake and the appearance of a new island in Milne Bay, with a tidal wave which would submerge the coast for two or three months. Thus complete destruction would come upon those refusing to obey the behests of the prophet.

First and foremost no man might possess anything introduced by the *dimdim* (white man). He must part with his treasures – matchboxes, tomahawks, knives, and other appliances which rendered his life pleasant or reduced toil ... there would be a reversion to the stone age, implying the revival of ancient wont and customs ... of their forefathers. New things must pass away and the Golden Age of the past must be resuscitated in the present. ... The faithful villagers of Gabugabula actually left their old village on the shore ... they were told to go inland and they did. ... When the catastrophe was past the wind would change to the south-east ... and the land would be covered with gardens of yams, taro and other native food, and the trees would be laden with delicious fruit. The south-east wind would waft a huge vessel into the vicinity crowded with the spirits of the dead. ... So firm was the belief of these trustful people ... that all the food in their gardens was consumed and ordinary gardening operations ceased. ... 300 or 400 of their beloved pigs were killed and eaten.[15]

There is nothing in the contemporary accounts to suggest that those who believed in Tokerua had trembling fits, became unconscious, or showed any of the usual signs of dissociation. A fair number of people were prepared more or less to accept his statements, and his own village to act on them, but in spite of the apocalyptic element in his prophecy there is no evidence of the establishment of any cult, indeed the whole affair seems to have occupied no more than a few weeks. On the other hand the element of race conflict is very evident.

CONCLUSIONS

(1) The population studied, i.e. of that part of Papua known until a few years ago as British New Guinea, is admittedly of an excitable and extrovert disposition.

(2) In spite of this and the frequency of suicide, both impulsive and ceremonial, there is no evidence of the occurrence of mental derangement, other than brief outbursts of maniacal excitement, among natives who have not been associated with White Civilisation.

(3) Fatal instances of insanity are cited in which the immediate cause (as evidenced by the history and delusions) was financial responsibility in connection with Europeans.

(4) In other instances (non-fatal) the difficulty has been in the religious fold.

(5) Of late years a series of religious cults has arisen. These are charac-

terised by hysterical dissociation and mass contagion, and in all except one there is evidence of the important part played by the conflict between old and new religious ideas.

INTRODUCTION REFERENCE

World Health Organisation (1973) *The International Pilot Study of Schizophrenia.* Geneva: WHO.

NOTES

1. I have purposely used the rather sensational term 'stone-age population' to accentuate the small amount of white influence to which these Papuasians had been subjected a quarter of a century ago. I do not wish to imply that their mental make-up is necessarily simpler or less advanced than that of a number of iron-using African tribes, but I lay stress on the fact that they are or recently were neolithic because it constitutes a proof of the absence of European influence.

     I am greatly indebted to my old friend Dr W. Marsh Strong, now P.M.O. of Papua, for patiently answering enquiries and providing part of the material used in this paper, while in this country Dr R. D. Gillespie has greatly assisted me by criticism and advice.

2. For further information see my *Melanesians of British New Guinea* (1910), Chapter 1.

3. 'The moral characteristics of the Papuan appear to me to separate him as distinctly from the Malay as do his form and features. He is impulsive and demonstrative in speech and action. His emotions and passions express themselves in shouts and laughter, in yells and frantic leapings. Women and children take their share in every discussion, and seem little alarmed at the sight of strangers and Europeans. ... It appears therefore, that, whether we consider their physical conformation, their moral characteristics, or their intellectual capacities, the Malay and Papuan races offer remarkable differences and striking contrasts. ... The Malay is bashful, cold, undemonstrative, and quiet; the Papuan is bold, impetuous, excitable, and noisy. The former is grave and seldom laughs; the latter is joyous and laughter loving – the one conceals his emotions, the other displays them' (*The Malay Archipelago* [London: 1894], pp. 449–50). Wallace is here writing of the true Papuan; my experience leads me to think that his remarks are applicable to Papuo-Melanesians, perhaps to an even greater extent.

4. *Annual Report*, 1902–3.

5. *Annual Report*, 1902–3.

6. Bronislaw Malinowski, *Crime and Custom in Savage Society* (1926), p. 97.

7. A girl of the Southern Massim prefers the *kanioga* root to any other food; her mother and her aunts twice eat the *kanioga* she had collected for herself. When they ask her to come with them to collect more of the desired root she refuses: 'Then she laid out all her ornaments and finery and put them on, necklaces of shell beads and quills, shell armlets, anklets and a new grass petticoat, then taking her pet dog in her arms she began to sing slowly, "Because of the lily rot, because of the lily root am I going." Presently she went into the bush

weeping. ... When the girl came to a lofty *wakola* tree which was easy to climb, she climbed it, and her mother, running up, saw her. "Come down, deary, come down," she said, but the girl answered: "No, too late," and then looking down she saw a crocodile in the sea close beneath her. ... Then she took off her ornaments one by one and threw them to the crocodile who snapped them down hungrily; she then threw her dog, and finally her petticoat until, when naked, she threw herself down and the crocodile took her' (Seligman, op. cit., pp. 395–6).

8. This remark of Dr Strong's raises the whole question of the relation of yaws to syphilis and whether yaws is capable of producing G.P.I. I will only record my belief that although as I know from personal experience, yaws in New Guinea and yaws in the southern Nilotic Sudan present very different clinical pictures, neither 'disease' is syphilis, and it is for this reason in my opinion that the late nervous manifestations of syphilis whether cerebral or spinal are absent, as they certainly are in the southern Sudan and, as I do not hesitate to say, they were in Papua twenty-five years ago.

9. In this country, if death in such cases as those outlined occurred in spite of careful nursing, it would, I suppose, have an organic origin, toxic or structural. In Papua prolonged delirium or mania might, I think, lead to death from exhaustion.

10. They thus differ entirely from the Malay *amok*. Dr Strong took a good deal of trouble making enquiries as to injuries inflicted, and the only instances brought to his notice seemed to him as likely to have been incurred during the struggle to restrain the patient as by the active agency of the latter.

11. Dr Strong's account seems to imply that there was a permanent change of character. Dr Gillespie has pointed out to me that the schizophrenic psychoses in Europeans may begin with hallucinations and later produce a change of character. The fact is suggestive, and investigation of similar cases by competent observers is much to be desired. At the same time due weight must be given to the severe effects known to be produced in other non-European races by injustice (sense of wrongful treatment) or by ridicule, even though these races have not the particular mental make-up of the Papuasian. I have been assured by those who best know the Naga tribes of Assam that laughing at a Naga may make him really ill.

The next case, Dr Strong's orderly who 'on another occasion seemed unduly upset at some trivial rebuke', bears on what has just been said, though here it must be remembered that fever may release paranoid tendencies otherwise controlled.

12. E. W. P. Chinnery and A. C. Haddon, 'Five new religious cults in British New Guinea', *Hibbert Journal* (April 1917): 448–83.

13. *Territory of Papua*, Report No. 4. 'The Vailala madness and the destruction of native ceremonies in the Gulf Division', 1923.

14. Chinnery and Haddon, op. cit., p. 452.

15. op. cit., pp. 458–9.

CHAPTER EIGHT

The Social Function of Anxiety in a Primitive Society (1941)

A. Irving Hallowell

Hallowell, Professor of Anthropology at the University of Pennsylvania, was one of the pioneers in American ethnography to use Rorschach tests and psychoanalytic theory with his informants (Stocking 1986; Wallace 1983). In this chapter, starting from a Freudian distinction between real and neurotic anxiety, Hallowell shows the circumstances under which the Saulteaux Indians (Ojibwa of Lake Superior) understand and indeed 'use' anxiety, dealing primarily – as we might expect – with sexual transgressions. He was one of the leading figures in the Committee on Personality in Relation to Culture, the founding body of what has become known as the 'Culture and Personality' school of American anthropology.

In his discussion of anxiety, Freud emphasises the fact that it is essentially an affective reaction to danger.[1] The relationship of anxiety to danger is anticipatory, the affect is a signal: 'one feels anxiety *lest* something occur.'[2] Anxiety is not confined to the human species. Freud states that it 'is a reaction characteristic of probably all organisms, certainly of all of the higher ones'.[3] He further suggests that since it has an indispensable biological function, anxiety may have developed differently in different organisms.[4] Freud does not elaborate the point, but I think it follows from the biological role he assigns to anxiety that it must be conceived as a function of the particular danger situations that the organism faces. These vary from species to species. What is dangerous for one species of animal would not necessarily be equivalent for another species, and danger situations in the human species may differ again from those faced by infrahuman animals. For the human species itself, Freud stresses another variable. Danger situations vary ontogenetically[5] and the birth process is the 'prototype of anxiety in man'.[6]

What Freud does not explicitly recognise is that the occurrence of anxiety in the human species is further complicated by another variable that I shall call 'cultural'. However, his assumption that anxiety reactions in man are based on experience and are in that sense learned,[7] leaves the door open for an evaluation of such variables within the framework of psychoanalytic principles. These cultural variables operate through the socialisation process that all human beings undergo and result in the definition of situations as dangerous in one society which, in another, may be viewed as less dangerous or not dangerous at all. This means that individuals may manifest anxiety reactions that are appropriate in a particular culture but not in another.

Such cultural variables are of importance with respect to two problems: first, the basic question in which Freud himself was particularly interested, viz., the relation between anxiety and neurosis; secondly, the *positive* role of anxiety. This social function of anxiety is definitely linked, in principle, with the biological role which Freud stresses as a generic function of anxiety. I mean that an affective reaction to danger situations, as culturally defined, may motivate behavior on the part of individuals which is as significant in terms of societal values as comparable reactions are valuable in terms of biological utility. Anxiety-preparedness in the face of any danger is a very adaptive reaction.[8]

Before discussing this second problem, however, I wish to return to the first one, the relation between anxiety and neurosis. In this connection, Freud asks, 'why it is that not all anxiety reactions are neurotic, why we recognise so many of them as normal', and he emphasises the need for distinguishing between true anxiety (*Realangst*) and neurotic anxiety.[9] The conclusion to which he comes is this:

> A *real* danger is a danger which we know, a true anxiety the anxiety in regard to such a known danger. Neurotic anxiety is anxiety in regard to a danger which we do not know. The neurotic danger must first be sought, therefore: Analysis has taught us that it is an instinctual danger (that is, fear of the intensity of one's own impulses).[10]

This differentiation led to the terminological distinction often made between fear, i.e., real or objective anxiety, and neurotic anxiety. I shall continue to use anxiety in its widest connotation, qualifying it with the adjectives 'neurotic' or 'objective' according to the meaning intended. In fact, I think there is a considerable conceptual advantage in considering fear-anxiety reactions as a broad affective continuum and not attempting to make categorical distinctions except in terms of known etiological factors, since what may seem to be instances of 'pure' objective anxiety actually may have neurotic involvements when all the facts are known. On the other hand, as will appear later, there may be analogies to neurotic involvements in anxiety-laden situations which, in a particular culture, may present real objective dangers to the individual concerned.

Let us turn now to the second problem, the positive role of anxiety. I wish to show how anxiety is instigated and reduced among the Saulteaux through the operation of cultural factors (beliefs and institutionalised procedures) which define certain situations as dangerous, how the motivations of individuals are affected, and how the resulting behavior is related to the maintenance of the approved social code. The beliefs relevant to our discussion still flourish today and the more recent changes in their social system have not essentially affected their functioning.

One of the striking features of Saulteaux society is the anxiety with which certain disease situations are invested.[11] In order to understand *why* such situations are the focus of so much affect, we have to know something about native theories of disease. These theories reflect traditional notions. They represent an ideology which is culturally derived and they involve fundamental assumptions about the nature of the universe. From the standpoint of the Saulteaux themselves, such assumptions are taken a priori and are unchallengeable. They not only represent beliefs but are also a basis for action. The affect which arises in certain disease situations is a product of reflection upon the symptoms observed in the patient and the cause of the illness interpreted in terms of the native notions of disease causation. Thus, the anxiety aroused is intimately connected with a cultural variable.

There is a correlative fact, however, which gives *social* significance to the affect generated. Disease situations of any seriousness carry the implication that something wrong has been done. Illness is the penalty. Consequently, it is easy to see why illness tends to precipitate an affective reaction to a culturally defined danger situation. Furthermore, a closer examination of the dynamics of Saulteaux society reveals the fact that fear of disease is the major social sanction operative among these Indians. In this society, certain classes of sexual behavior[12] (incest, the so-called perversions in heterosexual intercourse, homosexuality, autoerotism, bestiality), various kinds of aggressive behavior (cruelty to animals, homicide, cruelty toward human beings, the use of bad medicine to cause suffering, rough or inconsiderate treatment of the dead, theft, and a number of ego injuries like insult and ridicule, failure to share freely etc.), behavior prescribed by guardian spirits, the acquisition of power to render specialised services to others (i.e., curing or clairvoyance), all fall under a disease sanction.

This leads us directly to the heart of one of the basic problems in the social sciences, viz., the determination of the specific conditions under which social codes are maintained and the means by which they operate under different cultural frames of reference. For despite the widest cultural variability in *homo sapiens*, we observe that all human societies are characterised by norms of conduct which, in MacIver's words 'assure some regularity, uniformity and predictability of behavior on the part of the members of a community'.[13] Sheer anarchy, or literal rampant individualism, is unknown.

But this problem is not wholly a sociological one. It has important and far-reaching psychological implications, particularly in view of the fact that in many nonliterate societies, the institutions we associate with the maintenance of 'law and order' are unelaborated or even absent. In the case of the Saulteaux, e.g., there were no chiefs nor any kind of political organisation in aboriginal days. Nor were there any institutionalised juridical procedures or jails.

The psychological aspects of social control become evident when we examine the relation between the social sanctions operative in a given society and the motivations of individuals instigated by the prevailing sanctions. As Radcliffe-Brown has pointed out,[14] 'the sanctions existing in a community constitute motives in the individual for the regulation of his conduct in conformity with usage'. Hence, there is an integral, inextricable relationship between sociological and psychological factors.

In Saulteaux society, it is not fear of the gods or fear of punishment by the state that is the major sanction: it is the fear of disease.[15] Or, putting it in the terminology already employed, the motivating factor is the affect connected with certain disease situations. Individuals in Saulteaux society are highly sensitised to anxiety as an emotional reaction to a danger signal, the precipitating cause being illness interpreted as punishment. The manifest danger to which the anxiety is directed is the direct threat to someone's well-being or even life. But there is also a menace to the social code which is implied because some dissocial act has been committed. Insofar as individuals are motivated to avoid such acts through fear of disease, anxiety performs a distinct social function.

With this thesis in mind I should now like to analyse in more detail how disease operates as a social sanction in Saulteaux society in connection with anxiety-laden situations. (See also Chapter 13.)

In the first place, health and a long life are very positive values to the Saulteaux. *Pïmädazïwin*, life in the fullest sense, is stressed again and again in their ceremonies. The supernaturals are asked for it. It is a prime value. In psychological terms, it is a major goal response. Disease interferes with achieving this goal. Ordinary cases of illness, however, colds, headaches, etc., do not arouse anxiety among the Saulteaux any more than they do among ourselves. They are not danger situations. But the nature of disease is such that it may become a threat to life itself, may be a real danger to the human organism. Real or 'normal' anxiety is appropriate in such circumstances.[16]

A comparable affect under equivalent circumstances is found among the Saulteaux and ourselves. In both cases, the danger threatened is met with what are thought to be appropriate measures. Most disease situations

among the Saulteaux, however, do not conform to this type. They correspond either to the nondangerous variety or they rapidly pass from this
type into situations where the anxiety level is not only high, but where the
quality of the affect suggests neurotic anxiety without its actually being so.
What are the conditions that bring this about? It is here that native beliefs
about disease causation enter the picture.

In Saulteaux belief, one of the major causes of illness arises from what
they term 'bad conduct' (*madjīijiwé bazīwin*). 'Because a person does bad
things, that is where sickness (*ákwazīwin*) starts', is the way one informant
phrased it. In other words, a person may fall ill because of some transgression he has committed in the past. It is also possible that an individual
may be suffering because of the bad conduct of his parents. 'When a man
is young he may do something to cause his children trouble. They will
suffer for this.' Illness derived from this source is designated by a special
native term (*odjīneaúwaso*). Consequently, if a child falls seriously ill, it is
often attributed to the transgression of a parent. It is easy to see the
anxiety-provoking possibilities in this theory of disease causation. In
addition to the normal anxiety that the objective factors of the disease
situation may stimulate, a sense of guilt may be aroused in one or both
parents. They are bound to reflect upon what they may have done to cause
their child's suffering, or even death. Their own acts are entangled with the
disease situation.

Another cause of illness is witchcraft, the hostile action of some other
human being. The significant fact to be observed in cases of this class is
that the sick person almost always believes that his sickness is due to
revenge. Some previous act of *his* has provoked retaliation in this form.
Here the patient's own impulses, previously expressed in some form of
dissocial behaviour, are projected into the situation just as they are in
those instances where disease is thought to have resulted from 'bad
conduct'. In cases of witchcraft, the penalty that threatens has acted in a
mediate fashion instead of automatically as in the instances where bad
conduct is thought to be the source.

An illuminating clue to the psychological significance of disease situations interpreted as a result of the causes just cited is obtained if we follow
Freud's differentiation of what he terms a *traumatic* situation from a
simple *danger* situation. He introduces this distinction by asking what the
kernel of the danger situation is.[17] He finds that it revolves about the
estimation of our strength in relation to the danger. If we feel a sense of
helplessness in the face of it, an inability to cope with it, then he calls the
situation *traumatic*. This is precisely the differentiation that applies to
those disease situations among the Saulteaux where the cause of the illness
is uncertain and obscure. In these situations, the quality of the anxiety
aroused is different from that where illness is faced in the same way any

danger situation is faced. It is disease situations of this *traumatic* type that operate as a social sanction.

The qualitative aspects of the anxiety aroused emerge from the combination of two determinants. The first is purely objective: ordinary medical treatment of the sick person has failed to produce improvement. The symptoms persist or the person gets worse. It is at this point that the situation becomes serious. Prior to this, the illness may not even have been considered dangerous, but when the medicine does not work, the situation rapidly becomes traumatic. This is because the suspicion is aroused in the patient or his associates that the cause of the illness is hidden. It may be a penalty for something done in the past. It may be due to bad conduct or witchcraft. But who knows? Yet if this is so, his very life is in jeopardy. Consequently, a feeling of helplessness arises which can only be alleviated if the precise cause of the sickness is discovered. Otherwise, appropriate measures cannot be undertaken. Meanwhile, the source of the danger remains uncertain and obscure; further suffering, even death, menaces the patient.

Thus, while from an objective point of view we often may have displayed what seems to be a 'disproportionality of affect' in disease situations, at the same time the definition of such situations in terms of Saulteaux beliefs presents dangers that are not comparable to those we would recognise in similar situations. This is an important qualitative difference. The affective reactions of the Saulteaux are a function of this difference.[28]

It would also appear that there are some analogies, although by no means an identity, between the anxiety created in some of these traumatic disease situations among the Saulteaux and neurotic anxiety. This is true, at least, in the cases where the danger that threatens is believed to have arisen out of the patient's own acts, so there is the closest integral relation between inner and outer danger as in neurotic anxiety, but there are no substitute formations in the individual which project the danger outwards, as in animal phobias, while the real source of danger remains unknown. Nevertheless, it is true that the impulses of the individual become the sine qua non of the external danger, just as in neurotic anxiety. Consequently, these impulses are the ultimate source of the danger itself. The disease is not considered to be impersonal and objective in origin and for this reason it cannot be faced in the same terms as other kinds of illness or other objective hazards of life. The real source of danger is from within and, like neurotic anxiety, it is connected with forbidden acts.

Take the case of an Indian who believes himself bewitched, for example. At the first appearance of his illness, he may not have been worried because he may have thought that there was some other cause of his trouble, but as soon as he believes he is the victim of a hostile attack, he gets anxious. Why? Because he believes his illness is in retaliation for some previous act of aggression he has perpetrated. The assertion of these aggressive impulses on his part has led to a feeling of guilt and the illness from which he is suffering has aroused anxiety because he senses danger. His very life may be threatened. What this man fears is that he had endangered his life by acting as he did. He is afraid of the consequences of his own impulses. The source of the outwardly sensed danger lies in his own hostile impulses.

So far I have tried to explain how anxiety is integrated in disease situations among the Saulteaux and why it is that the emotion generated has qualitative features which suggest neurotic anxiety. I hope that I have made it clear, however, that these features are only analogies deduced from the manner in which the belief system of the Saulteaux compels the individual to interpret the objective aspects of disease situations under certain conditions. What we actually appear to have exhibited in these cases is an affective reaction on a fear-anxiety continuum that lies somewhere between true objective anxiety and real neurotic anxiety.[19] That this is indeed the case is supported by the fact that, on the one hand, we can point to occurrences of real anxiety in danger situations among the Saulteaux and, on the other, to cases of neurotic anxiety. An instance of the latter is the behavior of a man I have described at some length in Chapter 13. Among other things he had severe phobic symptoms, a kind of agoraphobia and fear of the dark.

The point I wish to emphasise particularly is that at both extremes of the fear-anxiety continuum the main function of the affect has reference to the individual alone. This is true whether he runs away from some objective danger or develops phobias which are reaction formations in self-defense against some instinctual danger. The anxiety associated with disease situations among the Saulteaux, on the other hand, has a social function insofar as it motivates individuals to avoid the danger (disease) by conforming so the dictates of the social code. This is accomplished by forcing the individual to reflect upon disapproved acts under the stress of the anxiety aroused by a disease situation or to anticipate possible discomfort through a knowledge of the experience of others. In either case, the disease sanction encourages the individual to be responsible for his own conduct.

The full implication of the social function of anxiety in Saulteaux society can best be exposed, however, if we return to the traumatic disease situation and inquire what steps are taken to reduce anxiety in the individual. I have already pointed out that, in such situations, the cause of the disease is at first problematical though the suspicion is aroused that the patient himself or some other person is responsible for the illness. This means that the true cause of the trouble must be sought before the disease can be alleviated. Once the cause of the illness is discovered, the disease situation loses some of its traumatic quality because the danger can be squarely faced like any other danger and some action taken to meet it. The therapeutic measures employed can be looked upon as anxiety-reducing devices.

Now one of the distinctive features of the Saulteaux belief system is this: if one who is ill because of 'bad conduct' *confesses* his transgression, the medicine will then do its work and the patient will recover. This notion is the most typical feature of the operation of the disease sanction in cases where the penalty threatened is automatically induced. In fact, it adds considerable force to the sanction so far as the individual is concerned. It means that deviant conduct may not only lead to subsequent illness but that in order to get well one has to suffer the shame of self-exposure involved in confession. This is part of the punishment. Since it is also believed that the medicine man's guardian spirits (*pawáganak*) will inform him of the cause of the trouble, there is no use withholding anything.[20] At the same time, confession provides the means of alleviating the guilt and anxiety of the individual, because, if a feeling of helplessness or being trapped is an intrinsic factor in these traumatic situations (or in any severe anxiety situation), confession provides a method of escape according to both Saulteaux belief and sound psychological principle.

From the standpoint of Saulteaux society as a whole, confession is also a means by which knowledge of confessed transgressions is put into social circulation. Confession among the Saulteaux is not equivalent to confession to a priest, a friend, or a psychoanalyst in Western culture. In our society, it is assumed that what is exposed will be held in absolute confidence,[21] but among these Indians the notion is held that the very secrecy of the transgressions is one of the things that makes them particularly bad. This explains why it is that when one person, confesses a sexual transgression in which he or she has participated with a second person, the latter will not become ill subsequently or have to confess. Once the transgression has been publicised, it is washed away or, as the Saulteaux phrase it, 'bad conduct will not follow you any more'.

Perhaps this attitude towards what is secret is connected with the lack of privacy that is intrinsic to the manner in which these people live. Anything that smacks of secrecy is always suspect. There is even an aura of potential menace about such things, fortified no doubt by the covert practice of magic and sorcery. Consequently, in disease situations where any hidden transgression is thought to be the cause of the trouble what is in effect a public exposure is a necessary step to regaining health.

In actual practice, this works out in a very simple way. When anyone is sick, there is no isolation of the patient; on the contrary, the wigwam is always full of people. Any statement on the part of the patient, although it may be made to the doctor, is not only public but also very quickly may become a matter of common gossip. Where conjuring is resorted to, in cases where all other efforts have failed to reveal the hidden cause of the malady,[22] almost the whole community may be present *en masse*. Under these conditions, to confess a transgression is to reveal publicly a secret 'sin'. Consequently, the resistance to self-exposure is very great and the shame experienced by the individual extremely poignant. In terms of our own society it is as if the transgressions committed were exposed in open court or published in the newspapers so that everyone knew that Jerry had slept with his sister or that Kate had murdered her child. Among the Saulteaux, however, it is only after such a confession is made that the usual medicine can do its work and the patient can recover. In one case, three children of a married couple were all suffering from a discharge of mucous through the nose and mouth. They had been treated by a native doctor who was also a conjurer but his medicine had done no good. Finally, a conjuring performance was held. Despite the fact that the woman's husband, who was present, had threatened her with death if she ever told, she broke down in a flood of tears and confessed to everyone that he had forced fellatio upon her.

This public aspect of confession is one of the channels through which individuals growing up in Saulteaux society and overhearing the gossip of their elders *sense*, even though they may fail to understand fully, the general typology of disapproved patterns of behavior. Children do not have to be taught a concrete panel of transgressions in Saulteaux society any more than in our own. Nor does it have to be assumed that they have been present on numerous occasions when transgressions have been confessed. Even if they are present, they may not always understand what is meant. Yet some feeling is gained of the kind of conduct that is disapproved. The informant who told me about the case of fellatio was present at the conjuring performance when this was confessed. She was about ten years old at the time and did not understand what was meant until later when her stepmother enlightened her.

In actual operation, the disease sanction among the Saulteaux does not completely deter individuals from committing socially disapproved acts but it functions as a brake by arousing anxiety at the very thought of such conduct. Functionally viewed, a society can well tolerate a few breaches of the rules if, through some means such as confession, a knowledge of dissocial conduct is publicised with the result that a large majority of individuals follow the approved types of behavior.

These deductions are by no means theoretical. That individuals in Saulteaux society actually are deterred from acting in forbidden ways by the disease sanction is illustrated by the following story.[23] In this case, illness did not follow incestuous intercourse. Perhaps this was because it occurred only once. In fact, this may be the moral of the story from the point of view of the Saulteaux themselves. At any rate, it gives a very clear picture of the conscious conflict between the impulses of the individual and socially sanctioned modes of conduct.

> An unmarried woman had 'adopted' her brother's son, a boy who was already a fairly good hunter.[24] They were camping by themselves alone in the bush. The boy had shot some meat and they were drying it. One night after they both lay down to sleep, he began to think about his *kisagwas*.[25] After a while he spoke to her. 'How's chances?' he said.[26] 'Are you crazy,' she replied, 'to talk like that? You are my brother's son.' 'Nothing will happen to us,' the boy said. 'Yes, there will,' said his aunt, 'we might suffer.' 'No we won't. Nothing will happen,' her nephew replied.
>
> Then he got up, went over to where she was lying and managed to get what he wanted, After he had finished, he went back to his own place and lay down again. He could not go to sleep. He began to worry about what he had done to his father's sister.
>
> In the morning he said to her, 'I'm going now.' 'Where?' she asked. 'I'm going to live somewhere else, I'm ashamed of what I did. I'm going away. If I starve to death, all right.' 'No! No! Don't go,' said his aunt. 'If you leave who is going to make a living for me? I'll starve to death. It's not the first time people did what we did. It has happened elsewhere.'
>
> But the young man was much worried and determined to go. 'No, you can't leave me,' said his aunt. 'I've brought you up and you must stay here.' 'I'll go for a while, anyway,' the boy said. 'All right,' said his aunt, 'just for a short time. NO one knows and I'll never tell anyone. There might come a time to say it, but not now.'
>
> So the young fellow went off. He came to a high rock and sat down there. He thought over what he had done. He was sorry that he did it. He pulled out his penis and looked at it. He found a hair. He said to himself, 'This is *nisagwas*, her hair.' He threw it away.
>
> That night he camped by himself, half thinking all the time that he would go back to his aunt. In the morning, he did go back to where they had their camp. He arrived at sundown.
>
> All during the night he was away his aunt had been crying. He was so very glad to see him now. He said to her, 'I wonder if it wold be all right if we lived together, just as if we were man and wife." I don't think so,' the woman said. 'It would not look

right if we did that. If you want a woman you better get one for
yourself and if I want a man I better get one.'

The trouble was this young man had tasted something new
and he wanted more of it. He found a girl and got married in
the spring. He and his wife lived with his aunt. Later his aunt
got married, too.

The narrator commented that the boy's aunt was a sensible woman.
They just made one slip and then stopped. This may explain why nothing
happened to them, i.e., neither one got sick and had to confess.

Among the Saulteaux, then, desire for *pimädaziwin* can be assumed to be
a major goal response. Everyone wants to be healthy, to live long, and to
enjoy life as much as possible. In order to achieve this aim, certain kinds
of conduct should be avoided, not only for one's own sake, but for the
sake of one's children. If one does commit transgression and then falls ill,
or if one's children become ill, it is better to suffer shame than more
suffering or even death. This is the setting of confession and its individual
motivation.[27] Confession, in turn, by making public the transgression
committed permits the individual to recover. This is its ostensible purpose.
But confession has a wider social function. It makes others aware of disapproved types of conduct which act as a warning to them. At the same time,
since patients who confess usually recover, the publicity given to such cases
supports both the native theory of disease causation on which the sanction
rests, and the efficacy of confession itself. So while most individuals are
motivated to avoid the risk of illness, there is consolation in the fact that
even if one's sins find one out, there still is a means of regaining health.

In some traumatic disease situations where witchcraft is thought to be
the cause of the illness, the anxiety of the patient and his associates is
relieved by the removal of a material object from the patient's body by the
doctor. This type of therapy is based upon the belief that it is possible to
project material objects into the body of a person that will cause illness.
Once the object is removed the patient is supposed to recover. The sociopsychological reverberations of cases diagnosed as due to witchcraft are
much the same, however, as those in which confession has occurred. This
follows because the same factors are involved: (a) a disease situation that
requires explanation in terms of some previous behavior on the part of the
patient; (b) the selection, perhaps with the help of the doctor, of some
offensive act that is brought forward because the patient feels guilty about
it; (c) the dissemination of the cause of the illness through gossip about the
case; (d) the resulting publicity given to socially disapproved types of
conduct that act as a warning to others.

We can see, then how the therapeutic measures utilised by these Indians
in traumatic disease situations have the social function of anxiety-reduc-

tion, although this is not their ostensible purpose from the standpoint of the Saulteaux themselves. We can likewise understand how it is that in a society where so much anxiety is associated with disease the persons who specialise in curative methods are individuals who enjoy the highest prestige. In psychological terms, this prestige accrues to those who are instrumental in reducing anxiety.

It is impossible to discuss here all the further ramifications of the functional aspects of anxiety, but we may point out that the whole magico-religious apparatus of the Saulteaux is a complex anxiety-reducing device.[28]

In summary, the thesis developed here is that, by its very nature, disease may arouse 'normal' or objective anxiety, but among the Saulteaux, native theories of disease causation invest certain disease situations with a traumatic quality which is a function of the beliefs held rather than of the actual danger threatened by the illness itself. The quality of the anxiety precipitated in the individuals affected by such situations suggests neurotic rather than objective anxiety because the ultimate cause of the disease is attributed to the expression of dissocial impulses. The illness is viewed as a punishment for such acts and the anxiety is a danger signal that heralds the imminence of this penalty. Insofar as individuals are motivated to avoid dissocial acts because of the penalty anticipated, the pseudoneurotic anxiety aroused in disease situations has a positive social function. It is a psychic mechanism that acts as a reinforcing agent in upholding the social code. Thus, in a society with such a relatively simple culture and one in which formalised institutions and devices for penalising the individual for dissocial conduct are absent, the utilisation of anxiety in connection with disease is an extremely effective means for supporting the patterns of interpersonal behavior that make Saulteaux society a going concern.

Finally, I should like to point out that this role of anxiety in Saulteaux society is consonant with the results that are emerging from certain researches in contemporary experimental psychology.[29] It has been found possible, in Mowrer's view, to recast the Freudian theory of anxiety in stimulus-response terms and to set up hypotheses which can be tested. In this paper, I have attempted to show how such a hypothesis is useful in interpreting observations made in a primitive society.

INTRODUCTION: REFERENCES

Stocking, G. W. (1986) *Malinowski, Rivers, Benedict and Others: Essays on Culture and Personality*. Madison: University of Wisconsin Press.

Wallace, E. R. (1983) *Freud and Anthropology: A History and Reappraisal*. New York: International University Press.

NOTES

1. S. Freud, *The Problem of Anxiety*, trans. H. A. Bunker (New York: 1936), pp. 94, 121.
2. ibid., p. 147.
3. ibid., p. 93.
4. ibid., p. 94.
5. ibid., p. 116. Cf. p. 108: 'Psychic helplessness is the danger which is consonant with the period of immaturity of the ego, as object loss is the danger appertaining to the state of dependence of early childhood, the danger of castration to the phallic phase, and dread of the superego to the latency period. And yet all these danger situations and anxiety determinants may persist alongside one another and cause the ego to react with anxiety at a later period also than the appropriate one; or several of them may become operative simultaneously.'
6. ibid., p. 94. But Freud rejects O. Rank's theory 'that those persons become neurotic who on account of the severity of the birth trauma have never succeeded in abreacting it completely' (p. 123).
7. Cf. O. H. Mowrer, 'A stimulus-response analysis of anxiety, and its role as a reinforcing agent', *Psychological Review*, XLVI (1939): 554 n.
8. ibid., p. 563. 'Anxiety is thus basically anticipatory in nature and has great biological utility in that it adaptively motivates living organisms to deal with (prepare for or feel from) traumatic events in advance of their actual occurrence, thereby diminishing their harmful effects.' According to Mowrer, anxiety may be viewed as 'the conditioned form of the pain reaction' (p. 555).
9. Freud, op. cit., p. 147.
10. Freud, op. cit., p. 147. In this paper, reference is made throughout to Freud's revised theory of anxiety. A discussion of the difference between his first and second theories will be found in *New Introductory Lectures on Psycho-Analysis* (New York: 1933), Chap. 4.
11. In Chap. 13 I called attention to this affective differential as an explicit example of how cultural variables not only define situations for the individual but structuralise them emotionally.
12. Cf. A. I. Hallowell, 'Sin, sex and sickness in Saulteaux relief', *Brit. J. Med. Psychol*, 18 (1989): 191–9.
13. R. M. MacIver, *Society, its Structure and Changes* (New York: 1931), p. 248.
14. A. R. Radcliffe-Brown, 'Sanctions' in *Encyclopedia of the Social Sciences*: 'What is called conscience is thus in the widest sense the reflex in the individual of the sanctions of the society.'
15. In Radcliffe-Brown's terminology, disease is an example of a diffuse, negative sanction. Curiously enough, he does not mention disease at all in his article, despite the fact that it operates to some degree in many societies. Systematic attention has not been given to it as a sanction.

    On the basis of the sketch of the Ojibwa given by Ruth Landes in *Co-operation and Competition among Primitive Peoples* (New York: 1937), Margaret Mead concludes (p. 468) that: 'Although they know of and sometimes act in reference to concepts of social behavior characteristic of adjacent societies with higher integrations, they (the Ojibwa) lack effective sanctions to enforce any rule, either in mourning obligations or against incest or murder.' Although Landes described Ojibwa in a different locale, the belief system and institutional setup is equivalent to that of the Saulteaux. Mead's statement is, to my mind, completely misleading. A closer analysis would show, I think, that the diseases sanction is both important and effective among all Ojibwa peoples.

16. Cf. Joseph C. Yaskin, 'The psychobiology of anxiety', *Psychoanalytic Review*, XXIV (1937), Supplement: 53.

17. Freud, op. cit., p. 149.

18. Cf. Mowrer, op. cit., pp. 563–4, who points out that '...experienced anxiety does not always vary in direct proportion to the objective danger in a given situation, with the result that living organisms, and human beings in particular, show tendencies to behave "irrationally", i.e., to have anxiety in situations that are not dangerous or to have no anxiety in situations that are dangerous. Such a 'disproportionality of affect" may come about for a variety of reasons, and the analyses of these reasons throw light upon such diverse phenomena as magic, superstition, social exploitation, and the psychoneuroses.'

19. While not offered in direct support of our contention, the following remarks of Freud (op. cit., p. 148) seem worth citing: 'There are cases in which the attributes of true and of neurotic anxiety are intermingled. The danger is known and of the real type, but the anxiety in regard to it is disproportionately great, greater than in our judgment it ought to be. It is by this excess that the neurotic element stands revealed. But these cases contribute nothing which is new in principle. Analysis shows that involved with the known reality danger is an unrecognised instinctual danger.'

20. There seems no doubt that this belief also opens the door wide to the use of suggestion on the part of the native doctor.

21. R. Pettazzoni, reviewing the ethnography of confession (*La Confession des Péchés* [Paris: 1931]), making the point that 'la confession des primitifs en général n'est pas secrète', pp. 128 ff.

22. Conjuring involves appeal to supernatural entities. The 'bad conduct' of parent may be discovered by this means and sometimes the spirits of the dead may be invoked for consultation if this seems relevant. Cf. Hallowell, and Chap. 7.

23. Cf. Mowrer, op. cit., p. 558. 'This capacity to be made uncomfortable by the mere prospect of traumatic experiences, in advance of their actual occurrence, (or recurrence), and to be motivated thereby to take realistic precautions against them, is unquestionably a tremendously important and useful psychological mechanism, and the fact that the forward-looking, anxiety-arousing propensity of the human mind is more highly developed than it is in lower animals probably accounts for many of man's unique accomplishments. But it also accounts for some of his most conspicuous failures.'

24. Probably seventeen or eighteen years of age. His aunt was not an 'old' woman, I was told.

25. The term for father's sister and also for mother-in-law. Because of mother-in-law avoidance there was a double barrier to any erotic behavior.

26. The local English vernacular.

27. Among the Saulteaux there is absolutely no connection between confession and the Supreme Being, so that the disease sanction is not in any sense religious. Attention is drawn to this fact because of P. W. Schmidt's categorical interpretation of certain religious aspects of the *Urkulturen* to which, in his opinion, the Northern Algonkian peoples belong. Cf. Pettazzoni, op. cit., pp. 151–2, who discusses this problem. He stresses the dissociation of confession from supreme deities or supernaturals of lesser rank except in a few cases. After referring to these, he goes on to say that 'dans le reste des cas dont nous avons connais-

sance – c'est-à-dire le plus souvent – la confession a lieu en dehors de toute intervention directe ou indirecte d'êtres divins'.

28. Cf. R. R. Willoughby, 'Magic and cognate phenomena: an hypothesis', in *A Handbook of Social Psychology*, ed. Carl Murchison (Worcester: 1935).

29. Cf. O. H. Mowrer, op. cit., p. 564, and his 'Preparatory set (expectancy): some methods of measurement', *Psychological Monographs*, LII (no. 2, 1940): 1–2, 39; and 'Preparatory set (expectancy): a determinant in motivation and learning', *Psychological Review*, XLV (183): 62–91).

CHAPTER NINE

Psychopathology, Primitive Medicine and Primitive Culture (1943)

Erwin H. Ackerknecht

Ackerknecht here cautions care in lumping together a wide set of local insti-tutions and labelling them with a term derived from Western hospital psychiatry. He proposes that in looking at phenomena that overlap the inter-ests of anthropologists and psychiatrists, we need to evaluate them in two distinct ways: on whether they are locally regarded as abnormal (autopatho-logical); and on whether they can be seen as abnormal in relation to medical criteria (heteropathological). This approach we might now term the emic and the etic (Littlewood 1990). He leaves open Seligman's question about the absence of psychosis in small-scale communities, but is broadly sympa-thetic, arguing that in many cases the apparently high rate of illness may be an acculturation (social change) phenomenon.

ON PSYCHOPATHOLOGICAL LABELS

One of the characteristic mental traits of our culture is the labelling of phenomena with psychiatric diagnoses. This trait has become so very common that we are hardly any more aware of it. Persons and crowds, historic personalities and periods, cultures and societies, magic procedures and religions are 'neurotic', 'sadistic', 'schizophrenic', etc., or in the plain and less dignified vocabulary of the common man 'mad', 'lunatic' and 'crazy'. Even the child in the cradle has not been spared and is supposed by some to undergo a 'normal neurosis'.

This trait is not so very new. Vesalius was called Vesanus. Goethe complained about its occurrence in literary criticism. As a more general phenomenon it may be traced back at least to the beginning of the last century, to the reactionary French historians, to Chateaubriand and his generation, and later on to Taine and his school.[1] Full of the strongest moral indignation against the revolution of 1789, but lacking already at that time a common moral basis, as e.g. religion, from which to appeal to the public, they arrived, probably rather unconsciously, at the ingenious solution of condemning the revolution as a case of mental illness. In a culture oriented towards and penetrated by an almost religious respect for science, deeply impressed by great medical progress, the procedure proved to be efficient and has thus survived in full vigor. Their adversaries did not remain inactive and devoted much time to a pious analysis of the more or less authentic mental defects of dead monarchs. Both parties immediately mobilised against the other the meanwhile rather outmoded but once so handy psychological and anatomical concept of the 'degenerated'.[2]

This quality of a hidden moral judgment may still be easily detected in a number of contemporary, apparently objective and scientific psychopathological labels.[3] The deep resentment against our own culture is very often manifested in this way. To avoid misunderstandings: we are not opposed to moral judgments at all. On the contrary, we cannot resign to this modern 'Ersatz' for moral norms and judgments. We think that the custom of covering moral judgments with a pseudoscientific psychopathological nomenclature is no advance at all and is equally bad for both of them: morals and science. But quite apart from the scientific 'value' of this labeling, by the development of our attitude towards the mentally ill the once powerful weapon has paradoxically become very often a weapon against the one who uses it. It makes him now powerless instead of more efficient. Transferring a famous dictator, for instance, out of the political into the psychopathological sphere means to transfer him out of the field of normal political action. We pity the ill, and to fight and to hate one who is insane has become utterly unfair and senseless in our society. Thus from being an instrument of intolerance, psychopathological labeling has sometimes become an expression of tolerance or even over-tolerance. It may, on the other hand, serve just the opposite purpose and soothe moral scruples for ruthlessness following the old French dictum: Si on veut tuer son chien, on dit qi'il a la rage.

Psychopathological labeling is in part simply an expression of the very old penetration of our entire speech and thought by medical, physiological and anatomical terms and metaphors. Today it is to a large extent an involuntary tribute to the great achievements of psychiatrists in the field of general psychology during the last decades.[4] We cannot blame psychiatrists like Freud or Kretschmer[5] that they made their great discoveries with ill people. But we suffer from the fact that this procedure has formed the terminology. 'Paranoids', 'schizoids', 'sado-masochistic characters' to us are unfortunately much less primary normal forms than people suffering from an extremely mild degree of mental disease. Looking at a character and classifying him as 'paranoid', 'schizoid', etc., we usually see in him at least the potential paranoiac, schizophrenic, etc., while the actual probability that he ever will develop a psychosis is infinitesimal.[6] Of course, there are authors who, speaking e.g. of paranoid or megalomanic traits[7] in cultures or individuals, are fully aware of the fact that they deal with normal and not pathological phenomena; but in this awareness unfortunately they seem to represent rather the exception than the rule. Attempts by modern psychologists to change the terminology are therefore far from being vain stylistic exercises and deserve the fullest approval and encouragement.[8] This part of the history of psychopathological labels is almost tragicomic. The pathologists, embittered by the pertinacious lack of anatomical findings in certain mental and other diseases, had stigmatised them as 'functional', had deprived them (and the unfortunate sufferers from them) of the legitimate title of honest diseases and driven them out of the realm of the scientifically abnormal; but the functional diseases have returned by the backdoor and have not only reconquered their deserved places, but also inundate the normal world with their terminology.

In psychopathological labeling there is also much lingering of older psychiatric thought. Older psychiatry was based on a concept of 'normal' mentality which became not less efficient by the fact that it was never clearly formulated. From the counterparts of the pathological symptoms, from the ideals of past philosophers there was constructed an ideal 'mentally normal' man who, every much like certain 'ideal' anatomical pictures, has never existed and compared to whom not only every one of us but also – as the study of numerous 'historical' psychiatric or psychological articles shows – every outstanding personality of the past is hopelessly 'psychotic' or 'neurotic'. It is still not yet realised how extremely difficult it was to gain a realistic concept of the normal in a field as inaccessible to morphological, physical, chemical, even statistical methods, and what enormous an advance in our understanding of the mentally normal and abnormal has been reached by the functional method, the introduction of the notion of 'integration', 'adjustment', etc.

Nevertheless, all these explanations, true as they are, do not touch the fundamentals of our phenomenon. *Psychopathological labeling seems to be foremost an expression for helplessness, a specific attitude of our culture towards the unknown.* While the savage regards the incomprehensible as supernatural, the 'civilised' Western man regards it as psychopathological. This reaction of our culture seems to occur in whatever field it may be. Whether Moreau de Tours declares 'le géie n'est qu'une névrose' or one of our most intelligent and influential businessmen can see in the economic crisis of 1929 but 'crowd madness',[9] in both cases the psychopathological 'diagnosis' gives, perhaps, emotional relief, but not a scientific solution of the incomprehensible.

Our culture is unique in its consequent outlawing of the irrational, the emotional, the ecstatic. These phenomena have thus become most uncomprehensible and unknown to our society.[10] The bedroom, the liquor store and the office of the psychiatrist are their last sanctuaries, but only the last of these three places is not tabooed for public expression. Thus it is no wonder that an almost unlimited number of phenomena have acquired a psychopathological label.[11] Without hesitation the irrational is now very often called simply psychopathological and sometimes actually made psychopathological by this procedure. The same banishment of the irrational into the barren fields of psychopathology explains also the unmeasured and otherwise almost incomprehensible interest of the large public in psychopathology as the only means of satisfying an innate metaphysical need.[12]

We cannot agree with those who see in psychopathological labeling but a mere variant of the 'psychological manoeuvres' of 'bourgeois ideologists' to hide fundamental economic facts. Social psychology in itself did by no means ignore those facts and was on the contrary born out of the impotence of exclusive biological or economical materialism to explain fully the social process in past and present. As long as it does not fall into the monopolistic attitude of its forerunners it is a sound reaction.

The mechanism of psychopathological labeling in itself is obvious and the paralogism very easy to detect. The concept of the *different* is simply identified with the concept of the pathological although the latter should be limited to the socially incompatible. But we are very far from underestimating the attractiveness of this trend, from despising its followers. Its emotional roots are too deep, the step from analysing analogies between psychopathological thought and other forms of behavior to identifying those phenomena is too short and easy, that it should not be a very great temptation to make it. But, as we have already seen, it is very bad for the labeled, for the labeler and – what we are most concerned about here – *for science.* Once we stop at a typical statement of the 'psychopathological school' as the following: '*(Primitive) religion and in general "quaint" primitive areas are organized schizophrenia*',[13] and think it over, it is not very difficult to realise the full consequences[14] of this tendency for science. When (primitive) religion is but 'organised schizophrenia', then there is left no room or necessity for history, anthropology, sociology, etc. God's earth was, and is, but a gigantic state hospital and pathography becomes the unique and universal science. Absolute subjectivism has thus conquered science again. It needs the gigantic helplessness and vanity, the terrible 'uniqueness' of our culture to come to such statements.

One of the main contributions of anthropology was to throw new light on the concept of the abnormal[15] and to invalidate older misconceptions of an universal type of 'abnormality'. The tendency of psychopathological labeling in our culture and science is thus a challenge to medical anthropologists to begin charity at home and to reexamine their material to find out the actual role psychopathology plays in primitive medicine and primitive cultures.

THE MEDICINE MAN AND PSYCHOPATHOLOGY

When the medicine man first became known to Europeans, he generally was regarded as a humbug. With an increasing knowledge and understanding of primitive cultures this opinion has since been abandoned.[16] But it is still quite usual to see the medicine man characterised as a kind of madman. The diagnosis varies from epilepsy[17] to hysteria,[18] from fear neurosis[19] to 'veritable idiocy'.[20] As a matter of fact he is one of the preferred targets of psychopathological labeling in anthropology. We observe in his case again the passing from moral judgment to clinical diagnosis already described above.

Before analysing how far the mentality of the medicine men may be regarded as abnormal or psychopathological, it may be useful to define how in our sense this diagnosis can only be applied in a legitimate sense. From the medical point of view mental diseases have the great disadvantage that the overwhelming majority of them cannot be defined in terms of anatomy or biochemistry. A cancer or a diabetes is everywhere the same, not only in its disabling consequences, but also in its objective symptoms and bodily changes.[21] A neurosis or a psychosis most probably has also an organic basis or components,[22] but those are not known to us and we can diagnose mental disease exclusively by observation of changes in behavior and mental content, incompatible with successful social activity; such changes are not biological but socio-cultural phenomena. Our psychiatrists have empirically classified as special diseases and belonging to the realm of abnormality and psychopathology a number of such changes and attitudes which (and because they) are incompatible with normal functioning in our society. The anthropological study of other cultures has now produced the great surprise that these notions of abnormality judged from the only possible criterion, social integration, deserve by no means the absolute value we imputed to them. A man, e.g., with paranoid behavior and ideas, unlike a man suffering from tuberculosis, may in another cultural set-up where almost everybody shares his attitude, be by no means socially disabled, but a normal and even ideal participant of his society.[23] Ruth Benedict has analysed in her 'Anthropology and the Abnormal' and *Patterns of Culture* trances in the Shasta, Zulus and Siberians, homosexuality in the berdache-customs, paranoiac behavior in Dobu and 'megalomania' among the Kwakiutl, and shown that the normals of those cultures look like abnormals in our culture while the abnormals in Dobu, among the Crow and Zuñi, could be perfectly normal with us.[24] '*Normality within a very wide range is culturally defined.*'[25] That means that we cannot any longer regard as abnormal a person only on the basis of certain fixed symptoms, disregarding the historical and cultural place of this person, but that we can only regard as abnormal a person whose character reactions hinder social integration in a given period and society.

As anthropologists we deal with societies, cultures separated in space. But the same is true for separation in time, for different periods of the 'same' culture. A normal of the Middle Ages would easily be an abnormal today.[26] This statement even holds good for the different horizontal culture areas[27] or subcultures,[28] in stratified (non-primitive) societies, in which for normality only 'social personalities of the same level'[29] or 'status'[30] should be compared.[31] We call in the following '*autonormal*' and *autopathological*', *those who are defined in their normality and abnormality by their own society, the only true definition of normality we recognise.*

We call '*heteronormal*' or '*heteropathological*' *those who are regarded as normal or pathological according to the scale of our society,* a scale which is inadequate as long as we lack truly general notions of human psychopathology. We would like to warn from the very beginning that of course even the 'autopathological' in a non-literate society is never to his brethren 'mentally ill' in our sense, as these societies lack the conception of special mental or bodily diseases. He is simply 'ill' and his illness is explained by the general disease concept, in the respective society. But for our purpose here it is essential that he is regarded as pathological and it would be an unnecessary burden for our present study, to analyse in every case the exact meaning of his disease in his society.

We are fully aware of the intricacies of the problem. We know that our solution is a provisory one and an expression of our limited knowledge. Our knowledge allows us to see that those members of primitive societies who behave like our psychopaths may be perfectly normal. But there may be a fundamental state of mental disease, common to all those who are mentally ill, as after all we are all men.[32] But we ignore it. There may be a morbid type condemned to become mentally ill in every society and changing only the forms of his disintegration in difficult cultures. But we are unable to diagnose this type, as we do not even know truly and to a necessary extent the normal of our own society. We are only able to state integration and non-integration every time they occur. It is almost certain that among the members, e.g., of a culture with paranoid or schizoid orientation there are those who are simply following the pattern[33] and there are those who are following it by 'vocation', by inner structure, by a kind of organic necessity, and that both types, though normal, are different. But we have no instruments to differentiate them in quantity and quality.[34] We know that while between the former type and our paranoiac and schizophrenic there exists *but one analogy*[35] because their 'delusions' grow from different sources, *the one being formed by society, the other having grown against society,*[36] there may be more intimate relations between the latter and our psychopath. But without new criteria we can but produce more or less meaningless speculations on the problems. We are fortunate enough to have learned at least that the member of a primitive society, although he behaves exactly like the psychopath of our own society, may be perfectly normal (auto-normal) because functioning well in his society, while the abnormal, the non-integrated of this society may be normal (heteronormal) in the eyes of another society. The insight in the incompleteness of our equipment must not stop our endeavor, but encourage us to clear and prepare the field for new advances by using the valuable although limited criteria we already have for analysing concrete material.

For some decades now it has become customary to apply to medicine men all over the world the Siberian term 'shaman'. This use of terminology – or more exactly, misuse, as a rapid examination of the peculiarities of the shaman will show immediately – has undoubtedly to a very large extent contributed towards creating the psychopathological reputation of the medicine man. It seems too late to attempt or to obtain a change of this terminology; but an exposition of the facts may perhaps help to reduce the faulty conclusions springing from an uncritical use of the term shaman.

The Siberian shaman, as a matter of fact, is by no means the model of a medicine man, but a very special type of medicine man. Loeb[37] asked in 1929 that a differentiation at least be made between 'shaman' and 'seer'. He wanted to retain the term 'shaman' for the inspirational type of medicine man; the (voluntarily) possessed, *through* whom the spirit speaks; the man, who exercises and prophesies; as he occurs in Siberia, Asia, Africa, among the Dravidian tribes of India, the Veddhas, in Melanesia, Fiji and Polynesia. He created the term 'seer' for those 'non-inspirational' non-possessed medicine men, *with* whom the guardian spirit speaks and who do not exorcise or prophesy: the medicine men of North and South America, Australia, New Guinea, and of the Negritoes. He observed personally both types in Indonesia.[38] The proposition of Loeb becomes particularly important when his opinion can be confirmed that the seer is an earlier type and the shaman a later product of development.[39]

But not only in this sense is the Siberian shaman different from a great number of other medicine men. Not only is his possession of such a peculiar type (ventriloquism) that Oesterreich in his fundamental book – it is true on the basis of very incomplete material – even denies to him the character of possession.[40] Not only does the Siberian shaman belong to that restricted group of medicine men where previous illness in general is a condition of his vocation[41] where the vocation has an absolutely compulsory and obsessional character,[42] but he is the *outstanding representative of that small group of medicine men where the medicine man passes indeed through a stage of grave mental illness* before becoming a shaman. This fact has undoubtedly given more than anything else the special psychopathological tint to the term 'shaman'.

Of course mental illness is not the only way to become a shaman.

Young orphans may voluntarily become shamans.[43] A special adventure accompanied by great danger may lead to shamanism.[44] Shamanism, e.g., among the Buriats may be simply hereditary and transmitted by instruction.[45] Or the 'inspiration' may even be sold (Ostjak).[46] But as far as we are able to judge from the scanty documents mostly collected in a period of decay of shamanism,[47] a kind of mental disease seems to be most common during the preparatory period of the shaman. The first signs may appear in childhood. The outbreak occurs generally in the late puberty. 'The preparatory period is compared by the Chukchee to a long severe illness and the acquirement of inspiration to a recovery.'[48] 'He who is to become a shaman begins to rage like a raving madman. He suddenly utters incoherent words, falls unconscious, runs through the forests, lives on the bark of trees, throws himself into fire and water, lays hold on weapons and wounds himself, in such wise that his family is obliged to keep watch on him. By these signs it is recognised that he will become a shaman.'[49] Bogoras knew a woman shaman who had been violently mad for 3 years and whose hands were mutilated[50] as a consequence of these paroxysms. He reports of this tendency towards isolation, the changing periods of excitement and calm. One man slept during two months.[51] Sternberg reports a Giljak who was 'unconscious' during two months.[52] Sieroszewski tells the story of Tiuspuit who had auditory and visual hallucinations during 9 years before recovering by becoming a shaman.[53] 'If the man designed to become a shaman (by the spirits of dead shamans) opposes the will of the predecessors and refuses to shamanize, he exposes himself to terrible afflictions which either end in the victim losing all his mental powers and becoming imbecile and dull or else going raving mad and generally after a short time doing himself an injury or dying in a fit.'[54] It is clear why a person should try to avoid the terrible shamanistic call and in spite of Radloff's general statement a few succeed in recovering without becoming shamans.[55]

It is not quite clear which one among the numerous Siberian psychoses the pre-shamanic psychosis is, nor can it be classified exactly as one of our mental diseases; it is not the convulsionary disease called epilepsia by Sieroszewski and Bogoras, and leading more or less rapidly to death.[56] It is certainly not amürakh, the 'arctic hysteria' (see following chapter). On the contrary an amürakh cannot become a shaman and a shaman who gets amürakh has to give up his profession.[57] It seems to come closest to what Sieroszewski calls the 'crying disease'.[58] He saw these lunatics guarded in cages because they sometimes kill, and it sometimes seems necessary to kill them.[59] Although the preparatory madness of the Siberian shaman is generally regarded as hysteria, these descriptions would rather fit into our picture of schizophrenia insofar as they fit into one of our pictures at all.

Similar phenomena may occasionally be observed with Eskimo medicine men,[60] or in Indonesia.[61] They seem to have been rather common in the life history of medieval saints.[62] But *with a like clearness we have found the preshamanistic psychosis only among South African Bantu tribes.* We have the old but very graphic description of Rev. C. H. Calloway in his *Religious System of the Amazulu.*[63] A man falls ill, does not eat, becomes 'a house of dreams', weeps, has convulsions. He is treated for years, all his wealth is eaten up by the practitioners. He is but skin and bones. His death is daily expected. But then he becomes able to detect hidden (or stolen) things and after a purification ceremony he is a medicine man (inyanga) and well again. 'If the relatives of the man who has been made ill by the Itongo do not wish him to become a diviner, they call a great doctor to treat him, to lay the spirit that he may not divine. But although the man no longer divines, he is not well; he continues to be always out of health.'

Laubscher's[64] very recent studies among the Tembu and Fingu tribes present a rather similar picture. Numerous people fall in a state called 'ukutwasa'[65] where they undergo a call from the mythical 'River People; to become a 'Doctor'. They have visions, run wild, some commit suicide in this state. If one is refrained during ukutwasa from becoming a 'Doctor', or if he is not properly treated by native methods he becomes mad. It is not quite clear if ukutwasa is already definitely regarded by the Tembu as mental illness or more as a mental state comparative to those of our examination candidates; but anyway the consequences of an ukutwasa not ending in doctoring activity are clearly hetero- and autopathological.

Mention should here also be made of the Wyo, male and female mediums among the Ga people of the Gold Coast.[66] Although not medicine men themselves, they are important assistants of both, medicine men and priests. They also pass through a preparatory state of mental disturbance (in this case closer to our 'hysteria') and if their call is not followed they become plain mad (The Ga themselves differentiate between plain undirected madness and spirit possession.) Following their call they undergo a long training period by a medicine man ('treatment'?) and function then as full-fledged mediums, being able to undergo voluntary possession, and being otherwise perfectly normal![67]

Among the South African Thonga the ordinary medicine man is highly 'non-inspirational'. His office is purely hereditary. But those who have suffered from possession by a spirit ('bubayiby psikwembu' = 'the madness of gods') enter after the exorcism a special group of practitioners, who now themselves treat possession.[68] The possessing spirit has been won as a friend and protector.

This recovery by becoming a shaman is certainly a very strange fact. While it is easy enough to understand in simple hysteria-like states of possession where conversion to a creed and becoming an exorciser is well known to heal (Thonga, Ga),[69] it is rather difficult to do so in the above-described Siberian, Tembu and Zulu cases. But even Laubscher who generally is rather inclined to diagnose full-blown schizophrenia everywhere, states: 'The "witch doctors" conform broadly to the class of abnormal characters known in our culture as psychopaths. They display in conduct all shades of deviation from the average person and it is not unlikely that many of them are psychotic persons in remissive phases or *improved or relieved without insight*.'[70] He even recognises that a whole category of them (the isanuse – they all have gone through ukutwasa!) is *not psychotic or psychopathic at all*.[71] We cannot adopt Nietzsche's principal refusal to recognise religious healing as real healing which is based on the very personal philosophy of a minister's son, but he incidentally has pointed to an important, special trait of these healings: they rather stupefy than eradicate the evil.[72] In our cases too it is symbolical that the disease spirits are not 'expulsed' but only pacified and even worshipped.[73] This seems to explain in a certain way why during old age some shamans seem to have a relapse,[74] while others retire, completely calmed.[75] On the other hand we cannot disregard the fact that the shaman is functioning socially while those who do not become shamans stay unadapted. We have to remember what a tremendous psycho-therapeutic power magic has not only for those for whom it is performed, but above all for the performer himself.[76] It is a kind of psychological safety valve where too strong psychic pressure can be released. We thus have to recognise that in primitive societies there perhaps exist outlets for mental conditions with which we are not able to deal. It seems as if we will have to accept the fact that *shamanism is not disease but being healed from disease*.

In stating that the shaman after having passed through an autopathological stage is autonormal[77] we could stop our argument. But in order to convince sceptics we would like to discuss some points which show how little the shaman fits even in our scheme of a psychopathological (disintegrated) personality, as soon as we study not only some traits analogous to those of our psychopaths but his whole (integrated) personality. Although the preshamanistic mental crisis during puberty is unparalleled elsewhere in its deepness, we would become perhaps somewhat more comprehensive towards it, if we would remember that even in our society we accord to youngsters of that age an amount of mental unbalance, which is by no means physiologically justified but culturally conditioned.[76] The prophetic crisis is regarded as non-pathological, is highly respected and looked for; it is *voluntarily induced, prepared and always kept in certain limits*. Some minutes afterwards the shaman is perfectly calm, without signs of exhaustion. 'Although hysteria lies at the bottom of the shaman's vocation, yet at the same time the shaman differs from an ordinary patient suffering from this illness in possessing an extremely great power of mastering himself in the periods between the actual fits which occur during the ceremonies.'[79]

The professional shaman besides is not such an exceptional being in his culture, he is only a variety of the family-shaman. Where family-shamanism still exists, to a certain extent everybody shamanises. Noise is as comforting to the Siberian in case of illness, as calm is to us.[80] Bogoras, who always insists on the nervosity of the shaman, reports himself a very rare act of self-control in Chukchee land: the refusal of alcohol perpetrated by a shaman (Scratching Woman). The existence of *self-control* is also evident in the rules for a model shaman: 'Un véritable chamane doit posséder les vertus qui forment le trésor du cœur humain; il doit être sérieux, avoir du tact, savoir convaincre son entourage; surtout il ne doit pas se montret présomptueux, fier, emporté!'[81] 'In answer to persons seeking advice Chukchee shamans often display much wisdom and circumspection.'[82] In refusing to treat tuberculosis, dysentery, scarlet fever, measles, syphilis and other diseases inaccessible to their therapeutic means they certainly display a good deal of *judgment*.[83] Perhaps they would be better understood if one would realise that they are not only priests and healers but also great dramatic artists.[84] This trait has impressed observers from the very beginning (v̇. Wrangel [no title given] 1839, Castren [no title given] 1853). One of the preferred arguments for the psychopathology of the shaman is his bad economic status. One forgets too easily that this poverty is imposed on the shaman by society. The mentally similar Eskimo angagok and Bantu isanuses by no means suffer from this evil for the simple reason that they are not instructed like the Siberian shaman to go first to the poor and not even to ask much from the rich![85] The adoption of woman's clothes by the shaman, another 'psychopathological' trait, appears after closer examination in the overwhelming majority of cases socially conditioned and not temperamentally. Very few of these transvestites are true homosexuals and marry another man.[86] And besides even homosexuals are rather biological variants and by no means psychopaths by nature, but only become psychopathic through their outlawed position in our society.[87] Just the two latter points remind us to what an extent the shaman is formed by society, how impossible it is to identify his socially created mentality with that of our psychopath which has grown asocial. it is typical that he cannot work in a trance without an 'ocitkolin', a person who gives him answers and applause during the séance.[89] As elsewhere he probably could not give up his wretched profession even if he wanted to do so.[90] 'The magician is a being determined by society and pushed by it to fulfill its rôle.'[91]

Certainly the shaman is very sensitive, nervous, has a special look, etc. He may be called supernormal, an 'abnormal of fulfillment' as Benedict terms it,[92] but he cannot be regarded as subnormal, abnormal in the psychopathological sense. He is not an outcast, but privileged by the gods. He is normal in the sense of being well adapted to his society. He is 'autonormal', and even those who would like to have him heteropathological, cannot deny that he is far from presenting the disintegrated personality which our psychopaths present.

Already the rest of the inspirational medicine men, although they undergo ritual possession, offer much less difficulty to our psychological understanding than the real 'shaman' type. Possession may be a mental disease among primitives, truly autopathological and most often compared to our hysteria (see following chapter). But the *ritual possession* of the medicine man is *autonormal*. Melanesians clearly differentiate it from the possession-disease (and other pathological conditions: fever-delirium, etc.).[93] As already described, it is voluntarily induced by drumming, singing, dancing, gazing, etc., and rather well controlled. It may even be of actual value 'setting free the healing instinct'.[94] It seems to be a state of *autohypnosis* and even quite far from hysteria (not to speak of epilepsy).[95] Hysteria or other psychoneuroses may be entirely absent in the tribe where ritual possession is practised.[96] On the other hand death from exhaustion and over-exertion of the devoted medicine man has been described, a trait rather inconsistent with our conception of hysteria.[97] While the possessed medicine man by his technique comes thus rather close to our spiritual mediums, he does not participate in their psychopathology. This is not so very surprising if we remember that the psychopathology of our mediums is due – as the psychology, e.g., of our homosexuals, mulattoes, hunchbacks and not so long ago onanists – much more to their ambiguous position in society than to their organic structure. *Where possession does not occur as an illness but as a requisite of the 'medical' profession, it neither needs an ill person to become possessed nor does it make one mentally ill.* The missionary Warneck in his *Die Religion der Batak*, (Göttingen: 1909), p. 8, on the basis of long personal experience makes the following clear statement: 'This state *in a person otherwise completely sane* has nothing to do with epilepsy or other nervous affections, for those who suffer from mental troubles are well known and clearly distinguished from the shamans; no one of the diseases of the mind, found among the Bataks, presents the same symptoms.'

Mariner[98] says in his classic, *Account of the Natives of the Tonga Islands*, concerning the 'inspirational' medicine men: 'If there was any difference between them and the rest of the natives, it was that they were rather more given to reflection and somewhat more taciturn and probably greater observers of what was going forward.' The Seligmans found no special nervous irritability either among the Vedda medicine men or their pupils.[99] The confusion between them and the spontaneously possessed (mentally ill) seems to be the main source for the myth of 'veneration of the insane and his sayings' by the primitives.

With the 'non-inspirational' medicine man (the non-possessed, Loeb's 'seer') the elements which may suggest psychopathological conditions fade out still more. Their visions and trances lack almost all objective 'symptoms' like fits and seizures. They are easier to understand as the effects of an early implanted conception of a world where the natural and supernatural are not firmly separated, as dramatised day-dreams than as 'auditory and visual hallucinations' in otherwise normal persons. A real analysis of our normal individuals would perhaps reveal even there a surprising number of such tendencies, hidden only by the structure of our culture pattern. Besides, the ways of producing these experiences are very often frankly artificial, from fasting to alcohol and other drugs, and show them as momentary consequences of intoxication in normal people. Or we deal with simple dreams which are not different from ours, but are only differently interpreted. The strange standardisation, the stereotype of these subjective experiences betrays also their social origins. The elements of tradition, social heredity, and learning – objectively decisive in the making of every medicine man – also become officially more prevalent and visible. In the procedure of these medicine men the accent is more on the objective and fixed parts of their rite: spells, drugs, fetish objects than on their inspiration, their state of mind.

Of course the activity even of the most 'non-inspirational' medicine man still involves magico-religious acts which appear strange enough to us. Fundamentally, the medicine man as the outstanding representative of primitive mentality can only be understood by those who have grasped the essentials of this mentality. But as long as one does not make the rather radical step of regarding the belief in magic qua such as pathological, these magic acts do not justify heteropathological evaluation.

The strongholds of the 'non-inspirational' medicine man are, as mentioned above, America and Australia. Already Bourke stated, that 'our native tribes do not believe that the mildly insane are gifted with medical or spiritual power'.[100] Autopathological and even heteropathological behavior is not very likely when a majority performs the acts in question and as a matter of fact is absent in all those Indian cultures where leechdom is not hierarchised, where almost everybody in reaching adulthood has a vision governing his future behavior, and where the vision of the 'medicine man', who stays a rather common man, differs only slightly from the other visions.[101]

But more psychopathological traits are not observable when the medicine man becomes the leader, as, e.g., among the Cherokees.[101] Among Olbrechts' numerous and detailed character studies of Cherokee medicine men there is not a single psychopath.[103] The fact that only such individuals are accepted as pupils who seem apt to live up to the high moral standards of the profession,[104] that, e.g., the quarrelsome and the lazy are excluded in advance[105] is of course a very efficient preventive measure in this direction. A. J. Hallowell states expressly of Salteaux conjurers: 'My impression of Salteaux conjurers were quite the reverse (of Bogoras' impressions concerning Chukchee shamans). Nothing seems to distinguish them, as a group from other Indians in respect to psychological type or psychic peculiarities of major significance.'[106]

Even in Mohave culture where dream experience is so dominant that it is actually confused with ordinary life experience,[107] where the medicine man seems to occupy a peculiar position, going into a special heaven[108] and provoking his own murder,[109] Devereux comes to the following result: 'Under ordinary circumstances Mohave shamans seem as extroverted as any run-of-the-mill Mohave. The average Mohave shaman is neither obviously neurotic nor obviously maladjusted.'[110]

Concerning Australian medicine men B. Spencer and I. G. Gillen in their classical book on the native tribes of Central Australia state that 'the medicine men are characteristically the reverse of nervous and excitable in temperament'.[111] Recent studies among the Murngin by so sophisticated an observer as W. L. Warner bring out the same results. The white magician among the Murngins has such supernatural qualities as seeing the spirits of the killer near the dead man; he prophesies, sucks out disease objects, etc. Nevertheless: 'The individuality of the white magician is not different from that of the ordinary man. The only noticeable tendency in all the observed healers was their joviality and pleasantness in their ordinary social relations. There were no indications of the psychopathic personality, for psychologically and physically they were a very normal group.'[112]

And even the black magician who daydreams the most awful magic murders, 'is individually not different from the ordinary men in the community. He participates in the culture and in the daily round of affairs exactly like other men.'[113] Of one of these men (Laindjura) Warner states expressly: 'There was nothing sinister, peculiar or psychopathic about him; he was perfectly normal in his behaviour.'[114]

When the call for the medical profession is absolutely hereditary, when the (magic but mostly objectively efficient) drug is more important than the medicine man, as among the Manos of Liberia, where advanced techniques and elementary ignorance (no method of lighting a fire) are strangely mixed his behavior may take the following forms: 'In treating disease . . there is no special dress, no fuss, no shouting, singing or chanting. There is even a bedside manner, dignified, confident. . .'[115]

The mentality of medicine men all over the world, conditioned by their respective culture patterns, can hardly be caught by one general label, and least of all by the term 'shaman' (the healed madman, as we have seen) or other psychopathological labels like epilepsy, hysteria, etc. (Nor can the different mentalities be arranged in an evolutionary scheme.) It is more or less in the nature of things that the medicine men are autonormal. Closer analysis shows the psychological soundness of such an approach, in revealing a surprising amount even of heteronormalcy, where superficial and premature labeling had seen but psychopathology.

PRIMITIVE CULTURE AND PSYCHOPATHOLOGY

The medicine man owed his psychopathological label mostly to the fact that he was the best known representative of primitive mentality. When this mentality became better known as a whole, the same 'logic' which had made him a madman, characterised also primitive mentality, especially the belief in magic and primitive cultures as psychopathological.[116]

Of course primitive mentality looks at first glance strange enough to those who are brought up only with the (incomplete) knowledge of the 'white, adult and civilised' man. There is no limit between the natural and the supernatural. The natural is supernatural and the supernatural is quite natural.[117] Perception may not be different,[118] but values are just the reverse of those of our culture.[119] 'What high cultures stigmatize as purely personal, non-real and non-social, abnormal and pathological, lower cultures treat as objective, socially useful, and conducive to special ability.'[120] The ideas concerning 'causality' which are generated by this approach are of course as different from ours as possible.

But being different is not yet being psychopathological. To regard primitive culture and the primitive qua such as 'neurotic' because of certain analogies is as intelligent as to regard childhood as a kind of neurosis.

As long as there are no more objective criteria for mental health in cultures as in individuals our main criterion has to be the criterion of *function*.[121] Now, primitive cultures, in spite of numerous supernaturally conditioned regulations which seem to 'work against the practical wisdom of conservation',[122] have well sustained the ordeal of existence. Cultures, where the fear complex and the corresponding 'regulations' are much more overt than in our own, like Navaho, Apache, Eskimo society,[123] have even proved to be extremely vigorous. *A culture cannot be called pathological except under one condition: when the culture is driven to self-destruction by its own mental structure or by changes in its mental structure.*[124] Such cases and 'diseases' exist, as we will see, but they are very rare – their diagnosis is mostly possible only post mortem – and have nothing to do with the superficial and fashionable talk of 'neurotic cultures'.[125]

The faulty conclusions spring from the supposition that a society is only able to function normally insofar as it is rational. History proves that this 'criterion of rationality' is but a delusion. As Kroeber has pointed out again and again, in this belief our difference from the primitive consists not so much in the complete absence of magico-irrational attitudes in our own culture, than in our bias of not seeing in our own culture, what we so easily discover and condemn in others.[126] Only a society which is based entirely on rationality according to plan would be entitled to apply the criterion of rationality in stigmatising others as abnormals. Whether such a society will ever exist is unknown. But one has only to look at the history of the two great revolutions started under the banner of rationality, the French and the Russian, both of which proved to be such a deadly surprise in the most literal sense of the word to their initiators, to know that it certainly has not yet arrived.

The problem of psychopathology in primitive culture cannot be solved by cheap generalisations and paralogisms. It has to be approached by an examination of the existing material, scanty and highly contradictory as it unfortunately still is. While the psychopathological labels have suggested nothing but madmen among our august ancestors and their primitive cousins, the first exact researches have put quite another problem: *does mental illness exist to any considerable extent among primitives?*

A fact which badly hampers every study in this field, is that most cultures that we regard as still primitive have already entered the stage of *acculturation* when they become observable. It is now well known, for individual as well as mass psychoses, from ethnographical studies as well as from 'transition periods' of our own history or between our different subcultures, that man in such situations – 'marginal man' in the terminology of R. Park[127] is particularly liable to fall a victim of disease in general and especially of mental disease.[128] As soon as it is thus possible to prove that a primitive culture is definitely in an acculturation situation, a large occurrence of mental disease in such a culture loses every relevance to the problem of frequency of mental disease in actual primitive societies.

The mere existence of mental disease in primitive societies is, of course, established beyond doubt.[129] For those who have realised the impact of social factors on the genesis of mental disease, this fact is not surprising or mysterious. One would be a belated victim of the belief in the 'good savage' to think that primitive society does not also contain sufficient psychic tensions to produce mental disease.[130] Hallowell has well pointed to the ambivalent character of primitive society in this behalf: 'It is quite possible that the decline of supernaturalism in Western society has forever undermined the status of a generic culture pattern which, in a multitude of forms, has been an effective, although to us naive authority, previously available to the individual as a means of resolving various forms of psychic stresses. *At the same time, certainly, one must not forget the potent rôle that supernaturalism has played in causing psychic stresses.*[131]

While there is no doubt concerning the existence of mental disease in primitive society, its frequency, especially in *its Western forms has become extremely questionable.* Seligman's statement[132] that among Papua–Melanesians, schizophrenia is absent, neuroses are rare, and only occasional manic conditions are observable, has raised great interest. But there are and have been already rather numerous similar statements concerning the scarcity of mental disease among primitives.[133] On the other hand primitive tribes are sometimes reported as presenting a particular high incidence of mental disease.[134] Hirsch quotes both kinds of sources.[135] All these statements are too vague to enable us to reach any definite conclusions. Fortunately we dispose at least of one document based on the records and observations of 80 years in the District of Astrachan which gives some more articulate *local* conclusions (N. Skliar and K. Starikowa, 'Zur vergleichenden Psychiatrie', *Arch. f. Psych. und Nervkrkh.*, 88 (1929): 554–85. Skliar and Starikowa compare the psychopathology of seven nations among which two: the Kalmucks (100,000) and the Kirghizes (300,000) were at least primitive for a long time. Their research brings out the following results:

1. The incidence of mental disease was extremely low, almost non-existing among these tribes (Kalmucks 1850; 0.01 per cent; Kirghiz admission rate 1890: 0.4: 100,000).
2. Contact with civilisation, established around 1850, means steady increase of disease rates (Kalmucks 1898: 0.07 per cent; Kirghiz admission rate 1927 from 0.9–3.0: 100,000). The farther a Kalmuck division is from civilised areas, the less the disease rate. The disease rate in both tribes is still far below that of the surrounding civilised people (Kalmuck 2–14: 100,000; Tartars 30–60, Armenians 90, Jews 50, Russians and Persians 100: 100,000). The influence of civilisation is independent of alcohol and syphilis. In both tribes syphilis is endemic but both lack general paresis. The Kalmucks were always alcoholics, the (Islamic) Kirghizes still do not drink alcohol.
3. Dementia praecox is still rare (Kalmucks 2.6 per cent of all mental diseases; Kirghizes 1.9 per cent compared to 6.4 per cent among the Russians and 20 per cent among Armenians). There is no hysteria and no general paralysis.
4. While these tendencies are common to both tribes there are considerable differences in frequency and male-female ratio. While among the Kalmucks there are twice as many insane women as men, the Kirghizes have the usual higher male ratio (8 times

more diseased Kirghiz men than women). Between 1890 and 1902 there were from 5 to 30 times more admissions among the Kalmucks than the Kirghizes, in 1925 to 1927, from 3 to 10 times more.

These conclusions emphasise the scarcity of mental disease in certain primitive tribes and the differences in this belief among primitives themselves. They confirm the statements of Revesz, Seligman, Gordon, Lopez, Dhunijibhoy, Overbeck-Wright, Faris, Cooper[136] about the absence of schizophrenia among primitives and relative prevalence of manic-depressive conditions, if there is any psychopathology at all.[137] Devereux has built on these facts a rather speculative 'Sociological Theory of Schizophrenia' which comes close to Donnison's thought of the diseasing effect of isolation in civilisation[138] and to the older sociological ideas on psychopathology expressed by the late Charles Blondel.[139]

These reports on the scarcity of mental disease in *certain* primitive societies may partly be due to the fact that for social or biological reasons some cultures actually enjoy a greater *mental health* (with some it seems to be just the opposite). In others it may be due to a more effective psychotherapy[140] (the wealth of psychotherapeutical methods in primitive medicine, although such methods are of course also efficient in 'pure' bodily disease, nevertheless suggests a certain amount of mental disease). But those reports may also sometimes be the result of misunderstandings. In a culture where there are a number of 'native' forms of mental disease and a lack of its western forms, two observers may come to opposite results, the one including, the other excluding the former cases. The main source of misunderstanding is probably the fact that *the primitive not only in his medical concepts[141] does not separate diseases of the body and the mind, but also does not produce such separate units.* His 'body' ailments may very often hide very strong 'mental' elements[142] which may have escaped some observers.

That such 'native' mental diseases, as alluded to above, exist, mental diseases which do not fit into our classification, seems by now fairly certain. The best known is the almost proverbial *amok* or amuck of men, first described among Malays, but meanwhile observed in other different parts of the world: among Fuegians, who ask to be bound before the onset of the attack,[143] among Melanesians, where the maniacs seem to be less murderous and consequently are not killed,[144] among Siberians,[145] among Kalmucks and Kirghizes,[146] in India.[147] The very fact that amok has been so differently classified, is to a certain extent in favor of its being a special disease.[148] Another Malay disease mostly mentioned together with amok is *lattah*, which also was first studied in Indonesia and later detected in Siberia and among Eskimos as so-called 'arctic hysteria'.[149] A similar disease was also found in the Philippines.[150] Lattah is mostly a disease of women and characterised by echolalia and echopraxia. To call it hysteria, as Kraepelin did, is insofar not very enlightening as our hysteria just lacks these two main traits of lattah. It has more than only a local connection with amok insofar as an attack of lattah may end with amok-like paroxysms, e.g., in its Ainu form Imu.[151] Winiarz and Wielawski identify not only Imu with lattah, but also the Meriachenie of the Siberian Russians, the Ramaneniana of Madagascar, the Yuan of Burma and the Bah-tchi of Siam. Revesz mentions also the Mali-mali of the Tagals. Lattah is a rather serious condition insofar as it may lead to considerable damage of the victim itself or that done by the victim to others. The *Piblokto* of Eskimo men and women[152] comes closer to our own hysteria and seems on the other hand related to the Saki-si-djoendai of Sumatra.[153]

While we probably are not entitled to classify the 'madness of starvation and cannibalism'[154] among the hungry Eskimos as a special *cannibalistic psychosis*, such psychoses seem to exist elsewhere among primitives where the food supply is satisfactory[155] and to a larger extent than among us. The relatively best known is the *windigo psychosis* of the Cree and Ojibwa Indians.[156]

Devereux has recently described the 'Hiwa-Itck' of deserted older Mohave men[157] and Linton, the tromba, a dancing mania among the Tanala of Madagascar.[158] There are special psychoses on the basis of exotic narcotics like the Indian hemp, etc. If the problem would be followed up by field workers, probably many more such diseases would be discovered and thus the basis created for a more satisfactory discussion of the problem.

While we much more often regard as heteropathological what is autonormal, the case also occurs that the primitive sees disease where we see only character difficulties. A. I. Hallowell has described a very interesting case of this sort in his: 'Shabwan, a dissocial Indian girl' (*Am. J. Orthopsych.*, 8, 1938: 329) and M. J. Field gives very plastic descriptions of the treatment of such cases among the Ga people (*l. c.*, pp. 94–6). In general this field of the autopathological and heteronormal states is still less studied than the 'native' diseases which are auto- and heteropathological.

To us perhaps the most interesting native 'mental disease' is what the late W. E. Roth called '*thanatomania*',[159] the death from magic, the death from autosuggestion without other visible pathological reason. The importance of autosuggestion for health and disease of primitives has always been emphasised,[160] striking examples have been quoted.[161] But in thanatomania undoubtedly the phenomenon reaches a magnificence which can only be compared with the voluntary sterility of Polynesian women[163] probably based on the stopping of ovulation.[163] *Thanatomania seems to illustrate best what we meant when we spoke of the impossibility of separ-*

ating mental and body diseases in primitive man (a separation which, of course, even with us is only gradually less artificial). Thanatomania makes Bilby[164] say concerning the medicine man: 'Apropos of the extraordinary command the conjurors universally exercise over the people and of the paramount psychic influence they establish in the community, it is not much to say that they hold every man's life in their hands.' Suicide may also sometimes be effectuated by the mechanism of thanatomania.[165] But otherwise we are not entitled to list *suicide* – unknown to some primitives[166] – under mental disease except in the rare cases when it is attributed by the primitives themselves to insanity.[167] We have already quoted Czaplicka's judgment: 'But neither to the institution of voluntary death nor to the hysterical fits of the shamans are we justified in applying the name of disease since these are not so considered by the natives themselves.'

The 'hysterical fits' of the shamans of which Czaplicka is speaking, are the cases of artificial, ritual 'possession' already discussed in the previous chapter and which we think to be autonormal as well as heteronormal. But there is another form of *possession*, involuntary, spontaneous, distinguished from the former even by the natives, which we think is clearly heteropathological as well as autopathological and which is generally regarded as a form of hysteria. The 'asocial' tendencies of the individual becoming too strong, they get split off and speak with another voice out of the mouth of the innocent 'patient'. It is thus no wonder that *periods and situations of heightened social tension like acculturation make for a tremendous increase in possession.*[168] But possession, although very widespread among primitives, does not belong to the discussed 'native' mental diseases, as it also pervades all civilisations through antiquity up to the middle of the last century.

Possession epidemics are only one subspecies of other 'pathological' mass movements, 'psychic epidemics', as our forefathers used to call them. They certainly are not specific for primitive society as the history of civilisations in transition periods abundantly proves. It is even highly *doubtful* if they exist in *primitive* societies properly speaking although they too have had their transition periods; in any case we lack pertinent material. The twenty messianic movements occurring among American Indians prior to 1890 and listed by Barber,[169] the Melanesian 'mass neuroses' mentioned by Seligman,[170] the Madagascan dancing mania of 1863[171] are all *typical acculturation phenomena* and another attempt of the natives besides rebellion and depopulation to deal with the new situation. It is highly doubtful if they deserve the title of 'neuroses'. When they are autopathological the case is, of course, clear. But most of them are autonormal. Concerning the psychopathological character of historical as well as exotic 'psychic epidemics' even conservative authors such as Friedman, Hirsch, Ireland or

Oesterreich[172] have been extremely sceptical. Lowie, treating two of the outstanding ones: the Ghost Dance and the Peyot cult purely as religious phenomena, seems to have hit the right point.[173] Much more for the understanding of *most of them is gained if we regard them as attempts of a disturbed culture to produce a new equilibrium by producing a new religion*.[174] Nothing in their forms is found which could not be found in the rite of other religions: dances, trances, etc.[175] The fact, so often quoted against them, that they are caused by suggestion, they partake with numerous other normal beliefs and ideologies, even scientific ones. (The pathological character of some *sects* is not based on these elements, but on their living outside of society.) The clearly self-destructive messianic movements which could be regarded at least as heteropathological, are extremely rare.[176] And even those like the mass suicide of Caribbean Indians[177] bear sometimes rather the mark of a rational decision than of neurosis.

In speaking of *sorcery* too many are somewhat hypnotised by the great witch-smelling wave in our renaissance or in some African cultures, probably both acculturational.[178] And they forget too easily that the belief in magic and sorcery and its execution are common to the majority of mankind and thus already most unlikely to be psychopathological.[179]

The fear complex, expressed in some cultures by the sorcery belief (by no means in all),[189] is after all rather well founded and its expression a matter of convention. While for some renaissance witches the psycho-pathological assumption can at least be based on reports of hysteric stigmata, we know already of the perfect mental health of numerous primitive black magicians.[181] Others should rather be regarded in the same way as primitives do for them; as criminals, choosing the best known native way of crime. And the criminal is until further notice not yet identical with the psychopath, sometimes rather an alternative. On the other hand, the black magician, far from being antisocial, may just enforce the tribal law by his threats and maintain the public order without coercion.[182] Even the enormous acculturation increase of sorcery[183] would perhaps sometimes be better understood when regarded as a kind of *'negative' new religion*, as Michelet did, than as 'neurosis'. A heteropathological element may indeed pervade the strange, *spontaneous self-accusations* of witches and sorcerers which must have clearly self-destructive consequence[184] and form one of the most disturbing psychological problems of all time. But Lowie has given a rational explanation even to them, which may fit some cases, others not.[185] Here in the sorcery question as everywhere in anthropology, things are complex and not very accessible to generalisations and it is always wiser to look first for a normal explanation instead of choosing the way of least resistance in ceding too quickly to fashion and adopting a probably erroneous psychopathological one.

We do not know enough of the so-called 'disease worship' to decide whether it belongs at least heteropathologically to native mental diseases. Caution seems necessary since we have lately learned that there is no disease worship at all in some of the cases. 'Small pox as such is not worshipped. It is the earth gods who are worshipped. Small pox is merely their most severe penalty for wrong doing.'[186]

We have thus come to the end of our short survey of psychopathology in primitive society.[187] We have tried to correct some current prejudices by confronting them with facts. We are very well aware of the shortcomings of our essay, conditioned to a certain extent by the scarcity of good material. Psychiatry and anthropology have many common problems and are even genetically closely connected. Suffice it to recall the names of Benjamin Rush and J. C. Prichard. The collaboration of psychiatry and anthropology has yielded rich results, but it also threatens now to produce, from a scientific point of view, rather unwelcome consequences. This is a problem coming up everywhere where sciences try to collaborate. It would perhaps be useful to remember what Kroeber once wrote (in another context, concerning the scientific and historic approach in anthropology): 'But precisely if they are to cooperate, it seems that they should recognize and tolerate each other's individuality. It is hard to see good coming out of a mixture of approaches, whose aims are different.'[188] Just because we believe in the necessity of cooperation between the two sciences we have tried to eliminate some misconceptions, and we sincerely hope to have thus furnished a modest contribution to a future fertile collaboration of psychiatry and anthropology.

INTRODUCTION: REFERENCE

Littlewood, R. (1990) 'From categories to contexts: a decade of the "new cross-cultural psychiatry"', *British Journal of Psychiatry*, 156: 300–27.

NOTES

1. A. Cabanès, *L'histoire éclairée par la clinique* (Paris: 1920), pp. 13, 230.
2. See for this side of psychopathological labeling the masterly study of O. Bumke: *Kultur und Entartung* (Berlin: 1922); G. L. Walton, 'The prevailing conception of degeneracy', *Boston M. Soc. J.* (1904): N. 3.
3. A very meritorious contemporary sociologist still thinks that 'the normal is but a variant of the concept of the good and the proper'. Kimball Young, *Personality and Problems of Adjustment* (New York: 1940), p. 736. But William James already has shown that the mere fact even of a true psychopathological origin decides nothing concerning the value of a phenomenon (*The Varieties of Religious Experience*, Lecture I: 'Religion and neurology').
4. Zilboorg in his paper 'Overestimation of psychopathology' (*The Am. J. of Orthopsych.*, 9 [1937]: 86–94) seems to look mainly in this direction for the

reasons of psychopathological labeling and calls it 'an expression of the fundamental narcism of man who naively overestimates the arms he himself has invented'.

5. It is interesting to notice that Kretschmer created the unequivocal normal notion of the 'schizothym', but the pathological 'schizoid' became the usual term.

6. This procedure has of course served the understanding of the insane, being regarded so far as something absolutely unhuman. But it has had ugly consequences for the normal, after all the majority.

7. E.g. Ruth Benedict, *Patterns of Culture* (New York: 1934), pp. 151, 190, 216, 222.

8. E. Fromm, *Escape from Freedom* (New York: 1941), p. 164.

9. Bernard Baruch, Foreword to Mackay: *Extraordinary Popular Delusions and the Madness of Crowds* (Boston: 1932), p. XIV.

10. And this in spite of the most extensive and intensive study of these phenomena and in spite of the official, scientific recognition, nay, overemphasising of the role of the emotional in our psychic economy!

11. 'Many psychiatrists, including psychoanalysts, have painted the picture of a "normal" personality which is never too sad, too angry or too excited. They use words like "infantile" or "neurotic" to demonstrate traits or types of personalities that do not conform with the conventional pattern of a "normal' individual. This kind of influence is in a way more dangerous than the older and franker forms of name-calling. Then the individual knew at least that there was some person or some doctrine which criticized him and he could fight back. But who can fight back at "science"?' Fromm, loc. cit., p. 246.

12. Concerning the problem of the metaphysical need see E. H. Ackerknecht: 'Problems of primitive medicine', *Bull. Hist. Med.*, 11 (1942): 516–18.

13. G. Devereux, 'A sociological theory of schizophrenia', *Psychoanal. Rev.*, 26 (1939): 338. It is sad to see – but one reason more to take up the problem – that this statement – apparently an 'improvement' of the older slogan that religion is a neurosis – comes from an author who, on the other hand, has done so much to elucidate problems of primitive psychopathology (e.g. 'Mohave culture and personality', *Character and Personality*, 8: 91–109; 'Primitive psychiatry', *Bull. Hist. Med.*, 7 [1942]: 1194 ff.; 'Mental hygiene of the American Indian', *Mental Hygiene* [1942], pp. 71 ff.).

14. An analysis of the degree of reality in such a statement is not the object of these short introductory notes, but of the whole article.

15. See E. Sapir, *Journal Abn. Soc. Psych.*, **27** (1932): 325; A. I. Hallowell, *J. Abn. Soc. Psych.*, 29, (1934): 1–9; *Am. J. of Psychiatry*, 92, (1936): 1291–30; A. L. Kroeber in Bentley, *The Problem of Mental Disorder* (New York: 1934); but especially Ruth Benedict, 'Anthropology and the abnormal', *J. of Gen. Psychol.* 10, (1934): 59–82 and her *Patterns of Culture* pp. 258–88. In 1930 in his 'Psychopathologie und Kulturwissenschaft' (*Abh. aus der Neur., Psychiatrie, Psychol. und Grenzgebieten*, Heft 61, pp. 140–6), H. E. Sigerist already warned against the projection of present psychopathological notions into history very much on the line of argumentation which was developed here by anthropologists. The above-mentioned article of Zilboorg and remarks of Fromm, loc. cit., p. 140), A. Kardiner, *The Individual and His Society* (New York: 1939), pp. 84, 418, seem to show that at least some more 'enlightened' psychoanalysts become aware of the danger.

16. Concerning the problem of the sincerity of the medicine man see Ackerknecht, loc. cit., p. 510.

17. D. McKenzie, *The Infancy of Medicine* (London: 1927), p. 8; J. Gillin, 'Personality in preliterate societies', *Am. Sociol. Rev.*, 4, (1939): M. Bartels, *Die Medizin der Naturvölker* (Leipzig: 1893), p. 79. The epilepsy diagnosis implies besides the appreciation of the medicine man as mentally ill, which we are discussing, a special psychiatric error. Closer examination of these cases hardly ever reveals true epilepsy, but symptoms which would be classified in our society either among schizophrenic or hysteric syndromes. We will discuss this problem all the less as the identical error of historians is dealt with in great detail in Dr O. Temkin's forthcoming 'History of Epilepsy'. We want to express to Dr Temkin here our gratitude and indebtedness for many stimulating discussions on our problems. We also are very grateful to Dr H. A. Loewald for his inspiring criticism of the psychiatric implications of this article, for which, of course, the author is only responsible.

18. D. Jennes, *The People of the Twilight* (New York: 1938), p. 52; (J. Maddox, *The Medicine Man* (New York: 1923), p. 40.

19. W. D. Hambly, *Origins of Education among Primitive Peoples* (London: 1926).

20. C. Wissler, *The American Indian* (New York: 1922), p. 204.

21. Of course so many social and cultural factors enter directly and by psychological ways even the genesis and effects of these diseases that the above statement is only valid in the limited context of the artificial confrontation of mental and bodily disease!! *Primarily every disease is a social phenomenon and is defined socially.* Then only the incapacitated or maladjusted are analysed in terms of anatomy or biochemistry. Thus the paradox occurs that an anatomically slight deformation is 'disease', while a much graver one like the deformed feet of Chinese women never is regarded as such, because it is never socially singled out to be submitted to pathologico-anatomical analysis.

22. Those mental diseases where organic changes are well known like general paralysis, alcoholic psychoses, have played the trick on us of appearing only in our civilisation, thus stressing the importance of the cultural component even in those mental diseases where the organic basis is obvious, but depriving us again of possibilities of comparative study of mental diseases on a given organic basis.

23. 'It is clear that culture may value and make socially available even highly unstable human types. If it chooses to treat their peculiarities as the most valued variants of human behaviour, the individuals in question will rise to the occasion and perform their social roles without reference to our usual ideas of the types who can make social adjustments and those who cannot. Those who function inadequately in any society are not those with certain fixed abnormal traits, but may be well those whose responses have received no support in the institutions of their cultures. The weakness of these aberrants is in great measure illusory. It springs not from the fact that they are lacking in necessary vigour but that they are individuals whose native responses are not reaffirmed by society. They are as Sapir phrases it "alienated from an impossible world".' Benedict, *Patterns*, p. 270.

24. Benedict, *Patterns*, pp. 258–60. See also M. Mead, *Sex and Temperament in Three Primitive Cultures* (New York: 1935), Ch.: 'The deviant', pp. 290 ff.

25. Benedict, *J. of. Gen. Psych.*, I (1934): 73; 'Psychiatric diagnosis cannot be made without regard to cultural environment'. A. L. Kroeber in Bentley: *The*

Problem of Mental Disorder (New York: 1934), p. 347; 'Psychosis can only be stated in relation to culture pattern', Hallowell, *J. Abnorm. Soc. Psych.*, 29 (1934): 3.

26. See Sigerist, loc. cit., p. 145. Only such an approach elucidates the paradox why the majority of us, through apparently descendants of (pseudo) 'neurotics' and 'psychotics' are nevertheless rather normal persons.
27. Benedict, *Patterns*, p. 230.
28. E. Sapir, loc. cit., p. 36 ff.
29. L. Warner, *Am. J. Psych.*, 19, (1939): 280.
30. R. Linton, Introduction of Kardiner, loc. cit., p. xiv.
31. See also G. Scheunert, 'Kultur and Neurose am Ausgang das 19. Jahrhunderts', *Kyklos*, 3 (1930): 258–72, Leipzig; K. Davis, 'Mental hygiene and the class structure', *Psychiatry*, 1 (1938): 55–65.
32. 'The problem of understanding abnormal human behavior in any absolute sense independent of cultural factors is still far in the future. . . When data are available in psychiatry, this minimum definition of abnormal human tendencies will be probably quite unlike our culturally conditioned, highly elaborated psychoses such as those that are described, for instance, under the terms of schizophrenia and manic-depressive.' Benedict, *J. Gen. Psychol.*, I (1934): 79.
33. 'The small proportion of the number of the deviants in any culture is not a function of the sure instinct with which society has built itself upon the fundamental sanities, but of the universal fact, that, happily the majority of mankind quite readily take any shape that is presented to them.' Benedict, loc. cit., p. 75.
34. This field of research has so far not yet been explored. It is not surprising that a single attempt on a dogmatic basis (W. Sachs: *Black Hamlet* [London: 1937], being the psychoanalysis of a South African Medicine Man) has not yielded many results.
35. Hallowell, *Am. J. Psychiatry*, 92 (1936): 1294; H. J. Wegrocki, *J. Abnorm. Soc. Psychol.*, vol. 34 (1939): 169–70.
36. A. Gallinek ('Psychogenic disorders and the civilization of the Middle Ages', *Am. J. of Psychiatry*, 99 [1942]: 54) in spite of using the heteropathological terminology, observes this fact very clearly on a historical level: This hysteria was productive and of cultural significance in contrast to modern hysteria. It was different and it affected other personalities, personalities, who nowadays hardly would have a tendency towards hysteria and psychogenic disturbances. It affected those persons who needed a stimulus and a tool in order to embody and express completely the essence of their era.'
37. E. Loeb, 'Shaman and seer', *Am. Anthr.*, 31 (1929): 61–2.
38. It seems not to be the place here to discuss in detail Loeb's classification. It is obvious that of course Africa and Asia are full of non-inspirational medicine men and that in North and South America, in New Guinea and among the Negritoes exist some rather rare occurrences of inspirational medicine men.
39. The study of disease concept distribution by Clements (*Univ. Cal. Publ. Am. Arch. Ethn.*, 32 (1932): 223 leads to similar results.
40. T. K. Osterreich, *Possession*, Eng. transl. (London: 1930), p. 305.
41. As e.g. among the Zuñi: Benedict, *Patterns*, p. 72; Kwakiutl: Benedict, loc. cit., p. 211; Pawnee: Linton, *Field Mus. Leafl.* VIII: 5; Africans: G. Harley, *Native African Medicine* (Cambridge, Mass: 1941), p. 199.
42. L. Sternberg, 'Divine election in primitive religion', XXXI, *Congr. Intern.*

Américanistes (Göteborg: 1924), pp. 472–512; Yakuts: W. Sieroszewski, 'Du shamanisme d'après les croyances des Yakuts', *Rev. Histoire Rel.*, 46 (1902): 311; Abyssinians: M, Leiris, 'Le culte des Zärs', *Aethiopica*, (Paris: 1934), Vol. II, n. 4; Yavapeis: B. Aitken, *JAI*, LX, (1930): 370; Maida: W. Th. Corlett, *The Medicine Man of the American Indian* (Springfield-Baltimore [no date given]), loc. cit., p. 92; Mentawei: E. Loeb, p. 62.

43. W. Bogoras, 'The Chukchee', *Mem. Am. Mus. Nat. Hist.*, XI (Leiden/New York: 1904–9), p. 424.
44. ibid., p. 421.
45. D. Klementz, 'Buriats', *Hastings Enc. Rel. Eth.*, 3: 15.
46. M. A. Czaplicka, *Aboriginal Siberia* (Oxford: 1914), p. 178.
47. Bogoras, loc. cit., p. 444.
48. ibid., p. 421.
49. V. M. Mikhailowsky, *JAI*, 24, (1895): 85.
50. Bogoras, loc. cit., p. 43.
51. Czaplicka, loc. cit., p. 181.
52. ibid., p. 420; see also W. I. Jochelson, *The Koryak* (New York: 1905–8), p. 47.
53. loc. cit., p. 310.
54. W. Radloff, *Aus Sibirien*, (Leipzig: 1884), 2: 16.
55. Czaplicka, loc. cit., p. 173.
56. Sieroszewski, loc. cit., p. 218; Bogoras, loc. cit., p. 42; see concerning a similar disease in Fiji, D. M. Spencer, *Disease, Religion and Society in the Fiji Islands* (New York: 1941), pp. 29–30.
57. Czaplicka, loc. cit., pp. 320, 325.
58. Sieroszewski, loc. cit., p. 229.
59. Bogoras, loc. cit., p. 43.
60. Kind of Amok of the future Anjagok. Ch. F. Hall, *Life with the Esquimaux* (London: 1864), 2: 251; E. M. Weyer, *The Eskimos* (New Haven: 1932), p. 431.
61. Loeb, loc. cit., p. 67.
62. Oesterreich, loc. cit., p. 85; Gallinek, loc. cit.
63. London (1870), pp. 259–67.
64. B. J. Laubscher, *Sex, Custom and Psychopathology* (London: 1937).
65. See also W. Hoernle, in J. Schapera, *The Bantu Speaking Tribes of South Africa* (london: 1937), p. 231.
66. M. Field, *Religion and Medicine among the Ga People* (New York: 1937), pp. 100–9.
67. 'Anyone who gets to know Wyei in their everyday lives cannot but be struck with the *lack* of any imbalance or hysteria in their everyday behavior. They are often serene and good tempered and not selfish or in the least "difficult". Seeing them again when excited by the spirit one cannot doubt that they are working off volumes of "steam" which others must dispose of quietly and perhaps less thoroughly: the Wyo system is probably satisfactory from the Western medical point of view, as well as having the social satisfactoriness of providing a dignified niche for the type of person who in Europe would be the unfit and plague of society.' Field, loc. cit., p. 109.
68. H. A. Junod, *The Life of a South African Tribe* (London: 1913), 2: 439.
69. Oesterreich, loc. cit., pp. 272, 219 ff.' E. H. Ackerknecht, 'Primitive medicine and culture pattern', *Bull. Hist. Med.*, 12 (1942): 571.
70. Laubscher, loc. cit., p. 227.
71. ibid., p. 32. Similar preshamanistic pathological stages exist among tribes of

Southern California (A. L. Kroeber, 'Psychosis or social sanction', *Char. and Personal*, 8 [1939–40]: 205; ibid., 'Handb. of the Ind. of Calif', *B A E Bull.*, 78 [1925}: 425). Devereux (*Ment. Hyg.*, 26 [1942]: 82 seems to allude to these tribes in the following rather sensational statement: 'Many native tribes believe that a seizure of insanity precedes the acquisition of shamanistic powers, and that a person receiving these powers, but unwilling to practice will become psychotic. One cannot but wonder how many Indian psychotics have turned into shamans while hospitalized in an institution, and been retained here, although they are ready to return to their tribes and to function as useful members thereof.'

72. F. Nietzsche, *Zur Genealogie der Moral* (Leipzig: Reclam), p. 160.
73. Junod, loc. cit., 2: 454.
74. 'Des qie ;'âge affaiblit les sorciers, les esprits se vengent de l'abaissement dans lequel ils les ont tenus. Ils les tourmentent, les agacent, les empêchent de dormir, volent incessament autour d'eux en criant, en les raillant, en les mordant, en les piquant. Personne ne les entend, à l'exception du chamane qui souffre en silence, en général délaissé lêchement de tous.' Sieroszewski, loc. cit., p. 324.
75. Bogoras, loc. cit., p. 419. Bogoras regards this as complete 'recovery from nervous conditions'.
76. E. J. Kempf, 'The probable origin of man's belief in sympathetic magic', *Med. Jour. and Rec.*, 33 (1931): 25.
77. 'But neither to the institution of voluntary death nor to the hysterical of the shamans are we justified in applying the name of disease since these are not so considered by the natives themselves.' Czaplicka, loc. cit., p. 319.
78. See M. Mead, *Coming of Age in Samoa* (New York: 1928).
79. Czaplicka, loc. cit., p. 169.
80. Bogoras, loc. cit., p. 463.
81. Sieroszewski, loc. cit., p. 318.
82. Bogoras, loc. cit., p. 429.
83. Sieroszewski, loc. cit., p. 323.
84. ibid., p. 325. We accord even to our own artists a certain amount of ecstatic behavior as normal.
85. Klementz, loc. cit., p. 16.
86. Bogoras, loc. cit., p. 450.
87. Benedict, *Patterns*, p. 262 ff.
88. [No note 88 appears in the original paper.]
89. Bogoras, loc. cit., p. 434.
90. Summer-Keller, *The Science of Society* (New haven: 1927), 2: 1368, 4: 747.
91. Hubert-Mauss, *Année social*, 7 (1907); Benedict, *Journ. Gen. Psych.*, 10 (1934): 76.
92. The Giljak quite naively symbolise this in according him four souls instead of one (Czaplicka, loc. cit., p. 272), the Samoyeds in singling him out for a life after death (ibid., p. 163).
93. R. H. Codrington, *The Melanesians* (Oxford: 1891), p. 218; W. Müller-Wismar, *Yap* (Hamburg: 1917), Vol. 1, p. 378.
94. P. Saintyves, *Les origines de la médecline* (Paris: 1920), p. 83.
95. Intoxication, probably the active factor in epilepsy, is by no means the only agent able to mobilise the *latent tendency towards convulsion*, present in every brain. Bumke, loc. cit., p. 29.
96. C. G. and B. Seligman, *The Veddas* (Cambridge: 1911), p. 135.

97. Field, p. 105; Oesterreich, loc. cit., p. 272.
98. 'London: 1817), Vol. II, p. 146.
99. Seligman, loc. cit., p. 129.
100. I. G. Bourke, *The Medicine Men of the Apache* (BAE-R: 1892), p. 460.
101. E.g. Cheyenne: Ackerknecht, *Bull. Hist. Med.*, 12 (1942): 556; Chiricahua Apache: M. E. Opler, *An Apache Life-Way* (Chicago: 1941), p. 200.
102. F. Elbrechts and J. Massey, 'The swimmer manuscript' (*BAEB*, 99 [1932]: 83.
103. loc. cit., p. 109 ff.
104. loc. cit., p. 95.
105. loc. cit., p. 99.
106. *The Role of Conjuring in Salteaux Society* (Philadelphia: 1942), p. 13.
107. Kroeber, *Handb.*, p. 754.
108. Bourke, loc. cit., p. 470.
109. G. Devereux, *Bull. Hist. Med.*, XI [no date given]: 529.
110. ibid., *Char. and Personality*, 8 [no date given]: 107.
111. (London: 1899), p. 278.
112. W. L. Warner, *A Black Civilization* (New York: 1937), p. 210.
113. ibid., p. 197.
114. ibid., p. 198.
115. Harley, loc. cit., p. 39.
116. See e.g. an outstanding psychiatrist as A. Hesnard, *Les psychoses et les frontières de la folie* (paris: 1924). But even A. L. Kroeber occasionally speaks of 'magic as the pathology of culture' and of 'the abnormal primitive cultures, which are perhaps less numerous than the normal ones' (in Bentley, loc. cit., p. 350). Mr Roger Money Kyrle (*Superstition and Society* [London: 1939], p. 71) states bluntly: 'The savage is indeed an obsessional neurotic', with the benediction of the *Psychoanalytic Quarterly* indeed (11 [1942]: 563).
117. F. H. Garrison, *An Introd. to the Hist. of med.* (Philadelphia: 1929, p. 20; see also the whole work of Lucien Lévy-Bruhl.
118. But even in the field of perception differences often enough develop, e.g. 'To the Tanala ghosts are thoroughly individualized and entirely real. Every native will report seeing ghosts and talking with them. It is very often difficult for the people to distinguish between dream states and waking states. Hearing ghosts talk to one is so common an experience that natives often will not pay attention to you if you call them only once. If you call twice, they will know it is a man and pay attention, since ghosts call only once.' Linton in Kardiner, loc. cit., p. 269. See also for the Mohave, Kroeber, Handb., p. 754, etc.
119. Kroeber, *Char. and Pers.*, loc. cit., p. 209. See also Warner, p. 24: 'I had not been able to obtain this information (the ideas on natural conception) earlier because the ordinary savage is far more interested in the child's spiritual conception. . . He would far rather talk about ritual and myth than about ordinary human affairs.'
120. Kroeber, *Char. and Pers.*, p. 205.
121. See Fromm, loc. cit., p. 140.
122. Weyer, loc. cit., p. 455; such regulations are besides by no means lacking in our 'rational' society.
123. A. and D. Leighton, *Psychiatry*, 4 (1941): 517; M. E. Opler, *Am. J. Psychiatry*; 92 (1936): 1374; Weyer, loc. cit., p. 238.
124. In culture there is so far only the possibility of differentiating between these two tendencies: life or death, but no objective criterion for judgments of

neuroticism as those proposed by Devereux (if energy expenditure is 'most fruitful' or less or 'permits an optimum survival in proportion to the energy expended' or less than an optimum, etc.).

125. Kardiner has rightly opposed to this conception the genetic criterion. 'The elaboration of these basic frustrations in neurosis and in a cultural trait are very different. In neurosis the representations of frustrated needs usually indicate coexisting inhibitions; in cultural constellations they depend on actual or institutional harriers.' loc. cit., p. 418.

126. Kroeber in Bentley, loc. cit., p. 346. *Char. and Pers.*, loc. cit., p. 205.

127. R. E. Park, *Am. J. Soc.*, 33 (1928): 881; E. V. Stonequist, *The Marginal Man* (new York: 1937).

128. See Bumke, loc. cit., p. 87; Hallowell, *J. Abnorm. Soc. Psych.*, loc. cit., p. 6; H. D. Lamson, *Social Pathology in China* (1935); M. Mead, *The Changing Culture of an Indian Tribe* (1932); B. Revesz, 'Rassen u. Geisteskrankh', *Arch. für Anthr.*, 6 (1907): 180, and E. D. Baumann, *Medisch. Historische Studien* (Arnheim: 1934), p. 57, concerning Japan. It is noteworthy that magic in such situations not only generally becomes relatively stronger in relation to religion as has been pointed out, e.g., by R. Benedict (*Encyl. Soc. Sc.*, Vol. X, p. 41) or M. Field ('If centralised, disciplined faith is weaker, vagrant credulity is stronger', loc. cit., p. 133), but undergoes a definite change, gaining all the characteristics, which differentiate so strongly, e.g., medieval from primitive magic. (For an excellent description of this process see R. Redfield, *The Folk Culture of Yucatan* [Chicago: 1942].) It would perhaps be useful to differentiate this kind of magic as '*secondary magic*' from primitive magic, as generalisations on magic often suffer from a confusion of the two types.

129. For collection of data see M. Bartels, *Die Medizin der Naturvölker* (Leipzig: 1893); E. Westermarck, *Origin and Development of Moral Ideas* (London: 1906–10), II, p. 269; Brinton, Nervous Dis. among Low Races, *Science*, XX; A. E. Crawley, 'Sexual taboo', *JAI*, 24 [1937]: 223; especially J. Koty, *Die Behandlung der Alten und Kranken bei d. Naturvölkern* (Stuttgart: 1934); see also E. Winston, *Am. Anthr.*, 36, (1934): 234 (the second part of W's article which tries to solve the problem on the basis of five (5) cases is valueless).

130. Such a naive assumption has existed at least concerning suicide, making part of the degeneration 'myth'. G. Zilboorg ('Suicide among civilized and primitive races', *Am. J. Psych.*, 92, 1936): 1347, has demolished the equation suicide – mental disease – civilisation. The equation seems by now as wrong in its second as in its first part and the existence of mental disease is no more an exclusive feature of our society than is suicide.

131. loc. cit., 1308.

132. 'Temperament, conflict and psychosis in a stone age population', *Brit. J. Med. Psychol.*, 9 (1926): 196.

133. E.g. F. Plehn, *Die Kamerunküste* (Berlin: 1898), p. 271; F. Krause, *In den Wildnissen Brasiliens* (Leipzig: 1911), p. 338; E. Faris, *The Nature of Human Nature* (New York: 1937), p. 286 (concerns the Forest Bantus); C. P. Donnison, *Civilization and Disease* (London: 1937); J. Dhunijibloy, *J. Ment. Sc.*, 76 (1930): 254.

134. E.g. G. Devereux, 'A sociol. theory of schizophrenia', *Psychoanal. Rev.* (1939): 316 (Indoch. Moi); Klementz, *ERE*, 3 (Siberia); M. Cooper, 'Ment. dis. sit. in certain cultures', *J. Soc. Abn. Psych.*, 29 (1934): 14.

135. *Handb. d. histor-geogr. Path.* (Stuttgart: 1886), Vol. III, p. 361.

136. Revesz. Djimokonhoy, Seligman, loc. cit., A. W. Overbeck-Wright, *Lunacy in India* (London: 1921), P. 3; Gordon at Donnison, loc. cit., pp. 33–4; C. Lopez, 'Ethnogr. Betrachtg. Schizophrenie', *Zschr. ges. Neur. Psych.*, 142 (1932): 706; Faris, *REL*, 'Some obser. on the incidence of schizophrenia in primitive soc., *J. Abn. Soc. Psych.*, 98 (1942): 5.

137. It is easy to rule out the opposite thesis of L. Stern ('Kulturkreis und Form der geistigen Erkrankung', *Sammlg. zwangl., Abh. Geb. Nerven Geisteskrkh,* 10 [1913]: 1–62) as it is definitely based on irrelevant acculturation material like Kraepelin's Java observations, etc. More difficult is the case of Laubscher who after very extensive studies among the Tembu has concluded to an enormous incidence of schizophrenia among the Tembu and the black race in general (the latter statement is certainly wrong; see J. H. Lewis, *The Biology of the Negro* [Chicago: 1942], p. 260). One could easily oppose to Laubscher that his Tembus are acculturated. But to me the error seems still deeper and Laubscher's whole study the result of a gigantic misunderstanding produced by his bias towards an exclusive 'heredity' theory of schizophrenia. To him ukutwasa (see above), a very frequent phenomenon, is equal to mental disease and particularly to schizophrenia. Thus he obtains his result. But is very doubtful whether in most cases ukutwasa is a disease at all. It is even very doubtful if his 'schizophrenics', who are, e.g. 'rarely ever readmitted to the hospital' and *obey* generally tribal interdiction of suicide, are schizophrenics at all! Laubscher basing his whole thesis on the frequency of ukutwasa in the family of his 'schizophrenics' has even omitted the most elementary controls on the frequency of ukutwasa in the family of normals which probably would have ruined his whole theory from the very beginning.

138. loc. cit., p. 134; on the problems of isolation see also Fromm, loc. cit.

139. Ch. Blondel, *La conscience morbide* (Paris: 1913).

140. In this connection see also O. Klineberg on Buddhism and schizophrenia (*Social Psychology*, [New York: 1940], p. 510).

141. Ackerknecht, *Problems* loc. cit., p. 514.

142. Laubscher, loc. cit., p. 28.

143. F. H. Coriat, Psychoneur. among prim. tribes', *J. Abn. Psych* 10 (1915): 201.

144. Seligman, loc. cit., p. 198; R. Fortune, *The Sorcerers of Dobu* (New York: 1932), p. 55.

145. Czaplicka, loc. cit., p. 310.

146. Skliar and Starikowa, loc. cit., p. 573.

147. Overbeck-Wright, loc. cit., p. 46.

148. Gimlette (*Med. Arch. Fed. Mal. St.* [1901]) considers it a form of somnabulism. Kraepelin thought it to be epilepsy. F. H. G. Van Loon ('Amok and lattah', *J. Abn. Soc. Psych.*, 21 [1926–7]: 435) calls it 'an agony of fear on the basis of fever'. Cooper (loc. cit., p. 13) doubts whether it is a disease at all or simply a custom, which seems unlikely.

149. Not all cases of 'arctic hysteria' in the literature are 'lattah'. Czaplicka warns rightly (loc. cit., p. 320): 'It would seem that the name "arctic hysteria" has been given by travellers partly to religio-magical phenomena and partly to the nervous ailments which are considered by the natives to be disease.'

150. J. Deniker, *Les races et les peuples de la terre* (paris: 1926).

151. W. Winiarz and J. Wielawski, 'Imu – a psychoneurosis occurring among the Ainus', *Psychoanal. Rev.*, 23, (1936): 181. Imu, sometimes very frequent (12 cases in a village of 100 inhabitants), is regarded as possessions by a serpent spirit *and as healing another morbid state.*

152. A. Brill, Piblokto', *J. Nerv. Ment. Dis.*, 40 (1913): 514; Czaplicka, loc. cit., p. 314.

153. Bartels, loc. cit., p. 215.

154. Weyer, loc. cit., p. 118.

155. Marquesas; Linton in Kardiner, p. 142; Kwakiutl; cannibalistic possession during initiation, Kardiner, loc. cit., p. 118.

156. Hallowell, *J. Abn. Soc. Psych.*, 29, loc. cit., ibid., *Am. J. Psych.*, 92, loc. cit.; J. M. Cooper, *J. Abn. Soc. Psych.*, 29, loc. cit.; ibid., 'The Cree Witiko psychosis', *Prim. Man*, VI (1933). The renaissance has known mental epidemics with similar contents: the Vaudoisie of 1436, etc. See H. Cesbron, *Histoire critique de l'hystérie* (Paris: 1909), p. 134 ff.

157. *Bull. Hist. Med.*, 8: 1198.

158. Linton in Kardiner, loc. cit., p. 270.

159. W. B. Cannon has collected in a recent article 'Voodo death' (*Am. Anthr.*, 44 1942: 169) the material of Soares de Souza and Varnhagen for South America; Mirolla and Leonard for Africa; Brown for New Zealand; Lambert, Cleland, W. E. Roth, Basedow, Warner (interesting for a social theory of thanatomania, loc. cit., p. 242), Porteus for Australia, and tried to give a physiological explanation of the phenomenon. Besides the material collected by Cannon and another collection in Sumner-Keller, pp. 1326 ff. or H. Webster, *Taboo* (Stanford: 1942), pp. 24 ff., further cases may be found, e.g., in Brough-Smyth (loc. cit., II: 468), Codrington (206), Czaplicka (260), Field (118), Fortune ([no publication details given in this paper] 284) Howitt (*J A I* 16 [no publication details given in this paper]: 42), Laubscher (105), Linton in Kardiner (187), Mariner, Seligman (192), Weyer (237, 460). Benedict's cases of shamans dying of shame (*Pattern*, 210, 214) probably also belong here.

160. E.g. B. Malinowski, *Argonauts of the Western Pacific* (London: 1922), p. 465. See the surgery by Otto Stoll: *Suggestion und Hypnotismus in der Völkerpsychologie* (Leipzig: 1904).

161. E.g. suggested dumbness in taboo transgressors, Harley, loc. cit., p. 127; rashes in food-taboo transgression, M. J. Herskovits, *Dahomey* (New York: 1938), Vol. 1, p. 161; an incurable 'trembling sickness' as consequences of taboo transgression among the Batamba (Uganda), M. A. Condon, *Anthropos*, 6 (1911): 377, etc.

162. G. H. L. F. Pitt-Rivers, *The Clash of Cultures* (London: 1927), p. 147.

163. Personal communication Dr J. Gillman, Johannesburg.

164. Weyer, loc. cit., p. 459.

165. Zilboorg, loc. cit., p. 1353. For the strange suicides by conscious taboo violation which then kills by autosuggestion, see E. S. C. Handy, 'The native culture in the Marquesas', *Berenice P. Bishop Mus. Bull.*, 9 [no year given]: 279; W. G. Ivens, *The Melanesians of the S. E. Solomons* (London: 1927), p. 121.

166. Kardiner, loc. cit., p. 113.

167. Linton in Kardiner, loc. cit., p. 275 (Tanala of Madagascar).

168. Oesterreich, loc. cit., pp. 137, 139. Historically speaking, *epidemics* of possession are limited to a period between the thirteenth and the eighteenth century!

169. B. Barber, 'Acculturation and messianic movements', *Amer. Soc. Rev.*, 6 (1941): 663; see also: J. Mooney, 'The Ghost Dance', *BAER*, XIV, 2 (1893); A. C. Parker 'The code of a Seneca prophet', *N. Y. St. Mus. Bull.*, 163 (1913); Phister, 'The Indian Messiah', *Am. Anthr.* (1891); V. F. Ray, 'The Kolaskin

cult', *Am. Anthr.*, n.s., 38 (1936); L. Spier, 'The Prophet Dance of the N. W.', *Gen. Ser. Anthr.*, 1 (1935).

170. E. W. P. Chinnery and A. C. Haddon, 'Five religious cults in New Guinea', *Hibbert J.* (1917): 446; F. W. Williams, 'The Vailala madness', *Terr. of Papua Rep.*, 4 (1923).
171. Hirsch, loc. cit., 3: 367.
172. M. Friedmann, *Über Wahanideen i. Völkerleben* (Wiesbaden: 1901), p. 20; Hirsch, loc. cit., p. 363; W. W. Ireland, 'Psychology of the crusades', *J. Ment. Sc.*, 53 (1906–7): 322; Oesterreich, loc. cit., p. 190.
173. R. H. Lowrie, *Primitive Religion* (London: 1936), p. 88 ff.
174. E. D. Chapple and C. S. Coon *Principles of Anthropology* (New York: 1942), p. 411.
175. Concerning dance see, e.g., Herskovits, loc. cit., 1: 133; dance is by now even regarded as a very valuable psychotherapeutic element of group treatment (Marsh, L. C., Group Psychotherapy, *J. Ment. Nerv. Dis.*, 82 [1935]: 389).
176. Only one of the five cults reported by Chinnery and Haddon (loc. cit., p. 458) is self-destructive; then of course the two famous African catastrophes of Usambar (C. Meinhof, *Relig. d. Afr.* [Oslo: 1926], p. 6) and of Mulakaza (J. Schapera, *The Bantu speak. tr. of S. Afr.* [London: 1937], p. 253; Ch. Brownlee, *Reminiscences of Kafir Life and History* [Lovedale: 1898]). In the former case the seed was stopped, in the latter all cattle slain, in both famine followed.
177. Zilboorg, loc. cit., p. 1352.
178. For self-destructive witch hunt in Africa see Sumner-Keller, p. 1321; P. A. Talbot, *South Nigeria* (London: 1926), 2: 219.
179. For Laubscher, of course, 'Witchcraft and mental disorder are practically synonymous' (p. 29) and 'a study of the histories of a few witches bore ample evidence that they were suffering from schizophrenia' (loc. cit., p. 17).
180. 'When a man suffers from misfortune due to witchcraft his emotional reactions generally range from annoyance to anger rather than from fear to terror.' E. D. Evans-Pritchard, *Witchcraft, Oracles, Magic among the Azande* (Oxford: 1937), p. 84. See also C. G. Seligman, *Melanesians of Br. N. Guinea* (Cambridge: 1910), p. 279.
181. Warner, loc. cit., pp. 197–8; Fortune, loc. cit., p. 163.
182. E.g., Fortune, loc. cit. [see above, n. 159], p. 175; Loeb, loc. cit., p. 83; Linton in Kardiner, loc. cit., p. 139; Pitt-Rivers, loc. cit., p. 201; W. H. R. Rivers, *Psychology and Ethnology* (London: 1926), p. 87; D. M. Spencer [no publication details given in this paper], loc. cit., p. 76; J. W. M. Whiting, *Becoming a Kwoma* (New Haven: 1941), p. 219.
183. Friedman, loc. cit., p. 247; Junod, loc. cit., 2: 488; Evans-Pritchard, loc. cit., p. 446; Field, loc. cit., p. 135; Redfield, loc. cit., p. xx. This kind of sorcery is the cornerstone of 'secondary magic' (see above).
184. For those confessions see for Africa, Harley, loc. cit., p. 27; Field, loc. cit., p. 128; 139; Lowie, loc. cit., p. 37; D. A. Talbot, *Woman's Mysteries* (London: 1915), p. 50; C. K. Meek, *Law and Authority in a Nig. Tribe* (London: 1936), p. 84; for America: Summer, Coll. Essays, I, Ch. IV; R. Karsten, *The Civilis of the S. Am. Ind.* (London: 1926), p. 492. Here belong also the self-provoked murder of the Mohave sorcerer (Devereux, *Bull. Hist. Med.*, 11 [no date given]: 529) and the self-execution of the New Caledonian sorcerer (G. Turner, *Samoa* [London: 1889]).
185. Lowie, loc. cit., p. 39.

186. Herkovits, loc. cit., 2: 136, for a similar statement concerning the Shilluk where a god and illness bear the same name, because the god gives it, see D. Westermann, *The Shilluk* (Philadelphia: 1912), XL. See, e.g., also for leprosy in Bali, which is called the 'holy disease' while being the most terrible punishment of the gods: W. Weck, *Heilkunde u. Volkstum auf Bali* (Stuttgart: 1937), p. 159.

187. The fact that 'race' was not mentioned at all in this article is by no means caused by forgetfulness or because we deny in advance the possibility of racial factors in mental disease. It is exclusively conditioned by our inability to find during our research a single reliable fact which actually demonstrates the influence of race on mental disease.

188. *Am. Anthr.*, 37 (1935): 547.

CHAPTER TEN

The Effectiveness of Symbols (1949)

Claude Lévi-Strauss

In this paper Lévi-Strauss (1908–), the founder of anthropological structuralism, offers a model of shamanic healing which owes much to Mauss. As a number of commentators have argued, the essential mechanism – 'as if [comme ci] to abolish in the mind' – is rather mysterious. What actually is the link between the physiological and social bodies? Is it really as 'tight' as argued here and did the woman actually understand the song (Laderman 1987) or can fairly non-specific factors such as relaxation or avoidance of fear play a part? Dow (1986) has developed Lévi-Strauss' idea into a more generalised notion of healing in which a pre-existing social 'mythic model' already contains possible modes of distress and their symbolic resolution.

The first important South American magico-religious text to be known, published by Wassén and Holmer,[1] throws new light on certain aspects of shamanistic curing and raises problems of theoretical interpretation by no means exhaustively treated in the editors' excellent commentary. We will re-examine this text for its more general implications, rather than from the linguistic or Americanist perspective primarily employed by the authors.

The text is a long incantation, covering eighteen pages in the native version, divided into 535 sections. It was obtained by the Cuna Indian Guillermo Haya from an elderly informant of his tribe. The Cuna, who live within the Panama Republic, received special attention from the late Erland Nordenskiöld, who even succeeded in training collaborators among the natives. After Nordenskiöld's death, Haya forwarded the text to Nordenskiöld's successor, Dr Wassén. The text was taken down in the original language and accompanied by a Spanish translation, which Holmer revised with great care.

The purpose of the song is to facilitate difficult childbirth. Its use is somewhat exceptional, since native women of Central and South America have easier deliveries than women of Western societies. The intervention of the shaman is thus rare and occurs in case of failure, at the request of the midwife. The song begins with a picture of the midwife's confusion and describes her visit to the shaman, the latter's departure for the hut of the woman in labor, his arrival, and his preparations – consisting of fumiga-

162

tions of burnt cocoa-nibs, invocations, and the making of sacred figures, or *nuchu*. These images, carved from prescribed kinds of wood which lend them their effectiveness, represent tutelary spirits whom the shaman makes his assistants and whom he leads to the abode of Muu, the power responsible for the formation of the fetus. A difficult childbirth results when Muu has exceeded her functions and captured the *purba*, or 'soul', of the mother-to-be. Thus the song expresses a quest: the quest for the lost *purba*, which will be restored after many vicissitudes, such as the overcoming of obstacles, a victory over wild beasts, and, finally, a great contest waged by the shaman and his tutelary spirits against Muu and her daughters, with the help of magical hats whose weight the latter are not able to bear. Muu, once she has been defeated, allows the *purba* of the ailing woman to be discovered and freed. The delivery takes place, and the song ends with a statement of the precautions taken so that Muu will not escape and pursue her visitors. The fight is not waged against Muu herself, who is indispensable to procreation, but only against her abuses of power. Once these have been corrected, relations become friendly, and Muu's parting words to the shaman almost correspond to an invitation: 'Friend *nele*, when do you think to visit me again?' (413)[2]

Thus far we have rendered the term *nele* as shaman, which might seem incorrect, since the cure does not appear to require the officiant to experience ecstasy or a transition to another psychic state. Yet the smoke of the cocoa beans aims primarily at 'strengthening his garments' and 'strengthening' the *nele* himself, 'making him brave in front of Muu' (65–6). And above all, the Cuna classification, which distinguishes between several types of medicine men, shows that the power of the *nele* has supernatural sources. The native medicine men are divided into *nele*, *inatuledi* and *absogedi*. The functions of the *inatuledi* and *absogedi* are based on knowledge of songs and cures, acquired through study and validated by examinations, while the talent of the *nele*, considered innate, consists of supernatural sight, which instantly discovers the cause of the illness – that is, the whereabouts of the vital forces, whether particular or generalised, that have been carried off by evil spirits. For the *nele* can recruit these spirits, making them his protectors or assistants.[3] There is no doubt, therefore, that he is actually a shaman, even if his intervention in childbirth does not present all the traits which ordinarily accompany this function. And the *nuchu*, protective spirits who at the shaman's bidding become embodied in the figurines he has carved, receive from him – along with invisibility and clairvoyance – *niga*. *Niga* is 'vitality' and 'resistance',[4] which makes these spirits *nelegan* (plural of *nele*) 'in the service of men' or in the 'likeness of human beings' (235–7), although endowed with exceptional powers.

From our brief synopsis, the song appears to be rather commonplace.

The sick woman suffers because she has lost her spiritual double or, more correctly, one of the specific doubles which together constitute her vital strength. (We shall return to this point.) The shaman, assisted by his tutelary spirits, undertakes a journey to the supernatural world in order to snatch the double from the malevolent spirit who has captured it; by restoring it to its owner, he achieves the cure. The exceptional interest of this text does not lie in this formal framework, but, rather, in the discovery – stemming no doubt from a reading of the text, but for which Holmer and Wassén deserve, nonetheless, full credit – that *Mu-Igala*, that is, 'Muu's way', and the abode of Muu are not, to the native mind, simply a mythical itinerary and dwelling-place. They represent, literally, the vagina and uterus of the pregnant woman, which are explored by the shaman and *nuchu* and in whose depths they wage their victorious combat.

This interpretation is based first of all on an analysis of the concept of *purba*. The *purba* is a different spiritual principle from the *niga*, which we defined above. Unlike the *purba* the *niga* cannot be stolen from its possessor, and only human beings and animals own one. A plant or a stone has a *purba* but not a *niga*. The same is true of a corpse; and in a child, the *niga* only develops with age. It seems, therefore, that one could, without too much inaccuracy, interpret *niga* as 'vital strength', and *purba* as 'double' or 'soul', with the understanding that these words do not imply a distinction between animate and inanimate (since everything is animate for the Cuna) but correspond rather to the Platonic notion of 'idea' or 'archetype' of which every being or object is the material expression.

The sick woman of the song has lost more than her *purba*: the native text attributes fever to her – 'the hot garments of the disease' (1 and *passim*) – and the loss or impairment of her sight – 'staring . . sleep on Muu Puklip's path' (97). Above all, as she declares to the shaman who questions her, 'It is Muu Puklip who has come to me. She wants to take my *niga purbalele* for good' (98). Holmer proposes translating *niga* as physical strength and *purba* (*lele*) as soul or essence, whence 'the soul of her life'.[5] It would perhaps be bold to suggest that the *niga*, an attribute of the living being, results from the existence of not one but several *purba*, which are functionally interrelated. Yet each part of the body has its own *purba*, and the *niga* seems to constitute, on the spiritual level, the equivalent of the concept of organism. Just as life results from the cooperation of the organs, so 'vital strength' would be none other than the harmonious concurrence of all the *purba*, each of which governs the functions of a specific organ.

As a matter of fact, not only does the shaman retrieve the *niga purbalele*; his discovery is followed immediately by the recapture of other *purba*, those of the heart, bones, teeth, hair, nails, and feet (401–8, 435–42). The omission here of the *purba* governing the most affected organs – the generative organs – might come as a surprise. As the editors of the text emphasise, this is because the *purba* of the uterus is not considered as a victim but as responsible for the pathological disorder. Muu and her daughters, the *muugan*, are, as Nordenskiöld pointed out, the forces that preside over the development of the fetus and that give it its *kurgin*, the natural capacities.[6] The text does not refer to these positive attributes. In it Muu appears as an instigator of disorder, a special 'souls', thus destroying the cooperation which insures the integrity of the chief body' (*cuerpo jefe* in Spanish, 430, 435) from which it draws its *niga*. But at the same time, Muu must stay put, for the expedition undertaken to liberate the *purba* might provoke Muu's escape by the road which temporarily remains open; hence the precautions whose details fill the last part of the song. The shaman mobilises the Lords of the wild animals to guard the way, the road is entangled, golden and silver nets are fastened, and, for four days, the *nelegan* stand watch and beat their sticks (505–35). Muu, therefore, is not a fundamentally evil force: she is a force gone awry. In a difficult delivery the 'soul' of the uterus has led astray all the 'souls' belonging to other parts of the body. Once these souls are liberated, the soul of the uterus can and must resume its cooperation. Let us emphasise right here the clarity with which the native ideology delineates the emotional content of the physiological disturbance, as it might appear, in an implicit way, to the mind of the sick woman.

To reach Muu, the shaman and his assistants must follow a road, 'Muu's way', which may be identified from the many allusions in the text. When the shaman, crouching beneath the sick woman's hammock, has finished carving the *nuchu*, the latter rise up 'at the extremity of the road' (72, 83) and the shaman exhorts them in these terms:

> The (sick) woman lies in the hammock in front of you.
> Her white tissue lies in her lap, her white tissues move softly.
> [1]The (sick) woman's body lies weak.
> When they light up (along) Muu's way, it runs over with exudations and like blood.
> Her exudations drip down below the hammock all like blood, all red.
> The inner white tissue extends to the bosom of the earth.
> Into the middle of the woman's white tissue a human being descends.
> (84–90)

The translators are doubtful as to the meaning of the last two sentences, yet they refer to another native text, published by Nordenskiöld, which leaves no doubt as to the identification of the 'white inner tissue' with the vulva:

sibugua	*molul*	*arkaali*		
blanca	tela	abriendo		
sibugua	*molul*	*akinnali*		
blanca	tela	extendiendo		

. . .

sibugua	*molul*	*abalase*	*tulapurua*	*ekuanali*
blanca	tela	centro	feto	caer haciendo[7]

'Muu's way', darkened and completely covered with blood owing to the difficult labor, and which the *nuchu* have to find by the white sheen of their clothes and magical hats, is thus unquestionably the vagina of the sick woman. And 'Muu's abode', the "dark whirlpool' where she dwells, corresponds to the uterus, since the native informant comments on the name of this abode, *Amukkapiryawila*, in terms of *omegan purba amurrequedi*, that is, 'woman's turbid menstruation', also called 'the dark deep whirlpool' (250–1) and 'the dark inner place' (32).[8]

The original character of this text gives it a special place among the shamanistic cures ordinarily described. These cures are of three types, which are not, however, mutually exclusive. The sick organ or member may be physically involved, through a manipulation or suction which aims at extracting the cause of the illness – usually a thorn, crystal, or feather made to appear at the opportune moment, as in tropical America, Australia, and Alaska. Curing may also revolve, as among the Araucanians, around a sham battle, waged in the hut and then outdoors, against harmful spirits. Or, as among the Navaho, the officiant may recite incantations and prescribe actions (such as placing the sick person on different parts of a painting traced on the ground with colored sands and pollens) which bear no direct relationship to the specific disturbance to be cured. In all these cases, the therapeutic method (which as we know is often effective) is difficult to interpret. When it deals directly with the unhealthy organ, it is too grossly concrete (generally, pure deceit) to be granted intrinsic value. And when it consists in the repetition of often highly abstract ritual, it is difficult for us to understand its direct bearing on the illness. It would be convenient to dismiss these difficulties by declaring that we are dealing with psychological cures. But this term will remain meaningless unless we can explain how specific psychological representations are invoked to combat equally specific physiological disturbances. The text that we have analysed offers a striking contribution to the solution of this problem. The song constitutes a purely psychological treatment, for the shaman does not touch the body of the sick woman and administers no remedy. Nevertheless it involves, directly and explicitly, the pathological condition and its locus. In our view, the song constitutes a *psychological manipulation* of the sick organ, and it is precisely from this manipulation that a cure is expected.

To begin, let us demonstrate the existence and the characteristics of this manipulation. Then we shall ask what its purpose and its effectiveness are. First, we are surprised to find that the song, whose subject is a dramatic struggle between helpful and malevolent spirits for the reconquest of a 'soul', devotes very little attention to action proper. In eighteen pages of text the contest occupies less than one page and the meeting with Muu Puklip scarcely two pages. The preliminaries, on the other hand, are highly developed and the preparations, the outfitting of the *nuchu*, the itinerary, and the sites are described with a great wealth of detail. Such is the case, at the beginning, for the midwife's visit to the shaman. The conversation between the sick woman and the midwife, followed by that between the midwife and the shaman, recurs twice, for each speaker repeats exactly the utterance of the other before answering him:

> The (sick) woman speaks to the midwife: 'I am indeed being dressed in the hot garment of the disease.'
> The midwife answers her (sick woman): 'You are indeed being dressed in the hot garment of the disease, I also hear you say.' (1–2)

It might be argued[9] that this stylistic device is common among the Cuna and stems from the necessity, among peoples bound to oral tradition, of memorising exactly what has been said. And yet here this device is applied not only to speech but to actions:

> The midwife turns about in the hut.
> The midwife looks for some beads.
> The midwife turns about (in order to leave).
> The midwife puts one foot in front of the other.
> The midwife touches the ground with her foot.
> The midwife puts her other foot forward.
> The midwife pushes open the door of the hut; the door of her hut creaks.
> The midwife goes out. . . (7–14)

This minute description of her departure is repeated when she arrives at the shaman's, when she returns to the sick woman, when the shaman departs, and when he arrives. Sometimes the same description is repeated twice in the same terms (37–9 and 45–7 reproduce 33–5). The cure thus begins with a historical account of the events that preceded it, and some elements which might appear secondary ('arrivals' and 'departures') are treated with luxuriant detail as if they were, so to speak, filmed in slow-motion. We encounter this technique throughout the text, but it is nowhere applied as systematically as at the beginning and to describe incidents of retrospective interest.

Everything occurs as though the shaman were trying to induce the sick woman – whose contact with reality is no doubt impaired and whose sensitivity is exacerbated – to relive the initial situation through pain, in a very precise and intense way, and to become psychologically aware of its smallest details. Actually this situation sets off a series of events of which the body and internal organs of the sick woman will be the assumed setting. A transition will thus be made from the most prosaic reality to myth, from the physical universe to the physiological universe, from the external world to the internal body. And the myth being enacted in the internal body must retain throughout the vividness and the character of lived experience prescribed by the shaman in the light of the pathological state and through an appropriate obsessions technique.

The next ten pages offer, in breathless rhythm, a more and more rapid oscillation between mythical and physiological themes, as if to abolish in the mind of the sick woman the distinction which separates them, and to make it impossible to differentiate their respective attributes. First there is a description of the woman lying in her hammock or in the native obstetrical position, facing eastward, knees parted, groaning, losing her blood, the vulva dilated and moving (84–92, 123–4, 134–5, 152, 158, 173, 177–8, 202–4). Then the shaman calls by name the spirits of intoxicating drinks; of the winds, waters, and woods, and even – precious testimony to the plasticity of the myth – the spirit of the 'silver steamer of the white man' (187). The themes converge: like the sick woman, the *nuchu* are dripping with blood; and the pains of the woman assume cosmic proportions: 'The inner white tissue extends to the bosom of the earth. . . Into the bosom of the earth her exudations gather into a pool, all like blood, all red' (84–92). At the same time, each spirit, when it appears, is carefully described, and the magical equipment which he receives from the shaman is enumerated at great length: black beads, flame-colored beads, dark beads, ring-shaped beads, tiger bones, rounded bones, throat bones, and many other bones, silver necklaces, armadillo bones, bones of the bird *kerkettoli* woodpecker bones, bones for flutes, silver beads (104–18). Then general recruitment begins anew, as if these guarantees were still inadequate and all forces, known or unknown to the sick woman, were to be rallied for the invasion (119–229).

Yet we are released to such a small extent into the realm of myth that the penetration of the vagina, mythical though it be, is proposed to the sick woman in concrete and familiar terms. On two occasions, moreover, 'muu' designates the uterus directly, and not the spiritual principle which governs its activity ('the sick woman's muu', 204, 453).[10] Here the *nelegan*, in order to enter Muu's way, take on the appearance and the motions of the erect penis:

> The *nelegan*'s hats are shining white, the *nelegan*'s hats are whitish.
> The *nelegan* are becoming flat and low (?), all like bits, all straight.
> The *nelegan* are beginning to become terrifying (?), the *nelegan* are becoming all terrifying (?), for the sake of the (sick) woman's *iga purbalele*. (230–2)

And further, below:

> The *nelegan* go balancing up on top of the hammock, they go moving upward like *nusupane*. (239)[11]

The technique of the narrative thus aims at recreating a real experience in which the myth merely shifts the protagonists. The *nelegan* enter the natural orifice, and we can imagine that after all this psychological preparation the sick woman actually feels them entering. Not only does she feel them, but they 'light up' the route they are preparing to follow – for their own sake, no doubt, and to find the way, but also to make the center of inexpressible and painful sensations 'clear' for her and accessible to her consciousness.

'The *nelegan* put good sight into the sick woman, the *nelegan* light good eyes in the (sick) woman . .' (238).

And this 'illuminating sight', to paraphrase an expression in the text, enables them to relate in detail a complicated itinerary that is a true mythical anatomy, corresponding less to the real structure of the genital organs than to a kind of emotional geography, identifying each point of resistance and each thrust:

> The *nelegan* set out, the *nelegan* march in a single file along Muu's road, as far as the Low Mountain,
> The *nelegan* set out, etc., as far as the Short Mountain,
> The *nelegan*, etc., as far as the Long Mountain,
> The *nelegan*, etc., (to) Yala Pokuna Yala, (not translated)
> The *nelegan*, etc., (to) Yala Akkwatallekun Yala, (not translated)
> The *nelegan*, etc., (to) Yala Ilamalisuikun Yala, (not translated)
> The *nelegan*, etc., into the center of the Flat Mountain
> The *nelegan* set out, the *nelegan* march in a single file along Muu's road. (241–8)

The picture of the uterine world, peopled with fantastic monsters and dangerous animals, is amenable to the same interpretation – which is, moreover, confirmed by the native informant: 'It is the animals', he said, 'who decrease the diseases of the laboring woman'; that is, the pains themselves are personified. And here again, the song seems to have as its principal aim the description of these pains to the sick woman and the naming of them, that is, their presentation to her in a form accessible to conscious or unconscious thought: Uncle Alligator, who moves about with his bulging eyes, his striped and variegated body, crouching and wriggling his tail; Uncle Alligator Tiikwalele, with glistening body, who moves his glistening flippers, whose flippers conquer the place, push everything aside, drag everything; Nele Ki(k)kirpanalele, the Octopus, whose stick tentacles are alternately opening and closing, and many others besides: He-who-has-a-hat-that-is-soft, He-who-has-a-red-colored-hat, He-who-has-a-variegated-hat, etc., and the guardian animals: the black tiger, the red animal, the two-colored animal, the dust-colored animal; each is tied with an iron chain, the tongue hanging down, the tongue hanging out, saliva dripping, saliva foaming, with flourishing tail, the claws coming out and tearing things 'all like blood, all red' (253–98).

To enter into this hell *à la* Hieronymus Bosch and reach its owner, the *nelegan* have to overcome other obstacles, this time material: fibers, loose threads, fastened threads, successive curtains – rainbow-colored, golden, silvery, red, black, maroon, blue, white, wormlike, 'like neckties', yellow, twisted, thick (305–30); and for this purpose, the shaman calls reinforcements: Lords of the wood-boring insects, who are to 'cut, gather, wind and reduce' the threads, which Holmer and Wassén identify as the internal tissues of the uterus.[12]

The *nelegan*'s invasion follows the downfall of these last obstacles, and here the tournament of the hats takes place. A discussion of this would lead us too far from the immediate purpose of this study. After the liberation of the *niga purbalele* comes the descent, which is just as dangerous as the ascent, since the purpose of the whole undertaking is to induce childbirth – precisely, a difficult descent. The shaman counts his helpers and encourages his troops; still he must summon other reinforcements: the 'clearers of the way', Lords-of-the-burrowing animals, such as the armadillo. The *niga* is exhorted to make its way toward the orifice:

Your body lies in front of you in the hammock,
(Her) white tissue lies in her lap,
The white inner tissue moves softly,
Your (sick) woman lies in your midst. .
. . thinking she cannot see.
Into her body they put again (her) *niga purbalele*. . . (430–5)

The episode that follows is obscure. It would seem that the sick woman is not yet cured. The shaman leaves for the mountains with people of the village to gather medicinal plants, and he returns to the attack in a different way. This time it is he who, by imitating the penis, penetrates the 'opening of muu' and moves in it 'like *nusupane* . . completely drying the inner place' (453–4). Yet the use of astringents suggests that the delivery has taken place. Finally, before the account of the precautions taken to impede Muu's escape, which we have already described, we find the shaman calling for help from a people of Bowmen. Since their task consists in raising a cloud of dust 'to obscure . . Muu's way' (464), and to defend all of Muu's crossroads and byroads (468), their intervention probably also pertains to the conclusion.

The previous episode perhaps refers to a second curing technique, with organ manipulation and the administration of remedies. Or it may perhaps match, in equally metaphorical terms, the first journey, which is more highly elaborated in the text. Two lines of attack would thus have been developed for the assistance to the sick woman, one of which is supported by a psychophysiological mythology and the other by a psychosocial mythology – indicated by the shaman's call on the inhabitants of the village – which, however, remains undeveloped. At any rate, it should be observed that the song ends after the delivery, just as it had begun before the cure. Both antecedent and subsequent events are carefully related. But it is not only Muu's elusive stray impulses that the cure must, through careful procedures, be effected; the efficacy of the cure would be jeopardised if, even before any results were to be expected, it failed to offer the sick woman a resolution, that is, a situation wherein all the protagonists have resumed their places and returned to an order which is no longer threatened.

The cure would consist, therefore, in making explicit a situation originally existing on the emotional level and in rendering acceptable to the mind pains which the body refuses to tolerate. That the mythology of the shaman does not correspond to an objective reality does not matter. The sick woman believes in the myth and belongs to a society which believes in it. The tutelary spirits and malevolent spirits, the supernatural monsters and magical animals, are all part of a coherent system on which the native conception of the universe is founded. The sick woman accepts these mythical beings or, more accurately, she has never questioned their existence. What she does not accept are the incoherent and arbitrary pains, which are an alien element in her system but which the shaman, calling upon myth, will reintegrate within a whole where everything is meaningful.

Once the sick woman understands, however, she does more than resign herself; she gets well. But no such thing happens to our sick when the causes of their diseases have been explained to them in terms of secretions, germs, or viruses. We shall perhaps be accused of paradox if we answer that the reason lies in the fact that microbes exist and disease is external to the mind of the patient, for it is a cause-and-effect relationship; whereas the relationship between monster and disease is internal to his mind, whether conscious or unconscious: It is a relationship between cymbol and thing symbolised, or, to use the terminology of linguists, between sign and meaning. The shaman provides the sick woman with a *language*, by means of which unexpressed, and otherwise inexpressible, psychic states can be immediately expressed. And it is the transition to this verbal expression – at the same time making it possible to undergo in an ordered and intelligible form a real experience that would otherwise be chaotic and inexpressible – which induces the release of the physiological process, that is, the reorganisation, in a favorable direction, of the process to which the sick woman is subjected.

In this respect, the shamanistic cure lies on the borderline between our contemporary physical medicine and such psychological therapies as psychoanalysis. Its originality stems from the application to an organic condition of a method related to psychotherapy. How is this possible? A closer comparison between shamanism and psychoanalysis – which in our view implies no slight to psychoanalysis – will enable us to clarify this point.

In both cases the purpose is to bring to a conscious level conflicts and resistances which have remained unconscious, owing either to their repression by other psychological forces or – in the case of childbirth – to their own specific nature, which is not psychic but organic or even simply mechanical. In both cases also, the conflicts and resistances are resolved, not because of the knowledge, real or alleged, which the sick woman progressively acquires of them, but because this knowledge makes possible a specific experience, in the course of which conflicts materialise in an order and on a level permitting their free development and leading to their resolution. This vital experience is called *abreaction* in psychoanalysis. We know that its precondition is the unprovoked intervention of the analyst, who appears in the conflicts of the patient through a double transference mechanism, as a flesh-and-blood protagonist and in relation to whom the patient can restore and clarify an initial situation which has remained unexpressed or unformulated.

All these characteristics can be found in the shamanistic cure. Here, too, it is a matter of provoking an experience; as this experience becomes structured, regulatory mechanisms beyond the subject's control are spontaneously set in motion and lead to an orderly functioning. The shaman plays the same dual role as the psychoanalyst. A prerequisite role – that of listener for the psychoanalyst and of orator for the shaman – establishes a direct relationship with the patient's conscious and an indirect relationship with his unconscious. This is the function of the incantation proper. But the shaman does more than utter the incantation; he is its hero, for it is he who, at the head of a supernatural battalion of spirits, penetrates the endangered organs and frees the captive soul. In this way he, like the psychoanalyst, becomes the object of transference and, through the representations induced in the patient's mind, the real protagonist of the conflict which the latter experiences on the border between the physical world and the psychic world. The patient suffering from neurosis eliminates an individual myth by facing a 'real' psychoanalyst; the native woman in childbed overcomes a true organic disorder by identifying with a 'mythically transmuted' shaman.

This parallelism does not exclude certain differences, which are not surprising if we note the character – psychological in the one case and organic in the other – of the ailment to be cured. Actually the shamanistic cure seems to be the exact counterpart to the psychoanalytic cure, but with an inversion of all the elements. Both cures aim at inducing an experience, and both succeed by recreating a myth which the patient has to live or relive. But in one case, the patient constructs an individual myth with elements drawn from his past; in the other case, the patient receives from the outside a social myth which does not correspond to a former personal state. To prepare for the abreaction, which then becomes an 'adreaction', the psychoanalyst listens, whereas the shaman speaks. Better still: when a transference is established, the patient puts words into the mouth of the psychoanalyst by attributing to him alleged feelings and intentions; in the incantation, on the contrary, the shaman speaks for his patient. He questions her and puts into her mouth answers that correspond to the interpretation of her condition, with which she must become imbued:

> My eyesight is straying, it is asleep on Muu Puklip's path.
> It is Muu Puklip who has come to me. She wants to take my *niga purbalele* for good.
> Muu Nauryaiti has come to me. She wants to possess my *niga purbalele* for good.
> etc. (97–101)

Furthermore, the resemblance becomes even more striking when we compare the shaman's method with certain recent therapeutic techniques of psychoanalysis. R. Desoille, in his research on daydreaming,[13] emphasised that psychopathological disturbances are accessible only through the language of symbols. Thus he speaks to his patients by means of symbols, which remain, nonetheless, verbal metaphors. In a more recent work, with which we were not acquainted when we began this study, M. A. Sechehaye goes much further.[14] It seems to us that the results which she obtained while treating a case of schizophrenia considered incurable fully confirm our preceding views on the similarities between psychoanalysis and shamanism. For Sechehaye became aware that speech, no matter how symbolic it might be, still could not penetrate beyond the conscious and that she could reach deeply buried complexes only through acts. Thus to resolve a weaning complex, the analyst must assume a maternal role, carried out not by a literal reproduction of the appropriate behavior but by means of actions which are, as it were, discontinuous, each symbolising a fundamental element of the situation – for instance, putting the cheek of the patient in contact with the breast of the analyst. The symbolic load of such acts qualifies them as a language. Actually, the therapist holds a dialogue with the patient, not through the spoken word, but by concrete actions, that is, genuine rites which penetrate the screen of consciousness to carry their message directly to the unconscious.

Here we again encounter the concept of manipulation, which appeared so essential to an understanding of the shamanistic cure but whose traditional definition we must broaden considerably. For it may at one time involve a manipulation of ideas and, at another time a manipulation of organs. But the basic condition remains that the manipulation must be carried out through symbols, that is, through meaningful equivalents of things meant which belong to another order of reality. The *gestures* of Sechehaye reverberate in the unconscious *mind* of the schizophrenic just as the *representations* evoked by the shaman bring about a modification in the organic *functions* of the woman in childbirth. Labor is impeded at the beginning of the song, the delivery takes place at the end, and the progress of childbirth is reflected in successive stages of the myth. The first penetration of the vagina by the *nelegan* is carried out in Indian file (241) and, since it is an ascent, with the help of magical hats which clear and light up the way. The return corresponds to the second phase of the myth, but to the first phase of the physiological process, since the child must be made to come down. Attention turns toward the *nelegan*'s feet. We are told that they have shoes (494–6). When they invade Muu's abode, they no longer march in single file but in 'rows of four; (388); and, to come out again in the open air, they go 'in a row' (248). No doubt the purpose of such an alteration in the details of the myth is to elicit the corresponding organic reaction, but the sick woman could not integrate it as experience if it were not associated with a true increase in dilatation. It is the effectiveness of symbols which guarantees the harmonious parallel development of myth and action. And myth and action form a pair always associated with the duality of patient and healer. In the schizophrenic cure the healer performs the actions and the patient produces his myth; in the shamanistic cure the healer supplies the myth and the patient performs the actions.

The analogy between these two methods would be even more complete if we could admit, as Freud seems to have suggested on two different occasions,[15] that the description in psychological terms of the structure of psychoses and neuroses must one day be replaced by physiological, or even biochemical, concepts. This possibility may be at hand, since recent Swedish research[16] has demonstrated chemical differences resulting from the amounts of polynucleids in the nerve cells of the normal individual and those of the psychotic. Given this hypothesis or any other of the same type, the shamanistic cure and the psychoanalytic cure would become strictly parallel. It would be a matter, either way, of stimulating an organic transformation which would consist essentially in a structural reorganisation, by inducing the patient intensively to live out a myth – either received or created by him – whose structure would be, at the unconscious level, analogous to the structure whose genesis is sought on the organic level. The effectiveness of symbols would consist precisely in this 'inductive property', by which formally homologous structures, built out of different materials at different levels of life – organic processes, unconscious mind, rational thought – are related to one another. Poetic metaphor provides a familiar example of this inductive process, but as a rule it does not transcend the unconscious level. Thus we note the significance of Rimbaud's intuition that metaphor can change the world.

The comparison with psychoanalysis has allowed us to shed light on some aspects of shamanistic curing. Conversely, it is not improbable that the study of shamanism may one day serve to elucidate obscure points of Freudian theory. We are thinking specifically of the concepts of myth and the unconscious.

We saw that the only difference between the two methods that would outlive the discovery of a physiological substratum of neurosis concerns the origin of the myth, which in the one case is recovered as an individual possession and in the other case is received from collective tradition. Actually, many psychoanalysts would refuse to admit that the psychic constellations which reappear in the patient's conscious could constitute a myth. These represent, they say, real events which it is sometimes possible to date and whose authenticity can be verified by checking with relatives or servants.[17] We do not question these facts. But we should ask ourselves whether the therapeutic value of the cure depends on the actual character of remembered situations, or whether the traumatising power of those situations stems from the fact that at the moment when they appear, the subject experiences them immediately as living myth. By this we mean that the traumatising power of any situation cannot result from its intrinsic features but must, rather, result from the capacity of certain events, appearing within an appropriate psychological, historical, and social context, to induce an emotional crystallisation which is molded by a pre-existing structure. In relation to the event or anecdote, these structures – or, more accurately, these structural laws – are truly atemporal. For the neurotic, all psychic life and all subsequent experiences are organised in terms of an exclusive or predominant structure, under the catalytic action of the initial myth. But this structure, as well as other structures which the neurotic relegates to a subordinate position, are to be fund also in the normal human being, whether primitive or civilised. These structures as an aggregate form what we call the unconscious. The last difference between the theory of shamanism and psychoanalytic theory would, then, vanish. The unconscious ceases to be the ultimate haven of individual peculiarities – the repository of a unique history which makes each of us an irreplaceable being. It is reducible to a function – the symbolic function, which no doubt is specifically human, and which is carried out according to the same laws among all men, and actually corresponds to the aggregate of these laws.

If this view is correct, it will probably be necessary to re-establish a more marked distinction between the unconscious and the preconscious than has been customary in psychology. For the preconscious, as a reservoir of recollections and images amassed in the course of a lifetime,[18] is merely an aspect of memory. While perennial in character, the preconscious also has limitations, once the term refers to the fact that even though memories are preserved they are not always available to the individual. The unconscious, on the other hand, is always empty – or, more accurately, it is as alien to mental images as is the stomach to the foods which pass through it. As the organ of a specific function, the unconscious merely imposes structural laws upon inarticulated elements which originate elsewhere – impulses, emotions, representations, and memories. We might say, therefore, that the preconscious is the individual lexicon where each of us accumulates the vocabulary of his personal history, but that this vocabulary becomes significant, for us and for others, only to the extent that the unconscious structures it according to its laws and thus transforms it into language. Since these laws are the same for all individuals an din all instances where the unconscious pursues its activity, the problem which arose in the preceding paragraph can easily be resolved. The vocabulary matters less than the structure. Whether the myth is re-created by the individual or borrowed from tradition, it derives form its sources – individual or collective (between which interpenetrations and exchanges constantly occur) – only the stock of representations with which it operates. But the structure remains the same, and through it the symbolic function is fulfilled.

If we add that these structures are not only the same for everyone and for all areas to which the function applies, but that they are few in number, we shall understand why the world of symbolism is infinitely varied in content, but always limited in its laws. There are many languages, but very few structural laws which are valid for all languages. A compilation of known tales and myths would fill an imposing number of volumes. But they can be reduced to a small number of simple types if we abstract, from among the diversity of characters, a few elementary functions. As for the complexes – those individual myths – they also correspond to a few simple types, which mold the fluid multiplicity of cases.

Since the shaman does not psychoanalyse his patient, we may conclude that remembrance of things past, considered by some the key to psychoanalytic therapy, is only one expression (whose value and results are hardly negligible) of a more fundamental method, which must be defined without considering the individual or collective genesis of the myth. For the myth *form* takes precedence over the *content* of the narrative. This is, at any rate, what the analysis of a native text seems to have taught us. But also, from another perspective, we know that any myth represents a quest for the remembrance of things past. The modern version of shamanistic technique called psychoanalysis thus derives its specific characteristics from the fact that in industrial civilisation there is no longer any room for mythical time, except within man himself. From this observation, psychoanalysis can draw confirmation of its validity, as well as hope of strengthening its theoretical foundations and understanding better the reasons for its effectiveness, by comparing its methods and goals with those of its precursors, the shamans and sorcerers.

INTRODUCTION: REFERENCES

Dow, J. (1986) 'Universal aspects of symbolic healing: a theoretical synthesis', *American Anthropologist* 88: 56–69.
Laderman, C. (1987) 'The ambiguity of symbols in the structure of healing', *Social Science and Medicine*, 24: 293–301.

NOTES

1. Nils M. Holmer and Henry Wassén, *Mu-Igala or the Way of Muu, a Medicine Song from the Cunas of Panama* (Göteborg: 1947).
2. The numbers in parentheses refer to the numbered sections in the song.
3. E. Nordenskiöld, *An Historical and Ethnological Survey of the Cuna Indians*, ed. Henry Wassén, Vol. X of *Comparative Ethnographical Studies* (Göteborg: 1938), pp. 80 ff.
4. ibid., pp. 360 ff., Holmer and Wassén, op. cit., pp. 78–9.
5. Holmer and Wassén, op. cit., p. 38, n. 44.
6. Nordenskiöld, op. cit., p. 364 ff.
7. ibid., pp. 607–8; Holmer and Wassén, op. cit., p. 38, nn. 35–9.
8. The translation of *ti ipya* as 'whirlpool' seems to be strained. For certain South American natives, as also in the languages of the Iberian peninsula (cf. the Portuguese *olho d'agua*), a 'water eye' is a spring.

9. Holmer and Wassén, op. cit., pp. 65–6.
10. ibid., p. 45, n. 219; p. 57, n. 539.
11. The question marks are Holmer and Wassén's, *nusupane* derives from *nusu*, 'worm', and is commonly used for 'penis' (see Holmer and Wassén, p. 47, n. 280; p. 57, n. 540; and p. 82).
12. ibid., p. 85.
13. R. Desoille, *Le Rêve éveillé en psychothérapie* (Paris: 1945).
14. M. A. Sechehaye, *La Réalisation symbolique*, Supplement No. 12 to *Revue suisse de psychologie et de psychologie appliquée* (Berne: 1947).
15. In *Beyond the Pleasure Principle* p. 79, and *New Conferences on Psychoanalysis*, p. 198, cited by E. Kris, 'The nature of psychoanalytic propositions and their validation', in *Freedom and Experience, Essays presented to H. M. Kallen* (Ithaca, NY: 1947), p. 244.
16. Caspersson and Hyden, at the Karolinska Institute in Stockholm.
17. Marie Bonaparte, 'Notes on the analytical discovery of a primal scene'. In *The Psychoanalytic Study of the Child*, Vol. I (New York: 1945).
18. This definition, which was subjected to considerable criticism, acquires a new meaning through the radical distinction between preconscious and unconscious.

CHAPTER ELEVEN

Mental Diseases Peculiar to Certain Cultures: a Survey of Comparative Psychiatry (1951)

P.-M. Yap

It was from the colony of Hong Kong that a British-trained Chinese psychia-trist, Yap, first articulated a more self-conscious cultural psychiatry which looked at the criteria of definition used by different theoreticians. Yap who was to coin the term 'culture-bound syndromes' here uses Ackerknecht's double system of defining abnormality ('theirs', 'ours') rather than a hypothetical mechanism to sketch out various culture-specific patterns. As was common, until the 1970s, he does not touch on 'Western-specific' patterns, and most of his argument follows the problem of Western percep-tion: how does it seem abnormal to the European? Yet he does not consider how certain patterns such as miryachit may be in part a communication or response to relative power between local and European.

Modern psychiatry has developed in Western Europe, largely under French and German aegis, and latterly in the United States. It is pertinent to ask, since it deals with human behaviour in all its variety, if the concepts, working principles and empirically derived conclusions of psychiatry possess universal validity, wherever it might be practised. As one instance of the influence of cultural environment on psychiatric symptomatology (and also psychiatric practice), we may point to the 'hysterogenic points' so often found in French hysterics by the Salpêtrière school of neurologists, who could provoke an hysterical attack or sometimes abort one by pressing on these points. Just across the Channel in England, among English hysterics, these phenomena could not be repro-duced; they were, of course, special features of the disease, exhibited only in the atmosphere created by Charcot and his colleagues at that period. The psychiatrist in cultures farther removed from the civilisation of Western Europe may well have reason to pause and ask if the principles and practice of orthodox psychiatry possess the same degree of truth or usefulness elsewhere than in Western Europe or America.

Margaret Mead recently spoke of 'psychiatric imperialism' on the part of her American colleagues[1] – a peculiarly trans-Atlantic phrase, but one perhaps effective in emphasising that psychiatric thought originating in

Euro-American culture, need not be the alpha and omega of psychiatry everywhere. Another American, E. H. Acker[k]necht, protests against the egocentricity of Western thought: 'Our culture', he says, 'is unique in its outlawing of the irrational, the emotional, the ecstatic. These phenomena have thus become most incomprehensible and unknown to our society. The bedroom, the liquor store and the office of the psychiatrist are their last sanctuaries, but only the last of these three places is not tabooed for public expression. Thus it is no wonder that an almost unlimited number of phenomena have acquired a psychopathological label.' He mentions how primitive religion has been called 'organized schizophrenia', magic 'the pathology of culture', the savage 'an obsessional neurotic', and the medicine man of primitive tribes described variously as epileptic, hysterical, or suffering from neurosis[2]. He concludes: 'It needs the gigantic helplessness and vanity, the terrible uniqueness of our culture to come to such statements.'

Emil Kraepelin, the founder of modern psychiatry, was probably also the first to inquire into the possibility of a science of comparative psychiatry. He introduced that term (*vergleichende psychiatrie*) in 1904 to denote the study of mental diseases as they manifested themselves in different cultural groups[3]. He himself, a lover of travel, had spent some time in Java and India studying insanity. Following the example of his classical *Lehrbuch*, most text-books devoted a section to the influence of culture on mental disease, but more often than not this contained merely an undigested and ill-assorted miscellany of observations by untrained or poorly trained workers, too ready to see correlations where there were none, or draw conclusions where none could be inferred. For example, ever since Krafft-Ebbing's famous observation on 'civilisation and syphilisation' many curious statements have been made on the alleged absence or rarity of general paralysis of the insane in non-Western cultures.

Moreover, attention was paid to the nutritional, toxic and climatic aetiological factors, rather than to the strictly sociological factors of psychological significance which may cause or modify the picture of insanity. The latter are no doubt much more difficult to investigate.

THE MEANING OF THE NORMAL

The problem of the definition of abnormality comes to the fore, once we turn from the organic reaction types to the schizophrenic and affective reactions, where reactive psychogenic factors play a significant part in the pathogenesis. Here no simple physico-chemical, biological or anatomical test can establish an abnormality. The disease itself can only be defined against the social background; thus even the deformed foot caused by the practice of foot-binding – specimens of which grace many a pathological museum in the West – cannot be simply regarded as abnormal without taking into account the social and cultural *milieu*.

Theoretically, the concept of abnormality is both peculiar and confused, because in it are contained two different notions; on the one hand, there is a judgment of value, of goodness or badness; on the other, there is a reference to the statistical average. If we keep in view the *ideal* functioning of body and mind, then the actuality must fall short of the ideal, since the majority of men and women cannot possibly function in the ideal manner. The majority also constitute the average, which is, from the statistical point of view, the normal or the healthy. Paradoxically, then, the normal or healthy is that which is not functioning in the ideal manner. (For a full discussion of this theme see K. Jaspers[4].)

It is desirable, therefore, when we say that a man is abnormal, to specify, firstly, how he departs from the average; and secondly, how he falls short of the ideal, then we are immediately faced with the problem, what average? and whose ideal?

To answer the first question, we may draw some help from the work of the school of anthropologists associated with the names of Mead, Benedict, Bateson, Boas and Linton. These workers attempt to describe the psychological characteristics of various patterns of culture, and even attempt to classify the latter into various psychopathological categories (e.g. as paranoid, aggressive, introvert or extrovert, megalomanic, etc.). We may agree with B. Malinowski[5] (p. 206, f.) that this approach is lacking in scientific objectivity* and that the writers fall into the error of thinking that psychological normality is a special attribute of Western civilisation. Clearly, the recognition of differences in the temperamental make-up of various peoples is of fundamental importance for comparative psychiatry.

What is needed is not a total rejection of this method of study, but the use of ordinary descriptive terms which do not drag in psychopathology, and, consequently, implicit reference to an arbitrary norm of human behaviour.

It would be a grievous error to suppose that if a certain form of behaviour in some culture or other resembles insane behaviour it is necessarily abnormal. For instance, if a Hindu fakir behaves much like a catatonic schizophrenic in Britain, he need not necessarily be insane; since not only can he begin or stop his apparently catatonic behaviour at will, but such behaviour has a recognised place, and possesses some degree of social approbation, in his own culture. Similarly, the Siberian shaman may fall into a state of partial hysterical dissociation like the hysteric in, say, Britain, but this state he voluntarily seeks, and in doing so he obtains authority and respect from the tribe.

---

*Professor C. G. Seligman, for example, relates how with practical experience of the Chinese people he had to change his impression of them as introvert to the opposite view[6] (p. 86).

It is essential, therefore, to look beyond appearance and form, and inquire into function. We are brought back to the question, what is normal behaviour from the ideal point of view?

We need to concern ourselves with functional concepts like 'adjustment', 'integration', 'adaptation', and 'survival'. In organic medicine the problem of what is not normal or ideal is relatively simple; he is not ideally normal, i.e. he is ill, who feels pain or fatigue, who does not live reasonably long, who cannot work or reproduce, etc. In psychiatry we tread on uncertain ground. Even within one culture, as Jaspers has pointed out, ideas of what constitutes abnormality may vary. Thus the patient with an hysterical headache following injury to the head during work, and expecting compensation, will be regarded as ill by the psychiatrist, but not so by the insurance company.

It is still possible to reach a conclusion as to normality or otherwise by thinking in terms of 'adjustment' or 'adaptation' of the individual to his environment. In social anthropology this method of approach has its exponent in B. Malinowski (op. cit.), who insists that every anthropological fact has meaning only when its function in the culture is appreciated. With this attitude, of course, the question whether any behaviour characteristic of a given culture is normal or not becomes meaningless, just as with the advent of psychoanalysis the difference between normal and abnormal behaviour is largely obliterated (cf. Freud's *Psychopathology of Everyday Life*). Deviation from the mean of any form of behaviour is unimportant, but rather why the deviation occurs. The quintessence of abnormality, as H. J. Wegrocki[7] points out, is the choice of a type of reaction which enables the individual to escape or fly away from a difficult situation instead of facing it squarely. The choice resulting from the conflict is, moreover, unconscious, and apparently beyond the will or purpose of the patient. It must be noted that the reaction which takes the form of flight must, according to the values of the society, be regarded as useless, non-productive, non-constructive behaviour. If this were not so, if it had instead social approbation, then it would probably be a form of 'sublimation' (see later). In point of fact, social attitudes towards unusual behaviour are changeable, and also often uncertain, so that it is not always clear whether a form of abnormal and unusual behaviour is diseased or not.

We need to consider here briefly the distinction between genius and lunacy. Both are departures from the mean. Unlike lunacy, genius is constructive, it extends the range of human experience, and it is valued and sought after by the community. A single individual may at one time produce work bearing the stamp of genius, and at other times fall into behaviour characteristic of insanity; and society may mistake genius for insanity or vice versa.

From the psychoanalytical point of view, a case can be made out for regarding the behaviour of genius as a 'sublimation' of internal psychic conflicts. Unfortunately the concept of sublimation is far from generally accepted. Sublimated behaviour is simply by definition, socially valued behaviour substituted for similarly determined but less desirable behaviour, so that in the end we are not much nearer an understanding of the nature of genius. The philosopher C. Delisle Burns has tried to analyse the difference between genius and lunacy in general terms[8]. He thinks that the genius is more co-ordinated in his behaviour, is more in equilibrium, makes more use of the conscious mind, and is generally more in contact with his fellow men than the lunatic. These distinctions are difficult to apply to concrete cases. They are probably true at their own conceptual level, but they cannot explain why, for instance, a dissociated person like the shaman is treated as a genius in Siberia (see below), but would be regarded as a madman in Europe. The cultural background cannot be ignored. Both genius and madman are abnormal, since they are unusual as well as functionally unable or unwilling to adapt themselves to Society. Society, however, adapts itself eventually to the genius, but does not do so in regard to the lunatic. However, each culture has *within limits* its own idea of what genius and lunacy consists in, and these ideas may also change with the times.

MENTAL DISEASES PECULIAR TO CERTAIN CULTURES

We are now in a position to study various mental diseases recognised as specific to particular cultural groups. For the purpose of classification I propose to adopt E. M. Ackerknecht's terminology (ibid.). He suggests the term 'autopathological' to describe those conditions abnormal in the culture in which they are found, but normal in other cultures; and the term 'autonormal' to cover those forms of behaviour, normal in their own cultural *milieu*, but which, occurring in other cultures, would be regarded as abnormal, i.e. the behaviour is also 'heteropathological'. Similarly, the term 'heteronormal' is self-explanatory.

(a) Autopathological and Heteropathological Behaviour

This class is the most important, since it comprises the majority of mental diseases universally recognised as such, at least, in their developed forms.

Among this group are also certain diseases distinguishable from the accepted major reaction types, which are peculiar to particular cultures, but which, if they appeared in other cultural groups would, I think, also be called abnormal. These have been called 'fashions in disease'. It is characteristic of fashions that they change with time, and it is better to use that phrase for those mass hysterical outbreaks which, for instance, afflicted the medieval Europeans.

Psychic contagions – These hysterical 'contagions' were frequent in medieval societies, and still to be found now and then in closed, fervently religious communities like nunneries, where belief in possession by external agencies exists, or in small, compact communities of easily excited and emotional people, like girls' boarding schools. Thus there were in Europe dancing manias, children's crusades (cf. the legend of the Pied Piper of Hamelin), the Tarantism (a 'dancing mania' provoked by the belief that such exertions will ward off death from the bite of the poisonous tarantula spider), and the choreomania or St Vitus' Dance of those times. For a list of these epidemics in Europe from the later Middle Ages to fairly recent times, we may turn to K. Osterreich[9] (p. 187, f.). This author also mentions (p. 192) a case of epidemic zooanthropy occurring in a German convent, when the nuns believed themselves possessed by cats (or changed into cats), and behaved accordingly. Related to these are the epidemic hysterias manifested by the 'Jumpers' and 'Barkers' of the eastern part of the United States. These assumed extreme and grotesque proportions at the turn of the eighteenth century, when, at revival meetings by camp-fires, tens of thousands of people, stirred by fiery oration, would jump, shout, bark and roll about in extreme religious fervour (D. W. Yandell[10]). Of the 'Jumpers' and 'Barkers' I shall have more to say later. To come to our own times, the occurrence of an epidemic of hysterical convulsions among the inmates of a girls' boarding school in Louisiana has been reported at length by E. A. Schuler and U. J. Parenton[11].

These epidemics must have been considered abnormal by many in their own times and within their own cultural settings. As psychological phenomena they are no doubt traceable to certain prevalent social attitudes and beliefs; and if these ideas, beliefs and attitudes become fixed so as to assume the significance of culture traits with some degree of permanence, it is conceivable that they may give rise to certain aberrations, which, persisting while the society as a whole undergoes development and change, and while knowledge advances, will become increasingly unusual and grotesque. The so-called possession by animals or the devil, accepted as part of the natural order of things in olden days, appears to us educated moderns as something definitely insane, although the idea of possession by the spirits of the departed still exists among the spiritualists in Europe, and among a rather larger proportion of the people of China, and is in no way regarded as a disease. The idea of the abnormal varies with the times.

An excellent example of a disease shaped largely by prevailing folk-beliefs is *Koro* or (in Chinese) *Su Yang*.

Koro or Su Yang – This illness is known by the former name among the Malays, and by the latter among the Southern Chinese, especially the

Cantonese. It has not been recorded among other peoples. The patient, usually a neurotic with sexual conflicts, e.g. over-impotence or masturbation, suddenly becomes seized with the conviction that his penis is shrinking into his abdomen. According to popular belief, if this is allowed to happen, death ensues; and the patient falls into a state of panic. He hastily resorts to various remedies. The orthodox way to forestall death is to clamp the penis in a wooden case used for holding a jeweller's balance (called in Cantonese *Leh Teug Hup*); or failing this, to tie round the penis a red string (among the chinese), red being the colour successful in warding off evil. Sometimes instead of the above measures the wife immediately practices *fellatio*. Inevitably a great commotion is caused and the patient may be carried in distress to hospital.

That it is a psychogenic illness resting on superstition there can be no doubt. There is a wealth of folk-lore in connection with this disease, but it is probable that actual hysterical anaesthesia of the penis, or some disturbance of the 'body image' occurs. G. Bychowski has described a case in a European corresponding exactly to *Koro*[12]. It is said that a female form of the disease consisting in fear of shrinking of the breasts and genitalia also occurs. The best account of *Koro* is probably that of van Wulfften-Palthe's[13]. Nosologically, *Koro* is, I believe, an acute anxiety state (panic) in persons with sexual conflicts and preoccupations.

Latah – This is a comparatively well-known disease, first described among the Malay races, but it has become apparent that essentially similar diseases occur in many of the simpler societies under local names; for example, as *imu* among the Ainus of North Japan, as *myriachit*, *ikota* or *arctic hysteria* among the Siberian tribes, as *mali-mali* in the Philippines, *yaun* in Burma and *bah-tsi* in Siam. It has also been described in the Sahara desert, Italian North Africa, and the Yemen. (See R[14–20]).

The disease is probably a fright neurosis with marked hysterical features; it is certainly not simple hysteria, as Kraepelin supposed it to be ([21] p. 157). The patient, usually a middle-aged woman, when suddenly frightened, falls into a trance-like state in which she exhibits automatic obedience, echolalia and echopraxia. The stimulus may be of the most trivial kind, e.g. a sudden touch, the ringing of a passing bicycle bell, or even the mention of the name of a dangerous animal. In the latah state the patient is completely at the mercy of those who surround her, doing almost anything they command her to do, imitating all their actions, and, it is said, even the swaying of a tree bough or the mewing of a cat – but this is probably not true.

There is perhaps a special predisposition to fear, as van Wulfften-Palthe points out (op. cit.), but in younger women a brief exhibition of echo-symptoms when startled or suddenly embarrassed, as, for instance, when tickled, may simply be a sort of affectation designed to attract attention.

(*Latah* in Malay means ticklish, *bah-tsi* in Siamese means 'tickling madness'). Many Malay women in the countryside show this and nothing more; but some cases gradually progress until they become after many years, permanently latah and prone to automatic obedience and echo-reactions, and they then tend to hide themselves from other people. These cases remind one of the 'degenerative hysteria' of German authors.

It is possible that the social and cultural conditions in places where the disease occurs are such as to produce a certain passivity of mind and an unpreparedness for sudden decision and action, since they are far removed from the noise and competition of modern civilisations, but are at the same time not wild and menacing to their inhabitants. As regards proneness to fear, this is clearly seen among the Ainus. According to W. Winiarz and J. Wielawski (ibid.), these people have a special fear of serpents, and if one of them steps on a (serpent-like) snake, he will throw a full hysterical fit. It is possible to see how an hysterical attack can easily acquire mimic features when it is accompanied by some clouding of consciousness, as in this case, where the provoking cause is fear. The attack may become standardised by repetition, so that it may even become, in a sense, a culture trait.

Some authors, e.g. Manson-Bahr, van Loon and W. McDougall[16] (p. 324, f.n.) have pointed out that the disease only affects Mongolian peoples, and point to race as a causal factor in its pathogenesis. That this cannot be so is proven by the occurrence of an exactly similar type of illness among the 'jumping Frenchmen' of Maine (Beard[22]), sufferers from a curious disease, misidentified as convulsive tics, and as such repeated parrot-fashion from book to book, but entirely neglected by writers on latah. That this disease was described in temperate North America also dispose of the theory that extremes of climates are causative factors.

Miryachit may occur in epidemic form. An example is recorded of a regiment of Transbaikal cavalrymen who suddenly became echolalic and began to repeat the commands of their officer, and the more vehemently the officer reiterated his commands the more readily they were repeated (quoted by Czaplicka, op. cit., p. 313). This resembles the psychic contagions, or mass hysterias.

The primitive hysterical outburst of undifferentiated excitement, weeping, laughter and running away, with or without hiding has been described among many of the simpler people, e.g. as *piblokto* among the Eskimos (A. A. Brill[23]) and as *misala* among the natives of Nyasaland (R. Howard[24]). The hysterical outburst (from which the lay connotation of the word 'hysterical' is derived) also occurs in more advanced societies, though usually among the less intelligent and the poorly educated.

Amok – This is an acute outburst of unrestrained violence associated with homicidal attacks, preceded by a period of brooding, and ending with exhaustion and amnesia. The fury of the patient may be quite undirected and he may strike down animals and men indiscriminately in his path. Such an acute reaction can obviously arise from many underlying causes. It has been ascribed to epilepsy by Kraepelin[21] (p. 157), confusion from malaria or cerebral lues by F. H. G. van Loon[25], and by others to hashish poisoning, sunstroke and mania. It has been suggested that this may be a primitive reaction corresponding to the outbursts of psychopathic persons in more developed cultures (J. C. Carothers[26]). Thus very similar attacks have been described in Polynesia and in the Sahara (*cafard*, *soudanite*). There is no doubt that amok-like attacks occur both in Europe and America.

Some authors, like van Loon (ibid.), believe that the reaction is specific to the Malays, but the ascription to race as such of definite causal significance is always dubious. Perhaps the more correct view is that of van Wulfften-Palthe (ibid.), who calls amok a standardised form of emotional release, accepted by the community, and indeed expected of the individual who is placed for some reason or other in an intolerably embarrassing or shameful situation. It is not simply a lack of power of self-control, since it is a mistake to equate deficient powers of inhibition as such with so-called primitiveness. Many outlandish tribes exhibit the greatest self-control, for example, when undergoing ritual tortures.

We should probably distinguish true amok as it occurs among the Malays from cases of acute confusion with paranoid and homicidal trends arising *per se* or as episodes in many different psychiatric reactions. The amok of the Malays probably has a social significance; for example, among the Moros of the Philippines cases of amok have been recorded which had worked themselves up by religious incantation and other prescribed rituals.

The Wihtigo Psychosis – This is an illness confined to the Cree, Ojibway and Salteaux Indians of North America. These people believe in the possibility of being transformed into a *wihtigo*, a giant creature with a heart of ice, who eats human flesh for food. During times of starvation, a man may suddenly develop a craving for human flesh, and also develop the delusion that he has been transformed into a *wihtigo*. This mythological creature is greatly feared, but sometimes actual cannibalism takes place, as though the patient were impelled towards the very behaviour that is feared. The belief is so strongly held that sometimes alimentary symptoms like loss of appetite or nausea arising from quite ordinary reasons causes the patient to fall into great excitement for fear of being transformed.

This illness is a good illustration of the effect of mythology and environment on insanity. Nosologically, it may perhaps be essentially hysterical in nature, like demoniacal possession. For an account see A. Irving Hallowel[l][27].

(b) Autonormal and Heteropathological Forms of Behaviour

Among those types of behaviour which are normal in their own cultural settings, but which would be regarded as diseased in Euro-American civilisations, or for that matter, in Chinese civilisation, are the following:

Homosexuality – That homosexuality is accepted openly as a normal mode of behaviour in certain cultures, and also certain sub-cultures within Euro-American civilisation is well-known. It was so accepted in ancient Greece, and if not accepted, it is at least looked upon with less distaste or surprise among, for example, the Turks and the Bengalis. The English public school system provides a *milieu* conducive to it. The degree to which it is regarded as an abnormality in various countries may be gauged by the attitude of the law towards it; I believe it is true to say that the Anglo-Saxon countries adopt a rather harsher attitude towards it than the Latin countries, and that Chinese law is rather more tolerant.

In certain cultures not only is the homosexual tolerated, but the homosexual actually obtains a position of power and prestige. Thus in North-Siberia the shaman (or medicine-man *cum* oracle) of the Chukchis, are men who, in the process of acquiring shamanistic powers have, often suddenly, turned homosexual. More rarely, a woman may also become homosexual and then acquire all the prestige and influence of the shaman (quoted by H. Klineberg[28], p. 272).

Possession – Many of the tribal medicine-man-oracles among primitive peoples fall into a state of trance, when they are believed to be 'possessed' by a spirit, who speaks through them. The medicine-men of the Bataks of Borneo are of this type, though the majority of the Siberian shamans are not. The phenomenon of possession is doubtless hysterical in basis; indeed, Osterreich in his classic book on this subject[9] (Chap. 3) says it is identical with the phenomenon of somnambulism, a form of hysterical dissociation. In Euro-American civilisation such a form of behaviour would be labelled pathological, except by cultural sub-groups like the spiritualists, or the Roman Catholic Church, which, I think, still believes in possession by the devil. It may here be pointed out that in China a form of possession-shamanism, the (Taoistic-Buddhistic) *Moh* or *Wu* priests, exists (see Osterreich, op. cit., p. 355, f.). Similar phenomena are also found in India and Japan.

The Potlatch of British Columbia – Among the Indians of British Columbia there is an institution called the 'Potlatch' which is a recognised way of settling a quarrel by the destruction or distribution of property of any sort. The persons involved challenge each other to a duel in which each tries to destroy or give away more property than the other, and the one who succeeds in doing so is acclaimed the winner. This method of 'fighting with property' is also known in Alaska.

During the potlatch the contestants make long speeches referring to themselves in excessively grandiose terms, which the orthodox psychiatrist might well describe as paranoid and megalomanic. Moreover, among these people there is a great sensitivity to insult, so much so that every little misfortune or accident is looked upon in terms of an attempt to insult them. The only redress then is to challenge their fancied enemy to a potlatch. This kind of behaviour corresponds to that of a lunatic in a paranoid state in advanced cultures elsewhere.

Whether or not paranoia and paranoid states occur among them I do not know, but if they do there can, under such circumstances, be abnormal and deviant behaviour only if they are extreme or associated with definite depressive or schizophrenic symptoms.

An account of the potlatch may be found in a paper by R. Benedict[29].

The Touch taboos of the Dobuan Islanders – Among the inhabitants of the Dobuan Islands there exists a general attitude of fear and suspicion each towards his neighbour. No one, for example, will touch or eat the food of another in case it might have been magically poisoned (see R. Fortune[30]). This is but one example of the many taboo systems commonly found in Polynesian cultures. The touch taboos are reminiscent of the rituals and prohibitions of our obsessional-compulsive neurotics (more especially if *défense de toucher*). Indeed the psychoanalytic theory of this neurosis takes into account the remarkable similarity.

Thanatomania – This term has been used to describe cases of death occurring for no other reason than auto-suggestion, following the breaking of a taboo, the consequence of which is known to be death. Thus an untutored Maori may pine and die if he discovers that he has taken the chief's food, an infringement of a taboo which is known to be followed by death. This remarkable phenomenon is thoroughly authenticated, and has been the subject of a paper by W. B. Cannon[31]. Such a method of death, accepted almost as a matter of course by the Polynesians, would, if it occurred among us, arouse all the curiosity and amazement associated with the abnormal.

Yogism – In spite of its exposition by many popular writers, there are included under this term phenomena of great psychiatric interest. Such, for example, are the catatonia-like postures assumed by the fakirs for long periods, sometimes for days on end, until, it is said, structural changes take place. By dint of long practice they are able to withdraw their attention from the environment, to remain in a state of intense self-absorption, in complete immobility, and apparently with suspension of basic physiological needs (see quotation from F. Alexander by Klineberg, op. cit., p. 253). It may be pointed out that yoga practices also have a following among certain Taoist-Buddhistic sects in China. (C. G. Jung has studied this from the point of view of analytical psychology[32].)

The Western psychiatrist would, if he took the static, structuralist point of view, classify all the above with the pathological. Conversely, many primitives would, according to their own standards and values, regard as diseased or abnormal certain forms of behaviour which are in the West regarded only as personality aberrations or, indeed, as entirely normal personality and character traits.

Under this heading might be mentioned the case of the unsociable girl of the Ga people (North American Indians) described by A. I. Hallowel[l][33]. She was regarded as ill and needing treatment, but such a girl in Europe or America would only be thought of as shy and retiring, perhaps a little schizoid.

R. Benedict[29] has also pointed out that the initiative and energy of the American considered as a virtue by them, might well be regarded by the Zuni Indians as an illness or at least something abnormal (indeed, it would so be regarded by many Chinese of the old school!). Similarly the North-West Coast Indians, used to throwing away their property at the potlatches, will not take for granted that the acquisitiveness of the modern civilisation, East and West, is something only to be expected of human nature, as we ourselves implicitly do; to them our greed may savour of lunacy.

CERTAIN OBSERVATIONS AND GENERALISATIONS

We have already mentioned that the old notion that G.P.I. is rare in non-Western countries is no longer tenable. There is no better illustration of the dangers of generalisation about the incidence of a disease than in this instance. The exponents of the original view failed to take into account the many complex factors in the social environment that determine whether or not patients will present themselves at clinics for observation, and also the facilities which exist for such observation. For similar reasons, the parallel observation that the disease is more common among the educated (cf. van Wulfften-Palthe[13]) is suspect, because in societies like that of Java the educated classes are doubtless more ready to present themselves at hospitals, and being urban, can do so more easily. It must be remembered that folk-ideas and superstitious ways of thought, as well as fear, are apt to cling round mental diseases more tenaciously than round bodily illnesses.

The reluctance of children to send their aged parents into a mental hospital arising from the tradition of filial piety, as well as the relatively smaller development of compact and restricted flat-life in cities, probably explain the apparent rarity of senile dementia in China; although it is true that care and comfort in old age may ward off senile dementia to a great extent. It is difficult to know what reliance can be placed on observations like that of J. C. Carothers[26] when he maintains that there is little hypertension and arteriosclerosis among the negroes of Kenya because there is seldom anxiety of any duration occurring in these people. Even if there is little arteriosclerotic dementia, the reason adduced for this is probably not true. It is facile to assume that because a society is primitive, it is necessarily less complex and that there are fewer causes for insecurity and anxiety. The savage seldom lives in noble and idyllic simplicity, either from the sociological or from the psychological point of view.

Many observers have pointed out that in the more primitive cultures schizophrenia is quieter, less florid, and is, in the words of Gordon, 'a poor imitation of European forms' (cf., for example, H. L. Gordon34], can Wulfften-Palthe, op. cit.). This is possibly true, since the richness of psychiatric symptomatology is dependent on the intellectual and cultural resources of the patient: the same difference is found between the educated and uneducated in any cultures, and sometimes the barrenness in clinical picture of insane Chinese peasants in striking. It must be pointed out that the psychiatrist studying patients whose language is unfamiliar to him is bound to miss a great deal in the way of symptoms. There is also a notion that paranoid schizophrenia is rare among the simpler peoples, in contrast to the catatonic variety. This could only be true if the people concerned were so primitive as to have only the rudiments of language. The more likely explanation for the difference, supposing it were true, is that the observer cannot understand what the patient says, and that possibly the patient is thereby discouraged from communicating his thoughts to him in speech.

The frame-work of the schizophrenic process remains the same wherever it is found. The classical dissociation of mood from thought, the ideas of influence and of passivity, the hallucinations and delusions, are constantly found. (For a study of the content of thought among Chinese schizophrenics see C. C. Kao *et al.*[35], Chap. 11.) Laubscher[36] has noted that among the Tembus in S. Africa schizophrenic delusions show a regression to tribal beliefs (the patient presumably having previously taken over modern or 'Western' ideas in varying degrees).

Van Wulfften-Palthe agrees with Gordon that in Java and Kenya respectively, true manic-depressive insanity of the cyclic type is rare. Both van Wulfften-Palthe and Carothers (the latter working in Kenya) observe that mania is more common than depression, the first worker noting that mania is often associated with mental defect, and the second attributing the difference in incidence to the weak repressive powers of his patients. Van Wulfften-Palthe also mentions that in Java melancholia (depression) is rather commoner among the Chinese. Carothers finds that in his involutional melancholics there is little idea or feeling of guilt, and he compares this fact to the observation of C. G. Seligman that in Japan delusions of a religious nature with guilt are practically absent, probably because Japanese religion is cheerful and not centred round the idea of sin.

Whether Carothers' thesis is true, that mania is rare among negro patients because they can so readily fulfil their desire in phantasy, thanks to the weakness of their repressive mechanisms, is certainly open to question. Carothers also declares that obsessional-compulsive illness is uncommon in Kenya because the society itself is obsessional-compulsive in nature, i.e. full of rituals and prohibitions. Here again language difficulty may obscure the recognition of obsessional symptoms, just as a stupid patient may be unable to describe his obsessional symptoms to the doctor, thereby helping give rise to the impression that unintelligent subjects do not suffer from obsessional illness, a point which Aubrey Lewis emphasises.

We must finally mention an important psychiatric generalisation which affirms that there is an analogy between schizophrenic and primitive ways of thought. This was first exhaustively studied by A. Stroch[37] more than twenty-five years ago, but for a recent study see J. Burstin[38]. Where the Tembu schizophrenic regresses to his own tribal beliefs, the European schizophrenic regresses to what is very like superstition and primitive folk-lore a magic. The Chinese patient in his turn becomes preoccupied with ideas possession by animal familiars, gods and devils, of magical influence, and communication with many unseen spirits, all drawn from the animistic element still so strong in Chinese culture. There is a large literature on the nature of schizophrenic thought processes, and the *analogy* between primitive savage thinking and the regressed schizophrenic thinking is often striking. To say this, of course, is not necessarily to imply that the savage is diseased; but both he and the schizophrenic in fact do not make use of, or lack, the logic, the concept of causality and the capacity for abstract thought of the normal educated modern man.

PRONENESS TO CONFLICT

Having seen how standards of normality differ from one culture to another, and how cultural conditions can influence the form and incidence of disease, we may now proceed to a more detailed consideration of the nature of 'unhealthy' situations in various cultures.

Every cultural group contains within itself possibilities of mental conflict. While Freud holds the view that increasing civilisation, since it is associated with various prohibitions, must be attended by discontent and mental conflict, he also points out that of the three sources of human suffering – that from our body, from the environment, and from our relations with other men – the most painful is the last[39] (p. 28). It would be a mistake to think that 'uncivilised cultures are, therefore, necessarily simple in their interpersonal relationship and that this source of pain is in them negligible.

Malinowski's study of the Trobriand and the Amphlett Islanders[40] has demonstrated that comparatively undeveloped societies may yet show a distinct difference in the incidence of psychoneurotic illness among them. Both these peoples are of similar race and language. The former have generally a loose morality, with their children permitted a great deal of sexual experimentation, but the latter neither permit pre-nuptial inter-course, nor have they institutions to maintain what might be termed sexual license. Malinowski observed that the former people showed little in the way of neurasthenia, tic, or hysteria, compared with the latter.

Certain social customs and institutions serve to relieve accumulated anxiety, or prevent anxiety from accumulating, by making possible the expression of biological drives. Such are the cultivation of games of aggression, like boxing or wrestling, the toleration of adolescent sex-play, of organised prostitution, and of the orgy in various forms. Here we may also mention the use of intoxicants and other drugs like opium, which help to produce a withdrawal from the harshness of reality and soften the pain of emotional conflict.

That the above factors have an influence on the occurrence of psychological illness there can be little doubt; but probably a rather more significant and important factor is the nature of the prevailing parental attitudes towards the infant, forming as they do the psychological environment of the latter. The Freudians place much emphasis on the effect on character and personality of early upbringing in such matters as control of urination and defaecation, breast-feeding and opportunity for the expression of early aggressiveness. The work of psychoanalytically orientated anthropologists in interpreting the character-structure of various peoples is as interesting as it is important; such observations have been made on the Chinese by Weston La Barre[41].

In advanced societies it has been pointed out that the stability of inter-parental and parent–child relationships are a more important factor in maintaining mental health than is economic well-being. This is the conclusion of W. L. Neutstatter after studying fifty poor families in London[42] (p. 37, f.), although some American work appears to show that mental disease is definitely related to poverty [e.g.[43]]. There are many fallacies in statistical studies of the latter kind, but it seems true, on theoretical ground, that wealth must help to relieve conflict that is not strictly intra-psychic, since it enables one to satisfy one's needs, and execute one's pleasures.

An important aspect of the problem of proneness to conflict is the nature of the personality of the average individual in different societies. The 'previous personality' determines not only the liability to neurotic or psychotic breakdown, but also the nature of the psychiatric reaction that ensues when disease sets in. Little or nothing is known of the relation of the prepsychotic personality to mental disease in cultures other than the Euro-American, but it appears that among Chinese schizophrenics the schizothymic type of temperament, identified by means of Kretschmer's self-rating scale, is common, as is the case with Western schizophrenics[35]. In regard to the milder psychoneurotic complaints and personality inadequacies in northern Chinese, these have been the subject of study by B. Dai, who analysed the case histories of 2,400 Peking patients, and concluded that such abnormalities arose on a basis of conflict between the immediate social environment and the personality organisation, which had been largely moulded by the individual's conception of himself in early life ([44]; also [45]). In this connection we might also note the approach of L. K. Tao, who attempts to relate such Chinese traits as stubbornness, dependence, lack of power of organisation, and 'suppression of the personality' to the peculiar stability and influence of the family institution in China[46]. We may disagree with his delineation of Chinese character, but his method of analysis is not necessarily a sterile one. The structure of the family, the attitudes of parents to children, and the child's conception of his own self are inextricably mixed.

Several workers have obtained interesting results by making comparative studies of the incidence of neuroticism, in the sense of the frequency of occurrence of neurotic traits, in Chinese and Americans. Making use of Thurstone's Neurotic Inventory, S. K. Chou and C. Y. Mi[47] found that Chinese students were 'more neurotic' than American students. A similar conclusion was arrived at by E. Shen, using the Bernreuter Personality Inventory[48]. These results can only be of suggestive value, since traits considered neurotic or deviant in America may not be so regarded in China, and, moreover, in translating the inventories, changes in nuance and emphasis might have been introduced. However, T. Pai *et al.*[49] have shown by the criterion of internal consistency that the most diagnostic items in the Thurstone inventory are the same for both Chinese and Americans, thus indicating that it may be useful among the former. Even if the Chinese show a higher neurotic score, it may mean, not that the race of society is less healthy, but that the lack of psychiatric services allow[s] more individuals to remain neurotic than need be.

CONCLUSION

It clearly emerges from the extension of the psychiatrist's interest to cultures other than his own that there are basic pathological processes to be found in insanity everywhere; processes such as the fragmentation and regression in schizophrenia, to be found in many aspects of the patient's thought and behaviour; the primary changes in mood and in tempo of psychophysiological functioning of the affective reactions; and the psychological and physiological defects and deficiencies of the organic reactions. These are seen everywhere, but the detailed symptomatology of these broad syndromes may vary from one culture to another, reflecting as they do prevailing beliefs, customs, interests and conflicts.

We discern, on turning our attention to the psychoneuroses, all the complexities of the interaction of the individual with his environment. Personality is shaped by cultural environment, and in each culture one or more types of personality may be allowed freer and more healthy expression. Cultures vary in the amount of latitude they allow for change from one sex role to another, and the same applies to roles identified by age, occupation or class. Moreover, there are great variations in the opportunities allowed for the satisfaction of fundamental drives. Man is to a remarkable extent pliable, and 'human nature' is not the clear-cut and easily delineated entity it is commonly thought to be.

We obtain a clearer view of the nature of abnormality, and see how much it is dependent on cultural standards. The form of behaviour in Euro-American cultures maybe conveniently used for comparison with behaviour elsewhere in order to enlarge our understanding of them all, but they are neither necessarily the commonest nor the most healthy, and they do not possess the finality that might come, for instance, from basically biological norms.

I am indebted to Dr the Hon. I. Newton, Director of Medical Services, Hong Kong, for permission to publish this paper.

REFERENCES

1. Mead, M. (1948) *Lancet*, 21.
2. Ackerknecht, E. H. (1943) *Bull. Hist. of Med.*, 14: 30.
3. Kraepelin, E. (1904) *Zentralbl. f. Nervenheilk. u. psychiat.*, 27: 433.
4. Jaspers, K. (1928) *Allgeneriae Psychopathologie.* (French translation, Paris).
5. Malinowski, B. (1938) *Human Affairs* ed. R. B. Cattell, London.
6. Seligman, C. G. (1935) *Psychology and Modern Problems*, ed. J. A. Hadfield, London.
7. Wegrocki, H. J. (1939) *J. Abnorm. and Social Psychol.*, 34: 166.
8. Delisle Burns, C. (1933) *The Horizons of Experience.* London.
9. Osterreich, K. (1930) *Possession, Demoniacal and Other.* London.
10. Yandell, D. W. (1881) *Brain*, 4: 339.
11. Schuler, E. A. and Parenton, U. J. (1943) *J. Social Psychol.*, 17: 221.
12. Bychowski, G. (1943) *J. Nerv. and Ment. Dis.*, 97: 310.
13. Wulfften-Palthe, P. M. van (1936) *Text-book of Tropical Medicine*, by C. D. de Langen and A. Lichtenstein. Batavia.
14. ibid., op. cit., chapter on latah.
15. Winiarz, W. and Wielawski, J. (1936) *Psychoanal. Rev.* 23: 181.
16. Czaplicka, M. A. (1914) *Aboriginal Siberia.* Oxford, 309 f.
17. Repond, A. (1940) *Ann. Méd-Psychol.*, 98: 311.
18. Musgrave, W. E. and Sison, A. G. (1910) *Philippine J. Sc.*, 5: 335 (B).

19. Matoli, A. (1937) *Gior. Ital. de Clin. Trop.*, 1: 20.
20. Scheube, B. (1903) *Diseases of Warm Countries*, 3rd edn. London, 514 f.
21. Kraepelin, E. (1909) *Psychiatrie*, Bd I. 8th edn.
22. Beard (1880) *J. Nerv. Ment. Dis.*, 7: 487.
23. Brill, A. A. (1913) *J. Nerv. Ment. Dis.*, 40: 518.
24. Howard, R. (1910) *J. Trop. Med.*, 13: 269.
25. Loon, F. H. G. van (1927) *J. Abnorm. Psychol.*, 21: 434.
26. Carothers, J. C. (1947) *J. Ment. Sci.*, 93: 549.
27. Irving Hallowell, A. (1934) *J. Abnorm. and Social Psychol.*, 29: I.
28. Klineberg, O. (1935) *Race Differences.* New York.
29. Benedict, R. F. (1934) *J. Genet. Psychol.*, 10: 59.
30. Fortune, R. (1932) *The Sorcerers of Dobu.* London.
31. Cannon, W. B. (1942) *Amer. Anthrop.*, 44: 169.
32. Jung, C. G. and Welhelm, R. (1942) *The Secret of the Golden Flower.* London.
33. Irving Hallowell, A. (1938) *Amer. J. Orthopsychiat.*, 8: 329.
34. Gordon, H. L. (1933) *J. Ment. Sci.*, 79: 712.
35. Kao, C. C., Ting, T. and Hsu, E. H. (1939) *Neuropsychiatry in China*, ed. R. S. Lyman. Peking.
36. Laubscher, B. I. F. (1937) *Sex, Custom and Psychopathology.* London.
37. Storch, A. (1924) *The Primitive, Archaic Forms of Inner Experience and Thought in Schizophrenia.* Washington.
38. Burstin, J. (1935) *Schizophénie et Mentalité Primitive.* Paris.
39. Freud, S. (1946) *Civilization and Its Discontents.* London.
40. Malinowski, B. (1927) *Sex and Repression in Savage Society.*
41. La Barre, Weston 91946) *Psychiatry.* 9: 375.
42. Neustatter, W. L. (1940 *Early Treatment of Nervous and Mental Disorders.* London.
43. Hyde, R. W. and Kingsley, I. U. (1944) *The New England J. Med.*, 231: 543–8.
44. Dai, B. (1941) *Am. Sociol. Rev.*, 16: 680.
45. ibid., (1943) *Asia.* 43: 616.
46. Tao, L. K. (1934) *Essays Presented to C. G. Seligman*, ed. Evans Prichard *et al.* London.
47. Chou, S. K. and Mi, C. Y. (1937) *J. Social Psychol.*, 8: 155.
48. Shen, E. (1936) *J. Social Psychol.*, 7: 471.
49. Pai, T., Sung, S. M. and Hsu, E. H. (1937) *J. Social Psychol.*, 8: 47.

CHAPTER TWELVE

Daru and Bhang (1951)

George M. Carstairs

Carstairs (1917–91), the son of Scottish missionary parents in India, became Professor of Psychiatry at Edinburgh and then first Vice-Chancellor of York University (England). In this paper he deals with a commonplace of the study of psychoactive substance use, indeed of any comparative psychiatry. How much do patterns of psychopathological interest reflect the society in which they are found? Carstairs argues that alcohol, chosen by the Rajput caste, fits well with their valuing of militaristic values, whilst cannabis goes better with the contemplative life followed by the Brahmin priests. Do societies choose their substances, or do substances choose their societies – in other words, are cultural patterns chosen by history, trade, the economics of power and actual psychophysiological property (Douglas 1986, Furst 1972)?

---

1 THE PROBLEM

Throughout the year 1951 the writer of this article was engaged in a field study which involved his living in intimate daily contact with the inhabitants of a large village in the State of Rajasthan, in northern India. In the course of that year, he got to know this community fairly well; and he was struck by one unexpected aspect of the caste system which permeates Hindu society. This was the violent antithesis shown in the community's attitudes toward the two most prevalent forms of intoxication – that caused by drinking *daru*, a potent distilled alcohol derived from the flowers of the mahwa tree (*Bassia latifundia*) and that due to *bhang*, which is the local name for an infusion of the leaves and stems of Indian hemp (*Cannabis indica*) which is readily cultivable in this region. Each had its partisans, and each decried the other faction.

It may be noted, in passing, that these were not the only forms of *nasha*, or intoxication, recognised. Villagers frequently spoke of the nasha caused by drinking cups of sickly-sweet tea infused in milk. Some went so far as to blame the break-down of traditional piety on this modern indulgence in 'English tea'. They would also describe the nasha induced by a few puffs from a communally shared cigarette, and of that brought about by an unaccustomed feast of meat. Instances were cited of men who had become

197

addicted to chewing opium; but in recent years this has become so prohibitively expensive as to have dropped out of the picture. It was remembered by the warrior-caste, the Rajputs, one of whom explained that in the old days they would take opium before a battle in order to steady their nerves and to inhibit untimely bowel movements. Another Rajput, of humbler rank, put it more prosaically: 'Yes, they'd issue a lump of opium to every man in those days, and glad to get it. – Might as well enjoy it now – may not be here tomorrow.'

Here in Rajasthan the Rajput caste held a position of social supremacy. It is they who are the *Rajahs*, the rulers. For centuries their semifeudal authority has governed the State, which was divided into a number of kingdoms, each with a hierarchy of subordinate rulers, down to the village *Thakur*, who is a Rajput squire of a few acres. They traditionally justified their wealth and prestige by their willingness to fight in defense of their land and their religion. On the smallest scale, it was to the Thakur and his kinsmen that the ordinary villagers turned for protection against marauding bands, especially in times of famine or of war.

As fighting men, the Rajputs had certain special prerogatives, notably the right to eat meat and drink alcohol. These privileges, as well as their forefathers' bravery in battle, are commemorated in a rich store of poetry and song. The writer recalls many evenings spent listening to minstrels reciting epics of war and of the hunting field, while drummers played and strident women's voices sang with the refrain: *Pi lo, pi lo manna Raja!* (Drink on, drink on, oh King!) His Rajput hosts were careful to point out on such occasions that daru should be taken with circumspection, only in the proper measure (*niyam se*) and with due formality. Yet for all their protestations, 'Oaths are but straw to the fire i' the blood', and a typical Rajput party tends to become boisterous, bawdy and unbridled.

Besides the Rajputs, only the *Sudras* (the artisan castes) and the Untouchables – and not all of them – are accustomed to take meat and alcohol. These lower orders also observe a certain formality in their drinking. Usually they go in a group to the village grogshop, and there the daru is passed from hand to hand in a small brass bowl. Each man, before taking his first drink, lets fall a drop or two and says, '*Jai Matajai!*' – invoking the demon-goddess Kali in her local embodiment. In so doing, they fortify themselves with the knowledge that that great goddess, mother and destroyer in one, relishes a diet of blood and alcohol.

In striking contrast, the members of the other top caste-group in the village, the Brahmins, unequivocally denounce the use of daru. It is, they say, utterly inimical to the religious life – and in matters of religion the Brahmins speak with authority. Certainly begin to devote themselves seriously to religion is always: 'Abhor meat and wine.' Priests and holy men insist that a *darulia* (an alcoholic) is beyond the pale of possible salvation. And yet again and again the writer was able to see respectable Brahmins and holy *Saddhus* who were benignly and conspicuously fuddled with bhang. To his eye, they were drunk as lords – drunk as Rajputs – and yet they would have been mortally offended if the comparison had been drawn, because this form of intoxication they believed to be not only no disgrace, but actually an enhancement of the spiritual life.

It might have been thought that if one form of intoxicant were condemned, so would be the other. In time, however, the writer was able to learn not only the subjective characteristics which distinguish these two states, but also the important cultural values which are associated with their use, and a solution to the riddle began to emerge.

2 DIFFERENT EFFECTS OF DARU AND BHANG INTOXICATION

The physiological and psychological effects of the ingestion of alcohol are sufficiently familiar to require no further elaboration. As Ravi Varma[1] has shown, the stages of inebriation have also been described in ancient Sanskrit texts. He quotes the pre-Medieval writer Susruta as distinguishing three phases: first, elation and conviviality with increase in sexual desire; next, a progressive loss of sense of propriety with overactivity and failing coordination; and finally a comatose, dead-drunk state, 'like a felled tree', in which, 'though alive, one is as it were dead'. As will be shown below, the Rajputs were vividly aware of the 'release of sexual and aggressive impulses' which Horton[2] has shown to be the basic role of alcohol in every community which resorts to its use.

The effect of taking *Cannabis indica* in one or other of its preparations is less familiar to occidental readers; and yet it is an intoxicant which is second only to alcohol in the volume of its use, the variety of its recipes, and the profusion of its names. Descriptions of its effect show a number of discrepancies, which may be attributed in part to the varying concentration of the drug in different preparations, and also to the fact that it is often taken in conjunction with other drugs. Thus Porot[3] reports that most North African cannabists are also alcoholics. In the Middle East it is used often in conjunction with an aphrodisiac.

When a Cannabis preparation is taken alone and in moderate strength (as is the case with the village bhang drinkers), Porot describes the following sequence of events: (*a*) A transient euphoria, a rich, lively, internal experience, in which ideas rush through the mind and there is an enormous feeling of superiority, of superhuman clarity of insight. (*b*) Sensory hyperesthesia, and coenesthesias: sights and sounds become unusually vivid and meaningful. (*c*) Distortion of sense of time and space. (*d*) Loss of judgment. (*e*) Exaggeration of affects, both of sympathy and of antipathy. (*f*) The phase of excitement is succeeded by one of placid ecstasy, known to Moslems as *el kif* or 'blessed repose'. The 'will to act' becomes annihilated. (g) After some hours of the trancelike state, sleep supervenes.

As a Frenchman, Porot was interested in the cult of cannabism which was created by a circle of writers and painters in Paris during the 1840s: an intellectual vogue which has enriched medical literature with some vivid accounts of the subjective aspects of the intoxication. This reportage was facilitated by the fact that the condition does not interfere with self-awareness, so that the participants had the sensation of being onlookers at the same time as actors in the scene. As Théophile Gautier wrote[4]: 'Je voyais mes camarades à certains instants, mais défigurés, moitié hommes, noitié plantes, avec des airs pensifs d'ibis debout sur une patte l'autruche.'

But Gautier, as Guilly[5] has pointed out in a recent essay on the 'Club des Hachischins', was not altogether a reliable witness. His account was frankly embellished, designed to exaggerate the bizarre and the orgiastic elements of the situation; and in so doing he illustrates a finding of his contemporary, Baudelaire, who also was fascinated by the effects of the drug and carried his experiments to extreme lengths. Baudelaire[6] pointed out that Cannabis affected people differently according to their degree of intellectual refinement. He distinguished 'spiritual' from merely material or brutish intoxication; and to this one can add that the quality of the intoxication can be influenced by the expectations with which the subject enters into it. For example, Tunisian addicts would smoke their *takrouri* in a quiet room, scented and decorated with flowers and with erotic prints calculated to stimulate hallucinations proper to their self-induced anticipation of paradise.

Frivolous though his interest was, Gautier seems to have tasted enough of the drug to have experienced the state of lethargic ecstasy – in Baudelaire's words, 'l'apothéose de l'Homme-Dieu' – which he described as follows: 'Je ne sentais plus mon corps; les liens de la matière et de l'esprit étaient déliés; je me mouvais par ma seule volonté dans un milieu qui n'offrait pas de résistance. ... Rien de matériel ne se mêlait à cette extase: aucun désir terrestre n'en altérait la pureté....'

There have been other European experimenters who have described the effects of cannabism but none who have been outspoken in its praise. Walter de la Mare[7] wrote that, 'Like opium, it induces an extravagant sense of isolation', and he went on to quote the experience of his friend Redwood Anderson, who reported on the effect of taking small doses of the drug. He was able to describe the euphoria, the rush of ideas and the intense subjective feelings of awareness and heightened significance of all his perceptions; but he was not seduced by this near-ecstasy, rather struggling to resist the weakening of voluntary control and to repudiate these illusions of godlike intuition.

In this he was at one with Baudelaire, who indulged very profoundly in this as in other forms of intoxication and, in the end, like a true Westerner, protested against any drug which would hamper the exercise of free, individual assertion and volition. He wrote: 'Je ne comprends pas pourquoi l'homme rationnel et spiritual se sert de moyens artificiels pour arriver à la béatitude poétique, puisque l'enthousiasme et la volonté suffisent pour l'élever à une existence supra-naturelle. Les grands poètes, les philosophes, les prophétes sont des êtres qui, par le pur et libre exercice de leur volonté, parviennent à un état où ils sont à la fois cause et effet, sujet et objet, magnétiseur et somnambule.'

It is necessary to refer at length to these subjective experiences because, although to the superficial observer the behavior of the bhang drinker might seem not unlike that of an alcoholic (except that the progress of intoxication is at first delayed, for up to 90 minutes, and then proceeds by rapid stages to a profound stupor), the subject's inner experiences are very different. To quote an early medical investigator, Hesnard[8]: 'Ses symptomes en sont bien plus riches pour celui qui l'éprouve que pour l'observateur.' This was convincingly demonstrated to the present writer when he was prevailed upon to share in the Brahmin group's potations on two occasions. He experienced the time distortion, the tumbling rush of ideas, the intensified significance of sights, sounds and tastes and, more strongly than anything else, the feeling of existing on two planes at once. His body sat or lay in a state of voluptuous indifference to its surroundings, while consciousness alternated between a timeless trancelike state and a painful struggle to keep awake, to keep on observing, and acting (in this case, to keep on writing down notes on his introspective experiences). It became clear to him, in retrospect, that throughout the intoxication of his bias of personality, and perhaps his less conscious fears of surrendering to a dreamlike state, resisted the somatic pull of the drug; and yet he was able to enter sufficiently into the fringe of the real ecstasy to quicken his future appreciation of what the experience meant to those who welcomed and valued it.

Hitherto, it will be noted, the state induced by bhang has been discussed in the terms of reference used by Western observers. The writer's own experience confirmed their clinical accounts, with emphasis on feelings of detachment, of extreme introspection, of the loss of volition coupled with a dreamlike impression of heightened reality. Moreover, the recognition of his own fear and repudiation of the state opened his eyes to two possibilities: (*a*) that other Western observers might have shared his own reluctance, if not inability, fully to submit to this intoxication; and (*b*) that to Hindus, with their different cultural heritage and personality bias, the experience might represent something different, at once less frightening and more congenial. It was with this in mind that he reviewed his notes of some hundreds of conversations with villagers, in order to consider what were their associations to daru and to bhang respectively.

It should be pointed out that this discussion concerns the use rather than the abuse of these intoxicants. There were many habitual drinkers of both, and instances of alcoholic delirium were described by several Rajputs, though not witnessed by the writer. The only Brahmin who could be called an addict to bhang in the strict sense was also an opium eater, and at 75 was one of the oldest men in the village. It is a vexed question as to whether cannabism, when carried to extremes, incites to crimes of violence, as Wolff[9], Dhunjibhoy[10] and Porot[3] assert, or whether, as Bromberg and Rodgers[11] and Wallace[12] have shown in careful statistical this association is not supported by the facts. The present writer's study of the literature supports the view that crime (even the berserk attacks on the Crusaders by the hashish-inspired followers of the Mohammedan Old Man of the Mountains, from which the word assassin is said to be derived) is, like the voluptuous daydreams of the Tunisians, merely one of the ends which cannabism can be made to serve during its brief phase of excitement, and not a necessary consequence of taking the drug. In this village, at any rate, there were no instances of crimes attributable to the drinking of bhang, nor was there any evidence to support the suggestion of Dhunjibhoy, among others, that it gives rise to a characteristic psychosis. It remains open to proof whether such cases are not, as Mayer-Gross[13] maintains, simply schizophrenic illnesses occurring in a Cannabis-taking population.

3 VILLAGERS' ASSOCIATIONS TO DARU AND BHANG

In the following series of quotations from a number of villagers' conversations, it will be helpful to bear in mind that Rajputs are distinguished by the addition of the title *Singh* (lion) to their name; among the Brahmins, a common second name is *Lal* (red, the auspicious color). For the sake of clarity all Brahmin names have been transcribed to conform to this rule.

The first obvious difference to emerge is that while the Brahmins are unanimous in their detestation of daru, the Rajputs do not present a united front in its defense. 'Some Rajputs', explained Himat Singh, 'those who are worshippers of God, they do not eat meat or drink wine – that is the first thing for them to give up. Wine spoils men's mind: some swear and give abuse, which is inimical to holiness.' Such Rajputs, however, are few and far between: 'The rest, they eat, drink and remain *must*.'[4]

Many Rajputs prided themselves on drinking with discrimination, a fixed measure every day. Thus Nahar Singh: 'My father used to drink a fixed quantity of daru, from a small measure, every night. It was his niyam, his rule.' A young man called Ragunath Singh was emphatic in asserting the warlike traditions of his caste, and their need for meat and drink: 'Panthers and tigers don't eat grass – and that's what Rajputs are like, a carnivorous race.' He also, however, stressed that liquor was a dangerous ally: 'If you take it to excess it destroys your semen, the good stuff, the strength of your body – but taken in right measure it builds it up.'

Gambhir Singh mentioned that his father, a former Inspector of Police, used to allow himself a generous measure every day: 'It helped him in his work, made him fierce and bold, ready to beat people when that was needed.'

This stress on restraint, and on small measures, soon tended to be forgotten in the course of an evening of Rajput hospitality, when glass after glass was filled and emptied at a draught. In his cups, Amar Singh used to boast of his ungovernable temper, of men he killed in the heat of anger, of his sexual prowess with prostitutes. His friend Gordhan Singh chipped in with a description of a typical Rajput celebration: 'They sit drinking heartily till they are senseless, and then they talk loudly and make fools of themselves, and spill their food down the front of their shirts, and shout to the dancing girls; and some of them pass out altogether – oh, it's a fine sight to see, it's good fun.'

The former Ruler of the village and of the surrounding principality expressed conflicting views on daru. On the one hand, he aspired to gain a 'spiritual rise' through the practice of prayers and austerities, and this necessitated a strict rationing of his customary indulgence in alcohol. Quite often, however, something would happen to interrupt his abstemious intensions, and on such a day his eloquence in praise of wine was noticeably stimulated: 'Red eyes are thought by us Rajputs to be very beautiful. They are the sign of lust. Those who have the good fortune to have red lines in the eyes, they are thought to be very lusty. Rajputs are very lusty, Sahib. It is because of their meat and drink: it makes them so that they have to have their lust, poor fellows.' At this point he began to quote verses in praise of wine: 'It makes the eyes red, it keeps the pleasure going between the pair, the husband and wife: how shall I praise you enough, oh twice-distilled!' And again: 'In time of war, when the drum beats, only opium and daru drive out fear.'

On another occasion, the Ruler quoted a ribald couplet to the effect that without meat all food is grass, and without daru even Ganges water has no virtue. But this blasphemy alarmed him into a momentary sobriety. He hastily repudiated the verse, but a few minutes later he was exuberantly describing the scene at a wealthy Rajput's wedding party: 'They will be sitting drinking far into the night, with dancing girls entertaining them. They will call the dancing girl to sit on their lap, then they will get stirred and take her into a room and bar the doors; and the others will beat upon the door and say, "Eh, Rao Sahib, we also want to see this girl." Poor girl, where can she go, all doors are locked! Enjoy till morning, she must do what you want.'

The Ruler's younger brother was emphatically not one of those Rajputs who renounced their pleasure in alcohol in the interests of religion: 'Sahib, I am not interested in these things. These religious matters, usually one begins to be interested in them after the age of fifty.'

And before then?

'Before then, Sahib, eat, drink and make merry.'

Rajputs not infrequently referred to bhang, but never with strong feelings either of approval or condemnation. It is mentioned as a refreshment given to guests who arrive after a long journey. An elderly retainer called Anop Singh said: 'We are not in the habit of drinking bhang, though we'll take it if it comes our way. Sometimes holy men come, and they are great ones for bhang, so you have to join them if they invite you, and have some too.' On one occasion the writer found a young Rajput landowner called Vijay Singh profoundly fuddled with a large dose of bhang which had been given to him, without his knowledge, in a spiced sweetmeat: 'I didn't know I was eating bhang or I wouldn't have taken it – it's not a thing I like. It makes you very sleepy and turns your throat dry. I don't like it, it makes you quite useless, unable to do anything. Daru is not like that: you get drunk but you can still carry on.'

The Brahmins, on the other hand, were quite unanimous in reviling daru and all those who indulged in it. They described it as foul, polluting, carnal, and destructive to that spark of Godhead which every man carries within him. As Shankar Lal put it: 'The result of eating meat and drinking liquor is that you get filled with passion, rage – and then what happens? The spirit of God flies out from you.'

The Ruler's own attempt to reconcile religious devotions with a measure of indulgence in alcohol was rejected with contumely by Mohan Lala, a scholarly teacher: 'He is all wrong: he is a bogus lecher. Always busy with wine and women, how can he find his way along this stony and thorny path?'

In their references to the use of bhang, the Brahmins were matter-of-fact rather than lyrical. 'It gives good *bhakti*', said Shankar Lal: 'You get a very good bhakti with bhang.' He went on to define bhakti as the sort of devotional act which consists in emptying the mind of all worldly distractions and thinking only of God. The 'arrived' devotee is able to keep his thoughts from straying off onto trivial or lustful topics; in his impersonal trance he becomes oblivious to mundane concerns so that you 'could hit him in the face with shoes a hundred times, and he would remain unmoved' (Mohan Lal).

Brahmin informants made many references to a nearby pilgrimage center presided over by a very influential priest. Both he and his predecessors were described, with admiration, as being mighty drinkers of bhang and heroic in the depth of their devotional trances. The chief object of worship at this place was an ancient phallic symbol of black stone, representing the God Shiva; and this God in turn was often cited as both a bhang drinker and a paragon of the contemplative life. It is by modeling themselves on his example that religious ascetics practice severe and prolonged austerities, training themselves to withdraw their entire attention from the distraction of the sensible world until they can exist for hours in an oblivious, inward-looking state. The ultimate reward of this asceticism is that the Saddhu is enabled to divest himself of his body (which becomes imperishable, though apparently lifeless) and to pass directly into reunion with the spirit of the universe. (One is reminded of Baudelaire's 'l'apothéose de l'Homme-Dieu'.) Bhang is highly regarded as conducting toward this condition and is taken regularly by most saddhus. In the precincts of the great Shiva temple, the writer frequently encountered holy men, dressed in little more than a coating of sacred ash, who staggered about in the early stages of bhang intoxication. If he addressed them, they would reply only with an elusive smile or with an exclamation like 'Hari, Hari, Hari!' – repeating one of the names of God. Ordinary village Brahmins, who did not aspire to such feats of asceticism, made a practice of devoting some minutes or hours every day to sitting in a state of abstraction and prayer, and in this exercise they found a modicum of bhang to be most helpful.

4 RELEVANT THEMES IN HINDU CULTURE PATTERN

Both the Rajput and the Brahmin castes, at least in this large village, belonged to the economically privileged section of the community. Their male members had all received at least enough education to make them literate in Hindu, and in an unsystematic way had been instructed in the fundamentals of their religion and made familiar with the main features of the Ramayana and Mahabharata epics which illustrate those teachings in a variety of dramatic episodes. Hinduism encompasses so wide a range of practical and philosophical beliefs, of myths and ritual ordinances, and contains so many contradictory elements, that one theologian, after 25 years of study, came to the conclusion that there were only two indispensable features in this religion: reverence of the Brahmin, and worship of the cow[14]. These features are epitomised in the formal greetings exchanged by Rajput and Brahmin. The former salutes the priestly caste with, 'I clasp your feet', and the latter replies, 'May you live long and protect the Brahmins and the cows'. In so doing, they acknowledge each other's caste in its respective status of spiritual and temporal primacy.

The fundamental orthodox Hindu beliefs, as Taylor[15] has pointed out in an analysis drawn from study of a community in an area contiguous with Rajasthan, stem from the concepts of *karma* (predestined lot), of the cycle of rebirth, and of *dharma* (right conduct), observance of which leads to promotion in one's next rebirth and ultimately to the goal of all human endeavor, which is *moksh*, or liberation from the cycle of reincarnation altogether. Socioeconomic relationships are accepted as inevitable, as is the hierarchic structure of caste. Indeed, 'the individual's security in this society comes from his acceptance of his insignificant part in a vast pre-ordained scheme: he has little anxiety, because he is not confronted with a variety of choice.' Rajputs and Brahmins are alike in knowing that virtue consists in performing the duties appropriate to that station in life into which one is born, and in minimising one's indulgence in sensual and emotional satisfactions of a private nature. Thus Nahar Sing, a Rajput renowned for his religious zeal, said: 'Those of us who take religion seriously, but have still not wholly renounced the world, we can do it by taking care not to let our affections become too deeply engaged in things of lesser importance. We should do our work, fulfill all our duties, and be affectionate to our families – but all that should be on the surface of our daily lives. Our real souls, deep down, should not be involved in any of these emotional ties. . . .'

Mohan Lal expressed similar views: 'The religious man lives in the world, but apart. He is like a drop of water on a lotus leaf, which moves over its surface but is not absorbed.' His caste-fellow Bhuri Lal described the ideal pattern of 'nonattachment', leading in the end to release: 'Moksh is obtained by purging the self of all carnal appetites and withdrawing from the illusions of this world. A wise man is cool-tempered.' Immediately after this, he went on to talk of sexual morality. Sex, he said, should be strictly controlled. It should be regarded as a duty, and used only for the purpose of perpetuating one's male line. He himself had been afflicted with four daughters before his two sons were born, and then, 'As soon as my second son was born, I gave up having sex. You say I look young? That's because I have practiced celibacy for years.'

This exaltation of asceticism, of self-deprivation, of trying to eliminate one's sensual appetites, is a basic theme. Again and again in Hindu mythology one encounters heroic figures (by no means always virtuous ones) who practice austerities so severe and prolonged that their spiritual power becomes prodigious: the gods themselves beg them to desist and offer to grant anything they ask. Taylor has related this to the absoluteness of paternal authority in the home; the pattern is firmly laid down that one can achieve success and recognition only by self-abnegation and prostration before the all-powerful father figure. A student of Kardiner[16] might be tempted to carry the analogy still farther back, to the Hindu child's wholly indulgent experience at the suckling stage, during which he actually usurps his father's place, because parents are not supposed to sleep together until the child is weaned. In this context, the *tapassya* which constrains even the gods can be seen as a return to the infant's fantasied omnipotence.

The values discussed thus far are held in common by both castes, with the difference that the Brahmins, being at the pinnacle of the spiritual hierarchy, have a special obligation to lead a pious life. More than ordinary men, they must pay constant attention to the fulfilling of religious duties. Their lives are beset with recurring threats of defilement and their days are punctuated with acts of absolution. Among the many forms of self-denial to which they are accustomed are the avoidance of anger or any other unseemly expression of personal feelings; and abstinence from meat and alcohol is a prime essential. They are rewarded by being regarded, simply by virtue of their birth in this high caste, as already quasi divine. Ordinary men address them as *Maharaj*, the greeting given to the gods. As one of them put it: 'Even now, when people see a man is a Brahmin, they pay much respect in comparison to other castes. He is much more closely related to God.'

In this region the Rajputs represent the temporal aristocracy, as the Brahmins do the spiritual. Their caste is one of warriors and landlords. Until the social reforms of 1948, their Rajahs exercised arbitrary and autocractic rule over the innumerable small principalities into which Rajasthan is divided. They owed allegiance in their turn to the Ruler of their State – in the case of this village, to their turn to the Ruler of their State – in the case of this village, to the Maharana of Udaipur. By virtue of their role as warriors, the Rajputs were accorded certain privileged relaxations of the orthodox Hindu rules: in particular, those prohibiting the use of force, the taking of life, the eating of meat and drinking of wine. These all represent violations of basic canons of Hindu dharm, and so they are hedged about with restrictions and formalities in order to minimise their evil effects. Violence is a part of their lives, but they are taught to exercise forbearance, to rebuke an offender twice before chastising him. In warfare they obeyed a code of chivalry not unlike that of the medieval knights. Similarly, the meat of only a few animals is counted fit to eat, and then only of the male of the species; and hence, also, the emphasis on restriction and invariable 'measure' in drinking daru.

The Rajputs find themselves in a curious position. Their social preeminence is due to their role as defenders of religion, and they are as conservative in belief as they are in politics; and yet their own cherished traditions emphasise their deviation from 'right living' in the orthodox Hindu sense. The conflict is heightened by the circumstance that in their caste, even more than in all the others, patriarchal authority is stressed. As the writer has pointed out elsewhere[17], both sons and younger brothers in Rajput families have to learn to defer in utter subservience to their fathers and elder brothers. Whereas in the Brahmin caste this domestic discipline is made tolerable by the fact that it is impersonal, simply a facet of a general obedience to propriety which the elders observe in their turn, among Rajputs it is different. There is a great difference between the status of the head of the family and that of his subordinates. For example, a younger son inherits an estate only one-twentieth the size of that which comes to the first-born. The head of a Rajput family is anything but an impersonal figure. Coached from infancy by a succession of sycophantic retainers, he has an inflated idea of his personal importance, coupled with an often well-founded suspicion that he is surrounded by rivals and enemies. The tensions which arise in such a setting explode from time to time in violent quarrels. Another corollary of the peculiar upbringing of the Rajputs is that they are taught to put great stress on individual bravery and ferocity in the face of danger. The test of real danger is all too seldom met with, but every young Rajput lives with the anxiety that he may not prove adequate to the occasion when it comes. As a result he tends to be boastful, touchy, and readily inclined to assuage his anxieties in the convivial relaxation of a drinking party.

5 DISCUSSION

In her much-quoted study of patterns of drinking in two South American villages, Bunzel[18] remarks, of such sociological appraisals in general: 'It should be borne in mind that each group represents a different problem: it is necessary in each case to find out what role alcohol plays *in that culture*.' She was able to demonstrate two widely differing ways of using alcohol. In Chamula there was little aggression or promiscuity or severity of discipline; there, heavy drinking was indulged in from childhood and was attended with no guilt. In Chichicastenango, on the other hand, she saw a strict paternal authority and an insistence on the repression of aggressive and sexual impulses, which found release in the course of occasional drinking sprees; and these were followed by feelings of severe guilt. The Rajput drinking pattern, obviously, has much in common with the latter.

A more general frame of reference has been given by Horton[2] in his survey of alcohol in primitive societies, which led to his drawing up three basic theorems: (*a*) The drinking of alcohol tends to be accompanied by release of sexual and aggressive impulses. (*b*) The strength of the drinking response in any society tends to vary directly with the level of anxiety in the society. (*c*) The strength of the drinking response tends to vary inversely with the strength of the counteranxiety elicited by painful experiences during and after drinking.

The first of these theorems is abundantly borne out by the behavior of Rajputs in their cups. It is clear also that the presence of socially approved prostitutes and lower-caste servants and dependants enables the carrying out of these impulses in a manner which excites no retribution, and so the third theorem operates in support of their drinking heavily. On the side of restraint is the knowledge that sensual indulgence is an offense against the Hindu code of asceticism; but this code not weigh heavily on most Rajputs.

On Brahmins, on the other hand, the code weighs very heavily indeed, being associated with their fondest claims to superiority over their fellow men. A Brahmin who gets drunk will be outcasted, condemned to associate with the lowest ranks of society. Consequently the threat of this 'counteranxiety' is sufficient to make the drinking of alcohol virtually impossible to Brahmins (at least in the village). There is no reason to suppose, however, that they, any more than the Rajputs, are devoid of anxiety. But the differences in emphasis on individual self-assertion (stressed by Rajput upbringing but constrained by their fiercely authoritarian disciplines) and on the unimportance of personal and sensual experiences (stressed in the Brahmin code) seem to imply that the anxieties of the Rajputs will be more acute while those of the Brahmins will be more diffuse and more readily sublimated in the religious exercises which play such a large part in their adult lives.

Another consideration is raised by Shalloo's[19] analysis of the way in which Jewish cultural values operate to minimise the incidence of alcoholism in their community. In his view, the Jews develop strong familial and communal ties and stress social conformity and conservatism in mores because they are aware of the critical and often hostile scrutiny of the Gentiles among whom they live. He concludes: 'Such an analysis indicated that we are dealing with an "isolated sacred society" as against a Gentile "accessible secular society"?'

In our Indian example, the Brahmins represented a 'sacred society' but not an isolated one. Far from being alien, they represent the ideal religious aspirations of the masses of ordinary Hindus, those who are obliged to 'eat, drink and keep their passions alive', as Shankar Lal once put it. If the Brahmins are abstemious, it is not through an exaggerated fear of the censure of their fellows. On the contrary, their consciousness of their exalted state often makes them high-handed and inconsiderate in their dealings with those of lower caste; and moreover, they are not abstemious. If Horton's theorems hold good for alcoholism, must a new set be constructed to account for cannabism?

The answer which the present writer would suggest to the problem posed at the outset of this paper would be on the following lines: There are alternative ways of dealing with sexual and aggressive impulses besides repressing them and then 'blowing them off' in abreactive drinking bouts in which the superego is temporarily dissolved in alcohol. The way which the Brahmins have selected consists in a playing down of all interpersonal relationships in obedience to a common, impersonal set of rules of Right Behavior. Not only feelings but also appetites are played down, as impediments to the one supreme end of union with God. Significantly, this goal of sublimated effort is often described in terms appropriate to sexual ecstasy, as is the case with the communications of ascetics and mystic in other parts of the world. Whereas the Rajput in his drinking bout knows that he is taking a holiday from his sober concerns, the Brahmin thinks of his intoxication with bhang as a flight not from but toward a more profound contact with reality.

Westerners, like the Rajputs, are committed to a life of action. They are brought up to regard individual achievement as important, and sensual indulgence to be not wholly wrong if it is enjoyed within socially prescribed limits. In spite of the existence among a sophisticated minority of the cult of nonattachment, the principles of *yoga* are unfamiliar to the West, and the experience of surrendering one's powers of volition is felt to be threatening and distasteful – as European experimenters with hashish (and the writer, with bhang) have found. Wolff[9] is, however, too sweeping in suggesting that cannabism is a peculiarly oriental taste. The Rajputs are far from being the only Easterners who dislike it or feel no need of it. Porot has pointed out that Indian hemp could easily be cultivated in the Far East, and yet it is practically unknown to the peoples of China and Japan. La Barre's[20] account of Chinese personality suggests that that people have little inclination to despite the material pleasures of this world; and the Japanese would be the last, one would suppose, to renounce the active life.

On the basis, presumably, of his own religious convictions, Wolff has implied that the ecstatic intuitions experienced through cannabism, far from having any validity, represent a flouting of 'an inviolable moral law'. This is the antithesis of cultural relativism. No one is left in doubt where Wolff takes his stand. Were the present writer to emulate this candor, he would have to say that of the two types of intoxication which he witnessed, and in a measure shared, in this Rajasthan village, he had no doubt that that which was indulged in by the Brahmins was the less socially disruptive, less unseemly, and more in harmony with the highest ideals of their race; and yet so alien to his own personal and cultural pattern of ego defenses, that he much preferred the other. It was a case of *video meliora proboque, deteriora sequor.*

POSTSCRIPT

Since the above article was written, Aldous Huxley[21] has published an eloquent and perceptive account of the experience of mescalin intoxication, which is shown to resemble that induced by bhang. Huxley was particularly struck by two aspects: in the initial stage, by the primordial vividness of visual impressions, in perceiving ordinarily commonplace objects; and in the later stages, by the feeling of superhuman insight into the nature of things, accompanied by a complete detachment both from his own self and from those of his fellow men. He regards mescalin as a 'gratuitous grace' which facilitates the sort of mystical experience which he finds both chastening and rewarding, in much the same way as Brahmins and Saddhus regard bhang as an aid to contemplation. Yet he is unrealistic enough to wish that Americans, and Westerners generally, should take to this drug in preference to alcohol and tobacco. If the thesis of this paper is valid, Westerners have refrained from taking mescalin (which has long been available to them) because its effect does not accord with their desires. Unless there is an unforeseen reversal of their basic values, they are as little likely to follow Huxley's advice as are the Brahmins to abandon bhang in favor of the Rajputs' daru, or vice versa.

SUMMARY

In a village in northern India, members of the two highest caste groups, Rajput and Brahmin, were found to differ in their choice of intoxicant, the one taking alcohol, the other a preparation of *Cannabis indica*. An explanation for this cleavage was sought in their own associations to the two drugs, in the psychological effects of either type of intoxication, and in the different values stressed by each group, both in their personality development and in their ideal patterns of behavior. The cultural uses of alcohol and of Cannabis intoxication are discussed in the light of this illustration.

INTRODUCTION: REFERENCES

Douglas, M. (ed.) (1988) *Constructive Drinking: Perspectives on Drink from Anthropology*. Cambridge: Cambridge University Press.
Furst, P. T. (ed.) (1972) *Flesh of the Gods: The Ritual Use of Hallucinogens*. London: Allen & Unwin.

REFERENCES

1. Ravi Varma, L. A., 'Alcoholism in Ayurveda', *Quart. J. Stud. Alc.*, 11 (1950): 484–91.
2. Horton, D., 'The Functions of alcohol in primitive societies: a cross-cultural study', *Quart. J. Stud. Alc.*, 4 (1943): 199–320.
3. Porot, A., 'Le cannabisme (haschich – kif – chira – marihuana)', *Ann. med. psychol.*, 100(1) (1942): 1–24.
4. Gautier, T., *Le club des hachischins*, paris: 1846.

5. Guilly, P., 'Le club de hachischins', *Encéphale* 39 (1950): 175–85.
6. Baudelaire, C. P., *Les paradis artificiels, opium et haschisch.* Paris: 1860.
7. De La Mare, W. J., *Desert Islands.* London: 1924.
8. Hesnard, A., 'Note sur les fumeurs de chanvre en Orient', *Encéphale*, 2 (1912): 40–6.
9. Wolff, P. O., 'Problems of drug addiction in South America', *Brit. J. Addiction,* 46 (1949): 66–78.
10. Dhunjibhoy, J. E., 'A brief résumé of the types of insanity commonly met with in India, with a full description of "Indian hemp insanity" peculiar to the country', *J. Ment. Sci.,* 76 (1930): 254–64.
11. Bromberg, W. and Rodgers, T. C., 'Marihuana and aggressive crime (in naval service)', *Amer. J. Psychiat.,* 102 (1946): 825–7.
12. New York City, Mayor's Committee of Marthuana (Wallace, G. B., Chairman), *The Marihuana Problem in the City of New York: Sociological, Medical, Psychological and Pharmacological Studies.* New York: Cattell, 1944.
13. Mayer-Gross, W., 'Die Auslösung durch seelische und körperliche Schädigungen'. In O. Bumke (ed.) *Handbuch der Geisteskrankheiten,* Vol. 9, spec. pt 5, pp. 112–34, 1932.
14. Carstairs, G., *The Hindu.* Edinburgh: 1926.
15. Taylor, W. S., 'Basic personality in orthodox Hindu culture patterns', *J. Abnorm. Soc. Psychol.,* 43 (1948): 3–12.
16. Kardiner, A., *The Psychological Frontiers of Society.* New York: Columbia University Press, 1945.
17. Carstairs, G. M., 'The case of Thakur Khuman Singh: a culture-conditioned crime', *Brit. J. Delinq.,* 4 (1953): 14–25.
18. Bunzel, R., 'Role of alcoholism in two Central American cultures', *Psychiatry,* 3 (1940): 361–87.
19. Shalloo, J. P., 'Some cultural factors in the etiology of alcoholism', *Quart. J. Stud. Alc.,* 2 (1941): 464–78.
20. La Barre, W., 'Some observations on character structure in the Orient. *II.* The Chinese', *Psychiatry,* 9 (1946): 215–37.
21. Huxley, A., *The Doors of Perception.* New York: Harper, 1954.

CHAPTER THIRTEEN

Normal and Abnormal (1956)

George Devereux

We have referred in the Introduction to the debate between Ackerknecht and Devereux. Devereux was a French-Hungarian anthropologist and psychoanalyst working in the United States (he was later professor at the Ecole des Hautes Etudes in Sciences Sociales). Devereux worked particularly among the Mohave of the Great Plain, but is known for his theoretical work on 'ethnopsychiatry' (Devereux 1961: he took the term from the Haitian Louis Mars). We have given his paper at length for its sophisticated psychodynamic of how we might evaluate the normality or otherwise of individuals, without recourse to the criteria of Western hospital psychiatry. His discussion of the shaman (inspirational and prophetic healer) may be faulted for his consideration of a unitary psychopathology; shamans in many situations have been found to be not so conspicuously abnormal whether in local or psychiatric terms. Similarly, his collecting together of 'ethnic disorders' (culture-bound syndromes) suggests more common ground between them than we would now generally allow. Nevertheless, this paper is a classic for first considering cultural psychiatry as a unified area, for its consideration of social change and for its incorporation of archaic European material.

PREFACE TO THE AMERICAN EDITION

The present volume contains a representative sample of my principal papers on the theory, methodology, and technique of a culturally nonrelativistic psychoanalytic ethnopsychiatry. Though these studies do not cover all aspects of this still relatively new discipline, they discuss enough of the salient features of *one* self-consistent operational theory of ethnopsychiatry to permit its – as yet not wholly foreseeable – further elaboration in one system-adequate manner only.

Though my system of ethnopsychiatry was developed conjointly with a specific epistemology (Devereux 1967a) and a complementaristic general theory and methodology (Devereux 1970 and 1978a) of the sciences of man over a period of several decades, the scheme here presented is wholly self-contained. It suffices to specify that the principle of complementarity presupposes the possibility of at least one (total/partial) psychological and one (total/partial) sociocultural explanation, defines the relationship between the two explanations, and permits the full scientific exploitation of the phenomena under consideration. It also abolishes the temptation to push any type of explanation beyond the point where the law of diminishing returns begins to operate. Above all, it explicitly admits the possibility and the legitimacy of formulating equally satisfactory alternative explanatory schemes.

Precisely because this book analyses disorder and delusion, it was necessary to follow scrupulously Lagrange's advice, 'Seek simplicity, but distrust it!' I have therefore endeavoured to bring to light the logic that subtends seemingly chaotic phenomena without trying to juggle out of sight what I still fail to comprehend. Unlike ancient oracles (Devereux 1968b) and fashionable profundity-mongers, I did not attempt to substitute for a meaningful, though as yet incomprehensible, reality a purely verbal rebus inherently devoid of sense.

Nearly all of the studies contained in this volume were originally written, and first published, in English.[1] Most of them appeared as journal articles, but some were contributions to multiauthored volumes. Revised and in some cases further expanded versions of these texts, translated into French, were published as a book, *Essais d'ethnopsychiatrie générale*, by Gallimard in 1970 (reprinted in 1973 and 1977). This French version was translated into Spanish (1973), German (1974), and Italian (1978) and has now been translated from French back into English, with a few further minor improvements, so that the present version is now the final one.[2]

The publication of this book in French marked a decisive turn of the tide in my professional life. I can only hope that its reception in the English-speaking world will be comparable to its reception elsewhere.

Professor Alain Besançon (Ecole des Hautes Etudes en Sciences Sociales), Mr Henri Gobard (Université de Paris VIII), and the late Professor Roger Bastide (Sorbonne) (who also wrote a Preface, both generous and insightful, for the original French edition) urged me to assemble these essays into a volume, whose publication was made possible by Professor Pierre Nogra (Ecole des Haute Etudes), general editor of the Gallimard series Bibliothèque des Sciences Humaines.

Ralph W. Nicholas and Raymond D. Fogelson (both of the University of Chicago brought this book to the attention of the University of Chicago Press.

Small grants from the National Institute of Mental Health (M-1669) and the Society for the Study of Human Ecology facilitated the writing of certain of the chapters.

Ms. Basia Miller Gulati translated with great care seven of the chapters (1, 2, 3, 5, 6, 9, and 15) and scrupulously took into account all my suggestions and preferences. I myself retranslated the remaining chapters into English.

In my Acknowledgments I list the copyright-holders of the first versions of the articles contained in this volume, which were reproduced with their permission in a revised form in the French edition and are further revised here.

George Devereux

ACKNOWLEDGMENTS

The acknowledgments below appeared in the French edition of this work. All of the essays have beeen further revised for the present publication.

Most of Chapter 1 appeared first in an article entitled 'Normal and abnormal' in J. Casagrande and T. Galwin (eds) *Some Uses of Anthropology, Theoretical and Applied* (Washington, DC:, 1956); it is reproduced with the permission of the Anthropological Society of Washington, DC. A few passages appeared first in a note entitled 'Shamans as neurotics', *American Anthropologist*, 63 (1961): 1088–90; they are reproduced with the permission of the American Anthropological Association. ...

INTRODUCTION

Each science has its key concept, or pair of key concepts, whose precise definition is the principal problem of that science and whose analysis is the best introduction to that field of inquiry. Thus, the key concept of anthropology is 'culture', and anyone who understands it may be said to possess the open sesame of this science. If, in addition, he uses it as a counterfoil to the concept 'society', he will soon strike an almost inexhaustible vein of productive research problems. The paired concepts 'normal' and 'abnormal' are the key concepts of psychiatry, and the determination of the exact locus of the boundary between them is the crucial problem of psychiatry, regardless of whether one views psychiatry as a 'pure' or as an 'applied' science. Yet, whereas anthropologists write a great deal about their key concept, the problem of what is 'normal' and what is 'abnormal' has received relatively little systematic attention in recent psychiatric literature. This is unfortunate, because the problem is still far from being satisfactorily solved.

Psychiatric anthropology, as a pluridisciplinary science must concern itself with the key concepts and key problems of both anthropology and psychiatry. It cannot simply borrow psychiatric techniques of investigation and explanation. Indeed, from the methodological point of view, one must differentiate between the *borrowing of techniques* and the complementaristic *conceptual cross-fertilisation* of sciences (Devereux 1945 [1978a, Chap. 4], 1961b [1978a, Chap. 5], 1967c). Truly pluridisciplinary sciences are characterised by this kind of conceptual cross-fertilisation – the concepts involved being those that are also the key problems of the several component sciences.

The autonomous science of ethnopsychiatry – that is, of psychiatric anthropology or anthropological psychiatry, the label chosen depending on the *use* to which this pluridisciplinary 'pure' science is put – must therefore have as its key problem the coordination of the concept of 'culture' with the paired concepts 'normal' and 'abnormal'. It must be brought to bear, first of all, on the problem of determining the exact locus of the boundary between 'normal' and 'abnormal'. This is the principal objective of the present chapter.

ADJUSTMENT AND SUBLIMATION

Since the problem of adjustment – which is not a concept of psychiatry, let it be said – has been thoroughly discussed elsewhere (Devereux 1939a), I shall content myself here with mentioning a few cases that show the logical flaw inherent in this diagnostic approach.

When E. H. Ackerknecht (1943) claims that the shaman, although objectively neurotic ('heteropathological') is nevertheless 'autonormal' to the extent that he is perfectly adjusted, he reduces the problem of diagnosis to testing degrees of adjustment. His reasoning leads to vicious circles, such as the following: 'In April 1945 the task of a German psychiatrist was completed the day his patient joined the Nazi party. In May 1945 it was finished the day he joined, if he lived in Frankfurt-am-Main, the Christian Democrat party, and, if he lived in Frankfurt-an-der-Oder, the Communist party' (Devereux 1951a [consult the 2nd rev. edn., 1969]). This thesis disregards the existence of societies so 'sick' that, in order to adjust to them, one has to be very sick indeed (Devereux 1939a). I hasten to add that I am not echoing here anything so controversial as Benedict's psychiatric diagnosis of different cultures (Benedict 1934[a]). What I have in mind is nothing more unusual than the matters discussed in any standard course in social pathology. Broadly speaking, there exist societies so enmeshed in a vicious circle that everything they do to save themselves only causes them to sink deeper into the quicksand. The Tonkawa, as Linton used to say, clung so tenaciously to cannibalism that finally most of their neighbors waged a war of extermination against them. Likewise, in seeking to uproot imaginary 'internal enemies' and to avoid encirclement, Germany created (real) enemies for itself on the inside and brought into being a worldwide alliance pledged to destroy Nazism (Devereux 1955a).

The social self-destructiveness of the South, which undermines the mental health of both its 'well-adjusted' whites and its Negroes, has been described by Dollard (1937). The case of Sparta, analysed elsewhere (Devereux 1965a), is similar in many respects. Also, the theory that makes adjustment the criterion of sanity is admittedly indefensible in view of Fromm's (1941) cogent distinction between healthy adjustment and sadomasochistic conformism. The crux of the matter is that there is a fairly simple distinction to be made between external (overt) and internal adjustment (Devereux 1939a). Some degree of overt adjustment is necessary for survival in any society. In a healthy society, the normal person is, in addition, in the fortunate position of being able to introject the norms of his group in the form of a subsidiary ego ideal. In a sick society, he cannot do so without becoming neurotic, if not worse (Devereux 1939a). On the other hand, if a man is rational enough to adjust overtly to a sick society *without also introjecting its norms*, he often experiences so much discomfort and feels so isolated that he eventually escapes for this 'double life', either by engaging in an ill-timed and therefore self-destructive rebellion or else by *forcing* himself to accept basically uncongenial norms and becoming a fanatic as a defensive reaction.

From a psychiatric point of view the valid criteria for normality are absolute, that is, they are independent of the norms of any given culture or society but are identical with the criteria for Culture as a universal human phenomenon.[1] Emotional maturity, a sense of reality, rationality, and the ability to sublimate can certainly contribute to the individual's adjustment in a healthy society and insure survival in a pathological one; they are nevertheless logically independent of adjustment itself.[2]

After these introductory remarks, I am ready to embark on a discussion of the problem of normality and abnormality in terms of the key *concept* of anthropology, which is Culture, and the key *problem* of psychiatry, which is the boundary between normality and abnormality.

I shall begin by defining as precisely as possible the aspects of the unconscious that are located within the framework of my own research. I shall examine the problem of trauma, not as a function of the absolute intensity of stress, but as a function of the availability of defenses for use in stress situations (Devereux 1966b [1978a, Chap. 2]).

TWO TYPES OF UNCONSCIOUS

The unconscious is composed of two elements: that which never was conscious – i.e., the psychic equivalent of the id – consisting of the psychic representatives or counterparts of instinctual forces,[3] and that which was conscious once upon a time but was subsequently repressed. The *repressed* material is made up partly of memory traces of both outer (objective) experiences and certain internal (subjective) experiences,[4] such as emotions, fantasies, and former bodily states, and includes also the defence mechanisms and a substantial portion of the superego.

I propose to concern myself exclusively with previously conscious but now repressed material, which, from the cultural point of view, can be divided into two groups: (1) the unconscious segment of the ethnic personality and (2) the idiosyncratic unconscious.

1. The *unconscious segment of the ethnic personality* must not be confused with Jung's 'racial unconscious'. I am speaking here of a *cultural*, not a *racial*, unconscious. The 'ethnic unconscious' is that portion of the total unconscious segment of the individual's psyche that he shares with most members of his given cultural community. It is composed of material that each generation teaches the next one to repress, in accordance with the basic demand patterns of the prevailing culture. It changes as culture itself changes. It is transmitted by a kind of 'teaching', as culture is transmitted, rather than biologically, as Jung's 'racial unconscious' is allegedly transmitted. In brief, it is acquired in exactly the same manner as the ethnic character is acquired – and in this context it does not matter in the least precisely whose theory of ethnic character formation one happens to subscribe to. Each ethnic character structure has both a conscious phase and an unconscious phase, the latter being complementary to the former (Devereux 1945 [1978a, Chap. 4], 1961b [1978a, Chap. 5], 1967c). Each culture permits certain impulses, fantasies, and the like to become and to remain conscious, while requiring others to be repressed. Hence, all members of a given culture will have certain unconscious conflicts in common.

The material composing the ethnic unconscious is maintained in a state of repression by means of various defense mechanisms, usually *strengthened and often even provided by cultural pressures*. Sometimes, however, the defensive devices that culture places at the disposal of the individual, to enable him to keep such culture-dystonic impulses in a state of repression, are not altogether adequate. In such instances more than just a few persons who have suffered early childhood traumata of an *atypical* sort find it almost impossible to master such impulses and to keep them safely out of sight. When this happens, culture often provides also a kind of *marginal* or halfhearted implementation for such impulses. The *berdache* (transvestite) complex in Plains Indian society (Devereux 1951a) is an example of an official, though marginal, recognition by Plains culture of a form of personality distortion that was in flagrant opposition to the ethnic ideal. Thus, even though the *berdache* grossly deviated from the 'heroic self-definition' of the Plains Indian, his (or 'her') status was nonetheless at least marginally implemented. However, the fact that it was implemented at all must not prevent one from realising that the implementation was marginal, amounting to an ex post facto sanctioning of the inevitable. In the last resort, though transvestism was often formally 'sanctioned' by a vision, there is irrefutable evidence that it was nonetheless both ego-dystonic and culture-dystonic. For example, when a vision instructed a certain Plains Indian to become a transvestite, the man committed suicide (Lowie 1924). This individual certainly had the impulse to become a trans-vestite, for otherwise his vision would not have 'given' him this particular directive. His (hidden) impulse was accepted by his culture, but it was ego-dystonic that the individual chose to kill himself rather than become a transvestite.

The institutionalisation – or excessive elaboration – of an abnormal impulse (see Chap. 16) emanating from the unconscious portio of the ethnic character must not blind one to its culturally dystonic character.

How culture-dystonic even highly institutionalised homosexuality is may be deduced from the fact that among the Mohave, who did highly institu-tionalise this deviation, the transvestite is subjected to ridicule and is goaded into scurrilous exhibitions of his deviation (Devereux 1937b). Likewise, the direct participation of a greater part of the group, either individually or collectively, in an activity that is basically abnormal although duly institutionalised cannot be held to imply that the activity is either psychologically normal or syntonic at the cultural level. Thus, Kroeber (1952) stressed that during 'epidemics' of sorcery a kind of low-grade paranoia of the laity as a whole is the counterpart of the witches' personal psychopathology.

To anticipate somewhat my later discussion of shamanistic disorders, I add here only that the shaman is exposed early in life to stress situations that are not only numerically *frequent* but culturally *typical*, that is, they originate in the cultural model. Thus his conflicts are permanently localised in his ethnic unconscious.

He also repatterns both his type conflicts (see below) and his subjective conflicts in cultural terms, either by using defenses the culture provides, such as visions, revelations, or initiation rites having palliative 'autothera-peutic' qualities, or by undergoing shamanistic treatment intended to cure an organic disease or psychic disorder.

2. *The idiosyncratic unconscious* is composed of elements that the unique and specific stresses the individual has experienced have obliged him to repress. These stresses can be of two types:

a) Stresses resulting from experiences that, without being typical of a given culture – that is, without reflecting the cultural model – occur frequently enough to be recognised and reformulated in cultural terms. Thus, in the *Iliad* (22.482 ff.), Hector was scarcely dead when Andromache was able to predict in detail the kinds of stress the fatherless Astyanax would experience, the way he would be traumatised, and the deviant behavior he would be forced to adopt. What is relevant here is that what

Andromache evokes is not Astyanax's future if Troy falls and he is captured by the enemy (*Iliad* 22. 487 ff.) but rather the fate of any orphan in Trojan society, regardless of rank. 'Ethnic neuroses' are produced by this kind of situation.

b) Stress resulting from experiences that are neither characteristic of a culture nor numerically frequent but that afflict some especially unfortunate individuals. Thersites' traumatising experiences (*Iliad* 2. 211 ff.) are in marked contrast to those predicted for Astyanax. The unhappy lot of the orphan, widow (*Iliad* 6. 407 ff.), and parents of a man fallen in battle is one of the recurrent themes of the *Iliad* because this type of trauma is a common occurrence in a warrior society. Thersites' woes, by contrast, are clearly quite unusual: he is the ugliest man in the Greek army; he is the only one who is glaringly deformed (bandy-legged, lame, and humpbacked). In a warrior society, which particularly admires strength and male beauty, a deformed boy suffers many completely atypical traumata. The *Iliad* itself (2. 211 ff.) suggests that Thersites' deformities are responsible for his disposition, which is perverse, envious, bitter, and hostile. Moreover, within an army of magnificent heroes, Thersites is doubly conspicuous and deviant. He reacts towards his marginal situation by exhibiting provocative behavior of an obviously neurotic kind, which in turn calls forth equally conspicuous and uncommon reprisals. If one disregards the beating Hera gives to Artemis during the battle of the gods (*Iliad* 21. 489 ff.), Thersites is the only free man in the *Iliad* (2. 265 ff.) who is physically punished by a member of his own group. Thus, idiosyncratic traumata produce conflicts that become permanently localised in the 'private' (idiosyncratic) unconscious.

It goes without saying that an individual does not have only an ethnic unconscious and an individual unconscious. He also experiences, in the course of his life, traumata that are in varying proportions both numerically frequent and typical of the culture. What matters here is that the *principal* conflicts of the shaman are localised chiefly in the ethnic unconscious, whereas those of the 'private' deviant are localised in the idiosyncratic unconscious.

A further exploration of these differences leads to a radical reappraisal of the concept 'trauma'.

TRAUMA AND THE UNAVAILABILITY OF CULTURAL DEFENSES

It is indispensable to distinguish systematically between stress – used in this chapter in its conventional sense and not in the strict sense I assign to this term elsewhere (Devereux 1966c [1978a, Chap. 2]) – and trauma. The term 'stress' is applied here only to the harmful *forces* that impinge upon the individual, the term 'trauma' to the harmful *results* of the impact of those forces. It is one of the main faults of psychiatric thinking that it considers only the absolute intensity of the stress-producing impact and forgets that the individual may have valuable resources at his disposal for resisting and overcoming the impact he has experienced.[5] In other words, an ordinary rifle bullet can penetrate the thin skin of a tiger and kill him, but it will only bounce off the back of a crocodile.

In human, that is, cultural, situations, stress will be traumatic only if it is atypical or if, though typical in its nature, it is abnormally intense or else premature. Stress is atypical if the culture has no 'mass-produced' defense available for relieving or buffering the shock. It is probable, therefore, that the Athenian mother was more traumatised than the Spartan mother by the loss of a son in battle, because the latter was conditioned by her culture to take pride and comfort in sacrificing a son to the city-state (Plutarch, *Apophthegms of Laconian Women*). A common stress may nevertheless be the source of trauma if it has a special intensity: it is one thing for a father to lose a son at war, but it is another to lose, as Priam did, nearly all fifty of his sons, including the famous Hector, or to lose, as Peleus did, an only son, when that son was Achilles. Finally, stress is traumatic when it occurs prematurely, that is, when it affects an individual who does *not yet* have access to the appropriate cultural defenses. A major variant of this kind of situation occurs among underprivileged classes, systematically denied access to the defenses the culture reserves exclusively for its privileged members. This matter will not be discussed here, because it has been analysed in sufficient detail elsewhere (Devereux 1965a).

The matters dealt with in the preceding paragraph sound somewhat complicated when expressed in a formal way, but what is actually implied is a fairly simple and obvious process. For example, a Bushman culture therefore probably does not provide a culturally standardised defense against the culturally atypical strain resulting from falling into deep water: the Bushman child is not taught to swim. Hence, if a Bushman does manage to fall into deep water, he will have to try to get himself out of his predicament by going through a series of idiosyncratic motions, such as calling for help and churning the water as best he can. In brief, falling into deep water is a trauma in Bushman society. It is not a trauma in Polynesian society, where every small child is provided by culture with the 'swimming defense'.

Even more striking is the contrast between the sequences of a leg wound for Tamerlane, on the one hand, and for a Crow warrior named Takes-the-Pipe, on the other. Since walking was nearly shameful in the steppe culture and no exploit had to be accomplished on foot, Tamerlane's wound, which left him lame for life (Timur-i-leng: Timur-the-Limper), did not prevent him from becoming the sovereign of his people and leader of an immense military empire. But Takes-the-Pipe's limp prevented him from accomplishing one of the exploits required of anyone aspiring to the rank of chieftain: he could not set out on foot and return astride a horse he had stolen from the enemy. He reacted to this form of stress – which in his case, but not in Tamerlane's, had produced trauma *stricto sensu* – by becoming a Crazy-Dog-Wishes-to-Die (Lowie 1925).

A culture or subculture can intentionally reject a defense that is potentially available. In the days when shipwrecks on the high seas were frequent, many sailors deliberately refused to learn to swim. They reasoned that in a shipwreck it would be better for them to sink immediately, without suffering, than to swim about for hours without hope of being rescued and then to drown.

For reasons of expository convenience, I have so far not differentiated between psychological defense mechanisms, such as projection, and cultural materials (or means) for strengthening and implementing such defense mechanisms – projection being implemented, e.g., by means of scapegoating. The defensive *use* of scapegoating can be taught. The defense *mechanism* of projection is not, properly speaking, taught, but it can be culturally developed and fostered – e.g. by teaching scapegoating. It is in this manner that each culture establishes a preferential hierarchy of defenses and patterns them. The chief result of this patterning is ethnic character. However, patterning can influence even broad social processes: identification with the enemy is a defense mechanism, which, on the cultural level, is implemented by 'antagonistic acculturation', i.e., by adopting the *means* used by the enemy in order to frustrate his *ends* (Devereux and Loeb 1943 [1978a, Chap. 8]).

These distinctions are important for understanding the concept of premature trauma. This term does not denote simply a chronologically early trauma but a trauma that occurs before the infant knows, and/or is capable of using, culturally provided defenses against an injury.[6] For a small child, unable to earn its living, the death of its parents is a premature trauma, since culture provides the child with only *external protection* – e.g., orphanages – but not with internal defenses, such as a sudden, culturally fostered, psychological maturation abolishing infantile dependent needs.[7]

This theory would also account for the fact that traumata causing severe psychoses occur very early in life – mostly at the oral stage, when the infant does not as yet have as its disposal the kind of culturally provided defense against traumata that would enable it to cope with them without sustaining serious permanent damage. Indeed, at this stage of its life – contrary to the assertions made by Kardiner – the infant does not experience the impact of '*cultural* materials' (or *culture* traits) but only the impact of the ethos (or culture pattern) reflected in the emotions and attitudes of its culture mediators: parents, older siblings, and others in its immediate surroundings. It must therefore improvise defenses against traumata. These defenses are necessarily of a strictly intrapsychic, affective-attitudinal type, since that is all the infant is capable of (Chap. 5). This view lends additional support to the thesis that psychosis – as distinct from neurosis – always entails a severe impairment of the ethnic personality, and this personality, as stated above, is produced by the impact of the culture pattern rather than by the impact of culture traits (child-rearing techniques) on the immature psyche (Devereux 1951a; Mead 1954). Last, but not least, it explains the singular stability of the ethnic character and its perpetuation, generation after generation, despite cultural change or even the pressures of brutal acculturation (Hallowell 1946; Devereux 1951a).[8]

This hypothesis casts doubt on the paramount importance of child-rearing techniques in the formation of ethnic character, as alleged by Kardiner (1939). Moreover, Linton himself subsequently partly repudiated their importance (1956). In fact, emotionally ill parents traumatise their children even if they follow all cultural rules governing child-rearing techniques, because the atypical affects of the parents mediate to the child a distorted ethos instead of conveying to him the affective equivalent of the real, undistorted ethos. Conversely, this hypothesis explains why children raised in a sick society by mentally healthy parents often become anxious or neurotic (Devereux 1956a).

These considerations account simultaneously for the notorious harmfulness of premature traumata and for the invariable impairment of the ethnic personality of the psychotic, which finds expression in a severe 'social negativism' (Chap. 3).

Premature traumata can also occur after infancy, e.g., at times when the child or adolescent is either still too young to be able to use certain culturally provided defenses or else – as in Samoa (Mead 1928) – is denied access to certain defenses on the ground that, in using them, he would 'presume above his age'. A functional equivalent of 'premature traumata' occurs also in the case of underprivileged minorities, whose characterological deviations and immaturities (Dollard 1937) I interpret as a consequence of their being denied access to many important cultural defenses, e.g., self-respect, the right to have 'honor', etc., that their culture makes available to members of the privileged group (Devereux 1965a). Hence, members of underprivileged minorities tend to be psychologically more vulnerable and are therefore more easily dominated than privileged individuals. The same is true of strangers, who have not yet acquired and/or have not as yet highly cathected the defenses that are most useful in their new environment. In brief, self-realisation (the Greek's *aretē*), *sublimation, maturity, real independence, and efficiency appear, in the light of this theory, as functions of a free access to all culturally provided defenses.*

Some cultural materials, such as myths – which from a certain point of view are defenses – may serve as a kind of impersonal 'cold storage' for a number of individual fantasies related to inner conflicts. These fantasies are too intensely laden with affect to be repressed but are also too ego-dystonic to be freely recognised as subjective and as pertaining to oneself. By putting, such fantasies into the 'cold storage' of culture, one gives them a formal and generalised expression within the impersonal body of culture but more or less keeps them out of idiosyncratic 'private circulation' (Chap. 16). Partly because the therapist himself knows and uses this 'cultural cold storage', these fantasies emerge on the individual level and, in particular, are recognised as pertaining to oneself and to one's own problems – and not merely to some mythical personage (projection supported by culture) – only at the end of an exceptionally successful psychoanalysis. This mechanism is particularly noticeable in the shaman, in whom such 'culturalised' fantasies emerge in the form of semisubjective and semipersonalised 'experiences', in which myths and subjective fanta-sies, rituals and idiosyncratic compulsive actions, etc., are inextricably interwoven. This view is perfectly in accordance with what will be said below about the culturally standardised 'type conflicts' and 'type solutions' of the shaman.

One way in which the individual subjected to a trauma seeks to escape from his difficulty is through the misuse of cultural material that, without such deformation, does not lend itself to symptomatic utilisation; or he may select some irrational culture traits that can be used symptomatically without any prior distortion (see below). This observation leads me to make a distinction between disorders that are prepatterned and those that are not.

ETHNOPSYCHIATRIC TYPOLOGY OF PERSONALITY DISORDERS

The preceding considerations require us to set up an ethnopsychiatric typology of neuroses and psychoses. The claim has been made that, since psychotics are desocialised, psychosis cannot have a sociocultural etiology.[9] This claim is untenable because desocialisation is not only a social process but one which is – as will be shown – susceptible of analysis in sociocultural terms.

I want to state once and for all that my ethnopsychiatric typology is perfectly compatible with scientific psychiatric nosologies. Every patient can be assigned a conventional diagnostic label *regardless* of the type of psychiatric disorder he represents within a given culture.

Personality disorders can be divided into four ethnopsychiatric categories:

1   'Type' disorders, relating to the type of social structure (see Chap. 10)

2　'Ethnic' disorders, relating to the specific culture pattern of the
　　group
3　'Sacred' disorders, of the shamanistic type
4　'Idiosyncratic' disorders

For the sake of clarity, these four types of 'illnesses' will be discussed in a
slightly different order.

'Sacred' Disorders, of the Shamanistic Type

The tendency of ethnologists to give far too much attention to the supernatural has considerably hampered our understanding of the shaman's
psychiatric status. While conceding that the supernatural is culturally often
highly elaborated, I feel that the degree of elaboration of a 'complex' –
whether a cultural one or a psychoanalytically defined one – is not prima
facie evidence of its nuclearity and functional importance. Without
accepting even for a moment the thesis of wholesale economic determinism
(defended today only by certain theoreticians of capitalism and anticapit-
alism and obsolete from both the scientific and the cultural standpoint,
since these theoreticians have not yet discovered the existence of man), I
maintain that earning a living, getting married, and other such 'pedestrian'
activities are far more unclear in any culture than complex fertility rites or
curing rituals, which are but the frosting on the cake. I wish to stress that
these remarks imply much more than Kardiner's 'genetic' classification of
institutions into 'primary' and 'secondary' ones (Kardiner and Linton
1939). I am specifically rank-ordering various segments of culture in terms
of their absolute importance for *all* members of a given culture.

The view just presented is materially strengthened by the factual observation that, whereas practically everyone gets married, raises children,
builds a hut, etc., only a small number of the persons composing a tribe
are engaged in shamanistic or other ritual activities on a full-time basis or
as a primary means of earning a living. The rest of the tribe are laymen or
at best 'consumers of the supernatural'. Similarly, the Mohave crowds
accompanying a transvestite on some scurrilous venture are only
audiences. Of course, the members of such crowds are willing to play this
role because it enables them to gratify vicariously, without conscious
commitment, their own latent homosexual impulses and, at the same time,
to gain further strength for fighting these impulses in themselves by witnessing the transvestite's discomfiture (Devereux 1937b).

These considerations are directly applicable also to the shaman. He, too,
is a person whose dominant conflicts lie in the realm of the unconscious
portion of the ethnic personality. He, too, experiences these impulses as
ego-dystonic. Many tribes stress the painfulness of the budding shaman's
psychic experiences, and some individuals who receive supernatural 'calls'

flatly refuse, like the prophet Jonah (Jonah 1:3), to comply with them, as the following examples show. A Plains Indian refused to obey the vision that instructed him to become a transvestite and killed himself instead (Lowie 1924). Among the Sedang Moi, a person who receives the 'call' may even drink his own urine in the hope that this act will so depreciate him in the sight of his divine sponsors that they will take back the power they had given him (Devereux 1933–45). The Mohave believe that a potential shaman who refuses to accept the call becomes insane. I personally interviewed such a man who had spent some time in a state hospital with the – to my mind questionable – diagnosis of manic-depressive psychosis. Both he and his tribe felt that his psychotic episode was due to his refusal to become a practicing shaman (Devereux 1961a).

Even those who do accept the 'call' occasionally feel that their mode of life is ego-dystonic and therefore commit vicarious suicide. Thus I am inclined to suspect that older healing shamans among the Mohave turn into witches precisely because witches are killed. In fact, society actually expects witches to incite others to kill them (Devereux 1937c, 1961a). There is no real psychological difference between this type of vicarious suicide and the suicide of the Plains Indian who refused to become a *berdache*.

In brief, there is no reason and no excuse for not considering the shaman to be a severe neurotic or even a psychotic in a state of temporary remission.

In addition, shamanism is often also culture-dystonic. This is a point that is amply documented but often systematically overlooked. Thus, the shaman is quite often what I have elsewhere called a 'trouble unit' in society (Devereux 1937a). The Mohave say that shamans are both crazy and cowardly. The Siberian shaman is often wretchedly poor and is not highly regarded. The Sedang bitterly resent their shamans, particularly because of their rapaciousness. This very human resentment – reflecting insight into the fact that the shaman is culturally dystonic – even contaminates the attitudes of members of 'higher' religions toward their truly saintly members, who are troublemakers from the viewpoint of workaday life. Even so gentle a man as Saint Francis of Assisi met with strong opposition, and the savior of France, Saint Joan of Arc, was burned at the stake as a heretic before being canonised. The opposition of primitive priesthoods to shamans is, moreover, conspicuous and chronic (Linton 1956).

Briefly stated, my position is that the shaman is mentally deranged. This is also the opinion of Kroeber (1952), Linton (1956), and La Barre (1966). By contrast, Ackerknecht (1943), who fails to differentiate between adjustment and sanity, is of the opinion that the shaman is 'autonormal' though heteropathological. I certainly do not challenge Ackerknecht's thesis that the shaman is to a certain extent 'adjusted'. However, as I have already pointed out, he is adjusted to a *relatively marginal segment* of his society and culture, and even though his position is institutionalised, it is ego-dystonic and often quite obviously culture-dystonic as well. The shaman is also much less realistic than ordinary people, and Kroeber (1952) specifically stressed that cultural development is in the direction of greater realism. This thesis – as Kroeber surely knew but did not say explicitly – expresses the classic psychoanalytic viewpoint, which systematically stresses the importance of reality acceptance.

However, Kroeber also held that the shaman is *less insane* than persons whom their own tribes consider psychotic, though he failed to explain what he meant by this specification. If he meant that the shaman's *symptoms* are less dramatic – or melodramatic – than those exhibited by recognised psychotics, his statement is definitely open to challenge, since it is hard to see how anyone's symptoms could be more strikingly florid than those of, e.g., the budding Siberian shaman (Czaplicka 1914). Also, the *obviousness* or *strikingness* of symptoms is not necessarily correlated with the *severity* of the underlying psychopathology. Thus, an acutely schizophrenic individual on a rampage in an acute ward is actually far less 'ill', and has a better prognosis, than a 'burnt-out' and tractable schizophrenic vegetating in a chronic ward.

Likewise, the diagnostic categories 'hysteria, phobia, obsessive-compulsive neurosis, character disorder' are here arranged in an *increasing* order of *severity* and in a *decreasing* order of *obtrusive* symptomatology. In fact, many character neurotics are often practically 'symptom free' in the ordinary sense. In other words, the obtrusiveness of symptoms gives no clue to the severity of the underlying psychopathology.

It is possible, of course, that Kroeber meant to contrast the shaman with the recognised neurotic or psychotic, not in terms of the obtrusiveness of symptoms, but in terms of the malignancy of the underlying psychopathology. In that case I can only say that his statement is far too general to be of practical use in the exploration of the shaman's distinctive psychopathology.

Linton (1956), who, like Kroeber, implied that the shaman is 'less crazy' than the recognised psychotic, advanced the thesis that he is usually a hysteric. This diagnosis has certain important implications:

a) It contrasts the (neurotic) shaman with the recognised psychotic on the basis of considerations related to the malignancy of the underlying psychopathology rather than to the obtrusiveness of symptoms.

b) The diagnosis 'hysteria' suggests a definite etiology and a definite psychodynamic configuration, susceptible of being tested by objective methods.

c) It places the relatively quite, even depressed, Sedang shaman

(Devereux 1933–5) and the violently disturbed Siberian shaman on the same continuum, presumably on the grounds that certain extreme types of hysteria verge on a genuine psychosis and are sometimes almost indistinguishable from certain forms of schizophrenia (Chap. 9).

d) It accounts for the florid and exhibitionistic symptomatology of many shamans.

From the strictly clinical point of view, Linton's diagnosis is probably correct and to the point. However, from the point of view of ethnopsychiatry, it fails to account for one crucial fact, namely, that some potential hysterics become shamans while others remain 'private' neurotics. Indeed, while it is possible that all shamans may be hysterics, it is quite certain that even in primitive society not all hysterics are shamans.

Theoretical considerations and firsthand observations suggest the same solution: the crucial difference between the shaman and the 'private' but recognised hysteric or psychotic lies in the fact that the *shaman's conflicts are characteristically located in the unconscious segment of his ethnic personality rather than in the idiosyncratic portion of his unconscious.* Unlike the 'private' neurotic or psychotic, he does not have to evolve most of his symptoms spontaneously. He can express, control, and redirect his impulses and conflicts by using the many – usually ritualised – devices that each culture places at the disposal of those whose conflicts are of the 'conventional' type. In brief, the shaman is psychologically ill for conventional reasons and in a conventional way. Quite often – though not always (see below – his conflicts are simply more intense than those of other members of his group, though fundamentally of the same type and involving the same segment of the personality, the ethnic unconscious. He is quite often like everyone else – 'only more so'. This explains why the normal members of the tribe echo the shaman's intrapsychic conflicts so readily and why they find his 'symptoms' (ritual acts) (Freud 1907) so reassuring. The normal primitive's readiness to respond to the shamans' and witches' conflicts and actions was pointed out by Kroeber (1952). In my opinion, this readiness is due to the fact that the shaman and his performance strike the 'normals' as 'uncanny' – i.e. as something that their *unconscious* experiences as 'disturbingly and unexpectedly familiar' (uncanny = *unheimlich*) in the Freudian sense (Freud 1919). Shamanistic treatment tends, moreover, to reproduce both the morbid process itself and the subjective process of cure (Lévi-Strauss 1958). This fact explains why the shaman's patient experiences the shaman's actions as reassuring.

The shaman provides his patient with a whole set of ethnopsychologically suitable and congenial and culturally recognised defenses (restitutional symptoms) against the idiosyncratic conflicts that torment him. In reality, the shaman does not perform a 'psychiatric cure' in the *strict* sense of the term. he simply provides a kind of 'corrective emotional experience', as the Chicago School of psychoanalysis calls it, that leads to a repatterning of the defenses without real curative insight. Thus, M. E. Opler (1936) reported that Apache shamans can cure tics (which are notoriously resistant to psychotherapy) by substituting a taboo for the tic.. These considerations also explain why, in so many primitive groups, the shaman is someone who has fallen ill and has then been successfully 'treated' by a shaman. The most detailed analysis of this kind of 'didactic' or 'initiatory' illness is to be found in the writings of Kilton Stewart (1954).[10] What seems to happen in such 'cures' is simply a change-over from idiosyncratic conflicts and defenses to culturally conventional conflicts and ritualised symptoms, without any real curative insight.

Thus, it is the conventional patterning of the shaman's conflicts and symptoms that differentiates him from the 'private' neurotic or psychotic. A careful comparison of the delusions of *a* paranoid Sedang Moi 'private' psychotic with the 'supernatural experiences' of *any*[11] Sedang Moi shaman shows that the two accounts contain identical elements and differ chiefly in their patterning and orientation, which in the shaman's case are of a conventional type while in the 'private' idiosyncratic ambulatory psychotic they are unconventional.. Similar correspondences and differences can be observed in our own society between certain socially approved personality types and their 'private' (idiosyncratic) counterparts in mental hospitals (Devereux 1955c).

The conventionality or unconventionality of a person's delusions is in itself a matter of considerable diagnostic significance. The patterning and orientation of every Sedang shaman's 'supernatural experience' – which is made up of elements identical with those of *a* certain Sedang psychotic's delusions – are the result of what is known as 'secondary elaboration', which also takes place – unwittingly – in the remembering and recounting of dreams (Devereux 1951a) and, of course, in culturally significant delusions as well. In the course of this secondary elaboration a conventional pattern is impressed on the (sometimes subverbal) material that emerges from the unconscious. This type of conventionalised secondary elaboration is possible only where 'social negativism' is not excessive and unmanageable and where there is still a residual need for remaining integrated, if only marginally, with society (Chap. 3).

What matters, psychiatrically is not so much the raw content of the unconscious – which is pretty much the same in every human being – but what the ego does with this material.[12] What differentiates the shaman from the 'private' psychotic is the conventional, though admittedly still abnormal, patterning of the material that emerges from the unconscious. It is this patterning that is lacking in the 'private' psychotic (Chap. 2).

As stated a moment ago, the patient who was ill, received shamanistic treatment, 'recovered', and became a shaman himself simply underwent a conventionalised repatterning of his conflicts and symptoms without gaining any real insight into his problems and without developing is capacity to sublimate. Ackerknecht (1943) also believed that the shaman is a mental patient 'cured without insight'; yet oddly enough, he attacked me for having said practically the same thing, more rigorously and before he did (Devereux 1942c, 1961a). This, however, is beside the point. What does matter is that Ackerknecht, as a physician, should have known better than to use the term 'cured' as loosely as he did. No real psychiatrist would ever call a 'remission without insight' a 'cure', because the patient in a state of 'social remission' remains vulnerable: his old conflicts can erupt anew at any time. No medical man considers a syphilitic really 'cured' until it is at least theoretically *possible* for him to contract syphilis a second time and to develop a second set of *primary* lesions. No shaman is 'cured' in this sense. He is simply in remission. When subjected to further strain, he does not evolve a *new* neurosis; he simply experiences a new breakthrough of his *old* conflicts and seeks to ward them off by means of the same old symptoms. In other instances his newly acquired defenses become 'stale' and lose their efficiency, forcing him to develop additional symptoms – most frequently cultural but occasionally idiosyncratic – exactly the way, after a syphilitic's primary lesions are suppressed by an *incomplete* (suppressive but not curative) treatment, he will eventually develop secondary or tertiary lesions.

The case of Black Elk, a Sioux shaman, illustrates this process in the clearest possible manner. Urged on by a variety of cultural 'type' conflicts, Black Elk had a shamanistic vision that received enough social approval and recognition to satisfy him and to relieve his tensions to the point where he could function for a while in a more or less normal manner. However, after a lapse of several years, this 'defense', too, became stale and no longer sufficed to hold his conflicts in check. He therefore felt impelled to enact publicly the ritual his vision had instructed him to perform – a task he had so far neglected (Neihardt 1932). In psychiatric terminology one could say that rumination was superseded by acting-out. This development is the typical *vicious circle* of psychopathology. The *primary* defense against a basic conflict creates a series of new difficulties,[13] against which further, *secondary*, defenses have to be developed. A similar process of deterioration can be observed in Mohave healing shamans who eventually become witches. Their initial conflicts are probably related to aggression. Hence, the primary defense consists not in attempts to sublimate but in a 'reaction formation' against hostile impulses: the budding shaman denies his sadistic impulses and – turning them around – specialises in healing. Then, when this defense – the therapeutic activity – becomes 'stale', a new breakthrough of hostility impels the healer to become a witch. The Mohave Indians understand this mechanism fairly well, since they specify that a shaman can cure *only* diseases that he is also *qualified to cause*, and vice versa, of course (Devereux 1961a). In the end, guilt over the overt manifestation of his hostility eventually impels the Mohave witch to commit vicarious suicide by inducing his victims' bereaved relatives to kill him. Characteristically, he does this in the most aggressive manner possible. He jeers at them, boasts of having killed their relatives by witchcraft, ridicules them for not killing him in revenge, and threatens to bewitch them too (Kroeber 1925; Devereux 1961a).[14] A more obvious example of the manner in which 'remission without insight' inevitably leads to a further exacerbation of the fundamental psychopathology, and of the way in which symptoms must be piled upon symptom and defense upon defense, would be hard to find. How anyone confronted with such classic manifestations of psychopathological dynamics can continue to speak of 'autonormality' or of '*cure* without insight' is hard to understand.

In the face of these observations, some ethnologists, taking refuge from the current disintegration of norms by adopting cultural relativism – whose motto is: 'Custom is King, and the King can do no wrong' – persist in denying the shaman's abnormality. Some of their arguments, specious at best and occasionally even false, barely deserve a footnote;[15] others must be systematically refuted.

M. K. Opler, for instance, seems to believe that any field worker is capable not simply of *observing* but of *diagnosing* unusual behavior (see below). This is obviously not the case, for in 1938, when my own psychiatric training was still quite incomplete, I wrote – thinking specifically of my Mohave shaman friend, Hivsū Tupōma – that the Mohave shaman was an exuberant extrovert. However, when, later that year, I did some additional field work, I had occasion to observe him one afternoon, quite drunk, pouring out to me a veritable torrent of frankly delusional material. The following day, when he was sober, he confirmed everything he had told me the day before and begged me to keep his secret because he was not yet prepared to be killed as a witch (Devereux 1961a). Likewise, until a certain night in 1934 I believed my Sedang Moi shaman friend, Hēang, to be a gay, bohemian character. That night, however, he experienced something more serious than a nightmare – he had a genuine psychotic episode (*bouffée délirante*). His shouts of 'Ghost! Ghost!' woke the whole village, and it required several men to hold him down while he fought the ghosts. Now, though it is generally understood that Sedang Moi shamans are on intimate terms with spirits, neither the villagers, unfamiliar with theories of cultural relativism, nor Hēang himself viewed his attack as 'normal'. All agreed that he had been temporarily insane (*rájok*). In short, unless, like occultists, one believes in the objective reality of spirit possession, one must view Hēang's attack as an expression of his latent psychological disturbance.

Opler also fails to understand that the diagnosis of normality is infinitely more difficult to make than the diagnosis of abnormality. A respected citizen may be a true paranoiac but reveal himself as such only when he decompensates and kills his entire family. It is known that a monosymptomatic hysteria or even a common torticollis[16] may mask a latent paranoid schizophrenia. Acute psychotic breaks can occur after cosmetic surgery – surgical correction of the nose, for instance – or after the healing of a neurodermatitis through hypnosis.

Newspapers, too, periodically carry stories about individuals who, considered cured and therefore returned to their families by first-rate psychiatric hospitals, murder someone or commit suicide as soon as they are at home. Nietzsche long ago wondered about the possibility of their being 'neuroses of sanity', and N. S. Reider (1950) published a brilliant paper on the neurotic compulsion to seem normal. In short, ethnologists, colonial civil servants, and missionaries, only slightly or incorrectly informed on psychiatric matters, can report any unusual behavior they had had a chance to observe. They do not have the training to make diagnoses; that is a task for trained clinicians. Hence Opler's statement that all the Ute shamans are normal no more deserved to be believed than I deserved belief when I wrote in 1938 – that is, at a time when my knowledge of psychiatry was still inadequate – that Mohave shamans are exuberant extroverts.

The preceding remarks pertain only to certain erroneous notions of a purely technical nature. The real source of the fallacious views held by cultural relativists is their refusal to distinguish between *belief* and *experience*. The Ute shaman whom Opler proposes to us as a model of balance and reson *felt* that he harbored within himself a spirit mannikin who swallows evil; he also felt that his shamanistic powers could turn against him and that he was incapable of controlling their inherently destructive tendencies. Finally, he would at times even plead in vain with the mannikin, urging him to refrain from using his malefic powers. Opler sees nothing abnormal in all of this because these beliefs are held by the Utes in general – and, one might add, by numerous other tribes as well. In support of his argument he also cites the misadventures of the son of a Ute shaman who wished to shorten, idiosyncratically, the normal cultural procedure for gaining shamanistic power and promptly had an attack of hysterical blindness. He owed the recovery of his sight to treatment of his father, a leading Ute shaman. Subsequently the young man was able to obtain shamanistic powers by recourse to regular, traditional methods (Opler 1959: 110). Since this account demonstrates that the acquisition of shamanistic powers is a 'restitutional process', it not only fails to support Opler's theory that the shaman is a normal individual but proves that he is not normal and that shamanism is a restitutional symptom, or, rather, syndrome, provided by the culture. The validity of this view is proved also by the widely held belief that the acquisition of shamanistic powers is always preceded by a psychotic incident.

I have nearly given up hope of convincing the apostles of cultural relativism – as impervious to facts as to logic – that the crux of the matter is simply the *difference between traditional belief and subjective experience*. It is one thing for a physicist to know the formula for the acceleration of a falling body: $s = \frac{1}{2} gt^{2}$, but it is quite another to experience this acceleration in the form of a hallucination (analogous to what one feels during a parachute jump) each time he utters the formula. Again, it is one thing to read about the Oedipus complex but quite another to *relive* one's own Oedipus complex on the psychoanalyst's couch. Today the Catholic Church itself acknowledges this distinction and consults with a psychiatrist before admitting the authenticity of a vision or other seemingly supernatural experience, even if it is in perfect conformity with dogma, with stereotypes, and with precedents of that 'spiritual' experience.

It is almost embarrassing to insist on a point that ought to go without saying, but the obstinacy of cultural relativist forces me to invent two fictitious cases that clearly emphasise the difference between a belief and a subjective experience conforming to that belief.

1. Any mullah knows that the houris in Paradise, as soon as they are deflowered, become virgins again. It is an article of faith for him: be believes it, teaches it, and expects the faithful to believe it. But should a certain Ali ben Mustapha, the village tinsmith, claim that his personal experience has confirmed the mullah's teachings – that he has visited Paradise, deflowered a houri, witnessed the renewal of her virginity, and deflowered her a second time – I do not doubt that the pious mallah would send him straight to a psychiatric hospital or its ritual equivalent.

2. Had Dante revealed in private – and therefore nonrepudiable – conversation what he said publicly in immortal – and therefore repudiable – verses, that is, that Virgil had led him, Dante Alighieri from Florence through Purgatory and Hell, his friend would have rushed him to a physician and an exorcist for fear that the Church might accuse him of necromancy and heresy.

To return to the Utes, the *belief* that the shaman harbors a spirit mannikin within himself is one thing; for a Ute shaman to *experience the presence* of that homunculus within himself is quite another. To confuse the one with the other amounts to a refusal to differentiate the sociological from the psychological (Devereux 1945 [1978a, Chap. 4], 1961b [1978a, Chap 5], 1967b). In short the shaman is not neurotic because he *shares* the *beliefs* of his tribe; he is neurotic because in *his own* case, and *only* in his case, this belief is transformed, for neurotic reasons, into a subjective *experience*, albeit a culturally patterned one, of a delusional type, which subsequently becomes part of the restitutional syndrome peculiar to shamanism.

It is no doubt even more significant that primitives themselves recognise the psychiatric abnormality of an abnormal condition even when that condition is fully integrated with, and indispensable for, some religious or supernatural rite. I might also add that Plato, who draws a distinction in the *Phaedrus* (244 ff.) between 'profane' insanity – insanity pure and simple, which is of concern only to the healer – and the 'mystical' seizure having a religious significance, suffered by the Pythia, knew perfectly well that both are cases of insanity. Plato sometimes even seems to wonder whether such episodes of spontaneous, nonritual exaltation are a 'divine' or a 'clinical' form of insanity. When in the *Cratylus* (386C ff.), for instance, Socrates, obviously in a hypomanic state, pours out a stream of etymological puns and compares his performance, half-respectfully, half-humorously, to a state of mantic exaltation, this seems to indicate that, even for Plato, the boundary between reverential belief and clinical diagnosis is less clear than his *Phaedrus* seems to imply. Furthermore, when he implies that Socrates' exhibition is at least partly abnormal, he is expressing a valid psychiatric opinion. No normal person – even one with the genius of Socrates, not even a Greek, incited by tradition to make etymological puns – could have intentionally released, without even catching his breath, such a barrage of improvised puns,[17] his exaltation increasing with each succeeding one. This kind of situation is psychologically conceivable only when there is a temporary eruption of the 'primary process' (Freud) or of the 'prelogical mentality' (Lévy-Bruhl).[18] I once analysed a borderline patient who compulsively broke words up into syllables and played on their etymology 'to understand the words', that is, in order to 'reconstitute' its meaning (Devereux 1966a, 1967a). I would therefore contend that, in the *Cratylus* Plato described a clinically abnormal aspect of his illustrious master's personality – and also an aspect of his own abnormality.[19]

What matters most, alas, is that, just like the apostles of cultural relativism, Plato and certain other Greeks formulated the difference between 'divine' and 'pathological' insanity in cultural rather than psychiatric terms.[20] For the clinician, both kinds of insanity are equally abnormal, and even ethnopsychiatry can say only that 'divine' madness is a special form of ethnic psychosis, while 'non-divine' madness is an idiosyncratic (individual) psychosis.

Even more interesting in many respects is the fact that in some tribes the shaman may be abnormal in two or even three ways. Thus, the acquisition of shamanistic powers is often preceded by a psychotic episode that, in spite of its supernatural overtones, is nonetheless, in the last analysis, a genuine 'clinical' disorder. The shaman may, moreover, be abnormal on both the shamanistic and the idiosyncratic levels. Thus the Mohave believe that all shamans are 'crazy', for the simple reason that they are shamans, but that they may, in addition, be victims of an ordinary ('clinical') abnormality. Besides, according to Mohave thought, these two forms of abnormality are mutually independent.[21] Thus, Tcāvākong was doubly 'mad': qua Mohave *shaman* and witch, he had a strictly shamanistic – i.e., destructive and self-destructive – madness, whereas, on the private level, he was *primarily* epileptic and his illness did not differ from the illness of any other epileptic and had, according to Mohave thought, absolutely nothing to do with his specifically shamanistic madness. Likewise, as I have mentioned above, the sudden nocturnal psychotic episode (*bouffée délirante*) of the shaman Hēang was interpreted by the Sedang Moi as an attack of ordinary madness, fitting their 'psychiatric' ideas rather than their beliefs about shamans and shamanism. The only difference was that, owing to his fortuitous status as a shaman, i.e., as an intimate of supernatural powers, in his hallucinations he necessarily fought off ghosts rather than, say, tigers.[22]

As for the threadbare argument that considers the shaman's 'social usefulness' a proof his normality, one might as well claim that the poet or the scientist is 'useful' because of his neurosis and then claim that his usefulness proves that he is not neurotic. This kind of circular reasoning does not deserve to be refuted, even apart form the fact that the truly creative poet or scientist is creative *in spite of* and not *because of* his neurosis (Devereux 1961c [1975, Chap 1]).[23]

Before appealing to the shaman's usefulness, I must first clarify the way in which he is useful. A stillborn two-headed calf can be more valuable than a normal living calf; as part of a traveling show it can bring in more money than a normal calf – even a prize-winning animal – at the county fair. This does not mean, however, that the two-headed calf is normal.

Wagner von Jauregg was able to arrest tertiary syphilis by inoculating syphilitic patients with malaria, but its usefulness in *this* context does not make malaria a nonillness; it continues to be an illness of which the patient must be cured. Similarly, some infectious diseases used to be cured by creating a fixation abscess, which subsequently had to be treated and cured.

The shaman's utility is of precisely the same order. Its nearest clinical equivalent is the utility of the psychotic child who plays the role of 'deputy lunatic' for a latently neurotic family. Here it is the family that is ill; the child's fever is not his own but his family's. The child who is a 'deputy lunatic' is, furthermore, so 'useful' to his family that he may literally be snatched out of the hands of the psychiatrist as soon as his state begins to improve. In fact, if this psychological scapegoat were cured, his family would soon become overtly neurotic (Devereux 1956a).[24] Yet, in spite of the evident 'utility' of these children to their families, child psychiatrists persist in thinking that both the 'deputy lunatic' child and the family should be treated. The psychic disorder of the shaman is 'useful' to the tribe in this sense *only*: like the child, he is mad in the name and on behalf of the 'others', whom his 'madness' enables to maintain a semblance of psychological stability. Modern society, too, has its 'deputy lunatics' (Devereux 1955c), but a discussion of this matter cannot be undertaken in the present study.

L.B. Boyer raises an altogether different problem in a study based on ethnographic work, psychoanalytic sessions, and clinical psychological tests. He convincingly demonstrates that within some rapidly disintegrating Apache tribes the shaman is, on the whole, less neurotic than the majority of the members of the tribe (Boyer 1961, 1962, 1964; Boyer, Klopfer and Kawai 1964). While I grant the validity of his findings, I think that Boyer is mistaken in considering that they weaken my theory of the shaman's abnormality. I even think that Boyer's findings could have been predicted by and deduced from my own theory, for which they provide the best confirmation available at present.

The crux of the matter is that today the Apache tribes are not simply disorganised but have almost ceased to function as autonomous societies animated by a vital and coherent ethos. Hence the average personality profile of a nonshaman Apache systematically reproduced, point for point and in an almost caricatural manner, my description of the disorganised and impoverished personality of the average reservation Indian (Devereux 1951a [consult 2nd edn, 1969]). In such a society the shaman is necessarily *less* disturbed than the nonshaman (even if one does not take into account the fact that he could scarcely be *more* disorganised without being hospitalised). In this type of society the shaman can still derive, from the previously stable but now disappearing aboriginal ethos of his tribe, the 'solution' (that is, the restitutional syndrome) for his neurotic conflicts. To put it another way, he still has available at least one type of model – a kind of matrix – that helps him to structure his defenses and restitutional symptoms. By contrast, the nonshaman no longer has access to ancient customs and is, from a psychological point of view, adrift.[25] Hence, 'being a shaman', which is a neurosis, has, for the Apache neurotic's total personality, precisely the same organising functions as those that I long ago ascribed to stabilised neurotics and psychotics (Chap. 2).

Nor is that all! Supernaturalism (which I shall show to be antisocial) is notoriously more resistant to even abrupt cultural change than are the practical areas of the culture, which fail when put to the test of daily life.[26]

By contrast the sole competitor of aboriginal supernaturalism is imported supernaturalism, which is just as unverifiable as the aboriginal one. This implies that more or less superficial and syncretistic religious conversions require no radical restructuring of the ethnic personality. The religious movement associated with the Ghost Dance has in no way intensified the Plains Indians' native ferocity, nor have cargo cults cooled that passion for property that characterises the Melanesians and the Papuans.[27] Finally, and this is the main point, a new ethos endowed with real vitality is seldom able to penetrate an oppressed group in a state of crisis.[28] This no doubt explains the relative impermeability of the ethnic personality to cultural change or decline, a fact emphasised by Hallowell (1945, 1946), Thompson (1948), Wallace (1951, 1961), and myself (1951a).

In short, the Apache shaman lives, even today, cloistered within the confines of his ethnic personality, which provides him with a relatively safe, although anachronistic, shelter. This is not true of the nonshaman Apache, who is forced to incorporate both conflictual and defensive new elements into his personality and even to reorganise, or, rather, first to disorganise, his character structure. In addition, the childhood conditioning he has undergone in a disorganised primitive tribe makes him apriori incapable of functioning well in a modern society that is still efficient. Obliged to improvise all his defensive maneuvers and 'solutions' by drawing almost entirely on his idiosyncratic resources, and to do this in a social environment that is affectively incomprehensible to him and to which his childhood conditioning absolutely prevents him from adapting, he will *inevitably* be more disturbed than the shaman, whose behavior is, on the whole, simply anachronistic.[29] The fact that the Apache shaman is psychologically less disturbed than the nonshaman in no way implies that he is not neurotic.[30]

The psychiatric problem of the normality or abnormality of the shaman is not in itself of prime importance. If it arouses so much anxiety, it is not only because, behind its commonplace façade, one can glimpse the immense and menacing phantom of our own sociocultural dereism (Devereux 1939a; cf. Chaps 9 and 10 below), our need for charismatic leadership (Devereux 1955c), and our own desperate and mostly fruitless attempts to adapt ourselves to the capriciousness of our times. These endeavors resemble those described with understanding and perspicacity by E. R. Dodds in his *Pagans and Christians in an Age of Anxiety* (1965). It is both saddening and humiliating that few ethnologists, psychiatrists, and sociologists are able to bring to their study of disintegrating cultures, including our own, the kind of realistic compassionateness that good historians of culture, such as Dodds, show spontaneously.

In the following pages I hope to show that the symptoms of 'sacred' disorders occupy a key position in the hierarchy of symptoms and reflect the most striking aspects of society's self-disavowal. But before examining the problem of the nature of symptoms, I must analyse the problem of ethnic disorders.

Ethnic Disorders

While ethnic disorders fit modern nosological categories fairly well, they are also structured and arranged by each culture and usually have a name.[31] Moreover, while some of these disorders are supposed to have supernatural causes or aspects and to be curable by esoteric means, they are, unlike shamanism, not directly integrated with tribal supernaturalism. It was no doubt the lack of true integration of epilepsy with Greek supernaturalism that enabled Hippocrates (*On the Sacred Illness*) to say that there was nothing particularly 'sacred' in the 'sacred illness': epilepsy.

One encounters a wide variety of ethnic disorders in the world. Each culture area, perhaps even each culture, has at least one and often several typical disorders of this kind. In fact, it is my impression, which I will not pause to discuss here, that the number and diversity of ethnic disorders in a given culture reflect its degree of psychological sophistication; that is, they offer an indication of the extent to which the society as a whole takes the individual and his personality into account (cf. note 31). It would thus have been easy to illustrate my theoretical views by choosing one example from central Africa and another from the Eskimos; but documenting a theory by such an assortment of far-flung examples, besides running the risk of disorienting the reader, would not have allowed me to emphasise two critical aspects of the problem, which are the complex patterning of ethnic disorders and their multidimensional character. I shall therefore support my argument with information about a limited number of ethnic disorders, all of which have been relatively well studied and which occur in societies with whose cultures I am particularly familiar.[32] The study in depth of a single ethnic disorder will produce the same results as the comparative – and therefore superficial – study of all disorders of this type (Devereux 1955b [2nd rev. edn 1969]), so that the deliberate restricting of my examples in no way prejudices the validity of my theoretical conclusions.

The ethnic disorders I will most frequently mention are the Malay's *amok* and *latah*, the ancient Scandinavian condition of *berserk*, the *imu* of the Ainus, the *windigo* of the Canadian Algonquians, the Crazy Dog syndrome of the Plains Indians, the heartbreak syndrome of the Mohaves, the transvestism of these last two groups, and a few others. In most cases the group has explicit theories about the nature and causes of a disorder and clear-cut ideas as to its symptoms, evolution, and prognosis. When a disorder of this type occurs in a particularly dramatic form or threatens to provoke a public crisis, or even when it simply stimulates the group's imagination, it acquires so great a 'social mass' (Devereux 1940 [1978a, Chap. 1]) that special measures may be taken to control it and possibly exploit it for the benefit of the group. Thus, on the eve of battle, the Vikings counted on some of them to go *berserk* in the heat of the fray and, in that state, to perform great feats of arms, insuring victory. The Crow Indians allotted a place in their battle array not only for the armed Crazy Dog but also for the exceptional one who chose to ride into combat unarmed, although the latter was of no military value to them. The *amok* attack is a recurrent theme in the Malay prose epic *Hikayat Hang Tuah* (Anonymous 1930), whose climax is doubtless the duel between Hang Tuah and his old friend Hang Jebat, who revolted against the king and became an *amok* runner. The cry '*Amok! Amok!*' was a socially recognised signal, to which the Malays reacted (Clifford 1922b) somewhat as we do when we hear an air-raid siren. In fact, the practice of *amok* even affected Malay technology. The *amok* runner who had been speared would press himself forward on the shaft of his enemy's spear until it transpierced his whole body; this enabled him to come close enough to his enemy to kill him with his *kris* (a dagger with a serpentine blade). Hence, the Malays began to make lances whose two blades, forming an acute angle with each other, prevented the frenzied man from closing the distance. This two-bladed spear reminds one of the boar spear of old, equipped at the base of the blade with a transverse bar that prevented the animal from getting dangerously close to the hunger by impaling himself on the spear. It has been claimed that the United States army exchanged the .38-caliber pistol for the more powerful .45 because a bullet from the latter will knock a man down even if he is only wounded in the hand, whereas the .38-caliber bullet will not make a suitably corseted *amok* runner (*juramentado*) double over, even if he is hit in the stomach or thorax (Hurley 1936). Finally, in many Malay cities, the municipalities used to place forked sticks at street corners to help people overpower the *amok* runner without having to come too close to him. These forked sticks played approximately the same role as call boxes do on our city streets, which permit citizens to alert the nearest police or fire station in an emergency.

Last, but not least, the cultural normalisation of such disorders not only allows them to be used as models for individuals who for some reason are physically disturbed; it also permits the same abnormality to be triggered by a wide variety of different stimuli, as is shown by the extreme diversity of situations that provide a Malay with a reason or incitement to run *amok* (see below).

In brief, ethnopsychiatry teaches – and this is one of its basic contributions – that particularly in stress situations, *culture itself provides the individual with directives for the misuse of cultural materials.* Linton (1936) called these directives 'patterns of misconduct'. It is as if the group said to the individual, 'Don't do it, but, if you do, go about it in this manner.' Before showing that ethnic disorders are indeed patterns of misconduct, I must examine more closely the conduct on which this type of 'pattern' is based.

One can criticise Linton on one score only: he applied his brilliant formula to individual deviant behavior only and did not even attempt to specify the nature of the social models by means of which society prepatterns individual misconduct. I was able to fill this gap only in part when, using Linton's views as my starting-point, I elaborated the concept of social negativism and suggested, timidly at first, that this negativism could manifest itself not only on the level of individual behavior but also on that of the social process (Chap. 3). This suggestion, which I made nearly forty years ago, I now propose to render explicit and to develop into a formal theory.

Every society not only has its functional aspects by means of which it affirms and maintains its integrity, but also has a certain number of beliefs, dogmas, and tendencies that contradict, deny, and undermine not only the essential operations and structure of the group but at times even its very existence. Hinduism, for instance, denies the reality of the sensible world, which is held to be pure illusion (*maya*). Platonism in many respects shares this way of conceiving reality, and Buddhism so strongly encourages men to shun existence, and detach themselves from their fellow men that Alexander (1931) could rightly claim that it constitutes a training for artificial catatonia. The same observations apply equally well to yoga, eremitism, and related attitudes.

On another level, medieval society condemned itself for not realising the theocratic ideal of the City of God, formulated by Saint Augustine. A number of illustrious popes and theologians maintained that all worldly government is fundamentally evil, and they condemned as sinful certain essential socioeconomic activities, indispensable to the survival of any society, on the pretext that they evidence a sinful attachment to worldly things. Because medieval society would have ceased to exist if these necessary tasks had not been performed, they were accomplished either by circuitous means or by requiring others – Jews, Saracens, and various pariahs – to do them. The Christian could live without sinning, as long as the 'sinful' pariah sinned in his stead, just as, until very recently, the prostitutes' sexual misconduct permitted girls from good families to remain virgins. In short, while claiming to aspire to the City of God, where these socially useful activities would no longer be necessary, medieval society still found ways to perform – or to have performed on its behalf – these impious activities, thus realising, *mutatis mutandis*, and in a caricatural manner, Augustine's famous prayer, 'Make me chaste, O Lord ... *but not yet.*'

The conflict between the socially negativistic ideal and the functional requirements of a society can also erupt at the individual level. Probably the best-known witness to a conflict of this type is Marcus Aurelius in his *Meditations*. This 'Stoic saint' (as J. H. Rose, 1960, calls him), although he fulfilled his imperial obligations not only conscientiously but brilliantly, never ceased to despise them and held them to be obstacles to the attainment of his Stoic ideal. Since it is quite clear that society's concept of its most useful activities, and of the persons who do perform them,[33] is an expression of its self-destructive tendencies, I hold that Marcus Aurclius's Stoicism suffices almost by itself to explain the decline and fall of the Roman Empire.

Though Linton was clearly not thinking of this type of *antisocial* social ideal when he formulated his concept of patterns of misconduct, it is evident that such attitudes also represent patterns of this type. Indeed, they constitute the pattern of misconduct *par excellence*, in the sense that they faithfully reflect society's attitude of social negativism and its self-disavowal.[34] Whatever prestige these ideals – or the people who champion them – may have, they represent, nonetheless, types of socially structured misconduct. Like the superstitions and beliefs of those who make up what Americans call 'the lunatic fringe' – which exists in every society – they satisfy simultaneously the subjective social negativism of the neurotic and his need to fit into at least one of the many marginal niches or statuses, which range from the ones occupied by the shaman, the Cynic philosopher, the hermit, and other individuals of this type, who are sometimes not considered psychotic by their own group; on through the niches occupied by persons like the *amok* runner or the Crazy Dog, whose condition their group views as an ethnic psychosis; and finally to the niches occupied by the genuinely idiosyncratic psychotics, who have managed to persuade their society that they are insane rather than criminals or sacrilegious persons (Chap. 13).

Cultural materials that reflect society's basic disavowal of itself are also precisely the ones that troubled individuals synthesise and give expression to by their behavior – and do this in a manner that can earn them either society's approval or its disapproval. These antisocial social values, which permit the individual to be antisocial in a socially approved and sometimes even prestigious manner, also have another important characteristic. Whereas the majority of cultural traits do not lend themselves to a symptomatic utilisation without first undergoing distortion (Chap. 2), cultural traits that reflect a society's self-disavowal can, as a rule, be used as symptoms *without* prior distortion.

Materials of this type have three further characteristics.

1. In order to turn them into symptoms, they need only to be hypercathected in a manner that transforms a popular belief into a subjective experience. This is what happens in the case of this shaman (see above).

2. One can transform *rational* cultural materials into symptoms by arbitrarily and illogically associating them with those *irrational* cultural materials that are part of any society's self-disavowal. Thus, when

members of a certain fanatical sect fall ill, they refuse medically indispensable blood transfusions on the ground that this is a form of 'cannibalism'.

3. Since these materials are fundamentally irrational, they can easily be articulated with modes of thinking and felling rooted in the primary process (Freud) and in prelogical thought (Lévy-Bruhl).

These findings also explain both the frequency of supernatural delusions in psychotics (Dumas 1946) and the fact that supernaturalism contains materials that clearly repudiate culture. It is obvious that every supernatural ritual is essentially opposed to the system of prevailing values of culture as a whole. In fact, the more 'sacred' and 'restrictive' an action is, the more horror it would inspire were it carried out in a profane context. In some Australian tribes, whose major ritual (*corroboree*) includes a period of sexual license, the ritually preferred sexual partner is often precisely the one who is the most strictly tabooed the rest of the time. At totemic banquets one eats the totemic animal, which is strictly taboo in all other circumstances (Durkheim 1912). After the ox sacrifice (*bouphonia*) the Athenians tried and condemned the knife that had killed the animal (Cook 1940). To insure victory of the Greek fleet over the Persians, Themistocles' soldiers *forced* him to make a human sacrifice (Plutarch, *Life of Aristides* 9. 1 f.; *Life of Themistocles* 13.2 f.). The Arcadian who was *forced* to eat the flesh of a child sacrificed to Zeus Lycaeus (Gk *lukos* = wolf) automatically became a werewolf for nine years; at the end of that time he became a man again, provided that, during his wolf period, he had abstained from eating human flesh (Cook 1914). In Rome the social hierarchy was completely inverted during the Saturnalia. In Africa there are even rituals of rebellion (Gluckman 1954). These examples, which could be endlessly multiplied, suffice to show that the majority of truly important supernatural rites break the rules and offend the values governing daily life; from a cultural point of view, they often constitute 'mirror-image' behavior.

Another expression of social negativism permeated with supernaturalism is a well-known but insufficiently analysed aspect of shamanism. Shamans are extreme individualists, notoriously hostile toward one another. The Mohave shaman sometimes bewitches one of his fellow shamans simply because the latter's beliefs and practices differ slightly from his own; he therefore refuses to talk about his powers in front of another shaman for fear that this will offend the latter and incite him to magic reprisals (Devereux 1957b). Trials of (magical) strength are very common between shamans. I shall cite, nearly at random, a Greek source (Apollodorus 6. 3–4), Crow data reported by Lowie (1925c), Róheim's (1950) data about Hungarian shamans, and more general data about the type of shaman found in the steppe tribes. In certain tribes the apprentice shaman must consent to the death of one of his kinfolk. Worse still, the Kuanyama

Ambo who wants to become a shaman must ask his mother to cohabit with him. If she consents, she dies because she has violated the incest taboo; if she refuses, she also dies, bewitched by her son (E. M. Loeb, personal communication). The relationship between incest and witchcraft is too well known to require further discussion in this context. All of this proves that even if the shaman is socially 'useful', as has been claimed (see above), he is also, in many respects, fundamentally 'antisocial'.

Practically the same thing can be said of hermits, ascetics, and other persons of this type, who must be treated with kid gloves because they are inclined to heap supernatural calamities on anyone who offends them. Although his tormentors were only children, the prophet Elisha cursed them and caused them to be torn apart by two bears (2 Kings 2:24). Similarly, just as shamans engage in trials of (magical) strength with each other, so, according to various important early Christian authors, some Christian ascetics were outrageously arrogant or exhibitionistic persons, competing with each other in 'saintliness' and 'self-mortification'. The data assembled and analysed by Dodds (1965) lead one to believe that this kind of misconduct was relatively common. During the Greek decadence, certain eminent men were not given to curbing their negativistic tendencies. The Greek Cynics, for example, ostentatiously violated all social conventions, and Lucian reports, in his *Death of Peregrinus*, that Peregrinus, who was first a Cynic and then a Christian before turning to still another creed, masturbated in public. Lucian then describes his suicide in detail: it was a spectacular self-immolation, heralded by flashy advance publicity and carried out during the Olympic festivals, with a stage setting that would outshine that of the greatest modern music halls.

In brief, however great may be their *apparent* integration with the rest of the culture, the supernatural and the irrational always preserve the imprint of their socially negativistic origins; all the sophistry of the apostles of cultural relativism will not convince me that they are a genuinely functional element of any and every genuine culture.

Hence, whatever superficial differences there may be between such generally respected persons as shamans, Stoic saints, and Cynics on the one hand, and the ridiculed Mohave transvestite and the despised prostitute on the other, both types constitute patterns of cultural misconduct within the sociological frame of reference, just as they constitute models of subjective social negativism within a psychological frame of reference. Nor is it at all certain that Stoic saints (and all their ilk) are socially and psychologically less ill than the Mohave transvestite or the prostitute (Chap. 7).

Whatever the case, these remarks prove once more that, far from being a marginal component of sociology, psychiatry is instead one of its most reliable grids, because no science can have a better grid than the concepts of another whose explanations stand in a relation of complementarity with its own (Devereux 1945 [1978a, Chap. 4], 1961b [1978a, Chap. 5], 1967c).

Since all patterns of misconduct belong in many ways to the same type, I can indicate more precisely, already at this juncture, the sense in which ethnic psychiatric disorders fit the patterns of misconduct defined by Linton and 'execute' their directives.

Sometimes culture itself provides explicit directives for the misuse of cultural materials, particularly in situations of frequent but atypical stress. The directive that is relevant here is the following: 'Don't go crazy, but, if you do, you must behave as follows.' Every society has definite ideas about 'how to act when crazy'. During funeral rites the Nyakyusa simulate insanity in a highly specific manner, since they believe that this prophylactic simulation will protect them from becoming actually insane later on (Wilson 1954). The prophylactic simulation of madness is also attested for other regions (A.F.C. Wallace 1958).

American Indian informants frequently say, 'The insane openly mention the names of their dead relatives.' Since this is not a common symptom in Occidental psychotics, one must conclude that this is a culturally predetermined form of misconduct and that many psychotic Indians do behave in just this manner. Modern society, too, has definite ideas of 'how to behave when insane'. People readily believe that the insane make faces, talk at random, get mixed up in their speech, and say 'brr' or 'b-b-b-b'. Scarcely less naive (and quite as cultural) preconceptions about how the insane 'should' behave, feel, and think are embedded in current legal theories. Hence, the psychiatrist appearing in court is often forced to answer questions that are psychiatrically senseless. I once had occasion to testify as an expert at the trial of a man who had shot his wife dead and then, turning the weapon against himself, had shot off a corner of his skull, knocking himself unconscious. The prosecution argued that the accused was sane and simply 'grossly selfish' because, when he recovered consciousness, he 'selfishly' called to his dead wife to help *him*. My testimony, that this in itself proved that the crime was committed during an epileptic figure and was completely blanketed by amnesia, was rejected out of hand because it did not dovetail with 'legal common-sense' views on how the 'insane' *should* behave. Actually, the kind of behavior commonly ascribed to the insane by both the legislator and the layman is seldom seen in mental hospitals. I add that, shortly after being sentenced to prison, the allegedly sane murderer became acutely psychotic.

A fairly good way to study cultural preconceptions about the 'proper way of being insane' is to examine the behavior of malingerers, for these persons usually try to conform to the *layman's* notion of how the insane behave and can therefore be shown up as frauds by an experienced psychiatrist.[35]

The earliest diagnosis of malingering was no doubt Palamedes' finding that Odysseus was simulating insanity in order not to have to fight in the Trojan War (Hyginus, *Fabulae* 95).

The fact that the impulse to malinger is in itself pathological may explain why one of the Esposito brothers tried to simulate psychosis by ostentatiously eating newspapers. He presumably *chose* this symptom because he was *sufficiently abnormal* to sense unconsciously that oral conflicts play an important role in most psychoses. An even more interesting problem is that of culturally expected and even prescribed transitory eruptions of abnormality. Linton once remarked to me that we will probably never know whether Mohammed was a real epileptic because convulsive seizures were, among the Arabs of his time, not only 'the' mental disorder *par excellence* but were, in addition, so consistently interpreted as tokens of divine backing that Arab chiefs often faked a 'fit' just before battle in order to encourage their followers. Odysseus likewise 'acted out' the Greek's idea of mental decay when he sought to deceive the suitors (*Odyssey* 17. 336 ff.), just as the fugitive David acted out the Judaic conception of lunacy by allowing his saliva to dribble on his beard (1 Sam. 21:13).

By contrast, the idiosyncratic psychotic tends to develop a symptomatology grossly at variance with cultural expectations and social demands, and, moreover, almost deliberately provocative, simply because his illness is itself an important manifestation of his 'social negativism' (Chap. 3).[36] Of course this does not mean that an ethnic disorder is to be interpreted as a case of pretense or malingering. *Amok* runners and Crazy Dogs seek a 'glorious' death and generally find it. Among the Plains Indians the coward either sacrifices glory, honored status, and heterosexual satisfactions or may even go so far as to commit suicide to avoid the official 'solution' to his problems, that is, transvestitism. In brief, the social stereotypes that determine 'how the insane behave' are drawn from 'patterns of misconduct', and individuals suffering from ethnic disorders shape their symptoms according to these patterns, which true malingerers in turn deliberately imitate to persuade others that they are really 'insane'.

In short, among some emotionally disturbed persons the unconscious segment of the ethnic personality is not so disorganised as to incite them to wholesale rebellion against *all* social norms. Although genuinely ill, such persons tend to borrow from culture the *means* permitting them to manifest their subjective derangement in a conventional way, if only to avoid being taken for criminals or witches (Chap. 13). This accounts for such 'exotic' ethnic neuroses as *amok, latah, imu, windigo, koro* and many others that are not found in our won cultural repertory. Aberle ingeniously demonstrated (1952) that even though the Siberian equivalent of *latah* in certain respects resembles Gilles de la Tourette's disease, it is nevertheless not identical with that syndrome. Likewise, although the newspaper s– and even some psychiatrists – wrote that the paranoid veteran who 'shot up the town' in Camden, New Jersey, 'was running amok', his psychosis was fundamentally different from that of a real Malay *amok* runner. In fact, his attack was purely idiosyncratic in both its motivations and its manifestations. No culture pattern influenced the course of events in Camden, and, contrary to what occurs in numerous cases of true *amok*, there was no cultural preparation – no premeditation, in the legal sense of the term. Moreover, premeditation plays an equally decisive role in the Crazy-Dog-Wishes-to-Die syndrome (Lowie 1925a and 1935), as well as in a number of other ethnic disorders.

In every ethnic disorder the behavior pattern of the abnormal person not only conforms to what *his* society expects – for instance, from the *amok* runner or the Crazy Dog – but his behavior is also quite often in complete contrast with *our* culturally determined notions of 'how the insane behave'. In fact the common 'lay' ideas on the subject are probably based on the symptomatology of different ethnic disorders obtaining at an earlier stage of our own culture.

If the symptomatology of ethnic psychoses fits cultural expectations, it is chiefly because conventional ideas on 'how to act when insane' reflect the specific nature of the conflicts prevailing within a culture – preconceptions determined by the nature of the defenses that that culture provides against culturally penalised conflicts and impulses. Thus, given the nature of Crow culture, the physically traumatised Crow Indian can, because of his distinctive ethnic makeup, find relief in 'being crazy' in accordance with the Crazy Dog pattern, whereas the Malay, because of his ethnic makeup and because of the nature of his culture, will relieve his tensions by becoming an *amok* runner.

This convergence of the states of tension characteristic of a culture and the defenses that it provides against these tensions, on the one hand, and the cultural preconceptions of 'how to act when insane', on the other, explains some important facts: the absence, or at least the extreme infrequency, of a certain syndrome in a given society, in which different syndromes proliferate; the variations, determined by the cultural environment, in the incidence and proportion of various syndromes; and, finally, the fact that in a given society the full range of all known psychiatric disorders is rarely observed. Thus, today, the Occidental psychiatrist practising in an urban environment rarely has occasion to encounter cases of *grande hystérie*, so common in Charcot's time.[37] Similarly, the Mohave Indians were totally *incapable* of understanding my descriptions of obsessive rumination and compulsive rituals. When questioned about obsessions, one of my Mohave informants replied: 'I see what you mean; it is like the chief's thinking constantly about the welfare of the tribe.' And when I mentioned compulsive rituals, I was told: 'So-and-so is always jingling the coins in his pocket.'[38] Nevertheless, the Mohave are so prone to 'psychological reflection' that it was from Mohave informants and not from psychiatric textbooks that I learned of the existence of *globus hystericus* and pseudo-cyesis (hysterical false pregnancy) at a time (1932–3) when I was unfamiliar with even the rudiments of psychiatry. This comes as no surprise from a culture in which training in sphincter control is remarkably casual and where avarice (anal retention) is one of the capital sins (Devereux 1951d). Moreover, I have so far encountered only a single case of hand-washing of a genuinely compulsive type in a primitive society: the Attawapiska Cree (Honigmann 1954). Finally, although I cannot diagnose with certainty the native of Dobu who could not stop working, discussed by Fortune (1932b), I am at least perfectly sure that this was not a case of true compulsive behavior.

I shall mention only in passing the absence of true schizophrenia among primitive peoples who have not been subjected to a brutal acculturation process, because I discuss the matter at length elsewhere (Chap. 9). In fact, what Occidental psychiatrists sometimes mistakenly diagnose as schizophrenia in a primitive belonging to an *intact* culture is usually a hysterical psychosis or a psychotic episode (*bouffée délirante*). As for Laubscher's (1937) numerous diagnoses of schizophrenia among the Tembu, their accuracy has been challenged even by psychiatrists without ethnological training and especially for those who had not simply read his book but had seen his film – and this in spite of the fact that, at the time Laubscher was working among the Tembu, the tribe was already undergoing a brutal acculturation process. A perspicacious psychiatrist (Domarus 1948), familiar with South African life, has suggested, no doubt correctly, that the Bantu have been able to survive psychologically in spite of very harsh oppression only because of the long period of nursing and relatively satisfactory mothering of infants.

Finally, and this observation is important, it appears that the authentic psychopath – who must be carefully distinguished both from the neurotic or nonneurotic criminal and from the illegalist[39] – is likewise quite rare in intact primitive societies.

The problem of historical change can be reviewed fairly briefly. I have already mentioned the quasi-disappearance of *grande hystérie* in modern urban environments and its persistence in less-developed societies. This is shown by the following incident.

A few years ago an eminent psychiatrist received a manuscript from a psychiatrist, born in the Middle East and practicing there, who had received his training in excellent European medical schools and psychiatric hospitals; the manuscript was so surprising that my colleague asked me to read it and give him my opinion. At first I thought it had been written by an eccentric or by someone trying to be original at all costs; but I gradually came to realise that the author had been treating patients who resembled those Charcot had studied a the Salpêtrière hospital but that, because of his Occidental training, he had tried to fit his clinical data into the straitjacket of contemporary psychiatric thought, whose main axis – or even obsession – is schizophrenia. His approach reminds one of current revisionist attempts to diagnose as latent schizophrenics certain patients whom Freud had diagnosed as hysterics. Such attempts are based not on clinical reality but on certain culturally determined psychiatric thought models (Devereux 1958a [1978a, Chap. 10]). One also notes that it has become a commonplace in psychoanalytic circles to say that, whereas the pioneers of psychoanalysis dealt primarily with symptom neuroses and the psychoanalysts of the thirties with character neuroses, the majority of those who consult the psychoanalyst today suffer from an alteration of the sense of their own identity (Lowenfeld 1944).[40]

There is noting surprising about the fact that the proportions of different psychiatric symptoms vary in terms of the cultural context. Until recently, *many* more men than women have had stomach ulcers. Social-class differences in the distribution of various psychiatric ailments are well documented (Hollingshead and Redlich 1958). In view of these findings, why should one be surprised to learn that the full gamut of psychiatric symptoms is rarely observed in a single society when one readily accepts the absence of malaria among the Eskimos and of snowblindness and frostbite among the Congolese?

Neither differences in the ratios of psychiatric syndromes that one can observe in various societies nor the absence of some known syndromes in every society affects the stability or variability, in a given society, of the proportion of 'abnormal' persons to those called 'normal'. It has been urged – whether rightly or wrongly matters little – that this proportion remains constant in every society and at every moment of history. What does matter is that some scholars (Eaton and Weil 1955) believe that one can conclude from this finding that psychiatric illnesses have a biological origin. This argument is, to say the least, specious. Were it acceptable, one would also have to suppose that physical illnesses do *not* have a biological origin, since the distribution of diseases and the percentage of premature deaths – that is, deaths not due to old age – vary greatly from one society to another. Moreover, the explanation of this fact about psychiatric illness, if indeed it is a fact, would be easy enough to find. If it is true that the percentage of physically incapacitated individuals may not exceed a critical threshold in a given society without causing that society to collapse, it is equally true that too high a ratio of psychiatrically ill persons would have similar consequences (Devereux 1956d).

Lastly, and above all, it is, sociologically speaking, absurd to try to draw rather complex conclusions from the simple ratio between *all* those who are psychiatrically normal and abnormal in a given society. In fact, a society may very well tolerate a relatively high proportion of 'abnormal persons' as long as the majority of them are, for instance, hysterics; it cannot survive if the majority are schizophrenic or feebleminded. Likewise, a society whose abnormal members were mostly mentally retarded persons, just below the normal range, would manage to survive, although with some difficulty, if the society were a simple agricultural one or if the majority of its feebleminded members constituted a class of unskilled laborers. This is the equivalent of the finding that if the Elmolo manage to survive in spite of so severe a calcium deficiency that the majority of its members have saber shins, their survival is due to their relatively protected geographical location, on the one hand, and, on the other, to their not being a warrior tribe (Dyson and Fuchs 1937). In a warrior society, such a rate of calcium deficiency would rapidly entail the tribe's extinction. Likewise Sparta, a highly militaristic and rigidly stratified state, was more severely endangered by the low birth-rate of its upper classes (Forrest 1968) than Hungary was by the massacre of the majority of its warrior caste during the disastrous battle of Mohács[41] simply because the Hungarians, unlike the Spartans, rapidly filled the decimated ranks of their warrior nobility with newly ennobled commoners.

To return to clinical problems, one cannot but be astonished when one sees psychiatrists misled by the cultural conformism of some of their neurotic or psychotic patients – even to the point of underestimating the seriousness of their fundamental pathology. The following example will demonstrate this.

An ambitious and educated white woman had married, on the rebound, an Indian farmer, an uneducated but honest and hard-working man. To compensate for her loss of status, she wanted her son to live like a white man and *be a success* in accordance with the standards of white society. In a word, she wanted to make him 'mother's hero'. However, this halfbreed, a remarkably gifted person, unconsciously identified himself with his father, whom he consciously despised, just as he despised all those of his race. He reacted against the conflicting demands of his mother in a very subtle way: he contrived to fail in everything he undertook in such a way that, by frustrating himself, he at the same time frustrated his mother's ambitions. Moreover, by making *himself* fail, it was first and foremost the despised part of himself, his Indian 'half', that he damaged. Thus, in spite of a brilliant freshman year at one of the best universities, when financial difficulties made it impossible for his parents to help him pursue his studies, he chose to leave the university and work in a factory, rather than accept help from one of his father's sisters, a 'lousy Indian' who had married a wealthy farmer. Also, though he complied with his mother's demand that he should not marry an Indian, he complied by marrying a white girl – but one as uneducated and 'primitive' as the most 'blanket' Indian. Having by his intelligence attracted the attention of his superiors, he was offered a foreman's job. He refused this promotion and, to justify his refusal, claimed that, if he became foreman, he would have to invite to his home not only his coworkers but also some of the office employees and lower-echelon bosses in the factory – and the latter would consider his apartment (which was in fact quite acceptable) the 'dirty wigwam' (sic!)[42] of a 'lousy Indian'. In short, he failed to achieve any of the typical middle-class values – 'education', 'success', and 'marriage to a white woman' – by setting up, in opposition to them, another white-middle-class value: racial prejudice. His behavior is therefore a typical example of 'mock compliance'.

Likewise, although he was beset by a severe Oedipal complex, he handled it by viewing his father as a 'lousy Indian'. He denied hating him or being jealous of him because he cohabited with his mother. He said that he was only 'indignant' that a 'lousy Indian' (his father) could defile 'a pure white woman' (his mother) by cohabiting with her (Chap. 2). This permitted him to face his Oedipal problems (under a cultural mask) without gaining insight into their subjective meaning. Moreover, although he was himself a halfbreed, he did *not* consider his own sexual relations with his (white) wife as a defilement of the white race – doubtless because, owing to her primitive and uncultivated behavior, his wife represented for him an Indian 'squaw' and, because of her race, his mother. From some of his allusions – too tenuous for me to cite here but sufficiently convincing to be taken into account – concluded, further, that it was as if his 'white' half made love with the white racial component – with the 'whiteness' of his wife – and his Indian half made love with her 'primitive', and therefore symbolically Indian, component.

In short, this halfbreed patient took advantage of the fact that race prejudice, like all prejudices, is a symptomatic defense that culture provides to neurotics and used it as a defense against insight into his Oedipal conflicts. Now, what betrayed the symptomatic character of his racial prejudice was the fact that he was a halfbreed, for it is particularly absurd for a halfbreed to profess to despise Indians. If he had been a simple southern white, obsessed with the desire to 'protect' the honor of white women, his neurosis, though equally pathognomonic, would have been less easy to discern, masked as it was by cultural prejudice.

This clinical observation strikingly demonstrates how a dual cultural allegiance may fit into the series conflict–defense–secondary conflict–secondary defense.[43] This schema provides a particularly fertile frame for the study of religious conversions and of conflicts triggered by acculturation.

Although a definition of ethnic disorders was given at the beginning of this chapter, so many marginal problems have now been raised that, before entering on a systematic study of the cultural patterning and organisation of these disorders, it seems appropriate to recapitulate the terms of the definition and to review the principal examples that have been cited.

Ethnic disorders resemble shamanistic derangements in that both use defenses and symptoms provided by culture and developed specifically for that purpose.[44] However, ethnic disorders derive their means of defense from one segment of culture, and shamanistic derangements derive theirs from another. Ethnic disorders differ from shamanistic derangements in the origin of their basic conflicts, which are rooted not in the ethnic unconscious but in idiosyncratic traumata *sufficiently prevalent* in a given culture to force that culture to take cognisance of them as soon as their frequency or intensity exceeds a certain threshold. When such is the case, the culture is obliged to create defenses against these disorders; one of these defenses is precisely the development of patterned symptoms, which, by permitting the externalisation of the disorders in standardised forms, render them, ipso facto, more easily controllable (see below). Otherwise expressed, only fairly recurrent types of traumata, which culture singles out for special notice and designates as 'traumata', elicit properly ethnic, as opposed to idiosyncratic, disorders, because culture places at the disposal of persons subjected to such strains a ready-made armamentarium of defenses in the form of prepatterned symptoms representing one kind of standardised 'pattern of misconduct'.

The preceding considerations permit a systematic examination of the origin, evolution, and manifestations of ethnic disorders. In what follows I shall examine all the significant problems except that of symptoms – of 'signals' (Chap. 13) – which are culturally formulated and by means of which the disturbed individual informs his society that he is 'crazy' and, at the same time, specifies that he is not a *non*crazy deviant – criminal or otherwise.

The main consequence of this cultural patterning of ethnic disorders is to render the behavior of the 'patient' not only predictable but, quite specifically, predictable in terms of the cultural frame of reference, whereas idiosyncratic disorders are predictable only in terms of a psychological frame of reference (Chap. 2). In the ethnic psychotic, the predictable segment of behavior will be the behavior exhibited by *any* ethnic psychotic of the same type. In Idiosyncratic disorders, on the contrary, it will be necessary to try to understand the psychology of the individual patient, and prediction made on this basis will apply only to the behavior of *a* (particular) paranoid individual, of *a* manic-depressive, and so forth. It must be remembered that this distinction between 'any' and 'a' has a crucial significance, not only, as Russell (1903, 1919) emphasises, in formal logic, but also in psychiatry (Devereux 1944b).

The (cultural) predictability of the actions of an individual suffering from ethnic disorders results from a powerful cultural conditioning. Of course the young Malay hopes he will never find himself in straits so desperate that only one acceptable solution remains open to him: running *amok*. He knows, however, that, should such a situation arise, he *will have to* become an *amok* runner and *he will know how* to conduct himself properly. Likewise it is probable that every young Viking not only hoped he would be capable of 'going berserk' in battle but even *learned* the behavior complex that constituted 'going berserk'. In Greek and Roman society, suicide, as a solution accessible to the individual in trouble with the law, was thoroughly regulated. The young Greek or Roman certainly hoped that he would never find himself in difficulties of the kind in which society would drive him to commit suicide or would suggest to him that he do so; nevertheless, when matters came to this pass, he did what was expected of him. Thus, although it had unjustly condemned them to death, society did not have to use force to make Theramenes or Socrates drink the hemlock. As for the Roman aristocrat, he was expected to anticipate his own execution – by committing suicide – in order to avoid the confiscation of his property by the state. And when the cowardly Paetus hesitated, his wife shamed him, and, to encourage him to kill himself, stabbed herself before his eyes, saying, 'Paetus, it doesn't hurt' (*Paete, non dolet*) (Pliny, *Epistles* 3. 16). I seriously doubt that a modern state could so easily persuade those it has condemned to death that it is their duty to carry out their own sentences so as to spare their countrymen the ritual pollution (*miasma*) of bloodshed.

The argument that ethnic disorders are culturally patterned not only does not contradict but considerably reinforces my fundamental view that, in the last resort, all psychic disorders involve impoverishment, dedifferentiation, and disindivudalisation. The Malay who runs *amok* ceases to be a highly differentiated individual; he is now nothing but an *amok* runner, his psychic disorder having obliterated and swallowed up everything that was unique in his personality.

The cultural patterning of ethnic disorders also allows two curious facts to be explained:

1. Whether provided by native informants, colonial officials, (Clifford 1898), planers (Fauconnier 1930), or psychiatrists (Van Loon 1926 [1920]; Yap 1952), descriptions of *latah* attacks are remarkably similar.[45] This tends to prove that Malay informants have not sought to force their accounts into the procrustean bed of the culturally imposed model of this disease. Similarly, the *amok* episodes described in the ancient Malay epic (Anonymous [1930] 1922) fit in even the minutest details with modern accounts (Clifford 1922) in regard to both the *amok* runner's behavior and the panic reaction of the civilian population and even of the soldiers sent against him.

2. This explains why nearly every case of *latah* and *amok* appears to be a 'classic' case, worthy of inclusion in a psychiatric textbook. The same cannot be said of the idiosyncratic psychotic, who generally does not have the good grace to facilitate the psychiatrist's task of diagnosis by exhibiting such 'textbook' syndromes. In fact, it may be that the relative uniformity of attacks of *grande hystérie*, as observed in Charcot's service, was due not only to the fact that in the 1880s hysteria was the ethnic type neurosis of the Western world but, even more, to the systematic inculcation of 'the right way to be a hysteric'.

In fact, victims of hysteria lend themselves particularly well to this kind of conditioning because they are notoriously prone to the theatrical behavior and are constantly invited to 'do their number' for the distinguished professional visitor. Proof that it was not a question of malingering was, moreover, explicitly provided by one of Charcot's 'prize patients', who muttered one day, 'You really have to be crazy to be able to play the part as expected.'

I shall not analyse separately the culturally prepatterned aspects of the various phases that occur in ethnic disorders.

Ethnic character and ethnic disorders. The wide variety of 'causes' that in a given society can produce a single type of patterned eruption is sufficient evidence that ethnic disorders are rooted chiefly in ethnic character (and not in the ethnic unconscious). At the risk of repeating myself, I shall state once again that the *amok* attack can result from the widest variety of causes: delirium due to a high fever, rumination of an insult, desire to perish in a glorious conflagration atop a heap of corpses, compliance with the orders of a hierarchical superior, fascination exerted by the *kris*, severe reactive depression, intentional anticipation of *amok* behavior, a kind of autohypnosis that takes the form of a litany on man's being fated to die and the futility of existence, and many others. Despite their statistical frequency, subjective conflicts ('traumata') of the individual *amok* runner trigger only a (temporary) psychosis in him. It is his ethnic character that causes him to become an *amok* runner rather than a catatonic or something else. *Mutatis mutandis*, the same remarks are applicable to other ethnic disorders.

Cultural-patterns and clinical labels. An ethnic disorder forms a coherent structure in its evolution, not only from its causes to its resolution, by way of its various manifestations, but also in its specific manifestations. It follows that specific expressions, such as 'to run *amok*' or 'to go *berserk*', should be used to designate only the specific disorders of Malays or Vikings, respectively. A Malay does not go *berserk*, nor does a Viking run *amok*. By contrast, in Occidental society only (idiosyncratic) paranoiacs or paranoid schizophrenics can become prey to a blind and uncontrollable homicidal rage. This finding absolutely does not authorise one, however, to conclude that the Malay *amok* runner, too, is paranoid. In fact, what underlies an ethnic disorder is not simply the specific psychodynamic configuration that determines its etiology, but a particular ethnic character as well – one so conditioned as to allow the subject to rid himself of a number of diversified subjective problems by means of one and the same complex of symptoms. This is shown by the fact that a mere attack of malaria may trigger an *amok* attack in a Malay, though it could not do this in a European, even if he had spent a long time among the Malays. I am therefore not convinced that the true *amok* can be observed (Teoh 1972) among Chinese and Tamil citizens of Malaysia.

This finding has an interesting implication: no one is entirely acculturated unless he has reacted to a culturally specific strain with the disorder culturally appropriate to that strain. Thus I have yet to hear of a squaw man (a white man married to an Indian and living as an Indian) who became a Crazy Dog or of a European living among the Malay who became an *amok* runner. In short, a given disorder must conform *in the smallest details* to the prescribed pattern if it is to be considered an ethnic disorder. Thus the term *amok* is inapplicable to the Melanesian's violent outburst, first, because he (usually) uses a lance (Chowning 1961) and not, like nearly all Malay *amok* runners, a *kris* or some other short sword or dagger and, second, because, unlike the Malay's fit, the Melanesian's fit does not always result in homicide. Nor can one compare to an *amok* attack the bloody outbreaks frequently observed among West African soldiers, because they do not use their bayonets but their army rifles and because their attacks do not appear to be culturally patterned (Aubin 1939; Dembowitz 1945). Finally, Sophocles' Ajax and Euripides' Orestes (in *Iphigenia among the Taurians*) are neither '*amok* runners' nor '*berserkers*' when, believing they are killing persons, they savagely slaughtered animals – even though the Malay *amok* runner sometimes incidentally kills animals that cross his path. I maintain that both Ajax and Orestes were 'werewolves', of the specifically Greek type described by Roscher (1896).

In short, whatever its frequency, a disorder is not an ethnic one as long as it has not undergone cultural patterning. Although in the nineteenth century the sepoys of the Indian army occasionally had seizures of murderous madness – the best-known case being that of Mangal Pande, whose execution was one of the direct causes of the great Sepoy Mutiny of 1857 – their fits were nonetheless idiosyncratic, because an ethnic disorder resembling *amok*, but culturally only slightly patterned, existed in only a few limited regions of the Indian subcontinent (Barbosa 1921; Correa (1858; *Encyclopaedia Britannica*, 1910, Vol. 1). Similarly, the British soldier described by Kipling ('In the matter of a private'), who went on a bloody rampage, exhibited neither a particularly thorough acculturation nor a desire to imitate Indian culture models. His homicidal psychosis was due to subjective causes and manifested itself in a subjective manner; in other words, he improvised his own symptoms in conformity with his own needs.

The ethnopsychiatrist must therefore reserve specific diagnostic terms for the manifestations corresponding to them: the term *amok*, for example, uniquely for the murderous outbursts of the Malay behaving in accordance with the traditional pattern. At the very most, he might also apply it to the behavior of a hypothetical Malay who, having no *kris* or other kind of knife but owning a revolver, runs through the streets shouting '*Amok!*' and shooting blindly into a crowd. My emphasis on the diagnostic importance of the appropriate model is justified by the following case. A particularly sensational psychotic crime – a virtual slaughter – sometimes triggers a 'fashion'; that is, the initial incident is soon transmuted into a sort of 'tradition' that is patterned, at least in part, by cultural values. A relatively recent example of this is furnished by the slaughter committed by a Texan who shot indiscriminately from a tower into a crowd – a crime that was followed by several similar outbursts of homicidal psychotic insanity. On the other hand, the at least equally sensational murder of eight Chicago nurses found no imitators, doubtless because the killer did not use a firearm. What is involved here is obviously a form of cultural conditioning: the 'proper' and 'honorable' American way to kill is to kill with a gun. To use a knife for the identical purpose is culturally 'despicable', good at best for 'dirty niggers', 'wops', and other un-American scum (Chap. 3).

Pattern and element. Numerous ethnic symptoms are readily mistaken for socially approved kinds of behavior. Thus the recklessness of the *amok* runner or *berserker* is only a paroxysmal manifestation of the courage so prized in the famous Malay or Viking warrior. What makes the *amok* runner's temerity pathological is its social uselessness and the fact that his victims are usually not his enemies but members of his own group. The case of the Crazy Dog is even more revealing. Though he was doubtless as eager as anyone to 'count coup' ('score' against the enemy), his ostentatious performance was, nonetheless, an act of pure self-glorification, because sometimes the Crazy Dog went into battle armed only with a quirt and a rattle. This egotistical display of courage had, moreover, a cultural model: it was that of the young daredevil Crow who, avid of glory, often betrayed a carefully laid ambush by riding out of it at breakneck speed so as to be the first to count coup on the enemy. It is to be noted that this practice of self-glorification often had disastrous military consequences.[46]

As for ethnic disorders of our own society, the similarities between the principal symptoms of schizophrenia and the patterns of behavior socially prized by our culture are discussed in Chapter 10.[47]

By contrast, the constituent symptoms of idiosyncratic disorders rarely coincide with elements of socially approved behavior. This finding justifies, I think, the utilisation of the word 'pattern' in Linton's formula 'patterns of misconduct', because in every ethnic disorder it is chiefly the pattern, rather than any one of its component elements, that is abnormal, and this abnormality is, in a way, a caricature of the total culture pattern.

Problems in the identification of symptoms. The champions of cultural relativism will predictably assert that the Crazy Dog is normal because his behavior is standardised and culturally controllable. I must therefore demonstrate that there is a parallelism between the definition of conduct qua 'symptom' in terms of the absolute criteria of normality and the definition of this same conduct formulated in cultural terms. Among the Plains Indians the coward had at his disposal the solution of becoming a transvestite, whereas, among the Tanala of Madagascar, transvestism was the refuge of the sexually deficient man, whose impotence, had he married, would have been made public by his unsatisfied wife (Linton 1933). The adoption of the same type of deviant behavior by two different types of individuals under stress proves that trasvestitism is a symptom even if it is culturally patterned and fitted into a social niche. Similarly, some notoriously irrational types of behavior that modern psychiatrists recognise as symptoms must necessarily be considered as such even if, in another society, they provide the constitutive elements of an ethnic (or 'sacred') psychosis. This is true for glossolalia, which is a clinical symptom for the modern psychiatrist but was a manifestation (a 'symptom') of 'divine madness' (Dodds 1951) for the Greeks. One can say at the most that the hallucinating Occidental psychotic is *more severely* disturbed than the Plains Indian, whose hallucinations are part of his vision quest (Chap. 15).

Trauma, motivation, and social justification. These factors practically coincide in ethnic disorders. Culture itself defines the nature and degree of intensity of the strain or trauma that justifies one's 'going crazy'. Among the Northern Algonquians only an 'extreme deprivation', acknowledged by the society to be of the requisite kind and intensity, justifies – and therefore gives rise to – the *windigo* seizure (Teicher 1960). What Crow culture defines as an 'intolerable disappointment' leads to the Crazy Dog syndrome (Lowie 1925a), and nothing it does not define in this manner is capable of motivating or eliciting this ethnic disorder.

If a Crow is to become insane in a *respectable* – that is, *ethnic* – manner, two conditions must be met:

1. The socially recognised stress must be experienced in a conventional manner and must be solved in an equally conventional way: the Crow Indian who fears death has the right to become a transvestite but not the right to declare himself a pacifist or 'conscientious objector'.

2. To an 'intolerable disappointment' of an 'appropriate' type, the Crow Indian may react by becoming a Crazy Dog and thus win the respect of the members of his tribe. Such may be his reaction, for instance, if his ambition to become a chief is frustrated (Lowie 1925a). But he is not

supposed to react to an 'intolerable disappointment' of a type *not acknowledged* as such by 'going crazy' in just 'any old way'; if caught in this second type of situation, he wins the respect of the others only if he ostentatiously reacts to it phlegmatically and displays exceptional stoicism and indifference toward what even his entourage admittedly recognises to be an atypical, though terrible, blow.

The following example will illustrate this point. Under certain conditions a Crow could claim the wife of another if he had had an affair with her. A thoroughly disreputable Crow once dared to claim the dearly beloved wife of another man by falsely alleging that he had had an affair with her. In spite of his wife' vehement denials, and even though both he and the rest of the tribe knew for a fact that the claimant was lying, the husband stoically commanded his weeping wife to follow the liar into his tent, thus gaining much prestige for himself (Lowie 1925b). Had he reacted by becoming a Crazy Dog, he would probably have been despised by all, simply because the trauma caused by this situation, though recognised as serious, was not of the 'right' kind.

Another telling example is the way in which the Mohave define personal loss and the appropriate response to it. The Mohave weep copiously at funerals and scorn the white man for not having wept at the god Matavilye's funeral (Devereux 1961a [consult 2nd rev. edn, 1969]). Though they ridicule the man who allows himself to become upset by the desertion of his wife or mistress, they readily accept that a woman should indulge in a violent display of emotion when abandoned by a husband or lover. In fact, the situation is even more subtly nuanced: the nature of Mohave culture explains why old men deserted by young wives suffer a transitory attack of *hīwa itck* (heartbreak) – a socially recognised but privately ridiculed disturbance – while old women abandoned by young husbands experience nothing of the kind, and why only widows – never widowers – try to commit suicide during the funeral of a spouse.[48]

In short, culturally acknowledged traumata generally provoke ethnic disorders; traumata in which the culture refuses to see a plausible cause of 'insanity' elicit idiosyncratic disorders. because these types of cultural definitions tend to change more slowly than social reality changes, a new ethnic disorder may become quite common before being acknowledged as a product of culture. Thus, because of the progressive disintegration of their social life, Mohave men commit suicide more and more frequently when faced with amorous difficulties, but the tribe as yet refuses to recognise in this emerging pattern the expression of a new ethnic disorder; it correctly perceives the correlation between this type of conduct and the acculturation process (Devereux 1961a [2nd rev. edn., 1969]), but it persists in viewing it simply as an idiosyncratic disorder.

The instigation – which must not be confused with motivation – is a formalised signal that triggers both 'sacred' and ethnic disorders. Sacred disorders are, moreover, socially functional only if they *can be elicited at will*. A seizure can be triggered either accidentally or intentionally; it can be either self-induced or elicited by an external cause. In a few cases the efficacy of triggering mechanisms can be partially explained in biochemical or neurophysiological terms, but in the majority of cases the sequence 'triggering–seizure' appears to be a 'conditioned reflex' of a purely cultural order. Furthermore, biochemical or physiological triggers may include cultural components, because, being integrated with a prescribed cultural sequence, they can considerably reinforce and even modify their inherent triggering capacity.

The most common biochemical triggers are alcohol and drugs. Given such well-known phenomena as the 'placebo effect' and the clear-cut influence of cultural anticipations and/or antecedent psychological states on the effects of alcohol and drugs, it is evident that this type of trigger needs to be studied also from an ethnopsychiatric viewpoint. As regards alcohol, I have noted elsewhere that the drunken Plains Indian is quarrelsome, whereas the drunken Mohave tends to fall into a sort of stupor (Devereux 1951a [2nd rev. edn, 1969]). An alcoholic American woman reacted to different types of alcohol in terms of their cultural definitions: under the influence of champagne she did her best to speak French and behaved like a cute lady's maid of the stage, but under the influence of gin she behaved and talked like an English charwoman, and so forth. Reliance on drugs or alcohol to induce certain particularly sought-after abnormal states is a commonplace phenomenon. Some specialists even think that Viking *berserk* behavior was artificially provoked by the consumption of poisonous mushrooms on the eve of battle (Fabing 1956). Like the modern gangsters who take cocaine or heroin before committing particularly audacious crimes, the dangerous Assassin sect in Persia and Syria consumed hashish.[49] In some modern armies a big shot of rum is regularly distributed to the soldiers before they are ordered to attack. Reliance on alcohol as a preliminary to coitus in puritanical societies is a particularly telling example of the influence of cultural factors on the consequences of intoxication. In fact, since one of alcohol's physiological effects is to decrease erectile potency, it cannot 'trigger' sexual behavior except by temporarily abolishing inhibitions; hence the saying 'The superego is soluble in alcohol'. I strongly suspect that the efficacy of the laurel leaves chewed by the Pythian priestess at Delphi was due less to the drug they contained than to the belief that Apollo's laurel was capable of inducing a 'mantic' state. In support of this interpretation I cite the fact that, contrary to the claims of some ancient authors, no trace of toxic telluric gas emanations, or of crevices that would permit such emanations, have been detected at Delphi by modern archeologists. I also interpret frenetic dancing – a frequently used technique for inducing abnormal states – in a similar manner: as a kind of self-intoxication, because physical exhaustion produces a state of self-intoxication (Chap. 11). Fasting is another physiological biochemical trigger.

Neurophysiological triggering. It was long believed that the state of ecstasy induced by the beat of a drum was a mere conditioned reflex. Today it is thought that the drumbeat is *also* a kind of auditory driving, which, like photic driving, modifies the brain waves, inducing an abnormal state explicable in electroneurophysiological terms (Neher 1961, 1962).

Certain kinds of seizure can be triggered either by a cultural stimulus of a conventional kind or by a drug. The Viking could go *berserk* either by ingesting toxic mushrooms or by listening to heroic ballads. An immensely strong but also prudent and good-natured Danish king, wishing to hear such ballads but knowing that they would put him into a state of *berserker* madness, asked his men to bind him hand and foot and watch over him so that, in the *berserk* state, he would not injure anyone (Bérard 1927). One may well wonder what was paramount in the king's mind: the desire to experience the *berserker* frenzy or the desire to hear the ballads. To my mind, his principal motive was doubtless the former. Likewise, the great khan Ogotai took the precaution of charging his men to ignore any death sentence he might pronounce under the influence of alcohol. This permitted him to become as drunk as he pleased without having to bear remorse the next day (Grousser 1941).

Among the Ainu, the *imu* seizure is triggered in a manifestly cultural way, since the standard trigger, 'snake', can be either a real snake, a toy snake, or even the simple exclamation 'Snake!' – and this in a region that is not infested with poisonous snakes (Winiarz and Wielawski 1936). Since these echolalic and echopraxic states (the Ainu's *imu*, the Malay's *latah*, and the Siberian's *myriachit*) are triggered by a stimulus that produces a startle-reaction, heartless people can amuse themselves at the expense of those afflicted with these disorders by startling them into a seizure. The same type of seizure may also be elicited accidentally and may even become contagious. By shouting at a regiment of Cossacks from Lake Baikal, a furious Russian colonel threw the whole regiment into a state of *myriachit*. Sometimes it is not even a man but an animal that triggers the *latah* attack. The imitative behavior of an old Malay woman who had been thrown into a *latah* seizure by the sudden appearance of a tiger so upset the animal that it fled (Adelman 1955). On the other hand, I know of no truly conclusive case of seizure provoked by a frightening object or by an unexpected noise of purely inanimate origin. This leads me to believe that a hysterical mechanism is at the root of these seizures. The fact that there is often an imitation of the instigator's behavior and that some individuals (a fact attested at least for the Siberians) become coprolalic during such attacks suggests the presence of another important mechanism: that of 'identification with the aggressor', so well described by Anna Freud (1946).

In the case of *amok*, a mere object can play the role of trigger. Thus, the *kris* (dagger, short sword) can excessively fascinate an individual about to run *amok* (Fauconnier 1930). Some data even suggest that in ancient Greece the mere fact of seating oneself on a tripod sufficed to induce a mantic attack. Thus, when the Pythia refused to prophesy for Heracles, he took away her tripod in order to set himself on it and prophesy for himself (Apollodorus 2. 6. 2). Similarly, when the Argonauts, who had lost their way on the sea, met the sea god Triton and gave him a tripod, the god sat down on it, went into a trance at once, and began to prophesy (Herodotus 4. 179).[50]

A particularly interesting triggering technique is the self-induction of the desired seizure by an anticipation of its symptoms or by a preparation for the seizure. When the prime minister of Madjapahit in Java ordered a group of soldiers to run *amok* against the embassy from Malacca, the soldiers started out by killing those of their fellow citizens who fell into their hands – in other words, by acting as if they were already in a state of *amok*. This then permitted them to become genuinely *amok* (Anonymous 1930). Among the Moro of the Philippines, the *juramentado* (*amok* runner) first asks his parents' permission; he then dresses in distinctive clothing, has himself tightly corseted, and performs various other acts, all of which facilitate the triggering of an authentic *amok* attack (Ewing 1955).

This brief survey of the data is far from exhaustive; it suggests, however, that many attacks, both sacred and ethnic, can be elicited by culturally standardised means. In other words, their onset is both positively and negatively controllable.

The manageableness of the patient. Ethnic neuroses are controllable; this is one of their distinctive traits. The instigator of the *imu* or *latah* seizure can, by his own behavior, which the patient will imitate, not only determine the specific manifestations of the seizure but also terminate it, simply by ceasing to goad the victim. The Crazy Dog is easy to control because, being consistently negativistic, he does the opposite of what he is told to do. Thus, when a mounted Crazy Dog gallops toward a group of people eating in front of their *tipi*, one need only shout, 'Come, trample on us', to make him turn aside. Moreover, the Crazy Dog is negativistic *only* to the extent to which he is expected to be. Thus, if a warrior wishing to pay homage to this hero, dedicated to glorious death, sends his wife to him for a night, the Crazy Dog proves normally cooperative and cohabits with her without needing the command, 'Don't cohabit with this woman!'

The fact that certain Occidental schizophrenics can also be manipulated by means of such 'reverse control' (Chap. 9) does not permit one to infer that the Crazy Dog is schizophrenic; he is only a Crazy Dog. What is more, his manipulability – his negatively patterned maneuverability – may even become blended with that of the negativistic psychotic. An example of this was provided by a Plains Indian woman belonging to a culture that includes the Crazy Dog pattern. Her psychotic behavior could *also* be controlled by ordering her to do the *opposite* of what one expected of her (Chap. 15). What matters, therefore, is that the ethnic psychotic is controllable by essentially cultural means, whereas the idiosyncratic psychotic is controllable only by psychological means.

Termination of the seizure. It is convenient to envisage the process of resolving the seizure in terms of prophylactic measures aimed at preventing symptomatic excesses, especially since data on this subject are relatively meager. Of course, the best way to end the seizure is to cure it. Some seizures are of predetermined length: the Crazy Dog who did not die in combat before the leaves turned yellow was free to give up being a Crazy Dog (Lowie 1935). The classical way of terminating a *latah* attack is to stop goading the subject, who, though sometimes perfectly conscious of what he is doing, cannot halt the seizure by himself and therefore begs the instigator to stop stimulating him. The classical way of terminating an *amok* attack is to kill the *amok* runner. According to Linton (personal communication), this was the situation in Indonesia until it occurred to the Dutch that they could prevent the *amok* runners from finding the glorious death they sought by sentencing to hard labor the ones they managed to capture; this markedly reduced the incidence of *amok* running. Some Northern Algonquians who felt a cannibalistic seizure – a *windigo* attack – to be imminent were so horrified that they begged to be killed (Landes 1938; Teicher 1960). I have noted elsewhere (Devereux 1961a [2nd rev. end, 1969]) that numerous suicides must be considered as attempts to forestall the onset of an acute psychosis.

Among clinical equivalents of social methods of resolving attacks one may mention such well-known techniques as slapping the hysterical patient or dousing him with cold water in order to end his seizure, or else simply leaving him to himself, because hysteria, being a 'social disorder' (G. Jaco, personal communication), requires a public. The clinical equivalent of the termination of the crisis by the neurotic subject himself, by recourse to culturally provided means, would be voluntary commitment to a mental hospital or a decision to undertake psychoanalytic treatment.

It goes without saying that my theory of ethnic psychoses in no way excludes the possibility of classifying these disorders also in terms of traditional psychiatric nosology. Thus, the Mohave 'heartbreak syndrome' is obviously a classic mourning depression,[51] *imu* and *latah* are almost certainly hysterias, and so on. This is not surprising, for fundamental psychodynamic processes have a universal character even if they express themselves in extremely varied forms. Whether normal or abnormal, whether belonging to one culture or another, the individual relies on defense mechanisms that are basically the same. The normal person differs from the abnormal and the Eskimo from the Bedouin, not in terms of the presence or absence of certain defense mechanisms, but through the patterning of the ensemble of these defenses and in terms of the relative importance his culture-assigns to each of them, though the attribution of a coefficient of importance is certainly not a deliberate act but a more or less inevitable byproduct of the prevailing cultural atmosphere.

'Type' Disorders

I designate by the term 'type disorder; the psychological illnesses peculiar to the type of society that produces them. From the ethnopsychiatric viewpoint, these are the most difficult to define and the least well known and studied. Some forty years ago (Chap. 9) I had already noted their existence (without, however, using the term 'type disorders'), but I neglected to follow up this finding, except incidentally. Moreover, the study of these disorders meets with a certain number of difficulties, of which I have singled out two for particular attention.

1. Only the distinction between community (*Gemeinschaft*), whose solidarity is organic, and society (*Gesellschaft*), whose solidarity is mechanical,[52] is workable in the ethnopsychiatric setting. The common distinctions between matrilineal society and patrilineal society or among types of activities (industrial, agricultural, pastoral, or hunting-fishing-gathering) are unusable for various reasons, the main one being that they do not exclude the intersecting and overlapping of categories. Thus the Mohave, who may appear next to the Crow insofar as they are a 'warrior' tribe, could equally well be listed alongside the peaceful Hopi, in that they too are 'farmers'. Given this situation, it is difficult to decide which of the two modes of classification is ethnopsychiatrically the most pertinent. Moreover, I cannot assert that these criteria really concern major types of social *structure* and not simply types of culture *patterns*. This is one of the many problems that arise from the difficulty of distinguishing with precision between what is social and what is cultural.

2. Research in social psychiatry rarely concerns the *total* social structure. Even the best analyses of categories of psychic disorders, considered in terms of 'urban zones', on the one hand (Faris [and Dunham] 1939), and 'social classes', on the other (Hollingshead [and Redlich] 1958), fail to specify, and are incapable of specifying, the correlation between a certain type of disorder and a certain type of *total* social structure. To be sure, every urban zone and every social class traumatises the individual in a different way. The disturbed person may therefore, precisely because of his difficulty, move automatically from one zone or class to another. In our

society, for example, a 'bourgeois' schizophrenic may finally land in a furnished room, while the alcoholic son of an aristocrat may become a tramp. By contrast, there is no segment of society in which the Sedang psychotic can 'end up'; his disorder does not wrench him from the setting of his regular life, nor does it cause him to 'lose status' in any sociologically significant way. At most, he may spontaneously leave his village to wander about in the jungle for a few days, until he dies from a snakebite, is devoured by a tiger, or perishes from simple exposure. Finally, and most important, it must be clearly understood that the 'rooming-house zone', just as 'lower class' (the poor) has meaning only in opposition to 'upper class' (the rich) – and *this within one and the same social structure*, characterised precisely by the multiplicity of its 'niches', that is, by what Durkheim called 'polysegmentation'. A simple example will facilitate understanding on this point. A Mohave of 1830, while objectively poor, was lord and master of his narrow *Lebenstraum* or social space. A Mohave of 1930, while objectively richer, was only a poor man, a nothing in the setting of the immense social space of the United States (Devereux 1961a). In short, psychologically, it is one thing to live in the finest hut in a primitive village and something again to live in a cabin (doubtless less rough and more comfortable than the hut) which is but a hovel when it is located at the edge of a city boasting luxurious private mansions.

I shall therefore pursue my analysis principally in terms of the typological opposition between *Gemeinschaft* and *Gesellschaft* and shall complete it with a discussion of the dichotomy peaceable/warlike and of different types of warlike conduct.

The ethnopsychiatrist will tackle the *Gemeinschaft/Gesellschaft* dichotomy in terms of the types of social relationships that play a key role in a given society. Parsons (1939) defines three types of social relationships: (1) the functionally specific, (2) the functionally diffuse, and (3) the functionally cumulative. Not being an ethnologist, he does not seem to have realised that none of these three types of relationships is decisive within the primitive *Gemeinschaft*, whose prevailing type of relationship I have called (4) *functionally multiple*. I shall discuss the first three types by following Parson's definitions closely but adding my own psychological commentary. As for the theory of functionally multiple relations, it is my own.

Functionally specific relationships play a preponderant role in all *Gesellschaften*, whose normal functioning they to a large extent insure. These relationships are segmental, often ephemeral, reduced to the essential, efficient, complete from their first moment to their last, and objective to the point of being impersonal – and therefore affectively frustrating. I even think that functionally diffuse relationships have been evolved to compensate people for the frustrations created by functionally specific relationships.

Functionally diffuse relationships often arise from trifles; but, once they are established, they are supposed to be stable, unlimited, and imbued with affective significance at every moment of their existence. A modern father cannot do what his Australian aborigine counterpart does during a famine: play lovingly with his young son all afternoon and then, in the evening, kill him and cook him for dinner (Róheim, personal communication).

Functionally cumulative relationships fall between the two preceding types. One can think, for instance of an affair between an employer and his secretary. Such 'office romances' are in fact common enough for modern society to take them into consideration and even to define how they 'ought' to develop. And yet they occur 'by accident' and are in principle 'optional'. If they constitute 'patterns of misconduct' (see below), it is chiefly because they juxtapose two types of theoretically incompatible segmental relationships. They can therefore be analysed sociologically, exactly in the way Davis (1937, 1939) analysed prostitution and illegitimate births. Like diffuse relationships, they probably result from unconscious efforts to extend and deepen skimpy and therefore frustrating specific relationships.

Since I discuss in Chapters 9 and 10 the important role that specific relationships play in the sociogenesis of schizophrenia, I shall add here only that the cleavage element – the *schizo* – of schizophrenia probably represents only a desperate attempt to reconcile mutually incompatible (cumulative) obligations, just as the schizophrenic's attitude of reserve and withdrawal represents an effort to inhibit the tendency, inherent in functionally specific relationships, to spread out of bounds – to become enlarged and transformed into functionally cumulative relationships.

Functionally multiple relationships, which constitute the fourth of the types of relationships under review, play a fundamental role in primitive societies with organic solidarity (*Gemeinschaft*). They differ from cumulative relationships in one essential aspect. Society recognised the 'naturalness' of each of the elements that constitute a cumulative relationship, but their *conjunction* may be viewed as a 'pattern of misconduct' because it is regarded as likely to hinder the correct functioning of each of the specific relationships that constitute it. Thus, the sexual nexus between an employer and his secretary is assumed to diminish the authority of the one and the efficiency of the other and therefore to impair the smooth functioning of the business. Now exactly the opposite is true of functionally multiple relationships in primitive societies, where it is precisely the pattern of the totality that is socially approved and held to make possible the functioning of each of the constituent relationships. As the Bible describes him, Abraham was simultaneously patriarch, paterfamilias, legislator, judge, executioner, tribal chieftain, generalissimo, high priest, and, in fact, 'Lord High Everything Else'. Therefore, by sharing the bed of his handmaiden, Hagar, he did not weaken his authority over her but, on the contrary, strengthened it: she did not become less submissive toward him, since his action only increased her desire to serve him. Moreover, if, seen superficially, Abraham can at a given moment act completely (or at least primarily) in but one of his multiple capacities, it is only because, at other times, he is able to act in a different one. He was able to be war chief only because, qua paterfamilias, he could mobilise all his kinsmen and, in his role as tribal chieftain, his whole clan. He could, moreover, raise an army because, as legislator, judge, and executioner, he could get his orders carried out; finally, he inspired confidence in his role as war chief because, in his role as high priest, he could persuade jehovah to favor his clan.

Functionally multiple relationships also differ from diffuse relationships. The constituent elements of a multiple relationship can, by definition, be enumerated, whereas those of a diffuse relationship cannot. In fact, as soon as one begins to enumerate the constituent elements of a diffuse relationship, one demonstrates by this very act that the relationship is on the point of disintegrating.[53]

Contrary to what happens in the *Gesellschaft*, the *Gemeinschaft* – and particularly the primitive *Gemeinschaft* – is often intolerant of functionally diffuse relationships; this is, in fact, one of its distinctive characteristics. Hence, in such societies passionate love, even between spouses, arouses violent disturbances and occasionally even ends in tragedy (Devereux 1961a). This finding may have some connection with what Mauss said of the relatively weak development of the role and concept of 'person' in primitive societies (1950).

Whereas in the *Gesellschaft* the average man is isolated and therefore runs the risk of becoming schizophrenic, in the *Gemeinschaft* he is almost forced into sociability and is in danger of becoming hysteric. These are the 'psychiatric type disorders' of these two kinds of societies; one will think of them first whenever one tries to make a psychiatric diagnosis. One must therefore think twice before diagnosing hysteria in an Occidental philosophy professor or schizophrenic in a North American Indian (even in one who is acculturated). Experienced psychiatrists sometimes seem to sense this without managing to formulate the principle clearly. Thus, faced with diagnosing a severely disturbed Indian woman patient who, though raised in a tribal society (*Gemeinschaft*), had later pursued fairly advanced studies and earned a university degree, the medical team was divided: the young psychiatrists were unanimous in diagnosing schizophrenia, whereas all the senior psychiatrists and psychoanalysts agreed on a diagnosis of hysterical psychosis. There is little doubt that this woman, who had suffered severe oral traumata (Chap. 15), would indeed have become schizophrenic *had she been raised* in a *Gesellschaft*. Nevertheless, it was fundamentally a case of hysteria overlain by schizophrenoid symptoms. Inversely, at the root of what has been called the 'three-day battlefield schizophrenia' of World War II American soldiers, there was a schizophrenic reaction, heavily overlain with hysterical elements. Though from a superficial point of view these two clinical pictures present certain similarities, the pathodynamics underlying them are nonetheless fundamentally different.

More generally, when a member of a *Gemeinschaft* – and particularly a primitive one – happens to suffer a trauma that in a member of a *Gesellschaft* would elicit schizophrenia, he will most often react with a hysteric disorder, but his hysteria will be overlain by symptoms improvised at the idiosyncratic level and resembling those of schizophrenia; the clinical picture will thus be that of a psychotic episode of, at most, a schizo-affective state. Conversely, a member of our society who accidentally suffers a trauma of a nature that would elicit hysteria in a primitive will nevertheless suffer from a form of schizophrenia overlain by improvised hysterical elements.[54] These remarks must not be misconstrued. I do not wish to encourage either the present tendency of making hysteria a catchall and holdall diagnostic label, universally valid the moment one deals with primitives, or the corresponding tendency of attaching the label 'schizophrenic' to every modern patient whose diagnosis is uncertain (Chap. 9). The psychiatrist's task is to diagnose human beings, not illnesses.

The way in which abnormal reactions are linked with types of societies – and perhaps even with culture patterns – may also be demonstrated by an analysis of the solutions the Crow, the Blackfoot, and the Mohave provided for the conflict between fear of death in battle in battle, on the one hand, and thirst for glory and social ambition, on the other. The Crow had only a single 'social ladder': an individual attained the rank of chief only by performing a particular *series* of warlike exploits. Further, it was their custom to work themselves into a state of blind recklessness by loudly claiming to be motivated only by sentiments of extreme altruism, a state that sometimes culminated in a 'heroic' and quasi-masochistic self-pity (Devereux 1951a). A Crow chief, about to lead his fierce warriors into battle against a hereditary enemy, made them a lachrymose speech, of almost Hitlerian sentimentality, in which he bewailed the wretched lot of Crow captives and portrayed both himself and his notoriously aggressive nation as a pitiful band of unjustly persecuted innocents, whose misfortunes he would now avenge (Lowie 1935). For the uninformed reader, his speech is touching, even poetic; it is absolutely grotesque for anyone who knows the ferocious aggressiveness of the Crow nation.

The conflict between fear of death and thirst for glory sometimes became so acute that Crow society was obliged to take it into consideration. Thus, those who, for one reason or another, were unable to perform *each* of the warlike feats required of a prospective chief could become

Crazy Dogs (Lowie 1925a), whereas those who dreaded death could become transvestites. In addition, the famous warrior who periodically acquired many horses taken from the enemy remained, nonetheless, quite poor because, in order to raise his status, he had to present the horses either to the needy or to those whom he wished to honor. In both cases his generosity à la Robin Hood – mad possible by 'heroic' banditry – brought him increased prestige.

In contrast to the Crow, the Blackfoot, another typical Plains Indian tribe, managed to reconcile economic preoccupations with martial ambitions. In their tribe, too, social advancement depended essentially on the ceremonial distribution of horses – but of *any horses whatsoever*. An ambitious but poor young man could procure the necessary horses only by raiding enemy territory, whereas a rich young man would be advised by his family to stay comfortably at home and choose from the family's herds all the horses he needed to distribute as prestige-earning gifts (Goldfrank 1945).

Among the Mohave, who are also a warrior tribe but outside the Plains Indian pattern, there were two forms of prestigious status, which, under certain circumstances, could merge: a kind of hereditary 'nobility' (*ipā tahāna*, 'real person') and an acquired 'nobility': that of the great commoner warriors who, on the strength of their feats, gained the status of *ipā tahāna* and could probably found new 'noble' lineages.

Now it would seem that certain 'noble' Mohave parents urged their sons to become transvestites (Fathauer 1954) in order to avoid the obligation to fight without, at the same time, risking total dishonor, because, except for transvestites, every Mohave man was expected to distinguish himself by some feat of arms. Still, according to all one can learn at present about this matter, a hereditary *ipā tahāna* who showed cowardice without, however, deciding to become a transvestite did not lose his status as a noble; he simply incurred the contempt of the rest of the tribe.[55]

A study of these facts shows that each of these three basically warlike tribes had, in terms of its distinctive social structure, resolved differently the conflict between the fear of death and the desire for prestige and glory. Among the Crow, the coward himself decided to become a transvestite. Among the Mohave, the young *ipā tahāna* was sometimes persuaded by his parents to adopt this solution. The parents of a rich Blackfoot youth advised him to stay quietly at home and increase his prestige by distributing his family's horses. The ambitious Crow who for one reason or another could not become a chieftain had the choice of acquiring an eminent, though marginal (nonnuclear), status by becoming a Crazy Dog. In a similar situation, the young Blackfoot could gain a socially *nuclear* type of prestige only if he was rich enough to distribute horses. It is unnecessary to dwell her on other obvious differences.

The presence or absence of war neuroses constitutes a third difference, which is often psychiatrically significant. It appears that primitive or semiprimitive *warrior* societies (which must not be confused with *militaristic* societies, such as Sparta) are not familiar with this type of neurosis. The relative brevity of primitive and semiprimitive military campaigns does not adequately explain its absence. Though Genghis Khan fought ceaselessly for many years, I have been unable, in spite of a close study of the relevant historical sources, to discover the slightest indication of war neuroses among his warriors. Nor have I been able to find among them even a hint of a simple slackening of enthusiasm for war, whereas at a certain moment the Macedonians of Alexander's army flatly refused to pursue their victorious advance (Plutarch, *Life of Alexander* 62), and Napoleon frequently had cause to reproach his generals for preferring the pleasures of their newly acquired wealth to camp life (von François 1929).[56] In fact, to speak of 'war neuroses' in primitive societies makes sense only in connection with two diametrically opposed phenomena: the technique that eliminates in advance every anxiety-producing war situation – as in the case of the transvestite – and the outbreak of battle madness of 'heroic' character – as in the cases of the *berserker*, the *ghazi* (heroes of Moslem holy wars), the *amok* runner, the *juramentado*, and some others.

These facts show that it is legitimate to speak of 'psychiatric type illnesses' determined not by the specific culture pattern of the group but rather by its *type* of social structure. Murdock is therefore right in saying that studies of 'culture and personality' should be completed by studies on 'social structure and personality' (1949). Now, if one accepts Murdock's suggestion, one is obliged to establish an explicit distinction between 'type disorder' and 'ethnic disorder'. The first is determined by the type of social structure and determines in turn the range of fundamental nosological categories, or pigeon-holes, into which real psychiatric disorders will fall. At this point the specific culture pattern intervenes and determines in turn the distinctive formulation ('ethnic disorder') of the type disorder peculiar to a given society. Thus, the short psychotic episode (*bouffée délirante*) is one of the type psychoses of relatively simple societies; when aggressive and self-destructive impulses are superimposed on it, it takes the form of an *amok* attack among the Malay, a Crazy Dog quasi-psychosis among the Crow, and so forth.

A last point now requires consideration. A society (or a culture) may be characterised precisely by the fact that it is highly typical – typical, for example, of societies with organic solidarity (*Gemeinschaft*) as opposed to societies with mechanical solidarity (*Gesellschaft*), or typical or warrior societies as opposed to militaristic societies. The principal characteristic of such a society will therefore be its tendency to incarnate a theoretical 'ideal type'. Thus, what is really significant about Sparta is the degree of perfection it brought to the realisation of the barracks state (considered as a type of social structure) rather than its manner of being militaristic (considered as a sociocultural pattern). What makes Tasmanian culture noteworthy is that it provides a perfect example of primitivism, while American culture is a close approximation of the 'ideal type' of industrial society. In extreme cases of this kind it is unlikely that valid *functional* differences can be established between 'type disorders' and 'ethnic disorders'. In any truly primitive society – for example, that of the Tasmanians (Roth 1899) or the Phi Tong Luangs (Bernatzik 1958) – hysteria will faithfully reproduce the theoretical conception of this illness as it appears in all the psychiatric textbooks. By contrast, an Occidental philosophy professor will have a form of schizophrenia that corresponds very closely to the 'ideal schizophrenia' of textbooks. In both cases the distinctive 'ethnic' formulation of the disorder comes close to merging with its basic 'type' structure.[57]

Nearly identical considerations permit one to explain why individual and collective neuroses observable in all societies undergoing brutal acculturation – the acculturation neuroses – resemble one another in a fundamental way; even a little probing reveals an undeniable psychological affinity between Melanesian cargo cults (Chap. 12) and, e.g., the Ghost Dance religion of the Plains Indians (La Barre 1970). In both cases, one is dealing with the type disorders of societies in a state of transition. These disorders are 'ethnic' only in their specific formulations.

When one is dealing with extreme cases, it is therefore difficult to differentiate on a *practical* level between 'type' disorders and 'ethnic' disorders, though from a *methodological* viewpoint the distinction remains a valid one. This implies that these double-edged disorders must be analysed in terms of each of the two frames of reference – and this even when the basic data are practically identical – and it explains why, although the facts and their interpretation involve numerous overlaps, I have though it necessary to analyse schizophrenia both as a 'type' disorder (Chap. 9) and as an 'ethnic' disorder (Chap. 10).

I conclude by stating that the etiology of *any* nonidiosyncratic disorder is essentially determined by the *type of social structure* in which that disorder arises, although its *clinical picture* is chiefly structured by the *ethnic culture pattern*. If the disorders characteristic of modern society – schizophrenia, psychopathic states, and obsessive-compulsive and character neuroses – are so resistant to psychotherapy, this is doubtless due to the fact that the psychotherapist does not realise that the disorders he is dealing with are not *simply* idiosyncratic disorders but are type disorders and ethnic disorders as well.

Our society has its share of ethnic disorders, among which schizophrenia, thoroughly discussed in Chapter 9 and 10, has a major place.

Psychopathy, which is no doubt another of them, is analysed in Chapters 2 and 7, though not as one of the ethnic disorders specific to our culture.

Idiosyncratic Disorders

The two types of traumata for which culture provides no defense and no symptoms that permit one to bind anxiety or face up to the conflicts that these traumata elicit are (a) those that, though statistically frequent, are culturally atypical, so that the culture takes no account of them, and (b) those that (whether culturally typical or atypical) are statistically rare. The individual who undergoes these types of traumata will exhibit an 'ordinary', nonethnic, neurosis or psychosis – that is, an idiosyncratic one. Idiosyncratic disorders are characterised by the improvisation of defenses and symptoms – an improvisation that usually operates, to start with, by deforming certain cultural items that originally were not intended to provide a defense against anxiety.

In Chapter 2, the four ways of distorting cultural material for symptomatic purposes are treated in detail, so there is no need to discuss them here. But I remind the reader once again that cultural materials that reflect a society's self-disavowal may be used as symptoms without undergoing a preliminary distortion, and they rank high as symptoms in the 'patterned' disorders of a given society, that is, in the 'patterns' that even idiosyncratic psychotics do not fail to imitate to a slight extent. Still, in the last analysis, the similarities between conventional or patterned disorders and idiosyncratic disorders are not due primarily to imitation or even to that relative uniformity of the ethnic character of all members of the same group. The essential cause of these similarities is the fact that cultural materials of this type lend themselves particularly well to symptomatic utilisation. This explains – among other things – why the supernatural is so often (Dumas 1946) and so easily incorporated into delusional systems.

None of this simplifies the task of the ethnopsychiatric diagnostician trying to determine whether a disorder is idiosyncratic or not. The complexity just mentioned may be deplored, but it may not be invoked to justify juggling out of sight the fundamental differences between idiosyncratic disorders and those that are not. It is for us to accommodate ourselves to the requirements of reality and not for reality to conform to our own requirements.

Having analysed

1. Shamanistic ('sacred') disorders
2. Ethnic disorders
3. Type disorders
4. Idiosyncratic disorders

I shall now briefly mention some of the clinical applications of this theoretical schema.

CLINICAL APPLICATIONS

The psychiatrist turns more and more to the ethnologist for help in diagnosing culturally atypical or marginal patients. Far too often the ethnologist contents himself with saying that 'among the Bonga Bonga this type of behavior is normal, this kind of belief is traditional' this sort of personality is well adjusted'. Though often true, such statements are almost always insufficient. It is not my intention to minimise the importance of this diagnostic approach, having myself often had occasion to rectify mistaken diagnoses of Indian veterans by stressing, e.g., the difference between delusion and belief (Devereux 1951a). I shall cite in this connection the case of an Indian veteran diagnosed in another hospital as a schizophrenic and subjected to electroshock treatment, which only caused him to become completely unmanageable. When he was finally transferred to Winter Veterans Administration Hospital, where I was working at that time, I was easily able to show that he was not schizophrenic but simply neurotic. Some supportive psychotherapy, given him by a young colleague, permitted him to leave the hospital within six months and return to normal life in the community. All this is routine.

Still, in a diagnostic report, it is not enough to stress the distinction between delusion and belief. The moment one adopts the standards implicit in this limited diagnostic procedure, one becomes unable to provide psychiatric help for an Indian who, after an initial psychotic episode or fugue, goes into remission and defines himself as a shaman (Devereux 1942b). In terms of the 'relativist' standards that govern the limited diagnostic technique just outlined, one would have to say that, because this Indian shaman could be considered 'culturally normal', he was not in need of psychiatric care; whereas I have demonstrated (see above) that the shaman is either a severe neurotic or a psychotic in a state of remission and is therefore still greatly in need of psychiatric help. Indeed, such a person is in emission *only* with reference to *a* particular social setting: his own tribe. He is more or less well adjusted to that setting and *only* to that setting. *He is not capable of adjusting and, above all, is not capable of readjusting.* By contrast, a normal Indian who is not a shaman may be well adjusted to his culture and yet retain the capacity to adjust to other situations as well (Devereux 1951a). To my mind, the crux of mental health is not adjustment per se but the capacity of the person to make successive readjustments without losing the sense of his own continuity in time (Devereux 1966d). Now, it is precisely this capacity that is so obviously lacking in the chronically hospitalised 'model patient': he is perfectly well adjusted to the hospital environment and seems rational and cooperative as long as he is in these surroundings, but he promptly 'cracks up' again when discharged from the hospital.[59]

To be effective, the psychotherapy of the shaman does not require that he be stripped of his ethnic character – de-Indianised – or that one persist in completing his acculturation. Nothing justifies such an attempt, not even the fact that, because of his origins – or, rather, because of discrimination – the Indian is clearly at a disadvantage when he tries to live in American society (Devereux 1951a). Moreover, it is not even culturally expedient to rob him of his ethnic character – to de-Indianise him; for every culture, including our own, grows and develops through contact with different cultures, and the Indian in our midst is an element of constant stimulation – a cultural yeast. The psychotherapy of a shaman must accomplish something entirely different. It must tackle only his shamanistic character – seek to deshamanise him – without attacking his ethnic character structure. It must seek to activate his capacity for readjustment by breaking down his pathologically rigid and relatively marginal and dereistic adjustment to his own tribal milieu *only*.

It may perhaps be objected that Indian tribes *still* need shamans and that, by treating the shaman's illness, one risks depriving the whole tribe of something it needs. I challenge the validity of this argument, for the simple reason that the *role* of an authentic shaman can be played just s well by an adaptable individual who only pretends to be a shaman and therefore does not risk contaminating his 'patients' by transmitting his own neurosis to them.

When I was working among the Sedang Moi of Indochina, like most field workers I sometimes practiced first-aid medicine. I soon discovered that, though my native patients were glad to receive Occidental drugs and dutifully swallowed them, they nevertheless went elsewhere for supplementary psychological (magical) support. Thus, after consulting me and receiving a pill and the advice to stay indoors and keep warm, they would proceed to call in a shaman who, on the pretext of a curative ritual, would drag them out into the rainy night – which generally aggravated the cold or indigestion from which they suffered. To put a stop to these harmful interferences, I simply declared that I, too, was a shaman.[60] Henceforth I did not limit myself to handing out drugs; I also performed certain traditional curing rituals, the only difference being that my rituals were performed, not in the rain, but indoors, and they cost nothing!

These practices gave the patients all the ritual (psychological) support they needed, even though I was not psychologically a shaman and therefore did not believe in the supernatural efficacy of these rites but viewed them simply as 'first-aid (supportive) psychotherapy' – in short, as a kind of reassuring bedside manner.

Although useful, the diagnostic technique that views the shaman as a neurotic or a psychotic in remission, adjusted *only* to a marginal segment of *his* culture, but considers the ethnic psychotic to be a genuine psychotic, adjusted to a given 'pattern of misconduct', is nevertheless related in many ways to the traditional diagnostic techniques founded on the criterion of adjustment, which consists of stating that 'among the Bonga Bonga, this is normal'. In both instances, the major risk is that of mistaking belief for delusion.

For a long time I believed that this limited refinements of diagnostic technique was sufficient for all purposes. Fortunately for two Acoma Indians, sentenced to die in the electric chair, I discovered just in time that even this more refined approach to the problems of adjustment was not entirely satisfactory. The prison psychiatrist charged with diagnosing the two Indians – who were half-brothers – was sufficiently familiar with ethnopsychiatry not to mistake ethnic character traits for psychotic manifestations. Hence, finding no *culturally neutral* evidence of psychological disorder, he felt obliged to declare them 'legally sane'. However, this astute diagnostician, who as a psychiatric resident had done a great deal of work with me on cultural problems arising in diagnostic work, continued to be disturbed by an indefinable feeling that he was overlooking something in these men, and he therefore asked me to come and see them at the Medical Center for Federal Prisoners at Springfield, Missouri.

In the presence of the prison psychiatrist, I conversed separately with the two half-brothers, who had not been able to communicate with each other, being confined to individual cells reserved for persons under sentence of death. In less than ten minutes, each, in turn, poured out a veritable flood of data about witchcraft, which perfectly fitted with Acoma belief but nonetheless left me feeling perplexed; for because of my experience in the field, I knew that this kind of material could normally be elicited from an informant only after much hard preliminary work. The point I am seeking to make is quite simple: a traditionally suspicious and distrustful Pueblo Indian – and one, moreover, under sentence of death – who after only ten minutes of conversation speaks freely of his esoteric beliefs and experiences, relating to witchcraft, to a person he is seeing for the first time is acting about as rationally as would a Navy cryptographer who discussed the Navy's secret code with a stranger he had just met in a bar. Following up this clue, I soon discovered that:

1. The two men had ceased to *experience* these cultural beliefs as objective cultural material and had begun to experience them in a delusional manner: 'The hand was Esau's, but the voice was Jacob's.'

2. Threatened by witchcraft, they had, in terms of Acoma culture, reacted in a wholly abnormal way: instead of ridding themselves of the witch in accordance with Acoma custom, by asking the help of ritual socie-

ties in charge of neutralising witches, they had sought to take the law into their own hands.

It is necessary to make clear the meaning of my statement that these men *experienced* their cultural beliefs in a delusional manner. A brilliant but paranoid electronics engineer ma believe that he is being persecuted by radar; he may even design the radar device that 'persecutes' him, and his blueprint may include real and considerable improvements on existing radar equipment. In short, his new apparatus may well do *everything* that other radar machines do and do it even better – but, *Whatever it does*, it certainly cannot persecute him. In this hypothetical instance, the cultural material is handled quite efficiently but nevertheless in a delusional manner, for in this man's mind electronics has ceased to belong to the realm of physics and has become part of the domain of supernatural persecutory devices.

Once I had determined the *manner* in which these two Indians had distorted cultural reality, it was easy for me to elicit from them personal and idiosyncratic delusional material as well – material that was at variance with the Acoma culture pattern and revelatory of a full-blown paranoid schizophrenia in one of the men and of a psychotically tinged psychopathy in the other.

In short, the idiosyncratic core of these psychoses was covered by a superficial layer of half-shamanistic and half-ethnopsychotic material. This finding, corroborated by a number of other observations of the same kind, suggests certain conclusions concerning ethnic and/or shamanistic psychoses.

1. They may be the first manifestation of an idiosyncratic psychoses.
2. At a later stage, they may mask an underlying idiosyncratic psychosis, in the sense in which a seemingly benign monosymptomatic hysteria may mask a schizophrenia.
3. In some instances, they constitute the terminal restitutional manifestation of an initially idiosyncratic psychosis (see above).

These three possibilities are not mutually exclusive; they represent alternatives that may occur either separately or in combinations of two or three in the development of a large number of obviously idiosyncratic derangements.

A certain number of observations support this hypothesis: a neurosis may be the initial manifestation of an illness that will develop into a psychosis; the psychotic may also present certain neurotic traits, and vice versa; a neurosis may sometimes mask a psychosis, and, in the course of recovery, a psychotic may sometimes become temporarily a neurotic or possibly a psychopath. If this hypothesis is valid, its systematic exploration should be productive.

To return to the diagnostic difficulties mentioned above, it is clear that, in the case of the two Acoma Indians, it was not a question of a belief being mistaken for a delusion but of a delusion that, because of its traditional content, was mistaken for a belief. What made me realise that I was dealing with a delusion was the deviant manner in which the two men handled cultural materials. Obviously, they neither *handled* nor *experienced* these materials according to the usual cultural norms or even in terms of culturally permissible 'alternatives' or of the kind of 'secondary meaning' that may become attached to a cultural item when it is assigned to a secondary or subordinate matrix (Chap. 16). In fact, these Acoma cultural items were not even handled in accordance with some marginal 'pattern of misconduct'. Traditional beliefs about witchcraft were handled in a purely arbitrary and idiosyncratic manner; the cultural items were 'deculturised' – stripped of their cultural content – in a way that is typically psychotic (Chap. 2).

I do not wish to leave this case history suspended in midair. The prison psychiatrist saw the validity of my findings and presented them so skillfully and competently to the court of appeals that the two men escaped capital punishment and were confined in the Medical center for Federal Prisoners.

CONCLUSION: THE PRACTICALITY OF THEORY

Nearly a dozen years of work in mental hospitals, more than thirty years of teaching psychoanalytic ethnopsychiatry, and years of psychoanalytic practice have convinced me that it is unfair and unreasonable to expect the psychiatrist to become an expert in ethnography (as distinct from ethnology). He cannot be expected to make a detailed study of the culture of each patient he must diagnose and treat. This makes it impossible for him to engage in the practice of what I have called 'cross-cultural psychiatry', which requires a thorough knowledge of the patient's culture and which is exemplified in my book *Reality and Dream* (Devereux 1951a, [2nd rev. edn, 1969]). Recognising the practical usefulness of this form of knowledge, I used to consider the impossibility of having a command of it as a calamity that might perhaps be palliated but never definitively remedied. I therefore cast about for some means that would allow psychiatrists to diagnose and treat even patients belonging to cultures of which they knew little or nothing.

As long as I looked for an answer to this problem in purely psychiatric or ethnographic terms, I came up against a blank wall. However, when I finally tackled the problem as an ethnologist, that is, not in terms of some particular culture but in terms of the *concept of culture*, the answer became obvious. This proves once more that the mathematician George Cantor was right in saying that it is more important to ask a question correctly than it is to answer it – presumably because a correctly asked question provides its own answer. The clue to the solution was the concept of culture as a lived experience, that is, as the *manner* in which the individual experiences and handles his culture both when he is psychically healthy and when he is psychically deranged. What remained to be seen was whether this theoretically correct solution could be effectively used when it became necessary to diagnose persons of whose culture I knew little or nothing. The fact that I had been able to diagnose the two Acoma Indians correctly in spite of my nearly total ignorance of their culture authorises me to conclude that this technique is valid not only logically but in practice.

In fact, at the time I interviewed the two Acoma prisoners, a diagnosis was so critically needed that I could not consult a treatise on Acoma ethnography. But though I knew little of their culture, I did know general ethnography and clearly understood the function of Culture per se and the nature of the 'universal culture pattern' (Wissler 1923). Thus, when these two man told me that they had gone after the witches with their guns, I did not know how the Acoma traditionally dealt with witches, but as an ethnologist I was certain that, *whatever* their specific custom of dealing with witches was, the Acoma, like most societies, had to have definite mechanisms for controlling them. Later on I discovered that the Acoma do, in fact, have ritual associations whose task it is to get rid of witches, just as the Sedang get rid of them by selling them as slaves to the Laotians, while the Mohave do it through witch-killing tribal champions or, more rarely, through lynchings (Devereux 1961a [2nd rev. edn, 1969]). I therefore formulated my diagnosis in terms of Culture per se and not specifically in terms of *Acoma* culture, which is but a particular version of a universal culture pattern – a version that was unknown to me at the time.

This experience suggests that a real analysis of the universal culture pattern and a full specification of its nature require that, in every study of culture, one should also take into account the psychiatric perspective. Indeed, regardless of the variety of cultures, the simple fact of having a culture is a genuinely universal experience, and man functions as a 'creator, creature, manipulator, and transmitter of culture' (Simmons 1942) everywhere and in the same way. *Pari passu* the Mohave feels about his culture the way the Eskimo feels abut his, and the way the American infantryman feels about his Garand rifle is probably identical with the way Rome's Balearic warrior felt about his slingshot.

To return for a moment to the hypothetical paranoid electronics engineer, one may say that his blueprint was *ethnographically* correct but *culturally* (ethnologically) delusional. To take a concrete example, Kempf (1920) described the case of a paranoid patient who, while delusional enough to cut off his penis, nevertheless continued to write articles for the prestigious *Oxford Dictionary*; yet, in stressing the objective quality of this performance, Kempf failed to ask himself what *subjective significance* this work – 'scientific' only ethnographically – could have had for the patient himself. I therefore agree with Dodds (1951) that Pythagoras was a shaman,[61] since I believe that his great mathematical discoveries were inspired more by mystical interests than by mathematical ones.

I once called the technique that approaches psychiatric problems in terms of the key concepts of culture 'transcultural psychiatry'; today I prefer the adjectives 'transethnographic', 'meta-ethnographic', or, more briefly, 'metacultural' (Devereux 1951a; [cf. 2nd rev. edn, 1969]), because those who borrowed the term – without, be it said in passing, ever acknowledging its source – have systematically deformed its meaning by applying it to what I myself have called 'cross-cultural' psychiatry (Devereux 1951a; [cf. 2nd rev. edn, 1969]).

Meta cultural psychiatry, then, does more than palliate the psychiatrist's *technical* inability to become a universal ethnographer. In fact, the approach that views psychiatric problems in terms of Culture rather than *cultures* is also more effective in a practical sense – that is, therapeutically – and is theoretically far superior to any other cultural approach; for it affords a deeper insight into psychodynamics, and this, in turn, leads to deeper ethnological insight into the nature of Culture. Moreover, it undermines once and for all the arrogant claims of the clique of neo-Freudian and pseudo-Freudian 'cultural psychoanalysts' who not only boast of their greater sophistication and ethnological flair but also claim that their views are more useful to the ethnologist than those of classical psychoanalysis.

The ethnologist cannot make a real contribution to psychiatric knowledge if he simply assimilates its jargon and, for the rest, is content to trot out his little ethnographic collection of esoteric 'curios'. He can make a real contribution to psychiatry only if he remains an ethnologist: a specialist of Culture, defined as a patterned way of experiencing both extrasocial and social reality. This, I feel, adequately answers Kroeber's (1948a) claim that ethnopsychiatry is not a part of real ethnology because it does not study Culture. Yet it is only the ethnopsychiatrist who studies both Culture and the manner in which the individual experiences his culture who completes and rounds out – precisely as it should be completed and rounded out – the science of Culture, which 'culturologists' (White 1969) sometimes seem to study as though Man did not exist.

As for myself, I feel that by also becoming a psychoanalyst I simply rounded out my training as an ethnologist – that is, a specialist of Culture and of Man. Had I begun as a psychoanalyst, I would certainly have felt the need to study ethnology also, to round out my training as a specialist of the human psyche. In the framework of an effort to understand man in a meaningful way, it is impossible to dissociate the study of Culture from the study of the psyche, precisely because psyche and Culture are two concepts that, while entirely distinct, stand to each other in a relationship of complementarity, in Heisenberg's and Bohr's sense (Devereux 1945 [1978a, Chap. 4], 1961b [1978a, Chap. 5], 1967c).[62]

INTRODUCTION: REFERENCES

Devereux, G. (1961) *Mohave Ethnopsychiatry and Suicide: The Psychiatric Knowledge and the Psychic Disturbances of an Indian Tribe.* Washington, DC: Smithsonian Institution.

NOTES

Preface
1   Chapter 11 was written in French; Chapters 8 and 10, though written in English, were first published in French translation.
2   Another volume of my selected papers has a similar history. *Ethno-psychoanalysis* (Devereux 1978a) originally appeared in book form as a French translation of a collection of papers most of which had originally been written and published in English. This French version was translated into Spanish (1975), Italian (1975), German (1978), and then back into English (1978).

Chapter One
1   For the concept of transcultural psychotherapy, see pp. 70 and 334, n. 4.
2   See Devereux 1961c [1975, Chap. 1] for a brief discussion of sublimation.
3   This is the classical view. In my opinion it needs some revisions, preferably in terms of the Hartmann–Kris–Loewenstein (1947, [Hartmann] 1950) theory of the undifferentiated infantile ego or even in terms of Fairbairn's (1954) view that it is the id that splits off from the infantile ego, not the ego that splits off from the infantile id. The classical view has to be refined in terms of a more sophisticated conception of the ego (Devereux 1966d), and particularly of the primitive ego of the infant. I mention this problem in order to indicate that I am aware of its existence, though I cannot discuss it in this context.
4   These are not pleonastic expressions (Devereux 1967c).
5   In a previously published article (Devereux and Hoffman 1961d) it was proposed that the diagnostician's principal task is to evaluate the patient's strengths rather than his weaknesses, his 'credit' rather than his 'debit' side.
6   This finding led me to propose (Devereux 1956a) that the superego contains the residual precipitate of those experiences a child cannot master with its own means at the time they occur.
7   This finding leads one to ask whether the early diffusion of emotional ties over a whole segment of society (kin group, village), which is so characteristic of primitive societies, may not be an (unconsciously evolved) prophylactic cultural defense, which, by decreasing the chid's exclusive emotional dependence on its parents – whose predictable life-span in primitive societies is often fairly short – reduces the intensity of the trauma resulting from the parents' death. This diffusion of emotional ties is socially fostered by establishing, e.g., a functional

equivalent between the mother and the mother's sister by means of a classificatory kinship system (Chap. 9). If correct, this hypothesis would account for some of the characterological differences between primitives, whose parents have a short life-span, and advanced groups, characterised by a greater longevity of the parent age group. Of course, in the latter types of societies, where the child's emotional ties are less diffuse (Devereux 1942c), becoming an orphan early in life is more likely to be an atypical experience and therefore more likely to be traumatic than among primitives, since in advanced societies children have few extrafamilial emotional ties and, in addition, remain socially immature for a long time.

8 I have discussed elsewhere (Devereux 1955c, 1965a) the breakdown of cultural defenses in situations of sudden historicocultural discontinuity.

9 Henri Ey, cited in Bastide 1965.

10 I refer here simply to Stewart's data and do not mean to endorse his highly heterodox interpretation of this phenomenon.

11 The distinction between 'a' and 'any' is to be taken in Bertrand Russell's sense (1903, 1919).

12 When I was still a relatively 'green' psychoanalytic candidate, I once remarked to my analytic supervisor that my patient 'had quite an Oedipus complex'. The supervisor very aptly replied, 'Who hasn't?'

13 By contrast, sublimations resulting from insight create no new problems and are therefore permanently effective (Jokl 1950).

14 The same kind of provocative and self-destructive behavior has been observed in witches of other culture areas as well.

15 The argument proposed by M. K. Opler (1959) is a case in point. He claims that Kroeber and I rely on material drawn exclusively from California Indians. This is simply not true; moreover, even if it were true, it would not be relevant, because similar data have been recorded in many other regions. Even Ackerknecht, the originator of the sophism that an individual can be simultaneously autonormal and heterogeneous, cites data from northern Eurasia, central Asia, India, Indonesia, Melanesia, Polynesia, South Africa, and other regions. Opler adds that some of the California tribes referred to by Kroeber were subjected to brutal oppression, and this is indeed true. By contrast, the Mohave were never persecuted. As for Genghis Khan's Mongols, Tamerlane's Turks, and the Bantu of Dingaan or Chaka, they were more aggressive than submissive. Further comment on this topic seems superfluous.

16 I am indebted to Harold Rosen, of the department of psychiatry at Johns Hopkins University, for detailed information about just such a case, which I have briefly summarised elsewhere (Devereux 1956a).

17 The brilliant punning intellectual described by Freud (1905b) did not manifest a comparable exaltation.

18 *Witzelsucht* (a 'toxicomania' of punning) may also be observed in some neurological illnesses, perhaps as a consequence of the 'dissolving' of higher functions, which entails the 'liberation' of interior functions, in Jackson's (1931–2) sense of the terms.

19 I hope to discuss on another occasion the way the *Cratylus* also reflects an abnormal aspect of Plato himself.

20 For a systematic presentation of Greek materials relative to this distinction, see Dodds 1951), especially Chapter 3. 'The blessings of madness'.

21 In the sense in which one may concurrently have both pneumonia and a broken leg.

22   It goes without saying that one need not be a shaman in order to dream in a hallucinatory manner that one is being attacked by ghosts, though the severely perturbed shaman will *no doubt* have hallucinations of this type more often and more systematically than other people do. The intrusion of irrational cultural beliefs into the delusional pattern of individuals who are not shamans will be discussed further on.

23   It is unnecessary to enumerate once more the great personages of the world of intelligence or of social history who confirm this rule.

24   Likewise, the patient and self-denying wife of a chronic alcoholic may turn into an alcoholic shrew as soon as her husband stops drinking.

25   Metaphorically speaking, the shaman still has at his disposal his grandfather's bow and arrows, whereas the nonshaman is obliged to try to shoot rifle bullets with a chid-size bow bought at the corner five-and-dime.

26   A bow cannot compete with a submachinegun, nor a horse with an airplane, nor the shamanistic curing ritual with penicillin, although the latter's supernaturalistic aspects may continue to coexist with penicillin treatments. Cf. my account of why I had to pretend to be a shaman when taking care of Sedang patients.

27   This explains the ease with which syncretistic cults – crisis cults – are born and spread and also the answer that Geza, the last of the pagan rules of ancient Hungary, made to a bishop who blamed him for serving Jehovah and his pagan gods at the same time: 'I am rich enough to serve them both.'

28   Pirenne (1939) correctly stressed the important role played by the Roman sociopolitical structure, on the one hand, and the tribal organisation of the barbarian invaders on the other, in the formation of the functional and active ethos underlying medieval 'Christian' society. He neglects to mention, however, how small a contribution was made to medieval society by the ethos and aspirations of the first oppressed Christians (slaves, poor people, publicans, and others). In my opinion, medieval society had only a thin veneer of true Christian spirit. Christianity, distorted in order to satisfy the demands of a system of brutal oppression, served only to rationalise fundamentally non-Christian sociopolitical models. The nostalgic dream of modern man, who sees medieval society as deeply inbued with the religion of Christ, is one thing, sociocultural reality is another.

29   See Chapter 2 for the various forms of neurotic manipulation of cultural materials.

30   After all, no ophthalmologist claims that, because 'in the kingdom of the blind the one-eyed man is king', being one-eyed is normal. Boyer is far too sophisticated a scholar to use this reasoning, but it is just the kind of thing, I am sure, that cultural relativists would not hesitate to advance.

31   I say 'usually' advisedly, for whereas the Mohave have a whole series of psychiatric labels of ('categories') (Devereux 1961a), the Sedang Moi, who show little interest in psychology, identify only the insane (*rájok*), the neurotic or eccentric or queer individual (*kok*), and the good-for-nothing (*plam ploy*).

32   These advantages outweigh the disadvantage – if indeed it is one – of being accused by the champions of cultural relativism (such as M. K. Opler) of proposing theories that apply only to those specific disorders and the cultures in which they occur. I have made only one concession in this respect: I cite only a very few examples drawn from my own field data.

33   This disdain is a far from recent development. Boardman (1964) notes that in ancient Egypt the greek colonist was as thoroughly hated as he was needed.

34 A partial analysis of the causes of a society's disavowal of itself, and specifically, the formulation of this in terms of *irrational ideologies,* is given below.

35 The situation is actually even more complex. Ganser's syndrome observed chiefly among imprisoned persons (who have a good 'obvious' reason for malingering), is often misdiagnosed as malingering because in many respects its symptoms fit the behaviour patterns that modern culture ascribed apriori to the insane. Since a detailed analysis of the psychodynamics of this similarity would take me too far afield, I will simply suggest that Ganser's syndrome may well be the 'ethnic psychosis' of imprisoned persons.

36 Some years after I developed this concept, Jenkins independently emphasised the *variable* importance of pure rebelliousness in different mental disorders (Jenkins and Glickman 1946, 1947).

37 A documentary film by Dr L. Chertok proves, however, that *la grande hystérie* still exists, even in Paris.

38 This example is of interest in that anality plays a decisive role in all obsessional neuroses and that money often symbolizes feces.

39 For these distinctions, see Chapter 7.

40 This perhaps explains why the psychoanalytic theory of hysteria has been on dead center for several decades. The course on the theory of hysteria that I took around 1950 was based almost exclusively on Freud's early writings about this syndrome.

41 It is claimed that fewer than sixty families of the Hungarian nobility can now trace their origins to the time prior to the battle of Mohács, at the beginning of the sixteenth century.

42 The tribe he belonged to lived formerly not in wigwams but in tipis.

43 Franz Alexander has reported a similar observation to me: the exploitation of a double cultural allegiance in a patient of Japanese descent, born in Hawaii.

44 Cultural items intended for quite other purposes can also be used as symptoms and defenses. This process will be examined later (Chap. 2).

45 Adelman (1955) also notes the uniformity of reports concerning the course of the *latah* attack.

46 Worse still, these flagrant violations of military discipline more often than not went unpunished, whereas anyone violating the discipline during a buffalo hunt was severely whipped by the tribe's police society.

47 The same is true of a number of traits characteristic of the psychopath (Chap. 2).

48 The only Mohave man who attempted to commit suicide during a funeral was a father who tried to throw himself on the funeral pyre of his son, whom his own hardheartedness had pushed to suicide (Devereux 1961a [2nd rev. edn, 1969]).

49 Compare: hashish – *hashshashin* (hashish addict)–assassin.

50 If this hypothesis proves correct, it would explain why the tripod was a particularly precious object as early as Homer. It was often dedicated to Apollo, god of prophecy.

51 Compare Aeschylus, *Agamemnon* 410 ff.: the mourning of Menelaus for his runaway wife (Devereux 1968c, 1976a).

52 This terminology differs intentionally from that of Durkheim.

53 This happens, for example, in the case of the marriage relationship. Only when a marriage is about to break up does one hear about the 'duties' of the spouses toward each other: the husband's 'duty' to provide for his wife and the wife's to behave in such-and-such ways toward her husband. This, incidentally, may be one of the reasons why divorce is less frequent in countries that permit

divorce by mutual consent than in those that require proof of a 'violation of contract'. Similarly, the pope ceased to exercise in fact an effective universal sovereignty as soon as the theologians felt impelled to specify that he is (1) a spiritual head and (2) a temporal leader and brought in, to support their propositions, a flagrant forgery – the *Donation* of the Emperor Constantine.

54 This is not to suggest that I am in agreement with those who claim to diagnose schizophrenia where Freud diagnosed hysteria. Vienna in 1890 is not New York or London in 1970.

55 The real natures and functions of the *ipā tahāna* status in Mohave society are rather poorly understood. One can be certain only of the fact that 'commemorative services' were celebrated solely in honor of the *ipā tahāna*, both those nobly born and those who had acquired noble status by their warlike feats. It is highly probably that a coward of noble origin incurred greater scorn than did one of common birth. Similarly, a French aristocrat of the sixteenth century who exhibited cowardice was more despised than an equally cowardly bourgeois, though he did not lose his title of nobility because of his cowardice.

56 For a description of the luxurious life of Alexander the Great's generals, see Plutarch, *Life of Alexander* 40.

57 Linton (1956) rightly complained that he could nowhere find a truly satisfactory definition of hysteria. This was no doubt due to the fact that our textbook definitions were based on Occidental clinical data. He would probably not have had this kind of difficulty while looking for a definition of so-called 'nuclear' schizophrenia, which is made especially explicit by Occidental clinical data.

58 In B. Russell's sense (1903, 1919).

59 I am indebted for this example to Richard L. Jenkins, MD, who discussed this paper when it was presented before the Anthropological Society of Washington, DC. I add that such cases confirm my view that the crux of mental health is the capacity to readjust.

60 I was duly recognised as a shaman becaues I twice found Neolithic stone axes, which only shamans are supposed to be able to locate (Devereux 1967c).

61 Similar considerations justify Burnet's opinion (1930 that Empedocles, too, was a shaman.

62 I can acknowledge in only a general way the influence of certain psychiatric and psychological writings of W. H. R. Rivers (1920, 1923, 1926) on the development of my ethnopsychiatric theories.

BIBLIOGRAPHY

This bibliography of works cited in the Preface and Chapter 1, 'Normal and abnormal', of George Devereux's *Basic Problems of Ethnopsychiatry*, trans. Basia Miller Gulati and George Devereux (Chicago and London University of Chicago Press, 1980), has been compiled from the bibliography provided for the whole book.

Works by George Devereux
Where republication data are given in parentheses at the end of an item, the later, revised edition should be consulted.

(1933–5)   Sednag field notes. Ms.

(1937a)   'Functioning units in Hå(rhn)de;a(ng) society', *Primitive Man*, 10: 1–7.
(1937b)   'Institutionalised homosexuality of the Mohave Indians', *Human Biology*, 9: 498–527.
(1937c)   'L'Envoûtement chez les Indiens mohave', *Journal de la Société des Américanistes de Paris*, n.s., 29: 405–12.
(1939a)   'Maladjustment and social neurosis', *American Sociological Review*, 4: 844–5.
(1939b)   'Mohave culture and personality', *Character and Personality*, 8: 91–109.
(1940)   'A conceptual scheme of society', *American Journal of Sociology*, 54: 687–607. (Now Chapter 1 of Devereux 1978a.)
(1942b)   'The mental hygiene of the American Indian', *Mental Hygiene*, 26: 71–84.
(1942c)   'Primitive psychiatry (Part 2)', *Bulletin of the History of Medicine*, 11: 522–42.
(1943)   (with E. M. Loeb) 'Antagonistic acculturation', *American Sociological Review*, 7: 133–47. (Now Chapter 8 of Devereux 1978a).
(1944b)   'The social structure of a schizophrenia ward and its therapeutic fitness', *Journal of Clinical Psychopathology*, 6: 231–65.
(1945)   'The logical foundations of culture and personality studies', *Transactions of the New York Academy of Sciences*, 2nd series, 7: 110–30. (Now Chapter 4 of Devereux 1978a.)
(1950a)   'Heterosexual behavior of the Mohave Indians'. In Géza Róheim (ed.) *Psychoanalysis and the Social Sciences*, Vol. 2. New York: International Universities Press.
(1951a)   *Reality and Dream: The Psychotherapy of a Plains Indian*. New York. (2nd rev. edn, New York: New York University Press and Anchor Books, 1969.)
(1951d)   'The primal scene and juvenile heterosexuality in Mohave society'. In G. B. Wilbur and Warner Muensterberger (eds) *Psychoanalysis and Culture*. New York.
(1955a)   'Anthropological data suggesting unexplored unconscious attitudes toward and in unwed mothers', *Archives of Criminal Psychodynamics*, 1: 564–76.
(1955b)   *A Study of Abortion in Primitive Societies*: New York: Julian. (Now see Devereux 1976c.)
(1955c)   'Charismatic leadership and crisis'. In Warner Muensterberger and Sidney Axelrad (eds) *Psychoanalysis and the Social Sciences*, Vol. 4. New York.
(1956a)   *Therapeutic Education*. New York: Harper & Bros.
(1956c)   'The origins of shamanistic power as reflected in a neurosis', *Revue internationale d'ethnopsychologie normale et pathologique*, 1: 19–28.
(1956d)   Review of Eaton and Weil 1955, *American Anthropologist* 58: 211–12.
(1957b)   'Dream learning and individual ritual differences in Mohave shamanism', *American Anthropologist*, 59: 1036–45. (Now Chapter 9 of Devereux 1978a.)
(1958a)   'Cultural thought models in primitive and modern psychiatric theories', *Psychiatry*, 21: 359–74. (Now Chapter 10 of Devereux 1978a.)
(1961a)   'Mohave ethnopsychiatry and suicide', *Bureau of American Ethnology Bulletin*, 175. (2nd rev. edn, Washington, DC: Smithsonian Institution, 1969.)
(1961b)   'Two types of modal personality models'. In Berk Kaplan (ed.)

Studying Personality Cross-Culturally. Evanston, IL: Row, Peterson. (Now Chapter 5 of Devereux 1978a.)

(1961c)   'Art and mythology: a general theory'. In Bert Kaplan (ed.) *Studying Personality Cross-Culturally.* Evanston, IL: Row, Peterson. (A French translation appears as Chapter 1 in *Tragédie et poésie grecques.* Paris: Flammarion, 1975.)

(1961d)   (with F. H. Hoffman) 'The non-recognition of the patient by the therapist', *Psychoanalysis and Psychoanalytic Review,* 48: 41–61.

(1965a)   'La Psychanalyse et l'histoire: Une application à l'histoire de Sparte', *Annales* 20: 18–44.

(1966a)   'Loss of identity, impairment of relationships, reading disability', *Psychoanalytic Quarterly,* 35: 18–39.

(1966c)   'La Nature de stress', *Revue de médecine psychosomatique,* 8: 103–13. (Appears in English as Chapter 2 of Devereux 1978a.)

(1966d)   'Transference, screen memory, and the temporal ego', *Journal of Nervous and Mental Disease,* 143: 318–23.

(1967a)   'Greek pseudo-homosexuality', *Symbolae Osloenses,* 42: 69–92.

(1967c)   *From Anxiety to Method in the Behavioral Sciences.* Paris and The Hague: Mouton.

(1968b)   'Considérations psychanalytiques sur la divination, particulièrement en Grèce'. In A. Caquot and M. Leibovici (eds) *La Divination,* Vol. 2. Paris: Presses universitaires de France.

(1968c)   'L'Etat dépressif et le rêve de Ménélas', *Revue des études grecques,* 81: 12–15. (Incorporated into Chapter 3 of Devereux 1976a.)

(1970)   'La Naissance d'Aphrodite'. In *Exchanges et communications (Mélanges Lévi-Strauss).* Paris and The Hague: Mouton.

(1975)   *Tragédie et poésie grecques.* Paris: Flammarion.

(1976a)   *Dreams in Greek Tragedy.* Oxford: Blackwell. Berkeley: University of California Press.

(1976c)   *A Study of Abortion in Primitive Societies,* 2nd rev. edn. New York: International Universities Press.

(1978a)   *Ethnopsychoanalysis: Psychoanalysis and Anthropology as Complementary Frames of Reference.* Berkeley: University of California Press.

Works by Other Authors

Aberle, D. F. (1952) 'Arctic hysteria and latah in Mongolia', *Transactions of the New York Academy of Sciences,* 2nd ser., 14: 291–7.

Ackerknecht, Erwin Heinz (1943) 'Psychopathology, primitive medicine and primitive culture', *Bulletin of the History of Medicine,* 14: 30–67.

Adelman, Fred (19550 'Toward a psycho-cultural interpretation of latah', *Davidson Journal of Anthropology,* 1: 69–76.

Alexander, Franz (1931) 'Buddhistic training as an artificial catatonia', *Psychoanalytic Review,* 18: 129–45.

Anonymous (1930) 'Hikayat Hang Toeah 3 vols. Java: Balei Poestaka Veltevreden. (German translation, *Hikayat Hang Tuah,* 2 vols. Munich: Georg Müller, 1922.)

Aubin, H. (1939) 'Introduction à l'etude de la psychiatrie chez les Noirs', *Annales médico-psychologiques* 97: 1–29, 181–213.

Barbosa, Duarte [d. 1521; supposed author' (1921) *The Book of Duarte Barbosa,* in 2 vols. Vol. 1, trans. from the Portuguese text and ed. Mansel Longworth Dames. London: the Hakluyt Society.

Bastide, Roger (1965) *Sociologie des maladies mentales*. Paris: Flammarion. (English-language translation, *The Sociology of Mental Disorders*, trans. Jean McNeil, London: Routledge & Kegan Paul, 1972.)

Benedict, Ruth (1934a) *Patterns of Culture*. Boston and New York: Houghton Mifflin. (Paperback edn, 1961.)

Bérard, Victor (1927–32) *Les Navigations d'Ulysse*, 5 vols. Paris: A. Colin.

Bernatzik, Hugo A. (1958) 'with the collaboration of Emmy Bernatzik' *The Spirits of the Yellow Leaves*. London: Robert Hale. (Published in German as *Die Gesiter der gelben Blätter*. Gütersloh: C. Bertelsmann, 1951.)

Boardman, John (1964) *The Greeks Overseas*. Harmondsworth, Mx: Pelican.

Boyer, L. B. (1961) 'Notes on the personality structure of a North American Indian shaman', *Journal of the Hillside Hospital*, 10: 14–23.

Boyer, L. B. (1962) 'Remarks on the personality of shamans'. In Warner Muensterberg and Sidney Axelrad (eds) *The Psychoanalytic Study of Society*, Vol. 2. New York: International Universities Press, pp. 233–54.

Boyer, L. B. (1964) 'Further remarks concerning shamans and shamanism', *Israel Annals of Psychiatry and Related Disciplines*, 2: 235–57.

Boyer, L. B., Klopfer, Bruno and Kawai, Hayao (1964) 'Comparisons of the shamans and pseudo-shamans of the Apaches of the Mescalero Indian reservation: a Rorschach study', *Journal of Projective Techniques* 28: 173–80.

Burnet, John (1930) *Early Greek Philosophy*. London: Black.

Chowning, Ann (1961) 'Amok and aggression in the d'Entrecasteaux'. In the *Proceedings* of the 1961 Annual Spring Meeting of the American Ethnological Society (Seattle, WA), pp. 78–83.

Clifford, Sir Hugh (1898) *Studies in Brown Humanity: Being Scrawls & Smudges in Sepia, White, and Yellow*. London: G. Richards.

Clifford, Sir Hugh (1922a) 'The amok of Dâto' Kâja Bĭji Ďerja'. In *The Further Side of Silence*. Garden City, NY: Doubleday, Page.

Clifford, Sir Hugh (1922b) 'The experiences of Râja Haji Hamid'. In *The Further Side of Silence*. Garden City, NY: Doubleday, Page.

Cook, A. B. (1914, 1940) *Zeus: A Study in Ancient Religion*, Vols. 1, 3. Cambridge: Cambridge University Press.

Correa, Gaspar [fl. sixteenth century] (1858) *Lendas da India*, 2 vols. London.

Czaplicka, Marie Antionette (1914) *Aboriginal Siberia: A Study in Social Anthropology*, with a preface by R. R. Marett. Oxford: Clarendon Press.

Davis, Kingsley (1937) 'The sociology of prostitution', *American Sociological Review*, 2: 744–55.

Davis, Kingsley (1939) 'Illegitimacy and the social structure', *American Journal of Sociology*, 45: 215–33.

Dembowitz, N. (1945) 'Psychiatry amongst West African troops', *Journal of the Royal Army Medical Corps*, 84: 70–4.

Dodds, E. R. (1951) *The Greeks and the Irrational*. Berkeley: University of California Press.

Dodds, E. R. (1965) *Pagan and Christian in an Age of anxiety: Some Aspects of Religious Experience from Marcus Aurelius to Constantine*. Cambridge: Cambridge University Press.

Dollard, John (1937) *Caste and Class in a Southern Town*. New Haven, CT: Yale University Press. London: Oxford University Press.

Domarus, Eilhard von (1948) 'Anthropology and psychotherapy', *American Journal of Psychotherapy*, 2: 603–14.

Dumas, Georges (1946) *Le Surnaturel et les dieux d'après la maladie mentale*. Paris.

Durkheim, Emile (1912) *Les Formes élémentaires de la vie religieuse*. Paris: Alcan. (English-language edn as *Elementary Forms of the Religious life*, trans. Joseph W. Swain. Glencoe, IL: Free Press, 1954. Reprinted London: Allen & Unwin, 1976.)

Dyson, W. S. and Fuchs, V. E. (1937) 'The Elmolo', *Journal of the Royal Anthropological Institute*, 67L 327–8.

Eaton, Joseph W. and Weil, Robert J. (1955) *Culture and Mental Disorders: A Comparative Study of the Hutterites and Other Populations*. Glencoe, IL: Free Press.

Ewing, J.E. (1955) 'Juramentado: institutionalized suicide among the Moros of the Philippines', *Anthropological Quarterly*, 28: 148–55.

Fabing, H. D. (1956) 'On going berserk: a neurochemical inquiry', *American Journal of Psychiatry*, 113: 409–15.

Fairbairn, W. R. D. (1954) *An Object-Relations Theory of the Personality*. New York: Basic Books.

Faris, Robert E. L. and Dunham, H. Warren (1939) *Mental Disorders in Urban Areas*. Chicago: University of Chicago Press.

Fathauer, George H. (1954) 'The structure and causation of Mohave warfare'. *South-western Journal of Anthropology*, 10: 97–118.

Fauconnier, Henri (1930) *Malaisie*. Paris. (English-language edn, *The Soul of Malaya*, trans. Eric Sutton. Oxford: Oxford University Press, 1965.)

Forrest, W. G. (1966) *The Emergence of Greek Democracy: The Character of Greek Politics, 800–400 BC*. London: Weidenfeld & Nicolson.

Forrest, W. G. (1968) *A History of Sparta, 950–192 BC*. London: Hutchinson.

Fortune, Reo F. (1932a) 'Omaha secret societies', *Columbia University Contributions to Anthropology*, Vol. 14. (Reprinted New York: AMS Press, 1976.)

Fortune, Reo F. (1932b) *Sorcerers of Dobu*, with an introduction by B. Malinowski. London: Routledge.

François, H. K. B. von (1929) *Napoleon I*. Berlin.

Freud, Anna (1946) *The Ego and the Mechanisms of Defense*, trans. Cecil Baines (from the German). New York: International Universities Press.

Freud, Sigmund (1905b) 'Jokes and their relations to the unconscious'. In the English *Standard Edition* of Freud's works, 24 vols, trans. (from the German) under the general editorship of James Strachey, in collaboration with Anna Freud. London: Hogarth Press, 1953–74. Hereafter SE.

Freud, Sigmund (1907) 'Obsessive actions and religious practices'. In *SE*, Vol. 9.

Freud, Sigmund (1919) 'The uncanny'. In *SE*, Vol. 17.

Fromm, Erich (1941) *Escape from Freedom*. New York: Farrar & Rinehart (Avon paperback edn, 1971.)

Gluckman, Max (1954) *Rituals of Rebellion in South-East Africa*. Manchester: Manchester University Press.

Goldfrank, Esther Schiff (1945) 'Changing configurations in the social organization of a Blackfoot tribe during the reserve period', *American Ethnological Society Monograph*, 8.

Grousset, René (1941) *L'Empire des steppes: Attila, Gengis-Khan, Tamarlan*. Paris: Payot. (English-language edn, *The Empire of the Steppes*, trans. Naomi Walford. New Brunswick, NJ: Rutgers University Press, 1970.)

Hallowell, A. I. (1945) 'Sociopsychological aspects of acculturation'. In Ralph Linton (ed.) *The Science of Man in the World Crisis*. New York: Columbia University Press.

Hallowell, A. I. (1946) 'Some psychological characteristics of the Northeastern

Indians'. In *Man in Northeastern North America: Papers of the Robert S. Peabody Foundation for Archaeology*, Vol. 3. Andover, MA.

Hartmann, Heinz (1950) 'Comments on the psychoanalytic theory of the ego'. In Ruth S. Eissler et al. (eds) *The Psychoanalytic Study of the Child*. New York: International Universities Press.

Hartmann, Heinz, Kris, Ernst and Loewenstein, Rudolph (1947) 'Comments on the formation of psychic structure'. In Ruth S. Eissler et al. (eds) *The Psychoanalytic Study of the Child*, Vol. 2. New York: International Universities Press.

Hollingshead, August de B. and Redlich, Frederick C. (1958) *Social Class and Mental Illness: A Community Study*. New York: Wiley.

Honigmann, John (1954) *Culture and Personality*. New York: Harper & Bros. (Reprinted, Westwood, CT: Greenwood press, 1973.)

Hurley, Victor (1936) *The Swish of the Kris: The Story of the Moros*. New York: Dutton.

Jackson, Hughlings (1931–2) *The Selected Writings*, 2 vols, ed. J. Taylor et al. London.

Jenkins, R. L. and Glickman, Sylvia (1946) 'Commons syndromes in child psychiatry', *American Journal of Orthopsychiatry*, 16: 244–61.

Jenkins, R. L. and Glickman, Sylvia (1947) 'Patterns of personality organization among delinquents', *The Nervous Child*, 6: 329–39.

Jokl, R. H. (1950) 'Psychic determinism and preservation of sublimation in classical psychoanalytic procedure', *Bulletin of the Menninger Clinic*, 14: 207–19.

Kardiner, Abram (1939) *The Individual and His Society: The Psychodynamics of Primitive Social Organization*, with a foreword and two ethnological reports by Ralph Linton. New York: Columbia University Press.

Kempf, Edward J. (1917) 'The social and sexual behavior of infrahuman primates, with some comparable facts in human behavior', *Psychoanalytic Review*, 4: 127–54.

Kempf, Edward J. (1920) *Psychopathology*. Saint Louis: Mosby.

Kroeber, A. L. (1925) Handbook of the Indians of California, Bureau of American Ethnology Bulletin, 78. Washington, DC. (Reprinted Saint Clair Shores, MI: Scholarly Press, 1972.)

Kroeber, A. L. (1948a) *Anthropology: Race, Language, Culture, Psychology, Prehistory*, rev. edn. New York: Harcourt Brace.

Kroeber, A. L. (1952) *The Nature of Culture*. Chicago: University of Chicago Press.

La Barre, Weston (1966) 'The dream, charisma, and the culture hero'. In G. E. von Grunebaum and Roger Caillois (eds) *The Dream and Human Societies*. Berkeley: University of California Press.

Le Barre, Weston (1970) *The Ghost Dance: The Origins of Religion*. New York: Doubleday.

Landes, Ruth (1938) 'The Ojibwa woman', *Columbia University Contributions to Anthropology*, 31. New York. (Reprinted, New York: AMS Press, 1969.)

Laubscher, B. J. F. (1937) *Sex, Custom, and Psychopathology*. London: Routledge & Kegan Paul.

Lévi-Strauss, Claude (1958) *Anthropologie structurale*. Paris: Plon. (English-language edn, *Structural Anthropology*. Vol. 1, trans. Claire Jacobson and Brooke Grundfest Schoepf. New York: Basic Books, 1963. Vol. 2, trans. M. Layton. New York: Basic Books, 1976.)

Linton, Ralph (1933) 'The Tanala, a hill tribe of Madagascar', *Field Museum of Natural History, Anthropological Series*, 22.

Linton, Ralph (1936) *The Study of Man* New York: Appleton-Century.

Linton, Ralph (1956) contribution to George Devereux (ed.) *Culture and Mental Disorders*. Springfield, IL: Thomas.

Lowenfeld, Henry (1944) 'Some aspects of a compulsion neurosis in a changing civilization', *Psychoanalytic Quarterly*, 13: 1–15.

Lowie, Robert H. (1924) *Primitive Religion*. New York: Boni & Liveright. (Paperback edn, New York: Liveright, 1970.)

Lowie, Robert H. (1925a) 'Takes-the-Pipe, a Crow warrior'. In Elsie C. Parsons (ed.) *American Indian Life*. New York: Viking Press. (Paperback edn, Lincoln: University of Nebraska Press, 1967.)

Lowie, Robert H. (1925b) 'A Crow woman's tale'. In Elsie C. Parsons (ed.) *American Indian Life*. New York: Viking Press. (Paperback edn, Lincoln: University of Nebraska Press, 1967.)

Lowie, Robert H. (1925c) 'A trial of shamans'. Elsie C. Parsons (ed.) *American Indian Life*. New York: Viking Press. (Paperback edn, Lincoln: University of Nebraska Press, 1967).

Lowie, Robert H. (1935) *The Crow Indians*. New York: Farrar & Rinehart. (Paperback edn, New York: Holt, Rinehart & Winston, 1956.)

Mauss, Marcel (1950) *Sociologie et anthropologie*, with an introduction by Claude Lévi-Strauss. Paris: Presses universitaires de France.

Mead, Margaret (1928) *Coming of Age in Samoa*. New York: Morrow. (Paperback edn, New York: Morrow, 1971.)

Mead, Margaret (1956) *New Lives for Old: Cultural Transformation – Manus 1928–53*. New York: Morrow. (Paperback edn, Morrow, 1976.)

Murdock, G. P. (1949) *Social Structure*. New York: Free Press. (Reprinted, New York: Free Press, 1965.)

Neher, Andrew (1961) 'Auditory driving observed with scalp electrodes in normal subjects', *Electroencephalography and Clinical Neurophysiology*, 13: 449–51.

Neher, Andrew (1962) 'A physiological explanation of unusual behavior in ceremonies involving drums', *Human Biology*, 34: 151–60.

Neihardt, J. G. (1932) *Black Elk Speaks* New York: Morrow. (Paperback edn, New York: Simon & Schuster Pocket Books.)

Opler, M. E. (1936) 'Some points of comparison and contrast between the treatment of functional disorders by Apache shamans and modern psychiatric practice', *American Journal of Psychiatry* 92: 1371–87.

Opler, M. K. (1959) 'Dream analysis in Ute Indian therapy'. In M. K. Opler (ed.) *Culture and Mental Health*. New York: Macmillan.

Parsons, Talcott (1939) 'The professions and social structure', *Social Forces*, 17: 457–67.

Pirenne, Henri (1939) *Mohammed and Charlemagne*, trans. Bernard Miall (from the French *Mahomet et Charlemagne*, 10th edn). New York: Norton.

Reider, N. S. (1950) 'The concept of normality', *Psychoanalytic Quarterly*, 19: 43–51.

Rivers, W. H. R. (1920) *Instinct and the Unconscious*. Cambridge: Cambridge University Press.

Rivers, W. H. R. (1923) *Conflict and Dream*. London: K. Paul, Trench, Trubner. New York: Harcourt Brace.

Rivers, W. H. R. (1926) *Psychology and Ethnology*, with a preface and introduction by G. Elliot Smith. London: K. Paul, Trench, Trubner. New York: Harcourt, Brace.

Róheim, Géza (1930) *Animism, Magic, and the Divine King*. New York: Knopf.

Róheim, Géza (1950) *Psychoanalysis and Anthropology*. New York: International Universities Press.

Roscher, W. H. (1896) 'Das von der "Kynanthropie" handelnde Fragment des Marcellus von Side', *Abhandlungen der philologisch-historischen Classe der Königlich Sächsischen Gesellschaft der Wissenschaften*, 17, 3.

Rose, H. J. (1960) *A Handbook of Greek Literature from Homer to the Age of Lucian*. New York: Dutton.

Roth, H. L. (1899) *The Aborigines of New Zealand*, 2nd edn. Halifax.

Russell, Bertrand (1903) *Principles of Mathematics*, Vol. 1. Cambridge: Cambridge University Press.

Russell, Bertrand (1919) *Introduction to Mathematical Philosophy*. London: Allen & Unwin. New York: Macmillan.

Simmons, Leo W. (ed.) (1942) *Sun Chief: The Autobiography of a Hopi Indian*, rev. edn. New Haven, CT: Yale University Press. (Paperback edn, 1963.)

Stewart, Kilton (1954) *Pygmies and Dream Giants*. New York: Norton. (Torchbook paperback edn, New York: Harper & Row, 1975.)

Teicher, M. I. (1960) 'The windigo psychosis'. In Proceedings of the 1960 Annual Spring Meeting of the American Ethnological Society (Seattle, WA).

Teoh, Jin-Inn (1972) 'The changing psychopathology of amok', *Psychiatry* 35: 345–50.

Thompson, Laura (1948) 'Attitudes and acculturation', *American Anthropologist*, n.s., 50: 200–15.

Van Loon, F. H. G. (1920) 'Amok and lattah', *Journal of Abnormal and Social Psychology*, 21: 434–44.

Wallace, Anthony F. C. (1951) 'Some psychological determinants of culture change in an Iroquoian community'. In *Symposium on Local Diversity in Iroquois Culture*, ed. W. N. Fenton. Bureau of American Ethnology Bulletin, 149. Washington, DC.

Wallace, Anthony F. C. (1958) 'Dreams and wishes of the soul', *American Anthropologist*, 60: 234–48.

Wallace, Anthony, F. C. (1961) *Culture and Personality*. New York: Random House. (2nd edn, 1970.)

White, L. A. (1969) *The Science of Culture: A Study of Man and Civilization*, 2nd edn. New York: Farrar, Straus & Giroux.

Wilson, Monica (1954) 'Nyakyusa ritual and symbolism', *American Anthropologist*, 56: 228–41.

Winiarz, Wiktot and Wielawski, Joseph (1936) 'Imu – a psychoneurosis occurring among the Ainus', *Psychoanalytic Review* 23: 181–6.

Wissler, Clark (1923) *Man and Culture*. New York: Crowell.

Yap, P. M. (1952) 'The latah reaction: its pathodynamics and nosological position', *Journal of Mental Science*, 98: 515–64.

CHAPTER FOURTEEN

Possession 'Hysteria' in a Kenya Tribe[1] (1957)
Grace Harris

Harris (1926–), a Cambridge anthropologist, here sets out what has become a commonplace in cultural psychiatry. Examining the particular example of saka among the Waitata, she examines in some detail how this sort of posses-sion state may be said to serve a social and psychological function: the possession allows women who have been disallowed access to the advantages of men to obtain some privileges by transferring agency onto possessing spirits. A similar model has been followed by Lewis (1969) and others, although criticism has been offered as to whether such female possession states are quite so transparently functional in allowing the voice of the subdo-minant to be heard (Boddy 1989).

I

In his monograph on the Akamba of Kenya, Gerhard Lindblom includes descriptions of spirit-possession and its treatment (1920: 230–40). After describing possession by the spirits of ancestors, called *aimu*, he discusses certain other spirits known as *mbeβo*, showing that the symptoms follow a characteristic pattern.

An mbeβo spirit, says Lindblom, makes its wishes known when a woman goes into a sort of ecstasy. While in this state she makes strange sounds which are said to be foreign words, for the mbeβo spirits come from other tribes. She not only speaks in a foreign tongue, but makes demands appropriate to the spirit's tribe. A woman possessed by a Masai spirit might demand a Masai spear or a piece of red cloth such as Masai wear. Sometimes the item requested is of European style, such as a shoe. Or the spirit may require meat, and an animal must be slaughtered to provide it.

There are two kinds of remedies. For temporary relief the spirit must be given what it asks, lest the seizures continue in the form of convulsions and ecstasy. This means that the woman's husband may be called on to make a considerable expenditure, for he must buy the cloth, slaughter the animal or do whatever else is required. Lindblom points out that in this way a woman is able to force her husband to give her something she wants. While many seizures are apparently quite spontaneous, Lindblom records an instance of deliberate fraud when a woman pretended to be possessed in order to extort a gift from her husband. Lindblom refers to 'deceitful feminine tactics'.

Akamba attempts at a permanent cure follow the general pattern of spirit exorcism for that people. The patient sits on the ground with her head covered by a dark cloth. Drums are beaten by men and songs are sung in which the foreign spirits are mentioned. After some time the woman gets up and begins to dance, going into an ecstasy and uttering weird noises. At last she sinks exhaustedly on the ground and water is poured on her head to revive her. Then the spirit, on being questioned, reveals its identity and desires. After more dancing the patient is treated with some of the standard medicaments, and then goes to sleep. Next day, says Lindblom, she goes about her work as though nothing had happened.

Lindhlom also mentions one other kind of spirit possession called *kiesu* or *kijesu*. Like others who observed it, he describes it as one of a series of ...remarkable psychical disturbances of a religious character which pass like epidemics over Kamba country'. Kiesu involved a new 'religious' dance and also the characteristic symptoms of possession. People went '...into convulsions at the sight of a European or even a pith helmet or a red fez such as is usually worn by the native Mohammedan. The afflicted one fell to the ground, writhing as if suffering from violent cramp, moaning, and groaning ... The Akamba themselves say that the spirits which (according to them) gave rise to *kiesu*, came from Ulaya (Europe)' (Lindblom 1920: 238–9).

Similar phenomena are found elsewhere in Africa. In Kenya, women's seizures occur in much the same form among at least two of the Coastal Bantu tribes, the Wagiriama and Waduruma.[2] They have also been observed among the Kikuyu, and Junod (1927: Vol. II, 435 ff.) has described something very like the Kamba possession for the Thonga. The Zulu,[3] Somali (Ross 1956), and Songhay (Rouch 1954: 52–3) are other groups displaying forms which show varying degrees of similarity, and certainly there are many others in various parts of Africa. In some cases only the women are affected, in others only the men, and in still others possession afflicts both sexes.

My own material is on the Wataita, or the Taita as I shall refer to them hereafter. They are situated in the Coast Province of Kenya, about a hundred miles up-country from Mombasa. One subgroup calls the spirit-possession afflicting women *pepo*, but it is known as *saka* to the larger portion of the tribe. In describing and analysing the saka complex among the Taita, I do not wish to imply that the details of my interpretation should be extended to cover similar situations elsewhere. However, I believe that the type of analysis applied here to one example of possession behavior in Africa may suggest ways of dealing with other cases, and perhaps lead to comparative treatment.

II

The Wataita are a hill people numbering about 53,000. They speak a Bantu language and follow a way of life somewhat similar to that of the Akamba. They live by cultivating the land and, these days, by considerable wage-labor outside the Reserve and by the sale of cash crops such as vegetables, wattle, chilis, and coffee. Livestock is kept in the form of small herds of cattle, goats, and sheep, with cattle in particular constituting the traditional form of wealth. Women cultivate the basic grain, legume, and root crops; men have other agricultural duties including especially the growing of cash crops, and they do most of the cattle-herding. In general the population lives in scattered clusters of homesteads, but there are also a number of large, compact villages. Localised descent groups are patrilineal but not exogamous. The people's own name for themselves is βadaβida.

What has already been referred to as the saka complex has several aspects: the set of symptoms to which people give the name saka; the distribution in the population of susceptibility to attacks; the immediate causes of the attacks; the form of treatment, and Taita notions about saka.

Women beginning to have attacks of saka sometimes show evident signs of a generalized restlessness and of anxiety. However, sometimes without any obvious warning a woman begins the characteristic convulsive movements. The upper part of the body trembles but often the head and shoulders are more affected so that, while the shoulders shake rapidly, the head is moved rhythmically from side to side. As the attack continues the eyes may close and the face become expressionless. Some women perform certain simple acts in monotonous repetition, or they repeat strange sounds which are supposed to be foreign words. If there is singing or drumming or other music, the woman in saka may move about as in a trance. There sometimes appears to be loss of consciousness, and at such times the woman becomes rigid, her teeth are clenched, and she must either be supported or gently helped to lie down.

Susceptibility to saka attacks is so common among married women that in some localities as many as half the married women are subject to them at least occasionally. Some women claim and are acknowledged by others to have saka very severely; others are subject to much milder attacks. Only three men were known to me who had analogous attacks or who had suffered from them previously. With respect to them I shall say simply that each of them was by Taita standards rather odd. A few unmarried girls have saka. In Taita, clearly, this kind of behavior can be treated as occurring primarily and characteristically among married women.

The immediate events which bring on an attack vary, for each woman has her own sensitivities, though all of these fall into a pattern. Sometimes a particular sight, smell, or sound is responsible: the sight of a motor car, the sound of a train whistle, the sight or smell of a cigarette, the sound of a match being struck, the sight of a bright piece of cloth, the smell, sight, or taste of bananas.

For example, one day in a remote part of the Taita Hills where Europeans are seldom seen, a woman saw a car parked where the road terminated, and went into convulsions. She began to dance back and forth, apparently trying to make herself go around the car and continue on her way. Trembling and with her head shaking in the saka fashion, she danced toward the car and then away from it, seeming to find it impossible to approach closely and go around. Eventually someone else held her arm and helped her to get by.

On another occasion a woman who was helping to prepare beer for a dance heard a match being struck, and immediately began to tremble. A child was sent to fetch a toy concertina which was kept for such times, and when this was brought the woman began to stroll about, playing the concertina's two notes over and over and making sounds which were supposed to be English words. The only intelligible ones were 'sit down' and 'thank you'. These she repeated in a monotonous tone, interrupting herself only to assure the two Europeans present, in Kiswahihi, that 'nothing was wrong'. When we left the village an hour or so later she was still walking about, jerkily playing the concertina and intoning the same words.

Sometimes an acute desire for a particular thing brings on an attack or threatens to do so. A woman went into saka because her husband, having no cash, would not buy her sugar; eventually he borrowed the money from me because the attack threatened to go on and on. The husband of another saka sufferer had small scars all over his forearms, for his wife demanded his blood and he had to make cuts for her to suck. Another woman demanded the water in which her mother's brother's son, of whom she was very fond, had washed himself. An unsatisfied craving for a cigarette often brings on an attack. Again, on a school sports day, the mother of one of the schoolboys arrived too late to hear the school band play its first group of tunes. When she was told that they would not play again for another hour, she went into saka. She lay on the grass supporting herself on her elbows, her head and shoulders shaking. She continued this until the band played again, whereupon she got up and staggered out on the playing field. Attended and supported by friends, she followed the band while they marched and played, her eyes closed and her face upturned. When the music ceased she lay down on the grass again and the trembling continued until she was led away about half an hour later. After a long attack like this one, some Taita women feel weak and unwell for a day or so. Others, like Lindblom's Akamba, go back to their work as though nothing has happened.

There are private and public forms of treatment. For private treatment, which is dispensed by men with the requisite knowledge, there are medicaments and treatment with the smoke from a fire on which certain herbs have been thrown. As in the Kamba procedure, drumming and singing may be involved. One standard prescription calls for drinking water in which a man's lower garment, whether shorts or wrapper, has been washed, or a woman may be told that she will be cured of saka if she becomes a Christian. Most frequently, attendance at a saka dance is deemed the most appropriate.

A saka dance is set for a time, usually night, when drummers are available. For a small dance, involving only one or two women, a single team of drummers is enough. For large dances, arranged for a number of women, there are two teams of drummers who play in turn, competing for the largest share of the beer which is their reward. Though the making of this beer is the work of the women who are going to dance, aided by their friends and kin, the husbands must pay for the sugar cane if the family fields do not supply enough for the brew. Husbands also arrange for the drummers to come.

The dance usually begins about nine in the evening and goes on all night. A crowd of varying size assembles, composed of men who hope to share the beer, and of women and girls who, if they have not come to dance themselves, desire to watch and perhaps to care for friends and kinswomen should they go into saka. The women who suffer from saka dance inside the ring of spectators, either in a line which shuffles back and forth to the drumming or in a circle which moves around and around. In either case they follow one another; they do not dance face-to-face.

Most of the dancers do not have saka attacks during the dance. They simply go on dancing in what is quite a dull way by comparison with other Taita dancing. As time wears on, a very few go into the typical ecstasy and their friends go out to them to prevent their falling. If women in the dance notice that one of their number is about to collapse, they go to her assistance. She is led aside and stretched on the ground. A lighted cigarette may be forced between her clenched teeth and this normally revives her, or her head is washed with suds made from a certain herb.

There is an accepted costume for these dances. Each woman wears a bright frock and a printed cloth over it. Usually the latter is tied under the armpits, the customary way for womwn, but occasionally it is tied like a man's waist-cloth. Both dress and cloth are supposed to be saved for use in saka dances. On the head is the red fez worn by African Muslims (few in number among the Taita) and by some Pagan elders, or else a man's felt hat. Across her breast the woman wears red and white cloth bandoliers,[4] and around her waist may be a man's belt. She carries either a wooden staff of the sort which formerly was a dancing accessory for men, or a wooden wand like the walking-sticks used by men who are not yet elders, and wears bells on one ankle. Her husband is supposed to furnish all the clothing and equipment.

The Taita say only that the spirits require the costume to be as it is. The purpose of the dance is sometimes said to be to allow the women to get 'all danced out' so that the will be prevented from having frequent or violent saka attacks. As we have seen, the dances themselves sometimes bring on severe attacks in a few individuals. Furthermore, there is no evidence that participation in dances really lessens susceptibility to attacks, and the same women take part over and over again.

Those who take saka seriously occasionally say that it is 'a matter of the heart'. This means that it belongs to one of the two main groupings into which Taita sort aberrations which they classify as psychological. Illnesses of the heart include anything involving abnormal cravings, fears, or urges. Thus *lwafuo*, which sometimes develops into a sort of kleptomania, is said to be one of these 'heart' illnesses. Saka is said to belong in this category because it is an illness of 'wanting and wanting'. It does not belong to the other category, illnesses of the head, which are called *isu*, madness.

Some men, particularly young ones, consider that saka is all pretense and they laugh at anyone who takes an interest in it. According to them, it is just one of those follies of women whose husbands ought to see through their 'deceitful feminine tactics'. Christian elders call it the work of the devil and when their own wives are afflicted forbid them to go to the dances. To Pagans, who are still in the majority, and to many Christians as well, saka is the product of foreign sorcery performed by tribes who wish to 'ruin' Taita women. One view is that foreigners covet the women for their beauty and hope to entice them away. More commonly it is said that the foreigners send saka to make the women barren. Impaired fertility is said to accompany saka, but supporting evidence is lacking.

III

In the saka attacks we see what appears at first to be a highly aberrant form of behavior. The symptoms strike one as being of an hysterical sort, using the term in an everyday rather than a technical psychiatric sense. The people themselves consider saka an illness; some women seek private (really semi-private) treatment, while most take part at least occasionally in the allegedly therapeutic dances. Shall we, on this basis, assume that saka is a genuine psychological disturbance and begin a search for explanations in terms of the life-circumstances of Taita women as these affect their psychological development? Even if one is to take this view, there is still the problem of why saka should take its particular form.

If for the present we ignore the symptoms of trembling and shaking, we can begin by noting that the same types of objects and events occur in all aspects of the complex – among the things fear of which or desire for which brings on an attack, among the objects or acts which bring women in saka ecstasy back to their normal state, and among items appearing in the dance costume.

All these objects, taken together, fall into three overlapping categories. The first includes things which are normally forbidden to women or which are usually the concern of men. These include: cigarettes, which women do not ordinarily smoke; the various items of clothing which they do not customarily wear; men's skills, such as playing the concertina (at local European-style dances known as *danzi*); bananas, which are one of the crops planted by men in the valuable valley-bottom fields; a husband's blood; a man's washing water or water in which his clothing has been laundered. The second category comprises purchased goods of a nondurable kind: clothing, sugar, cloth. The third category includes items of foreign provenance other than those falling into the other two categories. They are things which have not so far become part of everyday Taita life, and which therefore are more noticeably foreign: automobiles, fez, train whistle, foreign words.

Actually, not only the first category has to do with men or with the socially defined differences between men and women. The second category includes things which the Taita regard as women's special province – consumer goods for personal use. Though they are 'women's things', they are bought mainly with money earned by men. Finally, the foreign things and events refer to an area of activity, as well as a physical area, of which Taita women have little experience in comparison with men: the world of wage-labor outside the hills. Thus all the objects and acts which, in the context of saka, seem to excite strong fear and desire in women and which also appear to relieve the symptoms accompanying these emotions, have to do with the differences between men and women with respect to goods and activities.

The economic and jural distinctions between men and women need further exploration. The most fundamental difference concerns land and livestock, which cannot be inherited by women. A wife or widow has important rights respecting the use and disposition of both; she has the right to use enough land to supply her family with the bulk of their daily food, and she can also demand the use of one milch cow. A man is bound to consult his wife before lending or selling fields and livestock, and he depends on her to act as one of the main witnesses to important transactions. However, in addition to being debarred from a share in her father's estate, a woman has great difficulty keeping even a single goat, sheep, or calf which a kinsman may have given her. Men do not sell land or livestock to women, nor do they lend directly to them.

By contrast with their exclusion from the ownership of land and livestock, women are especially concerned with the acquisition of consumer goods. They sometimes have considerable control over household expenditure, a fact which is consistent in Taita thought with the role of women as controllers and producers of the daily household needs. At the same time, though women can earn small amounts of money through local trade in foodstuffs, baskets, beer, and pots, this trade is on a small scale and women have no entry into the field of wage-labor and large-scale trading.

This state of affairs is not wholly due to the limited opportunities open to untrained women in the labor market of Kenya, where men are preferred for domestic service as well as for other kinds of work. A woman is not free to engage in any money-making activities beyond minor local trading without her father's or husband's consent. Thus far there has been very strong opposition to the idea of women going into large-scale trade, which in any case requires capital that they cannot accumulate, or moving into the towns to work. Opposition to the latter is usually explained by Taita men on the grounds that unaccompanied women in the towns become prostitutes. For other reasons Taita womnen do not often accompany their husbands to the cities or towns on a permanent basis, though they may join them for a few weeks or even months. Therefore, Taita women generally have little experience of the world outside the Native Land Unit. There are individual exceptions, but on the whole their command of Kiswahili does not equal that of the men and few of them speak any other foreign language, African or European. Their familiarity with European machines and equipment is slight, and to many of them a camera is still an exceedingly sinister object.

These differences between men and women have special importance in many areas of social life. Land and livestock are the foci of rights and obligations which mark out enduring social relationships. Their status as actual or potential co-heir binds together the men of each localised patrilineal descent group and calls for a good deal of interaction among them. Furthermore, the exchange of these goods is of great social consequence in relations between different patrilineages. Men who are family heads, in particular men whose own fathers have died, control, subject to certain restrictions, the livestock and land which they have inherited from their fathers. Land is loaned, pawned, and in some areas sold, and these transfers not only take into account the relationships already existing between the parties, thereby marking them and maintaining them, but are also used to establish new relationships. Livestock also are fundamental to a series of exchanges, each with its own rules and social consequences. The result of this systematic exchange is that, from the point of view of a local community, kinsmen and neighbors are involved in a network of debtor-creditor relationships which have long-range implications. From the point of view of the status system, the exchange networks furnish the means by which a man, as he grows older, has the opportunity to acquire more land and livestock. These he can use in turn to acquire debtors of his own. Exchanges of land and livestock in this way are the means of acquiring prestige and also authority in the local group.

Women are completely excluded from this sphere of competition and achievement. Instead, they are the great producers of food. A vast amount of small-scale exchange of foodstuffs goes on among women, but the greatest amount of this is in the form of enjoined gift-exchange among kin and neighbors. In this exchange, important as it is for community good feeling, and vital though it may be to the balancing out of irregular household supplies, single gifts or sales do not establish long-term debtor-creditor relationships. Individual women cannot secure special positions as dispensers of food.

The basically different social consequences of exchange of men's property as against women's goods can be seen in the bride-wealth payments and gifts. The legitimation of children of a union depends on a certain livestock transfer from the husband or his father to the father of the bride. If the bride dies before bearing a child, or if the union breaks up before a birth, the livestock must be returned. In contrast, while the courtship foodstuffs exchanged by the women are important as demonstrations of good will and their acceptance entails specific duties, they need not be returned in these circumstances. Such gifts do not imply in themselves the establishment of any enduring bond, and therefore the failure of the bond to develop or to be maintained does not entail return of the goods.

As I have said, Taita consider that women's concern with housekeeping, including the production and allocation of food supplies, gives them a natural concern with money and with the consumer goods which money buys. Their interests are supposed to lie in the direction of teapots, crockery, and bright clothing, but such frippery is frowned on in any but young and unmarried men. Yet women cannot themselves earn more than a fraction of the money required to buy these things. They must depend on men, primarily their husbands, to provide them with cash earned by the sale of labor, land, cash-crops, and occasionally stock. Men have taken an increasing interest in using their money to acquire more durable goods such as metal roofing, maize-grinding machines, sewing machines, and so on, in addition to their desire to accumulate more land and cattle. Both the new and the old economic interests of men drain off cash which might otherwise be used to raise the level of household consumption.

In every-day life one sees something of the conflicts arising out of these different interests. It is expected by everyone that at least a part of the husband's earnings will be used to supply the household with consumer goods which men, as well as women, have come to look on as necessities: basic clothing, tea, sugar, matches, paraffin, blankets, a minimum of crockery or tin plates and mugs, and so on. But extra clothing, furnishings, and supplies – the things which women take pride in displaying and which are essential for entertainment – are often the subject of family disagreement. As one woman put it, 'Our children here have only one piece of clothing and that gets stiff with dirt and torn, but our husbands say, 'How can we have stock which begets stock if we sell our animals for money which is consumed in a day?'' '

The interests of women in consumables and the conflict between these interests and those of men in land and livestock, find expression in stereotyped descriptions of the female character. Women are said to have no head for land and cattle transactions. They do not have the right sort of minds for important community affairs because they have little control over their emotions and desires. Indeed, femininity is made synonymous with an uncontrolled desire to acquire and consume, with selfishness and the pursuit of trivial private interests.

Although they are accused by women of being lazy and of banding together to defraud women, men are also thought of as being concerned with the really important things in life, able to do without the present enjoyment of personal display (though unable to do without beer and interminable chat), for the sake of the greater benefits of planning and investment. These benefits are long-term relationships with other important men, enhanced prestige, provision for their sons' future, and a measure of authority in the community. Ultimnately, the result and the sign of the essential differentiation between men and women in terms of property, and therefore structurally, is the attribution of the greatest prestige to male rights, activities, and interests in general.

IV

Returning to the saka complex, we find that women afflicted with saka are thought of as having an inordinate desire for, or fear of, things or experiences normally pertaining to men; or they acutely desire things which they want and have normally to some degree, but which men supply for them. Saka is thought to result from spirit-possession, and it is considered an illness. Temporary relief is supposed to be achieved (1) by giving them the objects they desire, or allowing them to give free rein to their urges, or protecting them from what they fear; and (2) by having them take part in a public dance, the costume for which includes items which are distinctively male and also basic clothing which is distinctively female but finer and newer than what they wear ordinarily. (The semi-private treatment I consider a variant of the more public dance.) We may note that in acquiring or wearing items which are normally male perquisites, or in performing acts representing male achievements, there is no serious attempt to impersonate men. Desired objects and items of the costume are provided for women as women, by their husbands, in fulfillment of the general duty to succor an ailing wife.

One interpretation comes readily to mind, considering what has been said about the property system and its ramifications. That interpretation would stress the position of women in Taita society as 'deprived' persons. Saka behavior might then be thought symptomatic of psychological tensions arising from envy of men and involving ambivalence toward the feminine role. Here one would note the obviously Freudian symbolism of cigarettes, bananas, dirty water, blood, and dancing staves, as well as the appearance of both fear and desire accompanying the convulsive movements. Giving women the objects they desire, protecting them from what they fear, and giving them an opportunity to be the center of attention might then be thought compensatory or even therapeutic. Scope is left also for 'deceitful feminine tactics'; as with a European woman's 'sick headache', so also with saka: it may be used consciously or unconsciously to satisfy personal wishes.

At this point I do not wish to comment on the justification, or lack thereof, for such a view. Instead, I wish to demonstrate that a much fuller understanding of the symbolism of saka can be gained by treating it as a complex of ritual performances within the wider Taita ritual system, and by comparing it to one other complex within that system.

The view taken here is the one expressed by Leach: that there are ritual, i.e. customary, formalised, and symbolic aspects to virtually all actions, and that these ritual aspects symbolise 'socially approved "proper" relations between individuals and groups' (Leach 1954: 15). It is accepted that the actions performed by members of a society fall along a continuous scale; at one end are routine tasks with a minimum of ritual in the above sense, and at the other end are actions which are 'entirely sacred ... technically nonfunctional' (Leach 1954: 12). In saying that saka can be treated as a ritual complex, I am referring specifically to those actions performed by Taita which lie toward one end of the scale, and I am limiting the use of the word ritual to them. They are complexes of acts of the sort normally called rites or rituals and which, being bound up with notions of the mystical, are more than ceremonial performances.[6]

This paper, in its treatment of saka as a ritual complex, obviously cannot compare it with all or even many rituals within the Taita system. Instead, since saka involves women almost exclusively, it can most profitably be compared with rituals having to do specifically with men, ignoring the content of rites dealing with family relationships, community welfare, and so forth. In doing this I hope to throw light on the particular form of saka, the special way in which it may be said to symbolise and expound the social order. Such a procedure does not by itself imply rejection of psychological interpretations, or denial of the consequences of symbolic exposition for society. This is a point to be raised again at the end of the paper.

V

The Taita system of age-statuses gives attention to individual passage through the stages of the life-cycle, rather than to affiliation with a group of contemporaries passing through the stages together. The stages themselves are intimately related to the changing claims which an individual can make with respect to the acquisition and disposal of property, ritual, and other prerogatives. In this hierarchy of age-statuses, the highest position is that of old men who have grown sons and grandsons, who are independent householders in control of their own property in livestock and land, and who use this property to acquire debtors and followers. Their control over, and use of, property in particular ways may be viewed as the real basis for their joint exercise of authority in the community as elders meeting in ad hoc councils. But ritual prerogatives both validate their position and enhance it. These prerogatives consist of the ownership of private shrines and a share in the management of ritual performed in the community. The latter includes rites performed at the descent-group shrine-centers, each of which is supervised by a custodian who is *primus inter pares* among the elders of his own descent group. The system is egalitarian insofar as no man is barred initially from enhancing his status: there are no fixed or recognised status differences between the various descent groups. All depends on personal and family fortune, for though all men grow older, not all have flourishing families and not all grow rich. Women, of course, cannot become elders.

Until middle-age the careers of males and females follow something of the same course. Girls are circumcised (i.e. clitoridectomy is performed on them) in infancy, and boys are circumcised between the ages of five and twelve. For both, and especially for girls, the puberty rite known as *mwari* signifies transition from childhood to marriageability.[6] Marriage, which usually follows a more or less protracted period of courtship, brings only limited enhancement of status. The young couple live with the man's parents until the birth of two or three children or the marriage of a younger brother makes it imperative to set up by themselves. Householdership, though, is a privilege conferred by the man's parents. Economic and other kinds of independence come only gradually, in stages marked by ritual observances. Not until the couple themselves have a child ready for marriage is their position in the community at large much changed.

Even then, a man whose father is still alive is *mundu mlini*, an unimportant man. He is not in possession of his patrimonial livestock nor fully in control of the land which he and his wife cultivate. He is not supposed to compete openly for stock or for the prestige accruing to a man of wealth, for this would be to sin against his father. He and his wife are ritually dependent on his father and on other senior kinsmen for sacrifices to the dead, while they themselves can make certain other offerings only at the descent-group shrines through the custodian and his assistants. They can acquire only minor shrines having to do with garden and household prosperity. If his father is a rainmaker or one of the other ritual specialists known as 'protectors', the husband will usually learn the procedures but he cannot practice unless the father, becoming enfeebled, announces publicly that he wishes his son to act in his place.

After the death of his father, a man comes into his inheritance. This, together with independence from parental authority, makes it possible for him to lay claim to the visible signs of elderhood as he grows older, if he remains prosperous or attains greater wealth. These conditions fulfilled, he can proceed to acquire first the curing-kit shrine (*mfuko*), then the stool-shrine (*kifumbi*) and, in some parts of Taita, the bell-shrine (*mmanga*). Each shrine gives him additional rights in the management of the descent-group shrine-center.[7] He is also made progressively independent of the shrine-center, since he can now make important offerings at his own shrines which duplicate some of those in the center. As well as being a man of property, he is 'a man who knows medicines' (*wamanya buganga*) and his possession of ritual paraphernalia and knowledge is now spoken of as the basis for his influence in the community.

Shrines are not simply to be had for the asking. The rule in Taita is that no ritual steps are taken until divination reveals the mystical agency whose anger or desire has wrought some misfortune or has sent an omen warning of misfortune. By the signs, interpreted according to the known social situation of the suppliant, the individual diviner and then a group of elders performing haruspication prescribe the ritual remedy. Thus it is only when a man has arrived at a position of family headship, age, and wealth that illness or death among his family or his herd is interpreted as requiring the creation and/or consecration of a curing-kit shrine for him. The stool-shrine and perhaps the bell-shrine follow later in the same way. The men who are already elders determine the entry into their midst of a man who has become someone to reckon with. The rites by which shrines are acquired then translate his age, wealth, and practical influence into ritual possessions and knowledge, validating and enhancing his status. Many men acquire the curing-kit, quite a few can hope to have a stool-shrine, only a few live to possess a bell-shrine or its equivalent rights in the shrine-center.

The procedure of acquisition depends upon the shrine, for there are differences as to subsidiary paraphernalia, animals sacrificed, imparting of esoterica, steps in the consecration, and so on. However, certain common features are important to us here. As I have noted above, any shrine acquisition rite requires first a suitable diagnosis and prescription from a diviner and then a group of haruspicators. Second, a man who is already an elder must supervise the proceedings, always with the assistance of other elders who give their approval and can bear witness to the correctness of the performance. Third, an animal must be offered in sacrifice by the recipient of the new shrine. Meat from this animal is shared by all participants, along with the beer which is also provided by the new shrine owner. All the participating elders spray out beer in consecration of the shrine and in blessing of the owner, repeating prayers, invocations, and chants.

The phrases addressed to the shrine always have the same themes: the shrine is spoken to in a way which implies that even before its physical creation its anger caused the misfortune which required divination or haruspication; it is told that it is being consecrated and that henceforth it should be 'cool', i.e. beneficent toward its owner in order that he may prosper as the head of a numerous and healthy household and as the owner of a large, healthy, and fecund herd. Good will toward the shrine owner is also demonstrated by cursing all sorcerers who might be working against him. In doing this, each man in effect undertakes not to let envy or rivalry get the best of him to the extent of causing him to use sorcery against his fellow elder. The new elder himself is given a thong bracelet to wear for a certain number of days, during which he observes various restrictions. Beer is sprayed over him and other acts are performed to bless him and bring him prosperity.

Misfortunes may befall the new shrine owner in the future, both from ancestral anger and from the anger of the new shrine itself, but he can now placate the latter. He can make offerings to it when his herds or his human dependants suffer mishap – always provided that divination or haruspication indicates the shrine as the mystical agency responsible. Now he is recognised as a man who has acquired his wealth at the right time and in the right way. He has the right to possess and use his wealth, and therefore has the right to the means of protecting it. The ritual recognition adds further to his status.

VI

The saka complex and the rites of shrine acquisition and offerings may now be compared, with a view to understanding more completely what saka attacks and dances reveal about the Taita social system and women's place in it. Only brief mention of features which extend throughout the Taita ritual system is required for clarification.

As has been shown, rituals in Taita are not performed as a matter of course according to a cycle of ritual activities or as the necessary concomitant of particular events — excepting the blessings pronounced before meals and as part of salutations. Misfortunes or evil omens require visits to a diviner or haruspicator. The result is identification of the mystical agency which has sent the misfortune or omen, and prescription of suitable ritual measures. The exception to this rule is found in the activities of the persons called Dreamers (balodi, sing. Mlodi) whose visions are relied on to direct rituals of community-wide significance.[8]

One of the most basic features of the Taita ritual system is revealed by examination of the situations in which one or another mystical agency is (detected, and analysis of the patterns of participation in the corresponding rites. Rituals directed to a particular agency involve only certain social groups or persons standing in certain social relationships. The terms of a prescription given by a diviner, haruspicator, or Dreamer call attention to important aspects of the social relationships involved, and the ritual performances themselves do so as well. Each supernatural agency in the Taita roster thus becomes what might be called a ritual correlative for social relationships of a given order.

No doubt the reader will have applied the formula to the shrine rites, but both these and the saka complex need to be located precisely in the wider ritual system. More specifically, for men and women alike, misfortunes and evil omens are often attributed to the anger of deceased kin; examination of the situations in which this occurs shows that dead kin, identified by name or relationship, are the ritual correlatives for relationships within the circle of close consanguineous kin and affines. Situations involving relationships between persons, insofar as they are members of or closely linked to patrilineal descent groups, find their ritual correlative in the shrine centers. The Dreamers have visions of 'people of long ago' who direct crop-furtherance and rainmaking rites; these generalised ancestors make appropriate correlatives for relationships within a local community which is composite with respect to descent.[9]

For men who acquire most of their rights to property through membership in patrilineal descent groups (but who, rivalling each other, rise to positions of wealth and influence through controlled competition), individual shrines which duplicate one another and which are like some of those in the shrine center are suitable. But what is appropriate as a ritual correlative for the social differentiation of men from women? *Mlungu*, the Deity, creator of the world and man, might seem to be the answer. In Taita terms, however, Mlungu is not concerned with human relationships in their specific jural aspects, but only with the essential good and evil of mankind, with sin and purification from it. Not Mlungu, but foreign spirits are the ideal agencies on which to blame saka attacks. Like Mlungu, they are not involved in the particulars of the Taita social order and so can serve as correlatives for the basic social differentiation – that between the sexes, which is presupposed by all others. Unlike Mlungu, foreign spirits are of human origin and therefore can be concerned with human affairs.[10]

Thus both shrine rites and saka treatment are required for misfortune sent by a mystical agency; and choice of the latter is both suited to the social relationships involved and referred to by the ritual performance. The comparison can be extended beyond this point. Each man who attains the prerequisite social and economic standing acquires his own shrines, but each shrine has significance only in the total system of shrines. In the saka complex, an adult woman becomes possessed by a foreign spirit and all spirits, like all shrines, behave in the same general way. But each spirit has its own idiosyncrasies which distinguish it as a particular woman's spirit: one wants blood, another fears bananas or dislikes them, another is driven to play a concertina. In other words, these idiosyncrasies are functionally equivalent to the separate embodiments of shrines belonging to different men. They have meaning only within a system of possession which has one general theme.

The misfortunes sent by shrines, or by 'latent' shrines ivishing to be created, include illness of the man himself. More commonly, shrines are blamed for repeated illness and death among the man's human and animal dependants. The foreign spirits of saka, however, send an illness which attacks only the woman, causing her to behave in an abnormal way and perhaps causing her to be barren. These differences are consistent with the themes of the two ritual complexes: the property rights and economic position of men and women and their significance in the status system. Thus a shrine owner must be, ipso facto, head of a family and owner of a sizeable herd. That these can be affected by his shrine is itself diagnostic of his claims over them. A woman has no dependants or property in the same way as has a man. In this context she has, as it were, only her own person – with her own potentialities for action and her own childbearing capacity; these are the objects of the spirit's attack. The whole notion of persistent personal malady may indeed be taken to symbolise women's total exclusion from the sphere of male activities and perquisites. All men, as men, are potential family heads and owners of large herds; all are potential shrine owners, and many become such. All women, as women, are excluded from these prerogatives; all are viewed as susceptible to the attacks of foreign spirits and a large number do in fact succumb.

Once a man has acquired a shrine, later misfortunes can be attributed to his need for a more advanced shrine; and, as with the first shrine, acquisition of advanced shrines entails a publicly recognized rise in status. Alternatively, misfortunes can be blamed on a shrine already possessed; in this case offerings can be made to it, and these also involve other elders as witnesses and assistants, namely, they too have an element of publicity. There is a succession of occasions on which attention is called to a man's position as someone of property and consequence, and also to the entire system of elderhood in which men are rivals. Similarly, repeated saka attacks and successive saka dances depict over and over the nature of women's social position. No movement upward in status is involved, but merely repetition, in symbolic form, of the facts of that position. It is quite consistent that acquiescence to the spirits' demands and participation in numerous dances do not cure a woman of saka once and for all. It is also consistent that a woman who moves out of the Pagan ritual system by joining a church may be cured.

Looking again at the behavior characteristic of the two complexes, we see on the one hand that shrine rites demand of men that they behave in a calm and dignified way. Shrine owners are important and knowledgeable men, whose affairs are weighty and who are expected to conduct themselves with suitable moderation. On the other hand, a saka attack is signalised by shaking which, though it is in fact highly stylised, is supposed to be uncontrollable. The other acts, too, are supposed to indicate wild and ungovernable emotions. Indeed, the attacks present a highly colored view of what women are supposed to feel for the objects and acts involved. In so doing, they illustrate women's claims – or lack of claims – to such objects and activities. Some saka attacks depict women's demand for consumer goods; some express, in exaggerated form, female squeamishness when confronted with objects from the outside world. In others, things and acts representing the whole range of masculine prerogatives are shown as having for women an exaggerated interest, attraction, or repulsion. In saka attacks, then, women are caricatured as uncontrollable consumers; as persons without experience of the outside world; and as persons who, acknowledging the prestige attaching to masculine activities and possessions, can feel toward them any emotion except the calm and dignity consonant with an indisputable claim, which they do not have. In short, they are shown as contrasting in every way with men, and the contrast is symbolized as a personal malady.

The saka dance turns the saka attack on its head. Items of male attire and paraphernalia (including items of foreign provenance) dominate the costume, and the whole is composed of consumer goods in the form of finery. But now the behavior of women, except for the few who have a saka attack, is restrained and dignified. The costumes are becoming, and the women wear them with pride. The drummers take their work seriously and the onlookers are attentive. This does not imply that different meanings are attached to the three kinds of items in the context of the dance, but the feeling-tone is quite different from that of a saka attack — and this requires comment.

After all, the wild desires, fears, and urges of saka attacks are supposed to be the symptoms of an illness, and in such circumstances it is the duty of a husband to do what he can for his wife's relief. In saka attacks women show themselves as demanding that their whims be satisfied and their urges be given free play. In the saka dance, however, they are acknowledged to have the right to make these demands. Their appearance at the dance, in costumes for which their husbands have paid, accompanied by drummers the latter have hired, is evidence that their claims have met with success and that those claims are therefore just. But in both attack and dance, the essential nature of women's rights is presented: these are the rights of dependants (using the word in an economic and a jural sense, not a psychological sense). Lack of property, lack of experience of the outside world, and exclusion from other male prerogatives are aspects of their dependency; so also is the fact that they can acquire male prerogatives or the signs thereof only through illness. Attack and dance are two manifestations of a single situation. The first emphasises the negative aspects of women's social position in the guise of a malady; the second stresses the positive aspects in the form of deserved therapy, which is also a minor festivity. This makes understandable the fact that some women go into a saka attack in the midst of a dance or even at the sound of drumming which reminds them of a saka dance. Attack and dance can be translated into one another.

The place of saka in Taita ritual is most easily compared to the place given in American ceremonial to humorous dramas about pregnancy cravings. This situation seems to epitomise, for Americans, the ungovernable demands of dependent women and also the helplessness of the American male to resist those demands. The pregnancy is supposed to account for the quality and urgency of the demands, as is saka possession-illness. But it is surely not pregnancy itself which arouses response (and the fact that response takes the form of laughter should not obscure the meaning of the situation), but the spectacle of the male forced by the moral order to heed the demands of the dependent female. This spectacle is also presented by saka. Comparing the latter with play-acting in our own society may seem to imply that some of the Taita women who have saka attacks are only pretending, that their behavior does not indicate serious psychological disturbance. This brings us back to the question of alternative ways of looking at saka.

VII

In taking up briefly the relation between saka behavior and psychological disturbance, my contributions are those of an individual not trained professionally in medicine, psychology, or psychiatry. I was personally acquainted with perhaps twenty women who suffered saka attacks and I met many others casually. Among them were women whose everyday behavior ranged from mousy shyness to blustering aggressiveness, from habitual affability to sardonic cantankerousness. Observation of the saka attacks themselves led me to believe that some were set off by situations which had aroused genuine anxiety in the affected women. On other occasions women seemed to be pretending quite deliberately, at least at the beginning of an attack. Diminished self-control sometimes appeared quite real, but at other times it was obvious that the women had at least a measure of control over their movements and speech throughout the attack. I suggest that, on the level of personal tensions, attitudes, and feelings, saka may be many things to many women. Some affected women may even be severely neurotic, and in such cases susceptibility to saka attacks may be very closely bound up with their neuroses. I seriously doubt whether this is true of all or even most of them.

Of course, if one asserts that the symbolism of a performance carries meaning for the members of a society, one must assume some substratum of conscious or unconscious attitudes and feelings arising out of familiar social situations. From what I know of the rearing of Taita girls, their place in the family, their disciplining, and the development of attitudes toward marriage, childbearing, and domestic duties, I believe that many Taita women are made to feel hostile to men, that they come to envy their superordinate position, and that some wish they were men. In fact, it is not unusual to find Taita women ready to be very explicit on these points!

The feelings and attitudes common to many, most, or all Taita women; the neurotic elaboration of these in some women; and the part played by them in susceptibility to saka attacks, would be appropriate subjects for psychiatric study. Such a study could undoubtedly throw light on the apparently self-induced hypnotic states into which some saka attacks develop, and the psychotherapeutic value of the dances might also be assessed. Whatever the possible findings of psychiatrists, however, the point is that saka behavior in dance and attack carries meaning for all adult members of Taita society. Awareness of real tensions may well play a large part in the process whereby participants and spectators garner meaning from the performances, but the latter point directly to the jural relations between men and women of which all Taita are aware. The symbolism is part of the corpus of ritual language employed by Taita on many occasions to represent and expound the nature of their social relations.

Saka behavior is one of many examples of the expression of alleged feelings used to symbolise social situations which may generate such feelings. It is analogous, for example, to the habitual use in some societies of such phrases as 'I love my mother's brother'. The declaration may or may not represent true feeling in any particular instance, but it points to the existence of a type of structural relationship with the mother's brother which, it is thought, is likely to generate affection. Just as true feelings may be symbolised by actions, so real systems of action may be symbolised by the statement, in word or deed, of alleged feelings.

In basing my analysis on the conviction that ritual is expository of the social order and that the particular rituals considered here expound particular basic social relationships, I have said nothing about the possible function of symbolic expression. Most debates among social anthropologists about the nature of ritual are apparently no more than disagreements concerning either the consequences or the purposes of symbolic exposition. Some comments on ritual in relation to saka and shrine rites may clarify what I mean.

One purpose sometimes assigned to ritual might be called the *manipulative*. This aspect is stressed by Leach when he says that ritual 'serves to express the individual's status as a social person in the structural system in which he finds himself for the time being' (Leach 1954: 10–11). He points to the fact that an individual may manipulate the occasions of particular rituals, employing ritual assertions to maneuver himself into positions of higher status and prestige, or to validate such positions through ritual. Since other members of the society are doing the same thing, there is a scramble for positions which may ultimately alter the entire system of positions.

The manipulative side of ritual is surely of varying importance in different social systems and in different parts of the ritual order associated with those systems. Ritual may be manipulative in the sense that through it an individual claims the prerogatives of the social position he already occupies; this is part of what women do in saka. However, such manipulation serves only to maintain the status quo. The social position of women is not altered nor does any individual woman achieve higher status, though she may temporarily be the center of attention.[11] Men performing shrine-acquisition rites do assert higher status and are thereby accorded it; public acquiescence by participating elders endorses assumption of the new position.[12] Later offerings to shrines, however, serve only to maintain recognition and do not alter a man's position. In any event, all the men in Taita, striving to gain wealth, family headship, and the shrines which embody them, do nothing to alter the social structure. If the qualifications for elderhood were changed so as to 'pack the court' or if wealth came to be distributed in such a way that very few men qualified, there would be a real change in structure. At the present, neither rites of offering to shrines nor saka performances are manipulative in the sense of altering the system of social relationships.

Expository statements also have a *commendatory* aspect, pointed out by Leach when he says that rituals refer to the 'socially approved "proper" relations between individuals and groups' (Leach 1954: 15). The effects, however, may be of two sorts. On the one hand, establishment, maintenance, and recognition of a certain relationship between particular individuals and groups are commended – for example, the establishment of a particular man as an elder, or the observance by particular husbands of the duty to care for and protect their own wives. But, on the other hand, ritual goes beyond such particularisms to commend the *form* of relationships, the allocation of rights and duties in the way in which they are allocated. Any manner of allocating rights and duties entails some conflict, and the particular conflicts entailed in a relationship may receive special attention in its ritual exposition. Shrine rites do this through the prayers referring to potential sorcerers; saka does so in the symbolism of the attack, Real tensions, real conflicts, may be and probably are present, but ritual commends the whole of a relationship, with both its negative and positive aspects.

In this way participation in ritual indicates agreement on the forms of social relationships. This agreement may sometimes be given special recognition either in prohibitions on aggressive behavior during a rite, or in the assertion that the ritual performance (whether or not it includes symbolic representation of conflict) will result in benefit to the community at large. The saka attack allows a round-about acknowledgement of conflict, but in the saka dance the theme is again peace, dignity, and festivity. It is important in this respect that in some parts of Taita there is a tendency for saka dances to be incorporated in the rainmaking rites which bring prosperity to entire communities. On these occasions emphasis is placed on declarations of peace among the residents of such a community, who come from several descent groups and many villages. These declarations seem to me to represent agreement on the forms of the relationships binding people together, and it also seems logical that the Taita should start to include rituals which expound the form of the relationship between the sexes and thus to commend it and acknowledge agreement as to its nature.

If, without spelling out the whole matter of ritual commendation and social agreement, one simply says that such ritual occasions amount to expressions of harmony, there is room for misunderstanding. But if it is made clear what sort of harmony is referred to, no injustice is done to the facts. A more precise explanation would make it senseless to point only to the manipulative aspect of ritual, or only to the fact that ritual assertions may themselves generate and be indicative of real interpersonal conflict.

Ritual is surely both 'a language of argument' and a 'chorus of harmony' (see Leach 1954: 278).

Actual conflicts and tensions, some generated by ritual performances, have to be remembered when an *integrative* function is being assigned to the performances. If integration refers only to the maintenance of the current system of mutual expectations through ritual communication, that is one thing; we come back to commendation and agreement on the forms of relationships. However, if it is implied that ritual performances of themselves create solidarity, there are obvious difficulties.

Whatever the view taken of these matters, there remains the task of analysing rituals as expositions of particular jural relationships. These expositions are carried out in cultural forms which themselves become fully meaningful only in terms of the structural situations in which they are employed. It would seem that social anthropologists are well occupied when they work on this level, leaving the corresponding and equally valid psychological analyses to persons adequately trained for the appropriate investigations.

This suggestion is especially urgent with respect to such performances as those of saka, which seem bizarre to European or American eyes and which, on first sight, need immediate psychological interpretation. If all the women who have saka attacks are in fact severely neurotic, their behavior is carried out in the Taita idiom and in terms of Taita structural situations; if they are neurotic, it is in the Taita fashion. This applies also to individuals who are considered by the Taita as well as by the medical officers to be insane. They are mad in the Taita manner, expressing their madness in the same idiom which normal Taita employ. The particular idiom and the structural relations to which it refers need to be known if fuller understanding of the relationship between normal and abnormal behavior is to be achieved. This is a field of investigation to which social anthropologists can contribute much by the analysis and interpretation of behavior in social terms.

INTRODUCTION: REFERENCES

Boddy, J. (1989) *Wombs and Alien Spirits: Women, Men and the Zār Cult in Northern Sudan*. Madison: University of Wisconsin Press.
Lewis, I. (1969) 'Spirit possession in Northern Somaliland'. In T. Beattie and J. Middleton (eds), *Spirit Mediumship and Society in Africa*. London: Routledge.

NOTES

1 The field-work which is the basis for this paper was carried out from July 1950 to August 1952 under the auspices of the Colonial Social Science Research Council, to whom I offer my thanks. The original version was read to the

Anthropological Club of Cambridge University in May 1954 and in the following spring to Max Gluckman's seminar in the Department of Social Anthropology, Manchester University. Thanks are due for the criticisms and suggestions received on both occasions.

2 Information on the Wagiriama and Waduruma was secured from members of those tribes living in or visiting Taita. A retired Colonial Service official told me that in his opinion similar performances in Kikuyu country began to take place only in recent years and had been introduced from the Coast.

3 Various references bearing on the matter are given by Gluckman (1954) scattered through the text and notes. One of his references is to Lee's (1951) article. Lee has also written a relevant dissertation for the University of London which I have not seen.

4 Similar bandoliers form part of special costumes elsewhere in Africa. It seems possible that the idea was copied from early troops, European hunters, or explorers.

5 The distinction is Gluckman's (1045: 119). It is important to distinguish between performances as to whether or not they are connected explicitly with notions of the mystical. The extent to which such notions are present in some contexts and absent from others is surely related to significant differences among societies.

6 Boys participate in the last stage of *mwari* known as *kumaza ngasu*, the revelation wonders'.

7 If he is an eldest son he usually takes over the shrines of his father, but shrine-possession is not primarily a matter of replacing the father; each male member of a sibling group can acquire his own shrines if he achieves the prerequisites.

8 Dreamers are scattered about the country, the areas of their influence expanding and contracting according to the apparent success of the rites ordered by their visions, or according to the number of persons supposed to have suffered evil because of refusing to obey the Dreamer's words.

9 Diviners and haruspicators can be shown to alter interpretations according to the social situation. The system of signs is flexible enough to permit this to be done (Harris 1955: 114–31).

10 The inclusion of foreign sorcerers complements other Taita sorcery beliefs. It ties together fear of foreign influence and ideas about danger from the traitor within, the *mza kubi* or 'eater in two places'. This aspect is important, but full discussion would take us too far afield.

11 The situation is different elsewhere, as among the Wagiriama, where possession of this kind can result in entrance into the company of diviners.

12 The dance formation is significant. In much Taita dancing participants are paired in couples or lines, with the sexes facing each other. Or a group composed of one or both sexes forms a circle facing inward, with an individual or a couple dancing inside the circle from time to time. In either case, the dancers form an organized group. This is also true on occasions of bell-shrine acquisition, when the new owner dances with attending elders on a bull's hide, his aggregation to a group being symbolized in this way. In the saka dance, women are juxtaposed in such a way as to indicate only that they belong to the same social category. They follow one another in a line, taking either a straight or a circular path. Since they do not cluster or face each other, there is no implication of their forming an organized group, nor any indication of relationships which they may have among themselves.

REFERENCES

Gluckman, Max (1954) *Rituals of rebellion in South-east Africa*. The Frazer Lecture, 1952. Manchester University Press.

Harris, Grace (1955) The ritual system of the Wataita. Unpublished PhD thesis, Cambridge University

Junod, H. A. (1927) *The Life of a South African Tribe*. London: Macmillan.

Leach, E. R. (1954) *Political Systems of Highland Burma*. London, G. Bell & Sons (for London School of Economics and Political Science).

Lee, S. G. (1951) Some Zulu concepts of psychogenic disorder', *South African Journal for Social Research*: 9–16.

Lindblom, G (1920) *The Akamba*. Upsala.

Ross, A. D. (1956) Epileptiform attacks provoked by music (clinical note)', *British Journal of Delinquency*, VII, 1: 60–3.

Rouch, J. (1934) *Les Songhay*. Paris: Presses universitaires de France (for International African Institute).

CHAPTER FIFTEEN

Suicide and Risk-Taking in Tikopia Society*
(1961)
Raymond Firth[†]

Firth (1902–), one of Malinowski's pupils and later a professor at the London School of Economics, published extensively on fieldwork in the Polynesian island of Tikopia. He considers some of the possible objections to a straightforward application of Durkheim's (1897) classic typology to small-scale communities, and outlines the practice of suicide on Tikopia where it is relatively common. Of particular interest is the relationship between suicide, 'attempted suicide' and other risk-taking behaviours, particularly swimming towards the open sea (women) and hazardous solitary canoe trips (men). Firth places emphasis not only on risky behaviour as a communicative act, but on the variety of options which are available to the individual.

———

Ever since Henry Morselli suggested that in the 'so-called voluntary actions' of suicide there could be discerned regularities and uniformities which could be related to social factors, and Emile Durkheim brilliantly demonstrated some of the major relationships,[1] there have been many attempts to correlate suicide behavior and frequencies with states of society. In the enormous literature that has grown up there have been a number of studies of specific anthropological interest, including the general works of Steinmetz and Wisse, and localised analyses of varying detail such as those of Voegelin, Fenton, Elwin, Carstairs, and Bohannan – to mention only a few.[2] These studies contain very valuable material,

———

*I am indebted as a Fellow, 1958–9, of the Center for Advanced Study in the Behavioral Sciences, Palo Alto, California, for the facilities afforded me in the preparation of this article and for the helpful comments of colleagues, especially Lloyd A. Fallers, Clifford H. Geertz, Kaspar Naegele, and Seymour Perlin.
†BA 21, MA 22, University of New Zealand: PhD University of London 27, Lecturer, Acting Professor, Sydney University, Australia 30–2; London School of Economics 33–6; Reader 36–44, Professor of Anthropology 44, University of London. Secretary, Colonial Science Rsc. Council 44–6. Field Research: Tikopia, Western Pacific 28–9, 52; Malaya 39–40. Fellow, British Academy 49–.

especially on the etiology and mechanisms of suicide, its distribution, and the social reactions and events connected with it. But while one can accept Durkheim's general thesis about the social determination of suicide rates, there are still some difficulties – which I shall explore in this paper – about aspects of the theory which has been built upon it.

Durkheim's argument, in outline, was that in two types of suicide, anomic suicide and egoistic suicide, the social controls have been weak – in the first type because the individual has become detached from social institutions, and in the second because society itself has left the resolution of his personal affairs to him as a voluntary matter. In a third type, the altruistic suicide, the controls of society have been so ordered as to encourage and virtually dictate the individual's action.

SUICIDE AND STRENGTH OF SOCIAL CONTROLS

One argument that subsequent theory has made is that suicidal behavior is correlated positively with strength or completeness of social controls. Nadel[3] has argued with respect to the Nuba that where there is less latitude for misfits, the suicidal predisposition is fostered; where individuals deviating by choice or accident from normality are least able to find legitimate alternative ways of living in the group, they must lean most strongly toward ultimate escape by suicide. Straus and Straus,[4] using a comparative case study from Ceylon, hold that in a closely structured society, where reciprocal rights and duties are stressed and enforced, the identity of the individual merges with the group, and altruistic suicide occurs, even for seemingly trivial causes! But in a loosely structured society an offender can be reabsorbed into the family group and the society, or at any rate interpersonal relations are not so rigid that suicide ensues.

I find such propositions superficially plausible but not entirely satisfactory. In effect they fail to utilise some of the distinctions and the flexibility which Durkheim introduced as regards categories of persons concerned, and combinations of suicide types. Nadel regards a correlation between social rigidity and suicide incidence as an 'intrinsic and logical one'. I regard it as a tautology. If by definition suicide is an escape from society and its judgments, and if the society is so rigid that no other avenues of deviance from normality are open, the two variables are already interdependent, and the correlation is spurious. The *behavior* of suicide is an index of social rigidity, but the *incidence* – that is, rate – of suicide is an index of the degree of deviance in the society. With societies of equivalent rigidity in norms of conduct, there may be different degrees of deviance, depending, for example, upon the character of personal goals, variation in the resources available for satisfying them, and so forth. The model for theories of a direct relation between suicide and social rigidity seems to be of a rather simply mechanical kind – society is seen as a kind of vessel with apertures, and with a constant internal level of pressure from deviant behavior. In the case of the most rigid system, only one aperture is open, and pressure can be reduced only by use of the single outlet – that is, suicide, which therefore has a high rate. In less rigid, more loosely structured systems, there are presumably more apertures, and the rate of outlet through the suicide aperture is correspondingly lower.

I do not think that this simple conceptual model is a travesty, but there are objections to it. The first is that the notion of a social system which is rigid overall, in every particular of judging conduct and repressing deviance, seems unrealistic. Even in societies with a very elaborate and precise moral code, and very full mechanisms for dealing with breaches of the code, there still seem to be avenues for personal expression of deviant tendencies. Some of these may be in the direction of developing evasion techniques, or of the formation of deviationist subgroups, if the society has enough magnitude. Others may be in the direction of more positive outlets, possibly of a sublimatory kind, in the fields of art or religion.

A second objection lies in the type of argument which has been put forward with some cogency by Henry and Short,[5] to the effect that suicide varies *inversely* with the strength of external restraint over behavior. They point out, as did Morselli and Durkheim, that suicide is often a correlate of less responsibility – for example, of bachelors as against married men, of people of advancing age as against younger people. Even if it be found difficult to accept their general proposition comparatively, there is another alternative. In a society with more permissive, more flexible rules and treatment of deviance (and for brevity I am speaking here as if 'deviance' can be used as a unitary term, despite the differences in kind and degree), suicide incidence may be a semi-independent variable. It is conceivable that for reasons unconnected with the rigidity of social norms, suicide might be a preferred way of dealing with a situation, because of its assumed finality. If the character of the problem for an individual be seen not in the rigidity of society but in the very fact of having to cope with existence in society, then however easygoing the society, the individual may still prefer to escape from it altogether. Moreover, it could be argued that to some types of individuals – for instance, adolescents – it is not the rigor of social norms that is appalling, but the lack of firmness. They may commit suicide because they lack guidance, not because they have too much of it. As Kluckhohn has pointed out, the speculation that adolescent suicide occurs more often where marriage is late and premarital sexual expression is severely punished would be vindicated only if examination of the facts proved a higher rate in the more repressive societies and a lower one in the more permissive.[6] Empirical data may of course bear out the contention that lack of guidance leads to crime or some form of deviance other than suicide; yet though suicide and murder are usually seen in inverse relation, they are to some extent alternatives, as Elwin has mentioned for the Bison-horn Maria.[7]

Again, in a loosely structured society, in which considerable variation of individual behavior in general is sanctioned, there may be different views about the propriety of suicide. In one such society suicide may be strongly condemned, or, as among the Zũni or Tallensi,[8] it may be regarded as silly. In another, it may be tolerated, and if not actually praised, may be tacitly approved as a solution of personal difficulties. As Durkheim argued, the presence or absence of a religious sanction may not appear to affect greatly the actual volume of suicide. But it may be an indicator of the significance of more general social attitudes with more effect.

I put forward these views to indicate that it is logically possible for suicide to vary semi-independently with permissiveness, but I intend to offer later what may be concrete support for this theory. I would argue that the whole question of the incidence of suicide in relation to the state of society is much more complicated than is indicated by propositions such as I have cited earlier. Analysis is further complicated by one more element – the characterisation of 'suicide' itself. Most definitions of suicide refer to the death of a person through his intention to commit the act of self-destruction. Such a definition by intent is necessary for clear theoretical classification. Yet empirically the classification is in a sense *post hoc*. Where death has eventuated through an act initiated by the dead person, intention to self-destruction must be presumed. But where a similar act has been initiated, but for some reason death has not eventuated, there is often a question as to whether the person really intended to destroy himself and was prevented, or was feigning such intent and wished to be prevented. Some deaths classified as suicide were possibly acts which their initiators hoped would be prevented, but through miscalculation or other accident were not. As Weiss has pointed out, attempted suicide is often a different type of action from successful suicide.[9] Such situations are well known – for example, the rate of attempted suicide is much higher for women than men in Western society, though the incidence of actual suicide by men is higher. Involved in the suicide attempt is a distinct element of risk-taking. It is part of my argument that such risk-taking may be built into the structure of ideas about suicide, and may then have a bearing on the sociological interpretation of the volume of suicide.

SUICIDE METHODS IN A 'PRIMITIVE' COMMUNITY

I will illustrate this point of view by data from Tikopia, a Polynesian community in the Western Pacific.[10] With less than 2,000 people in all, Tikopia is politically part of the British Solomon Islands Protectorate, but has been so isolated that until very recently little effective administration has been given it and social control has been the responsibility of the local chiefs. The rate of suicide in this community has been relatively high. My figures on incidence relate to the period between 1929, after my first expedition, and the end of 1951, shortly before my second expedition (in March, 1952). Though not official, the figures may be taken as fairly accurate, since they were obtained primarily by comparison of the names in my sociological censuses at the two dates, and inquiry as to the cause of death of every person who appeared in the 1929 census but had not survived until 1952. The data on the second expedition were collected and analysed with the help of my colleague, James Spillius. Many of the people concerned had been known to be personally very well, and information about their deaths was obtained not from a questionnaire but as ordinary news, with much descriptive detail. Uncertainty in the classification of a death as suicide is therefore not due to lack of information about manner of death, but to uncertainty as to whether the death was intentional. The special physical circumstances of Tikopia offer, as it were, a wider arc than usual within which the ascription of death as self-destruction or not may swing.

Tikopia attitudes toward suicide are closely connected with their attitudes toward death in general. Summarily stated, these attitudes express regret concerning death rather than fear of it; the Tikopia view death realistically, both as a social and a personal phenomenon. There appears to be much sincere feeling expressed at the loss of close kin, but there is also much mourning of a more formal kind. The absence of the dead person, the social loss, receive ample emphasis; the personal terrors of physical dissolution do not seem to occupy much attention. The transient character of human life is accepted together with the idea of the continuity of the soul, consequently the timing of the moment of cessation of bodily functioning is not necessarily treated as a matter of crucial importance. To take one's own life is merely to anticipate the inevitable end. In some circumstances, death has an esthetic attraction. Judgment is primarily concerned with the circumstances of the death, rather than with the fact that it may have been self-inflicted.[11]

No term in Tikopia is the exact equivalent of 'suicide', but the expression *fakamate* (causing to die) is used reflexively and conveys the idea of devoting oneself to death. The descriptive terms for the various ways of putting an end to one's life are commonly used. Tikopia have sometimes chosen odd ways to commit suicide. About the oddest was that chosen by Pu Sao, who having broken wind in a public gathering, in his shame climbed a coconut palm and sat down on the sharp-pointed, hard flower spathe, which pierced his fundament and killed him – a bizarre case of making the punishment fit the crime. But the normal Tikopia ways of committing suicide are three, differentiated broadly according to age and sex: hanging (mainly by middle-aged and elderly people); swimming out to sea (women only, especially young women); putting off to sea by canoe (men only, especially young men). Hanging (*noa ua*, tying the neck) is usually fatal. The person makes a noose in a fishline or other fairly thin cord, ties the other end to a house beam, and then ruses to the end of the house, the violence and tightness of the noose apparently bringing death very quickly. The method is not completely reliable. One man looped a noose around his neck at the top of a coconut palm and leapt off, but the rope broke; he fell, but lived. In swimming out to sea (*kau ki moana*), the women, though good swimmers, soon seem to be overcome by heavy seas or by the sharks that are common off the coast; and mortality from such suicide attempts appears frequent. In accounts of Tikopia's past this method is mentioned very often, and the laconic *ne kau* (swam) is often used in discussions of a genealogy, indicating the fate of many unmarried young women.

Resort to either hanging or swimming out to sea may be classed (with a qualification discussed later) as a suicide attempt, since if straightforwardly accomplished without interference the result is death. But resort to putting off to sea in a canoe (*forau*) is more difficult to interpret. The Tikopia term in general indicates a sea voyage, and any canoe voyage from Tikopia is a hazardous undertaking. Tikopia is a mere dot in 40,000 square miles of ocean, with the nearest land, Anuta, equally isolated – only half a mile across and 70 miles away; larger land is more than 100 miles away and in some directions many hundreds of miles. With the alternation of storm and calm, especially in the monsoon season, to try to make a landfall from Tikopia is a great risk. Many would-be voyagers fail, and the chances for survival average considerably less than even. Yet spurred on by the desire to see the outside world, Tikopia men, especially young men, have been ready to take a chance. In many cases it is difficult to separate an attempt to escape from Tikopia to see the world, with a serious chance of not surviving, from an attempt to escape from Tikopia society with an intent to perish or an attitude of not caring whether one perishes or not. All these cases covered by the term *forau* involve a fatalism which is very strange to the Westerner. In effect, judgment of the canoe attempt as a suicide attempt or not is based by the Tikopia primarily on the conditions in which the person puts off to sea. Secrecy – often helped by a night departure – at the start of most such voyages is normal, to avoid being stopped not only by sorrowing relatives, but also by the canoe owner, who does not want to lose his property. But if a person puts off alone, in a high sea, after a scene in which he has been enraged or gravely embarrassed, in a tiny canoe ordinarily used for lake traffic, with no sail or provisions, then the integration is that he is a probable suicide. If, in contrast, he puts

off with other members of a crew, in a quiet sea, with no emotional scenes
preceding his departure, in a large seagoing craft, with some sort of sail
and provisions, then the interpretation is usually that he has made a deliberate ocean voyage. Yet it is possible for a man to take sail, club, bow and
arrows, coconuts and other food, but not intend to use them. When far
out at sea – perhaps having been afloat for days – and tired of life, he may
overturn his canoe or break it with his club, and go down to death or be
devoured by the sharks. The odds against survival, of the individual
hothead especially, are so high that it is reasonable to characterise *forau* of
this individual type from which young men did not return as 'suicide-risk'
or 'suicide' adventures in the pejorative sense of the term. But even in this
connection there is a qualification, especially in relation to the Tikopia
'rescue service', which will be discussed later.

In discussing Tikopia suicides, I give what seem to be predisposing
conditions, but I am not implying thereby that I have provided all the
elements for the final understanding of any case. Still, social factors are
clearly apparent both in the choice of method and in the attendant circumstances. In suicide at sea, an almost, complete sex differential is manifested:
a woman swims to her death, a man takes a canoe. Yet Tikopia men in
ordinary circumstances swim as well and as freely as women. Again, by
report a curious fastidiousness is sometimes displayed in committing
suicide. A person dying by hanging, it is said, excretes freely. If the deed is
committed without premeditation, the interior of the house is in a mess; in
the person's dying struggles mats and the interior of the house become
covered with excrement. People coming to release him are disgusted, and
before mourning begins women must clean up the disorder. For this
reason, I was told a person who is thinking of suicide by hanging may
refrain from food for a day or so, in order 'that his excrement may not be
laughed at'. It may seem to us unnecessary to be so finicky about the
manner of dying, yet this has a crude logic. If part of the reason for
destroying the body is to preserve the social personality intact – by
safeguarding it from disintegrating despair or shame – then the person
does not want his reputation to suffer by his death. Suicide in Tikopia is
thought to merit a certain dignity.

The physical details as such of the suicide do not seem to worry the
Tikopia. For a suicide at sea, the common fate is often discussed thus:
'The death of a woman, to be eaten by sharks; when a man voyages out in
a canoe, he goes on and on, his canoe overturns, he too is eaten by
sharks.' The details may be quite horrible to westerners, but the Tikopia
face them in a matter-of-fact way.

Attitudes Toward Suicide

The Tikopia attitude toward suicide of others is in general one of mild disapprobation. Among pagan Tikopia in 1952, according to information given by Pa Fenuatara, there was some religious sanction for this opinion. The gods dislike a man to kill himself by hanging, because their function is to take the soul at death, and a sudden death gives them no time for preparation. If a man commits suicide, his soul goes off and wanders about, and its ancestral spirits in the heavens must search for it to bring it safely to its spirit home. But if a man commits suicide by going off to sea in a canoe, or a woman by swimming out to sea, the result is 'a splendid death', a 'sweet death', to which the spirits do not object, and from which they can catch up the soul of the dead person. When the canoe of a man is engulfed at sea, he cries out to the spirits of his mother's lineage, who come and bear off his soul. The same is true for women, but in some groups there are special privileges. The Ariki Kafika – the chief – told me that when the women of his lineage swim out to sea they are clasped in the arms of their Female Deity, who pulls them down. They drown but are not eaten by sharks, while the goddess takes their souls. Similarly, the women of the allied lineage of Porima are protected by their Deity of the Woods, who spits in the eyes of the sharks.

Among Christian Tikopia in 1952 the orthodox view was that the soul of a suicide does not go to Paradise, but to Satan. The Bible says it is wrong for a man to die this way, and the church is opposed to the practice. But the common view seemed much more tolerant. Spillius was told that if a man commits suicide, the priest should make the proper prayers at the altar to insure that the soul goes to Heaven, but the families of suicides in fact seemed to go to little trouble to see that this was done. As Pa Raroifi said, the special prayers and services of the priest would cost the family a mat as a gift to the priest, and once the body of the man was in the ground people did not worry about him unless his ghost started to walk.[12] I myself have no record of any such special prayers.

In common with its condemnation of suicide, the church also condemned the *forau sora*, the secret voyage, holding that if a man wishes to undertake an overseas voyage he should wait for the Mission vessel or some other powered craft. The souls of people belong to God, and they should await the will of the Lord in respect to their time to die. Hence the more pious Christians held that the *forau* custom should be abandoned. Yet it is significant that the incidence of *forau* seemed to be much the same among Christian and pagan young men, and that among those who took canoes secretly in this way were two sons of the Mission priest, one of whom was lost at sea. In other words, the compulsive character of competitive adventure among the young men seemed to override all Christian teaching. The sanctions of the church had not yet been effectively internalised and integrated into the personality.

By 1952 no effective political sanction had been imposed on Tikopia canoe voyaging. But since at various times these voyages have given much trouble to the administration in searching for lost men and repatriating survivors, it is likely that before long some hindrances may be placed in the way of Tikopia risk-voyaging, and going off in a canoe may be declared an offense. Unless alternative outlets are provided at the same time, however, it may be very difficult to implement such a control.

In general, then, the Tikopia viewed suicide as no crime, and the church's doctrine that suicide was a sin was not influential enough to inhibit many Tikopia from risking their lives and some from deliberately sacrificing them. The disaprobation of suicide and the strenuous efforts to save those who had attempted it were based on social more than on religious reasons.

Suicide Rates

To consider Tikopia suicide rates more closely I give in the accompanying table the deaths between 1929 and 1951 from the three main methods as closely as could be ascertained by years.

Disregarding for the time being the deaths from canoe-voyaging, and considering only the indubitable suicides from hanging and swimming out to sea, for a mean population of 1,500, over a period of 23 years, the annual rate of suicide was 0.8 persons, or for comparative purposes, 53 suicides per 100,000 population. Even if in a mass suicide of 6 girls in 1950

Tikopia Suicides* and Possibly Suicidal voyages, 1929–51

| Year | Suicides according to Method | | |
	Hanging	Swimming to sea	Canoe-voyaging
Unclassified	3	1	26
1929–42	0	0	7
1943	0	0	6
1944	0	1	10
1945	0	0	2
1946	0	0	1
1947	0	3	6
1948	0	0	11
1949	0	0	8
1950	1	7	4
1951	2	0	0
Total	6	12	81

*Occasional suicides by odd methods are not included in this table.

by swimming out to sea, only the principal girl be counted (and her followers be put down to misadventure), the rate would still be about 37 suicides for annum per 100,000 population, which is considerably higher than that for most Western countries, where the yearly rate is between about 10 and 30 per 100,000 population.[13]

Now consider the deaths from sea-voyaging. The loss of 81 persons in 23 years includes 4 females who accompanied their male kin, either on an ordinary voyage overseas, or as part of a crew in a searching fleet, and at least 5 persons who died from exhaustion or other illness after landing on a foreign island. But the majority of those who perished must have set out under conditions so hazardous that their prospects of survival were slight, and their fear of self-destruction small. Since the Tikopia keep no precise annual records, a breakdown of the figures by years was not exact. But at least 30, and probably considerably more, were in the five years 1944–8, when the new experiences of the war had stimulated a high level of interest in overseas adventure. Despite their intense, almost obsessive interest in the novel, scarce goods of the Western world, the Tikopia did not develop a millenarian movement of the kind known as a 'cargo cult',[14] in which fantastic preparations were made to receive an expected bounty from heaven. a combination of reasons was probably responsible, but it may have been partly because of the outlet for their craving presented by the possibility of a voyage overseas. They could go to meet the millennium; they did not have to wait passively for it to arrive. In this connection it is significant that of the 55 persons whose loss could be dated with reasonable accuracy, about 40 were probably under 30 years of age when they died. In such young men the lust for adventure was greatest. But they tended also to be the more easily emotionally disturbed. From evidence about the nature of the flight and the preceding circumstances, it is clear that probably at least a dozen of these *forau* were deliberately suicidal attempts, and that the rate of effective suicide should perhaps be put at between 60 and 70 persons per annum per 100,000 population.

Types of suicidal situations

I have no systematic material of a quantitative kind on the causes of suicide in Tikopia, mainly because in many cases, often long after the event, it was not possible to get from the surviving kin any very clear-cut statement of all the reasons which led a person to self-destruction. It was evident, for instance, that many young men put off to sea following some degree of emotional disturbance, but the relatives and friends were not always sure exactly what the circumstances were leading up to this, and it was often impossible for me to discern how much shame, resentment, and frustration were intermingled. But the major types of situations apparently involved in suicide can be indicated, with ostensible cause.

One type of suicidal situation is that involving loss of spouse or other close relative. Pa Mukava, youngest son of the Ariki Tafua of 1929, some years after my first visit committed suicide on the death of his wife. 'He killed himself for his wife; he hanged himself. When she died, he wailed and wailed that day, his grief was great; then he went to hang himself – on the same day.' A similar case was that of Pa Nukusorokiraro; his wife died and he hanged himself on the same day. In 1929 I was told how one of my friends had earlier tried to commit suicide on the death of his son. In the darkness of the funeral house one of the mourners had felt someone crawl past. On inquiry, people discovered that the father was gone. One mourner, guessing that the father had gone to hang himself, ran out and saw him standing in a nearby canoe shed with a noose about his neck. The mourner dashed over, lifted him up and yelled to the others, who released him, worked over him, and revived him. Three points characterising this type of suicide are: action is taken by the grief-stricken person quite soon, with no more than a few hours for reflection; the method chosen is often hanging, which is fairly quick and certain; if the suicide is prevented, usually no further attempt is made.

Another type of situation is chronic or severe illness, including mental illness. In despair at the infirmities of old age (including, I was told, the disintegration of his body, so that his skin began to stick to the mat on which he lay), Pa Saukirima, the rather dour head of the lineage of Fusi in 1929, hanged himself in his house one evening, using a tough rope which had bound up a bundle of tobacco. Other suicides were by mentally ill people, as is illustrated by the following:

> The mother of Pa Ranginiumata was lunatic, and swam out to sea. A canoe party including the Ariki Kafika heard shrieks, eight or ten times, and then silence. Paddling to the spot, they found a basket with water bottles floating (a woman's equipment) and sharks poking up their heads from the water. The sea around was smooth and blood-stained, though waves were breaking elsewhere.

With regard to suicide from insanity, it is questionable how far the Tikopia would accept the old 'suicide while of unsound mind' formula of the English coroner. In general, the Tikopia draw a definite distinction between the suicides of insane persons, and those of persons who in their view have made a free choice voluntarily and consciously to take their lives. Here is an illustration:

> Pa Rangitoko went crazy, chasing children, fighting people who tried to restrain him, and trying to enter houses at random.

People tied him up at night by his wrists and ankles, and his wife, in fear of him, went to live with her daughter. This went on for a long time, with periods of lucidity intervening. At last his head cleared, and after living alone for a time, he wanted his wife to return. But his wife, still afraid that it might be a trick of the spirits to induce her to come back in order to wreak harm on her, did not come. His body pitiably wasted from lack of food, the man hanged himself, in the daytime, in his house.

I asked if his suicide had been brought about by spirits, since he had been so crazy. The reply was: 'Oh! It was his own doing! His being affected by the spirits, his shrieking, his madness, were over. When we used to come to him, he threw things at us, he fought us. But when his mind cleared, his wife didn't come and prepare food for the two of them, so he became angry, hanged himself and died.' Here then the Tikopia interpretation was that resentment against his wife took the form of an aggressive act against himself, a commingling of anger and despair. In such a case, too, the suicide is partly revenge against the person who has offended one.

But while the Tikopia distinguish suicides due to insanity from ordinary suicide, they are sometimes inclined to attribute the obsessional aspect of suicide to a temporary disturbance of the balance of the mind. They may even use the same expression (*vare*) as is used for insanity, although it is susceptible of a range of translation, and can also properly be interpreted in the relatively mild sense of plain silliness or stupidity. For instance, an old dirge voiced by a man for his sister can be rendered as follows:

> My sister, my nourisher
> You jumped into the sea
> Nor did you glance aside to shore
> The foolish thought was conveyed to your mind
> And you went to your death – whither?

Here the brother does not imply that the woman was actually insane, but stigmatises her idea of taking her life as stupid. Akin to this is the view traditionally taken when Tikopia chiefs at times insist on risking their lives on overseas voyages. A chief, especially the Ariki Kafika, the premier chief, should not voyage abroad for trivial reasons, such as a lust for adventure. If such a chief will not be held back by pleading and argument, but determinedly goes on a *forau* and is lost at sea, then it is thought his mind has been made up for him by the spirits. The expression is, 'His mind has been caused to be bound by the spirits.' His mental balance has been disturbed and his judgment affected.

Another type of situation sometimes leading to suicide is domestic discord. Not long before 1928 Nau Saraniu hanged herself because her husband was guilty of continued infidelity with a widow. In another case, some time after 1929, Pa Korofatu took a second wife, but fought with her so strenuously that both of them rushed off in opposite directions and committed suicide separately, by hanging. After the death of the Ariki Taumako, some time in the 1940s, the wife of Pa Nukuvakai insisted on keeping all the food taboos of mourning rigorously. Her husband tried to feed her with pudding and other good quality foods, but she refused. He objected, saying, 'Are we not married? And don't we eat together? Stay in your taboos. But I'm going and you can stay and keep your taboos for me.' By this he meant that she could now start mourning for him instead. He did not steal away secretly but ostensibly joined a searching fleet looking for three young women who had swum off to sea. Then he slipped away to pursue his own suicide attempt, and it was only discovered later that he had had a row with his wife. 'It's not certain if he died at sea or if he died on shore – he went in a small canoe, and with no provisions.'

The last case illustrates the pattern of many Tikopia suicides – the person feels himself or herself offended and frustrated, and flounces off in a rage, often hurling back some pointed 'last words' to make the survivors regretful. I did not actually witness any such departure, and it was not clear to me how far the subsequent reports tended to dramatise the final situation, or simply to reproduce in brief form the admittedly dramatic quality of much Tikopia behavior. While in general Tikopia manners are urbane, and the Tikopia are adept in concealing their thoughts, they often seem to lack self-control when frustrated. This is very much a matter of social conditioning, and their anger sometimes appears to an observer to be histrionic, and rapidly appeased by the recognised techniques of status enhancement. Yet they are capable in such conditions of radically destructive acts. The Tikopia well recognise and regret their propensity to take umbrage. As one of my informants said, 'This land is bad. Someone is angry, he goes then and hangs himself. Someone else is scolded by his family, thereupon there's a hanging.'

Under the general heading of suicides from domestic discord may be placed the consequences of revolt against parental authority. If a son is struck or strongly rebuked by his father, he may go off to sea with the intention of seeking his death. When the father finds out, he will wail for the son, and then go out to sea in search of him. If he finds the boy, he will bring him back, forgiven, the incident purged. If not, he may turn back to mourn in his house, or he may go on in his canoe to meet his own death. Such is the Tikopia stereotype. Actually, while most fathers go in search, few appear to have followed their missing sons to death. But by traditional account many sons have flung off in suicidal rage after reprimand from their fathers. Similarly, girls subjected to parental wrath are recorded to have reacted by swimming off to sea. Such suicide attempts by young people are part of the expected norms in Tikopia, and being feared by parents, help at times to mitigate parental discipline.[15]

Another type of suicide situation is shame at the unavoidable consequences of an act, which occasioned the curious death of Pu Sao, and also the mass swim out to sea, both mentioned earlier. The physical basis for the shame may vary through a wide range of circumstances. But with young women a common reason is pregnancy, if the lover either will not acknowledge himself as responsible, or will not marry his mistress. The circumstances of the mass swim were as follows.

> A granddaughter of the Ariki Kafika, Fakasuariki, 'swam out to sea because she was pregnant and ashamed'. She knew the father of her child, but, it was said, his family refused to allow him to marry her for reasons not known. She was afraid that if she revealed his name, he might be killed by the men of Kafika lineage, as he was a commoner and she was a woman of a chiefly family. Her father and mother were ignorant of her pregnancy, but her companions among the unmarried girls knew. When she decided to swim off to sea, many of them followed her. From Tuatekoro, the base of the cliff between Ravenga and Namo, they plunged into the sea. Some of them, perhaps a score in all, were held back on the beach by brothers and fathers who had obviously been alerted by the unusual sight, and others were pulled out of the sea. But not all could be rescued. It was a mid-morning on a sunny day, but with a very high wind and heavy, breaking seas. Those girls who succeeded in getting out beyond the reef were soon lost. A searching fleet of 10 canoes put out, but failed to find any of the girls who had evaded the first pursuit. One vessel of the fleet, containing three men and a girl as crew, was lost in the search, and one young man who had swum out to try to save his sister was also lost.

This tragedy cost 11 lives 6 of them with intent. The cause of the suicide of the girls who followed Fakasuariki may be broadly set down as loyalty, although from another point of view it may be termed anticipatory grief. Such loyalty is a complicated sentiment. In part it rests upon the notion that a person of high status should have a *following* when entering upon a new and critical experience (such as a voyage abroad, or a religious conversion), and in part here upon the peer-group attachment which obtains among young men or young women. Loyalty in another form is demonstrated by the traditional accounts of the death of bond-friends at sea, in which one will tie his wrist to that of his friend so that they may both perish together.[16] Still another type of loyalty suicide, according to Tikopia account, occurs when a sick elderly man, either because of food shortage, or because he believes that the time has come to hand over the responsibilities of office to his son, will refuse to take food, and starves himself (*fakapakupaku*) to death. It is difficult, however, to class such behavior simply as suicide, if only because the Tikopia are very sentimental about family relationships and may be inclined to attribute to suicidal starvation what is in fact mere physical weakness or inability to take nourishment. A type of suicide which may be linked with this category is that carried out from respect for authority. Such cases have occurred when an offender is ordered off to sea in a canoe; or when a man of rank, confronted with a woman who does not wish to marry him, has ordered her to swim to her death rather than allow her to marry another man. Such virtual executions have been regarded by the Tikopia as justified, and even the victims have acquiesced with regret rather than protest against their enforced suicide.

In this analysis my aim is not to make any particular psychological contribution, but to try to relate individual action more closely to social process. One might classify the motives for suicide in Tikopia into four general categories of a psychological order: (1) grief or despair, such as in suicide because of unrequited love, or love for a dead spouse; (2) anger, such as that resulting from domestic discord, including revolts against parental authority; (3) shame, such as occurs in the case of pregnancy of an unmarried girl; and (4) loyalty, such as is evident in suicides from friendship and peer-group attachment. How far do these relate to the sociological categories, for example, of Durkheim? Tikopia suicides hitherto mentioned do not fall easily into his 'anomic' type, characterised by loss of integration of the individual with society. Tikopia social values – as distinct from religious values – have been fairly well preserved, and even the upheavals consequent on the famine of 1952, or the loss of confidence in the state of Tikopia society when the division between paganism and Christianity seemed most acute, saw no outbreak of suicide. But anomic suicide is not unknown in Tikopia; at least one case is recorded in a previous famine of a man's taking his family in a canoe to sea rather than face starvation on shore. In general, suicides from motives of grief or anger may be regarded as falling under the heading of 'egoistic'; with regard to those in the category of response to shame, although they are in part egoistic, the strength of the shame may be related to the strength of the identification with the norms of the society. Suicide of the loyalty type clearly comes under Durkheim's 'altruistic' category.

Yet I find classification in his terms difficult. Every suicide is in some respects an egoistic act, yet nearly every suicide displays some regard for the norms of society, and a recognition that the person is not in a position or not willing to adapt to these norms. 'Detachment from society' or 'integration with society' seems very crude phrases, grossly oversimplified, for the description of states of interaction of the potential suicide with other members of his society.

Durkheim's notions of the relation of the suiciding individual to society are too naive. His statements, for example, about obligatory altruistic suicide, in which 'society' compels some of its members to kill themselves, raise a question of basic classification. If the individual has no choice, but is forced to his death as a duty, as in the case of a Tikopia criminal ordered off to sea, would not this be classed as execution rather than suicide? Even with the voluntary or 'optional' *(facultatif)* altruistic suicide, Durkheim misses an important point: that some *conflict* of obligations is usually involved. 'Society' is not united in praising the suicide; some sections of it may praise him, others – for example, members of his family – may condemn him, or at least anxiously try to stop him. Out of such situations of conflict the suicidal intent and much of the drama of the event arise. I would argue that at least for societies of the primitive order of Tikopia the potential suicide situation is one of much greater flexibility and even uncertainty than is usually stated in the theory of the subject.

One may first look at the suicide situation of going off to sea, either by swimming or in a canoe. As Halbwachs did,[17] I have drawn attention to the difficulty of classifying the empirical material in terms of knowing the actual intention of the person who died. Somewhat the same difficulty arises about Durkheim's famous principle of detachment, insofar as it refers to the initiative taken by the person concerned. Successful suicide is the only real detachment from society. People commit suicide in order to become detached from society, they need not, as Durkheim seems at times to have argued, first become detached from society and then commit suicide. If a person makes an attempt and does not die, is it because he was detached and made an error of judgment, or because he was not sufficiently detached and his nerve failed? Something like this quandary exists with the Tikopia. The problem is connected with what Weiss has termed the 'lethal probability' of the means used. For Tikopia the lethal probability of going off to die at sea, by either swimming or canoeing, is high, but not one hundred per cent. There are two major possibilities here. One is that the potential suicide has time, if not often much opportunity, to change his or her mind, and come back to shore. The Tikopia themselves are fully aware of this possibility, and take it into account in their calculation of motivation and outcome. One of my Tikopia friends put the matter in this form:

This land is sacred [in respect of] the women – a man does not make fighting gestures to a woman [this is not strictly true]. A woman who is reproved, scolded – an unmarried woman only is scolded by a man – desires to die, yet desires to live. Thereupon she goes to swim out to sea. Her thought is that she will go and swim, but be taken up in a canoe by men who will seek her out to find her. A woman desiring death swims to seawards; she acts to go out and die. But a woman who desires life swims within touch, behind the breakers. She goes and goes, and arrives at Tai here [the speaker was thinking of her starting from Ravenga a mile away] to emerge on shore. She then comes and deceives her relatives, 'I went and swam, swam, swam, to seawards, there, but I do not die.' Great is the mind of women!

The second major factor adding to the uncertainty of the situation is the searching fleet. The Tikopia have a very lively understanding of the whole situation of going off to sea, and a very energetic attitude toward rescue expeditions. As soon as news of a suicide swim or voyage is known, a searching fleet of canoes is organised and hastily paddles out in chase of the fugitive. If the attempt is really serious, the fleet's chances of success are not very high – the escapee goes off at night, or in a high wind, which militates against the likelihood of his being spotted and caught in those huge ocean wastes. But if the potential suicide rushes off in a rage at once, when sea conditions are good, or if his or her absence is noticed at once, or if the searching fleet is lucky or guesses well the effects of wind and current, the person may be recovered. For many of these attempts, especially by people who set of fin daylight or in good conditions of wind and sea, it is very difficult indeed to decide just what combination of motives and chances lay behind their calculations – or whether they made any conscious calculations at all. They may have thought that they stood a good chance of being picked up, and could return in restored equilibrium; they may have thought that their chances were slim, but were prepared to risk their lives for their reputations; or they may have thought that it as impossible for them to be located and stopped. All those who die are classed as suicides. Of those who are rescued, some can be classed almost certainly as intended suicides, some almost certainly as fakers; but for most of them the issue must remain very much in doubt. And it may be that this doubt is inherent also in the view of the escapee himself.

To illustrate these points, including the vivid appreciation of such a situation by the Tikopia themselves, I give the history of such a 'suicide' attempt.

Rather than live with a wife who had been forced upon him because it was understood that he had made her pregnant, Fakasauakipure, a man of Tafua in Namo, went off to sea in a commandeered canoe belonging to the Ariki Taumako. I was with the chief when the news came to him. He was sympathetic to the man, who was a matrilateral kinsman of his, and did not vent his displeasure upon the man's kinsfolk, as they had feared, but sent his son over to reassure them.[18] The Tikopia were sorry for the man on account of his flight to sea, but against him for the desertion of his wife. His family wept for him.

At this time the general fleet of canoes was engaged in diving for greens-nail, and it was thought that the news had not reached them. In any case, since the Namo people had already sent out a searching fleet, it was thought by senior men with whom I talked that many of the other craft would not leave their work and in fact few, if any, did so. The Ariki Taumako showed an adequate practical grasp of the situation. He asked whether the searching fleet was large, and on learning that it was, commented, 'Great is the number of the fleet! Oh! Then they will secure him.' He said that if the canoes of the fleet would spread out, starting from different places, they would have a better chance of seeing the wandered.

The man's flight and the search made good material for gossip, and people sat out on the beach until late that night discussing the case. The next day the chief and others were very ready to talk about such voyages and the action taken by the rest of the community in regard to them. First the constitution of the searching fleet was discussed. 'The married men mingle at intervals', it was explained; when the fleet responds to the news that someone is missing, the canoes are not allowed to start with crews of bachelors only, 'because their mind is different'. If left to themselves, fired by the spirit of adventure, and stimulated by the example of the man who is gone, these young men might quite likely start off on a voyage of their own. Hence the married men interpose themselves in ones and twos in each crew. The bachelors try to dissuade them, saying, 'Go and get a canoe for yourselves.' But the married men insist, for they know the minds of the young men. A very large fleet goes out in search only if the son of a chief has gone. In this case, 'Not a person may remain on shore', say the Tikopia in hyperbole. When such a fleet goes out, a woman may sometimes go with it – for instance, a mother wailing for her son may jump aboard and sit in the bottom of the canoe. She does not paddle, but merely wails. If the man is found, she may be of use in inducing him to return, for often be objects strenuously to being brought back.

If the weather is uncertain, the searching fleet goes out until the cliffs are lost to sight and the hill of Korofau and the peak of Reani alone show above the sea. But if the weather is good and the sea is calm, they go out until Korofau is lost and Reani (about 1,200 feet high) alone remains. They do not go out of sight of land altogether. All day they search, but if the man has had a long start they may not find him; at nightfall they abandon the attempt and return.

The attitude of the fugitive was also analysed by my informants. They gave three possible variations of motive for the voyage: an attempt to reach some other land in order to have the thrill of being a voyager and seeing the world; a deliberate attempt at suicide as a means of wiping out disgrace; or a feint at suicide, the man hoping to be pursued and caught before he get too far away. It was pointed out, too, that when a man is alone on the face of the ocean, anger and shame are apt to burn themselves out, and the initial urge to self-destruction might change to a desire for life. The putative situation of such a fugitive was outlined thus: if the man has affection and sympathy toward his island and his parents, then when he is out of sea he thinks of them, rests on his paddle, and wails, 'Oh! Alas, my land! Oh! Alas, my parents! Oh! Alas, my children!' – or similar thoughts. Then he stops his paddle and drifts, or starts to return. In this case he will probably be picked up by the searchers. But if a man is intent on his purpose he plies his paddle steadily, and soon gets beyond reach, so that he is not found.

There was much discussion of chances. It was said that Fakasauakipure had supplies, two pairs of coconuts. The Ariki Taumako said that even if he stayed at sea for a couple of days, if he drank from time to time to clear his throat and to strengthen his arms for the paddle he might be all right. People had found him missing in the morning, and had sought for him on shore without success. When they discovered that the canoe was gone, they knew he was at sea. When it is known that for any reason a man has become angry, a watch is kept upon him; if he says he is going anywhere, another man follows to prevent him. from taking a canoe. But in the present case, since the man had lived with his wife for some time, apparently amicably, and then had vanished suddenly without warning, no one was prepared.

Reference was also made to the actions of his kin on shore. Wailing was begun in his house after his departure was discovered, and should he finally not come back, the mourning ceremonies would follow a prescribed course, which was described to me. The *forau* continued to be a principal topic of conversation in the villages of the district, with much speculation on the man's fate. The Ariki Taumako said to me, 'I have sympathy for him, for the man who is drifting. We do not know if he is paddling, or if he is sleeping.' He illustrated each action in turn with his hands – paddling and then, with arms outflung, a man sleeping stretched over a thwart. General opinion was against the chances of his return. It was argued that if he had gone to the south, he might, considering the condition of wind and sea, reach another land. But if he had gone to the west, he would simply drift in the ocean spaces. Discussion also turned on the action of the chief's son, who, sent by his father to Namo, had gone in anger, inclined to smash one of the canoes there in revenge. Returning home without having done so (he discovered the canoe he proposed to smash belonged to his own clan), he was reproved by his mother, 'Why do you show anger? Look at your father! He is full of sympathy for the man. Why should you be angry about the canoe? Is it a man?' It was reported that the allegation of the woman's pregnancy had been untrue, and to that extent the man had been justified in rejecting her; but she was not criticised for having been the cause of his going off to sea.

The return of the wanderer put an end to speculation. Shortly after sunset, three days after he had gone, his canoe was sighted a long way off shore. There was great excitement. For a time he was lost to sight again, and it was not certain whether it was a canoe or a fish. The chief's wife said uncertainly, 'Perhaps it's a spirit!' Finally Fakasauakipure's identity was established. Five canoes hastily dragged down to the water's edge, ranged out for a couple of miles, with the rays of the setting sun full upon them, and at last they saw him. The nearest canoe closed in, and two of the crew jumped into his craft and paddled it back to shore. As they came into the shallows, people crowded down on to the beach, and some went into the water to press noses with the wanderer in greeting. He did not speak. He saw a chief, the Ariki Fangarere, seated near the edge of the beach, went over to him and pressed his nose to the chief's knee in token of abasement, was raised up by the chief, and pressed noses with him. The man who first reached the wanderer now led him off to his house by the wrist, in a conventional friendship sign, and put a new, dry, bark-cloth garment on him. The wanderer was then offered food, which he refused. Meanwhile the Ariki Taumako had been waiting in his canoe-yard to see the wanderer and hear his tale. He and his entourage examined the canoe, which had been carried up, and exclaimed about how the outrigger, which had been weak, had been strengthened with coconut fiber. They speculated whether the man had sat in the bow or the stern. Then the chief got impatient and angry at the delay, and stalked home, while children were hushed lest they annoy him further. The kind of remarks prevailing in the conversation were: 'Our friend is alive! If he had disappeared it would have been bad!' 'It is good that he has come in.'

Later the wanderer, accompanied by his brother and his friend, entered the chief's house. The chief greeted them crossly, saying, 'Why didn't you come before?' 'Shall he come wet to you?,' answered the friend (a cousin of the chief's) with spirit. As soon as they came in the door, the voyager then crawled to the chief, who was seated in the center of the house, lay at his knee, and pressed his nose against it. The chief raised up the bent head, and Fakasauakipure pressed his nose to the chief's face. Then, still lying at the chief's knee, he began to wail a dirge – the continuance of the formal token of abasement and apology. After a little the chief said, 'Sit still! Sit still!,' and the man stopped and went to sit at the side of the house. By this time a crowd had assembled.

Then he began to talk. First, he mentioned where he had been – out to the southeast – and then he spoke of the fish (he was not sure if they were sharks or not) – which had come and rested their snouts on the canoe outrigger. First he called on the Eel-god to chase them away, and then on the Taumako ancestor, upon which the fish disappeared. 'Ah! If you had called on him first!,' said the chief's wife; and the chief added, 'He it is who has given you to us again.' One of the first questions the chief asked was whether the man had lost sight of land, to which he answered in the affirmative; later the chief asked if he had seen any of the searching fleet, to which the answer was no. There were also several practical questions about mending the canoe. I noted particularly that throughout this discussion, which lasted a long time, the whole attitude was of interest in the man's journey – there was no reproach for the desertion of his wife, or for the trouble he had caused. The man himself related his experiences with considerable dramatic flair, and the audience listened quietly, with the chief doing most of the questioning. There was perhaps a kind of personal identification for each of the audience and suffered alone in the ocean wastes. A day or so later came a gift of atonement from the man's family to the chief for the abstraction of his canoe. I am not sure whether the customary rescue-payment was made to the first men to reach the wanderer and jump into his canoe.

Sociologically, two points of importance emerge from all this. The first is that the returned 'suicide' voyager by these procedures is completely reintegrated with society. His effort at detachment has failed, but he has succeeded in resolving his problem. He is once again absorbed and an effective catharsis has been obtained. The second point is that since a returned adventurer becomes the center of attention, a certain premium is attached to attempting a dramatic sea flight of this kind. The stakes are high: they involved a real gamble with death. But if a man can go out, stay away for a while, and then return, he has a windfall gain in immediate social status. Yet cases of return from a distance would appear to be very rare; usually if a man is not found in the course of the day, he is lost to Tikopia – although in rare instances he may fetch up on another island.

From the point of view of suicide interpretation, what such a person is doing is gambling on natural hazards and on his credit with society. If either nature or society is against him – if the weather is bad, or the searching fleet lethargic – he loses his life. As the figures on ocean voyages indicate about a four to one chance against survival in 1929–52, this is suicidal conduct, although not suicide in the accepted sense of the term.

What I am saying, then, amounts to this – that except where the lethal probability of the means employed is known to be almost complete (for example, with some poisons), there may not be a clear-cut line between the categories of suicide and nonsuicide, between intending to kill oneself and not. There may be instead a scale of intention-*cum*-risk-taking. At one end, no intention to lose one's life, and little risk; at the other end, the intention to kill oneself and the most grave risk of accomplishing it, or little risk of being prevented. In between there may be many degrees of partly formed intention mixed with reluctance to die and hope of being saved, with yet enough resolution to face the risk and abide by the outcome.

All this bears on the question of the rigidity or permissiveness of the society and the incidence of suicide. It is quite clear that no correlation between social rigidity and suicide rates can be effected without taking into consideration the efficiency of the rescue procedures. Whatever the rigidity of the society, if the rescue procedures are good, then the incidence of suicide may be relatively low, even though attempted suicides may be many. Moreover, the fact that the rescue procedures are good, and the suicide incidence low, may mean that the society is a firmly structured one. If the rescue procedures are poorly organised and ineffective, this may mean a more permissive, less rigid structuring of the society – associated with a higher, not a lower suicide rate.

Tikopia society may be regarded as firmly structured, even rigid, in some respects, as in the procedures concerned with lineage organisation and chieftainship, and the sense of social obligation is high. Yet in other respects it may be seen as a fairly permissive, tolerant society, with many alternative avenues of escape for offenders. Some kind of outlet for deviance is provided by spirit mediumship, which allows considerable personal expression outside the overt structural framework. Where frustration and aggression emerge in social relations, the Tikopia have well-developed techniques for smoothing over difficult situations and allowing aggrieved persons to retain their status. The expression *fakamatamata luai* (making the face good) refers to such techniques, which soften the rigor of social rules. In pregnancy, an unmarried woman has precedents for abortion or infanticide, or for bringing up her child out of wedlock – although this last is not common. For offenses against a chief, a man usually has the alternative of fleeing to another district and thence in time making his ceremonial apology. But the sea flight, with all its terrible risks, is part of the pattern of Tikopia behavior, associated for men, at least, not only with the commission of offenses but also with adventure and freedom of a positive, praiseworthy kind and the fascination of pushing back the limits of their universe. It is a case not of there being no other avenues of self-expression or expiation, but rather almost of seeking this avenue as a first resort rather than a last.

There is also a further factor linking the incidence of suicide and the permissiveness of Tikopia society. According to traditional Tikopia custom, the punishment for the most extreme offenses was for a chief's executive officer to drag the offender's canoe to the sea, and order him into it, to set out and either perish in the ocean or fetch up on a foreign land. The chances of survival being so small, the order was virtually equivalent to a demand for self-execution. Conversely, if a person offended a chief, he might announce or imply an intention to go off to sea. After allowing time for the intention to mature, a man of rank might step in and order the offender to stop. He could then acquiesce in obedience to the command, yet with the dignity of having been prepared to expiate his offense with his life. Into this situation enter some of the most delicate elements of Tikopia personal diplomacy. The person who had let it be known that he intended to put off to sea had no certainty of being stopped. Perhaps no one would take the initiative in getting him to desist, either because the responsibility was left by each man of rank to the others, or because there was not enough enthusiasm for his retention. In essence, then, the person placed his future in the hands of society. To what extent a given offender relied on not being allowed to proceed, it is impossible to say. But the whole situation of suicide attempts has this uncertainty of intervention as one of its parameters.

This may be illustrated further by a case which occurred during my first visit to Tikopia. A son of the Ariki Tafua fell seriously ill, and for a few days showed no signs of recovery, despite strenuous efforts by his family and others. The Ariki Tafua then attempted to commit suicide by hanging, to try to compel the gods to pay attention to the plight of his son. He was prevented from accomplishing his objective by two men, coming to him with a gift of food, who happened to enter the house just as the noose was settling over his head. They rushed to him, and while one supported him the other removed the fatal cord. I happened to visit the old chief shortly afterwards, and fund the household plunged in gloom. The chief soon began to speak, addressing his gods, upbraiding them for not curing his son and asking them to take his life instead, since he was an old man and could be more easily spared. It was a very serious, dramatic occasion. Shortly afterwards the old man did fall ill, it was believed in response to his appeal to the gods. But he was finally cured, and meanwhile his son had recovered also. The attempted suicide and the illness of the chief were the talk of the community, and great attention was paid to him, including ceremonial visit to him by the other chiefs. But I found that while the attempted suicide was treated as a very grave matter, some people questions whether the chief's action had perhaps been quite so spontaneous as it seemed – possibly he had chosen his time carefully, when the sound of approaching footsteps had notified him that rescue would be at hand. But this was no more than a breath of suspicion. Even had it been correct, the chief would have been taking a risk, since the newcomers might have been slow to take in the significance of the situation. But the mere existence of this suspicion indicates how far the notion of suicide as the outcome of a gamble is built into Tikopia conceptions.

In general, then, I would argue that the incidence of suicide is not a simple variable that can be correlated directly with another single feature of the society. From the Tikopia evidence it may be that not only the manner but also the fact of suicide is socially determined. The promptness of mobilisation of other members of the society and the efficiency of their rescue organisation have a definite bearing on the incidence of suicide. Moreover, the incidence of suicide is affected through the classification of acts. Where risk-taking assumes a proportion great enough to amount to a virtual throwing away of one's life, and there appears to be a complete intellectual and emotional acceptance of the virtual certainty of self-destruction, the sharpness of the boundaries of the suicide category become[s] blurred. Rigidity or permissiveness of the society, alone, then have little meaning in the interpretation. The Tikopia have a propensity to violent conduct in a variety of social situations in which their social status is threatened. There are a number of alternatives for the resolution of these situations. Even where the initial move is left to the person primarily affected and is in the direction of self-destruction, there are still some alternatives open. These are a product of natural forces, social forces, and the decision of the individual himself. Suicide, even if narrowly defined as persistence in conduct calculated to lead to self-destruction, is not a simple response to lack of alternatives, but to a selection of one alternative against others, for a complex of social reasons. The suicide of a person is a social act, to be understood only in the context of other social acts both of the person himself and of other members of his society.

INTRODUCTION: FURTHER READING

Durkheim, E. (1952) *Suicide: A Study in Sociology*. Originally published 1897. London: Routledge & Kegan Paul.

NOTES

1 Henry Morselli, *Suicide: An Essay on Comparative Moral Statistics* (London: Kegan Paul, 1881). Emile Durkheim, *Le Suicide: Etude de Sociologie* (Paris: Alcan, 1897), translated by John A. Spaulding and George Simpson as *Suicide: A Study in Sociology* (Glenco IL: Free Press, 1951).

2 S. Steinmetz, 'Suicide among primitive peoples'. *Amer. Anthropologist* 7 (1894): 53–60. J. Wiesse, *Selbstmord u. Todesfürch bei den Naturvølkern* (Zutphen: W. J. Thieme 1993) Erminie W. Voegelin, 'Suicide in northeastern California', *Amer. Anthropologist* 39 (1937): 445–56. William N. Fenton, *Iroquois Suicide: A Study in the Stability of a Culture Pattern* (Washington, DC: Smithsonian Inst. Bur. of Amer. Ethnology, Bull. No. 128, Anthrop. Papers No. 14, 194). Verrier Elwin, *Maria Murder and Suicide* (Bombay: Oxford University Press,

1943). G. M. Carstairs, 'Attitudes to death and suicide in an Indian cultural setting', *Internat. J. Social Psychiatry*, 1 (Winter 1955): 33–41. Paul Bohannan (ed.), *African Homicide and Suicide* (Princeton, NJ: Princeton University Press, 1960).

3   S. F. Nadel, *The Nuba* (London: Oxford University Press, 1947), pp. 173–4, 266. 480.

4   Jacqueline H. Straus and Murray A. Straus, 'Suicide homicide and social structure in Ceylon', *Amer. J. Sociology*, 58 (1953): 461–9.

5   Andrew F. Henry and James F. Short, Jr. *Suicide and Homicide* (Glencoe, IL: Free Press, 1954).

6   Clyde Kluckhohn, *Mirror for man* (New York: Whittlesey House, 1949), p. 170.

7   See Elwin, footnote 2.

8   M. Fortes, *The Web of Kinship Among the Talensi* (London: Oxford University Press, 1949), p. 168. But some Tallensi do commit suicide, as from grief at the death of a favorite child; and some may threaten suicide as a means of compulsion (p. 91).

9   James M. A. Weiss, 'The gamble with death in attempted suicide', *Psychiatry*, 20 (1957): 17–25.

10 General data about Tikopia are given in Firth, *We, the Tikopia: A Sociological Study of Kinship in Primitive Polynesia* (London: Allen & Unwin, 1936; 2nd edn with new introduction, 1958). For suicide, see this, pp. 473, 536; and Firth, *Social Change in Tikopia: Re-Study of a Polynesian Community After a Generation* (London: Allen & Unwin, 1959), pp. 55, 66, 309–10.

11 Tikopia attitudes toward death are illustrated in *We, the Tikopia* (footnote 10), pp. 20–1, 27 ff. Attitudes toward homicide are illustrated by a case in Firth, *History and Traditions of Tikopia* (Wellington, New Zealand: the Polynesian Society, 1961), p. 149.

12 Firth, *The Fate of the Soul: An Interpretation of Some Primitive Concepts* (New York: Cambridge Univ. Press, 1955).

13 For example: England and Wales, 10.6 (1947); United States, 11.5 (1946); Sweden, 15.0 (1930); Switzerland, 26.1 (1930); Austria, 39.9 (1930). From Straus and Straus, footnote 4; p. 462.

14 Firth, 'The theory of cargo cults: a note on Tikopia', *Man*, 55 (1955): 130–2.

15 For details of parental-filial relations see *We, the Tikopia*, footnote 10; pp. 178–88.

16 Firth, 'Bond-friendship in Tikopia', in *Custom is King: Essays Presented to R. R. Marett on his 70th Birthday*, ed. L. H. Dudley Buxton (London: Hutchinsons' Scientific and Technical Publications, 1936), pp. 259–69.

17 Maurice Halbwachs, *Les Causes du Suicide* (Paris: Alcan, 1930).

18 For more details on this case see *We, the Tikopia*, footnote 10; pp. 245–6.

CHAPTER SIXTEEN

An Ndembu Doctor in Practice (1964)

Victor W. Turner

Turner (1920–83) was a Scottish cognitive anthropologist who taught at Columbia. His model of Ndembu healing is essentially that of group therapy. Whilst local understanding implicates the ihamba tooth, his external understanding is that this idiom in therapy facilitates catharsis and reconciliation among the whole community (Scheff 1979). How much this is a general model of healing is open to question: what of illnesses less easily understood in collective terms? and what of healing that fails?

This chapter consists mainly of an extended case study of an Ndembu *chimbuki* (which I shall translate as 'doctor', though 'ritual specialist' or 'cult-adept' would be equally appropriate) at work. I knew Ihembi well and during a period of six months attended a number of curative rites over which he presided. He was a member of the Ndembu tribe of Mwinilunga District in the extreme northwest of Northern Rhodesia, among whom I did nearly two and a half years of fieldwork from 1950 to 1954 and about whom I have published a book and several articles.[1] The Ndembu are a relatively conservative people, an amalgam of Lunda invaders from the Katanga and a aytochthonous Mbwela and Lukolwe. They are matrilineal and virilocal;* have a senior chief and about a dozen subchiefs, four of whom are recognised by the British administration under the Native Authority; and grow cassava as their staple crop along with finger millet, maize, sweet potatoes, and a variety of cucurbits and other relish plants. They have no cattle and only a few sheep and goats (although large areas are free from tsetse-fly infestation). Until recently, hunting was the predominant male pursuit and was accompanied by a richly elaborated ritual system involving beliefs in the punitive and tutelary powers of hunter ancestors or 'shades' (as I shall call them henceforward). Ndembu live in small circular villages each of which consists of a nuclear group of matrikin, one of whom is headmass, surrounded by a fringe of cognatic and affinal kin.

---

*A system in which a woman normally resides in her husband's village.

These facts are relevant to the account that follows, for disease among the Ndembu must be viewed not only in a private or 'idiographic' but also in a 'public' or social structural framework. All societies have, of course, a functional interest in the minimisation of illness, as Parsons has pointed out.[2] But the Ndembu go further in positing a social explanation for illness itself. All persistent or severe sickness is believed to be caused either by the punitive action of ancestral shades or by the secret malevolence of male sorcerers or female witches. The shades punish their living kin, so the Ndembu declare, for negligence in making offerings at their village shrines, for breaches of ritual interdictions, or 'because kin are not living well together'. My own observations suggest that, whenever rites to propitiate or exorcise the shades – as distinct from private treatment by herbalists – are performed, there is a factor of social conflict present. The 'ritual of affliction', as I have called it,[3] constitutes, in fact, a phase in the complex process of corporate life and has a redressive function in interpersonal or factional disputes, many of which have long histories. Even when a person's fault has been slight, he may be 'caught by the shades', the Ndembu think, as a scapegoat for his group if it is full of 'grudges' (*yitela*) or 'quarreling' (*ndombu*). Therapy then becomes a matter of sealing up the breaches in social relationships simultaneously with ridding the patient (*muyeji*) of his pathological symptoms. Attributions of disease to sorcery or witchcraft are frequently made in the context of factional rivalry, especially when the factions support rival candidates for office during the old age of its incumbent, whether he be chief or village headman. All deaths are attributed to sorcery or witchcraft, but only those of structurally important individuals are singled out for special ritual attention. When minor personages die, the identities of their secret destroyers are left to speculative gossip and rumor, and no action is taken. But, in the course of lively factional struggle, the death of even an infant may precipitate accusations and counteraccusations. In villages that markedly exceed the average size of thirty men, women, and children, such accusations may precede schism – when a dissident faction leaves the parent village and builds elsewhere on the pretext that it is escaping from witchcraft, which is believed to have a limited geographical range of efficacy.

In their treatment of disease, the Ndembu, like ourselves, recognise symptoms and distinguish between diagnosis and therapy. But there the resemblance ends. Ndembu do not know of natural causes for diseases but, as we have seen, believe that either punitive shades or envious sorcerers produce them. Their diagnosticians are diviners, and their therapists are in effect masters of ceremonies.

DIVINATION

Divination is a phase in a social process that begins with a person's death, illness, reproductive trouble, or misfortune at hunting (for illness is only one class of misfortune that is mystically caused). It continues through discussion in the victim's kin-group or village about the steps to be taken next, the most important of which is a journey to consult a diviner (distant diviners are believed to give more reliable diagnoses than local ones). The fourth stage is the actual consultation or séance attended by the victim's kin and often by his neighbors. This séance is followed by remedial action according to the diviner's prescription. Such action may consist of the destruction or expulsion of a sorcerer or witch; the performance of ritual by cult specialists to propitiate or exorcise specific culturally defined manifestations of shades; or the application of herbal and other 'medicines' according to the diviner's advice by an herbalist or medicine man.

I have recently published an account of Ndembu leechcraft.[4] It is sufficient to state here that whatever may be the empirical benefits of certain treatments, the herbal medicines employed derive their efficacy, according to the Ndembu, from mystical notions, and native therapy is an intrinsic part of a whole magico-religious system.

The divinatory consultation is the central phase or episode in the total process of coping with misfortune, and it looks both backward to causation and forward to remedial measures. Since death, disease, and misfortune are, as we have noted, usually ascribed to exacerbated tensions in social relations, expressed as personal grudges charged with the mystical power of sorcery or witchcraft or as beliefs in the punitive action of ancestral shades intervening in the lives of their surviving kin, diviners try to elicit from their clients responses that give clues about the patterns of current tensions in their groups of origin. Divination therefore becomes a form of social analysis, in the course of which hidden struggles among individuals and factions are brought to light, so that they may be dealt with by traditional ritual procedures. It is in the light of this 'cybernetic' function of divination as a mechanism of social redress that we should consider its symbolism, the social composition of its consultative sessions, and its interrogation procedures.[5]

THERAPEUTIC RITES

The curative rites are performed by a number of cult associations, each devoted to a specific manifestation of the ancestral shades. Thus a shade that manifests itself as *nkula* afflicts its living kinswoman with menstrual disorders of various kinds, a shade that 'comes out [of the grave] in *isoma*' causes miscarriages, and so forth. The patient in any given cult ritual is a candidate for entry into that cult and, by passing through its rites, becomes a cult-adept. The particular shade that had afflicted him in the first instance, when propitiated, becomes a tutelary who confers on him health and curative powers for that particular mode of affliction. Although the tutelary shade is an adept's kinsman or kinswoman, cult membership cuts across membership of descent groups and territorial groups. Cult members make up associations of those who have suffered the same modes of affliction as the result of having been seized (perhaps 'elected' would be a more appropriate term) by deceased members of the cults. Since there are many cults and since the nuclear symbols of each refer to basic values and beliefs shared by all Ndembu, it may be said that the total system of cults of affliction keeps alive, through constant repetition, the sentiment of tribal unity. Ndembu secular society is characterised by the weakness of its political centralisation, by the high spatial mobility of its individual members and of its groups (due to shifting big areas of cultivation and the emphasis on hunting), and by the tendency of villages to split and reassemble. This secular mobility (and lability) is counteracted to some extent by the embodiment of tribal values of unity in the cults of affliction.

THE IHAMBA CULT

This necessarily truncated account of Ndembu divination and cult therapy must suffice as background to Ihembi's practice. Since this doctor specialised in the Ihamba cult, I shall briefly outline its characteristics. In the first place, the term *ihamba* refers among the Ndembu to an upper central incisor tooth of a deceased hunter. It forms an important element in a complex of beliefs and symbolic objects associated with hunting ritual — especially with ritual associated with those hunters who employ firearms. It is believed that the two upper front incisors of a gun-hunter (*chiyang'a*) contain much of his power to kill animals. If one of these teeth is knocked out or drops out as a result of pyorrhea, the hunter must preserve it. When a gun-hunter dies, these incisors are removed. The left incisor is said to belong to 'his mother's side', the right 'to his father's'. The teeth must be inherited by appropriate relatives who are initiated members of the gun-hunters' cult (*Wuyang'a*).

An inherited *ihamba* is carried in a pouch with a long sash of white or colored cloth. The pouch itself (called *mukata*) is made of white cloth. The *ihamba*, concealed beneath a long flap, is embedded in a paste of corn meal mixed with the blood of slaughtered game. Above it are inserted two cowrie shells (*mpashi*), which are known as 'the eyes' (*mesu*). With these *mesu* the hunter's shade is said to 'see animals' in the bush and to confer similar powers on their owner. The inheritor takes the *mukata* pouch into the bush with him when he goes hunting. With the carrying sash are folded strips of the dead hunter's clothing. When it is not in use, it is hung up in a shrine consecrated to hunters' shades. Women are forbidden to approach this shrine closely. Should they do so inadvertently, they are believed to develop menstrual disorders or to bleed to death after their next child-births. This prohibition derives from a basic principle of Ndembu ritual, that 'the blood of huntsmanship' (*mashi aWubinda*, from *Wubinda*, which stands for 'generic huntsmanship') must not be brought into contact with 'the blood of motherhood' (*mashi amama*) or 'the blood of procreation' (*mashi alusemu*). For example, when a hunter's wife is about to give birth he must remove all his hunting gear from his hut and its vicinity, lest it lose its efficacy. Behind this principle lies the notion that, for a child to be born, the maternal blood must coagulate around the fetus. Hunters shed blood and cause it to gush and flow. Again, women give life, while hunters take it. The two functions are antithetical.

It is necessary to distinguish between two ritual usages in connection with *mahamba* (the plural of *ihamba*). An *ihamba* may be inherited by a renowned hunter and then be used as a charm or amulet to bring him good fortune in the chase. On the other hand, some *mahamba* are believed to afflict the living by burying themselves in their bodies and causing them severe pains. In such cases the afflicting *mahamba* are believed to be of two kinds: some are from the corpses of hunters whose incisor teeth were lost before burial; others are 'escapees' from *mukata* pouches or from calabash containers in which they had been placed after extraction by Ihamba doctors. The Ihamba cult consists of male adepts, who must be initiated hunters of the gun-hunters' cult, and the purpose of the rites they perform is to extract *mahamba* from the bodies of persons afflicted by hunter-shades. The *mahamba* are said to be the incisors of the afflicting shades. To remove an *ihamba*, the senior adept or 'doctor' makes an incision on any part of the patient's body and applies to the cut a cupping horn (usually a goat's horn) from which the tip has been removed. After the horn (*kasumu*) has been sucked, it is plugged with beeswax. The doctor's intention is to 'catch' the *ihamba*, which is believed to 'wander about' subcutaneously.

What are the symptoms of *ihamba* affliction? Here are some of my infor-mants' comments. Nyamuvwila, the aged wife of a village headman, said that she had been 'eaten' (*ku-dya*) in the chest, neck, and shoulders by an *ihamba* that had 'fallen' into her body. The *ihamba* came from her uterine brother, a hunter whose *ihamba* tooth had not been removed before burial. After his death, 'it wandered about and went after meat'. Another woman from the same village had 'become sick' (*walata*) 'in the back', because an *ihamba* had 'started to bite' her. My best informant on ritual matters, Muchona, in describing to me the circumstances surrounding a particular case *ihamba* affliction, said

Chain [the patient] comes from the village of Makumela, his mother's village. That is also where the shade of *ihamba* [*mukishi wehamba*] has come from. His grandfather is the shade, the mother's brother of his mother. He is the one who has fallen on his grandson to obtain blood from him. He has come that he may be known [remembered]. When they have sucked him out [as an *ihamba*], they should offer him the blood of an animal [smear the *ihamba* with the blood of a kill after the hunt], so that they may stay well [live in health, mutual accord, and prosperity], and that the patient, who was sick, may also stay well. They pray to him that they may put him in a pouch of cloth and sing and dance with drums for him [at a gun hunters' rite].

According to other informants, an *ihamba* can be seen moving about under the patient's skin (muscular spasms, perhaps) 'like the movements of an insect' (*nyisesa yakabubu*). It is said to 'catch him with its teeth', the plural form *mazewu*, 'teeth', being sometimes used for the single tooth that has been extracted. It 'flies in the air' to reach its victim, whose blood it demands.

Its attributes suggest that the *ihamba* epitomises the aggressive power of the hunter. It also represents the harshness of internalised norms, since an *ihamba* only 'bites' when there has been transgression of moral or customary rules. At the unconscious level of meaning, behavior associated with *ihamba* – 'eating', 'biting', 'going after meat' – and its removal by 'sucking' and anointing with blood suggests that *ihamba* beliefs may be connected with the orally aggressive stage of infantile development.

An interesting feature of the Ihamba cult is its comparatively recent introduction into Ndembu territory. It has been grafted onto the rites of the long-established hunters' cult and shares much of its symbolism. But this cult, with many tribal variations, has a wide geographical range among the West Central and Central Bantu peoples. Certain linguistic features indicate that Ihamba was borrowed by Ndembu from the Luvale and Chokwe peoples in Angola. It has certainly spread rapidly in the postwar period. One major difference from the hunters' cult proper is that while the *ihamba* is almost invariably a manifestation of a male shade, its victims include at least as many women as men, although women may not become Ihamba doctors since membership in the curative cult is restricted to initiated hunters.

Two further features of Ihamba should be noted. The cult has spread precisely where hunting has been on the decline because of the increasing scarcity of game and the increase of population. Apparently, by frequently performing Ihamba, the Ndembu maintain in fantasy the values, symbols, and trappings of a highly ritualised activity that is rapidly losing its economic importance. The penetration of the modern cash economy into the pores of Ndembu social organisation, together with an accelerating rate of labor migration to the industrial towns of the Northern Rhodesian Copperbelt, have created new economic needs and new tensions in traditional social relationships, while new relationships based on trade and contract are insidiously undermining corporate bonds. Ihamba may, therefore, be seen as part of a rearguard action that Ndembu culture is fighting against change. In the projective systems of modern villagers, the shades of hunters may well represent, at one level of social experience, the guilts and anxieties of those who are compelled by changing conditions to act in contravention of traditional standards.

Another sign that Ihamba is a response to cultural change is reflected in the fact that the rite contains its own built-in phase of divination. The traditional diviner, it is true, may well diagnose a person's illness as due to an *ihamba* affliction, but it is not strictly necessary. It is enough for someone to dream of a hunter-shade when he is ill and then to consult an Ihamba doctor to have the rite performed for him. Furthermore, when the rite begins, the doctor divines by peering into medicated water in an old meal mortar, in which he claims to be able to see the 'shadow-soul' (*mwevulu*) of the afflicting hunter. By asking questions of the patient and his kin, he declares, he can then identify the particular relative who has 'come out in *ihamba*' (*wunedikili mwihamba*). He may also claim to detect sorcerers and witches who have seized the opportunity of patient's *ihamba*-caused debility to attack him. As we shall see, part of the process of removing the *ihamba* consists in the doctor's summoning kin of the patient to come before the improvised hunters' shrine (identical with that used in the hunters' cult) and inducing them to confess any grudges (*yitela*) and hard feelings they may nourish against the patient. The tooth will 'not allow itself to be caught', he will assert, until every ill-wisher in the village or kin-group has 'made his liver white' (or, as we would say, purified his intentions) toward the patient. The patient, too, must acknowledge his own grudges against his fellow villagers if he is to be rid of the 'bite' of *ihamba*. It is curious how the symbolism of oral aggression pervades our own speech-ways in the context of small-group behavior: 'envy's poisonous tooth', 'the bite of malice', 'the mordant utterance', 'back-biting', 'the sting of jealousy', 'being eaten up with jealousy', and so forth. There is a parallel here, too, between the Ndembu notion of the hunters' tooth preying on the living and our saying that someone is 'hounded by guilt' or 'a prey to remorse'.

Ihamba (as well as other Ndembu rites that involve the sucking of objects, including bones, graveyard-soil, and stones, from the bodies of patients) is a variation on that widespread theme of primitive medicine that Erwin Ackerknecht has called 'the stone of the medicine man'.[6] He quotes im Thurn that, for the Indians of Guiana at least, the foreign substance 'is often if not always regarded not simply a natural body but as the materialized form of a hostile spirit'. Given this premise, im Thurn goes on to argue, 'the procedure is perfectly sincere and in its way rational. An invisible force is dealt with visibly by means that are meant and upderstood to be symbolic.' Nevertheless, I can confirm that the Ndembu – except for the doctor – do believe that the *ihamba* tooth of a specific hunter relative is actually extracted from the patient's body. The doctor confines skepticism to the issue of whether the tooth is that of a human being or of an animal (like a monkey or a pig). He leaves untouched the question that sleight of hand may have been used in making the 'extraction' The doctors must themselves be aware of their own trickery, although I never managed to persuade one to admit that he had used deception. My own guess is that doctors sincerely believe that their therapy – which includes the use of washing and drinking medicines ('lotions' and 'potions') and of cupping techniques – has a positive efficacy and may also believe that in some mystical fashion they actually do withdraw an influence inimical to the patient's welfare from his person. At any rate, they are well aware of the benefits of their procedures for group relationships, and they go to endless trouble to make sure that they have brought into the open the main sources of latent hostility in group life.

THERAPEUTIC PROCEDURE

Before getting down to specific cases I shall briefly describe the manipulative techniques of an Ihamba doctor. We must consider, for example whether or not there may be certain unintended or inadvertent benign consequences for health from Ndembu practices that are overtly determined by magico-religious ideas without empirical foundation. It seems possible that the bloodletting that accompanies the doctor's efforts to 'capture' the elusive tooth may have beneficial effects on some patients. There may also be in the procedure something analogous to modern shock treatment – treatment that, as Lessa and Vogt have suggested, 'stimulates an internal reaction capable of returning the organism to health'.[7]

It is more difficult to establish whether or not the use of 'medicines' confers any physical benefit. The medicines employed are the leaves, bark scrapings, and roots of forest trees and bushes. The principles underlying their use are not derived from experiment but form part of a magical system, as is clear from a listing of the properties attributed to them by informants. I have collected a considerable body of this kind of exegetical material not only about Ihamba medicines but also about many other kinds of rite, and in almost every case notions of sympathetic or contagious magic control the selection of vegetable or animal medicines.

List of Ihamba Medicines

NDEMBU TERM	BOTANICAL NAME	INDIGENOUS EXPLANATIONS FOR USE
1 *Musoli*	*Vangueriopsis lanciflora*	(a) It comes from *ku-solola*, 'to make visible' or 'reveal'. (b) It has fruit that are eaten by *duiker* and other woodland game during the early rains. Ndembu say that the name is connected with the power of the tree to draw forth animals from their hiding places in the bush and make them visible to the hunter. What is made visible is good, what is concealed is often bad. *Musoli* medicine is given to barren women 'to make children visible'. (c) It is the senior (*mukulumpi*) medicine of Ihamba, the first to be collected. The doctor addresses the *musoli* tree and says: 'You *musoli* tree of animals (of huntsmanship), come quickly, may this *ihamba* come out quickly, so that the patient may get well soon.' He then guesses where the tap root lies and hoes up the ground. If he finds it at once, it augurs well that the tooth will be found quickly. (d) *Musoli* means 'to speak openly or publicly'. It refers to the confession of grudge described earlier.
2 *Museng'u*	(a) *Ochna pulchra*	(a) The name comes from *ku-seng'uka*, 'to multiply'. (b) It has many small black fruits – it stands for 'many animals' or 'many children'.
3 *Mututam-bululu*	*Xylopia adoratissima*	The name comes from *ambululu*, a small bee that makes nests in the ground or in old termite mounds. Such bees come in swarms to the *mututambululu* tree to gather its nectar. In the same way, many people will come to the drum (rite) at which it is used, and many animals will come near a hunter who has been washed with its medicine.

NDEMBU TERM	BOTANICAL NAME	INDIGENOUS EXPLANATIONS FOR USE
4 *Mufung'u*	*Anisophyllea boehmii*	From *ku-fung'a*, 'to gather together a herd of animals'.
5 *Mutata* This word means 'to heat huntsmanship' (*Ku-tatisha Wubinda*).	*Securidaca*	*longipedunculata*
6 *Muneku*	*Randia kuhniana*	It comes from *ku-nekama*, 'to sink down' – which means that a *mufu* or 'zombie' raised by a sorcerer's curse must ('change its mind' (*ku-nekuka*) about afflicting the patient and sink down into the grave again. It will be recalled that the grudges of the living must be confessed during Ihamba because the Ndembu believe that protracted grudges animate the mystical powers of sorcery and witchcraft if not brought into the open. In any case, sorcerers and witches and their familiars are always likely to be present in large assemblies of people or so the Ndembu think.

COMMENTARY

Other medicines employed in Ihamba have similar characteristics. They represent aspects of huntsmanship or protect the patient and the congregation from sorcery and witchcraft. Many of the medicines are borrowed directly from the hunters' cult rites and appear to represent *inter alia* the afflicting hunters' shades. At any rate, in other rites of affliction, the pieces of medicine leaves adhering to the patient's skin after he or she has been splashed by a leaf-broom are said to 'stand for the shade', in that each represents a cluster of values associated with the cult of hunters' shades, and, in a sense, to identify the patient with that shade. Other antisorcery medicines in Ihamba include a root dug up from under a path leading into the village. This root is used because Ndembu believe that sorcerers conceal destructive medicines beside or beneath paths to injure or slay their personal enemies. The root-medicine 'makes known' the sorcery and renders it innocuous. The doctor thus signifies that he has exposed the hidden sorcerers and can if necessary counter their malignant magic.

The main point to note in connection with these medicines (which are pounded by the doctor and his assistants in an old meal-mortar, soaked in water, and then both splashed on the patient's body and given to him to drink) is that they are ostensibly used because, through analogy, they confer on the patient certain powers and qualities conducive to strength, good luck, and health. The semantic links of analogy may derive from the name of the object used (by a species of serious 'punning') from its natural properties, as they are conceived by the Ndembu, or from both. But it is doubtful that the medicines have any pharmaceutical value at all; it is sufficient that they are not toxic.

IHEMBI, THE IHAMBA DOCTOR

This brief account of the cultural structure of Ihamba suggests that whatever efficacy the rite possesses – and it does have ameliorative effects on patients, as I can testify after witnessing more than a dozen performances, some of them in villages I knew really well – resides in the degree of skill wielded by the doctor in each instance of its performance. It is hardly likely to be attributable to the bloodletting and the application of medicines. We must therefore examine the form that Ihamba ritual takes in the light of what Radcliffe-Brown has called 'the actually existing network of social relations'. I propose therefore to say a few words about the personality of one Ihamba doctor, Ihembi, and then to describe his practice of his craft in two concrete situations.

Ihembi was a man about seventy years old, white-haired, dignified, but with a smile of singular sweetness and charm. He had the throaty voice characteristic of the Ndembu hunter, but he put it to lucid and eloquent use. I first met him at the court of a 'progressive' subchief, Ikelenge, when I was collecting from the chief and his councilors the official history of his chiefdom and the royal genealogy. There was a full muster of elders from the chief's area present, and they were encouraged to contribute to the discussion. Among the most vociferous was Ihembi, who tended to raise objections to the chief's narrative at crucial points. I found out afterward that Ihembi belonged to a branch of the royal lineage that had formerly supplied chiefs to the realm but had been permanently excluded from the succession several generations before after a bitter and unsuccessful dispute with another branch over the incumbency of the chieftainship. In compensation, the victors had given the defeated branch, that of Matembu, a ritual office. The members of Matembu resided in a single large village, several miles from the capital, and their headman performed important ritual functions in the installation of each new Ikelenge chief, at chiefs' funerals, and in periodically purifying the royal insignia. Ihembi thus belonged to a social group with ritual status that had nevertheless a permanently 'marginal' or 'outsider' quality in political terms. Within the Matembu matrilineage, Ihembi had further 'dispossessed' characteristics. Although he came from a senior branch of that lineage and was chronologically senior to its headman, he did not hold political office – probably because in his youth he had migrated to another Lunda subtribe, that of Shinde in Balovale District, many miles to the south of Mwinilunga District, where he had married and raised a family. There he had also practiced as a diviner. More important for this analysis, he had become initiated into the hunters' cult and had later learned the medicines and techniques of Ihamba, allegedly from the Luvale people who live intermingled with the Lunda in Balovale District. At a comparatively old age he had returned to the Ikelenge chiefdom, where he found the headmanship of Matembu already occupied. He did not fall into apathy but applied himself vigorously to his practice as an Ihamba doctor and earned quite a substantial income, for people were prepared to pay ten shillings or even a pound for an 'extraction'. Chief Ikelenge, who paid careful heed to the views of the Christian missionaries in his area, on more than one occassion fined Ihembi for fraudulently exploiting the people. Nevertheless Ihembi managed to carry on his practice and enjoyed a wide reputation. In many ways, he was typical of Ndembu doctors: capable, charismatic, authoritative, but excluded from secular office for a variety of reasons, some structural, some personal. He was the typical 'outsider' who achieves status in the ritual realm in compensation for his exclusion from authority in the political realm.

It was not long before Ihembi and I were on terms of friendship that soon developed into the 'joking relationship' between 'grandfather and grandson'. This friendship enabled us to speak very frankly to one another and to perform mutual services. I gave him gifts from time to time, and he allowed me to attend his Ihamba rites and explained much of their symbolism for my benefit. In this short paper, I can do no more than discuss briefly two performances. They were held for the same patient and formed part of a series of seven rites performed for him, of which I was fortunate to observe three in close detail. Three of the seven were Ihamba rites, two belonged to the hunters' generic cult of Wubinda (since the patient, though not a gunhunter, trapped and snared antelope), one was the antisorcery rite called *Kaneng'a* and one was a recently introduced rite called *Tukuka* in which the patient is believed to be possessed by the spirits of live Europeans or of alien tribesmen. The large number of these rites, all performed within a few months, indicates that the patient was seriously disturbed. Furthermore, as I have argued, it indicates that there was serious disturbance in his network of social relations.

IHEMBI AND THE CASE OF KAMAHASANYI

It is at this point unavoidable that I should deploy the divinatory apparatus of the social anthropologist: the genealogy, the hut plan, the village census data, and the condensed life history. For the events I shall discuss fall within a social field with many dimensions, several of which must be exhibited and scrutinised if we are to make any sense at all of the observed behavior and the monologues (the prayers and invocations) and dialogues of the participants. I may say, too that, in an intuitive or pragmatic fashion, the information and even analysis I shall submit were fully mastered by Ihembi, whose business it was to study social relationships in order to diagnose the incidence and pattern of tensions and to attempt to reduce them in his handling of the rites. We have noted earlier how Ihamba contains its own built-in system of divination. What I have written elsewhere of the divinatory process amomng the Ndembu holds true, therefore, *a fortiori* for the Ihamba doctor in his divining capacity. I wrote[8] that:

> the diviner clearly knows that he is investigating within a social context of a particular type. He first establishes his clients' locale – the Senior Chief's area, then the subchief's, then the vicinage (the cluster of neighboring villages), and finally the village of the victim. Each of these political units has its special characteristics: its factional divisions, its inter-village rivalries, its dominant personalities, its nucleated and dispersed groups of kin, all of them possessing a history of settlement or migration. An experienced diviner will have already familiarized himself with the contemporary state of these political sub-systems from previous consultations and from the voluminous gossip of travelers. Next he ascertains the relationships between the victim and those who have come to consult him. He is assisted in this task by his knowledge of the categories of persons who typically compose a village: the victim's matrilineal kin, his patrilateral kin, his affines, cognates and unrelated persons. He finds out the type and nature of the victim's relationship to the headman, then focuses his attention on the headman's matrilineage and discovers into how many sub-lineages it may be segmented. By the time he has finished his interrogation, he has a complete picture of the contemporaneous structure of the village, and of the position in its relational network occupied by the victim.

These remarks refer to diviners who are consulted by clients from distant regions and who operate by the manipulation of symbolic objects, as well as by the exhaustive interrogation that accompanies it. The clients try to trip up the diviner by feeding him false information, and it is the mark of a 'true diviner' if he avoids this pitfall. But the Ihamba doctor is in the more fortunate position of operating in a village not far from his own, whose inhabitants and their interpersonal relations are known to him, and of having had full access to the patient's dreams (which induced him and his kin to call in the Ihamba doctor in the first place) and to the gossip and opinions of the patient's neighbors and relatives. Nevertheless, he builds up his picture of the social field and its tensions in much the same way as the specialist diviner does and acts on this knowledge in his therapeutic practice. By tactful cross-examination of the participants and by keeping his eyes and ears open, he discovers the likes and dislikes of the patient, the village headman, the members of the patient's domestic family and matrilineage, and so forth.

In the case of Kamahasanyi, which I shall describe shortly, Ihembi already knew the principal participants, and his two assistants, Mundoyi and Mukeyi, had distant patrilateral ties with the patient. What is more, before the second performance of Ihamba he spent a day and night in the patient's village, where he was able to size up the situation.

My own acquaintance with Kamahasanyi's village had been long and close, for my first camp had been in the neighborhood, and my wife and I had attended a girl's puberty ritual there. Furthermore, I had collected census and budgetary information not only in this village of Nswanamundong'u but also in many other villages of the Mukang'ala chiefdom, of which it formed a part. It was while I had been visiting Nswanamundong'u that I first became aware of Kamahasanyi's troubles. His snares had failed to catch *duiker* antelope for many weeks, and he had had the hunting rite Mukala performed to placate the angry shade. This shade was that of his maternal grandfather, the late chief Mukang'ala, he told me, and the same shade had 'come out in Ihamba' to afflict him 'with pains in his whole body'. An Ihamba rite was to be performed for him the day after my arrival by a Luvale doctor temporarily residing in the neighborhood. I mentioned to the villagers that I knew Ihembi well, and they immediately besought me to bring the great doctor and his assistants (who helped him with the collection of medicines and with various ritual tasks) from the Ikelenge area in my car. He could 'help' the Luvale, they said, who was 'only a little doctor' – they even hinted that he might tactfully take over control of the rite. They also asked me to bring to the performance a man called Samuwinu, whom they described as 'the real headman' of the village. He had fled from the chiefdom at the accession of the present chief Mukang'ala Kambung'u, fearing the latter's sorcery. For Samuwinu had been a candidate for the chiefly 'chair', and, indeed, the male members of the nuclear matrilineage of Nswanamundong'u belonged to a branch of the royal patrilineage of Mukang'ala chiefdom. Their village was a 'royal village'. The villager told me that the shade afflicting Kamahasanyi 'in Mukala' and 'in Ihamba' was doing so because it was angry that a 'younger man' had become headman while a member of its own generation (genealogical generation) remained alive. A member of the junior adjacent generation to Samuwinu had been appointed as headman by the villagers. The shade was incensed too, they said, because it had been slain by the sorcery of the present chief, a slaying that had been unavenged for several years. Its wrath had been manifested in other ways. Once there had been a whirlwind that had ripped the thatch from the hut of the new headman Kachimba, and people claimed that they had seen flames leaping above it. Villagers said that they had dreamed that the late chiefs shade had come to reproach them. Not only was it aggrieved that it had been ensorcelled, they alleged, but also because the British authorities had a few years previously withdrawn recognition from the Mukang'ala chieftainship, which had been merged with that of Senior Chief Kanongesha. The shade, that of Mundong'u Kabong'u, blamed the people of the chiefdom and in particular those of his own village for merger to happen.

The persecution of Kamahasanyi by the late chief's shade was therefore not so much aimed at him personally as in his representative capacity. When I asked one informant why Mundong'u had not afflicted Kachimba, the acting headman, he replied that the shade 'wanted to shame' everyone by 'catching' one of the villagers. It was not Kachimba but the village folk (*enimukala*) as a whole who had behaved irresponsibly. They should have made Samuwinu headman, and the latter should have remained in the area to represent his matrilineage fittingly. Indeed, it was Kachimba himself who begged me earnestly to bring Samuwinu to the Ihamba performance so that Samuwinu could invoke the shade on Kamahasanyi's behalf. The shade, he said, would listen to Samuwinu, who was his uterine brother, as well as 'real headman' but might well reject his own intercession. I learned later that several villagers secretly despised Samuwinu for running away and indeed for not pressing his claim for the chieftainship with vigor while he could. As we shall see, this whole case history is pervaded by the theme of failure to undertake responsibility and failure to live up to expectation. Part of the work of a doctor is to encourage people to discharge the obligations of their status well and not seek escape from them.

But, while the villagers were sure that Mundong'u Kabong'u's shade was afflicting Kamahasanyi and that other misfortunes assailing them collectively at that time (like loss of crops because of wild pigs, quarrels between village sections, bad luck in hunting) could be laid at his door, it was thought highly probable that other mystical agencies were also at work. Some thought that Kamahasanyi was being bewitched by someone in the village, a line of inquiry that soon engaged Ihembi's attention and that he discussed with me. Others thought that the spirits of living Europeans were 'troubling' him. Kamahasanyi himself had recently gone to Angola to consult a diviner there and had been told that his own father's shade, as well as that of Kabong'u Mundong'u, had 'caught' him in Ihamba. This diagnosis, supported by the fact that Kamahasanyi had frequently dreamed of his father's shade, opens the way for an investigation of Kamahasanyi's life history and an analysis of his character and temperament that must be postponed until our sociological analysis has been made. The point I want to make here is that, when misfortune is attributed to mystical causes in Ndembu society, it is common for *many* sets of disturbed social relations to be scrutinised by the interested parties. The vagueness of the mystical beliefs enables them to be manipulated in relation to a great diversity of social situations. Eventually the crucial tension is isolated and dealt with.

THE STRUCTURAL CONTEXT OF THE CASE OF KAMAHASANYI

In order to give the reader a clear understanding of the social factors that Ihembi had to take into account in his handling of the two Ihamba performances he conducted for Kamahasanyi (in the first of which he removed what he claimed to be Mundong'u Kabong'u's *ihamba* and in the second of which he removed that of Kamahasanyi's father Mudyigita), I shall have to use a genealogy and a hut plan of Nswanamundong'u. Since the nuclear matrilineage of that village belonged to the royal matrilineage of the Mukang'ala chiefdom, I have included in the genealogy other branches of the royal lineage, for they are part of the total field influencing the behavior and ideas we are examining.

To simplify the analysis I shall subdivide the social field of Nswanamundong'u into its component social entities – various kinds of group, subgroup, category, and relationship – and exhibit them in a series of interpenetrating dimensions of relationships. These relationships consig of white–black relations; political relations between branches of the Mukang'ala royal lineage; intravilage relations; intrafamiial relations.

White–Black Relations
For the present analysis, this set of relations constitutes a set of perduring conditions full of chronic tension and conflict. The chieftainship of Mukang'ala had been abolished about four years before my arrival in the area. The area was in a state of seedy decrepitude. The court house at the capital village was falling into disrepair, as was the Mission Out-School, closed down after the abolition of the chief's chair. Those who had occupied paid positions under the Native Authority had returned to their villages of origin and reverted to the lives of peasants and hunters. Indeed, the 'primitive' appearance of Mukang'ala's chiefdom was the result of regression and of 'differentiation', of the breakdown of the modern political structure of Native Court and Treasury with their paid officials. It was not due to isolation from modern trends of change for the chiefdom

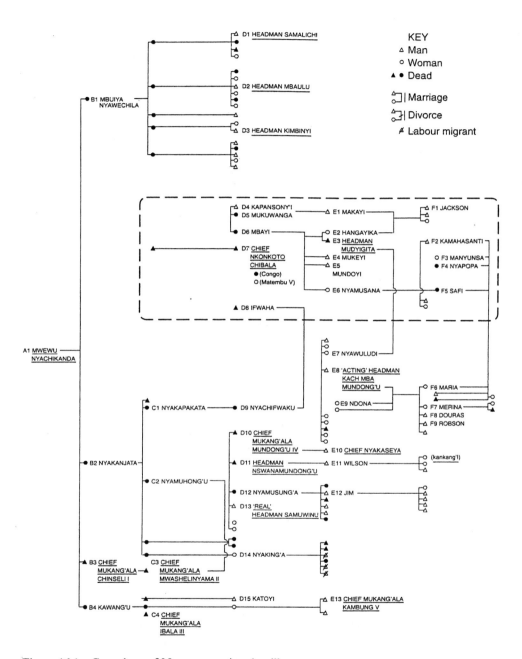

Figure 16.1   Genealogy of Nswanamundong'u village

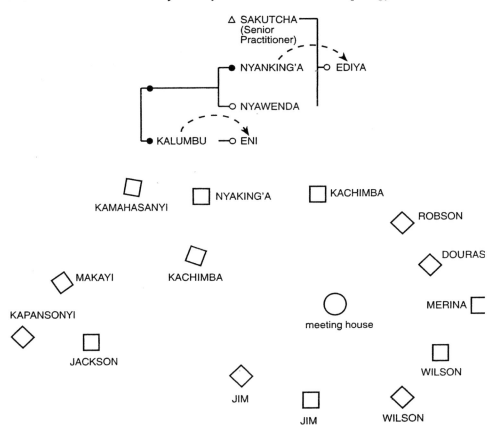

Figure 16.2   Hut plan of Nswanamundong'u village

extended almost to the British Adminstration Headquarters. Local sources
of cash income had dried up with the death of the local government. Men
had either to go to the Northern Rhodesia railway 300 miles away to find
paid work or to cultivate their cassava gardens and hunt in the bush –
mainly with traps, snares, bows, and spears, since they had not the cash to
buy guns nor the command of European and chiefly patronage to obtain
licenses to purchase ammunition.

Among those who had regressed to 'bush' life was Kachimba, the acting
headman of Nswanamundong'u. His smattering of literacy had been
enough to obtain him the post of court clerk in the days of the chiefdom's
official recognition. Now he had become a shy figure who normally evaded
a headman's duty of supplying hospitality to wayfarers and, as often as
not, was away in the bush when people called. His villagers and many

others in the former chiefdom used to blame him for the loss of his authority. He had been brusque and unco-operative toward European officials, it was said, and many stated that he had been considered 'dirty' and 'unhygienic' in the way he ran his capital village.

Relations Among Branches of the Mukang'ala Lineage

The abolition of black authority by white power had repercussions along several dimensions of social relations in the black sector. Among branches of the royal matrilineage, it led to widespread emigration of important men from the chief dom. Several went to Chief Ikelenge's area to the north. This area was highly prosperous in terms of modern cash economy. Several European traders and farmers held land there and offered opportunities for paid employment. Its chief was young, progressive, literate, and in favor with the government, in contrast to Mukang'ala. The dissident Mukang'ala royals, notably Samalichi (D1), Mbaulu (D2), and Kimbinyi (D3), all prospered and became headmen under Chief Ikelenge. Kimbinyi became, in addition, a wealthy trader. Samuwinu (D13), the 'real headman' of Nswanamundong'u, who had fled to Ikelenge's area before the abolition, had not prospered, but he was reckoned to be a man of weak character, who had failed to meet the crisis of his life with courage.

The defection of these royals left the Mukang'ala lineage divided into two branches: one descended from Nyakanjata (B2), the other from Kawang'u (B4). I shall call them the Nyakanjata and Kawang'u lineages. The incumbency of the chieftainship had alternated between these two lineages since Mukang'ala II — there had been earlier chiefs than those shown, but their genealogical connections are irrelevant to the present account. This alternation was never institutionalised but was the result of power struggles. Mukang'ala III, Ibala, who had fought against the British when they first came, had been slain, it is said, by the sorcery of Mundong'u Kabong'u (whose shade was believed to be afflicting Kamahasanyi). He was believed to have been ensorcelled in turn by Mukang'ala V, Ibala's sister's daughter's son, of Kawang'u lineage.

It is probably because Nyakanjata lineage, most of whose members resided in Nswanamundong'u, had in the past provided so many chiefs that its members did not emigrate but continued to stay in Mukang'ala's chiefdom. I do know that they cherished hopes that the chieftainship would be restored to official favor and recognition. Among those who hoped was Jim (E15), an intelligent, enterprising young man who had worked as a labor migrant in Southern Rhodesia. He was widely recognised as the likely heir of the present incumbent. In Nswanamundong'u, where he lived, it was Jim rather than Kachimba who took the lead in village matters and who offered hospitality to strangers. The biggest feather in his cap came when he sponsored a circumcision ceremony – a role normally performed by the chief in such a small chiefdom – at which three of his own sons were initiated. Jim's political strategy was twofold: to support the present incumbent in his frequent appeals to government for renewed recognition and to try to build up a following for himself from Nyakanjata lineage and from anyone else who could be induced to support his future claim for office. He had, therefore, a strong interest in preventing internecine strife in Nswanamundong'u and in maintaining friendly relations between it and other villages. It is hardly surprising therefore that he was among the foremost in asking for Ihembi to perform the Ihamba rite to propitiate his mother's brother's shade, a rite that was known to have beneficial effects on village relationships. It is also interesting that he performed the task at each ceremony of sucking the cupping horns of Kamahasanyi's body.

Intravillage Relations

Jim's concern that Nswanamundong'u should remain united sprang from a real fear that it would split. A comparison of the hut plan with the genealogy shows that, although the village is small, it is divided into two distinct sections. One is inhabited by Headman Kachimba (E8), his wife, and his adult children, Merina (F7), Douras (F8), and Robson (F9); by Jim (E12), his two wives, and his junior children; and by Wilson (E11), son of the late headman, and his two wives and junior children. The other is occupied by what I have called 'the Nkonkoto Group', consisting of a solitary old man, Kapansonyi (D4), his classificatory sister's son Makayi (E1) and his wife, and their adult son Jackson (F1). Between these sections are the two huts of Kamahasanyi (F2) and Nyakinga (D14), Kachimba's mother's mother's sister's daughter (whom he calls 'mother'). These siting arrangements reflect social structure. It seems that about thirty-five to forty years before the events I record, many members of the Mukang'ala lineage fled to Chief Nkonkoto's Ndembu chieftainship in what was then the Belgian Congo, probably to escape from the forces of the British South Africa Company, which Chief Mukang'ala Ibala (C4) had opposed. There they intermarried with some Nkonkoto villagers and made friends with others. Eventually they returned and, in the course of time Mundong'u Kabong'u (D10), the senior man in Nyankanjata lineage, succeeded to the chieftainship. Some Nkonkoto people tried to exploit their ties of affinity and friendship with Nyakanjata-lineage members to obtain paid employment under the Native Authority. They sought Mundong'u's patronage to get work in the Public Works Department or the Native Court. Makayi, one of this group, sent his son Jackson to the Mission Out-School at the capital village. They built their huts beside those of Nyakanjata people. For a time, all went well, but when I knew them the Nkonkoto group, reduced in number to those I have mentioned, were a pretty disgruntled bunch. They seemed to hold their fellow villagers from the Nyakanjata lineage, especially Kachimba, responsible for the decline in fortune of the chiefdom. And they had no good word to say of Samuwinu (D13), who had defected. Relations were particularly tense between Makayi and Kachimba. Neither would sit in a group when the other was present, although both were on good terms with Jim (E12), who made it his business to be friendly with everyone.

It was into this situation of strain between the Nyakanjata lineage and the Nkonkoto Group that Kamahasanyi arrived, a short time before my own first visit to the village. He, too, had come from Nkonkoto chiefdom, where his father Mudyigita (E3) had been a great headman and a famous hunter. Furthermore, Mudyigita was the son of a former Chief Nkonkoto (D7). Since Kamahasanyi's mother, as we have seen, belonged to the Mukang'ala royal lineage, he was certainly well connected on both sides. There are several peculiarities about Kamahasanyi's life history that made it most unfortunate for him that he had plunged into a situation that exacerbated conflicts between maternal and paternal loyalties. For it was as though his endopsychic conflict had been objectivised and given social form. Through his paternal link with the Nkonkoto group, Kamahasanyi was exposed to the grievances ventilated by Makayi and his people. As a member of Nyankanjata matrilineage, he heard the counteraccusations of his maternal kin. As can be seen from the hut plan, Kamahasanyi built his hut between those two groups, indicating his dual allegiance. A stronger character might have acted as a mediator between his matrilineal and patrilateral kin. Indeed, I have recorded several instances of men who played this very role. But Kamahasanyi 'retreated from the field' into what I can only think was neurotic illness. The key to an explanation of this illness may be found, I suggest, in the circumstances of his life and in his temperament.

KAMAHASANYI'S LIFE HISTORY

Kamahasanyi was exceptional in Ndembu society for the great length of time he had resided in the village of his father's nuclear matrilineage. When he finally came to settle with his mother's kin, he was past his fortieth year, and his father had been dead for several years. It not infrequently happens that sons reside with their fathers for some years after their own marriages, especially, as in Kamahasanyi's case, when the father is a headman and can extend to his son certain privileges and assistance in economic matters. But it is rare for a man in advanced middle life to do so, unless his mother is his father's slave (*ndung'u*). There was no evidence that Kamahasanyi's mother had been a slave, though it may well have been hushed up. If his mother had been a slave, Kamahasanyi, by matrilineal descent, would have inherited her status and would himself have been inherited by his father's matrilineal heir, unless his relatives had redeemed him by a substantial payment. Since they were too poor to have done so and since Kamahasanyi claimed to have made large payments of bridewealth for two of his wives in the Belgian Congo, he must have been a man of independent means. At all events, he seems, in his youth, to have been his father's favorite and to have received from him considerable assistance in accumulating bridewealth.

Members of the Nkonkoto group told me that Mudyigita, Kamahasanyi's father, was a man of great force of character. In this respect, he presented a sharp contrast to his son. Kamahasanyi was effeminate in manner and was reckoned to be 'womanish' (*neyi mumbanda*) by his fellow villagers. He plaited his hair in a feminine style known as *lumba*, and he spent much of his time gossiping with women in their kitchens. Furthermore, although he had been married four times, he had failed to beget children. An interesting feature of these marriages is that three of them were with cross-cousins. Two of the three were with patrilateral cross-cousins, that is, with members of his father's matrilineage. Such marriages are one means, in Ndembu society, of forging closer links with one's father, since one's children thus belong to one's father's matrilineage and will inherit and succeed within it. One will then live uxorilocally in one's father's village and not move to the village of one's maternal kin. Ndembu generally consider that men of mature years who live uxorilocally or patrilocally (with their father's kin), are men who evade their responsibilities, for the major sphere of a man's struggles for status and power is the village of his primary matrilineal kin. Here it is that a man may hope to become a headman or, if he is royal, to become a chief. Here it is, also, that a man is expected to help his matrikin in legal and ritual matters and to share his economic surplus. Kamahasanyi had shirked these duties and had obviously been dominated by his successful father. After Mudyigita's death, according to my informants (Ihembi's assistants, Mukeyi and, Mundoyi, who were Mudyigita's seminal brothers), Kamahasanyi's continued residence in his village aroused irritation and resentment. He had never really pulled his weight in corporate matters, and he was urged to return to 'his own people', to Mukang'ala's chiefdom. He paid several visits there, and on one visit married Kachimba's daughter Maria (F6), his first matrilateral cross-cousin. It is quite clear that unconscious incestuous drives influenced Kamahasanyi in his choice of mates. Cross-cousins are, it is true, preferred marital partners, but few Ndembu marry as many as three in a lifetime. They are the easiest partners to obtain, which would have been in accord with Kamahasanyi's tendency to take the line of least resistance. It is probable that his father and later his mother's brother had arranged these cross-cousin marriages for him. Like his father, his fourth wife Maria was a dominant personality who, both before and after her marriage to Kamaha-sanyi, took lovers when she felt like it. For a time she lived with her husband in Mudyigita's village, where she made large cassava gardens. The Belgian authorities paid relatively high prices for cassava meal, which went to feed the copper miners in the Katanga Union Minière belt, so that Maria, and through her Kamahasanyi, prospered for a while. But when Kamahasanyi's senior wife, his patrilateral cross-cousin Safi (F5), died, his patrilateral village kin demanded a large 'death payment' (*mpepi*) from him and from his matrilineal kin. The custom of paying *mpepi*, apparently intro-duced from the Luvale tribe, is a financially crippling one. It is connected with the notion that the matrilineal kin of the deceased have the duty of consulting a diviner about the cause of death to ascertain whose witchcraft or sorcery was responsible for it. Diviners charge high fees, and the surviving spouse and his kin are required to hand over a large payment in cash or kind to cover diviners' fees, as well as to compensate for the loss of the deceased's services. It is unusual, however, for *mpepi* to be demanded in the case of cross-cousin marriages, for the partners are considered kin as well as affines. But as Kamahasanyi had had to pay high bridewealth for his cross-cousin wives – again an unusual circumstance – so he was asked to pay a high *mpepi*. These facts indicate, I think, the villagers' dislike of the man. Kamahasanyi was dilatory in paying *mpepi*, and it was then alleged by his patrilateral kin that his wife Maria, with his connivance, had bewitched Safi to death, as cowives are often believed to do. The result was that Kamahasanyi and Maria were virtually forced to leave Nkonkoto chiefdom and return to Maria's village in Northern Rhodesia, although not before Maria had sold her cassava gardens at a profit, making Kamahasanyi more dependent upon her than ever.

Kamahasanyi had, therefore, returned at last to his own matrikin. But the fact that he was known to have been forced to do so and his reputation as a 'difficult' person to have around made his welcome a rather cool one. Again, as I have said, he was confronted in Nswanamundong'u with an external duplication of his own inner conflicts, for his new village was neatly divided into groups consisting respectively of his maternal and paternal kin. The Nkonkoto group not only felt grievances against the Nyakanjata lineage as a result of the 'putting down' of the chieftaincy as described, but they also shared the hostility of their Congolese kinfolk toward Kamahasanyi.

A further complication arose. Before her marriage to Kanahasanyi, Maria had taken as her lover one of the Nkonkoto group, Makayi's son Jackson, an educated young man who had hopes of employment as a clerk in a European enterprise. On her return to Nswanamundong'u Maria took up openly with Jackson again. So brazen was this relationship that several times when he was walking with me Jackson ostentatiously 'avoided'

Maria's mother Ndona (E8), rushing away from the path when he saw her advancing toward him – as though she were his mother-in-law! Kamahasanyi was said to be impotent, and to all appearances he was complaisant about the liaison. On the other hand, Maria fulfilled many of her wifely duties to Kamahasanyi. She worked beside him in his cassava gardens (indeed she did most of the work!), and she brewed finger-millet beer for his guests. She even accompanied him to Angola to consult a diviner about his health and fortune. This devotion may have been tendered because Kamahasanyi occupied a structural position of some importance in the village. As may be seen by consulting the genealogy, Kamahasanyi was a full member of Nyakanjata lineage and was therefore, according to Ndembu rules, a possible candidate both for the chieftainship of Mukang'ala and the village headmanship. In view of Jim's (E12) strong claims, by virtue of blood and intelligence to become chief in the future, it was unlikely that Kamahansanyi would succeed to the chair. But, on the other hand, since Jim, if he became a chief, would set up a capital village of his own, it was possible that Kamahasanyi would 'continue the name' of Nswanamundong'u by succeeding to its headmanship and scraping up a modest following of matrikin, cognates, affines, and anyone else he might persuade to reside with him. At least, Maria, with her strong will and energy, might do these things with her husband as nominal headman.

Despite his disadvantages, Kamahasanyi had a strong sense of his own importance. Even in a society whose members like to stress their connections with chiefs, Kamahasanyi was more snobbish than most. For example, when I discussed the history of the Mukang'ala chiefdom with senior men like Kachimba, Jim, and Wilson (E11), he would brush aside or interrupt their accounts and tell me 'what really happene'. He was the only one who could tell me the full, sonorous clan formula of the Saluseki clan to which the Mukang'ala royal lineage belonged – the clan ((*munyachi*) has ceased to have any political and has retained little social importance. He was also proud of his paternal link with the Nkonkoto chieftainship. He was, as I have said, conceited about his appearance, braiding his hair and oiling his body. He had brought with him from the Belgian Congo several dilapidated books in French, which he could not read but which he clearly considered to be status symbols. His attitude toward me was that we were both civilised men among barbarians, whom he despised and who could not understand him.

The symptoms of his illness consisted of rapid palpitations of the heart; severe pains in the back, limbs, and chest; and fatigue after short spells of work. He felt that 'people were always speaking things against' him – though he excepted Jim from blame – and finally he withdrew from all village affairs and shut himself up in his hut for long periods. He complained to me and to Ihembi that the villagers ignored his sufferings to the extent that no one had bothered to consult a diviner to find out what was wrong with him. In the end, ill though he was, he had had to travel many miles to Angola to consult a diviner himself. I cannot say with clinical certainty whether Kamahasanyi's symptoms were real or imaginary. My own feeling is that they were mainly neurotic. At any rate, when the ritual sequence was over, Kamahasanyi was perfectly able to cultivate his gardens, to set traps for game in the forest, and to travel considerable distances to visit kin and friends. And to all outward appearances there was nothing much the matter with him; he talked animatedly and at length to anyone whom, like Ihembi and myself, he considered sympathetic. It is probable that most of his symptoms were psychosomatic – with a few rheumatic pains, a common Ndembu ailment, in addition – and were an unconscious way of obtaining the attention of his fellow villagers.

THE PERFORMANCES OF IHAMBA

The material presented – and – and much more – was known to Ihembi, who discussed it with me and with his assistants Mundoyi and Mukeyi, who were themselves patrilaterally connected with Kamahasanyi and had grown up in the same part of the Belgian Congo. All of it was taken into account and put to therapeutic use by Ihembi, not only in the formalised situation of ritual performances, but also in the informal talks he held during his stay in Nswanamundong'u with Kamahasanyi, Maria, Jim, Kachimba, Makayi, and other interested parties. I would like, first of all, to present some of Ihembi's diagnoses of the causes of Kamahasanyi's illness and misfortune and then to consider his conduct of the Ihamba performances. Ihembi, like other Ndembu, believed that these causes were all of a mystical type. He was not at all like a Western psychiatrist working with the concept of mental illness.

After the first performance of Ihamba, in which he had, as anticipated, tactfully taken control of the proceedings from his Luvale colleague (with great delicacy he had first asked his permission to do so and later gave him a half-share of his ten-shilling fee), Ihembi told me that, while it was true that Kamahasanyi had been 'bitten' by the *ihamba* of his 'grandfather' Mundong'u Kabong'u, other entities had also been at work. He had himself removed the late chiefs incisor, and he had born correct, he said, in his view that the shade was angry because a proper headman had not been installed in Nswanamundong'u. He knew that he was correct, he went on, because the shade had caused the patient to 'tremble'* (*ku-zakuka*) after

---

*A sort of rhythmic shuddering, indicative of possession, which begins in time with the drum rhythm and afterwards may become uncontrollable.

Ihembi had 'addressed' (*kwinka nyikunyi*) the proper questions to it. But later he had divined by gazing into a meal mortar full of pounded medicines and sprinkled with powdered red clay (with the generic sense of 'blood') and white clay (which may mean 'innocence', 'health', 'strength', certain manifestations of ancestral shades, and so forth). There he had 'seen' another *ihamba*, probably that of the patient's father. Kamahasanyi, it may be recalled, had dreamed of his father's shade. Ihembi said that Mudyigita was angry with his son for having quarreled with his (Mudyigita's) matrikin. Since Kamahasanyi had dreamed on successive nights that the shade had stood between the forked branches of a hunters' shrine set up in front of his dwelling hut, Ihembi resolved to perform Ihamba at that very place.

But in addition to *mahamba* said Ihembi, sorcery and witchcraft were partly to blame for Kamahasanyi's troubles. When he first divined, he thought he saw in the medicated water the 'reflection' or 'shadow-soul' (*mwevulu*) of Wilson. He 'saw' further that Wilson had 'raised a *musala*', a kind of malignant ghost, by means of a curse, after quarreling with Kamahasanyi. I can confirm from my own information that Wilson strongly disliked Kamahasanyi and resented his coming to the village. Since he was not a matrilineal kinsman, Wilson was less constrained about expressing his hostility, for matrikin must in public maintain the fiction of amity in their relations. But, on going more deeply into the matter, Ihembi learned, since he was a great diviner and not easily deceived, that the 'reflection' of Wilson had been 'put in his *ng'ombu*' (his divining apparatus) by the 'real witches'. These witches were Kamahasanyi's wife Maria and her mother Ndona (E9), Kachimba's wife. They wanted to 'kill Kamahasanyi for his meat', since Ndembu witches are thought to be necrophagous. They had sent their familiars (malignant little beings known as *tuyebela*, who take the forms of small domestic anünals or tiny men with inverted feet) to 'beat' Kamahasanyi with hoe-handles. This behavior accounted for some of his symptoms. Beside, Ndona preferred Jackson to Kamahasanyi as a son-in-law and wanted the latter done away with.

He told me that he had informed the villagers that, before he could 'make another Ihamba', he would have to perform a rite known as Kaneng'a or Lukupu ('splashing with medicine'), to make the witches realise that in a general way 'they were known'. Lukupu also had the effect of driving off witches' familiars. He would not mention any names openly, since 'there was enough trouble in the village' but the performance of Lukupu would act as a sharp warning to the witches to call off their familiars, for otherwise he would expose them publicly and take drastic ritual remedial action. To perform Lukupu was also, in my opinion, Ihembi's way of sharply jolting the quarrelsome villagers into reconciling their differences and behaving better toward their kinsman Kamahasanyi. For to imply so bluntly that witchcraft was at work in the village was the sharpest rebuke Ihembi could make and played on the Ndembu villagers' deepest fears.

Ihembi told me that it was in his mind to advise Kamahasanyi to divorce Maria and to go to reside in Chief Ikelenge's area, where his widowed mother was now living with Kamahasanyi's younger brother – not far from the 'real headman' Samuwinu's hut (D13). He might thus hope to escape a horrible death. In the end, however, he decided against this course and worked to make 'the livers of the Nswanamundong'u people white towards one another', to remove the state of mutual ill-feeling. This removal would 'please the shade', which would stop afflicting Kamahasanyi.

In this projective guise, Ihembi was really dealing with the undercurrents of personal animosity and sectional rivalry in the village. He was also clearly trying to emancipate Kamahasanyi from the guilts and anxieties attendant upon his belated removal from his late father's sphere of influence. Kamahasanyi had to be made over, as it were, to the matrilineal sphere, which was also the arena of adult responsibility.

I shall pass over the events of the Lukupu rite, which I observed, except to note that Ihembi made Kachimba (E8) throw, on behalf of the whole village, a portion of white clay (*mpemba*) into the medicines which Kamahasanyi was washed to betoken that all had 'good feelings' toward him. Makayi, too, attended the rite, which was held in the bush far away from the village.

THE SECOND IHAMBA PERFORMANCE

I shall not give a 'blow by blow' account of the rite here but shall confine myself to its social implications. It is necessary to know, however, that, after certain ritual preliminaries, including the collecting of medicines in a prescribed formal manner, an Ihamba rite proceeds in a series of stops and starts. The 'stops' occur when the cupping horns (*tusumu*) are attached to the patient's body; then follows a phase of drumming and singing, in which all present join, and the patient goes into a trembling fit. If he shakes off a horn or two in his convulsions, the doctor bids the drummers stop playing, removes the horns, and investigates them. If he finds nothing in them, he makes a statement to the congregation about why the *ihamba* has not 'come out' – which usually entails a fairly detailed account of the patient's life story and of the group's inter-relations – then he invokes the shade, urging it to 'come quickly' and finally invites village members to come, in order of sex and seniority, to the improvised hunters' shrine set up for the shade and confess any secret ill-feeling they may have toward the patient. The patient himself may be invited as well. Then cupping horns are affixed once more, drumming and singing commence again, and the 'big doctor' passes the time until the next round of verbal behavior in dancing, purifying the village by ritually sweeping out huts and paths, or going out into the bush to bring back some new medicine plant.

Ihembi's greatest skill was in managing this stop-start routine so that, after several hours of it, the congregation felt nothing but a unanimous craving for the removal of the *ihamba* from the patient's body. The intense excitement whipped up by the drums; the patient's trembling; mass participation in the sad-sweet or rousing hunters' cult songs, which are sung to 'please *ihamba*', followed by the spate of confessions and the airing of grievances, the reverent or hortatory prayers addressed not only by the doctor but also by village elders to the shade to 'make our kinsman strong', the sight and smell of blood, which often pours in gouts from the horns: all these elements make a dialectical and dialogical pattern of activity that generates strong sentiments of corporateness, reduces skepticism, and maximises sympathy for the patient.

Ihembi was also skilled in allocating appropriate ritual tasks to the patient's kin. For example, he asked Nyaking'a (D14) to bring in a calabash of water to be consecrated to the making of Ihamba medicines. Nyaking'a had been a friend of Kamahasanyi's mother while both were married out in the Belgian Congo. She was Kamahasanyi's classificatory 'grandmother', and she had been ritual instructress to Maria some years earlier at her puberty rite. Because of its importance at life crises, Ndembu regard water as an 'elder' (*mukulumpi)* or most venerable 'thing' and Nyaking'a's friendly relationship with the disturbed marital pair was thus recognised.

Jim (E12), the tactful aspirant to the chief's chair, helped in the sucking of horns, thus demonstrating that he wanted to rid the patient (and his village) of troubles. Samuwinu was asked to invoke the shade before others did, since he was since he was 'the real headmatn'.

Wilson was asked by Ihembi to put a piece of white clay on the fork of a hunters' shrine-tree in token of his friendly and pure intentions toward Kamahasanyi, of which, as we have seen, there had been some doubt. Ihembi made the faithless Maria go into the bush to bring leaves from a *mudyi* tree (*Diplorrhyncus condylocarpon*). This tree, as I have shown elsewhere,[9] stands for 'motherhood' 'matriliny', and 'womanhood' (its white latex secretions are likened to mother's milk). It also stands for 'auspiciousness'. Maria chewed the leaves and spat the juice on her husband's temples, feet, and hands, centers of thought and activity, and tapped him smartly on the back and head with a small hand rattle – 'to give him strength'. By these acts, she reaffirmed her wifely duties toward the patient and her good will – the reverse of witchery.

Others too numerous to mention were assigned minor parts in this ritual drama by that old impresario Ihembi, who sought, as I have seen him do again and again in ritual contexts, to get everyone working together, despite the issues that divided them in secular life, 'to please the shade', and thus to cure the patient. Once when the women attenders did not sing loudly enough, Ihembi made them come closer to the compact men's group and exhorted them to sing up. It is very important', he said, 'that you should give your power to help Kamahasanyi.' For, in Ndembu belief, singing is not merely a pastime or aesthetic activity but a way of generating 'power' – which can be used by a doctor for healing purposes.

After a number of people had admitted to ill feeling or negligence toward Kamahasanyi, the patient himself spoke out. He complained vehemently that his matrilineal kin (*akumama*) had not moved a finger to help him when he was ill. He had been forced to go to a diviner himself, although he was unwell. It was fortunate, he said, that Maria, his wife, had gone with him. But, he added, now that he had told his grudge to everyone, he thought that all would be well. His hard thoughts had kept back his cure. It was also lucky that Mundoyi and Mukeyi, Ihembi's assistants (who had performed many ritual tasks) were present, for they were Kamahasanyi's (classificatory) 'fathers' (see genealogy) and it was his father who had been troubling him.

I should like to conclude my account of the performance with an extract from my field notes, written up shortly after I observed it in 1951, to convey something of its atmosphere and flavor:

> Mundoyi now took the *duiker* horn out of Kamahasanyi's hair over the brows, washed it, filled it with medicine, and replaced it at the back of his head. He did the same with the blue *duiker* horn at the back, replacing it at the front. He blew his whistle twice. Kamahasanyi started to quiver again violently, and the cupping horn on the left of his neck fell off, unpleasantly spilling what looked like a small chunk of flesh. Next the horn on his temple fell off. Ihembi sat very quietly, not registering any emotion at all. I felt strongly that what was being drawn out of this man Kamahasanyi was, in reality, the hidden animosities of the village. To all appearances, Kamahasanyo was in a state of complete dissociation.
>
> Now Ihembi fitted a long thin *duiker* horn on the little finger of his right hand, took a mongoose-skin purse in his left hand, and pointed the horn at one of the cupping horns, wiping the patient's skin just above it as he did so. The whole congregation rose to their feet as one man, and Ihembi fastened on the twitching Kamahasanyi, who fell on his side, writhing convulsively. Kamahasanyi cried out and sobbed when Lhembi

removed the blood-dripping horn in a large skin-purse. Mundoyi and Kachilewa (an Ihamba adept from a neighboring village) threw large quantities of medicine over the patient. Ihembi rushed to the small calabash (containing medicine and blood from other cuppings) and threw the cupping horn now concealed by the purse into it. He then spat powdered white clay on the really ugly bulge on Kamahasanyi's neck where the horn had been, 'to cool and purify it'. Kachilewa now held his hand poised over the leaf-concealed calabash while all of us waited intently. He removed the leaves and dredged with his hand in the bloody mixture. After a while he shook his head and said 'Mwosi' ('Nothing in here'). We were all disappointed. But Ihembi with a gentle smile took over. He plunged his fingers into the gruesome liquid and when he brought them up I saw a flash of white. Then he rushed with what was in his fingers out of the avid circle of onlookers. From the edge of the village, he beckoned to the elders and to me. Led by Samuwinu and Kachimba, we went one by one to Ihembi. It was indeed a human tooth, we had to say. It was no bush-pig's tooth, nor a monkey's. Jubilantly we told the women, who all trilled with joy. Men and women who had been on cool terms with one another until recently, shook hands warmly and beamed with happiness. Kachimba even smiled at Makayi, who smiled back. Several hours later a mood of quiet satisfaction still seemed to emanate from the villagers.

These events took place toward the end of my first field trip. More than a year later, when I visited the village again during my second tour, I found that several changes had occurred in its composition. Of the Nkonkoto group none remained in Nswanamundong'u. Old Kapansonyi had died, and Makayi had emigrated to Chief Ikelenge's area, while Maria's lover Jackson had gone as a labor migrant to the Copperbelt mining town of Chingola (where I met him by chance in the street one day – he said he was never going back to village life). Kachimba's sons Douras and Robson had built new huts elsewhere in Mukang'ala Chiefdom. But Kamahasanyi was still in residence, Maria was still his wife, and indeed he had added to his personal following by persuading his younger brother and sister to reside in Nswanamundong'u. Furthermore, he had increased his prestige by becoming an adept in some of the cults into which he had been initiated through suffering – though not in Ihamba, for he was not a gun-hunter. In terms of social morphology, therefore, Nswanamundong'u had shed its patrilateral attachments and was reduced to its matrilineal nucleus, although it had increased in size. Kamahasanyi gave me the impression that he was enjoying life, was accepted by his fellow villagers, and was liked by his wife. He showed me with pride his new cassava gardens and told me that he was now successfully snaring game. It looked as though Ihembi's 'therapy' had 'worked', if only for a time!

CONCLUSION

It seems that the Ndembu 'doctor' sees his task less as curing an individual patient than as remedying the ills of a corporate group. The sickness of a patient is mainly a sign that 'something is rotten' in the corporate body. The patient will not get better until all the tensions and aggressions in the group's interrelations have been brought to light and exposed to ritual treatment. I have shown how complex these interrelations can be and how conflicts in one social dimension may reverberate through others. The doctor's task is to tap the various streams of affect associated with these conflicts and with the social and interpersonal disputes in which they are manifested – and to channel them in a socially positive direction. The raw energies of conflict are thus domesticated in the service of the traditional social order. Once the various causes of ill feeling against Kamahasanyi and of his ill feeling against others had been 'made visible' (to use the Ndembu idiom), the doctor Ihembi was able, through the cultural mechanism of Ihamba, with its bloodlettings, confessions, purifications, prayers to the traditional dead, tooth-drawings, and build-up of expectations, to transform the ill feeling into well wishing. Emotion is roused and then stripped of its illicit and antisocial quality, but nothing of its intensity, its quantitative aspect has been lost in the transformation. Ndembu social norms and values, expressed in symbolic objects and actions, are saturated with this generalised emotion, which itself becomes ennobled through contact with these norms and values. The sick individual, exposed to this process, is reintegrated into his group as, step by step, its members are reconciled with one another in emotionally charged circumstances.

Yet there is room within this communal and corporate process for the doctor to take fully into account the nuances and delicate distinctions of interpersonal relationships. Ihembi, for example, dealt with the idiosyncratic relationships between a father and a son, a husband and a wife, an uncle and a nephew. But his main endeavor was to see that individuals were capable of playing their social roles successfully in a traditional structure of social position. Illness was for him a mark of undue deviation from the norm. The shades punish such deviation. In this time of rapid change, the shades of old hunters are particularly likely to be sensitive to breaches of traditional norms, since hunting is for Ndembu the activity around which has formed the basic constellation of tribal values. It is therefore appropriate that hunters' shades should 'bite' those who are most exposed to modern changes.

Stripped of its supernatural guise, Ndembu therapy may well offer lessons for Western clinical practice. For relief might be given to many sufferers from neurotic illness if all those involved in their social networks could meet together and publicly confess their ill will toward the patient and endure in turn the recital of his grudges against them. But it is likely that nothing less than ritual sanctions for such behavior and belief in the doctor's mystical powers could bring about such humility and compel people to display charity toward their suffering 'neighbor'.

INTRODUCTION: REFERENCES

Scheff, T. J. (1979) *Catharsis in Healing, Ritual and Drama*. Berkeley: University of California Press.

NOTES

1   V. W. Turner, *Schism and Continuity in an African Society* (Manchester: Manchester University Press, 1957); Turner, *Ndembu Divination: its Symbolism and Techniques* (Rhodes-Livingstone Paper No. 31 [Manchester: Manchester University Press, 1961]); and Turner, *Lunda Medicine and the Treatment of Disease* (Rhodes-Livingstone Museum Paper No. 15 [Lusaka: Government Printing Office, 1963]).

2   T. Parsons, *The Social System* (New York: Free Press of Glencoe, 1951), p. 430.

3   Turner, *Schism*, p. 292.

4   Turner, *Ndembu Medicines*.

5   Turner, *Ndembu Divination*, p. 18.

6   Erwin Ackerknecht, 'Problems of primitive medicine', *Bulletin of the History of Medicine*, 11 (1942): 503–21.

7   W. A. Lessa and E. Z. Vogt (eds) *Reader In Comparative Religion* (New York: Harrper & Row, 1958), p. 343.

8   Turner, *Ndembu Divination*, p. 18.

9   Turner, *Ndembu Medicines*, pp. 131–7.

CHAPTER SEVENTEEN

History and the Evolution of Syndromes: the Striking Case of Latah and Amok (1971)

Henry B. M. Murphy

Murphy (1915–87) was one of the founders of the McGill school of transcultural psychiatry (indeed he popularised the use of the term in the title of its journal) along with his Canadian colleagues Eric Wittkower and Raymond Prince. His studies in Mauritius and the Virgin Islands first argued that the prognosis of schizophrenia was better in (what are now called) developing countries. This paper is valuable for being one of the first to consider change in the presentation and social reception of a defined illness. Amok he suggests becomes a gradually less motivated affair and more 'dissociative' with time; whilst latah he argues is a culture-contact syndrome, which he explores psychodynamically. Similar arguments have been advanced for piblokto (Arctic hysteria) (Neutra et al. 1977).

Psychiatry has made ample use of epidemiological approaches in its attempts to elucidate the etiology of mental illnesses, as numerous mental health surveys attest. Yet if one views epidemiology as being concerned with the distribution of disease through space and time, as is customary, then it must be admitted that the time dimension remains largely neglected. Change has been well documented for general paresis (Jacobowsky 1965), but very little use has been made of this finding. Change also appears to have occurred in what we call mania, but despite the considerable theoretical importance of this it seems never to have been properly documented and analysed. In part we can attribute such neglect to the very large volume of reading that a historic review of some syndromes would demand. There are a number of conditions, however, on which the historic evidence is reasonably limited and clear, so that a search for possible changes in incidence or in symptomatology is within modest reach.

The syndromes of *latah* and *amok*, to which my attention was drawn many years ago, fall into the latter category and have additional attractions for the researcher. Their key features are such as can be reported on as easily by the layman as by the professional; the literature on them is limited but represents many writers, so that the problem of observer bias is small; they are found almost exclusively in a single people or culture, a fact that makes them of special theoretical interest; and it needs only a brief search to reveal that quite definite changes in frequency have occurred.

In this chapter I propose to review these changes and then to discuss how such evidence may throw light on etiology.

AMOK

From the mid-seventeenth century the phrase 'running amuck' has been current in English, and from the mid-nineteenth century or earlier the term amok is to be found in medical textbooks. Since few professional men ever encounter a case, however, the popular usage has contaminated the medical one and the word is employed by many doctors to describe any episode of homicidal mania or panic. Such episodes occur in all parts of the world, and their manifestations, sequels, and etiology are so varied that there is little point in considering them as comprising a single syndrome. In the Malay peninsula and archipelago, however, 'amok' has had a much more restricted meaning, and for the nineteenth-century form the term syndrome is quite appropriate. At that time cases usually showed a prodromal period of brooding or depression, no immediate connection existed between the outbreak and any provoking situation, there were usually no paranoid delusions, the subject often had his eyes closed during the fighting, and amnesia always followed the event. It is this syndrome with which I am concerned here.

The term amok (or *amouco* in Portuguese) enters written literature in the mid-sixteenth century when European travelers began providing detailed first-hand descriptions of South Asia. Initially it referred only to groups of exceptionally courageous men who had taken a vow to sacrifice themselves in battle against an enemy, as in the following passage:

> All that night they shaved their heads (this being a superstitious practice of those who despise life, people whom they call in India Amaucos) and betook themselves to their mosque, and there devoted their persons to death ... and as an earnest of this vow, and an example of this resolution, the Captain ordered a great fire to be made, and cast into it his wife, and a little son he had, and all his household and his goods, in fear lest anything of his should fall into our possession. Others did the like, and then they fell on the Portuguese. (De Barros 1552, quoted by Yule and Burnell 1886, p. 13)*

---

*Yule and Burnell's book of Anglo-Indian words, quaintly entitled *Hobson-Jobson*, has been a most valuable source of information concerning the early usage of 'amok', even though not entirely accurate.

Later, the term came to be applied to an individual form of death-seeking activity, a form that earlier Europeans had found remarkable and that was specific to the Malaysian region[†], not being reported from India. In this connection Nicolo Conti wrote, in about 1430:

> Debtors are made over to their creditors as slaves, and some of these, preferring death to slavery, will with drawn swords rush on, stabbing all whom they fall in with of lesser strength than themselves, until they meet death at the hand of someone more than a match for them. This man the creditors then sue in court for the dead man's debt. (Yule and Burnell 1886: p. 13)

Almost a century later, Duarte Barbosa wrote similarly, again not using the term amok:

> If anyone of these Jaos [i.e., Javanese] falls sick of any illness he makes a vow to his God that if he restores him his health he will seek out another more honourable death in his service; and after that he is whole he takes a dagger in his hand with certain wavy edges which they have among them of very good quality, and going forth into the places and streets he slays whomsoever he meets, men, women or children letting none go; these men they call *Guanicos*. (Barbosa 1921: 177)

It is clearly this individual pattern of behavior, which by the sixteenth century had lost the name of *guanico* and acquired that of amok, that we are mainly concerned with here, but it must be understood that at this time there was justifiably recognised a connection between the two usages. The individual amoker, like the member of a consecrated band of fighters, initiated his action consciously and deliberately; he avoided attacking his own relatives and friends (unless in a preliminary attempt to save them further suffering); there is no record of him closing his eyes; it is easy to establish the connection between some precipitating event and the episode; he does not seem to have shown signs of mental illness either previously or, if he survived, subsequently; and society often gave approval to the act,

---

[†]Throughout this paper the term Malaysian will be used geographically to apply to the whole region of the Malay peninsula, the Malay archipelago, and Borneo, while culturally it will apply to all peoples speaking a tongue related to Malay and Javanese. This conflicts with present-day usage, which on the one hand restricts 'Malaysian' to the former British territories and on the other extends it to all peoples within these territories, regardless of language and culture; but the convention is convenient for our purposes.

with a survivor sometimes having 'the fame of being an invincible hero because he so manfully repulsed all those who tried to seize him' (Schulzens 1676: p. 20). Moreover, the term amok was not applied only to large groups or to individuals; it was applied also to two or three persons acting in consort – for instance, in revenge against a cruel master as in the legend of Hang Tuah (Sheppard n.d.).

We have no idea of the frequency of the individual form of the condition in these early days. In the seventeenth century Schulzens (1659) [see 1676] reported seeing three amok-runners broken on the wheel during his few months' stay in Batavia; this seems more than earlier writers had observed at first hand, but that is doubtful evidence. What is clearer is that by the seventeenth century the Dutch were coming round to the view that amok might he a form of insanity, perhaps caused by opium. At this time they were paying for the spices which they brought west with opium that they carried east from India (Goldsmith 1939). Schulzens (1659 [see 1676]) was the first to make reference to this, and the idea that some types of amok were caused by the misuse of opium persisted in Dutch writings until the late nineteenth century. The theory was never confirmed, however, and the possibility of a transient connection between opium and amok at that time is doubtful. Later, there was definitely no connection.

The eighteenth century yields almost nothing of interest on the subject, as far as I have been able to trace. In 1764 amok for the first time received separate legal recognition by the Governor General in Batavia (Van den Chijs 1890), but insanity as a possible cause was not mentioned in the announcement, which appears to be directed mainly at combating the traditional tendency to treat the surviving amok-runner as a hero. When the British returned to the region during the Napoleonic wars, however, they were able to view the condition with fresh eyes, and their descriptions tell us that it had been changing.

For Crawfurd, the first of the nineteenth-century reporters, the characteristic feature of the condition was 'the apparently unpremeditated, and always sudden and unexpected' (p. 68) manner in which it broke out (Crawfurd 1820). He told of a petty chief who had changed sides during a small local war and had made himself very useful to his new associates. As the war was ending and he could anticipate the rewards for his efforts, he suddenly arose from his sleep one night and ran amok within the house, killing or wounding many people, the majority of whom were of his own tribe and had changed sides with him. Crawfurd, on the scene the next morning, could get no indication that the man had been angry, depressed, or sick, or that anyone could have anticipated the attack. In this case, as in the others reported by Crawfurd, a loss of honor had previously occurred and was probably a factor, though there was a quiescent interval between the time at which the loss or insult should have been recognised and the onset of the amok. Opium and physical sickness are not mentioned in these cases, and neither is fighting with the eyes closed, but the amoker's family and intimates are now as exposed to the attack as his enemies.

Some 30 years after Crawfurd's initial, description, Oxley, Singapore's first medical officer, the first doctor to make a formal study of amok, and an oft-cited authority on the subject, reported on the condition. His amokers were not defeated warriors or persecuted slaves, as had still largely been true earlier in the century, but ordinary workmen and traders living in the peaceful settlements that the British had by then established, For Oxley the typical history was as follows:

> A man sitting quietly among his friends and relatives will without provocation suddenly start up, weapon in hand, and slay all within his reach ... The next day, when interrogated, the answer has inevitably been 'the devil entered into me, my eyes were darkened, I did not know what I was about.' I have received the same reply on at least twenty occasions ... On examination of these monomaniacs I have generally found them to be labouring under some gastric disease or troublesome ulcer, and these fearful ebullitions [i.e. the amok] break out upon some exacerbation of the disorder. (Oxley 1849: 532)

Here we see that two further changes have taken place. The main underlying frustration has become somatic instead of social, disease instead of insult; and the identification with the act is now denied, the primitive impulse being attributed to the devil. Symbolising this denial, these men now sometimes fought with the eyes closed (*mata gelap*). It is possible that these changes did not apply to the amokers who achieved death during their attack, for Oxley, like the other medical reporters after him, based his impressions on those who survived. This could have induced a distortion in the reported picture similar to that which occurred when people began interpreting consummated suicide on the basis of the characteristics of patients who had made suicidal gestures. What is clear, however, is that in Oxley's time a form of amok appeared which was different both from the earlier type and from that which later was found to be associated with psychosis. Oxley's patients conversed and behaved quite normally the day after the attack (apart from some reactive depression), and although one can infer some earlier mental disturbance in one or two cases the picture is not that of a chronic psychosis. There seems to be little doubt, therefore, that the character of amok had changed, at least among those who had elected to live peacefully by trade and labor in the protected ports rather than by war and piracy in the jungle and the narrow seas.

Since Oxley had had less than 10 years to make these observations, since the Singapore adult male Malay community at this time must have numbered fewer than 5,000, and since most amok-runners traditionally did not survive to be interrogated, we have for the first time the means of making a very rough estimate of the incidence of the condition. It could not have been less than 1 per 1,000 adult males per annum, and might easily have been twice or thrice that rate. Some 20 years later the famous naturalist Alfred Wallace stated that in the port of Makassar, in Celebes, 'there are said to be one or two a month on average, and five, ten or twenty persons are sometimes killed or wounded at one of them' (Wallace 1898: 273). If we give Makassar a population of 20,000. which is not unlikely for that time, the resultant rate is similar, and there is no doubt that this frequency was causing much alarm. Thus in the non-Europeanised areas a bankrupt gambler and a resentful slave are known to have been killed for merely suggesting that they might choose to run amok (Wallace 1898), while in the Straits Settlements the chief justice of that time announed in passing sentence on a case that he found amok 'frightfully common' (Norris 1849: 461). From Java, Swaving (1856) wrote a thesis on the legal aspects of the condition and also remarked on its frequency. In the mid-nineteenth century, therefore, we have evidence for a rise in the incidence of the condition. It is my impression, however, that, at least in the peaceful Straits Settlements, it was a transient rise that had built up during the 1830s and 1840s and was to fade away shortly thereafter, since before the end of the century it was recorded that there had been 'not more than three real cases in the last fifteen years for the whole Straits Settlements, despite the marked increase in the population there' (Swettenham 1900: 253).

In the second half of the nineteenth century, writing on amok increased, though with much at second hand. If we take only the first-hand reports, however, a fairly clear picture appears. In areas remote from European influence the condition is associated with slavery, warfare, or politics and can still be referred to as 'the national and therefore honourable mode of committing suicide' (Wallace 1898: 273). In rural Java and Sumatra, where slavery and warfare had nominally been suppressed, there is a fairly direct connection between amok and some obvious frustration, but now the frustration tends to arise within the family, there is a latent interval between the provocation and the outbreak, and some cases fight with their eyes closed (Metzger 1887). In neither area are insanity, sickness, or drugs alleged to be involved. In coastal areas of European settlement, however, somatic factors (Crawfurd 1856), opium (Heymann 1855; Breitenstein 1899), and residual insanity (Swaving 1856; Vogler 1853) are mentioned as causes, while social factors tend to be ignored unless the author also had experience in the interior. Moreover, it is suggested for the first time that the condition may develop during the course of chronic dementia or a febrile delirium (Vogler 1853).

Particularly interesting, though regrettably brief (the paper seems to be the summary of a doctoral thesis, but I have been unable to locate a copy of the latter), are Swaving's observations at this time (1856). Some of his cases are already showing mental disturbance (perhaps schizophrenia simplex) before the episode; others, though previously considered normal, report having had vivid dreams involving stab wounds or blood streaming down their bodies – dreams which led them to wake in great anxiety and to attack imaginary enemies. Of those who showed no mental derangement before the episodes, some now show it afterwards. As a lawyer Swaving is much concerned by the difficulty of distinguishing the genuine *mata gelaps* from instances in which it is feigned for the purpose of achieving revenge or gain, and he notes that some case studies yield the history of a man apparently taking strong drink or opium as a deliberate means of loosening ego controls. Also, he notes that most cases occur among men from the mountains who have come to the city, have little education, and apparently are of low intelligence. Thus amok is now acquiring a psychiatric character which had previously been absent. The picture is still mixed, however, and Clifford (1897) is skeptical regarding the degree to which conscious intention is absent.

By the end of the century psychiatrists had arrived in the region and gave support to the idea that amok was a mental rather than a social disorder. Van Brero (1896) is very cautious in regard to the matter and recognises that the cases he sees in his asylum may be unrepresentative, but does tell us that family members are now the commonest victims and that dissociation from the act is customary. Ellis (1893) is bolder, though with only three cases to work from, and adds a new element to the picture by referring to a condition that is commonly called *sakit hati* (literally, 'liver sickness', the liver being considered the seat of the emotions, but which he calls heart sickness) and which Gimlette (1901) states is best understood as spite, envy, or being affronted. It is a form of depression, with brooding over wrongs, which was common among Singapore Malays at this time and for which running amok was viewed by some, according to Clifford (1897), as a remedy. Two of Ellis' three cases seemed to have suffered from this condition before running amok, and Clifford describes sitting up all night with a depressed Selangor noble to dissuade him from running amok after his father died. Neither opium nor somatic illness is now seen as a factor, though both are mentioned. (At this time Malaysians rarely took opium, whereas the Chinese, who used it extensively, did not run amok.) Ellis does propose epilepsy as a factor, however, and this theory, though unsupported by his own material and most other studies, was taken up by Kraepelin, introducing a new confusion.

Ellis' three cases were all that he saw in his first five years in the region; and although I have read all the annual reports that he wrote during his remaining quarter-century there, I cannot remember him returning to the subject. We may infer, therefore, that before the turn of the century amok was becoming very rare in Singapore, with the same holding true of Batavia (Rasch 1894) and Penang (Fitzgerald 1923). Rasch and Fitzgerald, as well as Van Loon (1922), Gans (1922), and Galloway (1923), all tell us that cases were occurring in the interiors of Java and Malaya, and Fitzgerald writes casually about 'the last six persons' admitted to Johore jail for running amok; but they can gain us very little first-hand information.

There is no doubt, therefore, that the condition had become quite rare in the regions where European doctors were practicing, and such descriptions as we possess suggest that by 1920 its clinical character may have changed once more. Three of the four reports from this decade mention, quite independently of each other, a connection with malaria or other sources of acute febrile confusion. Thus Fitzgerald states that the six amok-runners admitted to the Johore jail were all tested and found to have quartan malaria in their blood, and the single case personally treated by Galloway was also suffering at the time of his amok from a malarial relapse, although it was not in the febrile phase. (Incidentally, that patient killed no one.) Van Loon groups amok with what he regards as other types of acute confusional state induced by diseases such as malaria and syphilis, and in a later paper (Van Loon 1927) addressed to an American audience goes so far as to call it 'infectious-murder' (p. 437).

In concordance with this etiological view, the three (Fitzgerald, Galloway, and Van Loon) also see the condition as treatable, with the patient recovering his normal personality when the febrile delirium is over. In their discussions of the condition, epilepsy and opium are dismissed as irrelevant, Oxley's nonfebrile somatic precipitants go unmentioned, social precipitants are discussed by Van Loon only to be rejected, and even *sakit hati* hardly receives recognition. The writers of this generation (with the exception of Gans, who saw only cases that reached his mental hospital after months or years of imprisonment) are relatively unanimous respecting the role of infection in the disorder.

By the 1930s, however, this theory was also on the wane. Amir (1939 and earlier) provides us with full clinical descriptions of five cases with which he was concerned, and in only one of these could recent infection be considered a partial factor. In most of his cases a more chronic process – organic brain syndrome or schizophrenia – was clearly of major importance, and the only patient who had no such chronic disorder developed a prison psychosis three weeks after being apprehended. To judge by these cases, therefore, amok has now become an episode in a chronic process, not appearing in persons who afterwards make a sane impression. Amir, however, was a hospital psychiatrist with a long but perhaps restricted experience, and Wulffen Palthe, the professor of psychiatry in Java, disagreed with his view, arguing that 'any native [i.e., Malaysian] may react with amok if only the emotional stimulus is strong enough' (Palthe 1933: 137). Unfortunately Palthe gives us only a single detailed case, omits telling us where and when he encountered others, and complicates matters by stating that the condition can occur in Chinese and Arabs. From conversation with him, however, I gather that he was wont to wander into little-changed parts of the interior of Java and Sumatra, where amok had remained comparatively more frequent. The more doubtfully genuine account of a case by Fauconnier (1930) fits Palthe's view.

Since the work of Palthe and Amir, there have been only two first-hand studies of amok in the region, although Yap (1951), Van Bergen (1953), and Pfeiffer (1971) have written on the subject from a general knowledge of the region and Burton-Bradley (1968) cites seven cases from the neighboring but non-Malaysian territory of New Guinea. The first of the two direct reports is by Zaguirre (1957), who deals with cases occurring in the Philippine army. Twelve of these soldiers actually went on a 'murderous spree', while another thirteen were halted on the verge of doing so; but some or perhaps most of Zaguirre's cases did not closely fit the amok picture, being indistinguishable from instances of homicidal mania occurring in other cultures. Zaguirre is of the opinion that amok does not constitute a distinct syndrome today and that many cases showing the behavior that he calls amok have other forms of pathology. He does not give sufficient details for one to be able to judge how many of his cases did show the classical syndrome, but in one instance, in which the soldier involved had recently lost his favorite child, the picture is suggestive. An interesting aspect of his report is the use of narcoanalysis.

Karl Schmidt, the other field researcher on the subject, has collected the records of 24 cases occurring over a 10-year period in Sarawak, but at the time this is being written has not completed his paper on them, so that the information is still incomplete. From a preliminary report most kindly shown to me, it is uncertain how many of Schmidt's cases conform to the classical picture. It is clear, however, that most of them exhibited other signs of psychopathology before or after the episode and also that a family history of mental disturbance was frequently to be found. A number of his cases were soldiers suffering from homesickness and one was a woman, although running amok is usually considered a male phenomenon and no one, to my knowledge, has been able to report details of any female case.

To summarise, then, amok has shown a marked decline in incidence from the mid-nineteenth century onward, this decline being most striking in the centers of European influence where previously (i.e., during the eighteenth and early nineteenth centuries) the incidence had probably increased. Over this period amok has shown a marked shift from being a consciously motivated form of behavior to being a dissociation reaction, and probably a further shift from a dissociation reaction in an otherwise sane individual to an episode in the course of a longer mental disorder. Whether its reported associations with opium in the eighteenth century, nonfebrile somatic diseases in the mid-nineteenth century, and febrile disease in the early twentieth century represent additional shifts is more doubtful; but some changes in both character and incidence have undoubtedly taken place. I will briefly consider the possible causes of these changes after reviewing the other syndrome, latah.

LATAH*

This syndrome is less well known than amok, and it may be helpful, therefore, to commence this section with a definition and brief descriptions. First, the definition:

> Latah is an affliction or a disease, one hardly knows what name to give it, which causes certain men and women to lose their self-control for shorter or longer periods whenever they are startled or receive any sudden shock. While in this condition they appear to be unable to realise their own identity or to employ any but imitative faculties, though they very frequently, nay almost invariably, make use of villainously bad language without anyone prompting them to do so. A complete stranger ... can induce the condition accidentally and without exercising any effort of will ... [so that] though latah resembles hypnotic suggestion in many respects it differs from it in the important respect that it in no way depends on an original voluntary surrender of willpower. (Clifford 1898: 189)

Two main subcategories of latah are recognized, though more have been proposed. One is a startle pattern that often involves coprolalia and may be induced not merely by a sudden shock but also by a key word or by the presence of a superior. The other is an imitative pattern wherein the subject seems forced to copy the actions of another person or animal, even when these are meaningless, indecorous, or dangerous.

---

*For reasons of space I am confining myself in this paper to latah among Malaysians and am ignoring the latah-like conditions – *myriachit, yaung da hte,* and so on – which have been recorded sporadically in many other peoples. The latter are germane to any general discussion of the syndrome (see Aberle 1952; Pfeiffer 1971; Yap 1952) but have been too irregularly noted for their frequency and distribution to be analysed.

An illustration of the first form has been provided by Ellis (1897), whose best mental hospital nurse was afflicted in the following fashion: 'Whenever I have occasion to admonish her she stands trembling for a few seconds, micturates and passes flatus, and then as if startled by the sound she loudly utters a filthy word and promptly apologises for her conduct' (p. 36).

The second form can he exemplified by a case of Clifford's, that of a cook who was watching the cookhouse fire and was startled by a pot toppling over. A boy sitting with him made a grab to save the pot; but whereas the boy's hand stopped before reaching it, the cook's hand, in imitation, went into the fire, grasping the scalding metal. 'With the wanton cruelty and mischief of his age, the boy once more made a feint at the smoking ricepot and again Sat's fingers glued themselves to the scalding metal. ... Sat's fingers were in a terribly lacerated condition when at last someone chanced to enter the cook-room and prevented the continuation of Sat's torture' (Clifford 1898: 191).

Latah is thus a quite dramatic condition, likely to excite comment from both medical and lay observers regardless of culture, a fact that makes the absence of descriptions before the mid-nineteenth century both surprising and significant. The word latah had been used before that time to mean jumpy or ticklish. Only one doubtful reference to a pathological state has ever been cited from an earlier date (Wilkinson 1957), however, and I have been unable to trace the original. Normally, as in the legend of Nakhoda Ragam (Hervey 1885), the word latah meant no more than to be easily startled.

The first description of a possible (but not probable) case does not use the word latah (Logan 1849), and neither the author nor his Malay guide appears to have been seen anything similar before (the predominant features were tics and obsequiousness), whereas if the two had known of the latah syndrome they would probably have referred to it. In the Strait Settlements at that time, therefore, the condition must have been unfamiliar or unknown. When the word latah first comes to be applied to the syndrome in a written text, however, it is apparent that in Batavia the condition had been known for some time, since Van Leent (1867) not only refers to it as a distinct entity but also remarks that the judiciary recognized acts committed during a latah episode to be involuntary. When it became commonly known is a different matter, for Van Leent's brief note* remains unique until the 1880s, when two nonmedical descriptions appear,

---

*Van Leent probably provided greater details in the book that he published in Dutch the year after the cited paper, but I have been unable to track down a copy of it.

the one (O'Brien 1883a, 1883b) stating that the condition is common and the other (Metzger 1882) implying that it is not. Moreover, despite the fact that O'Brien's excellent descriptions attracted much attention from Gilles de la Tourette (1884) and others in Europe, 15 years passed before the next first-hand report.

By the end of the nineteenth century, however, latah seems suddenly to have become very common. Thus, Van Brero (1895) tells us that in western Java 'the condition is so common that one can find many women with it any day in the streets' (p. 940); Swettenham (1896) states that in some parts of Perak one or two cases are seen in every village: Bordier (1894) (though with what authority is unclear) refers to it as sometimes taking on the character of an epidemic; and Clifford describes how, within his own large retinue of servants, its dramatic occurrence in one individual led to its appearing in others. Whereas O'Brien and Metzger had seemed in 1882 to be describing every case they had known, Clifford by 1898 claims to have seen so many that he could go on giving examples indefinitely. We thus must recognise either that there was a true, marked rise in incidence at this time, or that the condition became suddenly recognised in subjects among whom it had previously been ignored. Of these alternatives the former is much the more likely, not only because the condition is a difficult one to ignore but also because a description is available of its actual spread among a group of servants, a spread that might suggest some infection had the author not shrewdly added:

> I must not be understood as suggesting that they became infected with latah, for on enquiry I found that they had one and all been subject to occasional seizures [of latah] before they joined my people. But the presence of Sat [the cook referred to previously] seemed to cause them to lose the control which they had hitherto contrived to exercise over themselves. (Clifford 1898: 192)

Not all peoples within the region, however, were as yet affected; and, among those who were, our informants at this time recognised differences in susceptibility. Most vulnerable, apparently, were the Amboinese (Swettenham 1896), people who occupied a small island that the Dutch had used, since the seventeenth century, as the center for the spice trade and who had extensively converted to Christianity. Next came the Javanese and Malays around areas of European influence. Only an occasional case was reported among the Buginese, Sundanese, and Madurese, who had been more distant from that influence, and no cases at all were reported from the Achinese, who had been well studied by

Hurgronje (1906) and Jacobs (1894); or from the Bataks, among whom Christian missionaries had recently started working, or from the peoples of Borneo. The Achinese were at this time resisting Dutch penetration strongly, and the Bataks and Borneans had hardly experienced any contact at all. Apparently, therefore, the condition first became frequent in areas of European influence, though this association was later to change.

In Java latah commenced and remained almost wholly a female disorder, but in Malaya at this time almost as many male as female cases were reported. Ellis (1897) remarks that the advent of the Christian mission schools had not reduced its incidence; Fletcher (1908) suggests that it is quite as common in the educated and higher class as in the lower; and Ellis' colleague Fitzgerald claims 20 years later (1923, but based on earlier experience) that 'the latah sufferer is usually intellectually superior and more alert than his fellows' (p. 154). Most medical informants note that latah is absent in mental hospital patients, though present in the attendants, and that it is unassociated with epilepsy, mental deficiency, or hysteria. All informants remark that latah subjects are normal outside of their attacks.

After 1900, first-hand papers on latah decline sharply in number and quality for a time, but from the writings of Abraham (1911, 1912), Fletcher (1908), Gans (1922), Galloway (1922), and Fitzgerald (1923), as well as from the absence of mention of the condition in some locations where one would have expected it, some tentative deductions can be drawn. One is that the average age of latah subjects in Java is increasing. A second is that the proportion of male cases in Malaya, though still higher than in Java, is declining. A third is that the condition is moving away from the centers of European influence and into the countryside. According to Fletcher's account (1908), it is now quite frequent in such locations as Pahang and Upper Perak, with cases encountered every day in the streets and courtrooms there, whereas anecdotal sketches and medical reports from Singapore, Batavia, Penang, and Malacca almost cease to mention it. These impressions, at least in regard to the age distribution and the incidence in urban locations, are confirmed in the next major paper on the subject, that by Van Loon (1924).

Van Loon circularised 600 physicians in the Dutch East Indies, inquiring for information on latah cases they had seen, and received answers from 106. This is a low figure, considering that doctors in such countries tend to feel isolated from the mainstream of medicine and hence welcome inquiries from a university, and of these 106 only 13 claimed to have seen more than two cases. This suggests a considerable diminution since the time of Van Brero and Bordier, at least in the areas in which Western-trained doctors were practicing. Of the 169 cases reported by these doctors,* all were Malaysian or part Malaysian, most had had contact with Europeans, and all but 4 were female, thus confirming earlier observations. However, the great majority were servants (something that cannot be said of the earlier cases), most were over the age of 40, and 11 showed some signs of dementia or other chronic mental disturbance – and this is new. Attacks were most common in the presence of the master of the house, obscene wishes were sometimes expressed toward him during these attacks, and in 10 cases the condition is said to have started after a frightening and frankly sexual dream. Nevertheless, the great majority of these women were reported to be intelligent, efficient servants except when in the throes of an attack.

After Van Loon a quarter-century elapsed with virtually no original or useful contributions to the subject, and it therefore comes as little surprise that Yap, when he returned to the subject in his extensive thesis (1952), could report only 7 fresh cases. Latah, judging from his experience, was now disappearing, and such cases as remained were atypical insofar as his subjects did not appear to be intelligent or alert and the attacks tended to be incomplete. Yet this is misleading, perhaps because of the fact that Yap had to seek his cases in and near large towns, since the deeper countryside was still in political turmoil. Even as his paper was being published, the anthropologist Hildred Geertz was finding, without much intent or effort, some 13 cases in a small, central Javanese town (1968), and a few years later agricultural resettlement officers told me that they still regularly saw cases in some parts of Malaya. Since then Pfeiffer (1971) has written that the condition remains endemic in some parts of East Java and has reported on 22 cases in the area round Lawang; Chiu, Tong, and Schmidt have uncovered no fewer than 65 cases during the psychiatric survey in Borneo (1970); and Barnett has told me that in some parts of Malaya most villages have at least one publicly recognised case.† What has clearly happened, therefore, is not that the condition has disappeared (though it has undoubtedly diminished) but that it has shifted its location, abandoning the centers of social change where it was initially to be found, and moving into regions that previously seemed free of it, notably Borneo.

Grouping the data of Yap, Geertz, Pfeiffer, and Schmidt, one can compose a picture of the distribution of latah among the present genera-

---

*Since there are discrepancies between Van Loon's 1924 and 1927 papers, I have used mainly the earlier and fuller version, written in Dutch.

†These last two sets of observations are unpublished at the time of writing, and I am most grateful to the observers for making the data available.

tion which is considerably different not only from the one suggested by Yap alone but also from that reported at the beginning of the century. The picture is as follows. The condition is still quite frequent among rural Malays and Ibans who have moved into the area surrounding Kuching, the capital of Sarawak. The prevalence here seems to approach 1%, informants regard it as comparatively normal, and subjects seem relatively resigned to it. In central Javanese towns the prevalence is less and subjects seem to resist the condition more, but it still seems to affect mainly women who have moved from the countryside to the town and remains more frequent in towns than in remote villages. The areas around Malacca and Kuala Lumpur, where Yap found most of his cases, rank next in relative prevalence, and there, where European influence has been strong for some time, the subjects seem to fight the condition hardest, modifying it somewhat in the process. Finally, among some 4,000 rural Iban in Sarawak no case at all was found, although the Iban near the town were susceptible and regarded latah as an aspect of their own culture. Virtually none of this generation's subjects had worked with Europeans and few had been servants; their attacks seem milder than those reported at the beginning of the century, but this may be because their neighbors tease them less. Meanwhile the basic constellation of symptoms remains the same.

Summarising once more, one can say that latah appeared relatively suddenly during the second half of the nineteenth century, spread quite rapidly among the populations most exposed to European influence, and then moved in wave fashion away from these centers, so that today it is virtually absent in the locations where it was first observed but is present in more distant locations where it was previously absent. Throughout this period its symptoms have remained relatively stable; however, the earlier form in males has almost disappeared, the intensity of attacks has declined, and in areas from which it is disappearing the residual subjects seem less intelligent than the earlier ones.

DISCUSSION

The purpose of this paper has been not to review the total literature and all the theories on latah and amok but rather to explore whether the tracing of a mental disorder's distribution and characteristics through time can contribute a new tool to the science of psychopathology. Like most psychiatric syndromes, latah and amok have attracted many theories based mainly on the clinical characteristics of cases, but have elicited as yet no convincing explanation. Although the present review of only a part of the picture cannot provide such explanation, it has, I think, added a new element wherewith old theories can be tested and new ones fertilised.*

In most informed discussions of latah and amok the assumption is that those pathological syndromes are part of traditional Malaysian life now disappearing as a result of modernisation. This is stated explicitly by Galloway (1922) and is implicit in the views of Van Loon (1927) and Palthe (1933). The present review has shown, however, that the assumption is wrong. Latah seems to have been absent in Malaysian societies untouched by European influence, just as it is today absent among the rural Iban, though present in their suburban compatriots. Amok, similarly, can hardly be called a psychiatric syndrome before the nineteenth century, since it is only then that cases are encountered where the conscious intent to attack is absent and where social provocations seem insufficient to explain the behavior. The syndromes are thus best conceived not as offshoots from Malaysian cultural tradition but as transitional products of an interaction between that tradition and certain modernising influences. Why should this have been?

Amok provides the clearer clues to an answer. In its original, conscious form it was a recognised instrument of social control, restricting the abuse of power by chiefs and the wealthy (Gullick 1958; Haar 1948), sanctified by proverbs (Wilkinson 1925b), and endorsed by hero worship of the man who went amok and escaped the consequences. In tale after tale one reads of the courtier, the emissary, the debtor, the vassal, the slave threatening to run amok if traditional customs of fair dealing were abandoned by some superior; and the threat was no empty one. When less drastic forms of social control were demonstrated in the European settlements and when it proved more profitable to collaborate with the European trader than to pursue traditional methods of warfare and piracy, however, recourse to amok became not only unnecessary but also repulsive, and most individuals consciously rejected it as something which they themselves might undertake. It is at this point and in this setting that the pathological syndrome first appears, with the provocation (physical sickness, domestic troubles) quite insufficient by traditional standards and with the act dissociated from consciousness, but with the same underlying meaning of escaping from distress into death while at the same time taking revenge on the society that has permitted this distress. And as other means of escaping these distresses are learned and the social tradition of amok becomes

---

*In a paper 'Notes for a theory on latah' read at the Conference on Culture and Mental Health in Asia and the Pacific, and due to be published in *Mental Health Research in Asia and the Pacific*, Vol. 4, the total picture of latah is discussed in relation to the foregoing observations, and a tentative theory offered for it.

fainter in men's minds, this pathological distortion of that tradition dies away also.

For latah there is no prior model of conscious behavior that is really similar, but a widespread tradition existed of children submitting themselves to a dissociated hypersuggestibility state for the amusement of others, a state during which they would imitate whatever was suggested to them and carry out actions that would be seemingly impossible in their conscious state.* Hence hypersuggestibility was in a sense already being used for a vaguely social purpose; and my proposal is that, when it became desirable to learn rapidly some new but little understood custom, a mild degree of hypersuggestibility was again, though less consciously, called into service. It is a notable fact that, although European colonists found the Malaysians unreliable and apparently unintelligent when it came to general labor or working on their own, they admired and became greatly attached to those with whom they had close personal contact, finding the usually more enterprising Chinese and Indians quite inferior in such relationships; and I suggest that this may have been related to the Malaysian's readiness to subordinate his personal inclinations and prior training to an accepted superior. It is always easier, when called upon to learn rapidly some quite unfamiliar task, to do so by rote[†] or simple imitation rather than by understanding, and an ease of accepting and retaining suggestions facilitates this approach. Our data suggest that latah became most frequent when the need to rapidly learn new customs pressed heaviest on Malaysians. and I propose that it be seen as a by-product of the increased suggestibility with which many Malaysians responded to that need, one form of the disorder being merely an exaggeration of this suggestibility and another, involving coprolalia or swearing, representing in part the resentment usually aroused by such complete submission to the will of another.

That is not the whole story, either for amok or for latah. It ignores, for instance, the fact that when ego controls are partly renounced, as in hypersuggestibility, repressed desires are more likely to gain expression. Broadly, however, the combined data suggest that, when Malaysian society was

---

*These childhood games were described by Wilkinson (1925a), Hurgronje (1906), and others around the turn of the century and have been shown by Koentaraningat (1957) and McHugh (1955) to persist in the present generation. It seems likely that they are a vestige of adult religious ceremonies which still persist in Bali but which Mohammedanism has stamped out elsewhere in the archipelago.

†Most, though not all, of the situations in which latah-like syndromes have been found present a similar picture of a people being called upon to learn new customs rapidly. In many there has also been, as in the Koranic schools. a tradition of rote learning for children.

confronted by certain types of social problem, it responded by exploiting personal characteristics that were only partly egosyntonic. The explosive release of repressed resentment was exploited as a check on those who too freely used their power to arouse resentment; the suppression of personal inclinations and prior training at the suggestion of a superior was exploited as a means of rapid learning in unfamiliar conditions. But because each method involved to some extent the bypassing of ego controls, each also resulted in a certain amount of uncontrolled behavior in forms that served no social function, that is, each produced some individual psychopathology. This psychopathology reached its height when the demand for adaptive change was greatest; but as long as society perceived some value in the underlying characteristic it was not viewed as really egodystonic and the bearers of the pathology did not consider themselves markedly deviant, so that its presence did relatively little personal damage. Once society had mastered the problem or found more efficient methods of tackling it, however, the characteristics began to be seen as being undesirable and requiring suppression. Hence it was only when the ego was weakened by other means or when strong, repressed feelings sought to exploit the characteristic for their own ends that amok and latah still continued to be found. Moreover, in this later stage they were increasingly likely to be associated with other pathology.

But now, although the tracing of latah and amok across time and place has provided new clues to their natures, can it be said that the same would probably apply for other syndromes? Latah and amok, it might be argued, are both atypical and little known; have we any reason to think that similar results could be obtained with more typical disorders that have been more thoroughly explored? The question resolves itself into two parts, the one concerned with the approach that has been used and the other with the relationship between psychiatric symptomatology and social change to which the results have pointed.

In regard to the usefulness of the general approach the answer is, I believe, relatively simple. Once we cease to regard psychiatric syndromes as stable patterns to be found in all societies and epochs, it becomes quite easy to spot apparent shifts in incidence or in symptomatology, and the likelihood is that a study of these shifts would in some instances enlarge our understanding of the conditions involved. One such probable shift is that from the medieval acedia to the Protestant melancholia in Western Europe during the fourteenth to the seventeenth centuries. Another lies in the striking diminution of classical mania over the past hundred years or so. Yet another, only partly overlapping, involves the increased chronicity of hospitalised patients during the middle of the nineteenth century. Away from Europe and North America instances are more numerous, though lesser known. One group concerns the apparent increase of depression in many parts of Africa and Asia; another, the increase of schizophrenia in certain specific peoples, as I have discussed elsewhere (Murphy 1968). And of course within the neuroses the changes in the diagnosis of *la grande hystérie*, neurasthenia, the cardiac neuroses, and others should be known to every scholar of modern psychiatry. Although some of these changes will undoubtedly prove to have been no more than shifts in diagnostic fashion, all deserve more attention than they have received, and I believe that some will prove to represent genuine changes in symptomatology or frequency which our current theories are poorly designed to explain.

Such changes, even when proved, need not have in any way the same sort of connection to social change that has been hypothesised here to have existed in the cases of latah and amok. On the contrary, all our knowledge argues against the relationship between psychopathology and social change being so simple that a single hypothesis could cover it. Yet this is not to say that relationships analogous to those described here will not be found. Jaspers long ago, I believe, pointed out that the pathological significance of delusional beliefs depends greatly on how they are treated by surrounding society, and more recently I have argued that in many developing countries delusional systems may provide a means whereby the public can be induced to explore new concepts or unfamiliar ways of tackling new problems (Murphy 1967). Often, as with the Cargo Cult beliefs, those who produce socially useful delusions develop no further individual pathology but are accepted as leaders or heroes, just as the amokers were accepted as heroes if they survived, and the latah victims as clowns. When such beliefs serve less purpose, however, those who freshly produce them usually suffer from further pathology. Turning to a more familiar subject referred to above, namely, the alleged rarity of classical depression in some African and Asian groups earlier in this century and its increasing frequency in recent decades, one might also see this as the by-product of a type of social change which conditions were pressing on these people, the change from the collective superego of the tribe or family to the individual superego of modern man. And if this were the case, might one not interpret the apparent increase in depression in England during the seventeenth century as reflecting a similar shift?

These last suggestions may be treated as flights of fancy produced in response to the editors' request that I give some indication of how the conceptual approach employed in this paper might be more broadly applied 'toward a science of psychopathology'. It is impossible to say without a proper examination of the evidence whether a particular theory will apply in a given situation or not, and I have not subjected the evidence to such examination. I do propose, however, that our under-standing of psychopathology would be increased if we reviewed the history of different syndromes with open eyes, and that it might also enlarge our understanding if we thought of mental disorder as sometimes being the by-product of social problem-solving.

INTRODUCTION: REFERENCE

Neutra, R., Levy, J. E. and Porter, D. (1977) 'Cultural expectations versus reality in Navajo seizure patterns and sick roles', *Culture, Medicine and Psychiatry*, 1: 255–75.

NOTE

Some first-hand reports have been omitted from the following bibliography since they were in essential agreement with other reports cited from the same period.

REFERENCES

Aberle, D. F. (1952) 'Arctic hysteria', *Transactions of the New York Academy of Sciences* (Series 2), 14(7): 291–7.

Abraham, J. J. (1911) *The Surgeon's Log: being Impressions of the Far East*. New York: E. P. Dutton.

Abraham, J. J. (1912) 'Latah and amok', *British Medical Journal*, i: 438–9.

Amir, M. (1939) 'Over eenige gevallen van amok uit Nord-Sumatra', *Geneeskundig Tijdschrift voor Nederlandsch-Indië*, 79: 2786–97.

Barbosa, D. (1921) *The Book of Duarte Barbosa*. London: Hakluyt Society.

Bordier, A. (1894) *La géographie médicale*. Paris.

Breitenstein, H. (1899–1902) *Einundzwanzik Jahre in Indien. Aus dem Tagebuche eines Militärarztes*. Leipzig: T. Grieben.

Burton-Bradley, B. G. (1968) 'The amok syndrome in Papua and New Guinea', *The Medical Journal of Australia*, 1: 252–6.

Chiu, T. L., Tong, J. E. and Schmidt, K. E. A clinical and survey study of latah in Sarawak, Malaysia. Unpublished manuscript.

Clifford, H. (1897) *In Court & Kampong: being Tales and Sketches of Native Life in the Malay Peninsula*. London: G. Richards.

Clifford, H. (1898) *Studies in Brown Humanity: Being Scrawls and Smudges in Sepia, White and Yellow*. London: G. Richards.

Crawfurd, J. (1820) *History of the Indian Archipelago*, Vol. 1. Edinburgh: A. Constable.

Crawfurd, J. (1856) *A Descriptive Dictionary of the Indian Islands & Adjacent Countries*. London: Bradbury & Evans.

Ellis, W. G. (1893) 'The amok of the Malays', *Journal of Mental Science*, 39: 325–42.

Ellis, W. G. (1896) 'Latah, a mental malady of the Malays', *Journal of Mental Science*, 43: 33–40. (Also summary and discussion in same journal, 1896, 42: 209.)

Fauconnier, H. (1930) *Malaisie*. Paris: Stock.

Fitzgerald, R. D. (1923) 'A thesis on two tropical neuroses peculiar to the Malays', *Transactions of the 5th Congress of the Far-Eastern Association of Tropical Medicine*: 148–61.

Fletcher, W. (1908) 'Latah and crime', *Lancet*, 2: 254–5.

Galloway, D. J. (1922) 'A contribution to the psychology of latah', *Journal of the Straits Branch of the Royal Asiatic Society*, 85: 140–6.

Galloway, D. J. (1923) 'On amok', *Transactions of the 5th Congress of the Far-Eastern Association of Tropical Medicine*: 162–71.

Gans, A. (1922) 'Ein Beitrag zur Rassenpsychiatric', *Münchener Medizinische Wochenschrift*, 69: 1503–4.

Geertz, H. (1968) 'Latah in Java: a theoretical paradox', *Indonesia*, 5: 93–104.

Gilles de la Tourette, H. (1884) 'Jumping, latah, myriachit', *Archives de Neurologie*, 8: 68–74.

Gimlette, J. D. (1901) 'Notes on a case of amok', *Journal of Tropical Medicine*, 4: 195–9.

Goldsmith, M. L. (1939) *The Trail of Opium, the Eleventh Plague*. London: Ryerson Press.

Gullick, J. M. (1958) *Indigenous Political Systems of Western Malaya*. London: Humanities Press. (London University, London School of Economics and Political Science. Department of Anthropology Monographs on Social Anthropology, No. 17.)

Haar, B. ten (1948) *Adat Law in Indonesia*. New York: Institute of Pacific Relations.

Hervey, D. F. A. (1885) 'Malacca legends of Nakhoda Ragam', *Journal of the Straits Branch of the Royal Asiatic Society*, 15: 26 (Notes & Queries suppl. No. 2).

Heymann, S. L. (1855) *Versuch einer pathologisch-therapeutischen Darstellung der Krankheiten in den Tropen-Ländern*. Würzburg.

Hill, B. and Schmidt, K. E. Amok; a description of twenty-four cases. Unpublished manuscript.

Hurgronje, C. S. (1906) *The Achehnese*, English trans. A. W. S. O'Sullivan. London: Luzac.

Jacobowsky, B. (1965) 'General paresis and civilization', *Acta Psychiatrica Scandinavica*, 41: 267–73.

Jacobs, J. (1894) *Het Familie en Kampongleven op Groot-Atcheh*. Leiden.

Koentjaraningrat, R. M. (1957) *A Preliminary Description of the Javanese Kinship System*. New Haven, CT: Yale University, S. E. A. Studies Series, 1957.

Logan, J. R. (1849) 'Five days in Naning', *Journal of the Indian Archipelago and Eastern Asia*, 3: 24–41.

McHugh, J. N. (1955) *Hantu Hantu*. Singapore: Donald Moore.

Metzger, G. (1882) 'Sakit latah', *Globus*, 41: 381–3.

Metzger, G. (1887) 'Einiges über amok und mataglap', *Globus*, 52: 107–10.

Murphy, H. B. M. (1967) 'Cultural aspects of delusion', *Studium Generale*, 20(11): 684–92.

Murphy, H. B. M. (1968) 'Cultural factors in the genesis of schizophrenia'. In D. Rosenthal and S. S. Kety (eds) *The Transmission of Schizophrenia*. Oxford: Pergamon Press, pp. 137–53.

Norris, W. (1849) 'Sentence of death upon a Malay convicted of running amuck', *Journal of the Indian Archipelago and Eastern Asia*, 3: 460–3.

O'Brien, H. O. (1883a) 'Latah', *Journal of the Straits Branch of the Royal Asiatic Society*, 11: 143–53.

O'Brien, H. O. (1883b) 'Latah', *Journal of the Straits Branch of the Royal Asiatic Society*, 12: 283–5.

Oxley, J. (1849) Malay amoks. *Journal of the Indian Archipelago and Eastern Asia*, 1849, 3, 532–33.

Palthe, P. M. W. (1933) 'Psychiatry and neurology in the tropics', *Malayan Medical Journal*, 8: 133–9.

Pfeiffer, W. (1971) *Transkulturelle Psychiatrie – Ergebnisse und Probleme*. Stuttgart: Georg Thieme Verlag.

Rasch, C. (1894) 'Uber "amok" ', *Neurologisches Zentralblatt*, 13: 550–4.

Schulzens, W. (1676) *Walter Schulzens Ost-Indische Reise-Beschreibung*. Amsterdam, 1676. (Quoted in Yule and Burnell 1886.)

Sheppard, M. C. (n.d.) *The Adventures of Hang Tuah*. Singapore: Donald Moore.

Swaving, G. (1856) 'Geregtelijk-geneeskundige stellingen over den moordlust of mata glap bij den Inlander', *Regt in Nederlandsch-Indië*, 7: 125–30.

Swettenham, F. A. (1896) *Malay Sketches*. London: John Lane.

Swettenham, F. A. (1900) 'Betrachtungen öber amok', *Zeitschrift für Psychotherapie und Medizinische Psychologie*, 3: 226–31.

Can Brero, P. C. Z. (1895) 'Über das sogenannte latah', *Allgemeine Zeitschrift für Psychiatrie und ihre Grenzgebiete*, 51: 939–48.

Van Brero, P. C. Z. (1896) 'Einiges über die Geisteskrankheiten der Bevölkerung des Malayischen Archipels', *Allgemeine Zeitschrift für Psychiatrie und ihre Grenzgebiete*, 53: 25–33.

Van der Chijs, J. A. (1890) *Nederlandsch-Indisch plakaatboek*, Vol. 13. Batavia.

Van Leent, F. J. (1867) 'Contributions à la géographie médicale', *Archives de Médecine Navale*, 8: 172–3 (these pages refer only to the note on latah, not to the whole article, which is scattered over several numbers).

Van Leent, F. J. (1868) *Geneeskundig-topographische opmerkingen betrofiende Batavia, hare neede en het eiland Onnust*. The Hague.

Van Loon, F. G. H. (1922) 'Acute Verwardheidstoestanden in Nederlandsch-Indië', *Mededeelingen van het Burgerlijken Geneeskundigen Dienst in Nederlandsch-Indië*, 4: 658–90.

Van Loon, F. G. H. (1924) 'Lattah, eene psychoneurose der Maleische Rassen', *Geneeskundig Tijdschrift voor Nederlandsch-Indië*, 64: 59–82.

Van Loon, F. G. H. (1927) 'Amok and Latah', *Journal of Abnormal and Social Psychology*, 21: 434–44.

Vogler, W. (1853) 'Wenken omtrent mata-glap', *Tijdschrift der Vereeniging tot Bevordering der Geneeskundige Wetenschappen in Nederlandsch-Indië*, 2: 95–113.

Wallace, A. R. (1898) *The Malay Archipelago, the Land of the Orang-utan and the Bird of Paradise: a Narrative of Travel, with Studies of Man and Nature*. London: Macmillan.

Wilkinson ,R. J. (1925a) *Papers on Malay Subjects. Life and Customs – Part III: Malay Amusements*. Kuala Lumpur: F. M. S. Government Press.

Wilkinson, R. J. (1925b) *Papers on Malay Subjects. Malay Literature – Part III: Malay Proverbs on Malay Character*. Kuala Lumpur: F. M. S. Government Press.

Wilkinson, R. J. (1957) *A Malay-English Dictionary*. London: Macmillan.

Yap, P. M. (1951) 'Mental diseases peculiar to certain cultures', *Journal of Mental Science*, 97: 313–21.

Yap, P. M. (1952) 'The latah reactions', *Journal of Mental Science*, 98: 515–64.

Yule, H. and Burnell, A. C. (1886) *Hobson-Jobson: being a Glossary of Anglo-Indian Colloquial Words and Phrases, and of Kindred Terms: Etymological, Historical, Geographical and Discursive*. London: J. Murray.

Zaguirre, J. C. (1951) 'Amuck', *Journal of the Philippine Federation of Private Medical Practitioners*, 4: 1138–49.

Index

393